Historical Musicology

Eastman Studies in Music

Ralph P. Locke, Senior Editor
Eastman School of Music

(ISSN 1071–9989)

Additional Titles in Historical Musicology

*Analyzing Wagner's Operas:
Alfred Lorenz and German
Nationalist Ideology*
Stephen McClatchie

Berlioz: Past, Present, Future
Edited by Peter Bloom

Berlioz's Semi-Operas: Roméo et Juliette
and La damnation de Faust
Daniel Albright

*"The Broadway Sound":
The Autobiography and Selected Essays
of Robert Russell Bennett*
Edited by George J. Ferencz

*The Chansons of Orlando di Lasso and
Their Protestant Listeners: Music, Piety,
and Print in Sixteenth-Century France*
Richard Freedman

*Elliott Carter: Collected Essays and
Lectures, 1937–1995*
Edited by Jonathan W. Bernard

*French Organ Music from the
Revolution to Franck and Widor*
Edited by Lawrence Archbold
and William J. Peterson

*The Gardano Music Printing Firms,
1569–1611*
Richard J. Agee

*Music and Musicians in the Escorial
Liturgy under the Habsburgs,
1563–1700*
Michael Noone

*Music and the Occult:
French Musical Philosophies,
1750–1950*
Joscelyn Godwin

The Music of Luigi Dallapiccola
Raymond Fearn

*Music's Modern Muse: A Life of
Winnaretta Singer, Princesse de
Polignac*
Sylvia Kahan

*The Musical Madhouse
(Les Grotesques de la musique)*
Hector Berlioz
Translated and edited by Alastair Bruce
Introduction by Hugh Macdonald

Portrait of Percy Grainger
Malcolm Gillies and David Pear

*Theories of Fugue from the Age of
Josquin to the Age of Bach*
Paul Mark Walker

A complete list of titles in the Eastman Studies in Music series,
in order of publication, may be found at the end of this book.

Historical Musicology

Sources, Methods, Interpretations

Edited by

Stephen A.
Crist

Roberta Montemorra
Marvin

John Michael Cooper
Georgetown, Texas
18 April 2011

®R University of Rochester Press

The editors are grateful to the College and the Graduate School of Arts and Sciences at Emery University for providing financial support for this publication. We also thank The University of Iowa Obermann Center for Advanced Studies for providing various kinds of assistance during the preparation of this book.

First published 2004
by the University of Rochester Press
Reprinted and transferred to digital printing 2008

University of Rochester Press
668 Mt. Hope Avenue, Rochester, NY 14620, USA
www.urpress.com
and Boydell & Brewer Limited
PO Box 9, Woodbridge, Suffolk IP12 3DF, UK
www.boydellandbrewer.com

ISSN: 1071-9989
Hardcover ISBN-10: 1-58046-111-5
Paperback ISBN-13: 978-1-58046-301-0
Paperback ISBN-10: 1-58046-301-0

Library of Congress Cataloging-in-Publication Data

Historical musicology : sources, methods, interpretations / edited by
    Stephen A. Crist and Roberta Montemorra Marvin
        p. cm. — (Eastman studies in music, ISSN 1071-9989; v. 28)
    Festschrift for Robert L. Marshall.
    Includes bibliographical references and index.
    ISBN 1-58046-111-5 (hardcover: alk. paper)
        1. Music—History and criticism. I. Crist, Stephen A. II. Marvin,
    Roberta Montemorra. III. Marshall, Robert Lewis. IV. Series.

    ML55.M265H57 2004
    780'.9—dc22
                                                            2004008142

A catalogue record for this title is available from the British Library.

This publication is printed on acid-free paper.
Printed in the United States of America.

For
Robert L. Marshall
a trusted mentor, a valued colleague, a cherished friend

Contents

Introduction

Scholarly Inquiry in Historical Musicology: Sources, Methods, Interpretations

Roberta Montemorra Marvin

Interpreting sources by applying diverse methods to their study lies at the core of humanistic scholarship. In musicology, the so-called disciplines—historical method, theoretical and analytical method, textual scholarship, archival research, lexicography and terminology, organology and iconography, performing practice, aesthetics and criticism, socio-musicology, psychology and hearing, gender and sexual studies[1]—all rely, to varying degrees, on interpretations of source materials. Indeed, from the inception of historical musicology sources have played a decisive role, with many significant achievements of the discipline having been established on documentary foundations. At the beginning of the new millennium, the definition of "sources" has broadened, and, of even greater significance, a wealth of approaches has opened new and exciting methodological paths of inquiry, permitting innovative and multifaceted interpretations. The discipline is benefitting from an expansion that has enriched scholarship.

During the past two decades musicology has undergone several transformations. Source studies used to be at the very center of disciplinary studies, but in the mid-1980s, they came to be taken for granted, viewed as a "positivistic," empirical component in a loftier process (Joseph Kerman's "criticism").[2] Intrigued by theories and methods borrowed from its sister disciplines, musicology passed through a phase in which source research was considered passé; the issues of interest—and value—were considered to be more cultural, ideological, and interdisciplinary. Temporarily these enticing influences took hold, bringing the discipline to an extreme and compelling scholars to view themselves as participants either in the "new musicology," indulging in cultural and theoretical studies, or the "old," holding to the ways of the past. It seemed for a time in the early stages of this evolution that the very foundations upon which the discipline was built might be dislodged, for some of the "new" work was quickly shown to have been compromised by inattention to the traditional principles of source study, solid methodology, and supported interpretations.[3]

Fortunately, however, once the novelty subsided, the pendulum began to swing back to the center. Enriched by some of the newer approaches the field has developed over the past few years, the discipline of musicology has now reached a point where it can see afresh the importance of source studies. These studies, of course, always held the potential for various interpretations—even invited them, but in many instances scholars had not ventured where they might have. Now, traditional and contemporary approaches have recently come into balance: source studies have been enhanced by new theoretical applications and modes of inquiry and newer ideologies have incorporated documentary evidence.[4]

As our knowledge continues to be supplemented by broad, interdisciplinary or multidisciplinary approaches to the study and interpretation of source materials, it seems especially appropriate to take a broad view of source studies in general through considering the methods scholars apply in interpreting sources in the current scholarly environment. This collection of essays thus builds on the disciplinary foundations that have been laid, celebrating a diversity of interpretations through studies based on both traditional and contemporary methodologies applied to conventional and unconventional sources. The seventeen essays that comprise the present volume represent the work of recognized scholars in the field, who use a broad array of source material and adopt a considerable variety of approaches in probing a wide variety of issues pertaining to a cross section of musical works and musical life from the sixteenth through the twentieth centuries. Taken together the essays might therefore serve as models reflecting the pluralistic profile of musicology at the beginning of the twenty-first century. The topics treated in this collection are wide-ranging—performing practices and performance histories, interpretation and meaning, textual criticism and the history and reception of musical works. In presenting this diversity of perspectives and interpretations, these essays deal with the nature of the information contained in the sources, treat the manner in which information can be applied to specific situations, and present arguments for interpreting documents in new ways and in more inclusive contexts. Some of the studies follow "tried and true" paths; others venture into less explored territory. Many of them reflect precisely on the ways in which the sources themselves pose questions or illuminate the issues. All impact our understanding of the sphere of music: the composers, the works, the performance, the audience.

Proceeding more or less chronologically by century, the volume opens with a revealing and exemplary source study: "A Collaboration between Cipriano de Rore and Baldissera Donato?" by Jessie Ann Owens. By way of close reading of manuscript sources and detailed philological and paleographical work, Owens posits a significant new hypothesis concerning possible collaboration—either as student and teacher or as colleagues—between de Rore and Donato, thereby calling attention to the manner in which an important Renaissance composer learned and worked. Russell Stinson also deals with a composer at work in "New Perspectives on Bach's Great Eighteen Chorales." Culling information from the autograph and other manuscript sources for BWV 651–668 and summarizing the vast literature of the past dozen years concerning these works, he addresses the issues of their chronology and authenticity. Owens and Stinson show us that traditional approaches to manuscript study combined with direct and imaginative questioning reveal valuable information bearing on larger issues in music history.

J. S. Bach serves as the subject of two further essays, both seeking meaning in music, but each adopting a different approach. In "Historical Theology and Hymnology as Tools for Interpreting Bach's Church Cantatas: The Case of *Ich elender Mensch, wer wird mich erlösen*, BWV 48" Stephen A. Crist demonstrates how information gleaned both from traditional sources in musicology—manuscript scores in particular—and from "extra"-musicological ones—biblical and hymnological sources—can inform the interpretation of musical works. Drawing on evidence from biblical commentaries of the seventeenth and eighteenth centuries and eighteenth-century hymnals, as well as from Bach's autograph score and the manuscript performing parts for Cantata 48, within a theoretical and theological context Crist offers observations that decode the cantata's meaning in its historical context. Turning to instrumental genres, Michael Marissen probes the composer's music in "Performance Practice Issues That Affect Meaning in Two Bach Instrumental Works." He considers how ensemble size in the first movement of Brandenburg Concerto No. 5 and the significance of rhythm (specifically overdotting) in the augmentation canon from the *Musical Offering* can contribute to a better understanding of the works. Based on surviving original performing materials, verbal documents, and performance traditions, Marissen argues that reaching a valid interpretation of Bach's instrumental music requires a continual, mutually qualifying interplay between the sense of the whole and the understanding of the parts.

Performance practice, or perhaps better, performance *in* practice, is also the subject of Ellen T. Harris's essay "Mozart's *Mitridate*: Going beyond the Text." This essay, which derives from the author's experience preparing ornamentation and cadenzas for a 2001 production of Mozart's opera, "offers a case study in reading the text for the purpose of going beyond it."[5] Drawing on an eighteenth-century treatise by Domenico Corri, epistolary evidence, Mozart's musical ornamentation, and her own first-hand experience working with singers, Harris demonstrates how thorough research and interpretation of source materials can facilitate a creative leap from the music as written to the music in performance, thereby illustrating how scholarship and practice can and should influence each other.

Influence of another cast is Richard Kramer's concern in "Carl Philipp Emanuel Bach and the Aesthetics of Patricide." This essay offers a provocative view of what it may have been like to have been a composer son of the great Johann Sebastian Bach. With insights based on the writings of Kant, Lessing, and Freud, as well as epistolary evidence and musical analysis of a sonata by the younger composer written in 1775 (but unpublished until recently), Kramer tackles the question of how C. P. E. Bach dealt with his father's musical omnipresence. The influence of Haydn on a generation of symphonists is the focus of Lawrence F. Bernstein's "Joseph Haydn's Influence on the Symphonies of Antonio Rosetti." Through studying the musical milieu at the court of Oettingen-Wallerstein under Prince Kraft Ernst, especially the manuscripts and printed sources of Haydn's symphonies from the court's library, Bernstein identifies specific instances of Haydn's influence on one particular composer who worked at that princely establishment. Combining the documentary evidence with musical and stylistic analysis read against theoretical context, the author accounts for supposed anomalies in Rosetti's music, tracing what he calls the "formal subterfuge" in the composer's symphonic finales to features of specific works by Haydn. Bernstein argues for a betrayed influence in which Rosetti reworked borrowed ideas to such an extent that they seem to be innovative.

Beyond dealing with influence, Bernstein sheds light on how composers may have thought about their artworks in comparison with others of their own era through relying upon musical evidence. Maynard Solomon's "Reason and Imagination: Beethoven's Aesthetic Evolution" also concerns itself with a composer's views on works of musical art, but through verbal evidence. By attempting to locate an evolutionary pattern in Beethoven's aesthetic views on art and the artist, as extrapolated from letters, diaries, conversation books, etc., Solomon shows that Beethoven freely synthesized the ideas of his era. He concludes that the remarks are neither haphazard nor capricious but rather that they reflect the evolving tendencies among the composer's contemporaries and show a sympathy with Hoffmann and Marx. To learn of another musician's ideas about his own works, Lewis Lockwood, in "Schubert as Formal Architect: the *Quartettsatz*, D. 703," studies compositional modifications as a means of evaluating both Schubert's sense of proportions and his keen awareness of the expressive functions of formal segments. He considers the single quartet movement as the first of a projected four-movement cycle and interrogates what it reveals about Schubert's mature manner of shaping a sonata-form movement, drawing on its formal anomalies in light of a substantial revision Schubert made at the autograph stage. Interpreting this evidence, Lockwood proposes replacing the old view of Schubert struggling with larger formal structures with a new one stressing his originality, thus engaging anew in the longstanding debate about how source studies might illuminate musical content and engage us in a dialog with the composer.

nd embellishments. She suggests that the rationale for these changes temmed from efforts to "modernize" Mozart to reflect contemporary fashions in solo concerto playing and composition, exploit the new capabilities f the piano, and suit audiences of the time. A similar topic is tackled by Margaret Murata in "'Wo die Zitronen blühn': Re-Versions of *Arie antiche*." This critical history of late-nineteenth- and early-twentieth-century editions f solo songs and arias from seventeenth-century Italian operas and cantatas focuses on the evolving aesthetics and changing interests of editors as evealed in written prefaces to the editions and in the musical realizations hemselves. Murata seeks to understand the "traditions" of preparing these ditions and contemplates their implications for modern understanding of istorical performing practices. Both Macdonald and Murata deal with ssues surrounding accessibility, popularization, and consumerism.

Modern-day understanding of the "popular" also underlies Jann Pasler's essay, "Material Culture and Postmodern Positivism: Rethinking the 'Popular' in Late-Nineteenth-Century French Music." Pasler challenges the reader o rethink assumptions and scholarly methodologies with regard to popularization of culture, consumerism, concepts of center and periphery as well as of serious and popular. She seeks to extend archival research beyond the usual scores, manuscripts, letters, and first editions expanding her sources to popular music magazines, sheet music published in newspapers, military band transcriptions, and concert programs. Using these sources to investigate networks of relationships between various branches of concert life—connecting them specifically through *Samson et Dalila*—Pasler considers how music was used to mediate differences in class and culture. She presents different notions of "context" for the music scholar and new perspectives on the dissemination of musical works and musical knowledge.

The final essay in the volume reflects upon the life of a musicological scholar. Laurence Libin's "Otto Gombosi's Correspondence at the University of Chicago" recounts the life and work of an immigrant Central European scholar whose scholarship influenced American musicologists in the twentieth century including many of those who are contributors to this volume. Through Gombosi's letters, as well as reminiscences from people who knew and studied with the scholar, Libin seeks to understand the trials and tribulations of one musicologist as he sought to pursue his academic life in the twentieth century.

All of these essays demonstrate the diverse ways in which careful examination and bold questioning of source materials contribute to musicological discourse. Disparate in their subject matter and their methodology, they demonstrate that sources tell stories and that those stories might vary depending on the methodology applied to their study, yielding multiple interpretations.

How audiences perceived a composer and his works i
Jeffrey Kallberg in "Sex, Sexuality, and Schubert's Piano M
thor engages in the controversy over Schubert's sexual procli
possible relationship to his music by examining some of
issues under debate in historical context. Based on nineteent
ings, especially ascriptions of feminized characteristics to Sc
music, in addition to his own nuanced interpretive reading o
A Minor, D. 845, Kallberg seeks to understand how and wl
and music converged during Schubert's lifetime. Mark Kr(
Exécution': Johann Nepomuk Hummel's Treatise and the
the Pianoforte" also addresses issues surrounding the interpre
music in the early nineteenth century, but in more traditional v
performance techniques. He discusses the contents of Hum
*plete Theoretical and Practical Course of Instructions, on th
ing the Piano Forte* within the context of contemporary mu
in particular, as it relates to the composer's approach to the ir
his influence on the "romantic" style. Kroll uses Hummel
structions, lucid descriptions, and poignant artistic philosoph
nineteenth-century pianism and performing practice.

Moving on in the nineteenth century, the next two essays de
musical works, in particular, the effects of the verbal text on
on interpretation and reception of the work. In "'For You H
bellious against the Lord': The Jewish Image in Mendelssohr
Marx's *Mose*" Jeffrey S. Sposato unravels the traditional stc
ing the libretto's role in the breakdown in the relationship bet
composers and compares the librettos of the two works with
images of the Jews. In the process, he sheds light on the sensit
Mendelssohn's ways of disparaging his Jewish heritage and infc
how the shaping of the text can convey a personal message.
Maffei's 'Ugly Sin': The Libretto for Verdi's *I masnadie*
Montemorra Marvin provides a contextualized reading of (
evidence surrounding the shaping of the libretto for Verdi's fir
ated expressly for an audience outside Italy. Drawing on ep
dence, contemporary critiques and commentaries, autograpl
performing parts and early printed editions, she evaluates tl
attitude toward operatic texts, provides information bearing o
and reason for modifications Verdi and Maffei made to the
assesses the effect of the librettist's contribution in the recej
opera, arguing that one major reason for the opera's lack of
well have been its uneven, ill-paced, and all-too-literary librett

Reception is studied further in two additional essays—throu
editions. In "Mozart's Piano Concertos and the Romantic G
Claudia Macdonald surveys early nineteenth-century editions a
ments of those works and the modifications made to them in instr

A fascination with sources and the stories they might tell is a central commitment in the life's work of Robert L. Marshall. In 1972, with the publication of his monumental and ground-breaking *The Compositional Process of J. S. Bach,* Marshall furnished the discipline with an exemplar of interpretative scholarship; his two-volume study has become a classic, a "rock" in music scholarship. Indeed, Robert Marshall's entire career has been dedicated to the pursuit of excellence in every regard; he has inspired and influenced a brace of students and colleagues. His willingness to probe the issues that need attention and to do so through enduring methods has enriched musicology. His impact can be perceived in the essays in this volume. Even when the influence is not explicit in these studies, it is still there, for no one who has worked with him can have failed to learn from him. The former students and professional colleagues who have contributed to this volume honor Robert Marshall and thank him for his scholarship, his mentoring, his collegiality, and his humanity.

Notes

1. These categories follow those outlined in the entry "Musicology: Disciplines of Musicology" in *The New Grove Dictionary of Music and Musicians,* 2d ed., ed. Stanley Sadie and John Tyrrell (London: Macmillan, 2001), 17:492–507.

2. See, for example, Joseph Kerman, *Contemplating Music: Musicology in Context* (Cambridge, Mass.: Harvard University Press, 1985).

3. For a range of views on recent methodological challenges, see "Round Table 3: Directions in Musicology," especially the opening statements by Andrew Dell'Antonio and Stefano Castelvecchi, in *Musicology and Sister Disciplines: Past, Present, Future: Proceedings of the 16th International Congress of the International Musicological Society, London, 1997,* ed. David Greer, Ian Rumbold, and Jonathan King (London: Oxford University Press, 2000), 179–229.

4. See, for example, the discussion in *Criticism and Analysis* (New York: Garland, 1985), esp. Arthur Mendel, "Evidence and Explanation," 125–40; and Joseph Kerman, "How We Got into Analysis, and How to Get Out," pp. 103–24. The former was originally published in *Report of the Eighth Congress of the International Musicological Society, New York 1961,* ed. Jan LaRue (Kassel: Bärenreiter, 1962), 3–18; the latter appeared first in *Critical Inquiry* 7 (1980–81): 311–31.

5. Ellen T. Harris, "Mozart's *Mitridate*: Going beyond the Text," this volume, 95.

1

A Collaboration between Cipriano de Rore and Baldissera Donato?*

JESSIE ANN OWENS

Sources have stories to tell us, if only we can get them to give up their secrets. But in the case of many, if not most, Renaissance music manuscripts, their transfer from their place of origin to their current locations in libraries and archives all over the world has often erased important clues about provenance and function, and about dating and authorship. Despite concentrated scholarship on sources and scribes in the past three or four decades, identifying the hand responsible for writing the music often remains an unsolved problem. In the final analysis, however, the absence of evidence concerning scribal identity may prove beneficial because it forces us to focus less on the hands themselves and more on what the writing in the manuscripts can tell us about how the sources were used. Being able to put a label on a hand—to identify it with a particular scribe or composer—can be less interesting than getting the source to reveal its story.

A case in point is the sheaf of six leaves now in the Bavarian State Library in Munich (Mus Ms 1503f). Mus Ms 1503f (hereafter *Mu*) consists of six leaves, one for each voice of a six-voice madrigal, *Fiamm'amorosa.*[1] (See figures 1.1 and 1.2.) The paper is in oblong format, measuring 17 x 24.5 cm. It is ruled on both sides with a rastrum measuring 13.5 mm, six staves per page. The music is written on the front side only.

The composer is identified in the *canto* as "Balthesar Donato" [Baldissera Donato], written above the first staff in the usual place for a composer attribution.[2] That identification seems secure. The madrigal appears in four other sources under his name: Wolfenbüttel, Herzog August Bibliothek, Cod. Guelph 293 Mus. Hs. (hereafter *Wolf*) as "Baldisera Donato" and in the three editions of Donato's *Il primo libro d'i madregali a cinque & a sei uoci con tre dialoghi a sette nouamente dati in luce con gratia et privilegio a cinque voci* (Venice: Antonio Gardane, 1553; the Pietrasanta edition of 1557, and the Gardano edition of 1560).[3]

Figure 1.1. Munich, Bayerische Staatsbibliothek (D-Mbs), Mus Ms 1503f, 4 (tenore). Used by permission.

The writing is legible but casual in style, not characteristic of a professional scribe's calligraphic writing. While the notes are, for the most part, written neatly and evenly, the text strains at the available space and is frequently out of alignment, particularly at ends of phrases; it often spills over into the margin. In some nineteen passages there are signs of correction and revision—erasures, notes overwritten or squeezed in. These sorts of changes generally signal a composer in the process of working out his music.

It might be tempting to imagine that *Mu* is a Donato autograph, except that the writing of the text does not match the only known specimen of his

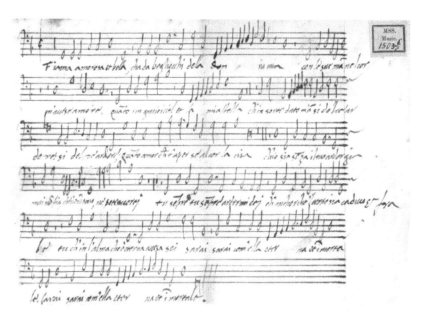

Figure 1.2. Munich, Bayerische Staatsbibliothek (D-Mbs), Mus Ms 1503f, 6 (basso).

handwriting (see figure 1.3). In this official Venetian tax document from 1566, Donato, writing in the first person, provides a declaration of the income he received from real estate.[4]

In fact, a different hypothesis about the identification of the hand of *Mu* takes us on a far more complex and intriguing journey than even the identification of *Mu* as a Donato autograph might have done. Mary Lewis wrote to me in 1980 that she and Joshua Rifkin had recognized the handwriting in *Mu* as identical to the hand found in a set of partbooks in Milan (Biblioteca Ambrosiana, A.10.sup).[5] (See figures 1.4 and 1.5.) Edmond vander Straeten was the first to identify these partbooks as autographs of Cipriano de Rore, thanks to an affidavit to that effect, written by de Rore's pupil Luzzasco Luzzaschi and bound with the partbooks.[6] My own work on the partbooks clarified their relationship to a composer's tablet (*cartella*) mentioned in the affidavit and focused on the ways in which de Rore had used them for composing two of his motets and a textless composition.[7]

From my investigation of the contents of the Milan partbooks, I was convinced that Cipriano de Rore had written all the music in the partbooks. But the handwriting does present problems. At first glance the manuscript appears to have been written by two hands, not one.[8] The first composition, *Miserere mei,* looks as though it had been written quickly. It uses a shorthand system for indicating the text (just the first letter of many of the words) and an informal form of the F clef (a simple line with two dots to

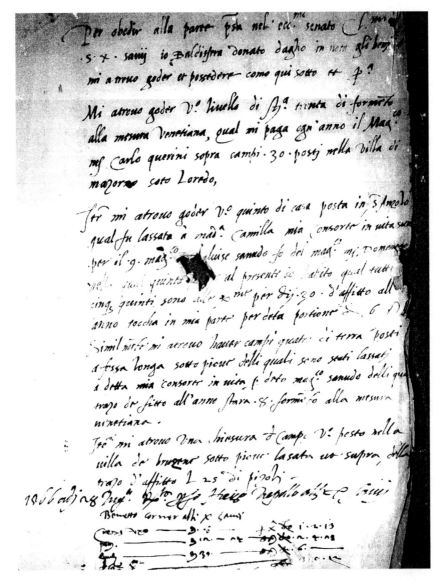

Figure 1.3. Venice, Archivio di Stato (I-Vas), X Savi alle Decime, busta 127, no. 600 (1566), Donato autograph. Used by permission.

indicate the F line).[9] (See figure 1.4.) The third piece is similar in appearance, except that there is no text at all, and the piece breaks off in the middle. In contrast, the second composition, *Sub tuum praesidium*, resembles a fair copy, with a complete text, carefully formed notes, and a more formal F clef (longa with opposing double minims; see figure 1.5).[10]

Figure 1.4. Milan, Biblioteca Ambrosiana (I-Ma), A.10.sup, *Miserere mei,* (basso), f. 18ʳ. Used by permission.

Closer inspection, however, reveals musical symbols that are identical in both styles of writing. The texts as well share letter forms that can in turn be found in de Rore's letters.

The connection between the formal and informal writing in the Milan partbooks becomes even clearer with the recognition of de Rore's hand in *Mu*. The hand in the Munich leaves, in effect, occupies a middle ground between the two extremes in the Milanese source. Taken together these manuscripts show one hand operating at different degrees of formality.[11]

If we accept that the Milan partbooks and the Munich leaves were both written by one hand and that the hand is de Rore's, we will need to consider a series of problems that have never been addressed.[12] After all, the Munich leaves contain music not by de Rore, but by Donato. How can we account for music by Donato in de Rore's hand or for the presence of corrections? What circumstances in the lives of these two composers might have produced the Munich leaves?

As a brief sketch of their lives will make clear, Cipriano de Rore and Baldissera Donato were both active in northern Italy; they interacted with some of the same patrons and were part of a larger group of musicians and composers with connections to Venice and its neighboring cities.[13]

Figure 1.5. Milan, Biblioteca Ambrosiana (I-Ma), A.10.sup, *Sub tuum praesidium* (basso), f. 20[r]. Used by permission.

De Rore, born in 1515 or 1516 in Flanders, had come to Italy, probably as early as the late 1530s. The earliest records we have of his whereabouts, from Strozzi correspondence, indicate that he was living in Brescia during the early 1540s, though he certainly visited Venice.[14] By spring 1546 he had secured the extremely prestigious position of *maestro di cappella* at the Este court in Ferrara. He continued to maintain strong connections with composers in Venice, the city where his music circulated in manuscript copies and where most of it was published. He returned to Venice in 1563 to succeed Adrian Willaert as *maestro di cappella* at San Marco, thereby becoming Donato's colleague. De Rore died at age 49 in 1565.

Donato was born, in all probability, sometime between 1526 and 1530, some ten to fifteen years after de Rore.[15] He began his lifelong service at San Marco in 1545 or 1546 as a *zago* or boy singer. He received a raise in 1547 and was entrusted with copying Willaert's music and reporting on Willaert's productivity to the *procuratori*. Donato's music appeared in print for the first time in 1548, in one of de Rore's madrigal books, the Scotto edition of his *Terzo libro*.[16] He would eventually assume the post held by de Rore, following the death of de Rore's successor, Zarlino. He died in 1603.

Table 1.1. Changes in *Mu*.

Note: Part names are C (canto), A (alto), Q (quinto), T (tenore), S (sesto), and B (basso). Note names are B (breve), M (minim), SB (semi-breve).

no.	m./voices	description of change	ink
1	4/A, S	erased E♭ in both parts	—
2	4/S	changed C to E	dark brown
3	5/S	uncertain	main (darker)
4	8–9/Q, B	rewrote cadence	main
5	11/B	changed rhythm and placement of bass entrance (erased rest, stem)	—
6	1–14/B	rewrote bass; original reading did not fit with other voices	dark brown
7	18–19/A, Q	voicing of sonority changed by switching pitches between A (G F C becomes D D C) and Q (D becomes G)	main
8	20/T	G A changed to B♭ B♭	dark brown
9	23–25/B 25/C	B rewritten [subsequently reworked in 1553], cadential ornament eliminated in C by erasure	dark brown
10	34/A	breve F changed to semibreve	main
11	41–42/Q	rewritten, repetition of "gia mai" squeezed in	red-brown
12	44/A; 43–44/B	reading uncertain	main; dark brown
13	45/S	m. 45/S changed one pitch from B♭ (third) to D (fifth)	main
14	47–48/B	rests rewritten (B B M to SB B SB M)	black
15	49/C	changed one pitch from G to B♭ [back to G in 1553]	dark brown
16	51/Q	parallel to no. 15 [back to G in 1553]	dark brown
17	58/C	C simplified	dark brown
18	59/S	changed one pitch from C to E♭	main
19	69/T	changed one pitch from Bb to G	main

The biographical details provide a chronological framework but little specificity about the nature of the possible connections between the two composers. *Mu* may be able to supply further information.

Table 1.1 lists the many changes found in *Mu*. The revisions range from single notes to entire phrases. They sometimes involve one voice, sometimes two. In the Appendix to this chapter (pp. 20–35) is an edition of *Fiamm'amorosa* as found in *Mu*, with the revisions on the main staff and the original version on small staves.

Ink color provides important clues to the character of the activity.[17] The main inks employed are grey for the music and brown for the text. The changes written in the prevailing grey ink constitute the first phase of activity. Some of the changes in the main ink seem to be copying mistakes. Examples from table 1.1 include no. 3 (de Rore may have omitted two notes and begun the dotted figure too soon) and no. 10 (he mistakenly wrote a breve instead of a semibreve). Possibly to be included in this category are the three instances where a single pitch was changed (nos. 13, 18, 19), but these could all be substantive corrections. The two changes in the main ink that involve two voices, however, clearly imply editing: rewriting a cadence (no. 4) and revoicing a sonority (no. 7).

A second phase is marked by the use of dark brown ink for the music. This may or may not have been close in time to the other corrections; since de Rore used brown ink for the text, he may simply have used that ink for some of the changes in the music. Given the difference in the color of ink from the rest of the music, however, it is not surprising that none of the mistakes seem like copying errors. They seem instead to be editorial (for example, nos. 2, 6, 8, 9, 15, 16, and 17). Two other colors may represent distinct passes over the music: the use of a red-brown ink to rewrite a phrase (no. 11) and the use of black ink to rewrite rests to show the tactus correctly (no. 14).

As a group the changes, apart from the possible copying errors, seem to represent an editorial process concerned with polishing the surface of the music: avoiding dissonance or adding it, eliminating fifths or octaves, adding or taking away passing notes, shifting the entrance of a voice, altering approaches to cadences, improving voice-leading, correcting the notation of rests, changing the voicing of a chord.

In effect, the Munich leaves preserve two versions of the madrigal, *A* and *B*. Version *A* consists of the original readings, some of which are no longer legible; Version *B*, the text closest to the surface, is the revised version. This account of the changes suggests that de Rore *copied* Donato's madrigal (Version *A*) and then *edited* it (Version *B*). Unfortunately, although the evidence in *Mu* suggests some form of collaboration, it does not reveal whether de Rore was acting in the role of teacher or of colleague.

The story does not end, however, with the revisions in *Mu*. Donato's *Fiamm'amorosa*, as I mentioned above, is also found in *Wolf*, a set of partbooks that contain music by de Rore as well as by Willaert and other composers associated with Venice. Mary Lewis has recently argued that these partbooks, once thought to be Ferrarese in origin, probably come from Venice.[18] She believes that they represent a composer/singer's personal collection of music that he encountered, primarily in manuscript form, probably between "ca. 1543/44 and 1557 or later." She offers as a candidate the composer Perissone Cambio.[19] I would add in support of this assertion the evidence of a (possibly autograph) handwritten correction to a copy of Cambio's 1545 publication that bears a strong resemblance to the hand of *Wolf*.[20]

Fiamm'amorosa offers another instance of Lewis's discovery that many of the compositions in *Wolf* were copied not from prints but from manuscripts containing independent readings.[21] A comparison of the readings of *Fiamm'amorosa* in the various sources shows that the edited version of *Mu* (Version *B*)—and not the 1553 printed version of the madrigal—served (directly or indirectly) as the source for *Wolf*. There is only one musical difference between *Mu* and *Wolf*: a flat (E♭) in the *sesto* (staff 3, m. 22) in *Mu* that is not found in *Wolf*. There are numerous minor textual differences in spelling and abbreviations, but they fall within normal ranges of

variation in orthography and are not significant for establishing relationships between sources.

One passage in particular suggests that *Wolf* could well have been copied directly from *Mu.* In staff 4 of the *tenore* in *Mu* (figure 1.1), de Rore
misjudged the space available for the phrase "sia senza il tuo ardor gia
maii," a problem aggravated by the number of elisions in the text:

> sia senza il tuo ardor giamai
> /　/　/　/　　/　/　/

His solution was to reduce the size of the text and squeeze it in. (This
passage suggests that he wrote out the notes first and then added the text,
another indication that the hand of *Mu,* if it turns out to be someone other
than de Rore, was copying, not composing.) The scribe of *Wolf* either had
to address the same problem independently, or, if he was copying from *Mu,*
was also misled by the spatial problem. In either event, he failed to come up
with an elegant solution and had to resort to writing "mai" under "gia-" (see
figure 1.6.)

While it is, of course, not possible to be certain that *Mu* itself, rather than
a copy of *Mu,* was the source for *Wolf,* there is additional evidence that makes
a direct connection more likely.[22] A set of parts for an anonymous five-voice
setting of *Bella guerriera* seems to share the same configuration of sources as
Fiamm'amorosa; in fact, *Bella guerriera* directly follows *Fiamm'amorosa* in
the Munich library (Mus Ms 1503g) and precedes it in *Wolf.* The Munich
source contains minor revisions, and these revisions are the readings adopted
by *Wolf.*[23] The connections between these two sets of leaves (Mus Ms 1503f
[=*Mu*] and Mus Ms 1503g) and *Wolf* increase the possibility that the Munich
sources are Venetian (or north Italian) in origin.[24]

The story still is not over. We know that de Rore liked to revise his music.
The 1542 letter from Pallazzo da Fano to Roberto Strozzi, placing him in
Brescia, contains the following tantalizing account: "I received yours with
the madrigal that Cipriano [de Rore] wrote for you, but now from lack of
time I can send you nothing in exchange, since I haven't been supplied with
the motet which Cipriano by now has in good shape after his return from
Venice."[25] Martha Feldman takes this to mean that de Rore "made one
documented trip to Venice—and probably many more—when he visited
[Neri] Capponi's salon, delivered madrigals to him, and apparently made
revisions (possibly with Willaert's advice)."[26] Although the letter stops well
short of any mention of Willaert, it does suggest a routine phase of revision
and editing that is attested to by other evidence as well.

There are important parallels between de Rore and Donato in the pro-
cesses both employ to reach a definitive version of their music. Lewis demonstrates that *Wolf* preserves early versions of music by de Rore, including

Figure 1.6. Wolfenbüttel, Herzog August Bibliothek (D-W), Cod. Guelph 293 Mus. Hs, sexta pars, f. 10ᵛ. Used by permission.

the *Vergine* cycle, which would reach its definitive form only in the 1552 edition of his *Terzo libro*.[27] Similarly, Donato's *Fiamm'amorosa* continued to undergo further revisions after the editing it received from de Rore that is recorded in *Mu* and *Wolf*, until its publication in 1553. Thereafter, the text remained stable in the subsequent two editions (Pietrasanta, 1557, and Gardano, 1560).[28]

Table 1.2. Changes between *Mu* and the Printed Editions (1553, 1557, 1560).

no.	m. (print)/voice(s)	description of changes
1	4–11/ALL	lengthened point by adding imitative treatment of motive; substituted a dissonant, syncopated entry at end to increase tension before cadence and eliminated a rather formulaic passing figure
2	13/S	changed voicing of chord
3	25–31/B, Q, A	avoided too many strong-beat arrivals on B♭; by substituting G-minor chord, made the B♭ stronger in m. 27, changed the figuration in the Q, changed the position of the text in the A
4	42/A	rewrote (changed figuration of) A
5	45/C	changed rhythm, adding syncopation
6	51/C	changed voicing of chord
7	53/A	changed rhythm
8	53/Q	parallel to no. 6
9	57/S	changed voicing of chord
10	59/S	changed voicing of chord
11	61–63/A, S	changed rhythm, voicing
12	67–69/C, A, Q, S, B	changed the position of passing notes, simplified the harmony
13	73/A	eliminated cadential ornament

Table 1.2 shows that most of the changes are minor, involving a single note. The second point of imitation, however, was substantially rewritten, lengthening it from five breves in *Mu/Wolf* to seven in the print (see the Appendix).[29] Donato also rewrote another point (mm. 25–28), which had also undergone revisions at de Rore's hands.

The date of publication fixes the endpoint of this process of revision, but the beginning is harder to determine. Feldman believes that Donato probably encountered the text, a twelve-line madrigal by Andrea Navagero (1483–1529), in the anthology *Rime diverse . . . libro primo* published in 1545.[29] If she is correct, then there was a narrow window of time for the various stages in the composition of *Fiamm'amorosa*. Between 1545 and 1553, Donato composed an early version of the madrigal; de Rore wrote it out in the Munich leaves and made corrections and revisions; the revised version circulated in Venice, where, if Lewis is correct, it was copied by Cambio into *Wolf*; and Donato continued to revise the piece until its publication. Musical compositions traveled in single sheets like *Mu*, so that they could be tried out and polished. They were copied into more durable collections like *Wolf*. And eventually they reached a wider audience through print.

As is so often the case in dealing with Renaissance sources, the evidence barely approaches the standards required for civil cases ("preponderance of evidence"), let alone the more stringent "beyond a reasonable doubt" required for criminal cases. It is not impossible that additional evidence may call into question the identification of the Milan partbooks and *Mu* with de Rore or challenge the assertion that the two sources share the same hand. Scholars will have to continue to try to build cases based on very slim evidence (recall, for example, that we have just one authentic document in Donato's hand). In the end, we may need to take comfort in the notion that the label we put on any source matters less than our interpretation of the significance of its contents. While I make a case here that *Mu* shows a collaboration between de Rore and Donato, as teacher-student or as colleagues, it seems prudent to leave the question mark in the title.

Appendix
Edition of Donato, *Fiamm'amorosa*[30]

Comments on the edition:

The first brace presents the edited (revised) version of the madrigal found in *Mu*. The parts are identified by the names found in the printed editions as well as by the modern pencil numbers in *Mu*. The ordering of voices from high to low corresponds to the modern edition (Donato, *Il primo libro di madrigali,* ed. Feldman [New York: Garland, 1991]). The edition retains original punctuation, capitalization, and spelling (except i/j and u/ v).

The original version of *Mu* is given on small staves directly above the main staves; the clef is the same as that of the main staff. The numbers in the boxes refer to table 1.1. The readings are difficult to discern in a number of instances and should be regarded as conjectural.

The second brace shows changes found in the printed editions. The numbers in boxes refer to table 1.2.

Because measure numbers are different between the *Mu* (revised) edition and the printed version, this edition divides the music into twelve distinct segments, each corresponding to a line of the text (and a musical unit), in order to make comparison easier between the manuscript and printed versions. For a continuous edition suitable for performing, see Feldman's edition.

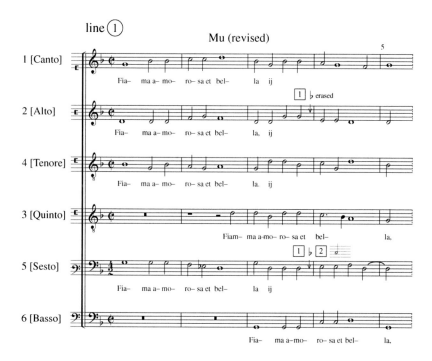

line ①

Mu (revised)

1553 (1557, 1560)

line ③

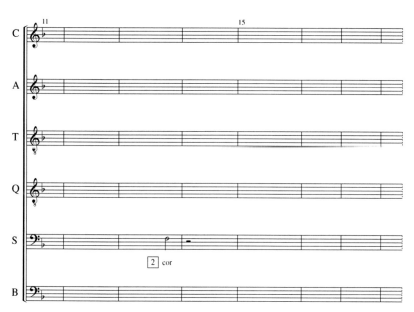

line ④

line (5)

(line 5 cont.)

line ⑥

(line 6 cont.)

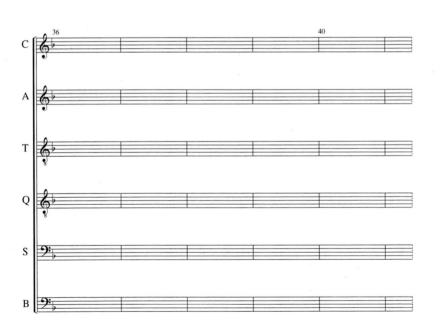

line ⑦

line ⑧

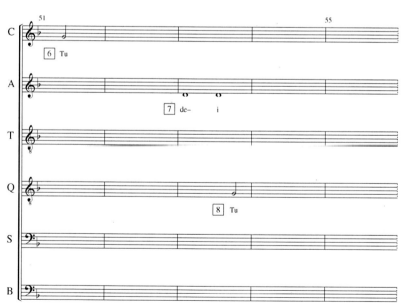

line ⑩

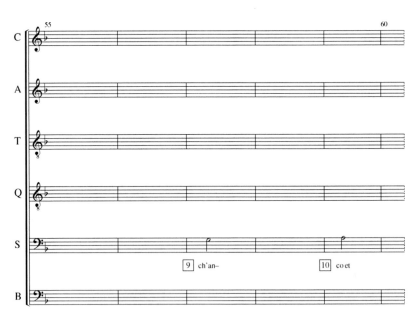

line ⑫

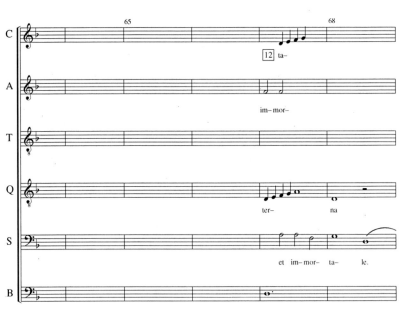

(line 12 cont.)

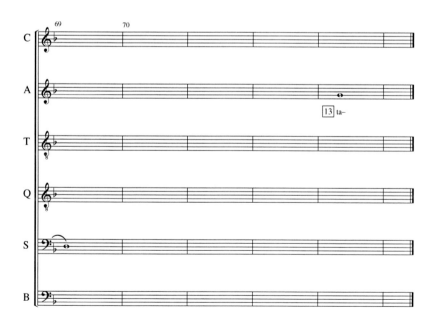

Notes

*I presented a version of this material in my paper "Identifying Composer Autographs in pre-1600 Manuscripts," read at the International Musicological Society Meeting (London, 1997). I am grateful to Ellen Harris, Mary Lewis, Lewis Lockwood, and Joshua Rifkin for commenting on a draft of this article.

1. Bayerische Staatsbibliothek, *Katalog der Musikhandschriften, 2: Tabulaturen und Stimmbücher bis zur Mitte des 17. Jahrhunderts,* ed. Marie Louise Göllner (Munich: G. Henle, 1979), 63.

2. There are no part names in the Munich leaves; the pages were numbered from 1 to 6 by a modern hand. I will refer to the parts by the conventional names found in Donato's own publication of the madrigal: 1 *canto* (c1, that is, a soprano or c-clef on the bottom line of the staff), 2 *alto* (c3), 3 *quinto* (c4), 4 *tenore* (c4), 5 *sesto* (F3), 6 *basso* (F4).

3. Mary Lewis, *Antonio Gardano, Venetian Music Printer, 1538–1569: A Descriptive Bibliography and Historical Study,* 2 vols. (New York: Garland, 1988, 1997), 2: #181; see also the discussion of Donato's publications, pp. 20–22. Concerning Donato's madrigals, see Baldassare Donato, *Il primo libro d'i madrigali a cinque & a sei voci, Venice, 1553, 1560,* ed. Martha Feldman, The Sixteenth-Century Madrigal, 10 (New York: Garland, 1991); Martha Feldman, *City Culture and the Madrigal at Venice* (Berkeley: University of California Press, 1995), 384–405; and Martha Feldman, "The Academy of Domenico Venier, Music's Literary Muse in Mid-Cinquecento Venice," *Renaissance Quarterly* 44 (1991): 476–512.

4. Venice, Archivio di Stato, X Savi alle Decime, busta 127, no. 600 (1566), registered on 28 June 1566. A full transcription can be found in Giulio Ongaro, "The Chapel of St. Mark's at the Time of Adrian Willaert (1527–1562): A Documentary Study" (Ph.D. diss., University of North Carolina at Chapel Hill, 1986), 214–15, and doc. 522, pp. 492–93; a synopsis is in Giulio Ongaro, "Sixteenth-Century Patronage at St. Mark's, Venice," *Early Music History* 8 (1988): 107–8. My thanks to Giulio Ongaro for identifying this document as autograph and to Jonathan Glixon for obtaining a microfilm.

5. Personal communication from Mary Lewis, 6 September 1980.

6. Edmond vander Straeten, *La Musique aux Pays-Bas avant le XIXe siècle,* 8 vols. (Brussels: G.-A. Van Trigt, 1867–88), 6:132–35. The partbooks were further scrutinized by Alvin H. Johnson, "The Liturgical Music of Cipriano de Rore," Ph.D. diss., Yale University, 1954, 14–19; and their contents were edited by Bernhard Meier in *Cipriani Rore Opera omnia,* Corpus mensurabilis musicae 14, 8 vols. ([Rome]: American Institute of Musicology, 1975), 6: xiii–xiv and xvi (reproduction of ff. 2^r, 3^v, and 4^r).

7. I first presented my work on the Milan partbooks at the 1980 Annual Meeting of the American Musicological Society and then published it in 1984 ("The Milan Partbooks: Evidence Concerning Cipriano de Rore's Compositional Process," *Journal of the American Musicological Society* 37 (1984): 270–98). I was able to provide a richer context for the Milan partbooks in *Composers at Work: The Craft of Musical Composition 1450–1600* (New York: Oxford University Press, 1997). I am indebted to Professor Robert Marshall for contributing "craft" to this title. When I was just beginning my work on compositional process, I made a pilgrimage from Florence to Bologna to consult a copy of *The Compositional Process of J. S.*

Bach: *A Study of the Autograph Scores of the Vocal Works,* 2 vols., (Princeton, N.J.: Princeton University Press, 1972); his framing of the questions and his methodologies were very helpful to me.

8. The entry for MilA 10 in the *Census-Catalogue of Manuscript Sources of Polyphonic Music, 1400–1550,* Renaissance Manuscript Studies, 1, 5 vols. (Neuhausen-Stuttgart: American Institute of Musicology, 1979–88), 2:142, states (with no authority listed): "Copied by two scribes, one of whom was Cipriano de Rore." In fact, Mary Lewis and I happened to be looking at the Milan partbooks at the same time (in June 1980); at that point she also believed that there were two scribes at work in the partbooks, one of whom was the Ferrarese court musician and copyist Jean Michel, at that time also a candidate for the scribe of *Wolf.* By 1985–86, Lewis had come to accept the partbooks as entirely written by de Rore ("Rore's Setting of Petrarch's 'Vergine Bella': A History of Its Composition and Early Transmission," *Journal of Musicology* 4 (1985–86): 391–92.

9. This feature of the writing has been commented on by everyone who has written about the partbooks. Vander Straeten, on 132–33 of *La Musique aux Pays Bas,* characterized the two forms of writing as "grande et ferme" ("large and well formed") as opposed to the "caractères minces et cursifs" ("thin and cursive characters"). "On y voit des ratures nombreuses, et, dans la rapidité de l'improvisation, le jeune musicien s'est contenté, pour plus de concision, de la première lettre de chaque mot tracé sous les notes voulues." ("One sees there a number of passages crossed out, and in the haste of improvisation the young musician decided to use just the first letter of each word under the proper note to save time.")

10. In *Composers at Work,* I employ "sketch," "draft," and "fair copy," terms that are commonplace in studies of compositional process. I am indebted to Joshua Rifkin, whose comments following a paper on Palestrina's process (now published as "Palestrina at Work," in *Papal Music and Musicians in Late Medieval and Renaissance Rome,* ed. Richard Sherr [Oxford: Clarendon Press in association with Library of Congress, Washington, 1998], 270–300) helped me to understand the usefulness of the concept "fair copy" for some of the manuscripts with which I had been working.

11. This sort of variety was part of the instruction of scribes (see, for example, the differing styles employed by Johannes Pollet, in *Vienna, Österreichische Nationalbibliothek, Mus. Hs. 18.744,* ed. Jessie Ann Owens, Renaissance Manuscripts in Facsimile, 25 (New York: Garland, 1986). Even today we are taught both to "print" (i.e., write with separated letters) and to write in cursive, using these styles for different purposes.

12. It is worth noting that there are two claims being made here, and that one or the other or both may be challenged. The first is that the same hand wrote both the Munich leaves and the Milan partbooks. The second is that the hand can be identified as Cipriano de Rore's. If de Rore is shown not to be the hand of *Mu,* and thus of the Milan partbooks as well, then much of what I have written about the Milan partbooks will have to be rethought; the observations about compositional process, of course, do not depend on the identification with de Rore.

13. On Venetian musical circles, see Jane Bernstein, *Music Printing in Renaissance Venice: The Scotto Press (1539–1572)* (New York: Oxford University Press, 1998); Feldman, *City Culture;* Lewis, *Antonio Gardano;* and Ongaro, "Sixteenth-Century Patronage."

14. On de Rore's biography, see my entry on the composer in *The New Grove Dictionary of Music and Musicians,* 2nd ed., ed. Stanley Sadie and John Tyrrell (London: Macmillan, 2001), 21:667–76. For the connections to Brescia, see Richard Agee, "Ruberto Strozzi and the Early Madrigal," *Journal of the American Musicological Society* 36 (1983): 12; Richard Agee, "Filippo Strozzi and the Early Madrigal," *Journal of the American Musicological Society* 38 (1985): 236; and Feldman, *City Culture,* 32.

15. Feldman, *City Culture,* 384; Lewis, *Antonio Gardano,* 2:20–22; Ongaro, "The Chapel," 88–91.

16. Concerning de Rore's *Terzo libro,* see Lewis, "Rore's Setting," 365–409, and Bernstein, *Music Printing,* no. 73.

17. I would like to thank Lewis Lockwood for verifying ink colors.

18. Lewis, *Antonio Gardano,* 2:19. Part of her evidence is the fact that the partbooks were bound by the Venetian "Apple Binder."

19. She cites as evidence the similarity between the hand of the manuscript and that in an autograph document signed by Cambio; none of Cambio's pieces in *Wolf* is provided with a composer attribution. Lewis's extended study of this manuscript is eagerly awaited.

20. The manuscript correction supplies music missing in the bass part of *Che cosa al mondo far potea* in Cambio's *Madrigali a cinque voci* (Venice: [Girolamo Scotto], 1545). According to Bernstein, *Music Printing,* no. 49, of the four surviving copies of the bass, two have printed corrections, one has a manuscript correction, and one has no correction at all.

21. Lewis, "Rore's Setting," 405–6.

22. It may also be significant that there are no part names on the Munich leaves. The scribe of *Wolf* was probably working from a source that did not give part names; with no guidance about how to interpret the cleffing of the lower inner voices, he placed what would later be called the quinta pars into the tenor partbook, the tenor into the sexta partbook, and the sexta pars into the quinta partbook.

23. The hand of Mus Ms 1503g has not been identified, though Lewis, in a 1987 paper, suggested that it was identical to the hand of *Wolf.* It is possible that Mus Ms 1503g will turn out to be a Cambio autograph and that he will be considered the composer of this five-voice setting of *Bella guerriera* (he published a four-voice setting in 1554).

24. Bayerische Staatsbibliothek, *Katalog,* 2, 63, lists the provenance as unknown ("Herkunft unbekannt, zweite Hälfte 16. Jh."). Iain Fenlon and John Milsom ("'Ruled Paper Imprinted': Music Paper and Patents in Sixteenth-Century England," *Journal of the American Musicological Society* 37 [1984]: 143–44) list *Mu* among the Herwart collection that came to Munich in 1585 and 1594. In addition to the bibliography cited by Fenlon and Milsom, see most recently Arthur J. Ness, "The Herwarth Lute Manuscripts at the Bavarian State Library, Munich: A Bibliographical Study with Emphasis on the Works of Marco dall'Aquila and Melchior Newsidler" (Ph.D. diss., New York University, 1984); Joshua Rifkin, "Jean Michel, Maistre Jhan and a Chorus of Beats," *Tijdschrift van de koninklijke vereniging voor nederlandse muziekgeschiedenis* 52 (2002): 69; and JoAnn Taricani, "A Renaissance Bibliophile as Musical Patron: The Evidence of the Herwart Sketchbooks," *Notes: Quarterly Journal of the Music Library Association* 49 (1993): 1357–89.

25. Agee, "Ruberto Strozzi," 12–13; translation by Agee; original text (based on Agee's published transcription, but with abbreviations expanded and u/v according to modern practice): "Ho rice[v]uto la sua con il madrigal che glie fece cipriano, che per non haver tempo hora non posso mandarli il cambio per non essere ancor fornito il mottetto qual cipriano ha ormai in bon essere, poi la sua tornata da Venetia." For an important emendation of Agee's reading of the letter, see Feldman, *City Culture*, 32; Feldman establishes the year of the letter as 1542.

26. Feldman, *City Culture*, 262.

27. Lewis, *Antonio Gardano*, 2: no. 177.

28. On Donato's first book of madrigals, see Feldman, *City Culture*, esp. 384–405.

29. Ibid., 395, and personal communication. I am grateful to Martha Feldman for sharing her discovery of the probable source of the text with me and for sending me a photocopy. The text was also set by Vincenzo Ruffo (1553, lines 1–9 only) and Aurelio Roccia (1571). See Emil Vogel et al., *Bibliografia della musica italiana vocale profana ("Il nuovo Vogel")* (Pomezia: Staderini, 1977).

30. I thank Hyungjung Choi for setting this complicated example with her customary flair.

2

New Perspectives on Bach's Great Eighteen Chorales

RUSSELL STINSON

J. S. Bach's "Great Eighteen" chorales, BWV 651–668, are undeniably among the composer's most celebrated works for the organ. The collection has long been championed by performers as church and concert repertory, and recognized by musicologists as a milestone in the history of the organ chorale. Not surprisingly, the music has also spawned a vast literature.

Over the past dozen years or so, these writings have dealt in particular with issues of chronology and authenticity. Since so much of this research has been published in piecemeal fashion, one suspects that even most Bach specialists are not fully aware of its importance. Thus one of the goals of this essay is to summarize the most significant of these findings. The other is to present some of my own research.[1]

To judge from the surviving manuscripts, these works originated not as a collection but as independent compositions. They evidently were composed no later than 1717, Bach's last year as court organist in Weimar, since virtually all the earliest manuscripts were penned by two members of Bach's Weimar circle: Johann Gottfried Walther and Johann Tobias Krebs.[2] These sources also transmit the chorales in versions that clearly predate those found in Bach's autograph of the collection, which he wrote out in Leipzig around 1740. On the basis of their relatively sophisticated musical style, none of the chorales could have been composed before Bach's Mühlhausen period, 1707–8.

Unfortunately, it is not possible to assign any of these Weimar sources to specific years within Bach's Weimar period (1708–17). Rather, in dating these early versions, matters of musical style are our best guide. To this end, we may turn to an impressive series of articles by Jean-Claude Zehnder on Bach's early style.[3] Zehnder has shown convincingly how the Great Eighteen relate to works by Bach's predecessors and contemporaries, and how they compare to other compositions by Bach himself. He has also proposed a chronology for the early versions.

Along these lines, let us consider six examples. The first three are the only examples in the collection of the chorale motet, whose modus operandi is to establish each phrase of the hymn tune as a point of imitation, always using the same basic rhythms for each imitative statement (as opposed to a concluding statement in augmentation, which is a hallmark of the cantus firmus chorale). Depending on the length of the tune, the technique can become monotonous, which might explain why Bach left behind only a few youthful specimens of this chorale type, including two ("Ehre sei dir, Christe, der du leidest Not" and "Nun lasst uns den Leib begraben") from the Neumeister Collection. Perhaps as he matured as a composer, Bach found the severity of the chorale motet a hindrance to his creativity.

The three chorale motets in question are the two settings of "Jesus Christus, unser Heiland," the first with pedal, the second for manuals alone; and the second setting of "Komm, Heiliger Geist, Herre Gott." As Zehnder has shown, they are probably among the first pieces in the collection to have been composed, and for reasons other than just the presence of this chorale type. For all three are very similar in style to church cantatas composed by Bach during his year in Mühlhausen. Accordingly, Zehnder dates these three organ chorales to this year as well.

One of the trademarks of these cantatas is the depiction of individual lines and even individual words of the text. Whereas this procedure achieves a particularly close correspondence between text and music, in agreement with Luther's notion of "the proclamation of the word,"[4] Bach often applies it with sufficient emphasis to fragment a single movement into several distinct sections. Two of the chorale motets from the Great Eighteen use similar techniques. The *pedaliter* "Jesus Christus, unser Heiland" changes countermelodies between phrases for the sake of text painting, while the "Komm, Heiliger Geist" arrangement ends with a veritable flurry of notes to symbolize the word "Hallelujah." That the bass voice of the *pedaliter* "Jesus Christus" vacillates between manual and pedal is a further sign of an early date.[5]

The last movement of the most famous of the Mühlhausen cantatas, *Gottes Zeit ist die allerbeste Zeit*, BWV 106, and the *manualiter* "Jesus Christus, unser Heiland" offer a further analogy. Both are chorale settings whose basic rhythm changes midway through from quarters and eighths, respectively, to sixteenth notes. (In neither instance, though, does this unusual acceleration seem textually motivated.)

Bach's organ chorale "Valet will ich dir geben," BWV 735a, whose earliest source dates from ca. 1708–10, provides additional evidence that the three chorale motets from the Great Eighteen are relatively early.[6] As Zehnder points out, not only is this work also a chorale motet, but much of its figuration is virtually identical to that of the *pedaliter* "Jesus Christus, unser Heiland." In both pieces the chorale tune tends to sound against the same two motives—a dotted rhythm and a disjunct, syncopated figure—which are integrated to produce continuous motion in sixteenth notes (see examples 2.1 and 2.2). Bach's model here with respect to form and figuration was probably Georg Böhm, organist at St. John's Church in Lüneburg

Example 2.1. "Valet will ich dir geben," BWV 735a, mm. 31–35. Hans Klotz, ed., *Johann Sebastian Bach: Neue Ausgabe sämtlicher Werke*, ser. IV, vol. 3 (*Die einzeln überlieferten Orgelchoräle*). Kassel: Bärenreiter, 1961, 82. Reprinted by permission.

Example 2.2. "Jesus Christus, unser Heiland," BWV 665a, mm. 22–25. Hans Klotz, ed., *Johann Sebastian Bach: Neue Ausgabe sämtlicher Werke,* ser. IV, vol. 2 (*Die Orgelchoräle aus der Leipziger Originalhandschrift*). Kassel: Bärenreiter, 1958, 188. Reprinted by permission.

while Bach was a student there from 1700 to 1702, and an important composer of chorale motets.[7]

A fourth work from the Great Eighteen consistent with Bach's Mühlhausen cantata style is the three-verse setting of "O Lamm Gottes, unschuldig." In verse 3, exactly where the word "verzagen" (despair) appears in the hymn text, descending chromatic lines suddenly appear, and the meter switches from compound to simple triple. Bach uses precisely this type of chromaticism to symbolize grief in the second movement of the Mühlhausen cantata *Gott ist mein König,* BWV 71, and in the *pedaliter* "Jesus Christus, unser Heiland" from the Great Eighteen. Because of its relationship to the Mühlhausen cantatas, Zehnder also assigns "O Lamm Gottes" to 1707–8.

A fifth work is the first setting of "Allein Gott in der Höh sei Ehr," which exemplifies the ornamental chorale. The ornamentation in this piece is for the most part not indicated by symbols but rather by runs in thirty-second and even sixty-fourth notes, much in the style of contemporary Italian violin music. These rhythms are extremely rare in Bach's Mühlhausen cantatas but standard in his earliest datable cantatas from Weimar, composed in 1713–14. One of these cantatas, *Ich hatte viel Bekümmernis,* BWV 21, offers an especially close parallel, since its introductory sinfonia—which makes regular use of these fast rhythms—includes in its penultimate measure a brief oboe cadenza. This setting of "Allein Gott" also concludes with a solo cadenza, a most unusual gesture for an organ chorale.

A further clue as to date of composition is the way in which the accompanimental voices of this chorale refer throughout to the two themes stated by the inner parts at the outset of the piece. Such unanimity immediately brings to mind Bach's *Orgelbüchlein,* a collection of organ chorales distinguished by motivically unified accompaniments. Bach probably began work on the *Orgelbüchlein* early during his Weimar period, but by 1712 at the latest.[8] On the basis of this correspondence, plus those involving the cantatas, Zehnder dates this arrangement of "Allein Gott" to 1711–13.

A sixth and final work is the trio on "Nun komm, der Heiden Heiland," which is the only one of the Great Eighteen to employ the "patented" ritornello formula of Antonio Vivaldi. This is a type of ritornello, appropriated by Bach on many occasions, consisting of three clearly differentiated and easily separated segments, each of which has its own function. The first segment grounds the tonality with mostly tonic and dominant harmonies, ending usually on the dominant; the second entails a sequence whose chords progress in the order of descending fifths; and the third concludes the theme with a satisfying dominant-tonic cadence. In the ritornello of his organ chorale, Bach follows this syntax to the letter (see example 2.3). The first segment (mm. 1–3), once it moves beyond the chorale tune, alternates between tonic and dominant harmonies, concluding on the

Example 2.3. "Nun komm, der Heiden Heiland," BWV 660a, mm. 1–8. Hans Klotz, ed., *Johann Sebastian Bach: Neue Ausgabe sämtlicher Werke*, ser. IV, vol. 2 (*Die Orgelchoräle aus der Leipziger Originalhandschrift*). Kassel: Bärenreiter, 1958, 160. Reprinted by permission.

dominant; the second (mm. 4–5) forms a "textbook" circle-of-fifths sequence (and adopts other Vivaldian traits such as motoric sixteenth notes and triadic contours); and the third (mm. 6–7) brings it to a close with an authentic cadence.

Regarding Bach's use of canon for the first three measures of his ritornello, one might assume this was the master contrapuntist's way of grafting his own style onto an otherwise "foreign" design. But Vivaldi was no stranger to this technique. Two of his most famous concertos open with canons, and both of them were transcribed for organ by Bach (BWV 594 and 596). The latter transcription, that of the D-Minor concerto, op. 3, no. 11, even begins, like our organ chorale, in trio texture and with canonic writing at the unison in the tenor and bass registers.

In light of this connection, it may be significant that Bach's autograph manuscript of this transcription originated during 1714–17, since this is also the date of his autograph of the early version of this organ chorale.[9]

(Incidentally, this is the only early version of any of the Great Eighteen chorales that exists in autograph.) Because the autograph of the organ chorale is not a composing score, this dating means only that 1717 is the latest possible year of composition. Considering Vivaldi's profound impact on the work, it can scarcely date from before 1713, the year in which Bach appears to have encountered Vivaldi's concertos for the first time.[10] Zehnder's findings indicate that Bach did not begin writing "Vivaldian" ritornellos until his church cantatas of 1715–16, suggesting that this chorale setting also stems from these years. If so, the trio on "Nun komm" was one of the last of the Great Eighteen to be composed.

To summarize Zehnder's research, Bach was involved intermittently with the composition of the Great Eighteen from 1707 to 1717. Decades later, as *Thomaskantor* and *Director Musices* in Leipzig, he decided to revise the works and assemble them into a collection, perhaps for the purpose of publication. His autograph manuscript, which is outlined in table 2.1, begins with his own entries of the first fifteen of the Great Eighteen, followed by the sixteenth and seventeenth chorales in the hand of Johann Christoph

Table 2.1. The Contents of the Autograph Manuscript of the Great Eighteen Chorales.

BWV No.	Title	Foliation	Scribe	Date of Entry
		f. 1^r (blank page)		
651	Komm, Heiliger Geist, Herre Gott	f. 1^v–3^r	Bach	ca. 1739–42
652	Komm, Heiliger Geist, Herre Gott	f. 3^v–5^v	Bach	ca. 1739–42
653	An Wasserflüssen Babylon	f. 5^v–6^v	Bach	ca. 1739–42
654	Schmücke dich, o liebe Seele	f. 6^v–7^v	Bach	ca. 1739–42
655	Herr Jesu Christ, dich zu uns wend	f. 7^v–9^r	Bach	ca. 1739–42
656	O Lamm Gottes, unschuldig	f. 9^r–10^r	Bach	ca. 1739–42
657	Nun danket alle Gott	f. 10^v–11^r	Bach	ca. 1739–42
658	Von Gott will ich nicht lassen	f. 11^v–12^r	Bach	ca. 1739–42
659	Nun komm, der Heiden Heiland	f. 12^r–13^r	Bach	ca. 1739–42
660	Nun komm, der Heiden Heiland	f. 13^r–13^v	Bach	ca. 1739–42
661	Nun komm, der Heiden Heiland	f. 13^v–14^v	Bach	ca. 1739–42
662	Allein Gott in der Höh sei Ehr	f. 15^r–15^v	Bach	ca. 1739–42
663	Allein Gott in der Höh sei Ehr	f. 15^v–17^v	Bach	ca. 1739–42
664	Allein Gott in der Höh sei Ehr	f. 17^v–19^r	Bach	ca. 1746–47
665	Jesus Christus, unser Heiland	f. 19^v–20^r	Bach	ca. 1746–47
666	Jesus Christus, unser Heiland	f. 20^v–21^r	Altnikol	August 1750–April 1751
667	Komm, Gott Schöpfer, Heiliger Geist	f. 21^v–22^r	Altnikol	August 1750–April 1751
769a	Canonic Variations on "Vom Himmel hoch"	f. 22^v–25^v	Bach	ca. 1747–48
668	Vor deinen Thron tret ich hiermit (incomplete)	f. 25^v	anonymous copyist	April-July 1750
		f. 26 (lost)		

Altnikol, a pupil of Bach's in Leipzig from 1744 to 1748. The Canonic Variations on "Vom Himmel hoch" next appear, in Bach's hand, followed by the eighteenth chorale ("Vor deinen Thron tret ich hiermit") in the hand of an anonymous scribe who belonged to Bach's Leipzig circle toward the end of the composer's life. This entry was presumably made, at Bach's request, between his first unsuccessful eye operation at the end of March 1750 and his death four months later.[11]

One of the most important findings registered in recent years about the Great Eighteen is Yoshitake Kobayashi's discovery that Bach began work on this manuscript around 1740, rather than about five years later, as was previously believed.[12] Kobayashi demonstrates on the basis of Bach's handwriting that he notated the first thirteen chorales around 1739–42, and the fourteenth and fifteenth chorales around 1746–47.

The different phases of Bach's script may be seen in figure 2.1. This page of the autograph begins with the last measures of the second setting of "Allein Gott," notated between ca. 1739 and 1742, and continues with the opening bars of the third setting, entered about four years later. Generally speaking, Bach's hand in the earlier entry tends to slant somewhat to the right, as opposed to the more vertical (and smaller) script of the later entry. Differences also exist with respect to particular symbols. A glance at the second, third, and fourth systems, for instance, reveals that the quarter rests of the earlier entry are relatively ornate. Most telling are the half notes with downward stems, which in the earlier entry have oval-shaped noteheads with stems on the left, and in the later entry have rounder noteheads (which are sometimes open at the top) with stems in the middle.

Bach's entry of the fifteenth chorale is followed on the next four pages by Altnikol's entries of the sixteenth and seventeenth chorales. The next seven pages contain Bach's entry of the Canonic Variations. This work was published in 1747, to commemorate Bach's induction in June of that year into Lorenz Mizler's Society of Musical Sciences (*Societät der Musicalischen Wissenschaften*). The published version (BWV 769) is clearly earlier than that found in the autograph (BWV 769a), which implies that the latter version did not originate before 1747. To judge from Bach's script, he entered this version into the autograph in either 1747 or 1748.[13]

To return to Altnikol, his presence in this manuscript raises a host of questions. Scholars have traditionally assumed that his two entries predate Bach's entry of the Canonic Variations, and this theory agrees both with Kobayashi's redating of the autograph and the time frame of Altnikol's study with Bach. The composer could have instructed his pupil to add these two compositions to the fifteen he had already notated.

Why, however, would Bach have entrusted this task to a student when he could have entered both works himself? In preparing this manuscript, he was not laboring under any time constraints, such as a Sunday deadline, that would have necessitated outside help. Rather, he was taking time to

Figure 2.1. Autograph Score of "Allein Gott in der Höh sei Ehr," BWV 663, mm. 120–127; and "Allein Gott in der Höh sei Ehr," BWV 664, mm. 1–16. Staatsbibliothek zu Berlin—Preussischer Kulturbesitz [D-Bsb], Musikabteilung mit Mendelssohn-Archiv, Mus. ms. Bach P 271, p. 90. Used by permission.

inscribe these works in a remarkably legible and even calligraphic fashion, and to revise the musical content of each and every one as well.

Moreover, recent investigations into Bach's musical estate raise the possibility that Altnikol could have entered both works sometime after Bach's death in 1750. For in 1749 he had married Bach's daughter Elisabeth Juliana Friederica, and there is reason to believe she inherited autograph manuscripts of her father's music.[14] If the autograph of the Great Eighteen was one of these, Altnikol had direct access to this source from 1750 until his death in 1759. Also suggestive in this regard is the fact that Bach's son Carl Philipp Emanuel Bach, at the time of his death in 1788, owned this autograph as well as several of Altnikol's J. S. Bach copies.[15] He may have come into the possession of all these sources through his stepsister, shortly after Altnikol's death.

Very recently, Peter Wollny has uncovered further evidence that points in this direction.[16] He has shown, first of all, that Altnikol's two entries in the autograph represent a different phase of his handwriting than do his Leipzig manuscripts that carry actual dates (1744 and 1748). Again, most revealing are the half notes with downward stems, which in the dated sources feature oval-shaped noteheads with stems on the left or right. As can be seen in figure 2.2, Altnikol's entry of the *manualiter* "Jesus Christus, unser Heiland," he draws these symbols in the autograph of the Great Eighteen with relatively large, round noteheads and with stems in the middle.[17]

Wollny also points out that the only Altnikol manuscripts that match his script in the Great Eighteen autograph are also partially in the hand of Bach's very last pupil, Johann Gottfried Müthel. During a year's leave of absence from the court at Schwerin, Müthel studied first with Bach in Leipzig from early May 1750 and then for a while with Altnikol in Naumburg. These jointly copied sources therefore could not have originated later than 1751. That they were prepared after Müthel left Leipzig—for Altnikol could have collaborated with him in Leipzig, say, while visiting his sick father-in-law—is indicated by their watermarks, which are atypical of that city.

We may conclude, then, that Altnikol made his two entries in Naumburg between August 1750—Bach died on July 28—and April 1751. Along with Kobayashi's redating of the autograph, the likelihood that Altnikol's portions of the manuscript originated after Bach's death significantly changes our understanding of the Great Eighteen as a collection, since Altnikol apparently added the sixteenth and seventeenth chorales without the composer's authorization. It follows that Bach left blank the four pages between the fifteenth chorale and the Canonic Variations simply as a means of separating the latter work—which is unquestionably an independent composition—from the preceding fifteen. Accordingly, Altnikol was careful in choosing two works of relatively modest size that would not exceed the available space. But size was obviously not the only criterion, since the first chorale he notated ("Jesus Christus, unser Heiland") is based on the same hymn as Bach's entry that precedes it.

Figure 2.2. Altnikol's entry of "Jesus Christus, unser Heiland," BWV 666, mm. 1–24. Staatsbibliothek zu Berlin—Preussischer Kulturbesitz [D-Bsb], Musikabteilung mit Mendelssohn-Archiv, Mus. ms. Bach P 271, p. 96. Used by permission.

To return to Kobayashi's redating of the autograph to around 1740, its most important implication is that Bach began the Great Eighteen shortly after completing Part III of the *Clavierübung,* published in 1739. Scholars have long recognized that Part III of the *Clavierübung* served as a model for the Great Eighteen in terms of its opening gesture (a majestic, *organo pleno* work), preference for multiple settings of the same chorale, use of certain musical devices to organize these multiple settings, and choice of particular hymns. But some striking differences suggest that he probably also regarded the two as complementary collections.

Consider, for instance, that they are quite distinct in the chorale types they employ. While the *Clavierübung* contains no fewer than seven specimens of the chorale fughetta—a brief fugue on the opening phrase of the chorale—the Great Eighteen contain none. Also completely absent from the Great Eighteen but represented in the *Clavierübung* by two large-scale works is the chorale canon, a canonic rendering of the entire chorale tune. Conversely, the ornamental chorale, which is the most common chorale type in the Great Eighteen, is not to be found in the earlier collection. The same goes for the chorale motet.

In more general terms, the assimilation of the *stile antico* in various works from the *Clavierübung,* the use of the chorale canon, and the choice of modal plainchant melodies give the collection a somewhat learned and anachronistic character.[18] Bach himself even seems to call attention to this by dedicating the collection to "Music Lovers and especially . . . Connoisseurs." Without question, the musical style of the Great Eighteen—with their tendency toward lyrical, dance-like settings of major-key tunes—makes them a more accessible group of pieces. Could it be that Bach intended them for a more dilettante audience?

Finally, let us consider the nature of the autograph manuscript. It is regularly cited in the literature as a fair copy (*Reinschrift*).[19] In truth, however, it contains many compositional revisions consistent with what Robert Marshall has termed a "revision copy," wherein the composer is copying from an existing source but simultaneously making compositional changes.[20]

A case in point is Bach's entry of the opening "fantasy" on "Komm, Heiliger Geist, Herre Gott." Its first page, given in figure 2.3, is a note-perfect reproduction of the early version.[21] Conversely, its fourth and final page (given in figure 2.4) contains enough compositional revisions to suggest a composing score, for the obvious reason that Bach is working here with thematic material not found in the early version. To set the word "Hallelujah," he introduces in m. 89 a fugue subject that he will manipulate for a full fifteen measures. Just as soon as the new theme appears for the first time, in the last measure of the top system, alto voice, Bach's script begins to lose its beautiful, calligraphic appearance, especially with regard to the placement of accidentals and spacing between notes.

Figure 2.3. Autograph score of "Komm, Heiliger Geist, Herre Gott," BWV 651, mm. 1–27. Staatsbibliothek zu Berlin—Preussischer Kulturbesitz [D-Bsb], Musikabteilung mit Mendelssohn-Archiv, Mus. ms. Bach P 271, p. 58. Used by permission.

Figure 2.4. Autograph score of "Komm, Heiliger Geist, Herre Gott," BWV 651, mm. 86–106. Staatsbibliothek zu Berlin—Preussischer Kulturbesitz [D-Bsb], Musikabteilung mit Mendelssohn-Archiv, Mus. ms. Bach P 271, p. 61. Used by permission.

To focus on the compositional revisions, the one in m. 98, which changed that inverted statement of the fugue subject from real to tonal, was dictated by the prevailing G-minor harmony. In five other instances a half note was fashioned from some faster note value. But it is impossible to say exactly which one, since all values less than a half note have the same size of notehead (and the same length of stem). Still, in all these revisions except the one in m. 102, the half note is preceded by the first seven sixteenth notes of the subject, in the same voice, implying eighths or sixteenths. An eighth note would have continued the theme, while a sixteenth would have allowed for back-to-back statements of its first half, as in mm. 90, 93–96, and 100.

Table 2.2 lists all of these revisions along with all of the other compositional revisions in this manuscript. An important conclusion to be drawn from Bach's compositional process is that his first three entries into this source are the only ones with a significant amount of added material. This statement suggests that when he began to compile the Great Eighteen chorales, Bach's energy was particularly high and that later on in the process his enthusiasm waned. This would explain not only the four-year hiatus between the thirteenth and fourteenth settings but also the likelihood that the collection was never properly completed.

It is infinitely more important, though, to realize that in no instance was Bach content just to copy a work: some inner force drove him as well to revise every one of the fifteen chorales he entered. This force, which may be regarded as the basic and final objective of the composer's methodology, is nothing less than the quest for perfection.[22] Accordingly, the revised versions of the Great Eighteen do not represent the "definitive" or "final" forms of these masterworks. They merely advance the music toward its ultimate goal.

Table 2.2. Compositional Revisions in the Autograph Manuscript of the Great Eighteen Chorales.

Measure	Beat	Voice	Revision
"Komm, Heiliger Geist, Herre Gott," BWV 651			
53	3–4	alto	half note changed to ♩♪♪
91	3–4	tenor	note originally faster rhythm than half note
97	1–2	soprano	note originally faster rhythm than half note
98	1	tenor	first note changed from a to g
101	1–2	alto	note originally faster rhythm than half note
102	3–4	alto	note originally faster rhythm than half note
103	1–2	soprano	note originally faster rhythm than half note
103	3	soprano	second note changed from b' to a'
"Komm, Heiliger Geist, Herre Gott," BWV 652			
118	2	alto	on second half of beat, eighth note on g' changed to two sixteenths on g' and f'
128	2	tenor	on second half of beat, eighth note on e' changed to two sixteenths on c#' and b
"An Wasserflüssen Babylon," BWV 653			
1	2	alto	rhythm changed from ♪♫ to ♫♪
2	1–2	alto	original reading is quarter note on g' followed by eighth note on f'
8	2	bass	pitch changed from A to e
39	2–3	soprano	original reading is half note on a'
79	1–2	soprano	original reading is half note on e''
"Schmücke dich, o liebe Seele," BWV 654			
80	3	soprano	rhythm changed from ♫. to .♫
86	1	soprano	rhythm changed from ♫ to ♫
105	1–2	bass	half note changed to quarter note followed by quarter rest
"Herr Jesu Christ, dich zu uns wend," BWV 655			
72	2	bass	original reading is eighth note on g followed by eighth rest
"O Lamm Gottes, unschuldig," BWV 656			
55	2	alto	both pitches (a' and e') originally half notes
61	1	soprano	original reading is half note on a'
70	2	alto	upper note (a') originally half note
128	9	alto	pitch changed from f' to g'
"Von Gott will ich nicht lassen," BWV 658			
7	3	soprano	original reading is four sixteenth notes on d'', b', g', and b'
"Nun komm, der Heiden Heiland," BWV 659			
5	2	soprano	original reading lacks appoggiatura on a'
16	3–4	soprano	quarter note changed to half note
24	3–4	soprano	quarter note changed to half note
"Nun komm, der Heiden Heiland," BWV 660			
25	3–4	left-hand	original reading is half note on g
"Allein Gott in der Höh sei Ehr," BWV 663			
26	1	alto	original reading is half note on g'
26	3	alto	original reading is half note on b
27	1	alto	original reading is half note on e'
"Jesus Christus, unser Heiland," BWV 665			
16	2	bass	second note changed from B to c#
29	1–2	soprano	half note changed to quarter note followed by quarter rest

Notes

This essay is a revised version of a paper delivered at the symposium "Bach in Leipzig—Bach und Leipzig," held in Leipzig in January 2000.

1. For a full discussion of all the issues raised here, see Russell Stinson, *J. S. Bach's Great Eighteen Organ Chorales* (New York: Oxford University Press, 2001).

2. On these manuscripts, see Hermann Zietz, *Quellenkritische Untersuchungen an den Bach-Handschriften P 801, P 802 und P 803 aus dem "Krebs'schen Nachlass" unter besonderer Berücksichtigung der Choralbearbeitungen des jungen J. S. Bach* (Hamburg: Karl Dieter Wagner, 1969); Stephen Daw, "Copies of J. S. Bach by Walther and Krebs: A Study of the Manuscripts P 801, P 802, and P 803," *The Organ Yearbook* 7 (1976): 31–58; and Kirsten Beißwenger, "Zur Chronologie der Notenhandschriften Johann Gottfried Walthers," in *Acht kleine Präludien und Studien über BACH: Georg von Dadelsen zum 70. Geburtstag am 17. November 1988* (Wiesbaden: Breitkopf & Härtel, 1988), 11–39.

3. Jean-Claude Zehnder, "Die Weimarer Orgelmusik Johann Sebastian Bachs im Spiegel seiner Kantaten," *Musik und Gottesdienst* 41 (1987): 149–62; Zehnder, "Georg Böhm und Johann Sebastian Bach: Zur Chronologie der Bachschen Stilentwicklung," *Bach-Jahrbuch* 74 (1988): 73–110; Zehnder, "Giuseppe Torelli und Johann Sebastian Bach: Zu Bachs Weimarer Konzertform," *Bach-Jahrbuch* 77 (1991): 33–95; Zehnder, "Zu Bachs Stilentwicklung in der Mühlhäuser und Weimarer Zeit," in *Das Frühwerk Johann Sebastian Bachs,* ed. Karl Heller and Hans-Joachim Schulze (Cologne: Studio, 1995), 311–38; and Zehnder, "Zum späten Weimarer Stil Johann Sebastian Bachs," in *Bachs Orchesterwerke: Bericht über das 1. Dortmunder Bach-Symposion 1996,* ed. Martin Geck, 89–124 (Witten: Klangfarben-Musikverlag, 1997).

4. Christoph Wolff et al., *The New Grove Bach Family* (New York: W. W. Norton, 1983), 124.

5. Because of its "migratory" bass line, this work is printed in the *Neue Bach-Ausgabe* on only two staves, with pedal cues. See Hans Klotz, ed., *Johann Sebastian Bach: Neue Ausgabe sämtlicher Werke,* ser. IV, vol. 2 (*Die Orgelchoräle aus der Leipziger Originalhandschrift*) (Kassel: Bärenreiter; Leipzig: VEB Deutscher Verlag für Musik, 1958); Klotz's *Kritischer Bericht* to this volume, p. 83; and Peter Williams, *The Organ Music of J. S. Bach,* 3 vols. (Cambridge: Cambridge University Press, 1980–84), 2:165.

6. See Zehnder, "Georg Böhm," 85–86. The source in question is the so-called *Plauener Orgelbuch.*

7. See ibid., 100–101; and Henning Müller-Buscher, *Georg Böhms Choralbearbeitungen für Tasteninstrumente* (Laaber: Laaber-Verlag, 1979), 95–105.

8. See Russell Stinson, "The Compositional History of Bach's *Orgelbüchlein* Reconsidered," *Bach Perspectives* 1 (1995): 43–78.

9. See Yoshitake Kobayashi, *Die Notenschrift Johann Sebastian Bachs: Dokumentation ihrer Entwicklung* (Kassel: Bärenreiter; Leipzig: VEB Deutscher Verlag für Musik, 1989), 207. (Kobayashi's study comprises ser. IX, vol. 2 of the *Neue Bach-Ausgabe.*)

10. See Hans-Joachim Schulze, *Studien zur Bach-Überlieferung im 18. Jahrhundert* (Leipzig: Edition Peters, 1984), 155–63.

11. See "The Deathbed Chorale: Exposing a Myth," in Christoph Wolff, *Bach: Essays on His Life and Music*, 282–94 (Cambridge, Mass.: Harvard University Press, 1991); and Yoshitake Kobayashi, "Zur Chronologie der Spätwerke Johann Sebastian Bachs: Kompositions- und Aufführungstätigkeit von 1736 bis 1750," *Bach-Jahrbuch* 74 (1988): 7–72.

12. Kobayashi, "Zur Chronologie der Spätwerke," 45, 56–57; and his *Die Notenschrift*, 207.

13. See Kobayashi, "Zur Chronologie der Spätwerke," 60.

14. See Yoshitake Kobayashi, "Zur Teilung des Bachschen Erbes," in *Acht kleine Präludien und Studien über BACH*, 67–75, esp. 69.

15. See Peter Wollny, "Zur Überlieferung der Instrumentalwerke Johann Sebastian Bachs: Der Quellenbesitz Carl Philipp Emanuel Bachs," *Bach-Jahrbuch* 82 (1996): 7–21, esp. 12–13.

16. See the preface to the facsimile edition of the autograph, *Johann Sebastian Bach: Die Achtzehn Grossen Orgelchoräle BWV 651–668 und Canonische Veränderungen über "Vom Himmel hoch" BWV 769* (Laaber: Laaber-Verlag, 1999).

17. The barely visible inscription *Von Altnikols Hand* at the top of figure 2.2 was penned by Georg Poelchau, the owner of this manuscript in the early nineteenth century; see Clark Kelly, "Johann Sebastian Bach's 'Eighteen Chorales,' BWV 651–668: Perspectives on Editions and Hymnology" (D.M.A. diss., Eastman School of Music, 1988), 87.

18. See Christoph Wolff, *Der stile antico in der Musik Johann Sebastian Bachs: Studien zu Bachs Spätwerk* (Wiesbaden: Franz Steiner, 1968).

19. See, for example, the *Kritischer Bericht* to ser. IV, vol. 2 of the *Neue Bach-Ausgabe*, 14.

20. Robert Lewis Marshall, *The Compositional Process of J. S. Bach: A Study of the Autograph Scores of the Vocal Works*, 2 vols. (Princeton: Princeton University Press, 1972), 1:4–5.

21. Looking back on my days as a graduate student at the University of Chicago, I fondly recall that a framed facsimile of this page of the autograph also adorned the Hyde Park home of Bob and Traute Marshall.

22. See Wolff et al., *The New Grove Bach Family*, 167.

3

Historical Theology and Hymnology as Tools for Interpreting Bach's Church Cantatas: The Case of *Ich elender Mensch, wer wird mich erlösen,* BWV 48

Stephen A. Crist

The purpose of this essay is to demonstrate, in the manner of a case study, how information from the disciplines of historical theology and hymnology can inform the interpretation of a church cantata by Johann Sebastian Bach. The work under consideration, *Ich elender Mensch, wer wird mich erlösen* (BWV 48), received its first performance in Leipzig on the Nineteenth Sunday after Trinity, 3 October 1723. I will draw attention to several remarkable features of this cantata and show how knowledge of its theological and liturgical contexts sheds new light on these compositional procedures. The primary sources consulted for this study are listed below. These items constitute a representative sample of the kinds of materials that can be brought to bear on the interpretation of Bach's cantatas. The commentaries and sermons are primarily from books in Bach's personal theological library or with demonstrably close connections to the composer.[1]

Musical, Theological, and Hymnological Sources for Interpreting Bach's Cantata 48

Music Manuscripts

(1) autograph score of BWV 48: Staatsbibliothek zu Berlin—Preussischer Kulturbesitz [D-Bsb], Musikabteilung mit Mendelssohn-Archiv, Mus. ms. Bach P 109
(2) original performance parts for BWV 48: D-Bsb, Musikabteilung mit Mendelssohn-Archiv, Mus. ms. Bach St 53

Biblical Commentaries

(3) Abraham Calov, *Das Neue Testament / verdeutschet durch D. Martin Luthern / Nach der eigentlichen Intention und Meinung des Heil. Geistes / Aus den Worten des Grund-Texts / Wie auch Aus dem Context, und Parallel-Sprüchen / und aus den Schrifften des theuren Mannes GOttes LUTHERI, in dem einigen waren Buchstäblichen-Verstande / zum heilsamen Gebrauch / mit Lehren / Widerlegen / Erinnerung / und Trost / fürgestellet* (Wittenberg: Christian Schrödter, 1682)

(4) Johann Olearius, *Biblischer Erklärung Fünfter und letzter Theil. Darinnen das gantze Neue Testament Nehmlich Die vier Evangelisten / Die Apostel-Geschichte / Die Apostolischen Episteln / und Die H. Offenbarung Johannis / enthalten / Ebenmäßig Aus der Grund-Sprache deß Heiligen Geistes betrachtet / und mit nothwendiger Lehre / Trost und Vermahnung / zu GOttes Ehre / und täglicher Beförderung der waren Gottseeligkeit / vorgestellet wird* (Leipzig: Johann Christoph Tarnoven, 1681)

(5) August Pfeiffer, *Kern und Safft der Bibel / Oder Kurtze / und nach dem Sinn des Heiligen Geistes durchgehends gründliche / auch deutliche Biblische Erklärung der auserlesensten Macht-Sprüche / nachdencklichen Redens-Arten und Krafft-Wörter, Welche in des / um die Kirche Christi hochverdienten gedachten Theologi, so wohl vor, als nach seinem Ableiben, in Druck gegebenen deutschen Schrifften vorkommen, Mit Fleiß ausgesucht, in Biblische Ordnung gebracht, und Mit nützlichen Registern ausgefertiget von Einem Evangelischen Prediger* (Dresden: Johann Christoph Zimmermann, 1718)

Sermons for the Nineteenth Sunday after Trinity

(6) Martin Luther, 26 October 1522[2]

(7) Luther, 2 October 1524;[3] reprinted in *Sommerpostille* 1526

(8) Luther, 5 October 1529;[4] reprinted in Cruciger's *Sommerpostille*

(9) Luther, 19 October 1533;[5] reworked into *Hauspostille* 1544 version[6]

(10) Heinrich Müller, *Evangelische Schluß-Kette / Und Krafft-Kern / Oder Gründliche Außlegung Der Sonn- und Fest-Tags-Evangelien / Worinnen nicht allein der Buchstab / nach dem Sinn deß Geistes / erkläret / sondern auch die Glaubens-Stärckung und Lebens-Besserung / auß den Krafft-Wörtern der Grund-Sprachen heraus gezogen / vorgetragen wird: Hiebevor in öffentlichen Predigten vorgestellet / hernach auff sehr vieler Gott-liebenden Hertzen flehentliches Anhalten zum Druck befördert* (Frankfurt am Main: Balthasar Christoph Wusten, 1698)

(11) August Hermann Francke, *Sonn- Fest- und Apostel-Tags-Predigten, darinnen die zum wahren Christenthum gehörige nöthigste und vornehmste Materien abgehandelt sind; nebst den darzu nützlichen Registern* (Halle: [Wäysen-Hause], 1709)

(12) August Hermann Francke, *Kurtze Sonn- und Fest[-]Tags-Predigten / Darinnen / Vornemlich zum wahren / lebendigen Kraft-vollen und in guten Früchten sich beweisenden Glauben, die nöthige Aufweckung und Anweisung gegeben wird, / Anderer Theil* (Halle: Wäysen-Hause, 1716)

(13) August Hermann Francke, *Sonn- und Fest-Tags-Predigten / Welche Theils in*

Halle / theils an verschiedenen auswärtigen Oertern von wichtigen und auserlesenen Materien gehalten worden, Nebst Vorbereitungen auf die hohen Feste und nützlichen Registern (Halle: Wäysen-Hause, 1724)

(14) Martin Geier, *Zeit und Ewigkeit, nach Gelegenheit der ordentlichen Sonntags-Evangelien in des HErrn Furcht hiebevor der Christlichen Gemeine in Leipzig Anno 1664. fürgestellet* (Leipzig: In Verlegung Friedrich Lanckischens sel. Erben, 1715)

Hymnological Sources

(15) Johann Christoph Olearius, *Evangelischer Lieder-Schatz: darinn allerhand auserlesene Gesänge, so sich auff alle Sonn- und Fest-Tags Evangelia schicken* (Jena: Johan Felix Bielcken, 1705-7)

(16) Johann Avenarius, *Evangelischer Lieder-Catechißmus Darinnen Die gantze Christliche Lehre nach Anweisung der Sechs Hauptstücke des H. Catechismi Lutheri durch erbauliche Lieder erläutert und mit raren Historien auch andern nachdencklichen Remarqven erkläret / Vormahls seiner anvertrauten Gemeinde in einen richtigen Jahrgang durch ordentliche Predigten vorgetragen / nunmehro aber auf Begehren in geschickten Dispositionibus dargestellet Und Mit vollständigen Registern versehen* (Frankfurt and Leipzig: In Verlegung Joh. Christoph. Stössels seel. Erben in Erffurth, 1714)

(17) Caspar Binder, *Historischer Erweiß Daß des bekandten Liedes unserer Kirchen: Ach GOtt und HErr, wie gros und schwer etc. wahrer Auctor sey M. MARTIN. RUTILIUS Ex matre nepos Georg. Rorarii, amanuensis Luthe[ri] weiland Archidiaconus bey der Haupt- und Pfarr[-]Kirchen zu Weimar; Gleichwie von dem Zusatz: Gleichwie sich fein ein Vögelein etc. Auctor ist M. JOHANN MAIOR t. t. Diaconus daselbst* (Jena: Mit Wertherischen Schrifften, 1726)

The Cantata *Ich elender Mench, wer wird mich erlösen*, BWV 48

BWV 48/1: Chorus

Text:

Ich elender Mensch, wer wird mich erlösen vom Leibe dieses Todes?

Wretched man that I am, who will deliver me from the body of this death? (Romans 7:24)[7]

The opening chorus is by far the most extensive movement. Bach's composition unites three separate musical complexes. The first is a haunting ritornello presented by the strings and continuo (mm. 1–12). The second is constituted by the choral parts, a series of canonic and fugal sections arranged as follows (the order in which the voices enter is given in parentheses):

mm. 13–21 = canon at the lower fourth (S, A)
mm. 31–44 = fugal exposition (B, T, S, A)
mm. 57–65 = canon at the lower fourth (T, B)
mm. 75–88 = fugal exposition (A, S, T, B)
mm. 89–107 = fugal exposition and episode (S, A, T, B)
mm. 114–120 = fugal exposition (S/A, T, B)
mm. 121–138 = fugal exposition and conclusion (T, B, S, A)

Superimposed on these two overlapping layers is a chorale melody, which is presented one phrase at a time in a canon at the lower fourth by the trumpet and first and second oboes in unison.

This imposing musical structure is based upon a short rhetorical question from St. Paul's Epistle to the Romans, an exclamation of despair over the strength and pervasiveness of sin. Earlier in Chapter 7, Paul describes his seeming powerlessness against it: "For what I do is not the good I want to do; no, the evil I do not want to do—this I keep on doing" (Romans 7:19). He then characterizes the life-long struggle between the flesh and the spirit as a battle between God's law (which rules the soul) and the opposing law of sin (which rules the body): "For in my inner being I delight in God's law; but I see another law at work in the members of my body, waging war against the law of my mind and making me a prisoner of the law of sin at work within my members" (Romans 7:22–23). Verse 24 is the climax of this discourse, expressing the apostle's profound distress about this situation.

In Cantata 48 the speaker of these words is not just St. Paul. A Gospel reading would have preceded the performance of the cantata. It tells the story of Jesus' healing of a paralytic:

> Jesus stepped into a boat, crossed over and came to his own town. Some men brought to him a paralytic, lying on a mat. When Jesus saw their faith, he said to the paralytic, "Take heart, son; your sins are forgiven." At this, some of the teachers of the law said to themselves, "This fellow is blaspheming!" Knowing their thoughts, Jesus said, "Why do you entertain evil thoughts in your hearts? Which is easier: to say, 'Your sins are forgiven,' or to say, 'Get up and walk'? But so that you may know that the Son of Man has authority on earth to forgive sins. . . ." Then he said to the paralytic, "Get up, take your mat and go home." And the man got up and went home. When the crowd saw this, they were filled with awe; and they praised God, who had given such authority to men (Matthew 9:1–8).[8]

It was generally understood among Lutheran theologians of Bach's time that the man's condition was the result of a stroke. For instance, in his commentary on verse 2, Calov noted that the paralysis stemmed from "a stroke."[9] Moreover, a stroke was considered to be an especially "dangerous" form of illness, because it is so sudden and unexpected and leaves people in such a "wretched" state. Francke articulated this as follows:

> παραλυτικος usually refers to one who has suffered a stroke, which is one of the most dangerous and most wretched diseases. That is why it is said of men who have suffered a stroke that they are touched by the hand of God; because the power that God has over life and death is revealed in a special way when it happens suddenly and unexpectedly that a man is placed in such a wretched state. For παραλυσις means essentially *solutio neruorum*, a disintegration of a man's nerves and veins that makes him incapable of all bodily tasks.[10]

Romans 7:24 not only represents the despair of St. Paul and the paralytic, it also constitutes the communal cry of all humanity. The continuation of the passage by Francke quoted above asserts that "this physical illness is an illustration of the sickness of our souls; we too suffer a stroke, so to speak."[11] This echoes a comment from Luther's 1533 sermon for the Nineteenth Sunday after Trinity: "The paralytic here is a picture of all sinners. For this is the kind of disease in which the limbs no longer can be used, and when one wants to move his foot or hand toward himself, he cannot do it and it just stretches farther away."[12]

Luther's and Francke's view that the paralytic and his illness are emblematic of mankind's universal spiritual malaise is rooted in the belief that the origin of human misery is original sin. This notion is reflected in Calov's parenthetical comment on the words "Ich elender Mensch": "who, because of his sinful, depraved nature, truly is wretched."[13] Likewise, Francke stated plainly that "sin is the cause of all our misery."[14] And in a similar vein, Müller wrote that "one flows from the other, misery from sin."[15]

Not only does sin inevitably lead to a state of "misery," but the struggle against sin continues through to the end of our earthly existence. The rubric at the beginning of the last section of Romans 7 (vv. 14–25) in the Calov Bible speaks of the believer's "constant battle" against fleshly desires: "How there may be with the reborn [i.e., Christians] great imperfection and a constant battle of the flesh with the spirit."[16] And Calov's commentary on St. Paul's expression "Leibe dieses Todes" contains an even clearer statement of this idea:

> That is, from this mortal body, which always carries death within itself (whether this be understood as natural or spiritual death), because of the remaining sinful desires that stick to us the whole time of this earthly life, even after rebirth, and always incite a believer of God to sin or to sinful longings.[17]

By interpreting Romans 7:24 as the cry of the paralytic in Matthew 9:1–8, Bach's anonymous librettist convincingly linked this verse with the Nineteenth Sunday after Trinity, despite the fact that it does not belong to the appointed readings. (The Epistle for this occasion was Ephesians 4:22–28.) But the librettist may also have been aware of a theological precedent connecting this verse with this specific Sunday. In his 1524 sermon for the Nineteenth Sunday after Trinity, Luther had alluded to Romans 7 in his remarks about the stubbornness of sin: "Sin, which sticks firmly to us, always hangs around our neck. St. Paul speaks to the Romans about this in the seventh chapter, but we will experience it in death."[18] Francke, perhaps picking up on this suggestion in Luther's sermon, went so far as to quote Romans 7:24 in full in connection with this liturgical occasion:

> Behold, when a man recognizes the problem of his sin, he yearns for salvation and a savior, and with Paul begins to sigh: Wretched man that I am, who will deliver me from the body of this death? Indeed, he yearns for the physician who can rescue him even from death.[19]

In view of the emphasis on law—both God's law and the opposing law of sin—in Romans 7, it is not surprising that Bach should have made extensive use of canon and fugue, two of the "strictest" contrapuntal procedures, in BWV 48/1. In this respect, the movement is similar to the chorus at the beginning of Cantata 77, which was first performed just six weeks earlier, on the Thirteenth Sunday after Trinity (22 August 1723). The contrapuntal artifice of BWV 77/1 includes a canon, in which each phrase of the chorale is first played by the trumpet, then imitated in augmentation at the lower fifth by the continuo instruments. In the earlier movement, the connection between Bach's use of strict counterpoint and the law is more overt than in BWV 48/1: the text is Luke 10:27 (summary of the Law), and the chorale melody (Luther's "Dies sind die heilgen Zehn Gebot") alludes to the Decalogue.

Since the melody of the four-part chorale at the end of Cantata 48 (movement 7) is the same as the one that is used as an instrumental cantus firmus in the opening chorus, it is meaningful to consider these two movements together. "Herr Jesu Christ, einiger Trost" (BWV 48/7) is stanza 12 of "Herr Jesu Christ, ich schrei zu dir":

Herr Jesu Christ, einiger Trost,	Lord Jesus Christ, my only comfort,
Zu dir will ich mich wenden;	To you will I turn;
Mein Herzleid ist dir wohl bewußt,	My heartache is well known to you,
Du kannst und wirst es enden.	You can and will end it.
In deinen Willen seis gestellt,	In your will may it be placed,
Mach's, lieber Gott, wie dir's gefällt:	Do, dear God, as it pleases you:
Dein bin und will ich bleiben.	Yours I am and yours will I remain.

The text of this hymn first appeared in a collection of songs for funerals with the following title:

THRENODIAE I Das ist: I Ausserlesene Trostreiche I Begräbnüß Gesänge / I So
bey Chur= vnd Fürstlichen Leichbe= I gängnüssen / vnd Beysetzungen / Wie auch
bey anderer im HERRN Christo seliglich entschlaffener I Bestattungen / in der
Churf. Sächs. freyen I HäuptBergkStadt Freybergk in I Meissen / üblichen / I
Beneben andern Christlichen meditatio- I nibus vnd Todesgedancken / I . . . / den
Verstorbenen zu Ehren / den Vberlebenden I aber zu Trost vnd linderung der
Trawrigkeit / . . . I gebrauchet werden / I Durch I CHRISTOPHORUM
DEMANTIUM. . . . Gedruckt zu Freybergk, bey Georg Hoffman, I Jm Jahr /
1620.

THRENODIAE That is: select comforting funeral songs, which are customary
at electoral and princely funerals, and burials, and also at the burials of others
departed this life in the Lord Christ, in the electoral Saxon free city of Freiberg in
Meissen, besides other Christian meditations and reflections on death, which are
used to honor the deceased, and for the consolation and easing of sadness of the
survivors, by CHRISTOPHORUS DEMANTIUS. . . . Printed in Freiberg, by
Georg Hoffman, in 1620.

Although unattributed, the heading "Ein ander schönes Christliches Lied,
Eines angefochten vnd betrübten Hertzens" ("Another fine Christian song,
of a troubled and distressed heart") indicates the song's sorrowful affect.
The same twelve-stanza version is found also in the *CANTIONAL* (Leipzig:
In Verlegung des Autoris, 1627) of Johann Hermann Schein, Bach's prede-
cessor as Cantor at St. Thomas's. The chorale next appears in the *New-
Zugerichtetes Lutherisches Gesang-Büchlein* (Leipzig: n.p., 1638) of
Jeremias Weber (1600–1643), a clergyman and professor of theology in
Leipzig. The rubric in Weber's hymnal is similar to the one in the 1620
publication:

Wider die Anfechtungen vnd versuchungen in schwermuth des
hertzens. Weh vnd angstklage elender betrübter seelen. Jm Thon: HErr
Jesu Christ ich weis gar, etc.

Against the doubts and temptations in sadness of the heart.
Lamentation of wretched, distressed souls. To the tune: HErr Jesu
Christ ich weis gar, etc.

Weber added two additional stanzas to the original twelve, marking them
as his own work with the heading "additamentum M. I. W."[20]
Although the melody given for "Herr Jesu Christ, ich schrei zu dir" in
the 1620 *Threnodiae* is the same as the one in Cantata 48, the tune originated over twenty-five years earlier than the text. It first appeared in the
Gesangbuch published in Dresden in 1593, with the text of Nicolaus
Herman's "Wenn mein Stündlein vorhanden ist."[21] The original four-stanza

version of Herman's chorale, in turn, dates back to a book of Bible stories, psalms, and spiritual songs for household use (*Die Historien von der Sindfludt, Joseph, Mose, Helie, Elisa, vnd der Susanna, sampt etlichen Historien aus den Evangelisten, Auch etliche Psalmen vnd geistliche Lieder, zu lesen vnd zu singen in Reyme gefasset, Fur Christliche Hausveter vnd jre Kinder . . .*), which appeared in Wittenberg in 1562. This song, too, is concerned with death and dying. Its heading reads "Ein geistlichs Lied, darin man bitt vmb ein seliges Stündlein" ("A spiritual song, in which one prays for a blessed final hour").[22] The same melody also appears with Bartholomäus Ringwald's "Herr Jesu Christ, ich weis gar wohl" in the Leipzig hymnals of Schein (1627) and Weber (1638). This text, too, is linked with death. The heading in the *Handbüchlin: Geistliche Lieder vnd Gebetlin* (Frankfurt an der Oder: n.p., 1586), where it is first found, reads "Noch ein Lied, vmb bestendigen Glauben, vnd vmb ein seliges ende" ("Yet another song [praying] for steadfast faith and a blessed end").[23] According to Zahn, however, this melody was most commonly associated not with these texts, but rather with Ringwald's "Herr Jesu Christ, du höchstes Gut," which originated in *Christliche Warnung des Trewen Eckarts . . .* (Frankfurt an der Oder: Eichorn, 1588).[24] Interestingly enough, this text has different connotations than the other three. Instead of being associated with death and dying, its heading reads "Ein Fein Liedt, vmb Vergebung der Sünden" ("A fine song, [praying] for forgiveness of sins").[25] And in Gottfried Vopelius' *Neu Leipziger Gesangbuch* (Leipzig: In Verlegung Christoph Klingers Buchb., 1682), it is included among the Catechism hymns concerning confession and repentance ("Von der Beicht und Busse"), immediately following "Ach Gott und Herr," the other chorale that is used in Cantata 48 (movement 3).

So, which words and associations did Bach have in mind when he incorporated this tune into BWV 48/1? This question has been answered differently by different scholars. As early as 1880, Philipp Spitta called attention to the instrumental chorale and noted: "In order to grasp its full poetic sense, one must know the words that go with the chorale melody."[26] He then printed the first stanza of "Herr Jesu Christ, ich schrei zu dir," but did not explore the implications of what this chorale might mean. Eighty years later, W. Gillies Whittaker followed Spitta's lead and cited (in English translation) the same chorale stanza. He noted, however, that the tune is the same as "Herr Jesu Christ, du höchstes gut," and suggested quite plausibly that the quotation of this melody supplies a kind of unspoken answer to the rhetorical question posed in Romans 7:24: "Where the librettist has provided only an agonized question, Bach has told his listeners where to look for succour."[27] Implicit in this view is the recognition that both of the chorales that are most likely to have come to mind when Bach's congregation heard the cantus firmus begin with the words "Herr Jesu Christ." But this is not merely Bach's personal answer to the question "Wer wird mich

erlösen?" For the sentence immediately following verse 24 in Romans 7—
i.e., St. Paul's own answer to his question—includes these very words: "Ich
dancke GOTT durch JEsum CHrist unsern HERRN" ("Thanks be to God—
through Jesus Christ our Lord!") (Romans 7:25a). The presence of the
instrumental chorale cantus firmus, then, provides an additional layer of
meaning in this movement. It simultaneously articulates despair over sla-
very to sin (and the physical and spiritual death that it brings) and points
toward the biblical solution, namely the Lord Jesus Christ.

BWV 48/2: Alto Recitative

Text:

O Schmerz, o Elend, so mich trifft,	O pain, O misery, which strikes me,
Indem der Sünden Gift	In that sin's poison
Bei mir in Brust und Adern wütet:	Does rage in my breast and veins:
Die Welt wird mir ein Siech- und Sterbehaus,	The world becomes for me a house of sickness and a house of death,
Der Leib muß seine Plagen	The body must carry its plagues
Bis zu dem Grabe mit sich tragen.	With it to the grave.
Allein die Seele fühlet den stärksten Gift,	But it is the soul that feels the strongest poison,
Damit sie angestecket;	With which it is infected;
Drum, wenn der Schmerz den Leib des Todes trifft,	Thus, when suffering strikes this body of death,
Wenn ihr der Kreuzkelch bitter schmecket,	When the cross's cup tastes bitter to the soul,
So treibt er ihr ein brünstig Seufzen aus.	Then that cup forces from the soul a passionate sigh.

   The most conspicuous musical feature of the alto recitative is its unusual
harmonic structure. Whittaker noted that "from bar 2 to 5 the key changes
rapidly from B-flat minor to the remote E major" but did not offer an
explanation. (He did mention, however, that "the tortuous solo line . . .
suggests the writhing of the body in acute pain.")[28] Eric Chafe argued plausibly that "the confrontation of extreme sharps and flats suggests the idea
of a 'separation of body and soul.'"[29] Indeed, the body/soul dichotomy is
an important theme both in this movement and throughout the libretto of
Cantata 48, as well as in contemporary Lutheran sermons and Biblical
commentaries (as we shall see later, in our discussion of the theological
background of the tenor aria, BWV 48/6). It may be, however, that the
double meaning of the word "Kreuz" (signifying both the Cross and the
musical sharp sign) in the phrase "Wenn ihr der Kreuzkelch bitter
schmecket" also influenced Bach's conception of the tonality of this
recitative.

BWV 48/2 develops several theological themes that we encountered in connection with the opening chorus. The "misery" in the first line of the text is the destructive power of sin on both body and soul. (This recalls Francke's and Müller's remarks about the causal connection between sin and misery.) Sin is likened to a poison that rages "in my breast and veins" and also infects the soul. This metaphor may have been inspired by Luther's notion of the forgiveness of sins as an antidote to the poison of sin: "For I have for them a priceless panacea and drug, which takes away the power and poison of sin and kills it. It is the word 'forgiveness,' before which sin dissolves like stubbles before the fire."[30] (Müller paraphrased this passage: "If sin is full of poison and death, then forgiveness is a priceless antidote to the poison, and it kills sin. Sin must dissolve before this word, like the stubbles before the fire.")[31] Likewise, the assertion in lines 5–6 that "the body must carry its plagues with it to the grave" echoes the end of Calov's commentary on Romans 7:24: "We will not get rid of this sinful behavior until we shed this mortal body. See Herr Luth. T. VII. Alt. p. 622."[32] This passage includes a reference to the Altenburg edition of Luther's writings, a copy of which Bach acquired in 1742.[33] Calov's commentary on Romans 7:24 also sheds light on the "passionate sigh" at the end of BWV 48/2. Immediately after the passage cited earlier, which explains that the believer experiences the temptation to sin throughout his entire earthly life (even after having been born again), Calov noted that the stress of this lifelong struggle against sin produces sighing.[34] And the words of the "sigh," which are cited thereafter, are none other than a literal quotation of Romans 7:24.

BWV 48/3: Chorale

Text:

Solls ja so sein,	If it then be so,
Daß Straf und Pein	That punishment and pain
Auf Sünde folgen müssen,	Must follow sin,
So fahr hie fort	Then proceed [to afflict me] here
Und schone dort	And spare over there
Und laß mich hie wohl büßen.	And let me indeed do penance here.

Although this movement is quite short (just ten measures), it has a prominent role in the unfolding of the message of Cantata 48. Alfred Dürr mentioned that this simple four-part chorale is "unerwartet" ("unexpected").[35] This modest remark calls attention to an important idiosyncrasy in the overall structure of the work. Movements 1–2 and 4–7 follow the six-movement design that is found in a number of other cantatas for the Trinity season in the first Leipzig cycle (BWV 136, 105, 46, 179, 69a, 77, 25, 109, 89):

Biblical Text–Recitative–Aria–Recitative–Aria–Chorale

Against this backdrop, movement 3 sticks out like an "extra" movement. (In the absence of any other sources for the libretto, it is impossible to determine whether the text of Cantata 48 represents its original form or is a variant. The possibility that Bach or his librettist may have added a chorale stanza to a preexistent six-movement structure should not, however, be dismissed out of hand.)

The unusual musical content of this chorale gives it special prominence as well and has caught the attention of many scholars. Spitta was perhaps the first to comment on its "modulatorischer Kühnheit" ("modulatory boldness"), which, he noted, "das Unglaubliche wirklich macht" ("makes the incredible real").[36] Schweitzer mentioned this movement as an example of Bach's willingness to contravene "the natural principles of pure composition" when this might enliven the meaning of the text. In his view, Bach's harmonization of this chorale "as pure music is indeed intolerable." He noted, however, that Bach's purpose in this case—i.e., the reason he composed such strange music (and, for Schweitzer, the justification for this approach)—was that he wanted "to express all the wild grief for sin that is suggested in the words."[37] In BWV 48/3, "the full sense of grief is given in the sinister harmonies."[38] Similarly, Whittaker characterized this chorale as "one of Bach's most amazing chromatic flights," and Dürr was impressed by its "kunstvolle Harmonisierung" ("elaborate harmonization"), especially at its end.[39]

It is perhaps worth noting that BWV 48/3 is the only setting of this chorale in the entire corpus of Bach's vocal music. A C-major version (BWV 255) is found, however, in the early collections of four-part chorales published by Birnstiel (Berlin and Leipzig, 1765) and Breitkopf (Leipzig, 1784). An organ version (BWV 714) also exists; until the discovery of the Neumeister chorales in the 1980s, only the last twenty-four measures of this sixty-one-measure piece were known. (Two other settings, BWV 692 and 693, are spurious.) In addition, "Ach Gott und Herr" is one of the many chorales whose text incipit was entered into the autograph of the *Orgelbüchlein* but not set. Even though "Ach Gott und Herr" is not one of the most famous chorales, Bach obviously considered it as belonging to the essential repertory of Lutheran hymnody.

The first time the text of "Ach Gott und Herr" appeared in print was in a broadsheet of a sermon preached in Jena by Johann Major (1564–1654) on 2 June 1613. The title of the original print describes the occasion in vivid detail:

Gedenck vnd Erinnerungs | Predigt / | Von dem grawsa= | men Gewitter / vnd schräcklichem | Gewässer / darmit Thüringen heimgesuchet | worden / am Sonnabend vor Trinitatis in der | Nacht / war der 29. May / dieses inste= | henden 1613. Jahrs. | Gehalten . . . zu | Jena den 2. Junij | Von | JOHANNE MAJORE . . . | Erstlichen gedruckt zu Jehna (1613).[40]

> Commemorative sermon on the terrible thunderstorm and dreadful flood that struck Thuringia on the Saturday before Trinity Sunday during the night, the 29th of May in the present year 1613. Preached . . . in Jena on 2 June by JOHANNES MAJOR . . . First printed in Jena.

The sermon was reprinted later the same year in Erfurt and Eisleben.[41] Because the fourth stanza of "Ach Gott und Herr" (the stanza in Cantata 48) is included in the Jena edition—and all six stanzas in the Eisleben edition—some hymnologists about a century ago (e.g., Fischer and Julian) concluded that the hymn was penned by Major.[42] It seems quite clear, however, that Major was simply quoting a chorale that had been written nine years earlier by his former colleague, Martin Rutilius (1551–1618).

The case for Rutilius' authorship of "Ach Gott und Herr" chiefly rests upon the testimony of Caspar Binder, a pastor in the Thuringian village of Mattstedt (near Apolda), who in 1726 published in Jena a thirty-two-page pamphlet "proving" that Rutilius was the chorale text's true author (see figure 3.1).

Binder reported that he had in his possession a handwritten album, which he had inherited. It had been compiled by an ancestor of his mother, Melchior Francke, who also had served as mayor of Weimar. According to Binder, the book contained under the heading "Ein Gebett vmb Vergebung der Sünden, vmb Gedult im Creutz, vnd vmb Erlassung ewiger Straffe" ("A prayer for the forgiveness of sins, for the bearing of one's cross with patience, and for the remission of eternal punishment") six stanzas of "Ach Gott und Herr," followed by the words "M. MARTINVS RVTILIVS, Diaconus Ecclesiae Vinariensis fecit & propria manu scripsit" and the date "den 29. Mey Ao. 1604."[43] Rutilius was a clergyman in Weimar from 1586 until his death in 1618. For a period of thirteen years, from Major's arrival in 1592 until 1605 when he moved away to become pastor, superintendent, and professor of theology in Jena, Rutilius and Major served together in Weimar.[44] "Ach Gott und Herr" was penned shortly before Major relocated to Jena, and he apparently remembered it (and had access to a copy of the words) when he wrote his commemorative sermon after the terrible storm several years later.

The question of the authorship of "Ach Gott und Herr" became even more complex over the course of the seventeenth and early eighteenth centuries. According to Julian, "Ach Gott und Herr" first passed into hymnals either as anonymous or signed "J. G." (these were the initials for "Johann Gross"; the surname was a German translation of "Major"). In the second edition of Joseph Clauder's *PSALMODIA NOVA* (Leipzig, 1630), however, it was signed "J. Gö.," which subsequently was taken to refer to "Johann Göldel," a pastor in the Thuringian village of Dinstätt (on the Ilm River).[45] This is indeed the case in Vopelius' *Neu Leipziger Gesangbuch* (Leipzig, 1682), where the heading for "Ach Gott und Herr" reads "Ein anders, Johannis Göldelii, Pfarrers zu Dinstätt an der Ilmen."[46] This is also

Historischer Erweiß

Daß des bekandten Liedes unserer Kirchen:

Ach GOtt und HErr, wie groß und schwer ꝛc.

wahrer Auctor sey

M. MARTIN. RUTILIUS

Ex matre nepos Georg. Rorarii, amanuensis Luther
weiland Archidiaconus bey der Haupt- und Pfarr
Kirchen zu Weimar;

Gleichwie von dem Zusatz

Gleichwie sich fein ein Vögelein ꝛc.

Auctor ist

M. JOHANN MAIOR

t. t. Diaconus daselbst,

gezeiget von

M. Caspar Binder, Vinariensi,

v. D. min. eccleſ. Mattſtad.

Jena, mit Wertherischen Schrifften.

Figure 3.1. Title page of Caspar Binder's 1726 treatise *Historischer Erweiß Daß des bekandten Liedes unserer Kirchen . . . .* Reproduced by permission of the Niedersächsiche Staats- und Universitätsbibliothek, Göttingen.

the point of departure for the study of "Ach Gott und Herr" in Part III of
Evangelischer Lieder-Schatz (Jena: Johann Felix Bielcken, 1706), a commentary on the principal hymns of the church year by Johann Christoph
Olearius, a distinguished hymnologist who served as deacon of the Neue
Kirche in Arnstadt during the time when Bach was organist there (1703–
7). Olearius' article begins: "The true author of this song is Johannes Göldel,
a pastor in Dinstett, on the Ilm, in Thuringia, but he only wrote the first six
stanzas, up through the words: 'Von Dir seyn abgescheiden.'"[47] Given his
strong interest in hymnody, Bach likely would have been aware of this
important publication by his colleague in Arnstadt, and perhaps even would
have read the commentary on "Ach Gott und Herr." It is also possible that
Bach knew of the controversy concerning the origin of "Ach Gott und
Herr" around the time he composed Cantata 48, since Binder's *Historischer
Erweiß* was dedicated to J. C. Olearius.

If nothing else, the title of Binder's treatise provides concrete evidence
that "Ach Gott und Herr" was "well known" in Jena in 1726, and it is,
therefore, likely also to have been familiar in Leipzig (only about 100 kilo-
meters to the northeast) when Cantata 48 was composed three years earlier. Indeed, this hymn was quite successful during the seventeenth century
and even well into the eighteenth. Not long after it appeared in Major's
1613 sermon, "Ach Gott und Herr" was published in Part I of Melchior
Franck's *Geistlichen musicalischen Lustgarten* (Nuremberg: Georg Leopold
Fuhrmann, 1616). Immediately preceding its six stanzas was a two-stanza
text: "GLeich wie sich fein" and "Also, HErr Christ." This brief chorale first
took on a life of its own and later intersected with "Ach Gott und Herr." The
subsequent history of these two hymns can be summarized as follows.

(1)   The two-stanza chorale appeared in Part I of Johann Staden's *Hauß
        MUSIC Geistlicher Gesäng* (Nuremberg: [M. Külssner?], 1623).
        Here the first line reads "GLeich wie sich ein Waldvögelein."

(2)   The two-stanza hymn appeared in the 1624 Erfurt hymnal with
        three additional stanzas (3 = "Die Seite mein"; 4 = "Meinr Händ
        Arbeit"; 5 = "Ehre sey Gott").

(3)   A different expansion of the two-stanza hymn was published in
        Leipzig in 1625, in Christian Gallo's *AS HYMNODUS SACER* (3 =
        "Darinn ich bleib"; 4 = "Ehre sey nun").

(4)   "Ach Gott und Herr," which last had appeared in 1616, finally
        turned up again in Joseph Clauder's *PSALMODIA NOVA*
        (Altenburg, 1627), but with an additional stanza (7 = "HErr JEsu
        Christ"). The second edition (Leipzig, 1630) included yet another
        stanza as well (8 = "Vntr des ich bitt").

(5)   The chorale "Gleichwie sich sein" also appeared in Clauder's 1627
        publication, with six stanzas (two each from Nuremberg 1616, Erfurt
        1624, and Leipzig 1625):

1 = "GLeich wie sich sein"
2 = "Also, HErr Christ"
3 = "Meinr Händ Arbeit"
4 = "Die Seite mein"
5 = "Darinn ich bleib"
6 = "Ehre sei nun"

These six stanzas follow directly after the seven of "Ach Gott und Herr," under the heading "Etliche thun hinzu:" ("Several add:").

(6) Finally, in the same year, in Johann Hermann Schein's CANTIONAL (Leipzig, 1627), the two hymns are joined into a single one of ten stanzas:
   1–6 = "Ach Gott und Herr," etc. (as in the original)
   7 = "Gleichwie sich fein"
   8 = "Also Herr Christ"
   9 = "Darin ich bleib"
   10 = "Ehre sei nun"

According to Fischer, it was this version that enjoyed the widest circulation.[48] Indeed, this is the form that is found in Vopelius' *Neu Leipziger Gesangbuch* (Leipzig, 1682), which is based in large part on Schein's hymnal.[49]

That "Ach Gott und Herr" still appeared in collections of chorales over a century-and-a-half after it was written (e.g., in the Heidelberg *Choralbuch* of 1766 and in Carl Immanuel Engel's manuscript *Choralbuch* of 1775) and that it was selected for inclusion in the *Evangelisches Kirchengesangbuch* (EKG) attests to the strength of its position within the vast repertory of Lutheran hymnody.[50]

The most striking feature of BWV 48/3, Bach's setting of stanza 4 of "Ach Gott und Herr," is the lengthy melisma on the final word "büßen." Bach called attention to this word by extending it for three measures, after setting the rest of the text in a predominantly syllabic manner. In addition, the use of chromaticism and minor-mode inflection (e.g., the pitches A flat and G flat in the context of B-flat major) reflects the "dark" affect of this word. The importance of the word "büßen" is reflected as well in the autograph score, which reveals that the melisma was revised and expanded from two measures to three.[51]

Bach lavished such care on the word "büßen" because it plays a pivotal role in proclaiming the theological message of Cantata 48. Both the liturgical occasion of this work and the chorale "Ach Gott und Herr" are closely connected with the themes of confession (*Beicht*) and penitence (*Buße*), as mentioned earlier. Günther Stiller noted, moreover, that the hymn schedules in Dresden and Leipzig specified the use of hymns "Von der Buße und Beichte" for the Nineteenth Sunday after Trinity.[52]

If movements 1 and 2 of Cantata 48 concern the deleterious effects of sin on the body and soul, movements 3 and 4 outline a response to sin's destructive power that entails penitence and the acceptance of suffering as the will of God. The first three lines of the chorale restate the theological premise discussed earlier, that misery (in this case, "Straf und Pein") is the inevitable result of sin. The words of line 4 ("so fahr hie fort") echo a passage from Luther's explanation of the Third Petition in the Lord's Prayer ("your will be done on earth as it is in heaven"). In *Ein kurz Begriff und Ordnung aller vorgeschriebenen Bitten* (1519), Luther prayed:

> O Vater, gib Gnad und hilf, daß wir deinen göttlichen Willen lassen in uns geschehen; ja ob es uns wehe tut, *so fahr du fort* [emphasis added], straf, stich, hau, und brenn, mach alles, was du willst, daß nur dein Will und ja nicht der unsere geschehe. Wehr, lieber Vater, und laß uns nichts nach unserm Gutdünken, Willen und Meinung fürnehmen und vollbringen. Denn unser und dein Will sind widereinander.[53]

> O Father, give grace and help that we may allow your divine will to be done in us; even if it hurts us, continue, punish, prick, hit, and burn; do everything you want to, so that only your will and not ours be done. Prevent, dear Father, and let us plan and achieve nothing according to our own discretion, will, and judgment. For our will and yours are against one another.

Luther's ardent desire that God's will ("dein Will") may come to pass, even if it involves suffering, is reflected as well in lines 1–2 of the alto aria (BWV 48/4): "Ach, lege das Sodom der sündlichen Glieder, / Wofern es *dein Wille* [emphasis added] zerstöret darnieder!" ("Destroy the Sodom of my sinful members, to the extent that it be Your will!")

The web of associations involving BWV 48/3 and the notion of penitence is, however, even more complex. Luther's explanation of the Third Petition (1519) includes a quotation from St. Augustine. Nearly a century later, in 1613, Johann Major, in turn, incorporated this passage into his commemorative sermon, immediately before quoting stanza 4 of Rutilius' chorale. The end of Major's sermon reads (the passage from St. Augustine is in Latin):

> Pray with David: O Lord, punish us not in your wrath [Psalm 38:1], with Jeremiah: Convert me, and I will be converted, for you are my God; since I was converted, I did penance [Jeremiah 31:18–19], for after I learned from experience, I strike myself on the hip. O bone Deus, hic ure, hic seca, hic pange, hic tunde, modo in aeternum parce.[54]

St. Augustine's prayer ("O gracious God, here burn, here plague, here hit, here crush; but spare in eternity") articulates virtually the same sentiments as the latter half of the stanza from "Ach Gott und Herr," as well as the alto aria (BWV 48/4), which concludes with the following petition: "Nur schone der

Seele und mache sie rein, / Um vor dir ein heiliges Zion zu sein" ("Only spare my soul and make it pure, so that it may be a holy Zion before thee.")

Of course, the idea of penitence is somewhat problematic within the context of Lutheran theology. In his commentary on "Ach Gott und Herr," Johann Christoph Olearius warned against misunderstanding the last line of stanza 4: "It is necessary to carefully explain the words 'und laß mich hier wohl büßen' in the fourth stanza, so that one doesn't get a popish interpretation out of it. 'Büßen' involves suffering, but it is not as though one could gain anything thereby."[55] Although Lutheran doctrine recognizes that "büßen" entails hardship, it differs from the Catholic view in denying that salvation can be earned. Olearius then quoted Johann Schmidt's definition of the word "büßen":

> The little word "Buß" is not used in the Scriptures as it commonly is in the world, so that it amounts to . . . reimbursing, settling, paying something that is due; but in God's Word "Busse thun" and "Büssen" means recognizing oneself as a poor sinner, humbling oneself before God in remorse and sorrow, regarding oneself as worthy of all punishment, disgrace, and wrath, and begging for and receiving pardon and forgiveness of sins for Christ's sake.[56]

Olearius' and Schmidt's remarks are rooted in Luther's understanding of "Buße," which he articulated as follows:

> The papacy holds instead . . . that if a person wants to have forgiveness of sins, he must confess and have remorse and do good works as satisfaction for his sins. That is what they have called "Buß." This is a very cunning theology, which makes the devil laugh, for it does him no harm. It is true that I should have remorse and be sincerely sorry for my sin. But I do not thereby receive forgiveness of sins. How do I receive it then? Only by relying on the Word and the promise, and by believing.[57]

According to Luther and his followers, then, one does not receive forgiveness of sins through confession, remorse, or good works, but rather simply by believing God's Word and promise.

Stanza 4 of "Ach Gott und Herr" brought into Cantata 48 an extensive network of associations, including a theology of suffering and penitence. Another important facet of the meaning of this movement involves the stories associated with the chorale. In Lutheran churches from the beginning of the Reformation through the first half of the eighteenth century, sermons often were preached using chorales (rather than Biblical passages) as their texts. One common approach, epitomized by Johann Avenarius in his *Evangelischer Lieder-Catechißmus* (Frankfurt and Leipzig: In Verlegung Joh. Christoph Stössels seel. Erben in Erffurth, 1714), was first to expound the relevant details concerning the authorship of the text and the main idea of the song and then to demonstrate the power of the chorale by relating some stories about it (see figure 3.2).[58]

M. JO. AVENARII
Evangelischer

Lieder-Catechißmus

Darinnen

Die gantze Christliche Lehre nach Anweisung der Sechs Hauptstücke des H. Catechismi Lutheri durch erbauliche Lieder erläutert und mit
raren Historien auch andern nachdencklichen
Remarqven erkläret/

Vormahls seiner anvertrauten Gemeinde in einen richtigen Jahrgang durch ordentliche Predigten
vorgetragen/ nunmehro aber auf Begehren in geschickten Dispositionibus dargestellet
Und
Mit vollständigen Registern versehen.

FRANCKFURTH und LEIPZIG,
In Verlegung Joh. Christoph. Stössels
seel. Erben in Erffurth/ Anno 1714.

Figure 3.2. Title page of Johann Avenarius, *Evangelischer Lieder-Catechißmus*. Reproduced by permission of the Bethany Lutheran Theological Seminary Library,
Mankato, Minnesota.

For instance, in his sermon on the Fifth Petition of the Lord's Prayer, Avenarius provided the following account:

> It was once reported to me by a distinguished preacher that he brought a very impatient sick person to patience and recognition of his sins with this song, especially the fourth and sixth stanzas. For when he had been laid low by painful gout for almost three whole months, he finally lost all his patience. But in order to preserve his faith and patience, he [the preacher] recommended this song to him; when the pain was at its worst, he should sing this song, particularly the words: "Solls ja so seyn" . . . Then he would find that God's grace would become mighty in him. The sick person did this; and even though his scornful wife and siblings wanted to laugh at him because of this, he overcame it, and when the pain raged most dreadfully, he shouted all the more: "Solls ja so seyn, daß Straff und Pein" . . . and he learned thereby that it was not in vain, for he always was powerfully strengthened and comforted in his heart by it.[59]

Eduard Emil Koch included in his discussion of "Ach Gott und Herr" a similar story, from an unidentified source. One night in the village of Steen (near Zwickau), a wealthy farmer by the name of Johann Schubart lost all of his possessions in a fire. This disaster nearly drove him to despair, and the village preacher, Martius, came to comfort him with the Word of God. When he found that the Scriptures would not sink into the heart of the unfortunate man, however, the godly pastor fell to his knees, shouted "Nun du lieber Gott," and then quoted stanza 4 of "Ach Gott und Herr."[60]

Both of these situations involve intense suffering: either chronic pain or the sudden and unexpected loss of all one's earthly possessions. The latter story implies that the chorale stanza had more power than even the Scriptures to console the bereaved man. Similarly, the former makes the astonishing claim that the two chorale stanzas had quasi-medicinal qualities: the sick man's pastor "prescribed" these words for their curative effect.

Although Avenarius' book is not listed among the volumes in his personal theological library, it seems likely that Bach (and his librettist) may have been aware of the healing powers associated with "Ach Gott und Herr." If this was the case, then perhaps stanza 4 of this chorale was incorporated into the libretto of Cantata 48 as a kind of remedy for the sin-induced sickness that is described so vividly in the alto recitative (movement 2).

BWV 48/4: Alto Aria

Text:

Ach, lege das Sodom der sündlichen Glieder,	Destroy the Sodom of my sinful members,
Wofern es dein Wille, zerstöret darnieder!	To the extent that it be Your will!

| Nur schone der Seele und mache sie rein, | Only spare my soul and make it pure, |
| Um vor dir ein heiliges Zion zu sein. | So that it may be a holy Zion before thee. |

We have already considered the theological content of the alto aria, in connection with our discussion of movement 3. While the contrast between the highly-charged language of the first two lines of the text and Bach's placid, dance-like music is initially puzzling, the movement's affect can perhaps be understood as reflecting the simple humility of true penitence, which was described above.

BWV 48/5: Tenor Recitative

Text:

Hier aber tut des Heilands Hand	Here, however, the Savior's hand does wonders
Auch unter denen Toten Wunder.	Even among the dead.
Scheint deine Seele gleich erstorben,	Though it seem as though your soul had died,
Der Leib geschwächt und ganz verdorben,	Your body weakened and completely ruined,
Doch wird uns Jesu Kraft bekannt:	Nevertheless Jesus' power is made known to us.
Er weiß im geistlich Schwachen	He knows how to make the body
Den Leib gesund, die Seele stark zu machen.	healthy, the soul strong in those who are spiritually weak.

The message of Cantata 48 takes a dramatic and unexpected turn in the tenor recitative with the miraculous intervention of the Savior. Here Jesus demonstrates His power ("Kraft") by both healing the body and strengthening the soul. The nature of Jesus' power, especially His ability to combat "misery," is again clarified by Francke:

> Now this power, which emanated from our Savior, Jesus Christ, in the days of his weakness, the same power is still in him, since he now sits in his glory at the right hand of power, and saves from their misery and distress all those who by faith in him are drawn to this power and partake of it.[61]

Although the libretto of Cantata 48 never refers directly to the healing of the paralytic in Matthew 9, knowledge of the Biblical story is taken for granted. Indeed, the shift from praying to God (movements 3 and 4) to addressing the congregation signals a contemporary application of the Biblical story in the tenor recitative. This movement affirms that, just as Jesus healed the paralytic's body and soul, He could do the same for Bach's congregation ("Doch wird uns Jesu Kraft bekannt").

BWV 48/6: Tenor Aria

Text:

Vergibt mir Jesus meine Sünden,	If Jesus forgives my sins,
So wird mir Leib und Seel gesund.	Then my body and soul become well.
Er kann die Toten lebend machen	He can make the dead alive
Und zeigt sich kräftig in den Schwachen,	And shows himself mighty in the weak,
Er hält den längst geschloßnen Bund,	He keeps the long-contracted covenant,
Daß wir im Glauben Hilfe finden.	So that we find salvation through faith.

In a sense, forgiveness can be considered the key word of the entire cantata. The first sentence (lines 1–2) asserts—not least through prominent placement of the word "vergibt" at the very beginning—that both the body and soul are healed when Jesus forgives a person's sins. Implicit in this statement is an observation about Matthew 9 that is articulated by several contemporary theologians: Jesus first healed the paralytic spiritually by forgiving his sins, and only after this matter of fundamental importance had been settled did He offer physical healing. The underlying assumption, of course, is that the soul is of greater importance than the body. This is because the soul is eternal, whereas the body is temporal.

This perspective is reflected in the capsule summary at the beginning of Matthew 9 in the Calov Bible: "When Christ returns from Capernaum, he heals a paralytic, first in soul and then in body."[62] It also is amplified in Calov's commentary on Jesus' statement to the paralytic, "your sins are forgiven" (v. 2): "This paralytic asked to be freed from his paralysis: but behold, the Lord first frees him from his sins, and delivers him first and foremost from its cause. For the cause of the disease must be dealt with first, if the disease is to be healed completely."[63] Similarly, Johann Olearius summarized the "Haupt-Lehre" ("main lesson") of Matthew 9 as "Christus hilfft an Seel und Leib" ("Christ helps in soul and body").[64] And in his commentary on verse 5, he posed the following rhetorical question: "Should not the soul's cure be more important than physical health?"[65] Francke's formulation resembles Calov's in its identification of sin as the "cause" of illness:

> Our dear Savior, when he had before him this sick person whom he should heal and actually did heal, did not look on the external illness alone but on the cause of the illness, namely sin. That is why, as a wise physician, he first healed his soul, before he freed him from his physical illness.[66]

A fascinating, and much more extensive, explanation of why Christ forgave the paralytic's sins first, before healing his body, is found in August Pfeiffer's commentary on Matthew 9:

> Now this may seem strange to some: Why did Christ not first make the poor man well? It seems that his answer does not match the request. Though the poor

man would have been glad if his limbs just became straight and healthy, the Lord spoke to him an absolution that he had not asked for. However, the Lord Jesus did not do anything inconsistent here, but he wants us to understand . . . the real origin of the illness and its obvious interpretation. As far as the first is concerned, the dear Savior does not want to be like a quack who heals the injury just superficially and does not touch the actual seat of the illness . . . but he wants to completely heal and eradicate the illness. Usually when a person wants to stop a flow of water, it is not enough just to cut off the stream, but he has to find the origin and main source and stop them up too. Now what else is sin than a mass of pus, the fountainhead of all diseases and of death? . . . Now the Savior first wants to stop up this source, he first wants to do away with paralysis of the soul, and therefore take away the inflow for paralysis of the limbs. He wants to say, "You miserable creature! I see your bodily need perfectly well, but first I want to do away with the evil source, so that you will become completely healthy in body and soul. First I will forgive all your sins, and then heal all your bodily afflictions."[67]

The most remarkable characteristic of the tenor aria is its unusual harmonic structure, which features two kinds of "upward" motion that are closely connected with its theological content. The first half of this movement (mm. 1–38) modulates from G minor (tonic—2 flats) to D minor (dominant—1 flat). The first part of the B section (mm. 45–57) continues the "upward" motion through the circle of fifths to A minor (no flats or sharps), a remote tonality outside the normal spectrum of modulatory possibilities for Bach arias (which includes the tonic, dominant, subdominant, and relative major or minor of these keys). The ritornello between the two vocal periods of the B section (mm. 58–68) includes a wrenching modulation upward a half-step from A minor to B-flat major (mediant). The large-scale motion through the circle of fifths and the abrupt shift both represent the idea of resurrection mentioned in the third line of the text: "Er kann die Toten lebend machen." The link between this theme and forgiveness of sins is illustrated powerfully in the following passage from a sermon by Francke, which concludes with a parable about a man who had been condemned to death but is pardoned at the last minute:

To know forgiveness of sins is not difficult; but to believe forgiveness of sins requires God's power and cannot be done naturally. But when God the Lord takes a man into the school of penitence, when his miserable condition is first set before his eyes, so that he learns to be shocked about the abomination of his sins, and then because of feeling his sins, the wrath of God, and the curse of the law does not know where he should turn for fear; but nevertheless has an ardent longing for salvation, and then the Holy Spirit plants in his heart the word of reconciliation, that for Christ's sake all his sins are forgiven, and because of that the power of Christ's blood, grasped by faith, penetrates his heart, so that his remembrance of sin fades like a mist, his conscience is freed from slavish and despairing fear and God takes away the feeling of sin's burden and his wrath, and causes the penitent sinner to taste again his love and grace; then he knows what justification means, then he believes the forgiveness of sins.

I have previously clarified this with a parable about a man who was sentenced to death: When he was led to his death, many people were gathered around who wanted to see how he would be brought from life to death. But when a messenger came from the high-ranking governmental authority who had pronounced over him the judgment of death, and he cried, "Grace! Grace! Grace!"—behold, who surely felt this word most deeply? To whom was it sweeter and more pleasant than to the evildoer who had been sentenced to death? For the others, it did not reach their hearts, they did not feel it so powerfully; but the one who was condemned to death, and now suddenly hears that he should receive grace, was, so to speak, brought out of death back to life.[68]

The imagery and language of this passage are so similar to the text of Cantata 48 that it appears likely that Bach's librettist, and perhaps the composer himself, knew this sermon and derived creative inspiration from it.

This paper has demonstrated the kinds of knowledge that can be gained by investigating the theological and hymnological sources of a Bach cantata, and the ways in which this material can inform interpretation of the work. Only by pursuing an integrated approach, which draws upon these sources as well as musical analysis and manuscript study, will it be possible to achieve a full-orbed understanding of these incomparably rich compositions.

Notes

1. I am grateful to the Staatsbibliothek zu Berlin, Preussischer Kulturbesitz, the Niedersächsische Staats- und Universitätsbibliothek (Göttingen), the Scheide Bach Archive at Princeton University, Concordia Theological Seminary (St. Louis), Bethany Lutheran Theological Seminary (Mankato, Minnesota), Don O. Franklin, and Robin A. Leaver for facilitating my work with these sources. Detailed bibliographical descriptions of items 3–5 and 10–14 can be found in Robin A. Leaver, *Bachs theologische Bibliothek: Eine kritische Bibliographie* (Neuhausen-Stuttgart: Hänssler, 1983). It is worth noting that not all scholars agree about the identity of some of Bach's books. For instance, Johannes Wallmann doubts that the octavo volume listed in the inventory of Bach's estate as "Francken Hauß Postilla" necessarily was authored by August Hermann Francke. See Johannes Wallmann, "Johann Sebastian Bach und die 'Geistlichen Bücher' seiner Bibliothek," *Pietismus und Neuzeit* 12 (1986):171–72.

2. *D. Martin Luthers Werke: Kritische Gesamtausgabe* [*Weimarer Ausgabe* = *WA*] (Weimar: Hermann Böhlaus Nachfolger, 1883–1983), 10/III, 394–99.

3. *WA* 15, 696–712.

4. *WA* 29, 562–82.

5. *WA* 37, 174–79.

6. *WA* 52, 497–504.

7. Translations of the texts for Cantata 48 are based on those in Melvin P. Unger, *Handbook to Bach's Sacred Cantata Texts* (Lanham, Md.: Scarecrow Press, 1996),

170–73. Quotations of Biblical passages other than Romans 7:24 are from the New International Version. All other translations are my own. I am grateful to Michael Marissen and Traute Marshall for their helpful suggestions concerning my translations.

8. Luther's translation in Bach's personal copy of the Bible (Abraham Calov, *Das Neue Testament* . . . [Wittenberg: Christian Schrödter, 1682], cols. 97–99) reads as follows: "Da trat Er in das Schiff, und fuhr wider herüber, und kam in seine Stadt. Und sihe, da brachten sie zu Ihm einen Gichtbrüchtigen, der lag auf einem Bette. Da nun JEsus ihren Glauben sahe, sprach Er zu dem Gichtbrüchtigen: Sey getrost Mein Sohn, Deine Sünde sind dir vergeben. Und sihe, etliche unter den Schrifftgelehrten sprachen bey sich selbst: Dieser lästert GOtt. Da aber JEsus ihre Gedancken sahe, spricht Er: Warumb dencket ihr so arges in euren Hertzen? Welches ist leichter zu sagen? Dir sind deine Sünde vergeben? oder zu sagen: Stehe auf, und wandele? Auf daß ihr aber wisset, daß des Menschen Sohn Macht habe auf Erden, die Sünde zu vergeben, sprach Er zu dem Gichtbrüchtigen: Stehe auf, hebe dein Bett auf, und gehe heim. Und er stund auf, und gieng heim. Da das Volck das sahe, verwundert es sich, und preisete GOtt, der solche Macht den Menschen gegeben hat."

9. Ibid., col. 97: ". . . welchen die Gicht, der kleine, oder halbe Schlag gerühret."

10. August Hermann Francke, *Sonn- Fest- und Apostel-Tags-Predigten* . . . (Halle: [Wäysen-Hause], 1709), 560: "Sonsten heißt παραλυτικος einer, der von dem Schlage gerühret worden, welches eine der gefährlichsten und elendesten Kranckheiten ist. Dahero man auch von solchen Menschen, so vom Schlage sind gerühret worden, zu sagen pfleget, daß sie von der Hand GOttes gerühret seyn; sintemal daran sonderlich die Macht GOttes, die er über Leben und Tod hat, erkannt wird, dieweil solches plötzlich und unversehens zu geschehen pfleget, daß ein Mensch in einen solchen elenden Zustand gesetzet wird. Denn παραλυσις heisset so viel als *solutio neruorum*, eine Auflösung der Nerven und Adern bey dem Menschen, dadurch er zu allen leiblichen Verrichtungen untüchtig wird."

11. Ibid.: "Diese leibliche Kranckheit ist demnach eine Abbildung unserer Seelen-Kranckheit, an welcher wir auch gleichsam vom Schlage gerühret sind."

12. *WA* 52, 503: "Der Gichtbrüchtige hie ist ein Bild aller sünder. Denn das ist diser kranckheit art, das man der glider nit mer brauchen kan, und wenn man den fuß oder die hand zu sich ziehen will, so kan mans nit unnd streckts nur ye mer von sich."

13. Calov, *Das Neue Testament*, col. 83: "der wegen der sündlichen verderbten Natur in Warheit elend ist."

14. Francke, *Sonn- Fest- und Apostel-Tags-Predigten* . . . , 565: "die Sünde die Ursache alles unsers Elendes ist."

15. Heinrich Müller, *Evangelische Schluß-Kette* . . . (Frankfurt am Main: Balthasar Christoph Wusten, 1698), 369: "Eins quillet auß dem andern, das Elend auß der Sünden."

16. Calov, *Das Neue Testament*, col. 79: "Wie bey den Widergebornen eine grosse Unvollkommenheit und steter Streit sey des Fleisches mit dem Geist."

17. Ibid., col. 83: "das ist, von diesem tödtlichen Leibe, welcher immerdar den Tod an sich träget, so vom natürlichen, oder vom geistlichen Tod mag verstanden werden, wegen der übrigen sündlichen Lüste, die uns die gantze Zeit dieses irrdischen Lebens, auch nach der Widergeburth, ankleben, und einen Gläubigen GOTTes stets zur Sünde, oder sündlichen Begierde, reitzen."

18. *WA* 15, 699: "Die sunde hanget uns noch allzeyt am halls, die uns hart anklebt. Wie S. Paulus davon redet zun Romern am 7., ym todt aber werden wyr es erfaren."

19. Francke, *Sonn- Fest- und Apostel-Tags-Predigten* . . . , 564: "Sehet, wenn nun der Mensch seine Sünden-Noth also erkennet, da sehnet er sich denn nach der Hulffe und einem Helffer, da fänget er an mit Paulo zu seuftzen: Ich elender Mensch, wer wird mich erlösen von dem Leibe dieses Todes? Ja da sehnet er sich nach dem Artzte, der ihn auch von dem Tode erretten kan."

20. Albert Fischer and Wilhelm Tümpel, *Das deutsche evangelische Kirchenlied des 17. Jahrhunderts*, 6 vols. (Gütersloh: C. Bertelsmann, 1904–16; reprint, Hildesheim: Georg Olms, 1964), 1:512–13 (no. 574).

21. Johannes Zahn, *Die Melodien der deutschen evangelischen Kirchenlieder*, 6 vols. (Gütersloh: C. Bertelsmann, 1889–93; reprint, Hildesheim: Georg Olms, 1997), 3:91 (no. 4486). According to the *Bach Compendium*, it is based on an earlier melody, published in Görlitz in 1587; see Hans-Joachim Schulze and Christoph Wolff, *Bach Compendium*, vol. 1, 4 parts (Leipzig: Edition Peters, 1985–89), 1:1369 (F 202).

22. Philipp Wackernagel, *Das deutsche Kirchenlied*, 5 vols. (Leipzig: B. G. Teubner, 1864–77; reprint, Hildesheim: Georg Olms, 1990), 3:1211 (no. 1414).

23. Ibid., 3:985–86 (no. 1473).

24. Zahn, *Die Melodien*, 3:91.

25. Wackernagel, *Das deutsche Kirchenlied*, 3:1028–29 (no. 1523).

26. Philipp Spitta, *Johann Sebastian Bach*, 2 vols. (Leipzig: Breitkopf & Härtel, 1873–80; reprint, Wiesbaden: Breitkopf & Härtel, 1979), 2:566: "Um den vollen poetischen Sinn zu fassen, muß man die der Choralmelodie zugehörigen Worte wissen."

27. W. Gillies Whittaker, *The Cantatas of Johann Sebastian Bach*, 2 vols. (London: Oxford University Press, 1959), 2:201.

28. Ibid., 2:34.

29. Eric Chafe, *Tonal Allegory in the Vocal Music of J. S. Bach* (Berkeley: University of California Press, 1991), 196.

30. *WA* 29, 574: "Denn ich habe dargegen ein köstlich tyriak und Apoteken, so der sunde yhr krafft und gifft nimpt und dazu tödtet, welchs ist das wort Vergebung, fur welchem die sund zurgehet wie die stoppeln, wenn das fewer drein kompt."

31. Müller, *Evangelische Schluß-Kette* . . . , 370: "Jst die Sünde voll Giffts und Todes, so ist die Vergebung ein köstlich Theriack wider den Gifft, und tödtet die Sünde. Für diesem Worte muß die Sünde zergehen, wie die Stoppeln, wann das Feuer kommt."

32. Calov, *Das Neue Testament*, col. 84: "Wir werden von dieser sündlichen Unart nicht eher los werden, bis daß wir diesen sterblichen Leib ablegen. Besiehe Herr Luth. T. VII. Alt. p. 622."

33. Leaver, *Bachs theologische Bibliothek*, 52–55; Robin A. Leaver, "Bach und die Lutherschriften seiner Bibliothek," *Bach-Jahrbuch* 61 (1975): 129.

34. Calov, *Das Neue Testament*, col. 83: "und daher seufftzen machen."

35. Alfred Dürr, *Johann Sebastian Bach: Die Kantaten*, 8th ed. (Kassel: Bärenreiter, 2000), 640.

36. Spitta, *Bach*, 2:566.

37. Albert Schweitzer, *J. S. Bach*, trans. Ernest Newman, 2 vols. (Leipzig: Breitkopf & Härtel, 1911; reprint, New York: Dover Publications, 1966), 2:31.

38. Ibid., 2:342.

39. Whittaker, *The Cantatas*, 2:201; Dürr, *Bach: Die Kantaten*, 640.

40. Fischer and Tümpel, *Das deutsche evangelische Kirchenlied*, 6:18.

41. Ibid., 1:39 (no. 52).

42. Ibid., 1:41; John Julian, *A Dictionary of Hymnology*, 2 vols. (London: John Murray, 1907; reprint, New York: Dover Publications, 1957), 2:983.

43. Caspar Binder, *Historischer Erweiß, Daß des bekandten Liedes unserer Kirchen: Ach Gott und Herr, wie gros und schwer . . . wahrer Auctor sey M. MARTIN. RUTILIUS . . .* (Jena: Mit Wertherischen Schrifften, 1726), 9–12.

44. Reinhold Jauernig, "Der Dichter des Liedes 'Ach Gott und Herr, wie groß und schwer . . .," *Jahrbuch für Liturgik und Hymnologie* 1 (1955): 107–9.

45. Julian, *A Dictionary of Hymnology*, 2:983.

46. Gottfried Vopelius, *Neu Leipziger Gesangbuch* (Leipzig: In Verlegung Christoph Klingers Buchb., 1682), 518.

47. Johann Christoph Olearius, *Evangelischer Lieder-Schatz*, 4 vols. (Jena: Johann Felix Bielcken, 1705–7), 3:26: "DIeses Liedes wahrer *Autor* ist *Johannes* Göldel, ein Pfarrherr zu Dinstett, an der Jlmen, in Thüringen, welcher aber nur die 6. ersten Strophen verfertiget, biß auf die Worte: Von Dir seyn abgeschieden."

48. Fischer and Tümpel, *Das deutsche evangelische Kirchenlied*, 1:40–41.

49. Vopelius, *Neu Leipziger Gesangbuch*, 518–20. See also Jürgen Grimm, *Das Neu Leipziger Gesangbuch des Gottfried Vopelius (Leipzig 1682): Untersuchungen zur Klärung seiner geschichtlichen Stellung* (Berlin: Merseburger, 1969).

50. Siegfried Hermelink, "Ein Heidelberger Choralbuch vom Jahre 1766," *Jahrbuch für Liturgik und Hymnologie* 15 (1970): 166; Konrad Ameln, "Das handschriftliche Choralbuch des Organisten C. I. Engel vom Jahre 1775," *Jahrbuch für Liturgik und Hymnologie* 12 (1967): 173.

51. Robert L. Marshall, *The Compositional Process of J. S. Bach*, 2 vols. (Princeton, N.J.: Princeton University Press, 1972), 1:76–77.

52. Günther Stiller, *Johann Sebastian Bach and Liturgical Life in Leipzig*, trans. Herbert J. A. Boumann et al. (St. Louis: Concordia, 1984), 246 and 252–53.

53. WA 2, 128. See Rudolf Köhler, *Die biblischen Quellen der Lieder (Handbuch zum Evangelischen Kirchengesangbuch*, Band I, Zweiter Teil; Göttingen: Vandenhoeck & Ruprecht, 1965), 289.

54. Johannes Kulp, *Die Lieder unserer Kirche (Handbuch zum Evangelischen Kirchengesangbuch*, Sonderband; Göttingen: Vandenhoeck & Ruprecht, 1958), 257: "Betet mit David: Ach Herr, strafe uns nicht in deinem Grimm [Psalm 38:1], mit Jeremia: Bekehre du mich, so werde ich bekehrt, denn du bist mein Gott; da ich bekehrt ward, tat ich Buße [Jeremiah 31:18–19], denn nachdem ich gewitzigt bin, schlage ich mich auf die Hüfte. O bone Deus, hic ure, hic seca, hic pange, hic tunde, modo in aeternum parce."

55. Olearius, *Evangelischer Lieder-Schatz*, 3:33: "Sonst aber ist nöthig im 4. Verß die Worte: und laß mich hier wohl büßen, behutsam zu erklären, damit nicht etwa ein Papistischer Verstand heraus komme. Büßen heist sonst auch leiden, aber nicht also, daß man etwas dadurch verdienen könne."

56. Ibid., 3:34: "Das Wörtlein Buß, das wird in H. Schrifft nicht also gebraucht, wie in Welt Händeln, da es so viel ist . . . als erstatten, bezahlen, gnug- und einen gebührlichen Abtrag thun; sondern in GOttes Wort heisset Busse thun und Büssen, sich für einen armen Sünder erkennen, in Reu und Leid sich für GOtt demüthigen,

aller Straff, Ungnad und Zorns sich würdig achten und ümb Christi willen Gnad und Vergebung der Sünden bitten und erlangen."

57. WA 52, 502: "Denn dafür helt mans im Bapstumb, . . . Wölle man vergebung der sünden haben, so müsse man beichten und rewen und für die sünde mit gutten wercken gnug thun. Denn das haben sie die Buß genennet. Das ist ein seer feien Theologi, welcher der Teuffel lachet, Denn sie thut jm kein schaden. War ist es, ich soll rewen und mir meine sünde hertzlich lassen layd sein, Aber dardurch kumme ich nicht zu vergebung der sünden. Wo durch denn? Allein dardurch, das ich auff das wort unnd verheyssung achtung habe und glaube."

58. Martin Rössler, *Die Liedpredigt: Geschichte einer Predigtgattung* (Göttingen: Vandenhoeck & Ruprecht, 1976), 243.

59. Johann Avenarius, *Evangelischer Lieder-Catechißmus . . .* (Frankfurt and Leipzig: In Verlegung Joh. Christoph Stössels seel. Erben in Erffurth, 1714), 130–31: "Von einem vornehmen Prediger ist mir ehemahls referiret worden, daß er einen sehr ungedultigen Patienten mit diesem Lied, und insonderheit mit dem 4. und 6. Vers zur Gedult und Erkäntnüß seiner Sünden gebracht. Denn da er fast auff ein gantz Viertel Jahr an dem schmertzhafften Podagra darnieder gelegen, hätte endlich alle Gedult bey ihm vergehen wollen. Ihn aber im Glauben und Gedult zu erhalten, hätte er ihn dieses Lied recommendiret; Wenn die Schmertzen am grösten wären, solt er dieses Lied singen, absonderlich die Worte: Solls ja so seyn, . . . so würde er finden, daß GOTTES Gnade in ihm würde mächtig werden. Der Patient thut es; Und ob gleich seine höhnische Frau und Geschwister ihn deßwegen wolten auslachen, so überwund er es doch, wenn die Schmertzen auffs grausamste tobeten, schrie er desto mehr: Solls ja so seyn, daß Straff und Pein, . . . und erfuhr dadurch, daß es nicht umsonst sei, denn er allezeit im Hertzen kräfftiglich dadurch gestärcket und getröstet worden."

60. Eduard Emil Koch, *Geschichte des Kirchenlieds und Kirchengesangs der christlichen, insbesondere der deutschen evangelischen Kirche*, 3rd ed., 9 vols. (Stuttgart: Belser, 1866–77), 8:227.

61. Francke, *Sonn- Fest- und Apostel-Tags-Predigten . . .* , 556: "Nun diese Kraft, die da ausgegangen ist von unserm Heilande, JEsu CHristo, in den Tagen seiner Schwachheit, dieselbige Kraft ist noch allezeit in ihm, da er nun in seiner Herrlichkeit zur Rechten der Kraft sitzet, und hilft allen denjenigen von ihrem Jammer und Elende, die durch den Glauben an ihn dieselbe an sich ziehen, und sich deren theilhaftig machen."

62. Calov, *Das Neue Testament*, cols. 97–98: "Alß Christus wider von Capernaum kommen, heilet Er einen Gichtbrüchtigen zuförderst an seiner Seelen, und denn am Leibe."

63. Ibid., col. 98: "Es hat dieser Gichtbrüchtige umb Befreyung von der Gicht angehalten: Aber sihe, der HERR befreyet ihn zuförderst von Sünden, und erlöset ihn für allen Dingen von derselben Ursach, weil doch erst die Ursach der Kranckheit muß abgethan werden, wenn die Kranckheit aus dem Grund soll geheilet werden."

64. Johann Olearius, *Biblischer Erklärung, Fünfter und letzter Theil. Darinnen das gantze Neue Testament . . . vorgestellet wird . . .* (Leipzig: Johann Christoph Tarnoven, 1681), 85.

65. Ibid., 80: "Solte nicht die Seelen-Cur wichtiger seyn als die leibliche Gesundheit?"

66. Francke, *Sonn- Fest- und Apostel-Tags-Predigten . . .* , 564: "Unser lieber Heiland, da er diesen Krancken, welchen er heilen solte und auch wircklich geheilet

hat, vor sich hatte, sahe nicht auf die äusserliche Kranckheit alleine; sondern auf die Ursach der Kranckheit, nemlich die Sünde. Daher er denn als ein weiser Artzt ihn erst an seiner Seelen heilete, ehe er ihn von der leiblichen Kranckheit befreyete."

67. August Pfeiffer, *Kern und Safft der Bibel* . . . (Dresden: Johann Christoph Zimmermann, 1718), 1190: "Das möchte nun wohl iemand wunderlich vorkommen, warum Christus den armen Menschen nicht erstlich gesund macht? Es scheint, das *redditivum,* oder die Antwort schicke sich nicht zum *Interrogativo,* zu der Bitte. Der arme Mann wäre gern an seinen Gliedern gerad und gesund gewesen, so spricht ihm der HErr eine Absolution dafür, die jener doch nicht gefodert hatte. Allein, der HErr JEsus thut hier nichts ungereimtes, sondern, er will uns zu Gemüthe führen, . . . den *eigentlichen Ursprung* der Kranckheit, und ihre *bequeme Deutung.* Was das erste anbetrifft, so wills der liebe Heyland nicht machen, wie ein *Seplasiarius* oder *Qvacksalber,* der nur den Schaden obenhin heilet und *curi*ret, und den eignen Sitz der Kranckheit nicht berühret, . . . sondern er will recht die Kranckheit aus dem Grund heilen und ausrotten. Wenn einer sonst einen Wasser-Fluß stillen will, so ists nicht gnug, daß er nur den Bach abschlage, sondern er muß auch zum Ursprung und Haupt-Qvelle kommen, und dieselbe zustopffen. Was ist nun aber die *Sünde* anders, als ein *Eiter-Stock,* als die Brünnqvell aller Kranckheiten und des Todes? . . . Dieselbe Qvelle will nun der Heyland am ersten zustopffen, er will die Seelen-Gicht zu erst abthun, und also der Glieder-Gicht ihren Zufluß benehmen; Er will sagen: *Du elende Creatur! Ich sehe dein Leibes-Anliegen gar wohl, allein, ich will zuvor die böse Qvelle abthun, damit du von Grund aus an Leib und Seel gesund werdest: Ich will dir erstlich alle deine Sünde vergeben, und sodenn heilen alle deine Leibes-Gebrechen.*"

68. Francke, *Sonn- Fest- und Apostel-Tags-Predigten* . . . , 568: "Eine Vergebung der Sünden zu wissen, ist nicht schwer; aber eine Vergebung der Sünden zu glauben, darzu gehöret GOttes Kraft, und das kan man von Natur nicht thun. Wenn aber GOtt der HErr den Menschen in die Buß-Schule führet, da ihm erst sein elender Zustand für Augen gestellet wird, daß er über dem Greuel seiner Sünden lernet erschrecken, und nun wegen Empfindung seiner Sünde, des Zorns GOttes, des Fluchs des Gesetzes für Angst nicht weiß, wo er sich hinwenden soll; gleichwol aber ein sehnliches Verlangen nach der Hülffe hat, und denn der heilige Geist das Wort der Versöhnung in sein Hertze leget, daß ihm um CHristi willen alle Sünden vergeben seyn, und darauf die Kraft des Blutes CHristi, im Glauben ergriffen, das Hertz durchdringet, daß der Sünden Gedächtniß wie ein Nebel vergehet, das Gewissen von der knechtischen und verzweiflenden Furcht frey wird und GOtt die Fühlung der Sünden-Last und seines Zorns wegnimmt, und den bußfertigen Sünder seine Liebe und Gnade wieder schmecken lässet; alsdann weiß er, was rechtfertigen sey, alsdenn glaubet er die Vergebung der Sünden.

"Ich habe es ehemals mit einem Gleichniß von einem zum Tode verurtheilten Menschen erläutert: Wenn dieser zum Tode hingeführt wird, so sind viele um ihn her, die zusehen wollen, wie er vom Leben zum Tode wird gebracht werden; Wenn aber von der hohen Landes-Obrigkeit, die das Urtheil des Todes über ihn gesprochen hat, ein Bothe kömmet, welcher ruffet: Gnade! Gnade! Gnade! sihe, wem ist das Wort wol am empfindlichsten? Wem ist es süsser und angenehmer, als dem zum Tode verurtheilten Ubelthäter? Den andern gehet das so nicht zu Hertzen, die fuhlen es nicht so kräftig; aber derjenige, der zum Tode verdammet ist, und jetzt plötzlich höret, daß ihm Gnade wiederfahren soll, der wird gleichsam aus dem Tode wieder lebendig gemacht."

4

Performance Practice Issues That Affect Meaning in Two Bach Instrumental Works

Michael Marissen

Much of the recent discussion concerning historically informed performance of J. S. Bach's music has focused on the factual matter of what he actually did in his performances, a problem assumed worth studying for its own sake. There are some works, however, for which performance practice issues could take on even greater interest and value, because they can affect what one might reasonably take to be the meanings of Bach's music. In this brief essay, I will consider two such examples: ensemble size in the first movement of the Fifth Brandenburg Concerto and the significance of rhythm in the augmentation canon from the *Musical Offering*.

At the outset of the Fifth Brandenburg Concerto, it appears as though some sort of contest may ensue between the flute and a conventional ripieno strings group: the strings perform a ritornello in repeated sixteenth notes, a militant style of writing in the tradition of Monteverdi's *stile concitato*. (See, for example, the Vivace section of the aria "Es ist vollbracht" in Bach's *St. John Passion,* where the words "Der Held aus Juda siegt mit Macht und schließt den Kampf" ["The hero from Judah triumphs with power and closes the battle"] are marked by repeated-sixteenth-note string writing in D major that is remarkably similar to the Fifth Brandenburg Concerto.) Since the only instrument not playing during the opening ritornello is the flute, we could be led visually from the scoring of the ritornello—with one instrument per line in the score: two violins, viola, and continuo—to expect a solo flute concerto, a scoring that would still have been novel for early-eighteenth-century German audiences. At the first episode, however, the harpsichord—now obbligato—and the first violin join the flute to form the concertino. (Bach had in fact entered only one ripieno violin line into his score, and only one separate performing part survives for this line.) It quickly becomes apparent that a rather different kind of struggle from that implied by the opening *concitato* string-ensemble writing will take place during the movement.[1]

A great deal of the surprise for Bach's subtle opening move depends on there being only one player per line in his score; the role of first violin line will not appear inherently ambiguous with multiple performers on the second violin line, because when the tutti has more than two violins in all, it will strike audiences as less improbable that one violin will emerge as a concertino member.[2] (This also assumes that Bach's groups performed either with all members apart from the bass instruments standing or with all seated, which are the ways ensembles are most often depicted in contemporary pictures.)[3]

Whatever one makes of the Fifth Brandenburg Concerto, many readers may find it interesting to consider carefully the issue of instrumental forces in Bach's music. There has been a great deal of controversy in the Bach literature over the size of Bach's *vocal* ensembles, and I will not enter into that discussion here.[4] Less attention has been given, however, to the question of Bach's instrumental groups. Hans-Joachim Schulze, focusing largely on verbal sources,[5] has argued for relatively larger ensembles, whereas Joshua Rifkin, focusing primarily on Bach's own performing materials, has argued for much smaller ones.[6] There is no need to repeat the details of their research here. Schulze's view ends up depending explicitly on invoking incomplete chapel records or lost duplicate performing materials and implicitly on players sharing their parts; Rifkin's depends explicitly on Bach's materials being mostly complete and implicitly on players not sharing their parts (as is evident, for example, from the corresponding ensemble sizes for the various recordings of Bach's vocal and instrumental music produced by Rifkin's group, *The Bach Ensemble*).

Bach's materials for the Fifth Brandenburg Concerto, written out at Köthen, survive with only one performing part for each line in the score. Schulze suggests that this set may not be complete and that it may have been broken up, for example, when Bach's estate was divided among his heirs.[7] This sounds reasonable enough on the face of it. Scholars have established that the materials for Bach's Leipzig church cantatas typically consisted of single parts per line in the score, except for the violins with two each and the continuo with three. Bach's heirs ordinarily received either the score along with the duplicate parts or a set of parts without the duplicates. It could be, then, that since Bach's own score to the Fifth Brandenburg Concerto does not survive (not to be confused with Bach's calligraphic score dedicated to the Margrave of Brandenburg in 1721), some duplicate parts to this concerto might also now be lost.

But we do not have to assume uncritically that Bach's practices in Leipzig's large churches corresponded to those in Köthen's small chamber music rooms. Consider Bach's materials for the Köthen secular cantata *Die Zeit, die Tag und Jahre macht*, BWV 134a.[8] For this work we have the score and single parts. (In this connection, it should be noted that the cantata's second *Continuo* part, marked in the score for violone, has some different readings from the first.) Each of the duplicate parts now associated with these materials was copied out for renderings of the Leipzig church cantata *Ein Herz, das seinen Jesum lebend weiß*, BWV 134 (a work that borrows vocal and instrumental lines from Cantata 134a but has new words). We have no reason to believe that Bach lost some duplicate Köthen parts before reusing the single parts in his Leipzig renderings. There is, in fact, no evidence to contradict the suggestion that it was Bach's general practice at Köthen to have single performing parts prepared.[9]

Bach's own performing materials for the remaining Brandenburg Concertos do not survive, but the other extant eighteenth-century sets of parts have typically come down to us without duplicates. The same holds true for the early parts to other Bach concertos that were performed outside the Leipzig churches. The A-Major harpsichord concerto, BWV 1055, for example, survives in autograph score and single parts, which makes the loss of duplicate parts not all that likely.[10]

If it seems that Bach's secular instrumental music was transmitted without duplicate parts, there remains the much more difficult question of how many players read from each performing part. To my knowledge, there are in all of Bach's output very few examples showing absolutely unambiguously that multiple players read from single parts. (What Bach's contemporaries did is perhaps another matter.) The upper parts, for example, in Bach's scorings provide some clear instances for and some fairly clear instances against sharing.[11]

The violin parts will naturally claim the greatest interest. Because in the Leipzig church cantatas there are two written-out parts for each of the two violin lines (designated simply *Violino 1* and *Violino 2*), Bach could have had as few as four and—theoretically—as many as twelve violins altogether in his ensemble (i.e., one to three per separate part, which means two to six per line in the score).[12] When, however, for a particular movement there is only a single violin in Bach's score, the music of this line will typically end up being copied into only one of the two separate Violin 1 parts, parts that elsewhere feature the first of the two violin lines in the cantata's movements scored with strings—which is to say that what have always been understood as solo violin obbligatos are not necessarily marked in any special way in the separate part. This could mean that the part was not shared and therefore did not need to be marked, or that multiple players of the first of the two separate Violin 1 parts would learn quickly and remember which arias were not scored for the entire violin group. There are, to my knowledge, no single parts that do call unambiguously for sharing by violinists.[13]

When Bach complained about his church ensembles to the Leipzig authorities in a memorandum of 23 August 1730, he mentioned that he required two or three players for each of his violin lines, two for the viola, and two for the cello.[14] Scholars have interpreted the entirety of Bach's arguably sometimes enigmatic document in such a wide variety of ways that the parts of it that might seem altogether clear when quoted in isolation—like Bach's passage about the size of the string ensemble—can become ambiguous in light of the whole. To gather what Bach's actual or desired instrumental practices were, then, we would appear to need more to go on than just Bach's memorandum. There is no escaping the necessity of scrutinizing the actual performing parts themselves.

There are only a few unambiguous examples of other treble instruments sharing their parts. For the wedding chorales *Was Gott tut, das ist wohlgetan, Sei Lob und Ehr dem höchsten Gut,* and *Nun danket alle Gott,* BWV 250–252, there are single instrumental parts for the soprano and alto lines marked *Violino è Hautbois 1* and *Violino è Hautbois 2. d'Amour.* And for the church cantata *Ich elender Mensch, wer wird mich erlösen,* BWV 48, the separate oboe part at first read *Hautbois 1* but was corrected to *Hautbois all unisono* so that Oboes 1 and 2 could read from one part. (The obbligato for the alto aria is marked *solo,* and presumably both oboists played together in the remaining movements scored with oboe.) In each of these cases where the sources unambiguously call for sharing parts, it involves a relatively simple melodic line. Bach's technically more difficult parts do not unambiguously call for sharing. Although schedules were very tight in Leipzig, with cantata renderings virtually every week and very little time between rehearsals and church services, perhaps Bach had separate parts prepared for each of his players so that they could practice at least a bit on their own.

It is not enough, then, to look at explicit evidence for sharing and apply the practice to other parts for which it would have been possible, however reasonable this may sound at first. We should also look into whether there is any evidence against sharing parts.

There are several instances of Bach's having prepared separately written-out woodwind parts that are melodically identical. This does not always necessarily mean, of course, that both instruments played together in unison. For the opening chorus and the obbligato in the alto aria from the cantata *Ihr werdet weinen und heulen,* BWV 103, for example, there is a separate virtuoso recorder part (notated in D minor in French violin clef, copied in the 1720s) that is duplicated in a part marked for flute or violin (notated in B minor in treble clef, copied in the 1730s). The flute part, sounding an octave lower, surely substitutes for, not supplements, the recorder part in a second rendering, when a recorder virtuoso (or the unusual recorder—in d'' rather than f' or f'') was presumably unavailable.

There are several cantatas, however, for which there are duplicate recorder parts when it would apparently have been much simpler for the players to share single parts. The separate parts to *Schauet doch und sehet, ob irgendein Schmerz sei,* BWV 46, call for the two oboists to take up recorders and double Recorders 1 and 2 for the relentless running sixteenth notes counterpoint of the closing chorale. (Whether this doubling stems from the first rendering or only from a later one is irrelevant to the present discussion.) Presumably Bach wanted four recorder players altogether—not two or three reading from each part, resulting in an ensemble with eight to twelve recorders (and four to six oboes, etc.). The two separate recorder parts to *Meine Seufzer, meine Tränen,* BWV 13, proceed in unison wherever the instruments play outside of the opening aria. Perhaps Bach wanted his players to be able to rehearse on their own the more difficult lines within these two works (i.e., the closing chorale from Cantata 46 and the bass aria from Cantata 13). In any event, the players do not appear to have shared parts here when it would have been easy, perhaps even expedient, to do so (i.e., if they were essentially sightreading anyway). For an example in the Bach sources of the more efficient notation to which I am alluding here (namely, an extended single part containing two melodic lines for only one of the movements), see the separate bassoon part at the "Quoniam" movement from the Missa, BWV 232[1].

One might object that Bach's young student copyists just more or less automatically copied out parts for each of the woodwind players, because, unlike string players, woodwinds simply did not share parts. We have seen from the oboe part to Cantata 48, though, that this was not necessarily the case; and, in any event, for the movements with duplicating recorders in Cantatas 13 and 46, one or the other line is, exceptionally, in Bach's own handwriting, not a student's.

A final and particularly telling example against sharing parts is provided by the church cantata *Gott der Herr ist Sonn und Schild,* BWV 79. At its first rendering, in the 1720s, Bach called for two oboes. For a 1730s rendering, he had flute parts copied out to double the oboe parts. Since he now wanted the obbligato in the alto aria to be taken by flute instead of oboe, however, the original Oboe 1 part was relabelled *Traversiere 1mo* and a new Oboe 1 part was copied directly from the original separate Oboe 1 part, this time without the aria. It would seem, then, that the flute parts supplement, not substitute for, the oboe parts. It would have been much simpler to have the flute and oboe players share the original oboe parts and, by analogy to Cantata 48, mark the alto aria for *Traversiere Solo*—unless, of course, which seems rather unlikely, Bach expected multiple players reading from each part, so that in the 1730s, Cantata 79 would feature eight to twelve woodwinds altogether, with four to six woodwinds playing each of the lines in unison.

It is not obvious, then, what Bach's general practice regarding sharing parts was, if there indeed was one. In the Fifth Brandenburg Concerto and elsewhere, we ought perhaps to make careful individual decisions by considering the original performing materials and studying the music.[15] Sometimes the issue of ensemble size will appear to be meaningful, and other times it will not.

In Frederick the Great's own copy of the 1747 print of Bach's *Musical Offering,* the following inscriptions appear next to the augmentation and modulating canons: "As the notes increase, so may the fortune of the king" ("Notulis crescentibus crescat Fortuna Regis") and "As the notes ascend, so may the glory of the king" ("Ascendenteque Modulatione ascendat Gloria Regis"). These two canons are evidently meant to be linked, for the word "king" ("Regis") appears only once, between the two canons and, uniquely, in bold script, to serve as the last word for both of the inscriptions.[16] Eric Chafe has recently pointed out that these canons show an opposition between their *Affect* and their external signs of glory.[17] In the first, the dichotomy appears between the usual significance of the majestic French dotted rhythms and the unmistakably melancholy tone, and in the second it appears between the evidently all-encompassing modulations and their deliberate registral finiteness. I would like to underscore and augment Chafe's observations by focusing on performance issues in the augmentation canon and on the wording of Bach's preface to the collection.

Towards the end of his preface, Bach uses some peculiar language that gets at the heart of the matter: "This resolve [to work out the *Musical Offering*] . . . has none other than this irreproachable intent, to glorify . . . the fame of a monarch" ("Er hat keine andere als nur diese untadelhafte Absicht, den Ruhm eines Monarchen . . . zu verherrlichen"). Both "rühmen" and "verherrlichen" mean "to glorify," and neither one of these words by itself would seem particularly significant. But to use them together, the one as the object of the other, would in the 1740s have seemed linguistically odd.[18] When Bach's text speaks of "glorifying the glory" of the king, it presumably refers to different notions of glory.

For help on this question, we can turn to the texts of Bach's surviving vocal works. The only instance there of "glorifying glory" is found in the opening chorus of the standard version of the *St. John Passion,* BWV 245. The text reads (my emphases): "Lord [*Herr*], our ruler [*Herr*scher], whose glory [in the sense of "praise" ("*Ruhm*")] is glorious [*herr*lich] in all the lands! Show us through your Passion that you, the true Son of God, at all times, *even in the greatest abasement,* have been glorified [ver*herr*licht]!"[19] Like Bach's preface to the *Musical Offering,* this text links "Ruhm" with "verherrlichen." The wording "Ruhm . . . verherrlicht" in the *St. John Passion* was presumably adopted deliberately, for the libretto otherwise quotes Psalm 8, a well-known psalm, whose text speaks of the glory of God's name ("Name," not "Ruhm").

The *St. John Passion* chorus reflects powerfully one of the central ideas in Lutheran theology, the notion that Jesus' glorification as the king of humanity centers on his suffering on the cross. This is not the place for a detailed consideration of Luther's "theology of the cross."[20] The only place God's glory is revealed to humans is, paradoxically, hidden in Jesus' suffering on the cross; and this in turn provides a model for how humans ought to live. This is why Bach's church cantatas can speak so often of people finding joy in suffering. For Lutherans, true knowledge of God and a right ethical attitude are not separate matters but one and the same. Seeking knowledge of God through philosophical speculation is in the same category as seeking salvation through good works. Both exalt humans to the level of God, and both use the same standard for God and our relationship to God: glory and power.

Glory, then, might be said to have two senses in Lutheranism, the one essentially spiritual and the other more worldly. Bach captures this in the *St. John Passion* and in the preface to the *Musical Offering* by using for the one "ver*herr*lichen" (literally, to glorify in the sense of "to make God-like"—to suffer) and for the other "rühmen" (to glorify in the sense of "praise," or "to make known").

It seems to me that Bach represents the spiritual glorification of worldly glory musically in a particularly striking and straightforward way in the augmentation canon from the *Musical Offering.* Here the bass line forcefully points to the French dotted style with its traditional baroque associations of majesty and glory. The realization of the canon, however, calls for augmentation and contrary motion. In its realization, the line becomes deregalized, because at half speed the rhythms can no longer give the impression of the majestic dotted style.

Some performers assimilate overdotting in the augmented voice with overdotting in the bass, so that thirty-second notes of the original voice become thirty-second notes in the augmented voice too[21]; the Bach literature has also recommended this solution.[22] An arguable virtue of this stylish manner of performance is that it heightens the piece's *Stylo Francese* qualities (cf. *Contrapunctus 6* in Bach's *Art of Fugue*)—which is not to say that overdotting has been incontrovertibly established as the right way to perform French baroque music or Bach's music in French styles.[23] Another virtue is that this manner of performance softens the rather strange dissonances that emerge in a realization featuring an augmentation of the entire bass line. Bach most probably meant only the first half of the bass line to be featured in the augmented realization, however, since, as few performers will have noticed from their modern editions, augmenting the entire line often involves changing the melodic readings and rhythms of Bach's print. (Many editions alter the print's rhythm at m. 7 by adding a dot to the first quarter note and changing the subsequent thirty-second notes to sixty-fourths, and some editions also read f–e♭–d–c at the last three notes of m. 8 and the first note of m. 9 rather than the a♭–g–f–e♭ of the print.)[24] The realization works unproblematically when only the first half of Bach's printed bass line is augmented, the type of solution encountered in Bach's own realizations of other augmentation canons.[25] I would argue that, no matter which canonic realization is employed, assimilated overdotting should not be adopted, because it goes against the letter and the spirit of the augmentation and its rubric. Although we might expect a historically informed performance style to be logically prior to a work's meaning, we could, in this instance at least, see the former governed by the latter.

In other words, the manifest worldly glory of Bach's original line is spiritually glorified by the canonic realization. The inscription for Frederick, "As the notes increase, so may the fortune of the king," in this context, has a rather different meaning from what is usually suggested (namely, "Vive le roi!").[26] The melancholy *Affect* and the deregalized canonic solution link regal fortune (worldly works—glory) not to splendor, might, and fame but to the "theology of the cross."[27] Performances with a more or less literal rhythmic augmentation will best reflect this understanding.

For each of the issues explored here, one might object that the method was circular: we should not allow various narrow performance practice questions to be answered via broader interpretation while the broad questions are also being answered via the narrow. The approach's circularity, however, is not necessarily problematic. It manifests Wilhelm Dilthey's celebrated "hermeneutic circle" of historical inquiry, whereby in order to understand the whole it is necessary to understand the parts, while to understand the parts it is necessary to have some comprehension of the whole.[28] The hermeneutic circle is not a vicious circle, in that we can come to valid interpretation through a continual, mutually qualifying interplay between our evolving sense of the whole and our retrospective understanding of its parts.

Notes

1. For the details of this interpretation, see Michael Marissen, *The Social and Religious Designs of J. S. Bach's Brandenburg Concertos* (Princeton, N.J.: Princeton University Press, 1995), 104–8.

2. The third movement of the First Brandenburg Concerto, whose original performing parts do not survive, also appears to make the most sense with one player per line; see ibid., 30–31.

3. See Heinrich Besseler, ed., *Musikgeschichte in Bildern*, Band IV, *Musik der Neuzeit*, Lieferung 3: Walter Salmen, *Haus- und Kammermusik* (Leipzig: VEB Deutscher Verlag für Musik, 1969).

4. For an extensive discussion and bibliography, see Andrew Parrott, *The Essential Bach Choir* (Woodbridge, U.K.: Boydell Press, 2000); see also Joshua Rifkin, *Bach's Choral Ideal* (Dortmund: Klangfarben Musikverlag, 2002).

5. Hans-Joachim Schulze, "Johann Sebastian Bach's Orchestra: Some Unanswered Questions," *Early Music* 17 (1989): 3–15.

6. Joshua Rifkin, "More (and Less) on Bach's Orchestra," *Performance Practice Review* 4 (1991): 5–13; Rifkin, "The Violins in Bach's *St. John Passion*," in *Critica*

Musica: Essays in Honor of Paul Brainard, ed. John Knowles (Amsterdam: Gordon & Breach, 1996), 307–32.

7. Schulze, "Johann Sebastian Bach's Orchestra," 9.

8. This example and several related ones are pointed out in Rifkin, "More (and Less)," 8. The present essay's information concerning Bach's performing materials has mostly been gleaned from the critical reports to the relevant volumes in the *Neue Bach-Ausgabe* (Johann Sebastian Bach, *Neue Ausgabe sämtlicher Werke* [Kassel: Bärenreiter, 1954–   ]).

9. This could well have also been the case for Bach's Weimar materials; see Rifkin, "More (and Less)," 8. When Bach used a different version of the first movement of the First Brandenburg Concerto at Leipzig as a sinfonia in the church cantata *Falsche Welt, dir trau ich nicht*, BWV 52, he had duplicate violin parts copied.

10. This and similar examples are mentioned by Rifkin, "More (and Less)," 8. Most of the contemporary Dresden concerto repertory also survives in single parts; see Ortrun Landmann, "The Dresden Hofkapelle during the Lifetime of Johann Sebastian Bach," *Early Music* 17 (1989): 17–30.

11. My thanks to Joshua Rifkin for communicating to me the examples of the former.

12. Reinhard Goebel, "Fragen der instrumentalen Solo- und Ensemblepraxis Bachs," in *Bericht über das wissenschaftliche Symposion anläßlich des 61. Bachfestes der Neuen Bachgesellschaft*, ed. Christoph Wolff (Kassel: Bärenreiter, 1988), 84–94, points out that Bach's concertato violin lines often contain detailed articulation markings whereas his ripieno lines are plainer. Such a functional distinction does not in itself necessarily tell us anything, however, about whether there would have been more than one player per ripieno line.

13. Regarding the confusing case of the duplicate *Violini Unisoni* parts in Bach's Sanctus in D Major, BWV 238, see Rifkin, "Violins in Bach's *St. John Passion*," 329.

14. See Hans-Joachim Schulze and Werner Neumann, eds., *Bach-Dokumente I: Schriftstücke von der Hand Johann Sebastian Bachs* (Kassel: Bärenreiter, 1963), 60–64.

15. Hans-Werner Boresch, *Besetzung und Instrumentation: Studien zur kompositorischen Praxis Johann Sebastian Bachs* (Kassel: Bärenreiter, 1993), 129–31, argues that, because of several *solo* markings in the ripieno violin line at the third movement of the Fifth Brandenburg Concerto (in Bach's own parts and in the score sent to the Margrave of Brandenburg; they do not appear in the earlier version of the concerto, BWV 1050a), there ought to be more than one player on this line. But these markings may well refer to corresponding episodic functions, not to the number of players on the line. Consider the fact that such markings also appear at the initial episodic passages in the concertato violin lines in Bach's or reliable early manuscripts of the Second and Fourth Brandenburg Concertos. Bach also provided in his separate performing part for harpsichord a *solo* marking at m. 154 of the first movement of the Fifth Concerto. Nobody has argued, or, presumably, would argue, that these lines ought to be taken by multiple performers. Consider, too, for example, the *solo* markings in the original flute part from the B-Minor suite, BWV 1067; this example was pointed out in Rifkin, "Bachs Chor—ein vorläufiger Bericht," *Basler Jahrbuch für historische Musikpraxis* 9 (1985): 141–55, at 147 n. 14. Another factor that has not been fully considered in the Bach literature concerns the page layouts of the original performing parts. It may be significant, for example, that Bach's performing parts for the Fifth Brandenburg Concerto were carefully designed to avoid difficult page turns;

this further suggests but of course does not prove that only one player may have been reading from each part.

16. Fortune and glory were commonly linked; this is true, for example, for the character *Schicksal* in Bach's cantata *Angenehmes Wiederau*, BWV 30a.

17. Eric Chafe, *Tonal Allegory in the Vocal Music of J. S. Bach* (Berkeley: University of California Press, 1991), 22–23, 213–15.

18. My thanks to Professor Emery Snyder (Princeton University), a specialist in eighteenth-century German literature, for confirming this suspicion. To give Bach's phrase in English as "to *extol* the fame" might seem on the face of it to be simpler and to make more sense, but, leaving aside the question of this translation's accuracy, we do in fact know that Bach took a rather dim view of extolling fame; see Howard H. Cox, ed., *The Calov Bible of J. S. Bach* (Ann Arbor, Mich.: UMI Research Press, 1985), 424.

19. "Herr, unser Herrscher, dessen Ruhm in allen Landen herrlich ist! Zeig uns durch deine Passion, daß du, der wahre Gottessohn, zu aller Zeit, auch in der größten Niedrigkeit, verrherrlicht worden bist!" This translation is taken from Marissen, *Lutheranism, Anti-Judaism, and Bach's St. John Passion—with an Annotated Literal Translation of the Libretto* (New York: Oxford University Press, 1998), 39.

20. For a convenient summary, see Paul Althaus, *The Theology of Martin Luther* (Philadelphia: Fortress Press, 1966), 25–34.

21. See, most notably, for example, the well-known 1970s recording directed by Gustav Leonhardt, released on various labels.

22. See Bernhard Kistler-Liebendörfer, *Quaerendo invenietis: Versuch über J. S. Bachs Musikalisches Opfer* (Frankfurt: Fischer, 1985), 14.

23. For a convenient overview of the issues and their bibliography, see Matthew Dirst, "Bach's French Overtures and the Politics of Overdotting," *Early Music* 25 (1997): 35–44.

24. Leonhardt's recording keeps the a♭–g–f–e♭, but brings the canon to a close by having the bass move down in eighth notes e♭–d–c (i.e., those latter notes and rhythms do not appear in Bach's print). The pitches are unlikely to have been miscopied in Bach's print, as it appears that the five numbered canons on this page of the original print were engraved by a tracing method; see Marissen, "More Source-Critical Research on Bach's *Musical Offering*," *Bach* 25, no. 1 (1994): 11–27, at 18–19.

25. For the details, see Christoph Wolff, ed., Johann Sebastian Bach, *Neue Ausgabe sämtlicher Werke*, VIII/1: *Kanons, Musikalisches Opfer, Kritischer Bericht* (Kassel: Bärenreiter, 1976), 114.

26. See, for example, Ursula Kirkendale, "The Source for Bach's *Musical Offering*: The *Institutio oratoria* of Quintilian," *Journal of the American Musicological Society* 33 (1980): 88–141, at 107, 110; and Lothar Hoffmann-Erbrecht, "Von der Urentsprechung zum Symbol: Versuch einer Systematisierung musikalischer Sinnbilder," in *Bachiana et alia Musicologica: Festschrift Alfred Dürr zum 65. Geburtstag,* ed. Wolfgang Rehm (Kassel: Bärenreiter, 1983), 116–25, at 118.

27. A much longer interpretation, including most but not all of the present material, appears in Marissen, "The Theological Character of J. S. Bach's *Musical Offering*," *Bach-Studies 2*, ed. Daniel R. Melamed (Cambridge: Cambridge University Press, 1995), 85–106.

28. For a far-reaching discussion of these issues, see David Couzens Hoy, *The Critical Circle: Literature, History, and Philosophical Hermeneutics* (Berkeley: University of California Press, 1978).

5

Mozart's *Mitridate*: Going beyond the Text

Ellen T. Harris

The performance of eighteenth-century opera seria demands more than an accurate text. In addition to the necessity for (preferably improvised) continuo realization, no opera seria is complete without vocal ornamentation. Indeed, without ornamentation and cadenzas, no da capo aria can make the desired intensification of dramatic effect. In the summer of 2001 I had the opportunity to serve as musicological consultant to the Santa Fe Opera performances of Mozart's *Mitridate*. My experience preparing ornamentation and cadenzas for this production offers a case study in reading the text for the purpose of going beyond it.[1]

Mitridate, Re di Ponto, Mozart's earliest essay in opera seria, was written for the Regio Ducal Teatro in Milan in 1770, when the composer was only fourteen. A corpus of significant research on this opera is available to the scholar or performer coming fresh to the work. The "Neue Mozart Ausgabe" (*NMA*) edition by Luigi Ferdinando Tagliavini provides an excellent text based largely on sources unknown or unavailable to the nineteenth-century edition that had appeared as part of *W. A. Mozarts Werke.*[2] The libretto by Vittorio Amedeo Cigna-Santi, based in part on Racine's *Mithridate,* was originally set by Quirino Gasparini in Turin in 1767.[3] Tagliavini postulated the importance of this earlier setting to Mozart's opera based on a study of the libretto and a surviving score in the Bibliothèque Nationale de France in Paris.[4] In 1991 Rita Peiretti discovered that the Turin copy of Gasparini's opera contained arias missing in the Paris copy, allowing her to identify Mozart's version of Mitridate's aria "Vado incontro al fate estremo" as an adapted borrowing of Gasparini's setting.[5]

Although no autograph exists of Mozart's *Mitridate,* autograph folios of discarded or alternate versions of arias from the opera survive in the Bibliothèque Nationale, all of which were published by Tagliavini in the NMA edition. Eight of the arias set by Mozart exist in at least one alternate version; in one case, Mitridate's entrance aria "Se di lauri," four alternate versions (in addition to the final version) survive. Peiretti's discovery of the

Turin score of Gasparini's opera enabled Harrison James Wignall in his dissertation to compare the Mozart and the Gasparini settings with a particular eye to the evolution of the preliminary versions of arias into their final form and to show definitively the significant impact of Gasparini's score on Mozart's composition.[6] Largely simultaneous with Wignall's work, Philip Adlung also completed a dissertation on Mozart's *Mitridate*.[7] Happily the two book-length studies are complementary. Wignall focuses his attention on the original singers of Mozart's opera (especially the lead tenor, Guglielmo d'Ettore) and on the discarded autograph versions, examining how Mozart recast his final versions to better suit his singers' voices and, at the same time, modeled them more closely on Gasparini's setting; Adlung provides in-depth analyses of the final versions, arguing that, however much Mozart may have been influenced by the singers or Gasparini's score, he also provided clear musical profiles of each dramatic character.

Despite this burst of scholarly interest in *Mitridate,* the necessity of composing (or improvising) ornamentation remains perpetually unresolved, arising anew for every performance. The creation of appropriate ornamentation requires preparation of various sorts. First, it is essential to be fully acquainted with the contemporary style, for Mozart's early opera seria ornamentation differs significantly from that of both earlier and later composers, such as Handel and Rossini. The most comprehensive sources for vocal ornamentation in the late eighteenth century are the volumes of examples published by composer Domenico Corri between 1780 and 1810: *A Select Collection of the Most Admired Songs, Duets, &c.,* volumes 1–4, and *The Singer's Preceptor.*[8] Corri writes in his "Explanation . . . of the following Work":

> When a person has purchased a book, would it not appear very extraordinary, if he should be under the necessity of applying to a master of language to correct the orthography, and to distinguish the members of every sentence by proper stops, in order to render the author's meaning intelligible? Just such an absurdity appears in written music,—vocal music in particular: for, notwithstanding the many alterations that are daily making, the manner of noting it, which remains nearly the same as it was in the infancy of the art, is quite insufficient to express the meaning, spirit, and peculiar delicacy of the composition.[9]

After discussing various performance indications and the use of appoggiaturas, he continues:

> We are now to take notice of the principal refinements in song; such as cadences, divisions, and all those intervening ornaments, the proper use of which alone can give to song its highest degree of grace and elegance. These ornaments, to the great disadvantage of composition, have never yet been written down. The Author has introduced into this work such as he judged proper, (and has distinguished them by notes of a smaller size than those which constitute the original

melody). As the invention of such ornaments is attended with difficulty, and as it is of great importance to know where and in what measure to introduce them, and where their application would be improper, the advantage of having them written down must be evident.[10]

As important as Corri's work is to eighteenth-century vocal music, of even more importance to vocal ornamentation in Mozart's early works in the opera seria form are the exemplars from the composer's own hand. In the late 1770s, Mozart prepared ornamentation and cadenzas for the da capo arias "Cara, la dolce fiamma" from *Adriano in Siria* (1765) by J. C. Bach and "Ah, se a morir mi chiama," from his own *Lucio Silla* (1772). Autograph cadenzas also survive for his rondo "L'amerò" from *Il rè pastore* (1775).[11]

Da capo arias, in which the first (A) section of the aria was wholly or partly repeated at the end, form the basis of Mozart's aria composition in *Mitridate* and demand additional ornamentation. Cadenzas should typically be added at the ends of the A section (each time) and B section, increasing in length and complexity. Mozart's ornamentation for the aria by J. C. Bach includes cadenzas for the two cadences in the A section (at the end of A_1 and A_2 in five-part da capo form: $A_1A_2\|B\|A_1A_2\|$) for both the first statement and the da capo, as well as two cadenzas for the B section, totaling six separate cadenzas in all, plus four alternative fermata embellishments for the opening motto. In *Mitridate,* Mozart marks these places for cadenzas with fermatas over the whole bar.[12] Surviving examples from the period indicate that cadenzas typically begin and end in the register notated in the score; further, they do not remain on a single chord but touch on a variety of harmonies; they contain striking rhythmic variety, often ranging from the sixteenth to the half note; and, although they may include sequential patterns, these are limited and rarely related to figuration from the aria. Although vocal tutors from this period sometimes state that cadenzas should be sung in one breath, infractions of this rule seem not only to have been relatively common, but also singers apparently "were trained to execute in a single breath passages that far exceed the capacity of most vocalists today."[13] It may perhaps be a better dictum today to say that classical cadenzas should be conceived as a single, coherent phrase without extensive patterning.

Embellishments within the aria, although focused on the repeated A section, were used sparingly in the first A section and the B section as well. Ornamentation made use of passing notes, sometimes further divided with turn or alternating-note figures, but large and distinctive leaps were generally not filled in. Generally, ornamentation increases the speed and intensity by the addition of smaller note values, in some cases moving through notated rests; however, a variety of rhythmic values occur here as well as in cadenzas, and syncopation seems to have been especially favored by Mozart.

Although the melodic shape of the line was normally maintained without octave transposition or the addition of high notes for their own sake, Mozart's variations did at times take the singer in one motion both below and above the written line by as much as an octave (see example 5.1).[14]

Example 5.1. J. C. Bach, "Cara, la dolce fiamma" with ornamentation by Mozart. From Will Crutchfield, "The Classical Era: Voices," in *The New Grove Handbooks in Music: Performance Practice* (London: Macmillan, 1989), vol. 2, *Music after 1600*, 307. Used by permission of Oxford University Press.

Recitative also requires ornamentation. With simple recitative, this means the addition of appoggiaturas; indeed, the use of appoggiaturas in both recitative and aria is critical to the style, as is clear in the examples provided by Domenico Corri, where both upper and lower appoggiaturas are used. As Crutchfield writes, "No Classical source suggests that there were exceptions to this practice or that these prosodic appoggiaturas were considered optional."[15] Accompanied recitative allowed for more elaborate flourishes when the affect was appropriate, and a surviving example of embellished cadences from Angelo Tarchi's *Mitridate* (1785) provides an example (see example 5.2).[16] In his treatise on singing from 1804, however, Johann Friedrich Schubert cautioned against using ornamentation in recitative when the text "has a meaning in which embellishment can find no place."[17]

Example 5.2. Angelo Tarchi, *Mitridate* (1785), ornamented accompanied recitative. From Will Crutchfield, "The Classical Era: Voices," in *The New Grove Handbooks in Music: Performance Practice* (London: Macmillan, 1989), vol. 2, *Music after 1600*, 296. Used by permission of Oxford University Press.

Beyond following contemporary style as indicated in the surviving musical texts, newly-composed embellishments, as Schubert's warning implies, have to take into account specific variables: that is, the finished ornamentation and cadenzas need to be consistent with the capabilities and strengths of the individual singers, the character being portrayed, and the emotion being expressed in the aria. Mozart followed this practice in composition, writing to his father (26 September 1781) of the aria "Ach, ich liebte" in *Die Entführung aus dem Serail*: "I have sacrificed Constanze's aria a little to the flexible throat of Mlle. Cavalieri [but] I have tried to express her feelings as far as an Italian bravura aria will allow it."[18] Ten years earlier, the composition history of *Mitridate* shows the same balance of concerns.

The story of King Mitridate of Pontus (now part of Turkey), who ruled from 124 B.C.E. to 88 B.C.E., takes place in the royal city of Nymphaea.[19] In Act I his two sons, Farnace and Sifare, have recently converged on the city, having heard a report that their father has been killed in battle. Farnace, who has treacherously sided with the Romans against his father, now desires to woo, by force if necessary, the Greek princess Aspasia who was betrothed to Mitridate and has already been proclaimed Queen. She turns for aid to Sifare, whom she had secretly loved before her betrothal. The brothers are ready to fight over Aspasia when they receive the news that their father is alive and has arrived in Nymphaea with Ismene, a Parthian princess betrothed to Farnace. Having spread the rumor of his own death in order to test his sons and confound his enemies, Mitridate quickly uncovers Farnace's traitorous allegiance to Rome and desire for Aspasia, and he determines fierce revenge.

In Act II, Farnace declares to Ismene that he no longer loves her, but she remains steadfast even when Mitridate suggests that Sifare might make her a better husband. Mitridate gives the care of his Queen to Sifare, and left alone together Aspasia and Sifare admit their mutual love, but struggle to renounce it in the name of duty. Mitridate publicly disarms and denounces Farnace, who then reveals the love between Sifare and Aspasia. In a rage, Mitridate condemns all three to death. The act ends with a duet for Sifare and Aspasia in which they express their hope that if they cannot live together they might at least die together.

Act III opens with Ismene and Aspasia, who has attempted suicide, pleading in vain for the lives of Farnace and Sifare, when the news arrives that a Roman military force has landed in Nymphaea. Events then quickly tumble over one another. Mitridate leaves for battle. Aspasia, still a condemned prisoner, is delivered poison, but the bowl is dashed from her hands by Sifare, who has been freed by Ismene. Sifare leaves to support his father. Farnace is freed from prison by the Romans, but suddenly repents of his disloyalty and assists in the Greek victory by setting the Roman fleet on fire. Before this turn in the battle, however, Mitridate, thinking he is about to fall into enemy hands, stabs himself rather than surrender and is carried dying into the royal courtyard. Before his death he recognizes Sifare's loyalty and courage and blesses his union with Aspasia. Then Ismene arrives with Farnace, revealing Farnace's repentance and bravery and their reconciliation, allowing Mitridate to die reconciled to both sons. The opera ends as the two pairs of lovers sing of their vow to continue the war for freedom against Rome.

Although Mozart's contract with the Regio Ducal Teatro of Milan for *Mitridate* does not survive, the contract of 1772 for the Milan production of *Lucia Silla* required that Mozart deliver all of the recitatives by the end of October and be in the city by the beginning of November to compose the arias.[20] The known sequence of composition for *Mitridate* follows that of *Lucia Silla* so closely that a similar contractual arrangement must have existed. Mozart began composition of the simple recitative on 29 September 1770 in Bologna.[21] He and his father arrived in Milan on 18 October, and two days later the young Mozart began a postscript to one of his father's letters: "My dear Mamma, I cannot write much, for my fingers are aching from composing so many recitatives. Mamma, I beg you to pray for me, that my opera may go well and that we may be happy together again."[22] Beginning in early November, and documented by the weekly letters of Mozart's father, Mozart composed the arias character by character, as each of the individual singers arrived in Milan.[23]

Leopold Mozart's letter of 10 November indicates that Wolfgang spent the previous week largely writing (and rewriting) the arias for the *prima donna*, Antonia Bernasconi, who played the role of Aspasia. According to Leopold, Bernasconi, soon after her arrival, was presented with a complete set of Aspasia's arias, presumably from Gasparini's opera, and encouraged to sing these rather than Mozart's settings.[24] Negotiations with Bernasconi led to Mozart's rewriting (and discarding his first versions of) the opening aria, "Al destin"; the first aria of the second act, "Nel grave tormento"; and the duet with Sifare that closes the second act, "Se viver non degg'io." In the end, Bernasconi used Gasparini's setting only for her final aria, "Secondi il ciel pietoso" (for which no Mozart setting survives), and otherwise sang what Mozart composed (four arias and a duet). Leopold writes exuberantly of winning her over:

> Thank God, we won the first battle, and defeated an enemy, who brought into the theater all of the arias for the prima donna that she is to sing in our opera, and tried to convince her not to sing any arias at all by Wolfgang. . . . However, . . . she denied this evil person, and she is completely beside herself with joy over the arias that Wolfgang composed for her, following her desires and preferences . . . she cannot praise Wolfgang's arias enough.[25]

Even so, he was aware that Wolfgang's troubles were not over: "There is, however, still another storm in the theatrical heavens, that we can already see from a distance. Nevertheless, with God's help, and good course of action, we will overcome it."[26] Indeed, this prediction turned out to be true. The following week, devoted to the composition of arias for the title character, was even more difficult.

Guglielmo d'Ettore, the tenor singing the role of Mitridate, was the only singer in Mozart's cast who had also sung in Gasparini's opera three years earlier in Turin. Apparently, Ettore arrived in Milan with the full expectation of singing Gasparini's arias, and it is likely that he was the "enemy" who provided Bernasconi with Gasparini's settings of Aspasia's arias. Ettore rejected the first four versions Mozart wrote of his opening aria, "Se di lauri." Mozart's setting of his final aria, "Vado incontro al fato estremo," was rejected out of hand, and the aria finally included in the opera was Mozart's reworking of Gasparini's aria—which, however, included a wholly new orchestration with added inner parts, some alterations to the vocal and bass lines, and the elimination of the B section. If Ettore was not as enthusiastic as Bernasconi, he was accommodated. Of his five arias, four were Mozart originals and one a significant Mozart adaptation. Leopold wrote home in his letter of 17 November: "Between yesterday and today we have overcome a second storm; and although one thing or another can possibly still take place, I hope that, with the help of God, everything will go well."[27] He concludes the letter with the news that he and Wolfgang have been given the opportunity to spend three days in the countryside outside Milan; undoubtedly this served as a needed respite from the tensions of the previous weeks.[28]

In the letter of 24 November about the preceding week, Leopold offers no report on continuing composition, but does state that the *primo uomo*, the castrato Pietro Benedetti who sang the role of Sifare, had not yet arrived. In the process he confirms once again the care the young Mozart was taking to suit the arias to the specific singers.

> Wolfgang has his hands full since the time is getting short and he has written only one aria for the *primo uomo*, since he has not arrived yet and [Wolfgang] doesn't want to do the work twice. Therefore, it is better to wait until he arrives in order to measure the suit correctly on the body.[29]

In the letter of 1 December, Leopold states, "as I write this, the *primo uomo* is still not here; he will certainly arrive today." However, he also implies that Mozart has continued to compose: "You think that the opera is already finished. You couldn't be more wrong. If it were up to our son, two operas would already have been written."[30]

Wignall's suggestion that these two weeks (18 November to 1 December) were devoted to the music for the other four singers left unmentioned by Leopold seems likely.[31] Farnace, sung by the alto castrato Giuseppe Cicognani, would have been the most important of these roles. Of his four arias, only one, "Son reo," exists in an earlier version; the revision reduces the full da capo into modified da capo form and lightens the orchestration by eliminating the trumpets, while adding a more lively violin accompaniment and a new countermelody in the oboes.[32] Ismene, sung by the soprano

Anna Francesca Varese, was the next role in importance with three arias, and Mozart completely rewrote the first of them, "In faccia all'oggetto." Arbate, soprano castrato, and Marzio, tenor, have one aria each, neither of which seems to have been revised. However, given the amount of rewriting that had been necessary for Bernasconi and Ettore and the worry over the late arrival of Benedetti, the third principal, the amount of composition required for the other four roles, including the two arias that were recomposed or significantly revised, would have given reason enough for Leopold to say "if it were up to our son, two operas would already have been written."

The letter of 8 December does not confirm the arrival of Benedetti, but it can be assumed: during this week the first two rehearsals, devoted to recitatives, took place. If, as seems likely, Mozart also completed Benedetti's arias during this time, then it was a busy period. Sifare has four arias and the duet with Aspasia. Perhaps his opening aria, "Soffre il mio cor," is the one Mozart tried to write in advance, as a draft of a discarded opening ritornello survives. In addition, the third aria, "Lungi da te," exists in three versions: an early, very different setting; a second setting largely representative of the final one; and a re-orchestration of the second version to include obbligato horn. Further, the rewriting of the duet had to have happened after Benedetti's arrival. Perhaps this took place in the next week, for in his letter of 15 December Leopold finally is able to state that all the singers were satisfied with their music.[33] He writes specifically of Benedetti: "The *primo uomo* said that if the duet did not please the public, he would have himself castrated a second time."[34] This week (9 December to 15 December) also saw the first orchestral rehearsals. The following week (16 December to 22 December) was devoted to stage rehearsals, and the next saw the opening of *Mitridate* on 26 December and the second and third performances on 27 and 29 December, all with Mozart directing from the first keyboard. (After the third performance the direction was taken over by Giovanni Battista Lampugnani.)

In his detailed comparisons of the early versions of the final arias, Wignall argues convincingly that Mozart was adjusting the music to the specific talents and requirements of the soloists, and he demonstrates in addition (a point surely not unrelated to the singers' requests) that in many cases Mozart's final versions are modeled on or more closely related to Gasparini's settings. Despite this evidence, or rather because of it, what remains most striking to me is the way Mozart carefully delineates the various roles in the final score. That is, despite any sacrifices to their demands (or to their "flexible throats"), Mozart succeeds in expressing the feelings of the character and the emotion of the aria.[35]

Each of Mitridate's five arias displays concision and directness. None is a full-fledged da capo. The first, "Se di lauri," is a written-out modified da capo following the typical form A_1BA_2: the A_1 section cadencing to the dominant, the B section to the relative minor, and A$_2$, of course, to the tonic. Mozart labels this aria "cavata," perhaps indicating that, despite its tripartite form, it should be thought of as short and through-composed. Such an intention may be signaled by the lack of any indication for a cadenza (a fermata over a bar with a pause in the orchestral accompaniment), although a small fermata on the final note of the B section suggests an ornamental flourish that could link to the "return" of A. The fourth aria, "Già di pietà mi spoglio," is also a modified da capo, and, like "Se di lauri," includes a possible indication of a (linking) flourish at the end of the B section but no indication for a cadenza. Mitridate's second, third, and final arias are all cavatinas (without B sections) in Mozart's opera, although Gasparini included the B sections in his setting; and the B section texts, although eliminated in the score, still appeared in the Milan libretto. Wignall hypothesizes that Ettore, who died a year after the *Mitridate* performance, "was unable to sing for extended periods and that the elimination of the B section (which of course dramatically shortens the aria) served to accommodate his limitations."[36] This may be. However, the arias are hardly "easy." They are full of extraordinary angularity created by large, almost ungainly, leaps of an octave, a twelfth, and two octaves, frequently one after another. And, lacking extensive figuration, the arias typically drive relentlessly forward. The musical result is that Mozart's arias for Mitridate depict him as bold, domineering, and brusque. Mitridate overpowers the other characters with the force of his utterance.

Sifare, in addition to his duet with Aspasia, sings four arias. In contrast to those of Mitridate, all are in some form of da capo. The first, "Soffre il mio cor," is a written-out half da capo (A$_1$A$_2$BA$_3$) with tonic closure before the B section, as in a full da capo, but only a single statement of the A text in the return; here the harmonic scheme of the four sections is V-I-iii-I. There is extensive figuration in a high register (repeatedly reaching b♭", sometimes by way of staccato repeated notes), in addition to passages in wide leaps. (One such passage proceeds directly through a descending minor seventh, rising octave, descending major ninth, ascending fifth, and ascending minor seventh, landing on the b♭". Mozart also calls for two cadenzas (at the end of A$_2$ and A$_3$). The third aria, "Lungi da te," also a written-out half da capo, includes similarly virtuosic figuration over a full two-octave range (low b♭ to high b♭") and, again, the indication for two cadenzas. Sifare's second and final arias are both written-out modified da capos (without any indications for cadenzas), but both include extensive figuration. Mozart characterizes Sifare as strong and forceful—perhaps the wide leaps are an indication that he is truly the bold son of the father—but emotionally torn. In his first aria, he grieves that Aspasia must deny him love but rages at his rival, shifting between long-held notes in a generally conjunct melodic line to disjunct dotted rhythms accented with *fp*'s; in his second, "Parto: nel gran cimento," a two-tempo A section expresses his agreement to stand by his brother Farnace but still remain loyal to their father; in his third, "Lungi da te," the A and B sections are characterized by different tempi (adagio cantabile and andante) and meters (C and 3/8), distinguishing Sifare's two statements that (1) he *will* leave if Aspasia wishes, but that (2) he *must* leave so as not to forget his duty. Throughout the opera, Sifare's arias make use of a syncopated rhythm that seems to symbolize his emotional turmoil (example 5.3).

Example 5.3a. "Soffre il mio cor" (Sifare). All quotations from Mozart's *Mitridate, re di Ponto*, Mozart, *Neue Ausgabe sämtlicher Werke* 2/5/4, ed. Luigi Ferdinando Tagliavini (Kassel: Bärenreiter, 1966). Used by permission.

Example 5.3b. "Parto: nel gran cimento" (Sifare)

Example 5.3c. "Lungi da te" (Sifare)

Example 5.3d. "Se il rigor d'ingrata sorte" (Sifare)

Farnace's four arias, like Sifare's, are all da capo forms: the first and last, half da capos, and the second and third, modified da capos. However, they are not typified by conflicting emotions. Farnace's one two-tempo aria (his one aria with alternating tempos in the A section), "Son reo; l'error confesso," is, like Mitridate's one two-tempo aria, imbued with fervor and incisiveness. Mitridate, in "Tu, che fedel mi sei," depicts with sharp precision his differing attitude toward Sifare and Aspasia, believing his son faithful to him and Aspasia ungrateful. Similarly, Farnace admits to Mitridate and the court his treachery ("I am guilty: I confess it"[37]), but then spins on his brother and identifies him as the king's rival in love ("but Sifare is guiltier than I am and shall not laugh at my misfortune"[38]). Neither aria expresses inner conflict. Similarly, in Farnace's first aria, "Venga pur," the A and B sections are contrasted with different tempos and meters (C—Allegro and 3/8—Andante) to depict Farnace's dual, but not conflicting, statements: "My father may threaten and rage, but he will be forced to respect and fear my alliance with Rome."[39] Farnace's arias, then, are distinct from those of his brother Sifare by their lack of inner emotional conflict. Rather, the contrasts within his arias depict strength and anger, usually with the formula: "I'll tolerate this, but you take that," as in the arias above and in his second aria, "Va, l'error mio palesa," where Farnace sings to Ismene: "O.K., you go reveal my offense, but you'll be sorry" (with a variation in vocal style but no change in tempo or meter).[40] In his final aria, "Già dagli occhi il velo è tolto," the pattern changes slightly to reflect his return to loyalty, but the contrast still depicts an unconflicted state: "I repent my base affections; now is the time to return to honor" (C—Andante and 2/4—Allegretto).[41]

If Mitridate, pig-headed and stubborn, acts before he thinks, and Sifare, the good son, finds himself rendered unable to act or speak due to the conflicts between his love for Aspasia, his rivalry with his brother, and his loyalty to his father, Farnace is the rebel, who strives to achieve independence through defiance. The figuration in his arias differs both from Mitridate's forthrightness (and consequent lack of ornamentation and cadenzas) and Sifare's conflict (with its rhythmic syncopation, lyrical phrase structure, and long, varied, and broken melismas). Farnace's arias depict his vitality in strong dotted figures and his impetuousness in short (often repeated) phrases and closely patterned figuration. The repetitions and patterning encourage the addition of ornamentation, and Mozart further suggests this by indicating more cadenzas for Farnace than for any other character. His first aria, "Venga pur," calls for four cadenzas, more than any other aria in the opera, and his last aria, "Già dagli occhi il velo è tolto," calls for three, which occurs in only one other aria, Aspasia's "Al destin." (In addition to these three arias, seven arias in *Mitridate* call for two cadenzas, five call for one, and nine call for none.) The implicit abundance of ornamentation in Farnace's arias through improvised embellishments and cadenzas helps to depict his dissimulation and cunning (in stark contrast to Mitridate's bluntness).

Although Mitridate and his two sons each encounter some alteration in attitude or experience—Mitridate realizes that his judgments have been too hasty and too severe, Farnace renounces his defiance and returns to loyalty, and Sifare struggles with the conflict between his love for Aspasia and obedience to his father, ultimately winning his father's blessing for their marriage—each is also given a largely stable and distinctive musical portrait. The musical characterization of Aspasia through her four arias differs from that of the men in depicting instead a personal and musical trajectory. Her first aria, "Al destin," sung at the point when the Queen believes Mitridate has died (Act I, scene 2), portrays her emotional response to the realization that not only is Farnace pressing his unwanted suit, but that Sifare, whom she has loved in secret, also loves her. It is a full da capo, richly ornamented throughout with extensive figuration and three indications for cadenzas. Her second aria, "Nel sen mi palpita," is a written-out modified da capo. Marked Allegro Agitato, it includes little embellishment, but is agitated and breathless with chromatic lines and strong off-beat accents; there are no cadenzas. Her third aria, "Nel grave tormento," a two-tempo cavatina, depicts her conflict between love to Sifare and her duty to marry Mitridate; her peace is overcome with torment (C—Adagio) and the struggle rends her soul (C—Allegro). Although there is more figuration, in both the slow and fast tempi, than in the previous aria, there is again no indication for cadenzas. The last aria Mozart wrote for Aspasia occurs as part of an extended *scena,* beginning and ending in accompanied recitative.[42] The central aria is a cavatina, in which the voice, moving largely in half notes against pulsating eighth notes in the accompaniment, seems to exist in a timeless realm.[43] There is no figuration and no cadenza. Leopold (as quoted above) directly compared writing arias to designing proper clothing for a character when he said that Mozart would wait until the arrival of Benedetti "to measure the suit correctly on the body."[44] At the beginning of Act III, the libretto describes Aspasia throwing away the torn bands of the royal diadem with which she has tried to hang herself (Act III, scene 1). Just as she discards this ornamental symbol of her former standing, Mozart strips away the ornamentation that had embellished her previous musical expression. As Aspasia descends from chosen Queen, to victim of Farnace's forced attentions, to tormented lover of Sifare, to prisoner condemned by Mitridate to die, she seems musically to discard the accouterments of her station until she is left in "Pallid'ombre" standing metaphorically naked and exposed before the image of her death.

Ismene, the only other female character, contrasts sharply with Aspasia. Although buffeted by war and rejection from her fiancé Farnace, she remains unconflicted and steadfast in her love. Her three arias are characterized by continual decoration that seems to represent her decorous femininity. Each is either in half or modified da capo form, and each calls for two cadenzas. Arbate (soprano castrato) and Marzio (tenor) have one aria apiece, and each is appropriate to the character. The aria for Arbate, governor of Nymphaea and ally of Sifare, is resolute and didactic as he urges the brothers to reconcile their differences and greet their father, and thus it is strongly differentiated from the arias of Sifare (the other soprano castrato in the cast). The aria includes figuration, largely limited to the word "peace," and indications for a closing cadenza and a fermata embellishment at the return to the A section. The aria for Marzio, a Roman tribune and ally of Farnace, is intense and virtuosic with extensive scalar figuration throughout, clearly contrasting this tenor aria from Mitridate's, and it drives forward with no pause for added cadenzas, as Marzio urges Farnace forward to accept the throne of Pontus from the hands of Rome.

The contemporary examples of cadenzas and embellishments and the analysis of musical characterization in *Mitridate* were the two guideposts in my preparation of ornamentation. Whereas the period examples provided a grounding in Classical ornamentation, the distinct musical portrayals apparent in Mozart's score suggested that the ornamentation for individual characters should be similarly differentiated, and also that it would be most appropriate to work through the opera by character rather than from beginning to end.[45] In the *NMA* edition of *Mitridate,* Tagliavini provided sample cadenzas of his own at all of the requisite spots, and he should be credited for recognizing the importance of cadential ornamentation and for preparing examples that were certainly corrective when they were composed almost forty years ago. More recently, however, Neumann has suggested, with unnecessary triple hesitation, that Tagliavini's cadenzas are "sometimes perhaps a little too long."[46] I believe, in addition, that they tend to be too closely modeled on figuration from the aria (which is like bringing coals to Newcastle); they are also sequentially repetitive, and the musical individuality of the characters seems to be lost. Example 5.4 compares Tagliavini's final cadenza (5.4a) for Sifare's "Soffre il mio cor" to my own version (5.4b). That Tagliavini fails to provide any sample ornamentation within the aria, or any indication of what kinds of ornamentation might have been improvised, also isolates the cadenzas unnaturally. Cadenzas make the most musical sense when they grow out of the previous ornamentation and when they and ornamentation are equally tailored to the singer, the character, and the emotion. My attempts to respond to these conclusions can be illustrated with excerpts from the ornamentation I wrote for specific characters.

The role of Mitridate calls for little addition of ornamentation. Only his entrance aria, "Se di lauri" (example 5.5, p. 109), a lyrical andante, allows for an extended embellished passage. The return of the A section material, beginning with an ornamented link from the B section, easily absorbs passing notes and turns, expressive of Mitridate's joy of homecoming, while

Example 5.4a. "Soffre il mio cor" (Sifare), final cadenza by Tagliavini.
Example 5.4b. "Soffre il mio cor" (Sifare), final cadenza by Harris.

still maintaining the integrity of his striding intervallic leaps.[47] The return of the adagio section in the two-tempo "Tu, che fedel mi sei" (example 5.6, p. 110) also suggests embellishment to emphasize the softness of Mitridate's love for Sifare as opposed to his hardened anger at Aspasia and to lead into the short cadential flourish. My suggestion for the brief cadenza eliminates the falling octave but includes the harmonically more distinctive leap of a minor sixth to the leading tone.[48] The accompanied recitative that precedes "Quel ribelle e quell'ingrato" (example 5.7, p. 110) ends angrily as Mitridate rages against his son Farnace: "If he has been traitorous, I will forget that I am his father."[49] This climactic line offers the opportunity for embellishments on "scordo" ("forget") and "padre" ("father") as Mitridate spits out his threats.[50] In Mitridate's last two arias, and especially in the adaptation from Gasparini, the ornamentation is largely reserved for variation of exact repetitions without the addition of diminutions to embellish (and dilute the virile strength of) the vocal line (see examples 5.8a and 5.8b, p. 111).

Farnace's arias call for more—and more elaborate—ornamentation. The return of the A section and the cadenzas of "Venga pur" (example 5.9, pp. 112–13) illustrate this difference. The acceleration begins in mm. 181 and 183 with the breaking up of the dotted quarter notes into militant quarters. Thereafter the quarter notes are increasingly broken down into still smaller values, and appoggiaturas add to the accents on "sdegno" ("disdain"). The triplets in m. 195 increase the energy of the rising line, and the figuration that follows is further accelerated in each iteration of the sequence. In the passage beginning in m. 204, the dotted figures add angularity and

Example 5.5. "Se di lauri" (Mitridate), ornamentation.

accent as they make the line more disjunct. In the repetition of the rising scalar passage (mm. 209 and 213), the anticipation of each note adds accent and articulation. In the first cadenza (not shown), at the end of the opening A section (m. 123), I attempted to depict Farnace's intransigence

Example 5.6. "Tu, che fedel mi sei" (Mitridate), ornamentation and cadenza.

Example 5.7. "Respira alfin, respira" (Mitridate), ornamentation of accompanied recitative.

and cunning with the leap of an octave and a sixth and step-wise chromaticism. In the B section the "preliminary" cadenza in m. 160 delineated the diminished seventh, while the following cadenza (m. 166) expanded the chromaticism out into a leap of a minor ninth from the dominant to its leading tone. The final cadenza (example 5.9, pp. 112–13) in the da capo (m. 226) leads through disjunct approaches to the leading tones of the dominant and tonic to *furioso* scales and a disjunct passage in insistent half notes closing in on the final cadence.

Sifare's ornamentation, in contrast, heightens the affective nature of his expression, longing, and inner conflict. In "Lungi da te" (example 5.10, p. 114), for example, the return to A material invites embellishment. My additions expand the repeated tones of the opening phrase "Lungi da te" ("Far from you") to a ninth, reaching upward on "te" ("you"). Small embellishments on the next line add plangent accents. The wide intervallic passage and following scale are not altered, but the word "cara" ("beloved") is preceded

Example 5.8a. "Già di pietà mi spoglio" (Mitridate), variation.
Example 5.8b. "Vado incontro al fato estremo" (Mitridate), variation.

and adorned with decoration. The cadenza (on "cara") embraces the beloved, reaching down an octave and rising stepwise an octave and a sixth, and then falls (despairingly) in syncopated falling tritones to the tonic.

Of Aspasia's arias, only the first, "Al destin" (example 5.11, p. 114), contains elaborate figuration and good opportunity for further embellishment. It is also her only aria to call for cadenzas: at the end of the A section each time and at the end of the B section. Because this aria presents the single opportunity for this kind of virtuosity by the *prima donna* and must

Example 5.9. "Venga pur" (Farnace), ornamentation and cadenza.

therefore be strongly contrasted with Aspasia's diminishing use of orna-mentation as the opera progresses, and because the text depicts stormy emotion, the cadenzas need to be strong and tempest-tossed. The first A-section cadenza might, as in example 5.11a, use disjunct angularity.[51] My B section cadenza (5.11b), in contrast, plunges rapidly down two octaves. The final A section cadenza (5.11c) needs to be the most spectacular, and here, after various of my attempts proved unsatisfactory for the singer, I returned to Mozart's own examples. A highly varied cadenza from his or-namented version of J.C. Bach's "Cara, la dolce fiamma" fit the situation extremely well (and was even in the correct key); its extension to high c'' demanded a slight expansion of the final cadence and allowed the addition of a leap down an octave and a diminished fifth to balance the pitch range before arriving at the tonic (example 5.11c).

The duet for Aspasia and Sifare, which closes the second act, is so virtuosic as to permit little, if anything, by way of added embellishment. A cadenza is, however, required (example 5.12, p. 115). I begin this with a solo "call and response" for the two lovers to express their longing. Then the voices come

Example 5.10. "Lungi da te" (Sifare), ornamentation and cadenza.

Example 5.11a. "Al destin" (Aspasia), A section cadenza, first time.
Example 5.11b. "Al destin" (Aspasia), B section cadenza.
Example 5.11c. "Al destin" (Aspasia), A section cadenza, second time, showing Mozart's original and adaptation.

Example 5.12. "Se viver non degg'io" (Aspasia and Sifare), cadenza.

together, tentatively at first, using pungent sighing motives that resolve a tritone to its third and rise through an octave and a sixth. The cadenza then ends with a strongly linked chain of suspensions falling to the lower tonic.

In the early 1780s Domenico Corri bemoaned that musical notation did not provide an accurate or complete text for musical performance, and, to remedy this failing, he provided the songs he published with such cadenzas, divisions, and intervening ornaments "as he judged proper." He also offered a significant caution, however, (referring to himself, as always, in the third person):

> At the same time, he hopes none of his readers have so much misunderstood him, as to conceive, he means these ornaments which he offers to the Public, as those only which can or ought to be made use of: Even within the limits of the strictest propriety, there is still left a very considerable latitude for the exertions of taste and fancy.[52]

In the case of the ornamentation I present here to the "Public," this caution should be doubled or trebled, for whereas Corri's work can be deemed both "authoritative" and "authentic" in the strictest sense of those words, deriving as it does from the period in question, ornamentation devised in the twenty-first century must obviously fail such a test. Nevertheless, my goals and Corri's have been similar. As Corri writes: "All he pretends to have done in this respect, is, to have adapted to the several pieces in this collection, such graces as are, in the first place, free from error with regard to the rules of music, and, in the next, proper to their respective characters." To which I can only add my hope that I have done the same. Indeed, what was most striking about preparing ornamentation for *Mitridate* was the sense that, regardless of the "authenticity" of the product, the exercise itself had an authentic ring, not just to the work of Corri, but also to that of Mozart.

Mozart at the time he wrote *Mitridate* was not the "Mozart" we know. Although a musical prodigy, he was only a boy of fourteen who needed to prove himself. Perhaps at no other time in his life was he so clearly a "working stiff."[53] When he was commissioned to write this opera, he was given a deadline by which the recitatives had to be sent to the singers. He wrote, revised, and rewrote the arias, adapting the music to the singers' voices and dealing with the desire on the part of some of the singers to substitute arias from another production. The cast and the music finally came together in early December, and the opera was premiered three and a half weeks later. My own experiences were strikingly parallel: a deadline by which the ornamentation had to be sent to the singers; the work of revising and rewriting after meeting and hearing the singers—both to accommodate individual voices and to deal with ornamentation brought into the rehearsals from other productions; and a three-and-a-half week preparation period beginning with rehearsals of the recitatives.

The process, hardly changed from 1770, is a productive one. Certainly, working with experienced and talented singers offers benefits to the final creation of appropriate ornamentation, and the rewriting and revisions created the opportunity for, and led to, improvements. It is also a benefit in today's world, I believe, to have someone engaged to oversee the addition of ornamentation. Whereas in Mozart's time, singers were drilled exclusively in the performance of contemporary style and embellishment, today's soloists move from the music of one century to the next in quick succession, each period with its own stylistic requirements. Although some singers have a good understanding of Classical style, others incline by preference or experience to more elaborate, early-nineteenth-century styles of ornamentation, and still others have no experience whatsoever. To leave embellishments and cadenzas to the singers today with no oversight means that while some soloists simply perform the text as written with no ornamentation, others may include excessive and anachronistic additions. By following the same process the fourteen-year-old Mozart was forced to use, not only can the ornamentation be tailored to fit the individual voice, but, as in the building of appropriate costumes, the ornamentation can help to create stylistic integrity for the performance.

Because music is a performative art, the study of archival documents and the close examination of the text cannot be ends in themselves. The productive use of detailed musicological research allows us to take the imaginative leap from the page to the stage, from the mind to the ear. By moving beyond the text we leave absolutes behind and operate rather, as Corri wrote, within boundaries of "strictest propriety" and "taste and fancy," as grounded in the documented practice. It is an exciting place to be.

Notes

1. My musical interpretations benefitted greatly from the collegial working environment of the Santa Fe Opera. I would like to thank particularly Kenneth Mont-

gomery, conductor, and Robert Tweten, assistant conductor, as well as the fine soloists with whom I worked: Laura Aikin, Celena Shafer, Kathleen Callahan, Nicolle Foland, Bejun Mehta and Donald Kaasch.

2. *Mitridate, re di Ponto*, Mozart, *Neue Ausgabe sämtlicher Werke* 2/5/4, ed. Luigi Ferdinando Tagliavini (Kassel: Bärenreiter, 1966); *Kritische Berichte* (Kassel: Bärenreiter, 1962). Used by permission. The previous edition appears in W. A. *Mozarts Werke* (Leipzig: Breitkopf & Härtel, 1881), 5/5.

3. Philip Adlung shows that Cigna-Santi's sources included Leopoldo Villati's 1750 libretto in addition to Racine's play; see his "Mozarts Opera Seria *Mitridate, Re di Ponto*" (Ph.D. diss., University of Hamburg, 1996; Hamburger Beiträge zur Musikwissenschaft, no. 46: Hamburg: Wagner, 1996). The libretto of Mozart's *Mitridate* is published in Ernest Warburton, ed., *The Librettos of Mozart's Operas* (New York: Garland, 1992), vol. 1, *The Works for Salzburg and Milan*; the text of Gasparini's *Mitridate* is published in vols. 6–7 of the same work: *The Sources*. A word-for-word translation of Mozart's *Mitridate* with a phonetic pronunciation guide for singers appears in Nico Castel, *The Libretti of Mozart's Completed Operas* (Geneseo, N.Y.: Leyerle, 1997–98).

4. Luigi Ferdinando Tagliavini, "Quirino Gasparini and Mozart," in *New Looks at Italian Opera: Essays in Honor of Donald J. Grout*, ed. William W. Austin (Ithaca, N.Y.: Cornell University Press, 1968), 151–71.

5. Rita Peiretti, "Storia di un prestito," *Diastema* 4 (May 1994): 55–56; see also *Diastema* 4 (October 1994): [2], for attribution of the contribution of Harrison James Wignall to the preceding; and Peiretti, "'Vado incontro al fate estremo': Eine bisher falschlich Mozart zugeschriebene Arie der Oper *Mitridate, re di Ponto*," *Mitteilungen der Internationalen Stiftung Mozarteum* 44/3–4 (1996): 40–41.

6. Harrison James Wignall, "Mozart, Guglielmo d'Ettore and the Composition of *Mitridate*" (Ph.D. diss., Brandeis University, 1995); Robert Marshall served as the primary advisor to this dissertation, and it seems particularly appropriate that, as his first Ph.D. student from 1976, I should now in writing this article in Professor Marshall's honor turn to a dissertation he shepherded some twenty years later.

7. Adlung, "Mozarts Opera Seria *Mitridate.*"

8. These are all available in facsimile together with facsimiles of the published scores (without ornamentation) from which Corri worked: *Domenico Corri's Treatises on Singing*, 4 vols., ed. Richard Maunder (New York: Garland Publishing, 1993–95).

9. Corri, *Domenico Corri's Treatises*, 1:[1].

10. Ibid., [4].

11. Frederick Neumann provides the original and ornamented versions of "Ah, se a morir mi chiama" (see his *Ornamentation and Improvisation in Mozart* [Princeton, N.J.: Princeton University Press, 1986], 231–33) and the cadenzas from "L'amerò" (ibid., 216). Will Crutchfield provides the written text and Mozart's ornamentation and cadenzas for both the first and second singing of the A section of J. C. Bach's "Cara, la dolce fiamma" (see his "The Classical Era: Voices," in *The New Grove Handbooks in Music: Performance Practice* [London: Macmillan, 1989], vol. 2, *Music after 1600*, 292–319), as well as the cadenzas for the B section (ibid., 305–10).

12. Neumann, *Ornamentation and Improvisation*, 218–21.

13. Crutchfield, "The Classical Era: Voices," 310–11, includes a summary list of cadenza characteristics on which my own is based.

14. Crutchfield's observations are necessarily similar (ibid., 305).

15. Ibid., 299.

16. The example is from ibid., 296.

17. Ibid., 297.

18. Quoted in Neumann, *Ornamentation and Improvisation,* 230. "[D]ie aria von der konstanze habe ich ein wenig der geläufigen gurgel der Mad:ᵉˡˡᵉ Cavallieri aufgeopfert. . . . habe ich, so viel es eine wälsche Bravour aria zulässt, auszudrücken gesucht;" *Mozart Briefe und Aufzeichungen,* ed. Wilhelm A. Bauer and Otto Erich Deutsch (Kassel: Bärenreiter, 1962–75), 3:163. All spellings and capitalizations are original.

19. In the following summary I have relied on the translation in Castel.

20. Wignall, "Mozart, Guglielmo d'Ettore and the Composition of *Mitridate,*" 62.

21. Ibid., 3. Wignall states this fact without providing any documentation. The statement that Mozart began the composition of the recitative "today" appears in a letter from Leopold Mozart from Bologna (29 September 1770). See *Mozart Briefe* 1:393; the specific line appears in translation in the section on the evolution of *Mitridate* in Robert L. Marshall, ed., *Mozart Speaks: Views on Music, Musicians, and the World* (New York: Schirmer Books, 1991), 256.

22. As translated in Emily Anderson, ed., *The Letters of Mozart and His Family* (London: Macmillan, 1938; reprint, New York: W. W. Norton & Company, 1989), 166. "Meine liebe Mama Ich kan nicht viell schreiben dann die finger thuen sehr weh von so viel Recitativ schreiben: Ich bitte bette die mama für mich daß die opera gut geht, und daß wir dan glücklich wieder beysamm seyn können;" *Mozart Briefe* 1:397.

23. I am indebted throughout the following discussion of the chronological order of composition of *Mitridate* to Wignall's "Mozart, Guglielmo d'Ettore and the Composition of *Mitridate*"; I refer the reader to his work in general, and I will limit citations to specific quotations.

24. Ibid., 64–65.

25. Letter of Leopold Mozart (10 November 1770) adapted from two separate translations in Wignall, "Mozart, Guglielmo d'Ettore and the Composition of *Mitridate,*" 64 and 307. At this point, the Mozarts and Bernasconi were not aware who had written these arias. "[D]ie erste Battaille haben wir, Gott Lob, gewonnen, und einen feind geschlagen, welcher der Prima Donna alle Arien ins Haus gebracht, die sie in unserer opera zu singen hat, und sie bereden wollte, keine Arien von Wolfg: zu singen. . . . sie hat es aber diesem bösen Menschen abgeschlagen, und ist ganz ausser sich für freuden über die Arien die ihr der Wolfg: nach ihrem Wille und Wunsch gemacht hat, . . . der des Wolfg: Arien nicht genug Loben kann"; *Mozart Briefe* 1:402.

26. As quoted and translated in Wignall, "Mozart, Guglielmo d'Ettore and the Composition of *Mitridate,*" 306. "Es stehet aber noch ein ander Sturm am Theatralischen Himmel, den wir schon in der ferne sehen. Allein, mit Gottes Hilfe, und guter Art werden wir uns wohl durchschlagen"; *Mozart Briefe* 1:402.

27. Wignall, "Mozart, Guglielmo d'Ettore and the Composition of *Mitridate,*" 306. "Einen zweyten Sturm haben wir zwischen gestern und heut abgeschlagen; und obwohl noch eins und das andere vorfallen wird, so hoffe, daß, mit der Hilfe Gottes, alles gut gehen wird"; *Mozart Briefe* 1:404.

28. Wignall, "Mozart, Guglielmo d'Ettore and the Composition of *Mitridate*," 73.

29. Ibid., 74. ". . .der Wolfg: hat itzt die Hände voll zu thun, indem nun die zeit anrücket, und er für den Primo uomo erst eine einzige Aria gemacht hat, weil er noch nicht hier ist, und doppelte arbeit, will er nicht haben, folglich lieber seine Gegenwart erwarten, um das Kleid recht an den Leib zu messen"; *Mozart Briefe* 1:405.

30. Wignall, "Mozart, Guglielmo d'Ettore and the Composition of *Mitridate*," 76–77. "Du glaubst die opera ist schon fertig. Du irrest dich sehr. wenn es an unserm Sohne gelegen wäre, so würden 2 opern fertig seyn. . . . da ich dieses schreibe, ist der Primo uomo noch nicht hier. heut soll er gewiß ankommen"; *Mozart Briefe* 1:406.

31. Wignall, "Mozart, Guglielmo d'Ettore and the Composition of *Mitridate*," 75.

32. Ibid., 162–64.

33. Ibid., 80.

34. Ibid., 234. ". . . der Primo uomo sagte, daß wenn dieses Duetto nicht gefalle, er sich noch einmal wolle *beschnatzeln* lassen"; *Mozart Briefe* 1:408.

35. Adlung also emphasizes this conclusion; see especially chapter 5 of his "Mozarts Opera Seria *Mitridate*": "Mozarts Musik zu *Mitridate*," 49–164, which includes a character-by-character analysis of the arias.

36. Wignall, "Mozart, Guglielmo d'Ettore and the Composition of *Mitridate*," 423.

37. "Son reo; l'error confesso."

38. "Ma reo di me peggiore il tuo rivale è questo . . . ; ridere ai danni miei Sifare non potrà."

39. "Venga pur, minacci e frema l'implacabil genitore . . . ; Roma in me rispetti e tema . . ."

40. "Va, l'error mio palesa e la mia pena affretta, ma forse la vendetta cara ti costerà."

41. "Già dagli occhi velo è tolto, vili affetti, io v'abbandono. . . . Già ricalco il bel sentiero della gloria e dell'onor."

42. The last aria for Aspasia in both the Milan and Turin librettos is "Secondi il Ciel pietoso" (Act III, scene 5). As Mozart did not set this text, it seems that Bernasconi sang the Gasparini aria at this point (Tagliavini, *Mitridate*, NMA, xi). In today's performances, Gasparini's aria is not inserted, making "Pallid'ombre" Aspasia's final aria.

43. E. Thomas Glasow suggests that Mozart in composing this aria was thinking of the nineteen-year-old Maria Martha Hagenauer, daughter of the Mozarts' land-lord and friend, who was seriously ill; see his "Jungfrau Martha: *Mitridate*'s 'Pallid Shade'?" *Opera Quarterly* 10/1 (1993): 13–22. Mozart adds postscripts to his father's letters of 4 August, 29 September, and 6 October hoping for her recovery, but add-ing at one point: "God's will is always best and He certainly knows best whether it is better for us to be in this world or in the next" (ibid., 16). The text of Aspasia's aria addresses the "Pallid shades of Elysium," asking that they "be merciful and restore to me my lost happiness" ("Pallid'ombre, che scorgete dagli Elisi . . . deh pietose a me . . ."), and depicts a young woman facing death and hoping for happi-ness in the world beyond; it could certainly have brought the plight of Martha Hagenauer to Mozart's mind. Father and son learned of her death at the end of

October, and Mozart pens a postscript to Leopold's letter of 20 October: "We have lost our good little Martha, but with God's help we shall meet her in a better place" (ibid., 16). "[W]ir haben die gute Martherl verloren, doch werden wir sie mit der hülf gottes in einen guten stande finden;" *Mozart Briefe* 1:397. Mozart wrote the arias for Aspasia between 5 and 10 November.

44. Wignall, "Mozart, Guglielmo d'Ettore and the Composition of *Mitridate,*" 74, and Adlung, "Mozarts Opera Seria *Mitridate,*" 49: "um das Kleid recht an den Leib zu messen."

45. I learned only after making this decision that Mozart composed the arias character by character. Indeed, Mozart's sequence of composition in this opera seria differs strikingly from the earlier practice followed by Handel, who composed the arias in sequence and only later filled in the recitatives that provided the harmonic continuity between the arias. It must be remembered, however, that Handel generally was writing for a known cast of singers, for many of whom he wrote over a period of years, so that he did not need to wait to learn of the strengths and weaknesses of individual performers before embarking on the composition of the arias. Nevertheless, the different sequence must have affected the finished compositions and surely is worth further study. Whereas Handel's practice emphasizes dramatic continuity and disjunction between contiguous arias, Mozart's practice more strongly combines the arias of a single character into a coherent musical portrait or individual trajectory.

46. Neumann, *Ornamentation and Improvisation,* 222.

47. The cadenza provided by Tagliavini at m. 42 is much longer (thirteen quarter-note beats compared to two beats in my ornamented link), more elaborate, and, it seems to me, quite out of character for Mitridate (*Mitridate, NMA,* xv).

48. Unaccountably, Tagliavini provides no cadenza at this point.

49. "Ah se mai l'ama Aspasia, se un affetto ei mi toglie a me dovuto, non speri il traditor da me perdono: per lui mi scordo già che padre io sono."

50. The addition of cadential ornamentation in accompanied recitative also seemed appropriate and worked well in "Qual tumulto nell'alma" (Sifare), "Non più, Regina" (Sifare), and "Vadasi, oh ciel" (Farnace).

51. In the Santa Fe Opera performances, this aria was shortened from its half da capo form ($A_1A_2BA_2$) to a modified da capo by a simple rearrangement (A_1BA_2); this eliminated the first cadenza.

52. Corri, *Domenico Corri's Treatises,* 1:[4].

53. The phrase is taken from Neal Zaslaw, "Mozart as a Working Stiff," in *On Mozart,* ed. James M. Morris (Washington, D.C.: Woodrow Wilson Center Press, 1994), 102–12.

6

Carl Philipp Emanuel Bach and the Aesthetics of Patricide

Richard Kramer

We have been taught by history to speak of Emanuel Bach as a function of, an exponent of, the great Bach. The name itself, those four sacred letters enshrined as a topos in the nineteenth century, insists that we do so. It signifies always the great Bach, and always an idealization of only a core of Bach's music that had come to stand for some transcendental power over the notes—a technical, intellectual, and spiritual power that everyone after Bach could only admire and seek to emulate. The weaving of these letters as actual tones into the fabric of some romantic homage—by Beethoven, by Liszt, by Schumann in the Six Fugues "über den Namen Bach," by Schoenberg in the Variations for Orchestra, op. 31—is only a symptom of this mythic aspect of Bach's preeminence. For old Bach, in his final months, these letters that encode the name of his dynasty also constitute what is arguably his last compositional act—the ultimate "theme" engraved as an emblem into the massive fragment with which the *Art of Fugue* breaks off. It was Emanuel Bach who seemed to testify to the act, in a note inscribed in the manuscript at just that point: "In the midst of this fugue, where the name B A C H is applied in countersubject, the composer died."[1] "*Seemed to testify*" means to raise the skeptic's flag, for Emanuel had been off in Berlin during Bach's death, and there is now legitimate reason to suppose that this apparent quietus in the manuscript signifies something quite different. Still, Emanuel had much to do with the posthumous publication of the work, and was responsible for the sale of the copper engraving plates in 1756, a few years after the second issue.[2] Perhaps this most oracular of fragments (or what Emanuel believed—or wished us to believe—to be a fragment), and its connection in Emanuel's mind with the rite of passage which he could not witness, intrude subconsciously in a miniature homage to that final fugue that Emanuel composed in the early 1770s as a kind of signature inscribed as a memento for his friends.[3] (This is shown in figure 6.1.) It is an intense little piece, contorted in all those fugal permutations that we associate with the father, and not with the son. The legacy of the

Figure 6.1. From Johann Friederich Reichardt, *Briefe eines aufmerksamen Reisenden die Musik betreffend*, 2 (1776), 22.

father hangs heavy over its notes, and it is only in the final dissonance, unresolved deep in the bass, that the real C. P. E. signs himself.

What can it have meant to have grown up in Bach's home, to have had Bach both as teacher and father, and at the same time to have been conscious of one's own claims to musical genius? Piecing together the evidence of Emanuel Bach's life, the scholar does not at once turn to the Oedipus myth as a model for illumination into the relationship with the father. By all accounts, his attitude toward the father, and his actions on behalf of the propagation both of Bach's music and of the legacy of his teaching, were altogether beyond reproach.[4] But even here, not everything is what it seems: beneath this impeccable decorum, one might imagine, is another Bach who had been more happily named anything else.

That there might be something behind the scrim of conventional evidence to wish to investigate seems to me manifest in the facts of the case, and imperative in the very act of biography. Evidence is of many kinds. The most intriguing, the most genuine in its aura of authenticity, is that elusive type which no one knows quite how to "read" as evidence pertinent to a biography. I mean of course the music itself, the most eloquent testimony to the deepest reaches of the mind.

In the 1770s and 1780s, it was Carl Philipp Emanuel Bach who was held by his critics to embody all those qualities which, for the philosophers of the Enlightenment, characterize the man of genius. The work of genius embodies, makes articulate, its own law: the creation of the superior mind gripped by some muse of which the mortal man of genius is himself only dimly conscious. Perhaps the most telling definition is Immanuel Kant's, in the *Kritik der Urteilskraft* (Berlin, 1790):

> Genius is an *aptitude* to produce something for which no definite rule can be postulated; it is not a capacity or skill for something that can be learnt from

some rule or other. Its prime quality, then, must be *originality*. . . . The aptitude cannot of itself describe how it creates its products, or demonstrate the process theoretically, though it provides the rules by itself being a part of Nature. Thus the progenitor of a work of art is indebted to his own genius and he does not himself know how the ideas for it came to him, nor does it lie within his power to calculate them methodically or, should he so wish, to communicate them to others by means of principles that would enable others to create works of equal quality. It is through genius that Nature prescribes the rules of art.[5]

The work of art, following its own rule, demands exegesis. This, precisely, is the task that a new criticism in the late eighteenth century set for itself: to develop an apparatus for construing such works. Here is how Carl Friedrich Cramer thought to introduce a long critical piece on a collection of keyboard sonatas, free fantasies, and rondos by Bach—the fourth in the famous series "für Kenner und Liebhaber," published in 1783:

> About certain men and their works, the judgment of the "Publicum"—that kernel of connoisseurs which unites a natural sensitivity with knowledge, taste, and experience—is so well established that a critic at the appearance of a new product of his genius, has almost nothing more to do than quite simply to indicate that it exists. If this were ever the case with an artist, it is so with Bach. . . . One can continue to apply to him what Herr Forkel, in his excellent review of an earlier collection, with such warm and well-founded enthusiasm, borrowed from Lessing on Shakespeare: "a stamp is imprinted on the tiniest of his beauties which calls forth to the entire world: Ich bin Bachs! and woe to the alien beauty that is inclined to place itself next to him."[6]

This "excellent review" by Herr Forkel, a critical account of two collections of accompanied keyboard sonatas—piano trios, we now call them— is in fact very much more than that. It appeared in 1778, in the second volume of Forkel's *Musikalisch-kritische Bibliothek,* and seeks at the outset to take the measure of Bach's genius:

> [T]hose few noble souls who still know how to value and take pleasure in true art repay [Bach] in the approval that the masses cannot give; and his irrepressible inner activity overpowers every obstacle that stands in the way of his creative outburst [*Ausbruch*] and communication. In this way a lively, fiery, and active spirit—even in a world which, in relation to him, is hardly better than a desert—is thus in a position to bring forth works of art which carry within them every characteristic of true original genius, and, as fruits of an inner compulsion of doubled strength, are of double worth to those few noble souls who, as Luther says, understand such things a little.
>
> We do not need to determine to what extent this is the case with the famous composer of these sonatas. Not, however, satisfied with that fame long ago established, not satisfied to have created a new taste, and through it, to have widened the musical terrain, he continues to enrich us with the fruits of his inexhaustible genius, and shows us that even in the evening of his life, his

imagination is still disposed toward the conception of those noble and stimulating ideas; so that now, as in the noontime of his life, one may say of him what
Lessing says of Shakespeare: . . .[7]

Lessing on Shakespeare is a central and very complex chapter in the
history of German literature. The passage in question comes from one of
the critical pieces published together under the title *Hamburgische
Dramaturgie* in 1769, and specifically from a review of Christian Felix
Weisse's *Richard III,* which Lessing took as a pretext to develop an essay
on the nature of tragic character and on the issue of imitation and borrowing in literature and the arts.[8] That Forkel, in writing about Emanuel Bach,
should have reached for this essay is in itself significant, and not, I think,
because Forkel intended to force an inconceivable comparison between
Bach's art and Shakespeare's. Rather, the coupling of this eminent critical
mind with the idea of Shakespeare conjured up the tone that Forkel wished
to set in contending with these trios by Bach, and to suggest by analogy the
relationship between the man of genius and his enlightened critic: Lessing
to Shakespeare is as Forkel to Bach. Tucked away in Göttingen, Forkel was
writing in the midst of a fervent mania for Shakespeare, whatever might
have been his actual experience of Shakespeare on the stage. More to the
point, Shakespeare figured prominently in the debate, some years earlier,
on the purity of classical tragedy. The complexity of Lessing's Shakespeare
criticism, of his brilliant and convoluted efforts to reconcile Shakespearean
tragedy with the Aristotelian principles of pure classical tragedy (and in
opposition to what Lessing held to be a misreading of those principles in
the tragedies of Corneille and Racine), need not obscure the intent of those
lines quoted by Forkel.[9] But it is in the following lines that Lessing's sense
of Shakespeare's creative originality, as a giver of rule, is implicit:

> Shakespeare must be studied, and not plundered. If we have genius, then
> Shakespeare must be to us what the *camera obscura* is to the landscape painter:
> he looks into it diligently to understand how Nature in all its conditions is pro-
> jected upon a *single* surface; but he borrows nothing from it.[10]

The originality of Shakespeare's work allows no imitation, a view consonant with
Kant's axiom that "it is through genius that Nature prescribes the rules of art."

For Forkel, it was Emanuel Bach's music, emphatically in all its inscru-
table originality, that served as a touchstone for the act of criticism. This
sense of Bach as law-giver comes through in Forkel's *Sendschreiben* in answer to some putative invitation to divulge the meaning of Bach's Sonata in
F Minor from the third collection "für Kenner und Liebhaber." Forkel turned
the opportunity toward nothing less than a disquisition on the concept of
sonata. There is talk here about neither thematic idea, nor modulation, nor
even harmony—except in some marginal comments that clearly reside outside the main argument. In principle, Forkel is concerned to demonstrate

the relationship between inspiration (*Begeisterung*) and the fire of imagination (*Feuer des Einbildungskraft*) on the one hand, and, on the other, "regulation [*Anordnung*], or the expedient and natural progression of feelings into similar, related or even into remote ones."

> A fine discrimination in uniting this refined [*gebildeten*] and abstract [*abgezogenen*] taste with fiery imagination, in bringing regulation and plan in the progression of *Empfindung*, is the pinnacle of art for the genuine composer of sonatas and the poet of odes. But it is also a difficulty which has always insured, and always will, that we have so few true and genuine composers of sonatas and poets of odes. The happy vanquishing of this difficulty is also why I hold the author of our Sonata in F Minor for a far greater musical ode-poet than we have ever had. . . . How precious, then, must be the products of a man who is the only one in his art who unites everything within it that Nature and taste can give to the artist, and who among the powerful lords of music stands thus alone in the heights, incomparable. No one can be set at his side, but rather (as Claudius says of Lessing) he sits on his own bank.[11]

Forkel was perhaps best known in the nineteenth century as the author of the first book-length biography of Sebastian Bach, published, finally, in 1802.[12] His work toward that end had begun in the 1770s, and the principal source of his information, both anecdotal and documentary, both archival and in actual musical texts of unknown works, was Carl Philipp Emanuel Bach. Some twenty-six letters from Bach to Forkel, dating from between 1773 and 1778—and a final one from 1786—have survived. Unwittingly, they capture a fundamental opposition in Bach's life: on the one hand, there is a deeply held obligation to the proper dissemination of the father's legacy, and on the other, the selling of a new aesthetic, one born in antipathy to that legacy. Here are two passages that convey this double mission, the first from a letter of 7 October 1774:

> In haste, dear friend, I have the satisfaction of sending you the remains of my Sebastianoren: namely, 11 trios, 3 pedal pieces, and Von Himmel Hoch etc. . . . The 6 keyboard trios . . . are among the best works of my dear, late father. They still sound very good, and bring me much satisfaction, even though they are more than 50 years old. There are a few adagios in them which even today could not have been composed in a more vocal style. . . . In the next letter, pure Emanueliana.[13]

And indeed the following letter, dated 10 February 1775, is three close pages of "pure Emanueliana." The following passage is well known, but worth retelling:

> Now one would like to have 6 or 12 fantasies from me, like the 18th "Probestück" in C Minor. I don't deny that I would love to do something in this genre, and perhaps I am not entirely ungifted in this. Besides, I have a good collection of them which . . . belong to the chapter on free fantasy in the second part of my *Essay* [*on*

the True Art of Playing Keyboard Instruments]. But how many people are there who love this kind of thing, who understand them, and who can play them well?[14]

What kind of music was Bach writing in the 1770s? We know from other letters that Bach made a distinction between music composed for the pleasure of a small circle of connoisseurs—music essentially for himself— and that which was intended for sale to a less endowed public. In the autobiographical notice written in 1773 for the German translation of Charles Burney's travel journals, Bach admitted as much:

> Because I have had to compose most of my works for specific individuals and for the public, I have always been more restrained in them than in the few pieces that I have written merely for myself. . . . Among all my works, especially those for clavier, only a few trios, solos and concertos were composed in complete freedom and for my own use.[15]

A sonata composed in 1775, and unpublished until very recently, displays that inimitable originality that had come to be prized as a defining attribute of genius. (Two movements of the sonata are given here as an Appendix to the chapter [pp. 132–36].) It has survived in Bach's autograph and in three contemporary copies, suggesting a wide circulation among the members of Bach's inner circle.[16]

One phrase in particular captures the ear. The most overtly coherent phrase in the piece (the only coherent one, by some measure), it occurs for the first time deep in the interior of the first movement, at mm. 33–37 (first beat), after the first double bar—outside, that is, the formal exposition. The intelligibility of the phrase, the sense that it makes within itself, is only exaggerated through a context that seems intent upon syntactical dislocation. Abruptly abandoned, the phrase suggests no self-evident relation to the immediate surface of the piece. Its significance refuses explanation: reason is not likely to get at the illogical aspect of its place in the course of things, nor to fathom the phrase in its gestural aspect.

This telling phrase returns, and when it does, it engages the narrative of the piece in ways that we could not have predicted. The opening idea, recapitulated at m. 60, is now reset in A-flat major, as though in search of this outcast phrase, and, finding it—see mm. 67–71 (first beat)—draws it into the immediate tonal motion of the piece. Set in the key of the flat submediant, the phrase seems to hover placidly for an instant before the inevitable augmented sixth at the cadence.

"Das Adagio fällt gleich ein," Bach instructs, at the end of the movement: "The Adagio begins straightaway." It is similar in kind, this Adagio, to any number of meditations in Bach's keyboard works that conjure some remote tonal landscape between the outer movements. This one opens its meditation on an isolated D flat. The tone itself, in its naked isolation, establishes a dissonance with the final cadence in the first movement, and therefore suggests a reaching back into the memory of the piece. Again, Bach's "Das Adagio fällt gleich ein" presses the point. Even the disposition of its first harmony is calculated to suggest a Neapolitan sixth in relation to the first movement.

The Adagio, too, has its luminous, telling phrase, and it flowers at just the point where the music begins its descent through the circle of fifths that winds inexorably from D flat to the half-cadence in C before the final movement. It is precisely at this moment of greatest remove (beginning at m. 10) that a phrase redolent of that expatriate phrase in the first movement is teased out of the narrative. The reciprocity between these moments is not casual, nor is it concrete in the manner of some thematic permutation. Rather, one gropes for the language to convey how they are related: for it is an evocative relationship of just this kind, with all that it suggests of the significatory power of an ambiguous phrase, that cries out for this new mode of criticism that Forkel and his contemporaries were struggling to develop.

On the clavichord, the inclination of those opening D flats toward some linguistic expression, however dimly felt, is palpable. On any other instrument, this eloquence is missed.[17] The harpsichord, innately antipathetic to such music, would trample on the nuances of what has been called its "*redende*" aspect—music as speech. Because the tangent remains in contact with the string, and establishes one node in the sounding structure, the finger controls the vibrating string as it can at no other keyboard instrument. Like no other keyboard instrument, the clavichord "speaks." And it is further in the nature of the instrument that it speaks directly to the player, and (because the instrument is nearly inaudible) only faintly to everyone else. It is the clavichord into which Emanuel Bach withdraws, into its world of near silence, where each tone is an *Empfindung*—expression itself— whose inaudibility only exaggerates its claim to speech. There is no grand splendor in music of this kind, but only a touching of sensibilities.

Less than a year before his own death, in a remarkable review of the first volume of Forkel's *Geschichte der Musik,* Bach affords us a rare insight into his understanding of the nature of musical expression:

> For a long time, one has referred to music as a language of feeling [*eine Sprache der Empfindung*], and consequently, that in which the similarity innate in the formulation of its expression and that of the ordinary language of speech has been darkly felt.[18]

This "*Sprache der Empfindung,*" and its darkly felt associations with linguistic expression, is at the core of Bach's aesthetic. To hear this music, we need to "feel" with it, to engage in what Herder would call *Einfühlung.*[19] The *Empfindungen* somehow conveyed through the syntaxes of this language do not open themselves up to conventional analysis. To seek to

explain such music in rational, equation-like syllogism as so many permutations of a *Grundgestalt,* is to miss its point. Analysis of this kind may tell
us something about certain aspects of the surface of the music, but it tells
us nothing of the essential inner core of it. It is Bach's "*dunkel gefühlt*" that
is suggestive of the critical process that will get us to the essence of the
piece.

How might we construe the language of a sonata such as this as testimony of a man whose only teacher, as he himself reverently claimed on
more than one occasion, was his father? Where is the patrimony in the
sonata? What heritage is this, in which all the old orthodoxies are repudi-
ated? The clichés of music history are not helpful. It will not do to speak of
"style change" as though it were some inexorable historical event to which
Emanuel Bach's music necessarily contributes. Bach's music sounds like no
one else's. It is radical and idiosyncratic beyond anything in the music of
even his closest contemporaries. Haydn, Mozart, and Beethoven, however
loudly their proclamation of Emanuel Bach as a spiritual father—and there
is no reason to doubt them—hardly knew what to make of it. Charles
Burney, who spent a good week with Emanuel Bach in 1772, and wrote
about it in his travel journals, published the following year, captured the
special quality of Bach's language as well as anyone:

> Emanuel Bach used to be censured for his extraneous modulations, crudities,
> and difficulties; but, like the hard words of Dr. Johnson, to which the public by
> degrees became reconciled, every German composer takes the same liberties now
> as Bach, and every English writer uses Johnson's language with impunity.[20]

It would be fatuous to suggest that Emanuel Bach's music could have
existed without the obscure patrimony to which I referred a moment ago.
The figure of Sebastian Bach, totem-like, was ubiquitous. Everywhere,
Emanuel felt the need to speak of his father. In his music, he fails to do so.
The patrimony is not acknowledged there. And when he speaks about the
father's music, it is the astounding technique that is admired, the awesome,
powerful control of musical forces—qualities that Emanuel Bach's music
does not seek. Even in the most lavish encomium to the father's art—the
comparison with Handel, written in 1788, provoked by an essay by Burney,
whose bias toward Handel was easily explained (he knew lots of Handel's
music, and very little of Sebastian Bach's)—even here, the praise is for Bach as
prestidigitator, both as an organist and as a contriver of fugal complexity.[21]

What I mean to suggest is that Emanuel Bach's music tells us something
about the relationship of the son to the father in this complex language of
signification, at once abstract and concrete, that is the deepest reflection of
feeling. What one reads there hews closely to what one has come to know,
through Freud, as an archetype for the ambivalence in the behavior of the
son toward the father. A revelatory passage from the third essay in *Moses*

and Monotheism, from a chapter titled "The Great Man," is very much to the point:

> And now it begins to dawn on us that all the features with which we furnish the great man are traits of the father, that in this similarity lies the essence of the great man. The decisiveness of thought, the strength of will, the forcefulness of his deeds, belong to the picture of the father; above all other things, however, the self-reliance and independence of the great man, his divine conviction of doing the right thing, which may pass into ruthlessness. He must be admired, he may be trusted, but one cannot help but fear him as well.[22]

Freud imagines Moses as a "tremendous father imago" to his people. "And when they killed this great man they only repeated an evil deed which in primeval times had been a law directed against the divine king, and which, as we know, derives from a still older prototype"—a reference to totemism among aboriginal tribes.[23]

Freud's own obsession with Moses is a topic in itself. The famous 1914 essay on the Moses of Michelangelo is rich in evidence for this, even in its misreadings. But it is also rich in what it suggests about the power of psychoanalytic scrutiny for the interpretation of art, for it forces us to separate out an analysis of the work, and the play of psyche within it, from an investigation of what Freud openly refers to as "the artist's intention." Freud's strategy calls for no such separating out, as I think is clear from a passage early on in the Michelangelo essay. "It can only be the artist's *intention,*" he writes, "in so far as he has succeeded in expressing it in his work and in conveying it to us, that grips us so powerfully. . . . It cannot be merely a matter of *intellectual* comprehension; what he aims at is to awaken in us the same emotional attitude, the same mental constellation as that which in him produced the impetus to create."[24]

But the impetus to create and the text of what is created are two very different phenomena, deeply related as they may be. This impetus, which the artist may sense only vaguely, does not readily translate into the substance of the work. How to read a psychoanalytic print of the author in the text, how the text itself constitutes evidence for such a reading, is a critical enterprise of a certain legitimacy. Its converse—how a psychoanalytic reading of the author might tell us of motives in the work—cannot lay claim to similar legitimacy: the work and the life are not interchangeable, are not the terms of a simple equation. In its unhinged, neurotic, fitful acts at speech, this isolated Sonata from 1775—he did not again write a solo sonata for keyboard until 1780—tells us something of Emanuel Bach's cast of mind, of an aesthetics born in some internalized revolt, in a playing out of a family romance, just as its inner coherence, however "darkly felt," speaks to that power of law-giving which Forkel senses in his lengthy communication on the Sonata in F Minor. That nostalgic phrase in the Adagio, for all its self-referentiality within the interiors of the piece, yet suggests something about its author. Recourse to a family romance can offer no more than the sketch of some internalized drama against which such a phrase might have been conceived. In the end, the piece must remain its own singular testimony to its meaning.

Sebastian Bach as Moses? In precisely how it has been made to signify in these past two hundred years, no repertory of music more nearly approaches the commandments engraved in those tablets that Moses holds than Bach's. There is a temptation to extend the simile to those "hundred-weight" copper plates—the tablets in which is engraved the *Art of Fugue*—which Emanuel Bach sold off after public advertisement, six years after his father's death.[25] *Kunst der Fuge*: the title itself has an Old Testament ring to it, some sort of cabbalah in search of the hermeneut. From a purely pragmatic point of view, Bach's decision to rid himself of these tablets seems entirely justifiable—and it must be said that the autograph score remained in his possession. But the ambivalent undercurrent in the act, its veiled suggestion of some public renunciation, has its place in the story as well.

A word about Bach's mother. If history tends to obliterate *this* aspect of the lineage, Emanuel Bach makes certain that she has her place. The opening lines of his autobiographical notice are unequivocal about that:

> I, Carl Philip Emanuel Bach, was born in Weimar, March 1714. My late father was Johann Sebastian, Kapellmeister at several courts and ultimately music director in Leipzig. My mother was Maria Barbara Bach, youngest daughter of Johann Michael Bach, a solidly founded composer.[26]

If we are ready to attribute Bach's musical gifts unconditionally to the father's side, the son corrects us. The mother died in July 1720. Sebastian Bach, knowing nothing of this, returned from a trip to Carlsbad to discover that her body had been interred. What can it have meant to a six-year-old to have been witness to that? Perhaps it is to the point to remind ourselves that Maria Barbara and Sebastian were related before marriage. Her father and Bach's father were first cousins. In this sense, too, the line between father's side and mother's side is blurred.

It was Forkel who, in the final lines of his biography of Sebastian Bach, established an hegemony of the father that necessarily set in subordination the works of his progeny—indeed, of all who were to follow. Forkel's mantic words have an evangelical ring:

> And this man, the greatest musical poet and the greatest musical orator that ever existed, and probably ever will exist, was a German. Let his country be proud of him; let it be proud, but, at the same time, worthy of him![27]

There was an agenda for the nineteenth century. In effect, the discovery and resurrection of Bach's music was an obsession with its own ambivalencies. The appropriation of Bach as the *Ur-romantiker* by composers as disparate as Beethoven, Schumann, Mendelssohn, Wagner, Brahms, and Schoenberg coincided with a stripping away of all such extravagant excess, in the endeavor to discover and scrape clean that enormous repertory whose magnitude Forkel could only vaguely surmise. It is not an exaggeration to say that the invention of a *Musikwissenschaft* at mid-century, along with a scholarly apparatus that vibrates sympathetically with all those other monumental achievements of the industrial revolution, was born of this moral necessity that Forkel preached: to be worthy of Bach. The *Gesamtausgabe* produced by the editorial staff of the Bach-Gesellschaft was an enterprise that consumed a half century, from its founding on the centennial of Bach's death to its completion in 1899.[28]

In the meantime, Emanuel Bach's music went the way of the clavichord. If Forkel, finding a language to convey Emanuel Bach's music even into the 1780s, felt the need to invoke Lessing on Shakespeare at a time when the call to write a biography of Sebastian Bach seemed driven more out of historical curiosity than a profound passion for the music, this assessment of their music would by 1800 have been turned on its head. How indeed could the imperious political and aesthetic agendas of the nineteenth century find a place for this idiosyncratic, heretical music which, when it can be heard at all, speaks out so eloquently against all such monument making? Its eccentricities touch the mind and the soul, and bring us close to the human condition in a way that Bach the father would not have wished to understand.

Appendix

C. P. E. Bach, *Sonata per il cembalo solo*, H. 248 (1775), first and second movements. From Carl Philipp Emanuel Bach, *Klaviersonaten: Auswahl,* ed. Darrell M. Berg, 3 vols. (Munich: G. Henle, 1986–89), 3:88–92. Used by permission.

Das Adagio fällt gleich ein

Notes

1. "Ueber dieser Fuge, wo der Nahme B A C H im Contrasubject angebracht worden, ist der Verfasser gestorben." For an illustration of the page, see Christoph Wolff, "Bach's Last Fugue: Unfinished?" in his *Bach: Essays on His Life and Music* (Cambridge, Mass.: Harvard University Press, 1991), 259. Wolff here (261) argues that the page was left unfinished because it had in likelihood been completed elsewhere—in a hypothetical "fragment x" in which Bach would have "worked out, or at least sketched, the combinatorial section of the quadruple fugue in a manuscript . . . that originally belonged together with [the surviving manuscript] but is now lost." We now know, thanks largely to Wolff's research, that the *Art of Fugue* was a work that occupied Bach from as early as 1742; see his "The Compositional History of the *Art of Fugue*," in *Bach: Essays*, 265–81. Still, this last fugue is on paper and in a hand that suggested to Wolff that "it is entirely possible that here we are dealing with one of the last documents of Bach's handwriting" (271).

2. The announcement by Emanuel Bach was printed in Friedrich Wilhelm Marpurg's *Historisch-kritische Beyträge zur Aufnahme der Musik*, 5 vols. (Berlin: Verlag Joh. Jacob Schützens sel. Wittwe[1], Gottlieb August Lange [2–5], 1754–78), 2 (1756): 575–76. The passage is reprinted in *Bach-Dokumente III: Dokumente zum Nachwirken Johann Sebastian Bachs, 1750–1800*, ed. Hans-Joachim Schulze (Kassel: Bärenreiter, 1972), 113–14 (item 683); an English version is given in Hans T. David and Arthur Mendel, eds., *The New Bach Reader: A Life of Johann Sebastian Bach in Letters and Documents*, revised and enlarged by Christoph Wolff (New York: W. W. Norton & Co., 1998), 377–78 (item 376).

3. Johann Friederich Reichardt, *Briefe eines aufmerksamen Reisenden die Musik betreffend*, 2 vols. (Frankfurt: An seine Freunde geschrieben von Johann Friedrich Reichardt, 1774–76), 2:22, at the end of a letter dated "Hamburg, den 12ten Julius, 1774." In precisely this way, Bach entered his signature in the "Stammbuch" of Carl Friedrich Cramer, dated 9 June 1774. The page is shown in *Carl Philipp Emanuel Bach: Musik und Literatur in Norddeutschland* (Heide in Holstein: Boyens & Co., 1988), 97; and in Ernst Suchalla, ed., *Carl Philipp Emanuel Bach: Briefe und Dokumente*, 2 vols. (Göttingen: Vandenhoeck & Ruprecht, 1994), 1:405 (item 169). For the facsimile of another, dated 3 November 1775, see Eva Badura-Skoda, "Eine private Briefsammlung," in *Festschrift Otto Erich Deutsch zum 80. Geburtstag am 5. September 1963*, ed. Walter Gestenberg, Jan LaRue, and Wolfgang Rehm (Kassel: Bärenreiter, 1963), plate 1 (after p. 288). In a letter dated "Hamburg, den 28. April 84," Bach appended a more elaborate composition in which the letters of his "Vornamen" are woven into the counterpoint. It is printed in C. H. Bitter, *Carl Philipp Emanuel und Wilhelm Friedemann Bach und deren Brüder*, 2 vols. (Berlin: Wilh. Müller, 1868), 2:303–4; and in Stephen L. Clark, trans. and ed., *The Letters of C. P. E. Bach* (Oxford: Oxford University Press, 1997), 204–5 (item 242).

4. This is poignantly evident in the letter written by Emanuel Bach in response to the unfavorable comparison of his father with Handel in Charles Burney's *An Account of the Musical Performances in Westminster Abbey in Commemoration of Handel* (London: T. Payne, 1785); Bach's response, published anonymously in Friedrich Nicolai's *Allgemeine deutsche Bibliothek*, vol. 81, pt. 1 (1788), 295–303, iterates the very points raised in a letter of 21 January 1786 from Bach to Johann Joachim Eschenburg, who translated Burney's *Account*; see Clark, *The Letters*, 243–

44 (item 287). The identification of Bach as the author of the published response to Burney was deduced by Dragan Plamenac in "New Light on the Last Years of Carl Philipp Emanuel Bach," *The Musical Quarterly* 35 (1949): 565–87, esp. 575–87.

5. The translation is from Peter le Huray and James Day, eds., *Music and Aesthetics in the Eighteenth and Early-Nineteenth Centuries* (Cambridge: Cambridge University Press, 1981), 228. For the notion of Bach as *Originalgenie,* see Hans-Günter Ottenberg, *C. P. E. Bach,* 2d ed. (Oxford: Oxford University Press, 1991), 1–5, 139–42; and Hans-Günter Klein, *"Er ist Original!": Carl Philipp Emanuel Bach. Sein musikalisches Werk in Autographen und Erstdrucken aus der Musikabteilung der Staatsbibliothek Preußischer Kulturbesitz Berlin* (Wiesbaden: Dr. Ludwig Reichert Verlag, 1988), 11–15.

6. "Ueber gewisse Männer und ihre Werke hat sich nun schon einmal das Urtheil des Publici (. . . den Kern der Kenner, die natürliches Gefühl mit Kenntniß, Geschmack und Erfahrung verbinden) so sehr fixirt, daß ein Recensent, bey der Erscheinung eines neuen Productes ihres Genius, beynahe nichts weiter zu thun hat, als nur ganz einfältiglich anzuzeigen: daß es da ist. . . . War dieß je bey einem Künstler so; so trift es bey Bachen zu. . . . Noch immer kann man das auf ihn anwenden, was Herr Forkel in seiner treflichen Recension einer frühern dieser Sammlungen, mit so warmen und gegründetem Enthusiasmus, Lessingen über Shakespearen aus dem Munde nahm: 'auf die geringste seiner Schönheiten ist ein Stempel gedruckt, welcher gleich der ganzen Welt zuruft: ich bin Bachs! Und wehe der fremden Schönheit, die das Herz hat, sich neben ihr zu stellen!'" Carl Friedrich Cramer, *Magazin der Musik,* 2 vols. (Kiel and Hamburg: Musikalische Niederlage bei Westphal und Comp., 1783–86; reprint, Hildesheim: Georg Olms, 1971), 1 (1783):1238–39.

7. "Jedoch, die kleine Anzahl derjenigen Edeln, welche die wahre Kunst noch zu schätzen und zu genießen wissen, halten ihn für den Beyfall des großen Haufens schadlos; und seine innere unaufhaltsame Wirksamkeit überwältigt jede Hinderniß, die seinem Ausbruch oder seiner Mittheilung im Wege steht. Auf diese Weise ist sodann ein lebhafter, feuriger und wirksamer Geist im Stande auch sogar in einer Welt, die in Beziehung auf ihn, beynahe nichts besser als eine Einöde ist, Werke der Kunst hervorzubringen, die jedes Merkmaal des wahren Originalgenies an sich tragen, und, als Früchte eines innern Drangs von doppelter Kraft, auch den wenigen Edeln, die, wie Luther sagt, solches ein wenig verstehen, doppelt schätzbar sind. . . . In wiefern dieses der Fall bey dem berühmten Verfasser dieser Sonaten ist, brauchen wir hier wohl nicht zu bestimmen. . . . Aber nicht zufrieden mit seinen längst gegründeten Ruhm, nicht zufrieden, uns einen neuen Geschmack geschaffen, und dadurch die musikalischen Gefilde erweitert zu haben, bereichert er uns noch immer mit den Früchten seines unerschöpflichen Genies, und zeigt uns, daß auch selbst am Abend seines Lebens seine Imagination zur Conception eines jeden edlen und reizenden Bildes noch aufgelegt sey; so, daß man noch jetzt, so gut wie am Mittage seines Lebens, von ihm sagen kann, was Lessing von Shakespear sagt: . . ." Johann Nikolaus Forkel, *Musikalisch-kritische Bibliothek,* 3 vols. (Gotha: C. W. Ettinger, 1778–79; reprint, Hildesheim: Georg Olms, 1964), 2:275–77. For more on Forkel's important review, see my "The New Modulation of the 1770s: C. P. E. Bach in Theory, Criticism, and Practice," *Journal of the American Musicological Society* 38 (1985): 551–92, esp. 573–74.

8. Lessing's line is "Auf die geringste von seinen Schönheiten ist ein Stempel gedruckt, welcher gleich der ganzen Welt zuruft: ich bin Shakespeares! Und wehe

der fremden Schönheit, die das Herz hat, sich neben ihr zu stellen"; it is found in the seventy-third number, "den 12. Januar 1768," of *Hamburgische Dramaturgie,* 2 vols. (Hamburg: In Commission bey J. H. Cramer, in Bremen, 1769), accessible in Karl Lachmann, ed., *Gotthold Ephraim Lessings sämtliche Schriften,* 3rd ed., 23 vols. in 24 (Stuttgart: G. J. Göschen'sche Verlagshandlung, 1886–1924; reprint, n.p.: Walter de Gruyter & Co., 1968), 10:95; and in English in G. E. Lessing, *Hamburg Dramaturgy,* trans. Helen Zimmern, with a new introduction by Victor Lange (New York: Dover Publications, 1962), 173.

9. "In the cult of Shakespeare Göttingen was only a pace behind Strassburg and Frankfurt. . . . The Göttingen students imitated the quips, phrases, and mannerisms of Shakespeare in 1772-1778 just as their contemporaries two years before had done in Strassburg," writes Lawrence Marsden Price, *The Reception of English Literature in Germany* (Berkeley: University of California Press, 1932; reprint, New York: Benjamin Blom, 1968), 34. On the complex topic of Shakespeare reception in Germany among Lessing's contemporaries, see ibid., 269–308. The topic has been addressed more recently in Elaine Sisman, "Haydn, Shakespeare, and the Rules of Originality," in *Haydn and His World,* ed. Elaine Sisman (Princeton, N.J.: Princeton University Press, 1997), 3–56, esp. 11–19.

10. "Shakespeare will studirt, nicht geplündert sein. Haben wir Genie, so muß uns Shakespeare das sein, was dem Landschaftsmaler die Camera obscura ist: er sehe fleißig hinein, um zu lernen, wie sich die Natur in allen Fällen auf eine Fläche projektiret; aber er borge nichts daraus." Lessing, *Hamburgische Dramaturgie,* in *Sämtliche Schriften,* 10:95; I have somewhat altered the translation given in *Hamburg Dramaturgy,* 173.

11. "Diese feine Beurtheilung, diesen gebildeten und abgezogenen Geschmack mit der feurigen Einbildungskraft zu verbinden, Ordnung und Plan in den Fortgang der Empfindung zu bringen, ist der Gipfel der Kunst eines ächten Sonatencomponisten und Odendichters, aber auch zugleich, eine Schwierigkeit, welche von jeher verursacht hat, und noch ferner verursachen wird, daß wir so wenig wahre und ächte Odendichter und Sonatencomponisten haben. Die glückliche Ueberwindung dieser Schwierigkeit ist es auch, warum ich den Verfasser unserer Sonate in F moll für einen weit größern musikalischen Odendichter halte, als es je einen gegeben hat. . . . Wie schätzbar müssen uns daher die Producte eines Mannes seyn, der der Einzige in seiner Art ist, der alles in sich vereiniget, was Natur und Geschmack dem Künstler zu geben vermag, der unter dem gewaltigen Heere von Musikern so ganz allein oben an steht, mit keinem verglichen, keinem an die Seite gesetzt werden kann, sondern (wie Claudius von Lessing sagt,) auf seiner eigenen Bank sitzt." [Johann Nikolaus Forkel,] "Ueber eine Sonate . . . Ein Sendschreiben," in *Musikalischer Almanach für Deutschland auf das Jahr 1784* (Leipzig: Schwickert, 1784), 28–29.

12. The work is available in English as Johann Nikolaus Forkel, *Johann Sebastian Bach: His Life, Art, and Work,* trans. with notes and appendices by Charles Sanford Terry (London: Constable & Co., 1920; reprint, New York: Vienna House, 1974); also in David and Mendel, eds., rev. Wolff, *New Bach Reader,* 415–82, as "On Johann Sebastian Bach's Life, Genius, and Works."

13. "In Eil habe ich das Vergnügen Ihnen, bester Freund, den Rest meiner Sebastianoren zu schicken, nehml. 11 Trii, 3 Pedalstücke u. Vom Himmel hoch p. . . . Die 6 Claviertrio . . . sind von den besten Arbeiten des seel. lieben Vaters. Sie klingen noch jetzt sehr gut, u. machen mir viel Vergnügen, ohngeacht sie über 50

Jahre alt sind. Es sind einige Adagii darin, die man heut zu Tage nicht sangbarer setzen kann. . . . Künftig kommen lauter Emanueliana." Suchalla, ed., *C. P. E. Bach: Dokumente,* 1:446–47 (item 190); my translation. For another, see Clark, *The Letters of C. P. E Bach,* 66–67 (item 71).

14. "Man will jetzt von mir 6 oder 12 Fantasien haben, wie das achtzehnte Probestücke aus dem C-moll ist; ich läugne nicht, dass ich in diesem Fache gerne etwas thun mögte, vielleicht wäre ich auch nicht ganz u. gar ungeschickt dazu, überdem habe ich ein Haufen collectanea dazu, welche . . . zu der Abhandlung von der freyen Fantasie meines zweyten Versuchs gehören: allein, wie viele sind derer, die dergleichen lieben, verstehen und gut spielen?" Suchalla, *C. P. E. Bach: Dokumente,* 1:486 (item 203); for another translation, see Clark, *The Letters of C. P. E. Bach,* 76 (item 77).

15. "Weil ich meine meisten Arbeiten für gewisse Personen und fürs Publikum habe machen müssen, so bin ich dadurch allezeit mehr gebunden gewesen, als bey den wenigen Stücken, welche ich bloß für mich verfertigt habe. . . . Unter allen meinen Arbeiten, besonders fürs Clavier, sind blos [*sic*] einige Trios, Solos und Concerte, welche ich mit aller Freyheit und zu meinem eignen Gebrauch gemacht habe." The Autobiography, written for the German translation of Charles Burney's *The Present State of Music in Germany, the Netherlands, and the United Provinces* (London: T. Becket, 1773), was published in Burney, *Tagebuch seiner Musikalischen Reisen,* 3 vols., trans. C. D. Ebeling and J. J. C. Bode (Hamburg: Bode, 1772–73), 3:198–209; that portion was reprinted in Carl Philipp Emanuel Bach, *Autobiography: Verzeichniß des musikalischen Nachlasses,* annotations in English and German by William S. Newman (Buren: Frits Knuf, 1991); the passages cited are on pp. 208 and 209. For an English version, see William S. Newman, "Emanuel Bach's Autobiography," *The Musical Quarterly* 51 (1965): 363–72, esp. 371 and 372.

16. *Sonata per il cembalo solo,* Helm 248 (Wotq. 65/47), now published in C. Ph. E. Bach, *Klaviersonaten: Auswahl,* ed. Darrell M. Berg, 3 vols. (Munich: G. Henle, [1989]), 3:88–95. A facsimile of the autograph is printed in Darrell Berg, ed., *The Collected Works for Solo Keyboard by Carl Philipp Emanuel Bach,* 6 vols. (New York: Garland Publishing, 1985), 4:217–22. Bach himself dated the work "1775" on the autograph, a date iterated in the *Verzeichniß des musikalischen Nachlasses des verstorbenen Capellmeisters Carl Philipp Emanuel Bach* (Hamburg: G. F. Schniebes, 1790), 22 (item 174); reprinted as *The Catalog of Carl Philipp Emanuel Bach's Estate: A Facsimile of the Edition by Schniebes, Hamburg, 1790,* annotated, with a preface, by Rachel W. Wade (New York: Garland Publishing, 1981).

17. In German usage in the late eighteenth century, "Cembalo" is the generic designation for any stringed keyboard instrument. On this point, see, among others, Herbert Grundmann, "Per il Clavicembalo o Piano-Forte," in *Colloquium Amicorum: Joseph Schmidt-Görg zum 70. Geburtstag,* ed. Siegfried Kross and Hans Schmidt (Bonn: Beethovenhaus Bonn, 1967), 100–117.

18. "Man hat die Musik schon lange eine Sprache der Empfindung genannt, folglich die in der Zusammensetzung ihrer und der Zusammensetzung der Sprachausdrücke liegende Aehnlichkeit dunkel gefühlt." The review appeared in the *Hamburgischen Unpartheyischen Correspondenten* for 9 January 1788, and is reprinted in Johann Nikolaus Forkel, *Allgemeine Geschichte der Musik,* 2 vols. (Leipzig: Schwickert, 1788–1801; reprint, Graz: Akademische Druck- und

Verlagsanstalt, 1967), 1:xvii-xviii; and in Bitter, *Carl Philipp Emanuel und Wilhelm Friedemann,* 2:109–11.

19. Isaiah Berlin writes of "this contrast between the sense of dialogue, communication, immediate understanding, achieved by what Herder was to call 'feeling into'(*Einfühlung*) a man, or a style or a period [or, one might add, a musical utterance], with rational, rule-dominated analysis," in Henry Hardy, ed., *The Magus of the North: J. G. Hamann and the Origins of Modern Irrationalism* (New York: Farrar, Straus and Giroux, 1993), 78–79. See also Berlin's "Herder and the Enlightenment," now reprinted in Berlin, *The Proper Study of Mankind: An Anthology of Essays,* ed. Henry Hardy and Roger Hausheer (New York: Farrar, Straus and Giroux, 1997), 403. Berlin's ideas are drawn primarily from Herder's *Auch eine Philosophie der Geschichte zur Bildung der Menschheit* (1774), reprinted in *Johann Gottfried Herder. Sämtliche Werke,* ed. Bernhard Suphan, 33 vols. (Berlin, 1877–1913; reprint, Hildesheim: Georg Olms, 1967–68), 5:503 in particular.

20. Charles Burney, *A General History of Music,* with critical and historical notes by Frank Mercer, 2 vols. (New York: Dover Publications, 1957), 2:955.

21. Plamenac, "New Light on the Last Years," 582–85; and see n. 4 above.

22. "Und nun mag uns die Erkenntnis dämmern, daß alle Züge, mit denen wir den großen Mann ausstatten, Vaterzüge sind, daß in dieser Übereinstimmung das von uns vergeblich gesuchte Wesen des großen Mannes besteht. Die Entschiedenheit der Gedanken, die Stärke des Willens, die Wucht der Taten gehören dem Vaterbilde zu, vor allem aber die Selbständigkeit und Unabhängigkeit des großen Mannes, seine göttliche Unbekümmertheit, die sich zur Rücksichtslosigkeit steigern darf. Man muß ihn bewundern, darf ihm vertrauen, aber man kann nicht umhin, ihn auch zu fürchten." Sigmund Freud, *Studienausgabe,* 11 vols., ed. Alexander Mitscherlich, Angela Richard, James Strachey, and Ilse Grubrich-Simitis (Frankfurt am Main: S. Fischer Verlag, 1969–79), 9:556. Sigmund Freud, *Moses and Monotheism,* trans. Katherine Jones (New York: Vintage Books, n.d.), 140. I have modified the translation slightly.

23. "Und wenn sie dann einmal diesen ihren großen Mann erschlugen, so wiederholten sie nur eine Untat, die sich in Urzeiten als Gesetz gegen den göttlichen König gerichtet hatte und die, wie wir wissen, auf ein noch älteres Vorbild zurückging." Freud, *Studienausgabe,* 9:556. Translation from Freud, *Moses and Monotheism,* 140–41. For a discussion of a variant of just this sentence, see Ilse Grubrich-Simitis, *Back to Freud's Texts: Making Silent Documents Speak,* trans. Philip Slotkin (New Haven, Conn.: Yale University Press, 1996), 174.

24. "Was uns so mächtig packt, kann nach meiner Auffassung doch nur die Absicht des Künstlers sein, insofern es ihm gelungen ist, sie in dem Werke auszudrücken und von uns erfassen zu lassen. Ich weiß, daß es sich um kein bloß verständnismäßiges Erfassen handeln kann; es soll die Affektlage, die psychische Konstellation, welche beim Künstler die Triebkraft zur Schöpfung abgab, bei uns wieder hervorgerufen werden." Freud, *Studienausgabe,* 10:198. Sigmund Freud, "The Moses of Michelangelo" (1914), in *The Standard Edition of the Complete Psychological Works of Sigmund Freud,* trans. and ed. James Strachey, in collaboration with Anna Freud, assisted by Alix Strachey and Alan Tyson, 24 vols. (London: The Hogarth Press and the Institute of Psycho-Analysis, 1953–74), 13:212; emphases in the original. I follow the phrasing in the translation of Joan Riviere, as reprinted in Sigmund Freud, *On Creativity and the Unconscious: Papers on the*

Psychology of Art, Literature, Love, Religion, selected, with introduction and annotations, by Benjamin Nelson (New York: Harper & Brothers, 1958), 12. For a
fascinating account of Freud's encounter with the *Moses* of Michelangelo, see Peter
Gay, *Freud: A Life for Our Time* (New York: W. W. Norton & Co., 1988), 314–17.

25. See above, n. 2.

26. "Ich, Carl Philip Emanuel Bach, bin 1714 im März, in Weimar gebohren.
Mein seliger Vater war Johann Sebastian, Kapellmeister einiger Höfe, und zuletzt
Musikdirektor in Leipzig. Meine Mutter war Maria Barbara Bachin, jüngste Tochter,
von Johann Michael Bachen, einen gründlichen Komponisten." Burney, *Tagebuch,*
3:199; Newman, "Autobiography," 366.

27. "Und dieser Mann—der größte musikalische Dichter und der größte
musikalische Declamator, den es je gegeben hat, und den es wahrscheinlich je geben
wird—war ein Deutscher. Sey stolz auf ihn, Vaterland; sey auf ihn stolz, aber, sey
auch seiner werth!" Johann Nikolaus Forkel, *Ueber Johann Sebastian Bachs Leben,
Kunst und Kunstwerke. Für patriotische Verehrer echter musikalischer Kunst*
(Leipzig: Hoffmeister & Kühnel, 1802; reprint, Kassel: Bärenreiter, 1999), 69. The
translation is from David and Mendel, eds., rev. Wolff, *New Bach Reader,* 479.

28. The final volume appeared, appropriately, in 1900. See David and Mendel,
eds., rev. Wolff, *New Bach Reader,* 504.

7

Joseph Haydn's Influence on the Symphonies of Antonio Rosetti

Lawrence F. Bernstein

Antonio Rosetti figures prominently among the many composers of the late eighteenth century whose emulation of the music of Haydn has been widely recognized. Born Anton Rösler, possibly in the Bohemian town of Litoměřice (Leitmeritz), about 1750, Rosetti needs to be carefully distinguished from at least six other musicians with identical or similar names, including the violinist Antonio Rosetti, who joined the Esterháza orchestra in 1766, and the Milanese composer of the same name whose operas were performed in the city of his birth. Our Rosetti became a member of the *Kapelle* at the South German court of Oettingen-Wallerstein in 1773, moving up to the post of *Kapellmeister* in 1785. In 1789, he assumed the same position at the court of the Duke of Mecklenburg-Schwerin at Ludwigslust, where he died in 1792. He was a prolific composer of symphonies recognized for their quality not only in the South German courts he served, but in Paris and London, too.[1]

As is well known, Oettingen-Wallerstein was a major center for the performance of Haydn's music. Prince Kraft Ernst systematically assembled there an extensive collection of Haydn symphonies.[2] By the end of the eighteenth century, his library included some eighty manuscripts and twenty printed sources of symphonies by the prince's favorite composer. It is preserved today in the collection of the Fürstlich Oettingen-Wallerstein'sche Bibliothek, formerly at Schloss Harburg, and now at the Universitätsbibliothek Augsburg.[3] The symphonic music from Wallerstein is particularly valuable as a potential source of evidence for Haydn's influence. At the very least, the scope and nature of the Haydn collection at this princely establishment enable us to demonstrate concretely the availability to the composers who worked there of singular models among the symphonies of Haydn. Indeed, the famous "Jena" Symphony, once thought to have been by Beethoven, but later shown to be the work of the Wallerstein composer and cellist, Friedrich Witt, is particularly rich in its reliance on thematic material from a number of Haydn symphonies. Virtually all of them can be found in the Wallerstein collection.[4]

Given the magnitude of the Haydn presence at Wallerstein, it is hardly surprising that evidence of the greater master's influence on the Rosetti symphonies was widely sought.[5] As early as 1782, Rosetti was subjected to charges of relying too heavily on Haydn. In that year, an anonymous piece in the *Musikalisches Almanach* (surely written by its editor, Carl Ludwig Junker) suggested that, "We have also often encountered Rosetti on the selfsame path with Haydn, almost to the point of risking plagiarism."[6]

The issue of plagiarism *vs.* influence, however, was as fraught with complexity in the eighteenth century as it is today.[7] Heinrich Philipp Bossler, the German music printer and publisher, soon came to Rosetti's defense:

> What the editor of the *Almanach* takes to be the risk of plagiarism is surely based on a misunderstanding. Musical reminiscences—phrases others have also used, and which, however, have served Rosetti in a totally different sense—these can, indeed, be found in his compositions. But a man as imaginative as Rosetti was not so impoverished as to appropriate other passages note for note and for similar artistic purposes.[8]

Another contemporary reference links Rosetti to Haydn. The Swedish composer Joseph Martin Kraus recorded in a diary his experiences during a visit to Vienna in 1783. He relates his reactions to the performance of a Rosetti symphony: "I arrived in Vienna on 1 April. On the same day, there was an *Akademie* at the *Hoftheater*. The Symphony in D Major by Rosetti was an imitation of the Haydn symphony I had heard in Regensburg."[9]

Writing in 1792, Ernst Ludwig Gerber characterized Rosetti as a composer who "modeled himself chiefly after the great Joseph Haydn of Vienna" ("bildete sich vorzüglich nach dem grossen Joseph Haydn zu Wien").[10] He went on to describe the essence of Rosetti's unique musical style:

> It is also not to be denied that in his works a characteristic pleasant, ingratiating, and sweetly flirtatious tone prevails, and his passages for wind instruments especially come off often as divinely beautiful, for he really knows how to utilize the orchestra masterfully.[11]

Having identified these attributes of sweetness and mastery of the orchestra as primary qualities of Rosetti's style, Gerber went on to suggest that his attempts to overstep the limitations of his own style could have significantly adverse effects:

> And so long as he abandons himself to his own genius in his compositions, he certainly merits our approval for his own style. This is, however, not the case when he has sought to follow in the lofty path of a Haydn; then he often sinks to the monotonous, artificial, and facile.[12]

Whether the comparisons with Haydn resulted in a favorable or an unfavorable view of Rosetti's music, his symphonies seem always to have

been considered in tandem with Haydn's, just as they were so often performed on the same programs—at Oettingen-Wallerstein, at the Concert
Spirituel (even before Rosetti's visit to Paris in October of 1781),[13] and at
the Professional, Mara, Pantheon, and Salomon subscription concert series
in London between 1786 and 1793. In the latter programs, the symphonies
by Rosetti exceeded in the actual number of performances those of any
other composer, save for Haydn and J. C. Bach.[14] Indeed, the extraordinary extent of Rosetti's popularity in London may well have come about
precisely because of similarities with Haydn that were not lost on discrimi-
nating London concert-goers. For all these reasons, the symphonies of
Antonio Rosetti would appear to offer a most promising source of evidence of Haydn's influence on his contemporary symphonists.

Among the Rosetti manuscripts from the Oettingen-Wallerstein collection
now preserved at the Universitätsbibliothek Augsburg is a Symphony in G
Minor (Murray A 42). It survives in an autograph score (MS III 4½ 2°
444), dated March, 1787. The finale of this symphony, as we shall see,
offers the best evidence of Haydn's influence. But before discussing its relationship to Haydn, we must first gain a sense of the nature of this movement itself. A diagram of its basic form appears in table 7.1.[15] One can
readily detect from this schema an initial thematic statement in binary form,
several reprises of that section, and the appearance of a fairly close variation of the opening material in the parallel major. The cyclical nature of the
reprise structure is evocative of a rondo-like form, and that is how many
listeners—certainly casual listeners—would be apt to regard the movement
as a whole. But the hybrid nature of the form actually can give rise to
higher levels of complexity. Indeed, the greater the listener's sensitivity to
late-eighteenth-century formal practices, the more complicated—perhaps
even the more ambiguous—a movement like this one can seem. Our interpretation of the music at hand approaches it from the perspective of the
listener whose command of the conventional formal paradigms can allow
him to grasp significant levels of ambiguity. The particular mixture of formal elements we encounter here is somewhat suggestive of the combinations of structural designs Elaine Sisman has found so extensively in the
music of Joseph Haydn. As we shall see, however, the particular pattern
Rosetti offers does not specifically match any of the hybrid paradigms Sisman
describes.[16]

The movement opens with a rounded binary form including repeats.
Often, symphonic finales in the second half of the eighteenth century that
begin with such closed forms turn out to be cast in cyclical designs like
rondo or sonata-rondo.[17] The presence of an initial thematic statement in
rounded binary form is no guarantee, however, that the movement will
actually adhere strictly to either of these formal schemes. Binary structures
initiate theme-and-variation forms, too, which make occasional, if rare,
appearances among symphonic finales.[18] And they also appear once in a

Table 7.1. Rosetti, Symphony A42 in G Minor/iv (1787). Formal Schema.

[A] Rounded binary (=P)

a	(motive 1; motive 2)		a	b	a	b	a	
1	(1–2	3–4	)	9	17	25	33	41

g

[B] "Exposition"-like Continuation

T	Tk	S	Sk	K1	Dvlp. of [A]a, mot. 1	Retransition ([A] a, both motives)
49	61	65	77	81	91	105

Eb–c–V/Bb Bb   g

[A'] Reprise

a	b	a
123	131	139

g

[C] "Maggiore" Variation of A

a	ak	b	a
147	155	159	169

G

[A"] Reprise

a	b	a		New Retransition (Rhythm of [A], mot. 2)
177	185	193		201

g

[Coda]

Anticipation	K2 ([A]a, mot. 1)	Rhythm of [A], mot. 2 as final K
209	231	248

G

while as the primary themes of movements cast in sonata form.[19] Thus, having heard the first forty-eight measures of this movement, we cannot be at all certain of what its overall form will ultimately turn out to be. This vacuum of information is discomforting, and it demands redoubled efforts to project and then interpret the next turn of events. This level of uncertainty is not uncommon at the beginning of a symphonic finale, where routinely the options for formal designs are greater in number than in any other movement of the four-movement cycle.[20] As we pursue the underlying formal paradigm in Rosetti's finale, at this juncture we are forced to focus intensely on what follows the reprise-like opening in rounded binary form.

At the beginning of the next passage (m. 49), the closed form of the initial section suddenly gives way to a more open-ended explosion of orchestral energy, accompanied by modulatory motion and development of the two principal motives of the rounded binary theme (see examples 7.1a and 7.1b). Inevitably, we identify these features as the conventional characteristics of the transitional material from a sonata exposition. The subsequent reiteration of the first of the two thematic motives just as the relative major is established (m. 65) projects an aura of secondary material—presented, however, in the "monomotivic" and somewhat restless manner Haydn often favored, and without clear articulation from the preceding

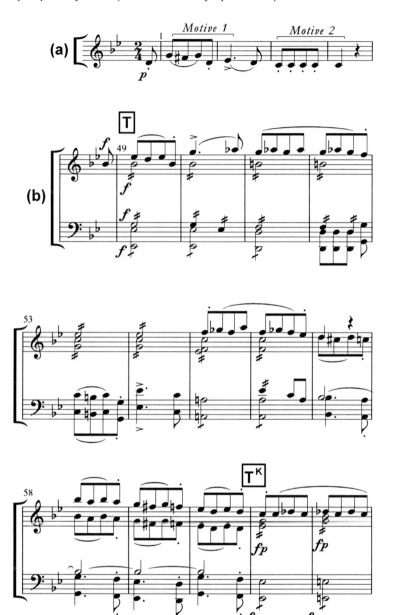

Example 7.1. Rosetti, Symphony A42/iv (a) mm. 1–4; (b) mm. 49–69, 81–89, after Oskar Kaul, ed., *Anton Rosetti (1750–1792): Ausgewählte Sinfonien*, rev. ed., *Denkmäler der Tonkunst in Bayern*, 22 (Wiesbaden: Breitkopf & Härtel, 1968). Used by kind permission of Breitkopf & Härtel.

Example 7.1. *(continued)*.

transitional material. In turn, this is followed by a short bank of closing gestures (also related to the opening motive). By m. 90, all the essential ingredients of a sonata exposition have been set forth, albeit in a context in which tight motivic homogeneity reins in the broader thematic differentiation and rhythmic articulation often encountered in sonata expositions.

The dynamic properties of the sonata-like exposition essentially rule out theme and variations as a governing formal design for this movement. All of the other options, however, are still viable. Sonata-rondo remains a distinct possibility. The case for sonata form is somewhat enhanced by the exposition-like functions just observed, although the closed binary form at the opening would remain a most unusual, albeit possible, feature of a sonata design. The movement could still turn out to be a rondo—but one with very strong sonata-like properties in its first episode. At the very least, Rosetti's deployment of a structure that has the shape of a sonata exposition awakens us to the possibility that we might expect some sort of continuing dynamic formal process, as opposed to greater reliance on the more quiescently predictable binary structures of a simple rondo.

At m. 90, Rosetti leaps back into G minor for fifteen measures, of which the structural function is not clear. The passage includes a fair amount of dominant harmony, along with some modest development of the opening motivic material (motive 1 of the rounded binary theme). Ultimately, it leads, beginning at m. 105, to a dominant pedal that ushers in a more traditional device, a lengthy retransition that unmistakably signals the need for return of the opening material in the tonic. The first passage (mm. 90–104) causes confusion by establishing G minor so clearly *before* the following retransition. Finally, the rounded binary theme, for which the retransition generates a clear expectation, does indeed return, at m. 123.

What we have heard thus far closely resembles the essential features of the first sections of a sonata-rondo.[21] That would lead us to expect in the next section some divergence from the structural and tonal stability inherent in the return of the opening theme—divergence that usually takes the form of a swing toward greater tension. In sonata-rondo designs, of course, this is generally achieved with the introduction of a more wide-ranging tonal discourse or of development.[22] Rosetti steers a different course here, however. At m. 147, he provides a brief rounded binary form without repeats in the parallel major; it bears a very close thematic relationship to the opening theme (see example 7.2). Our sense that this movement would continue in the manner of a sonata-rondo is rudely thwarted when this simple binary form in the tonic major takes the place of the markedly more unstable tonal and developmental disquisition we were expecting.

A more casual listener—one of many for whom sonata-rondo, in 1787, could be an arcane and relatively inaccessible construct—might continue to perceive this movement along the lines of a rondo. For such a listener, the G-major episode might be less surprising, but still not altogether devoid

Example 7.2. Rosetti, Symphony A42/iv (a) mm. 1–8; (b) mm. 147–154, after Oskar Kaul, ed., *Anton Rosetti (1750–1792): Ausgewählte Sinfonien*, rev. ed., *Denkmäler der Tonkunst in Bayern*, 22 (Wiesbaden: Breitkopf & Härtel, 1968). Used by kind permission of Breitkopf & Härtel.

of an element of confusion. What, after all, is the function of a rondo episode? Forkel spells this out with characteristic clarity and elegance. Its purpose is to enable each reprise to appear to the listener as a "newly strengthened phrase."[23] He goes on to recommend the means whereby this end can be achieved; it can be gained from a judicious balance between relatedness and contrast to the rondo refrain. The bonding to the rondo theme should arise from thematic and motivic resemblances to it, but that affiliation needs to be balanced by means of motivic variations ("Verän-derungen"), breaking down of thematic material ("Zergliederungen"), para-phrase ("Paraphrasieren"), or, when it is possible, by modulation to remote tonalities ("entfernte Tonarten von der Haupttonart").[24]

Rosetti's G-major couplet (beginning at m. 147) might technically qualify as an episode according to Forkel's definition, but it certainly seems to fall far short of the *balance* between resemblance and difference Forkel advo-cated. This "episode" is in the same key as the rounded binary theme. It maintains the same phrase structure and the same melodic motives, even disposing the latter in the same places within the phrase. Aside from the move to the opposing mode, the contrasting orchestration, and a bit of melodic inversion, very little has changed from the opening theme.

However we view the formal status of this movement, we will not have forgotten the first episode—the one that embodied the dynamic properties of a sonata exposition. In the course of doing so, it generated a significant need for the subsequent return of the stability associated with the follow-ing return of the opening theme. Significantly, Rosetti's very stable G-ma-jor "episode" fails at regenerating this need. It is too stable to imply a strong expectation for subsequent return. In this sense, it seems a step back from the success of the first (sonata-like) episode in "strengthening" the subsequent reprise, as Forkel recommends.[25] The abandonment of this ob-jective—so successfully achieved earlier—cannot but generate confusion.

Other aspects of the passage are perplexing as well. The content and structure of the *maggiore* section, especially its first strain, are so close to the opening theme that we cannot but flirt momentarily with the idea that Rosetti has initiated a strophic variation. To complicate matters even more, the switch to the opposing mode in this context is a hallmark of the alter-nating variation, a structural design of which Haydn was particularly fond. It entails the introduction and subsequent variation of a second theme in the opposing mode, in alternation with the theme first presented and its attendant variations. Often, the new material is totally independent the-matically. When it is related to the first theme, however, this affinity will generally take the shape of a motivic correspondence that still allows the contrasting elements of the new section to dominate. Of course, Rosetti's *maggiore* passage is much too closely related to the opening theme to pro-vide the "new" thematic material in the opposite mode that is characteris-tic of Haydn's variety of alternating variations. But we focus on the modal change first, and that is among the most vivid traits of the alternating variation. Thus, yet another strain of ambiguity enters our perception of this movement.[26] Altogether, then, this simple G-major couplet demonstrates a marked capacity to generate confusion. Of all the sources of ambiguity that contribute to this state, the central one is the notable step back from the more anticipatory character inherent in the first (exposition-like) episode.

In the next section (beginning at m. 177), Rosetti moves directly (i.e., with no preceding preparation) into a literal return of the binary theme, once again in G minor. This strategy seems highly problematical. In its immediate context, the return sounds stale, perhaps even cloying, for a number of reasons. First of all, this is the third time in succession the thematic material of the initial theme has been presented in the key of G. What is more, the last reprise (at m. 123) was heralded by an extended retransition. The relatively unceremonious manner with which the second reprise enters seems, by comparison, muted and lackluster. Moreover, the seemingly impromptu arrival of the second reprise flies in the face of the strong dynamic process inherent in the sonata-like exposition that followed the opening binary theme.

This overriding quality of stasis is, at first, somewhat bewildering, but, as the work proceeds, the *raison d'être* for Rosetti's plan eventually comes into focus. At m. 201, after the reprise is spent, a new retransition ensues, built on the second (repeated-note) motive of the opening rounded binary theme and couched in a series of highly punctuated secondary dominants. A significant event is clearly imminent. The anticipatory passage seems to find resolution in a somewhat dramatic turn of events: the unexpected return to the major mode at m. 209. But the material at this juncture is not stable. The harmonic resolution coincides with a highly directional and equally anticipatory scalar descent in the first violins, juxtaposed contrapuntally to the first of the two thematic motives in the second violins (see example 7.3a). The descending structural line ends on a' (in the first violin), one note short of the tonic, and that deprivation of closure is prolonged for another eight measures of animated cadential harmony (mm. 223–30). Whatever event was heralded by the preceding retransition obviously has not happened yet.

A coda seems to be taking shape, its objectives unfolding, but only gradually. Finally, all of this anticipatory material culminates in two successive closing gestures, based on each of the two motives of the original rounded binary theme (see example 7.3b). This point of arrival is richly satisfying, as fulfilling, in its own way, as the recapitulation of a sonata form. The simple reiteration once more of the two motives we have heard again and again throughout this movement has seemingly been invested with the capacity to stimulate the listener's impression of a major event. This is so owing to the formal strategies we observed earlier in the movement.

Example 7.3. Rosetti, Symphony A42/iv (a) mm. 211–223; (b) mm. 244–253, after Oskar Kaul, ed., *Anton Rosetti (1750–1792): Ausgewählte Sinfonien*, rev. ed., *Denkmäler der Tonkunst in Bayern*, 22 (Wiesbaden: Breitkopf & Härtel, 1968). Used by kind permission of Breitkopf & Härtel.

The second section of this finale (the "exposition"-like continuation), as we have seen, gave rise to an expectation for a continuing dynamic process. I take this to be a central rhetorical implication of the movement. Fulfillment of that expectation would normally lead first to one or the other of two unstable passages: a tonally discursive development section or a genuinely contrasting rondo episode.[27] The thematic restatement that normally follows either of these would stimulate a sense of high-level resolution—the one in the manner of a recapitulation, the other as a privileged reprise. Neither type of structural dynamism was provided by Rosetti.

Thus, the potent anticipatory passages beginning at m. 201 do more than merely create a need for the subsequent stable material at the local level. They reawaken recollections of the old, unpaid debt: that, in the wake of the sonata-like transition, this work was to have embodied a large-scale dynamic structural process. Given Rosetti's studied avoidance of that process in the *maggiore* couplet and the reprise that follows it immediately, the strong anticipatory elements of the coda and their resolution take on more global structural significance. The simple closing gestures satisfy greatly because they assume the guise of the covenanted dynamic structure: high-level, urgently anticipated return. It is not an accident that these closing devices incorporate a motivic synopsis.

In this movement, then, Rosetti has combined elements of different formal paradigms in ways that generate confusion. In the course of doing so, he mounts a large-scale prolongation, delaying until the very end of the movement the realization of its fundamental rhetorical objective. Rosetti's capacity to override the conventional centrality either of a recapitulation or a final (privileged) reprise in favor of a later capstone event—an end-oriented structure—will surely evoke thoughts of Haydn's influence in anyone who has read James Webster's incisive treatment of through-composition in that composer's music. Webster often sees in such through-composition a focus on high-level structural resolutions at the very end of the work.[28] Given Rosetti's access to specific Haydn symphonies at Wallerstein, it is tempting to seek out a particular composition from which he may have learned this approach, along with the other unique features of formal design cited above.

In pursuit of candidates for a specific model by Haydn, we would naturally incline to look first at symphonies in the minor mode. Eleven by Haydn survive, but only one exhibits enough surface similarity to Rosetti's finale to render it a reasonable starting place in the search for his model. This is Symphony 78, which Haydn appears to have composed in 1782, and which, like Rosetti's finale, begins in the minor mode and ends in major.[29] In addition, both Rosetti's finale and the last movement of Symphony 78 include *maggiore* sections in binary form that are scored almost identically (i.e., with the *a*-strain featuring solo oboe, the *b*-strain, solo flute). These exterior correspondences of form, modal design, and orchestration invite further comparison of the two movements. Significantly, moreover, the finale of Symphony 78 was demonstrably accessible to Rosetti within the appropriate time-frame, for Kraft Ernst's library included several copies of it, at least one of them acquired just a few years before Rosetti composed his G-Minor Symphony.[30]

The finale of Haydn's Symphony 78, like that of the Rosetti symphony just considered, begins with a rounded binary form. A basic diagram of the structure of the movement appears in table 7.2.[31] The second strain (*b*) of the opening binary form is long (twenty-four measures). It modulates securely to the relative major and encapsulates a pointed preparation for the return of the opening material, culminating in a unison dominant sustained with a fermata (mm. 25–32). The return of the *a*-material (m. 33), therefore, is a forceful event. Opening the movement with a rounded binary form must have conveyed the same range of projections with respect to the underlying design of the movement that we encountered in the Rosetti finale, which began with a similar structure. The more casual listener is apt to think along the lines of a cyclical, rondo-like form, while the more informed listener is more likely to entertain a wider range of possibilities: rondo, sonata-rondo, sonata, or theme and variations. Again, we shall track the movement bearing in mind the wider range of possibilities. As was so in our consideration of Rosetti's G-minor finale, this work, too, sets considerable store by the implications inherent in the section that follows the opening rounded binary theme.

What follows is the couplet in the parallel major that so closely resembles the G-major variation of Rosetti's finale. It is a brief rounded binary form

Table 7.2. Joseph Haydn, Symphony 78 in C Minor/iv (acquired 1784). Formal Schema

|A| Rounded binary
‖: a   :‖:   b   a   : ‖
   1   9   33
   c   E♭   c
|B| "Maggiore" Couplet (rounded binary)
‖: a   :‖:   b   a   :‖
   41   49   57
   C   C–G C
|A'| Reprise (with internal development)
   a | b | a   Dvlp. | Retransition | a |
   65   73   97 99   139   151 |
   c   E♭   →   V/c   c
|B'| "Maggiore" Couplet (repeated)
   a | a | b   a | b   a |
   159   167   175   183   191   199
   C   C   C–G   C   C–G   C
|Coda|
Fragment of a from Section |B| (anticipatory dissolution) | K (|B| a)
207   221
C   C

Example 7.4. Haydn, Symphony 78/iv, mm. 40–46, mm. 1–7, after H. C. Robbins
Landon, ed., *Joseph Haydn: Critical Edition of the Complete Symphonies,* vol. 8
(Vienna: Universal Edition, 1965). All examples from the *Critical Edition* (Volumes
5 and 8) are used by permission of European American Music Distributors LLC, US
and Canadian agent for Universal Edition, Vienna. © 1951, 1965 by Universal
Edition, A. G. Vienna. © renewed.

of almost identical proportions to the equivalent section in Rosetti's symphony, and, as we indicated above, it is scored exactly as is Rosetti's variation: solo oboe in the *a*-strain, solo flute in the *b*-strain. Our first impression is likely to be that this couplet in the contrasting mode is the first
episode of a rondo—perhaps a rondo variation, given its vague thematic
resemblance to the melody of the opening binary theme (see example 7.4).
The second section of the form is a little early, however, for the conversion
to the opposing mode. This usually occurs later in both rondos and variation forms (although one can cite examples of its appearance that early in
the movement). The resultant ambiguity gives rise to yet another possibility—that the combination of the shift to the opposing mode with an aura
of freshness might be suggestive of an alternating variation (just as it was
in the analogous place in the Rosetti finale). Confirmation of this design
would take the form of systematic variation alternately of the opening theme
and the *maggiore* passage.

   A return to the beginning of the opening couplet in C minor does follow.
The first half of the binary form is presented unaltered. This is consistent
with standard practice in alternating variations, where often variation is
first introduced only in the repeat of the first half of the binary structure (as

in Haydn's Symphonies 53/ii and 90/ii, for example). Up to this point, the potential for viewing this movement as an alternating variation, therefore, remains viable. Verification would come when the repeat of Section A is varied. That repeat is omitted entirely, however. In its place, the second half of the binary form is presented immediately, also unaltered from its original presentation, up to the fermata-blocked dominant unison that so strongly signals the return of the opening melody in C minor (m. 96). The absence of the repeat of Section A and, therefore, of the opportunity for variation, is sufficient to undermine the implication that alternating variation might serve as the model for this movement. That the section seems to proceed in its original binary form would appear to imply that the movement is couched as a fairly routine rondo.

Haydn does go on, however, to alter this binary form. He introduces change, but precisely where we least expect it: at the moment we have been led to expect the urgently anticipated return of the opening of the C-minor theme (m. 97). The melody with which the movement opened does, indeed, return, but only its first two measures (see example 7.5). Thereafter, unanticipated silences and sequences shake our confidence in the binary design of this section and in the implications for rondo structure inherent in it.

Furthermore, after a third moment of silence gives way to a third sequence (m. 109), the passage slips into conventional developmental activity: thematic manipulation of the opening motive in an active contrapuntal texture and in a rapidly moving tonal matrix. Thus, the closed and predictably simple structural pillar of the binary design has given way, without preparation, to the progressive, unpredictable character of a sizeable and decidedly sonata-like developmental passage (mm. 109–49). These changes are hardly the variations that might have provided the telltale earmark of alternating variation form. This movement has broken out of the bounds of binary form to turn into a much more dynamic, sonata-like process. (At least, so it would seem at this juncture.) The relatively high level of formal indeterminacy generates a significant need for a return to some level of stability, and that demand only intensifies with the arrival of a forceful and lengthy retransition (mm. 139–49).

The beginning of the C-minor binary melody—what we expected at m. 97—reappears right after this retransition. At first, it resounds with the force of the recapitulation of a sonata form. This is not surprising, for the material that prepares its arrival behaved precisely like the end of a sonata development. We were led thereby to expect that the architectonic consequence of this large body of developmental and retransitional anticipation would be a substantial formal entity. In fact, however, all that appears by way of returning material is the eight-measure *a*-strain of the binary unit. It is only when the next section of the movement commences and seems to interrupt the preceding theme that we realize retrospectively that the entire

Example 7.5. Haydn, Symphony 78/iv, mm. 97–112, after H. C. Robbins Landon, ed., *Joseph Haydn: Critical Edition of the Complete Symphonies*, vol. 8 (Vienna: Universal Edition, 1965).

sonata-like development was, in reality, simply a parenthetic extension of the second half of the opening theme. What seemed at its inception so much like a sonata recapitulation turns out, after all, to be no more than the significantly delayed return of the *a*-strain of the rounded binary form. We have been taken in again.

The latter realization dawns upon us at the instant of the initiation of the next section (m. 159). Having completely disabused the listener of any notion that this movement is cast as a set of alternating variations, Haydn now resuscitates that very idea by returning suddenly (at m. 159) to the *maggiore* passage that followed the opening couplet. Once again, the listener awaits the application to this material of classical variation technique. And once again, the expected variation does not seem to occur. Instead, the C-major theme is repeated literally. Indeed, Haydn, who often curtails internal repeats when a binary form returns, preserves them here in a manner that seems almost pedantic. Not only is the listener again denied confirmation that this might be alternating variation form; the elusive corroboration is this time withheld with a vengeance.

Actually, the preservation of the repeats serves a purpose that is realized beginning at m. 206 (see example 7.6). By this point, the entire *maggiore* passage has been replayed twice, but a prominent motive from just after its

Example 7.6. Haydn, Symphony 78/iv, mm. 207–222, after H. C. Robbins Landon, ed., *Joseph Haydn: Critical Edition of the Complete Symphonies*, vol. 8 (Vienna: Universal Edition, 1965).

beginning is repeated here again (it is the passage that appears in the upper staff of example 7.4, mm. 41–43). The listener has just heard this material a total of four times (in the *a*-strain and its repeat, and in both renderings of the return of the *a*-strain—beginning at mm. 160, 168, 184, and 200). In this context, yet another iteration seems redundant. But what begins (in m. 206) as merely another repeat of a prominent early motive of the *maggiore* passage changes dramatically in but an instant.

First, it is augmented (m. 208); then, it is interrupted by a series of silences and sequences very similar to those that interrupted the C-minor binary theme just before the developmental section (mm. 209–19). All sense of predictability is instantaneously eradicated, along with any hope that this movement would, indeed, turn out to be a set of alternating variations.

Not once have we been able to project accurately the outcome of Haydn's structural plans as they affect the overall form of this movement. The central strategic need has now become that of furnishing at least one transparently predictable high-level structural resolution before the end of the movement. Haydn provides it, at the eleventh hour, for the closing material that brings this finale to an end is manifestly, if not dramatically, the predictable consequent of the stuttering thematic splinters that precede it. Haydn sowed the seeds for this outcome much earlier. That is the point of the unusual frequency with which the reprise of the *maggiore* passage is repeated. At mm. 164, 172, 188, and 204 (not to mention the four times the same passage was heard earlier), we are emphatically instructed that the two notes in example 7.6, m. 217, inevitably lead to the descending scale at the end of the example.

Thus, at the very conclusion of the finale—and only there—Haydn offers nothing to contradict our sense of how an important structural implication of the movement will be realized. That is why the simple descending scales from a'' down to c'' with which the movement closes are so eminently satisfying, in the manner of a dénouement. No previous structural process in this movement at a level higher than that of an individual binary unit could have similar force, because each was undercut deceptively. The weightiest structural event in this movement is—as it was in Rosetti's finale—withheld until the very end of the movement. A local phenomenon, the simple closing gesture, is, in this way, catapulted into global structural prominence.

The finale of Rosetti's G-Minor Symphony and that of Haydn's Symphony 78, thus, have much in common. They both begin in the minor mode and end in the major (an exceptional procedure among Haydn's symphonic finales). They both combine elements of sonata-derived dynamism with the more relaxed predictability of conventional binary and rondo-like forms. They do so, moreover, without ultimately singling out the template of any one formal design as *the* paradigm for their respective movements. They impart the coded signals of a variety of formal designs (rondo, sonata, and sonata-rondo in Rosetti's finale; rondo, alternating variation, and sonata in Haydn's).[32] In the process, they inhibit the specific anchoring in any one of them that we tend to seek with particular urgency in our assimilation of symphonic finales. Both composers rescue us from the perils of unrelenting ambiguity at the eleventh hour by transferring global structural significance to capstone events. And for both composers the very quintessence of formal ambiguity resides in the strategies with which they manage the *maggiore* passage. Rosetti and Haydn alike seem to regard this unit as a kind of structural wildcard. Rosetti designs it so that it cannot comfortably fit any standard formal paradigm. Haydn uses it as the centerpiece of his deceptive rhetoric by creating with it the false impression that his movement might be an alternating variation. What Rosetti may well have learned from Haydn's model was how to use a couplet in the opposing mode specifically as a means of confusing the listener: by casting it in ways that run contrary to any of its conventional uses. The distinct similarities in these two passages with respect to form, length, modal character, and orchestration make it a certainty that Rosetti took a particularly long and hard look at Haydn's *maggiore* couplet. That he also learned from it a subtle approach to the generation of ambiguity seems, at the very least, a strong possibility.

Another Haydn symphony seems to have served Rosetti as a model for strategic emulation: Symphony 53. This work was composed near the end of the 1770s, just before the efflorescence of Rosetti's symphonic production. In its day, moreover, it appears to have been the most widely known of Haydn's symphonies, and so it remained for a number of years. Hoboken, for example, lists fourteen different instrumental arrangements of this symphony, along with a widely published version of the slow movement for voice and keyboard.[33] Haydn's Symphony "L'Impériale," as this work later came to be known, found its way into the court library at Oettingen-Wallerstein in 1779.[34]

As was so in the pair of symphonies discussed above, the relationship between Haydn's Symphony 53 and another work by Rosetti manifests itself in the last movements of the two symphonies. It links the redaction of the finale for Symphony 53 that is labeled "Capriccio" in its primary sources to the last movement of Rosetti's D-Major Symphony (Murray A 12), composed in Wallerstein in 1780, just a year after the court acquired its copy of Symphony 53.[35]

Haydn's "Capriccio" finale (Version A) for Symphony 53 and the last movement of Rosetti's Symphony A 12 both begin with rounded binary forms. In fact, the second strains of the binary forms in these two movements share a significant thematic resemblance, outlined in example 7.7. The two passages contain a series of wide downward leaps to sets of three

Example 7.7. Rosetti, Symphony A12/iv, mm. 9–14, after Oskar Kaul, ed., *Anton Rosetti (1750–1792): Ausgewählte Sinfonien*, rev. ed., *Denkmäler der Tonkunst in Bayern*, 22 (Wiesbaden: Breitkopf & Härtel, 1968); Haydn, Symphony 53/iv (Version A), mm. 15–18, after Helmut Schultz, ed., *Joseph Haydn: Critical Edition of the Complete Symphonies*, vol. 5 (Vienna: Universal Edition, 1965). Rosetti used by kind permission of Breitkopf & Härtel.

repeated notes, along with matching structural goals, consisting in motion first from D sharp to E, then from G sharp to A.

This substantive relationship helps to demonstrate Rosetti's familiarity with the work by Haydn. More significant, however, is a particular structural process in Symphony 53 that I believe informed the design of the last movement in Rosetti's Symphony A 12. Turning to the opening of Haydn's finale, we discover that its initial strain bears the form of the antecedent of a standard antecedent-consequent structure (see example 7.8).[36] The phrase closes on the dominant, prepared by an appoggiatura a half-step below.

Example 7.8. Haydn, Symphony 53/iv (Version A), mm. 1–5 (antecedent), after Helmut Schultz, ed., *Joseph Haydn: Critical Edition of the Complete Symphonies*, vol. 5 (Vienna: Universal Edition, 1965).

Critical to the implicative properties of this passage are the three anacrustic eighth notes that follow the half cadence in m. 5. Their anticipatory descent seems directed at the F sharp with which the melody began. Moreover, the alteration of the G sharp to a G natural forces the melodic descent to lean towards the F sharp just below, thereby confirming one's sense of this scale degree as destination. The return to the opening note of the phrase, of course, carries a strong implication that a traditional consequent phrase will follow.

Once m. 5 is perceived to be the dividing point between an antecedent and its consequent, the outcome of the subsequent phrase can readily be projected. Most likely, it will lead to tonic closure in m. 10 that is melodically

Example 7.9. Synthetic consequent for the opening antecedent melody of Haydn, Symphony 53/iv (Version A).

parallel to the half cadence in m. 5: a cadence on d', approached by a lower appoggiatura—as in the hypothetical solution in example 7.9.

As we might expect, this is not the route Haydn opts to follow. The leap up an octave in m. 6 (see example 7.10) at first seems quite disruptive. However, once the anticipated consequent phrase begins to repeat the melody of the antecedent in the higher range, we continue to project closure in the manner of a traditional antecedent-consequent structure; we simply expect it to occur an octave higher. In fact, as we see in the continuation of example 7.10, Haydn frustrates the melodic implications of the antecedent phrase, denying us the

Example 7.10. Haydn, Symphony 53/iv (Version A), mm. 5–10 (end of antecedent and consequent), after Helmut Schultz, ed., *Joseph Haydn: Critical Edition of the Complete Symphonies*, vol. 5 (Vienna: Universal Edition, 1965).

expected appoggiatura and propelling the closing gesture yet another octave higher with a D-major scale that tears upward like a loose cannon.

The effect of this is most destabilizing melodically (although the expected tonic closure is, in fact, provided harmonically). Nonetheless, latent within the large-scale formal process is the potential that the unrealized melodic implication will be provided in the return of the consequent at the end of the rounded binary form. Actually, however, at that point (m. 28), the same impulsive, upward gesture recurs. When it appears yet again in the reprise of the rounded binary form (beginning at m. 97), the debt to supply the level of stable melodic closure originally implied is even more powerfully reaffirmed.

The payment of this debt becomes a central concern of the coda in this finale, and Haydn discharges his obligations in two ways, as we see in example

7.11. First, he introduces a long structural descent that has the effect of re-versing (by literal inversion) the anomalous ascending D-major scale (the "loose

Example 7.11. Haydn, Symphony 53/iv (Version A), mm. 147–158, after Helmut Schultz, ed., *Joseph Haydn: Critical Edition of the Complete Symphonies*, vol. 5 (Vienna: Universal Edition, 1965).

cannon"). Second, the concluding gesture of the passage consists (at mm. 157–58) in motion from C sharp to D—the structural closure implied as early as the anacrustic pattern in m. 5, but withheld until this very late point in the movement. It occurs there, moreover, in the octave originally implied within the rounded binary form. Typically, this has the effect of emphasizing an end-oriented design at the highest structural level of this movement.

In the finale to Symphony A 12, Rosetti seems to employ a very similar process. As we see in example 7.12a, the *a*-strain of the opening rounded binary is set up like an antecedent-consequent structure.[37] It could just as readily have closed as it does in the synthesized version shown in example 7.12b, but Rosetti chose instead to end on the dominant (see example 7.12c). That choice enhances the implication that any return of the opening mate-rial at the end of the rounded binary form will, indeed, close along the lines of the synthesized version—that is, by way of descending motion to the tonic through its upper neighbor. Instead, Rosetti "closes" with an ascending D-major scale that is as destabilizing as the similar structure Haydn pro-vided at the end of his rounded binary form in the finale of Symphony 53 (see example 7.12d). Also like Haydn, Rosetti intensifies the need to realize the original implication (i.e., that closure will come by way of downward

Example 7.12. Rosetti, Symphony A12/iv: (a) mm. 1–4 (antecedent); (b) synthesized consequent; (c) mm. 5–8 (Rosetti's consequent); (d) mm. 21–24 (return of the opening material), after Oskar Kaul, ed., *Anton Rosetti (1750–1792): Ausgewählte Sinfonien*, rev. ed., *Denkmäler der Tonkunst in Bayern*, 22 (Wiesbaden: Breitkopf & Härtel, 1968). Used by kind permission of Breitkopf & Härtel.

motion to D) by repeating the upward motion at the end of the reprise of the rounded binary form (mm. 109–12). Rosetti's solution is almost identical to Haydn's. He provides a coda, the essential business of which is given over to embellishing a descending D-major scale that culminates in motion to D by way of its upper neighbor (see example 7.13).

Symphony A 12 may not be the only one by Rosetti to have been influenced by Haydn's Symphony 53. I believe that significant structural properties in the finale to Rosetti's Symphony A 9 in C Major may also have been designed with the "Capriccio Finale" of Haydn's "L'Impériale" as a prototype. The suggested relationship, in fact, turns on a particularly anomalous passage—a phrase that once led H. C. Robbins Landon to doubt the movement's authenticity:

> Proceeding further, we come to the very strange original finale, marked "Capriccio: Moderato." This is so contrary to every other symphonic movement of the period that one is seriously inclined to doubt its authenticity altogether. It may be that we are dealing with another hasty makeshift by one of Haydn's pupils, corrected here and there by the master himself. [The F-major melody at mm. 38–44 in example 7.14] . . . in its whole harmonic and melodic character is completely unlike Haydn.[38]

Example 7.13. Rosetti, Symphony A12/iv, mm. 176–183, after Oskar Kaul, ed., *Anton Rosetti (1750–1792): Ausgewählte Sinfonien*, rev. ed., *Denkmäler der Tonkunst in Bayern*, 22 (Wiesbaden: Breitkopf & Härtel, 1968). Used by kind permission of Breitkopf & Härtel.

Example 7.14. Haydn, Symphony 53/iv (Version A), mm. 38–44, after Helmut Schultz, ed., *Joseph Haydn: Critical Edition of the Complete Symphonies*, vol. 5 (Vienna: Universal Edition, 1965).

Table 7.3. Joseph Haydn, Symphony 53 in D Major/iv, Version A (acquired 1779). Formal Schema.

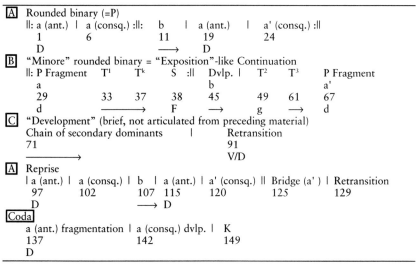

|A| Rounded binary (=P)

‖: a (ant.) | a (consq.) :‖: b | a (ant.) | a' (consq.) :‖
1 6 11 19 24
D ⟶ D

|B| "Minore" rounded binary = "Exposition"-like Continuation

‖: P Fragment T¹ Tᵏ S :‖ Dvlp. | T² T³ P Fragment
a b a'
29 33 37 38 45 49 61 67
d ⟶ F ⟶ g ⟶ d

|C| "Development" (brief, not articulated from preceding material)
Chain of secondary dominants | Retransition
71 91
⟶ V/D

|A| Reprise

| a (ant.) | a (consq.) | b | a (ant.) | a' (consq.) ‖ Bridge (a') | Retransition
97 102 107 115 120 125 129
D ⟶ D

|Coda|

a (ant.) fragmentation | a (consq.) dvlp. | K
137 142 149
D

Landon's concern is not unwarranted (even if he did not initially take adequately into account the implications of the attribution of this work to Haydn by Joseph Elssler, Sr.). The phrase does seem odd, at least on the surface. It consists in a brief, somewhat lyrical, and folk-like melody that spins out in an axial manner, rather than attempting any measure of self-containment. And it is poised over a tonic pedal on F that precludes the levels of stability that normally accrue from conventional movement between tonic and non-tonic harmonies. The melody takes us to a double bar, but it fails to close decisively.

However eccentric this excerpt may seem intrinsically, viewing it within the context of the structural plan for the movement helps us to understand the various anomalies inherent in the passage. The basic form of Finale A is schematized in table 7.3. Its underlying logic resembles in some respects that of Symphony 78/iv (discussed above). The movement opens with a complete rounded binary form, which, of course, conveys a wide range of implications regarding the structure of what will follow—the same wide range we encounter in all of the finales that begin this way. Again, we are made to focus on the beginning of the next section in search of clues regarding how to project subsequent musical events.

Haydn's shift to the parallel minor at the beginning of the subsequent section is suggestive of one of the more rigidly contained designs: rondo or alternating variation. The *minore* section would provide the first episode for the former, the new theme in the opposite mode for the latter. As in Symphony 78/iv, the modal conversion as early as the second unit of the

Example 7.15. Haydn, Symphony 53/iv (Version A), mm. 1–2 and 29–30 compared, after Helmut Schultz, ed., *Joseph Haydn: Critical Edition of the Complete Symphonies,* vol. 5 (Vienna: Universal Edition, 1965).

form is more strongly indicative of alternating variation than of rondo. This option may, indeed, be in the forefront of our consciousness, given the particularly transparent example of alternating-variation form that appears in the second movement of Symphony 53. That the *minore* section commences with a fragment of the beginning motive from the opening rounded binary theme (see example 7.15) only tends to enhance one's sense of an emerging set of alternating variations.[39] All this seems quite clear—at least through the first few bars of the passage.

At m. 33, however, the character of the music changes suddenly, if very briefly, to the characteristically nondescript and supercharged manner of a sonata transition (see example 7.16). Before we can fully absorb the shift to this more progressive dynamic, however, a modulation to the relative major (F) is achieved, and the section is neatly closed off. This happens so quickly that there is no time for the characteristic medial caesura that often is used to open space for a secondary theme.[40] Nonetheless, taken together, the latter transition-like features are distinctly implicative of the imminent arrival of subsequent thematic material, and we momentarily expect what follows to provide such a thematic event.

As we have seen, the subsequent passage (example 7.14) does gain our attention for the thematic quality of its lyricism, but its repetitive nature, its failure to achieve closure, and the monotonous harmonic quality that arises from its tonic pedal rob this material of any true sense of a secondary theme. From a tonal perspective, moreover, we know that it cannot really be a secondary theme in the key of the lowered third degree. The beauty of the process embedded in this passage—a passage we might characterize as a kind of postage-stamp "exposition"—resides precisely in its high level of ambiguity. In a manner distinctly reminiscent of the other finales we have considered, Haydn deploys structural ambiguity here to enliven what might otherwise be a rather static chain of highly predictable binary forms. What began as a *minore* variation is seemingly converted into a miniscule sonata-like exposition, only to leave us taken aback at the very notion that

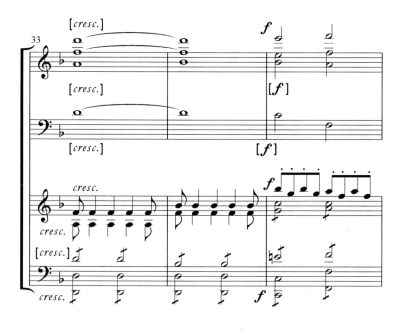

Example 7.16. Haydn, Symphony 53/iv (Version A), mm. 33–37, after Helmut Schultz, ed., *Joseph Haydn: Critical Edition of the Complete Symphonies*, vol. 5 (Vienna: Universal Edition, 1965).

we might have accepted as a secondary theme—even for an instant—melodic material in the relative major of the parallel minor.

Thereafter, the ambiguity only intensifies. Having offered the propulsive dynamic of sonata-like functions with one hand, Haydn withdraws it with the other by repeating the first strain of the *minore* section. Doing so reawakens our sensitivity to the binary design of this passage, but that awareness is not allowed to last long. The music becomes more discursive harmonically, beginning just after the repeat of the *a*-strain, at m. 45. At its inception, at least, this passage is suggestive of the second half of a binary unit, but as it goes on to modulate to G minor, it takes on more of the character of a sonata development. The return of the opening material that coincides with the modulation back to the tonic of D minor (m. 67), confirms that the *minore* section, at the highest level, has, in fact, remained a rounded binary form. But the reprise is a mere four measures long, and it provides no closure, nor is it followed by the expected repeat of the section (the first half of the form *did* repeat). Indeed, there is no articulation between this section and the next—a brief development in the form of a chain of secondary dominants, followed by a traditional retransition and, in turn, finally, by a reprise of the opening (*maggiore*) rounded binary form. The blurring of the seams between binary design and sonata-like development is distinctly reminiscent of what we observed in the finale of Symphony 78.

Like the last movement of Symphony 78 and so many other symphonic finales by Haydn, this movement escapes what could have been the rigid boundaries of successive binary units by transmitting mixed signals to the listener. Some of them are the traditional codes for closed binary structure (rondo or alternating variation); others prompt us to expect the more dynamic properties of sonata-like designs (the transition, developmental passages, and retransition embedded within the lengthy *minore* passage). The two sets of clues are mixed unpredictably, generating a high level of structural ambivalence, repeatedly undermining whatever conclusions we may draw with respect to what will follow, or regarding any assessment we might make regarding the overall formal design of the movement.

Seen against the backdrop of this processive context, the passage from the "Capriccio Finale" that Landon found so odd seems rather less anomalous than it does taken out of this context. It may be a somewhat extreme example. Still, this finale seems thoroughly compatible with Haydn's style—in its pursuit of ways to moderate the potential stasis of binary chains, and in its use of ambiguity and the combination of various formal stratagems as means toward that end.

We turn now to the Rosetti symphony I believe may have been informed by this very passage. Symphony A 9 was probably composed ca. 1783–84, but not later than 1785; thus, it appears to have been written four or five years after its putative (and famous) model was acquired at Oettingen-

Table 7.4. Antonio Rosetti, Symphony A9 in C Major/iv (ca. 1783–84). Formal Schema.

A	Rounded binary (=P)					
	a (ant.)	a (consq.)	| b |	a (consq.)		
	1	9	17	25		
	C	——→G		C		
B	"Minore" Rounded binary = "Exposition"-like Continuation					
	T^1	T^k	T^2 (P)	S (P)	T^3	S as K (P)
	a		b		a'	
	33	41	45	52	60	73	76
	c	——→Eb			——→	c
A	Reprise					
	a (ant.)	a (consq.)	| b |	a' (consq.)	| Sudden Modulation	
	85	93	101	109	116	
	C	——→	G	C	——→ a	
C	Development					
	P	P	Sequences	[A] b as Retransition		
	A!	a	C ——→	V/C		
	121	129	137	167		
A	Reprise					
	a (consq.)	| b |	fermata |	a' |	Coda on [A]	
	175	183	192	193	201	
	C					

Wallerstein.[41] A glance at the diagram of the form in table 7.4 reveals a number of striking tonal relationships, chief of which is the situation of what resembles a secondary theme on the lowered third degree (E flat in a work in C major, at m. 52). The passage in E-flat major needs to be contextualized. It appears, juxtaposed with its preparation, in example 7.17, which should be consulted in conjunction with the formal diagram in table 7.4.[42]

The movement begins with the traditional rounded binary form—briefer than the others considered heretofore, owing to its lack of repeats, and rather concise for its disposition of the first strain (the *a*-strain) as a conventional antecedent-consequent structure. Despite its brevity, the rounded binary design conveys the same wide range of options with respect to how the movement is apt to proceed that it did in all of the movements previously considered. We are made to attend carefully the subsequent material in pursuit of clarification. What appears next (in Section B) is remarkable for the magnitude of the ambiguity it generates.

A sudden shift to the tonic minor marks the beginning of the passage and is strongly suggestive of a standard *minore* couplet, of the sort one encounters in either rondo or alternating variation forms. In fact, this section of the movement *is* disposed in a rounded binary framework (albeit without repeats; see table 7.4, mm. 33, 45, and 73). But the passage also begins with the orchestral explosion that is characteristic of the initiation of sonata transitions, and it subjects the melody of the rounded binary theme to the sort of developmental fragmentation that inevitably heightens tension and is strongly suggestive of subsequent thematic stability. The

Example 7.17. Rosetti, Symphony A9/iv, mm. 33–60, after Oskar Kaul, ed., *Anton Rosetti (1750–1792): Ausgewählte Sinfonien*, rev. ed., *Denkmäler der Tonkunst in Bayern*, 22 (Wiesbaden: Breitkopf & Härtel, 1968). Used by kind permission of Breitkopf & Härtel.

Example 7.17. *(continued)*

explosive energy is articulated very clearly (m. 45), at which point modulation to the relative major of the parallel minor ensues, couched again in a context in which thematic material is rendered unstable through developmental permutation. We are led to expect the arrival of stable thematic material.

When the key of E flat—a natural tonal venue within a passage in C minor—is consolidated (at m. 52), the melodic character of the passage changes significantly. The essential thematic material of the rounded binary theme appears in the second violins, inverted and set against a slow-moving, lyrical counterpoint in the first violins. In the context of the preceding transitional material and its attendant implications, the material in E flat seems pointedly thematic and stable. The coordinated arrival of a contrasting tonality and relatively stable, more lyrical thematic writing is inescapably suggestive of secondary material. But the passage is Janus-faced in several important respects. That it is in the "wrong" key from the perspective of a sonata exposition hardly needs to be mentioned.[43] The "thematic" gesture itself is no more than that—a brief, if lyrical, motive that simply repeats itself, rather than attempting any measure of self-containment. Moreover, all of this is poised over an E-flat pedal that precludes the levels of stability that normally accrue from conventional movement between tonic and non-tonic harmonies. Finally, the passage returns to an anticipatory mode of writing, as it modulates back to C minor. Once the latter modulation is completed, the opening C-minor material returns, and the music is rounded off with the "secondary gesture" now deployed in C minor. This time, the latter material sounds very much like closing material. Upon hearing it in this context, we are apt to adjust our perception of the earlier rendering of this material in E flat retrospectively and regard it as having been more of a closing device for the first modulation. That is not, however, the manner in which the passage is likely to have been perceived on first hearing.

Another way to characterize the most fundamental ambiguity of this passage is to call attention to its internal formal conflict. Its essential design is similar to a rounded binary form without repeats, the return of the opening material at m. 73 coinciding with the return of C minor. Whatever happens in E flat in this context can be said to come about as part of the central tonal contrast of an internal *minore* unit in a composition in C major. On the other hand, the passage embodies several critical aspects of the functional character of a sonata exposition: transitional material of a relatively athematic and modulatory character, contrasting lyrical material (however weak and ambiguous), and a closing gesture. That is to say, it exhibits the features of what we called the "postage-stamp" exposition in the "Capriccio Finale" of Symphony 53.

The level of structural ambiguity in this passage is, thus, remarkably high. Depending upon the formal perspective that strikes one listener or another as more important, either its binary design or its sonata-like attributes may take precedence. In the face of a musical structure so markedly equivocal, we can seek clarification only in the subsequent material.

The parallels between the opening two sections of this movement and the "Capriccio Finale" of Haydn's Symphony 53 are striking. Both movements commence with rounded binary forms, of which the first member is an antecedent-consequent structure. In both finales, the second section shifts swiftly to the parallel minor, suggesting the characteristic *minore* couplet of alternating variation or rondo form. Both symphonies preserve binary form in the *minore* passage, but conceal it within an ongoing framework that avoids repeating either the *b*-strain (Haydn) or both strains (Rosetti). These similarities are common enough and could well be coincidental.

As the *minore* passage proceeds, however, both composers abrogate its tendency toward the relatively static properties of successive binary forms by embodying within it sonata-like transitional material, suggestive of the imminent arrival of thematic material. Both actually proceed, though, to provide a highly ambiguous, if stable, melodic statement in the key of the lowered third degree (i.e., the relative major of the parallel minor). The "thematic" statement, in each case, consists in a brief, lyrical motivic gesture, weakened, however, by its failure to attain formal self-containment and by the flat harmonic profile associated with the superposition of the motive over a tonic pedal. These similarities are sufficiently anomalous to suggest that Rosetti might well have emulated Haydn's model for the formal procedure he opted to follow in this section of the finale of Symphony A 9.[44]

These three finales Rosetti appears to have modeled on works of Haydn are veritable paradigms of formal subterfuge, of a sort that can often be traced to the particular Haydn symphonies he seems to have used as prototypes. By way of summary, the specific means of generating ambiguity Rosetti appears to have learned from Haydn symphonies include:

- the amalgamation of different formal paradigms to vitalize the structure of a movement by weakening our capacity to chart the course of the structure according to the template of any single formal design;
- the evisceration of traditional, internal points of arrival (e.g., recapitulation or weighty rondo reprise) in favor of a capstone, end-oriented event; and
- the endowment of various structures with clear formal implications that fail to achieve realization (e.g., couplets that portend alternating variation form, which, however, never materializes, or the conventional, sonata-like preparation of secondary themes that turn out on arrival to be weak melodically and in the "wrong" tonality).

Rosetti takes over from Haydn an occasional substantive fragment, enough to enhance the case for his familiarity with a particular model. But the essence of what he borrows from Haydn seems, rather, to be strategic in nature, and the objective of many of these strategies appears to be the enlivenment of the finale.[45] Of all the means both composers apply in the name of the latter goal, surely the most important is the combination of various formal paradigms to produce highly idiosyncratic mixtures of formal logistics. The objective of such formal coalescence seems less to be combination for the sake of innovation or variety than to bring about a collision of conflicting plans that often leaves the listener caught unawares, surprised, or bewildered—but always delighted at having been deceived.

For two hundred years, critics have been wedded to the notion that Rosetti was an emulator of Haydn. Their evidence in support of this claim, however, is rarely based on the unique properties of specific compositions. Early characterizations of the relationship between the two composers tend to be extremely subjective, as, for example, the following mid-nineteenth-century representation by Wilhelm Riehl:

> Rosetti sought to encompass everything of sweetness, gentleness, and lyricism from the Haydn epoch within a bright effusion of instrumental lyricism. . . . [He] sometimes copied Haydn intentionally, as nearly all his cohorts had, and he definitely stands closer to this model in delicacy of feeling and fineness of expression than other known [Haydn] students.[46]

More recent studies move into objective, technical realms and cite parallels between Rosetti's music and Haydn's with respect to such matters as thematic development, the rise of modern orchestration, number of movements in the cycle, the fusion of homophonic and contrapuntal textures, the use of the slow introduction, reliance on elaborate and florid baroque-like melodies in slow movements, and the use of musical humor in finales.[47] Undeniably, Rosetti must have assimilated much from Haydn in these spheres, but these criteria are geared to making comparisons among large numbers of compositions—to badly needed generalization, in short. As a result, they are necessarily not conducive to demonstrating the level of direct influence that would permit us to assert that Rosetti fashioned one symphonic movement or another in specific emulation of a given work by Haydn.[48]

But, if Rosetti was the imaginative composer Heinrich Philipp Bossler made him out to be, and he adapted his models from Haydn to new artistic objectives, as Bossler also claimed, the path from a specific model to its adaptation will not necessarily be explicitly inferable.[49] On the contrary, it is likely to remain bound by the subjective constraints of hermeneutic discourse.[50] One may suggest, for example, that Rosetti took from the finales of Haydn's Symphonies 53 and 78 the idea that one could combine different structural paradigms so as to confound the listener's expectations. To do so is, however, to interpret rather than to demonstrate. That carries risks—along with the hope that it may also offer the benefit of illuminating a small corner of the complexity inherent in the question of how eighteenth-century symphonists learned from Haydn.

There are, of course, no objective criteria for assessing whether or not the taking of such risks is worthwhile. But this particular interpretation rests upon a presumption: that both composers saw in their respective combinations of formal designs the capacity to generate what is, from the perspective of the listener's expectations, essentially a structure that rejects reliance on any one of the traditional forms. Surely, it would at least strengthen the argument on behalf of this interpretation if some objective support might be marshaled for the composers' actually having perceived this potential in their manipulation of musical structure. I believe that such external verification may, perhaps, reside in a particular feature of one of the pairs of finales we have considered.

Version A of the finale of Haydn's Symphony 53, as we have noted, is labeled "Capriccio" in the most authentic source of the movement (the manuscript copied by Elssler), and the Viennese copy of the work at Oettingen-Wallerstein—the one that was available to Rosetti—also preserves that rubric. This is the only symphonic finale by Haydn to have been so designated, although the term appears in connection with several other compositions by him. Those works reflect a notably wide variety of musical styles and of approaches to the concept of *capriccio*.[51]

The best-known among them is probably the G-Major Capriccio for keyboard of 1765, Hob. XVII:1, a lengthy rondo-like work loosely in the manner of C. P. E. Bach that traverses a notably wide tonal spectrum.[52] Such discursive and often unpredictable harmony surfaces also in the middle section of the second movement in Symphony 86, as it does in the slow movement of the String Quartet in C Major, op. 20, no. 2, two movements that are also called "Capriccio." The quartet movement is unique in other respects, too. It moves quixotically back and forth between a brooding, recitative-like unison passage and a lyrical, cantabile melody—the one in a manner that has been likened to a dramatic *scena*; the other, to a cavatina.[53] In a letter to Artaria, Haydn referred to his C-Major Keyboard Fantasia of 1789 as a "capriccio."[54] This work also meanders widely along the tonal spectrum, hinting structurally at a seemingly aberrant sonata-rondo design.

All of these works share a somewhat wayward approach to tonal process, and, in doing so, they reflect contemporary characterizations of *capriccio* as improvisatory in nature, in the manner of the fantasia. Johann Mattheson, for example, suggests that a *capriccio* "actually consists not so much in writing or composing with the pen, but appears to be a manner of singing and playing in a free spirit, or, as one says, *ex tempore*."[55] The same notion is conveyed in the letter of 20 July 1778 from Mozart to his father, describing the "little praeambulum" he had composed for Nannerl as "a sort of capriccio, with which to test a clavier. . . . This is a peculiar kind of piece. It's the kind of thing that may be played as you feel inclined."[56]

Not all of the pieces by Haydn called "capriccio" meander in this manner. The first movement of the Keyboard Trio in A Major, Hob. XV:35, for example, is labeled "Capriccio," but it is actually a relatively predictable sonata form in a conservative tonal style. What warrants the designation "Capriccio" for this movement is the presence within it of the kinds of figures that can serve to sharpen technical performance skills. In this sense, the first movement of Haydn's A-Major Trio serves as a perfect example for the keyboard of the type of *capriccio* Heinrich Christoph Koch described as "practice pieces for performers"—prototypes, we might say, of the emerging etude.[57]

Finale A of Symphony 53 is another work by Haydn that exhibits little by way of an improvisatory character. Its moments of greatest tonal activity, moreover, are reasonably predictable compared to the more vagrant modulations in most of the Haydn movements designated "Capriccio." Then why was the movement so designated? Perhaps the work was seen to fit yet another contemporary aesthetic associated with the *capriccio*—that of formlessness. Koch described the *capriccio* in this way, designating it "a piece, in which the composer is not bound by the forms and modulations of conventional compositions, but more just by his fantasy-driven moods than by an overarching design."[58] And Daniel Gottlob Türk described it similarly as "a type of fantasia, without a determined scheme."[59] These characterizations seems to fit Finale A of Symphony 53 aptly, for, as we have seen, in synthesizing elements of binary form, alternating variation, and sonata form in an uncommon combination, Haydn created an edifice that is really devoid of any one central, preexistent structural plan. It is, indeed, a work "without an established scheme." The Rosetti finale I believe was patterned after it combines various formal types to produce a similarly bewildering structure that stands apart from any conventional formal paradigm. Significantly, it too is called "Capriccio" in the composer's autograph score, as are both of the other Rosetti finales we have considered. In fact, altogether, five symphonic finales by Rosetti are designated "Capriccio," and all but one of these display highly idiosyncratic combinations of formal designs—each one unique unto itself.[60]

It seems reasonable to conclude that these symphonic finales cast as uncommon formal compounds and labeled "Capriccio" were so designated because they were meant to be perceived as works devoid of a central, preexistent architectural plan. To paraphrase Koch and Türk, they are lacking, in essence, a single, clear structural referent. If so, our contention that such amalgamation could have been intended, to some extent, to baffle the listener takes on a measure of support.

Finally, at least one contemporary writer seems to have regarded as the quintessential aspect of Haydn's music its ability to confound the listener's capacity to project future events. Writing at the very end of the eighteenth century, the English critic and prolific composer of symphonies, John Marsh, attributed to Haydn the bestowal of genuine substance upon the classical symphony. He specified the concrete means whereby Haydn achieved this success, expressing it in terms of the listener's grasp of Haydn's structure:

> Instead of being able, as was before the case, to anticipate in great measure the second part of any movement, from its uniform relation to the foregoing, it is on the contrary, in [Haydn's] works impossible to conceive what will follow, and a perpetual interest is kept up in much longer pieces than any of the same kind ever before composed.[61]

Rosetti appears to have learned the same lessons from the same master.

Notes

For their gracious assistance in reading the typescript of this article and offering numerous corrections and suggestions for improvements, I am deeply grateful to my late colleague, Dr. Eugene K. Wolf, and to Drs. Sterling E. Murray and Stephen C. Fisher.

1. Cf. Sterling E. Murray, *The Music of Antonio Rosetti (Anton Rösler), ca. 1750–1792: A Thematic Catalog,* Detroit Studies in Music Bibliography, no. 76 (Warren, Mich.: Harmonie Park Press, 1996), xvii–xx; Murray, "The Rösler-Rosetti Problem: A Confusion of Pseudonym and Mistaken Identity," *Music & Letters* 57 (1976): 130–43; and Murray, "Rosetti, Antonio," in *The New Grove Dictionary of Music and Musicians,* ed. Stanley Sadie, 2d ed., 29 vols. (New York: Grove, 2001), 21:704–6. For recently discovered biographical information, including speculation on Rosetti's whereabouts before joining the Wallerstein court, see Olaf Krone, "Antonio Rosetti (ca. 1750–1792): Neue Aspekte," *Concerto: Das Magazin für alte Musik* 15 (1998): 18–22.

2. For a summary of the correspondence between Kraft Ernst's agents and Haydn on the subject of the acquisition of Haydn's music, see Sterling E. Murray, "Antonio Rosetti (1750–1792) and His Symphonies" (Ph.D. diss., University of Michigan, 1973), 57–66. The letters are transcribed in Anton Diemand, "Josef Haydn und der Wallersteiner Hof," *Zeitschrift des Historischen Vereins für Schwaben und Neuberg* 45 (1921): 1–40.

3. Gertraut Haberkamp, *Thematischer Katalog der Musikhandschriften der Fürstlich Oettingen-Wallerstein'schen Bibliothek Schloss Harburg,* Kataloge Bayerischer Musiksammlungen (Munich: G. Henle, 1976).

4. On the "Jena" Symphony, see Fritz Stein, "Eine unbekannte Jugendsymphonie Beethoven's?" *Sammelbände der internationalen Musikgesellschaft* 13 (1911–12): 127–72; H. C. Robbins Landon, "The *Jena* Symphony," *The Music Review* 18 (1957): 108–13; reprinted in Landon, *Essays on the Viennese Classical Style* (London: Barrie & Rockliff, 1970), 152–59; and Stephen C. Fisher, ed., *Friedrich Witt (1770–*

1836): One Symphony, The Symphony, 1720–1840, ser. B, vol. 9 (New York: Garland Publishing, 1983), xvi. On the relationship of the "Jena" Symphony to the music of Haydn, see Ralph Leavis, "Die 'Beethovenianismen' der Jenaer Symphonie," *Die Musikforschung* 23 (1970): 297–302.

5. Another reason Haydn's putative influence on Rosetti seemed so likely surely resides in the long-held but mistaken belief that the Oettingen-Wallerstein *Kapellmeister* was the same Antonio Rosetti who served as a violinist at the Esterháza court, and who was thought to have studied composition with Haydn.

6. "Wir haben auch öfter Rosetti auf dem nämlichen Weg (bis zur Gefahr Plagiats) mit Haydn aufgetroffen." I owe my acquaintance with this quotation and with the following one to their citation in Oskar Kaul, ed., *Anton Rosetti (1750–1792): Ausgewählte Sinfonien,* rev. ed., Denkmäler der Tonkunst in Bayern, vol. 22 (Wiesbaden: Breitkopf & Härtel, 1968), xxxvii. The two passages also appear (with translation) in Murray, "Antonio Rosetti and His Symphonies," 18–19. Murray identifies the likely author of the excerpt from the *Musikalisches Almanach* as Junker.

7. On the emerging conflict in the late eighteenth century between the ideals of originality and emulation, see George J. Buelow, "Originality, Genius, Plagiarism in English Criticism of the Eighteenth Century," *International Review of the Aesthetics and Sociology of Music* 21 (1990): 117–28. For a broad study of the underlying aesthetic issues surrounding musical influence, see Charles Rosen, "Influence: Plagiarism and Inspiration," *19th Century Music* 4 (1980–81): 87–100.

8. "Was die Herausgeber des Almanachs Gefahr des Plagiums nennen, beruht sicherlich auf einem Misverstande. Musikalische Reminiscenzen, Phrasen, die andere auch gebraucht haben, deren sich aber Rosetti in einem ganz andern Sinne bedient, diese können sich wohl in seinen Stüken finden, aber um andern Passagen Note für Note und in ähnlichen Kunstintentionen abzuborgen, dazu ist so ein gedankenreicher Mann, wie Rosetti nicht arm genug." Heinrich Philipp Bossler, "Berichtigungen und Zusäze zu den musikalischen Almanachen auf die Jahre 1782, 1783, 1784," *Musikalische Korrespondenz der Teutschen Filarmonischen Gesellschaft* 5 (2 February 1791): cols. 34–35.

9. "Am 1. April in Wien angekommen. Am selben Tage war Akadamie im Hoftheater. Die Sinfonie von Rosetti aus D dur war eine Imitation von Haydns Sinfonie, die ich in Regensburg gehört hatte." Translated from the Swedish by Irmgard Leux-Henschen, *Joseph Martin Kraus in seinen Briefen* (Stockholm: Edition Reimers, 1978), 105. I am grateful to Prof. Sterling Murray for calling this reference to my attention.

10. Ernst Ludwig Gerber, *Historisch-biographisches Lexicon der Tonkünstler,* part 2 (Leipzig: Breitkopf, 1792; reprint, Graz: Akademische Druck- und Verlagsanstalt, 1977), col. 324.

11. "Es ist auch nicht zu leugnen, dass in seinen Werken ein eigener angenehm schmeichelnder und suss-tändelnder Ton herrscht und besonders fallen seine Sätze für Blase-Instrumente öfters himmlisch schön aus, die er überhaupt beym Orchester Meisterhaft zu benutzen weiss." Ibid., col. 325.

12. "Und so lange er sich in seinem Werken seinem eignen Genie überlässt, verdient er allerdings in seiner Manier unsern Beyfall. Dies ist aber nicht der Fall wenn er den erhabenen Pfad eines Haydn zu betreten gesucht hat, dann fällt er öfters ins monotonische, gekünstelte und spielende." Ibid.

13. A dozen performances of Rosetti symphonies are known to have been mounted

at the Concert Spirituel between 3 June 1781 and 17 May 1787. For a detailed account of Rosetti's Parisian tour including transcriptions of his letters to Kraft Ernst describing his success in Paris, see Kaul, ed., *Anton Rosetti: Ausgewählte Sinfonien,* xxi-xxiii. On the specific performances of Rosetti symphonies at the Concert Spirituel, see Constant Pierre, *Histoire du Concert spirituel, 1725–1790,* Publications de la Société française de musicologie, Sér. III, t. III (Paris: Société française de musicologie, 1975), 318 and passim.

14. Some forty-five performances of symphonies by Rosetti are known to have taken place in London between 1786 and 1793. For records of Rosetti's performances in London, see Simon McVeigh, "The Professional Concert and Rival Subscription Series in London, 1783–1793," *[R. M. A.] Research Chronicle* 22 (1989): 1–136.

Some of the Rosetti symphonies aired in London were surely performed from materials now preserved in the Royal Music Collection at the British Library. (Both of the Rosetti symphonies to be discussed in some detail below are represented in this collection.) These materials include about ten symphonies, a few in the composer's autograph, a few in the hands of known Oettingen-Wallerstein copyists, and several in multiple sets (Murray, *The Music of Antonio Rosetti: A Thematic Catalog,* 629–30). We cannot be sure how these performance materials found their way from the court of Kraft Ernst to London, but Sterling Murray speculates discerningly that Haydn, who stopped at Oettingen-Wallerstein on his way to London in 1792, may well have heard Rosetti's music there and requested copies to take with him to the British capital. I am very grateful to Prof. Murray for sharing this idea with me.

15. Musical examples of the details of the movements most germane to our discussion will be supplied below, often in condensed score. For the orchestration and for other references to the music for which examples have not been provided, the reader is urged to consult Kaul, *Anton Rosetti: Ausgewählte Sinfonien.* For this movement, see pp. 160–69.

16. For a detailed discussion of hybrid form in Haydn's instrumental music, see Elaine R. Sisman, *Haydn and the Classical Variation,* Studies in the History of Music, no. 5 (Cambridge, Mass.: Harvard University Press, 1993), 150–63, 265–70.

17. The structural meaning of sonata-rondo in the 1770s and 1780s—whether it should be regarded as a structural design or a formal process—remains controversial. On sonata-rondo as formal paradigm, see Malcolm S. Cole, "Sonata-Rondo: The Formulation of a Theoretical Concept in the 18th and 19th Centuries," *The Musical Quarterly* 55 (1969): 180–92; and Cole, "Haydn's Symphonic Rondo Finales: Their Structural Role and Stylistic Evolution," *The Haydn Yearbook* 13 (1982): 113–32. For the view of sonata-rondo as a broader, more variable process, see Stephen C. Fisher, "Sonata-Procedures in Haydn's Symphonic Rondo Finales of the 1770s," in *Haydn Studies: Proceedings of the International Haydn Conference, Washington, D. C., 1975,* ed. Jens Peter Larsen et al. (New York: W. W. Norton, 1981), 481–87; and Fisher, "Further Thoughts on Haydn's Symphonic Rondo Finales," *The Haydn Yearbook* 17 (1992): 85–107. Further details about the nature of the sonata-rondo concept, especially as it relates to the music of composers other than Haydn and Mozart, appear in my forthcoming study of Haydn's symphonic finales.

18. To date, only six mature eighteenth-century symphonies have been found that are known to close with a movement in theme-and-variation form: Joseph Haydn's Symphonies 31 and 72, a symphony by Florian Gassmann (Ab 65), one by

Carlo d'Ordonez (D 6), and two by Michael Haydn (MH 399 [= P 21] and MH 477 [= P 30]). On the symphonies by Gassmann and d'Ordonez, see Sisman, *Haydn and the Classical Variation,* 113.

19. The best-known example of a finale in sonata form that opens with a theme in rounded binary form is surely the last movement of Mozart's Symphony in G Minor, K. 550. Joseph Haydn also began a number of symphonic finales in sonata form with rounded binary themes, albeit in movements in which ambiguity between sonata and rondo design appears to have been among his central objectives. These include the finales of Symphonies 76, 77, 87, and (in a design that approximates rounded binary form in its opening theme) Symphony 50.

20. For a penetrating analysis of the uncertainties associated with the listener's surfeit of options at the beginning of a finale, and of the inspired manner in which Haydn can capitalize on them, see James Webster's discussion of the String Quartet in C Major, op. 54, no. 2 in his *Haydn's "Farewell" Symphony and the Idea of Classical Style,* Cambridge Studies in Music Theory and Analysis, no. 1 (Cambridge: Cambridge University Press, 1991), 300–313.

21. Among these features, the length of the retransition (twenty-three measures) is significant for differentiating sonata from sonata-rondo. A very brief retransition would not be readily distinguishable from the anticipatory closure that often occurs at the end of sonata expositions, generally in a briefly extended first ending that leads back to the repeat of the exposition, as in Haydn's Symphonies 88/i, 91/iv, 92/iv, and 93/i, among many others. In a sonata-like setting, only a retransition of reasonably substantial proportions can convince the listener that the rondo-like reprise of a sonata-rondo might be in store.

22. Even the less sophisticated listener, who perceives the movement along the lines of a rondo, would be awaiting a shift toward the contrast that is inherent in the beginning of an episode, which, itself, implies some measure of instability.

23. "[A]ls eine aufs neue bekräftigte Sentenz erscheinen lassen." Johann Nicolaus Forkel, *Musikalisch-kritische Bibliothek,* 3 vols. (Gotha: Carl Wilhelm Ettinger, 1778–79; reprint, Hildesheim: Georg Olms, 1964), 2:286.

24. Ibid.

25. Although the first episode enables the subsequent reprise to be perceived in a "renewed" manner, it does so by shaping the first episode in a way different from Forkel's model. Forkel requires that episodes should be succinct ("kurz und bündig" [*Musikalisch-kritische Bibliothek,* 2:286]), which presumably means closed. Clearly, he did not envision the sonata-like properties of Rosetti's first episode.

26. On Haydn's alternating variations and the balance between similitude and disparity within them, see Sisman, *Haydn and the Classical Variation,* 150–63. Generally, Haydn deploys alternating-variation form in second movements, but he is known to have used it in finales, too, as, for example, in the concluding movements of the String Quartet in D Major, op. 33, no. 6, and the Piano Sonatas, Hob. XVI:22, 33, 34, and 44. Most of these are couched in a relatively relaxed tempo— *allegretto* or *tempo di menuetto*—but the E-Minor Piano Sonata, Hob. XVI:34, which was probably composed in the 1780s (no later than 1784), more closely approximates in its tempo marking of *molto vivace* the vigorous character of a symphonic finale.

27. If Haydn's simple rondo finales are used as a comparative standard, we may note that the episodes most often generate contrast, not surprisingly, by moving to

contrasting keys (exactly as Forkel recommended). This stands in marked contra-distinction to Rosetti's approach. For examples of rondo episodes by Haydn that do modulate, see the minuet rondo of Haydn's Symphony 30/iii (both episodes); and the rondo finales of Symphonies 61 (episodes 2 and 3), 66 (both episodes), 68 (episodes 2 and 3), 69 (both episodes), 75 (episode 2), and 79 (episode 2). Similar tonal contrast may be noted in the rondo finales of several of the string quartets of op. 33: nos. 2 (episode 1), 3 (episode 1), and 4 (both episodes); and of that of op. 54, no. 1 (episode 2, in the second half of the binary form). Sisman regards most of the symphonic finales cited above as variation rondos (as opposed to rondo varia-tions). They are essentially simple rondos with incidental melodic figuration in the reprises. See Sisman, *Haydn and the Classical Variation*, 150.

28. Webster, *Haydn's "Farewell" Symphony*. "Through-composition" in Haydn is an important theme in that study. For a particularly trenchant example of its relationship to end-oriented structure, see Webster's ingenious analysis of the first movement of Symphony 92 (167–73).

29. Beginning the finale in minor and ending it in major is a relatively unusual solution, especially as early as 1782. The last movements of such minor-mode Haydn symphonies as Nos. 26, 39, 44, 49, and 52, for example, are entirely in the minor mode, while those of Symphonies 80, 83, and 95 are completely in the major mode. The finale of Symphony 45 (the "Farewell" Symphony) does begin in minor and end in major, but obviously for reasons linked to its programmatic agenda. The only other Haydn symphonic finale that begins in minor and ends in major disposes its modal configuration in a thoroughly anomalous manner. In Symphony 70, the last movement of a D-major symphony begins in D minor (the key of the slow movement), offering fugal treatment of three subjects, all of which comes to a close in a brief codetta in D major. In Symphony 26 ("Lamentatione"), it is the first movement that begins in minor and ends in major. But here, too, the change was probably made for extra-musical reasons—this time associated with the quotation and evocation of an old liturgical melody, the passion tone that represents the words of the Evangelist.

30. The performance materials for Symphony 78 at Oettingen-Wallerstein in-clude a set of manuscript parts largely in the hand of Johann Radnitsky, a copyist who did some work for Haydn in this period, as well as the Torricella print that offered Symphony 78 along with Symphonies 76 and 77. According to a payment record in the hand of Franz Xavier Link (principal copyist for Kraft Ernst's musical establishment), the Radnitsky parts now preserved in the Universitätsbibliothek Augsburg as MS III 4½ 2° 803 were acquired by the Oettingen-Wallerstein court in 1784, three years before Rosetti composed his G-Minor Symphony. See Haberkamp, *Thematischer Katalog der Musikhandschriften*, 99.

31. As in the previous movement, musical examples of the most germane sec-tions of the movement will be supplied below, some of them in condensed score. The reader is urged to consult the complete score of the symphony in *Joseph Haydn: Critical Edition of the Complete Symphonies*, 12 vols., ed. H. C. Robbins Landon (Vienna: Universal Edition, 1963–68), 8:207–52.

32. Sisman classifies Haydn's movement differently in separate studies: as an alternating strophic variation, and as a movement in "alternating rondo-variation style." In providing each designation, she goes on to underscore the presence of unusual or altered structure in the movement. The apparent incongruity in the two

classifications seems to me more the result of an accurate perception of the high level of ambiguity Haydn brings to this movement than of any methodological inconsistency. See Sisman, *Haydn and the Classical Variation*, 270; and Elaine Sisman, "Haydn's Hybrid Variations," in *Haydn Studies: Proceedings of the International Haydn Conference, Washington, D. C., 1975*, ed. Jens Peter Larsen et al. (New York: W. W. Norton, 1981), 513.

33. Anthony van Hoboken, *Joseph Haydn: Thematisch-bibliographisches Werkverzeichnis*, 3 vols. (Mainz: B. Schotts Söhne, 1957–78), 1:66–73.

34. The performance materials from Oettingen-Wallerstein are preserved today in the Universitätsbibliothek Augsburg in MS III 4½ 2° 876. Stephen Fisher has shown that the archival records of Kraft Ernst's court also preserve the bill that was submitted for this set of manuscript parts, which was purchased in Vienna. The invoice is in the hand of one of the scribes who prepared the copy and bears the date 1779. Stephen C. Fisher, "A Group of Haydn Copies for the Court of Spain: Fresh Sources, Rediscovered Works, and New Riddles," *Haydn-Studien* 4 (1976–80): 76 n. 56.

35. The autograph score of Rosetti's Symphony (A 12) may be found in MS III 4½ 2° 649 in the Universitätsbibliothek Augsburg, where it bears the rubric "Composto nel Messo d'Aprile 1780 a Wallerstein." Haydn's Symphony 53 presents a vexingly difficult source transmission, particularly with regard to its finale. Five different movements were used at one time or another to close this work. Three of these cannot contend seriously to represent Haydn's "real" intentions for the concluding movement of "L'Impériale." Of the other two (the "Capriccio Finale" [also known as Version A] and Version B), it is the "Capriccio Finale" that found its way into the collection at Oettingen-Wallerstein. Its primary source is in the hand of Joseph Elssler, Sr., Haydn's most trusted copyist at Esterháza, and it is now thought to embody Haydn's last thoughts on what should constitute the finale for Symphony 53. The morass of complexity surrounding the transmission of the finale for Symphony 53 and the equally tangled matter of its chronology are deftly unraveled in the *Kritische Berichte* accompanying the forthcoming editions by Stephen Fisher (in collaboration with Sonja Gerlach) of Symphony 53 and the Overture Hob. Ia:7. They appear in the *Joseph Haydn Werke*, ser. I, vol. 9, which was published after this study went into production. I am deeply grateful to Dr. Fisher for sharing this material with me prior to its publication.

36. Once more, musical examples of the most pertinent details of the movement will be supplied below, but the reader is urged to consult the complete score in the *Joseph Haydn Werke*, ser. I, vol. 9. Our examples were compiled before its appearance, however, and are based on the edition by Helmut Schultz in the *Joseph Haydn Gesamtausgabe*, ser. 1, vol. 5 (Boston and Vienna: The Haydn Society, in conjunction with Breitkopf & Härtel [Leipzig], 1951).

37. The most pertinent passages are given in examples below. The entire movement may be consulted in Kaul, *Anton Rosetti: Ausgewählte Sinfonien*, 64–73.

38. H. C. Robbins Landon, *The Symphonies of Joseph Haydn* (London: Universal Edition and Rockliff Publishing, 1955), 365. In subsequent discussions of this finale, Landon accepts its authenticity, either tacitly or explicitly. Cf. *Joseph Haydn: Critical Edition of the Complete Symphonies*, ed. Landon, 5:xiv; and Landon, *Haydn at Esterháza, 1766–1790*, Haydn: Chronicle and Works, vol. 2 (Bloomington: Indiana University Press, 1978), 562–63.

39. In alternating variations, as we have seen, the two themes are frequently related. For statistical data on how these levels of relationship play out in Haydn's alternating variations, see the table in Sisman, *Haydn and the Classical Variation*, 267–68.

40. For a detailed study of the function of the medial caesura in the classic sonata exposition, see James Hepokoski and Warren Darcy, "The Medial Caesura and Its Role in the Eighteenth-Century Sonata Exposition," *Music Theory Spectrum* 19 (1997): 115–54.

41. Murray (*The Music of Antonio Rosetti: A Thematic Catalog*, 23–24, 738) suggests the dates given above: "ca. 1783–84, but not later than 1785." Haberkamp (169) offers "ca. 1784." The work was printed by Artaria in 1786 and by Hummel in 1787, and it is cited in the supplement to the Breitkopf thematic catalogue of 1785–87. The flurry of interest in this symphony about 1786 suggests that its date of composition is roughly contemporaneous with that of its publication. On the citation in the Breitkopf catalogue, see Barry S. Brook, ed., *The Breitkopf Thematic Catalogue: The Six Parts and Sixteen Supplements* (New York: Dover Publications, 1966), 846.

42. As above, we provide the most important passages in condensed score, but the reader is urged to consult the full score of the entire movement in Kaul, *Anton Rosetti: Ausgewählte Sinfonien*, 95–105.

43. On the other hand, Rosetti's preoccupation with the importance of tonal relations at the distance of the third may be observed later in the movement (at m. 121), where the development section of this C-major symphony begins in A major.

44. The weak secondary theme in the relative major of the parallel minor is so curious a phenomenon that its common appearance in both of these finales almost begs to be considered a coincidence—merely a moment of stability in the contrasting area of a *minore* couplet, the contiguous sonata-like functions notwithstanding. That the device occurs in precisely the same way and in the same context in another Rosetti finale from the same time-frame, however, enhances one's conviction that this formal concept has some viability, and that Rosetti's borrowing of this procedure from Haydn in Symphony A 9 was intentional. The other finale is Rosetti's Symphony A 13 in D Major (ca. 1788–89). It offers what sounds very much like a brief secondary theme in F major that fails to close and that, like both of the examples just considered, is suspended over an F-pedal. For a modern edition of the latter finale, see Sterling E. Murray, ed., *Seven Symphonies from the Court of Oettingen-Wallerstein, 1773–1795*, The Symphony, 1720–1840, ser. C, vol. 6 (New York: Garland Publishing, 1981), 152–68. I rely on Professor Murray's assessment of the chronology of this work. In my forthcoming study of Haydn's symphonic finales, I cite still other examples of this phenomenon by other composers, including one by Ignace Pleyel.

45. This issue and its relationship to the broader question of the so-called "finale problem" are taken up in my forthcoming monograph on Haydn's symphonic finales.

46. "Alles Süsse, Milde, Sangreiche des Epikers Haydn sucht Rosetti in einen heiteren Erguss instrumentaler Lyrik umzugestalten. . . . [Er] copirte Haydn mitunter absichtlich, wie das fast alle seine Richtungsgenossen gethan, und jedenfalls stand er diesem Vorbild an Zartheit der Empfindung und Feinheit des Ausdruckes näher als andere bekanntere Schüler." Wilhelm Heinrich Riehl, *Musikalische Charakterköpfe: Ein kunstgeschichtliches Skizzenbuch*, 3d ed., 3 vols. (Stuttgart: J. G. Cotta, 1861–63), 1:235, 238.

47. Kaul, *Anton Rosetti: Ausgewählte Sinfonien*, xxxvi-l; Murray, "Antonio Rosetti and His Symphonies," 349, 434, 493.

48. An important exception to this may be found in Sterling Murray's discussion of Rosetti's approach to the minuet and trio, in which he relates the cancrizans treatment in the trio of Rosetti's Symphony A 29 in E-flat Major to the use of similar retrograde writing in the minuet of Haydn's Symphony 47. Murray, "Antonio Rosetti and His Symphonies," 475.

49. See Bossler's defense of Rosetti against charges of plagiarism quoted above, at n. 8.

50. The seminal study of this paradoxical circumstance, in which the most interesting sorts of influence are often the hardest to document, by virtue of the extent to which the model is transformed, may be read in Rosen, "Influence: Plagiarism and Inspiration." Mark Evan Bonds relies on the same methodological approach in "The Sincerest Form of Flattery? Mozart's 'Haydn' Quartets and the Question of Influence," *Studi musicali* 22 (1993): 365–409.

51. The single most complete survey of Haydn's capriccios may be found in A. Peter Brown, *Joseph Haydn's Keyboard Music: Sources and Style* (Bloomington: Indiana University Press, 1986), 221–26.

52. See the concise analysis in László Somfai, *The Keyboard Sonatas of Joseph Haydn: Instruments and Performance Practice, Genres and Styles,* trans. by the author in collaboration with Charlotte Greenspan (Chicago: University of Chicago Press, 1995), 348–49. Somfai traces some thirteen appearances of the primary melody in nine discrete tonal areas.

53. Carl Dahlhaus, *Analysis and Value Judgment,* trans. Siegmund Levarie, Monographs in Musicology, no. 1 (New York: Pendragon Press, 1983), 69–70; cf. Dahlhaus, *Analyse und Werturteil,* Musikpädagogik, no. 8 (Mainz: Schott, 1970), 79.

54. H. C. Robbins Landon, ed., *The Collected Correspondence and London Notebooks of Joseph Haydn* (London: Barrie & Rockliff, 1959), 83; for the original German, see H. C. Robbins Landon and Dénes Bartha, eds., *Joseph Haydn: Gesammelte Briefe und Aufzeichnungen* (Kassel: Bärenreiter, 1965), no. 118.

55. "Er bestehet eigentlich nicht sowol im Setzen oder Componiren mit der Feder, als in einem Singen und Spielen, das aus freiem Geiste, oder, wie man sagt, *ex tempore* geschiehet." Johann Mattheson, *Der vollkommene Capellmeister* (Hamburg: Christian Herold, 1739); facs., ed. Margarete Reimann, Documenta musicologica, ser. 1, vol. 5 (Kassel: Bärenreiter, 1954), 87.

56. "Nur so ein Capriccio—um das Clavier zu Probiren . . . es ist so eine gewisse sache,—Mann spiellt es nach eigenen gutachten." *Mozart: Briefe und Aufzeichnungen,* ed. Wilhelm Bauer and Otto Erich Deutsch, 7 vols. (Kassel: Bärenreiter, 1962–75), 2:409–11. The English translation is from Robert L. Marshall, *Mozart Speaks: Views on Music, Musicians, and the World* (New York: Schirmer Books, 1991), 293. Wolfgang Plath links the term *capriccio* to Mozart's four preludes of 1777, which would unfortunately relegate the piece mentioned in the letter to the list of Mozart's compositions known to be lost (*Klaviermusik,* Wolfgang Amadeus Mozart: *Neue Ausgabe sämtlicher Werke,* ser. IX, work group 27, vol. 2 [Kassel: Bärenreiter, 1982], xii-xiv).

57. Heinrich Christoph Koch, *Kurzgefasstes Handwörterbuch der Musik für praktische Tonkünstler und für Dilettanten* (Leipzig: Johann Hartknoch, 1807; re-

print, Hildesheim: Georg Olms, 1981), 74. For further discussion of Haydn's A-Major Keyboard Trio and additional examples of etude-like capriccios, see Jürgen Brauner, *Studien zu den Klaviertrios von Joseph Haydn,* Würzburger musikhistorische Beiträge, no. 15 (Tutzing: H. Schneider, 1995), 345–46.

58. "Ein Tonstück, bey welchem sich der Componist nicht an die bey den gewöhnlichen Tonstücken eingeführten Formen und Tonausweichungen bindet, sondern sich mehr der so eben in seiner Fantasie herrschenden Laune, als einem überdachten Plane überlässt." Heinrich Christoph Koch, *Musikalisches Lexikon* (Frankfurt: A. Hermann den jüngern, 1802; reprint, Hildesheim: Georg Olms, 1964), cols. 305–6.

59. ". . . eine art von Fantasie, ohne festgesetzten Plan." Daniel Gottlob Türk, *Klavierschule* (Leipzig and Halle: By the author, 1789), facs., ed. Edwin Jacobi, Documenta musicologica, ser. 1, vol. 23 (Kassel: Bärenreiter, 1962), 396. The English translation is after Daniel Gottlob Türk, *School of Clavier Playing,* trans. Raymond H. Haggh (Lincoln: University of Nebraska Press, 1982), 388.

60. Murray (*The Music of Antonio Rosetti: A Thematic Catalog*) lists the five symphonic finales by Rosetti designated "Capriccio": Symphonies A 8, A 9, A 12, A 42, and A 43. Of the five, the one movement not cast in a truly unique form is the finale of Symphony A 43. It is in sonata form but offers a vividly capricious element of its own. The second half of the movement, which is repeated, ends gently on an authentic cadence, played pianissimo in the strings, matching the closure of the exposition. Having heard the second half of the movement end this way when it was played the first time, we cannot but conclude that the movement (and the symphony) is over. After the repeat, however, a raucous coda follows, which develops the primary motive over diminished seventh chords and other relatively remote harmonies. The level of surprise is high and, for a few moments, we lose our structural bearings—much in the manner of the other movements designated "Capriccio." Surprise is also a component of the keyboard pieces by Rosetti called Capriccio (at least those available in modern editions: keyboard works E 44 and 45, for example). They are punctuated by dramatic changes in dynamics; unexpected fermatas; unprepared textural shifts; and the combination of exaggerated dynamics, accented offbeats, odd rhythmic figures, and eccentric harmonies.

Modern editions of Symphonies A 9, A 12, and A 42 appear in Kaul, *Anton Rosetti: Ausgewählte Sinfonien.* A modern score of Symphony A 43 may be consulted in Murray, ed., *Seven Symphonies from the Court of Oettingen-Wallerstein.* The Kaul edition of Symphony A 42 designates the finale "Allegro scherzante," which heading does appear in the autograph. The designation "Finale. Capriccio" is also given therein, but it is, for some reason, omitted in the modern edition. For the keyboard works, see *Antonio Rosetti (1746–1792): 12 leichte Klavierstücke,* ed. Bernhard Päuler (Zurich: Edition Eulenberg, ca. 1975), 18–19 (E 44) and 13–15 (E 45).

61. John Marsh, *Hints to Young Composers of Instrumental Music, Illustrated with 2 Movements for a Grand Orchestra in Score* (London: Clementi, Banger, Hyde, Collard & Davis, ca. 1805), quoted in Howard Irving, *Ancients and Moderns: William Crotch and the Development of Classical Music,* Music in 19th-Century Britain (Aldershot: Ashgate, 1999), 78. I am most grateful to Mr. Lloyd Frank for calling this reference to my attention.

8

Reason and Imagination: Beethoven's Aesthetic Evolution

MAYNARD SOLOMON

Beethoven left no connected writings on aesthetics, but his letters, diary, and conversation books contain a substantial number of comments, pronouncements, and aphoristic expressions which, taken together, offer insight into his views on the nature of art, creativity, and the responsibilities of the artist. They reveal that he absorbed a surprising number of current aesthetic ideas, mixing them freely, without apparent regard for consistency and without any thought of forming a systematic theory of art. These ideas, phrases, and fragments sometimes appealed to him as much for their sheer rhetoric as for their specific content. Furthermore, it remains open, especially in quotations drawn from Beethoven's letters, whether they are to be read as expressions of faith or primarily as conventional utterances intended to impress his correspondents with his devotion to high ideals in art. With due allowance for skeptical readings, however, it may be possible to find some order in this enthusiastic mélange of unelaborated ideas and, perhaps, to locate an evolutionary pattern in his conceptions of art and artist.

As befits a socially committed composer who came to maturity in the 1780s and early 1790s in a Rhenish principality where the dominant perspectives among young and radical intellectuals were shaped in unequal parts by the *philosophes,* the Austrian Aufklärung of Emperor Joseph II, Freemasonry, and the precepts of Kantian thought and Schillerian drama, Beethoven consciously and automatically stressed the pragmatic and altruistic purposes of art, seen variously to affect and instruct, to elevate taste and morality, to advance knowledge, to improve the social order, and to serve the divinity. Thus, he described his own purpose as being "to raise the taste of the public and to let his *genius* soar to greater heights and even to perfection";[1] he hoped that a time would come when, as he said, "my art will be exercised only for the benefit of the poor";[2] and he avowed, "Since I was a child my greatest happiness and pleasure have been to be able to do something for others."[3] Chiding Goethe for delighting "far too much in the court atmosphere than is becoming to a poet," he declared that poets "should be regarded as the leading teachers of the nation."[4] He often paired "Kunst und Wissenschaft" (the latter here probably signifying "learning" rather than "science") as fundamental shaping forces, and he attributed to them manifold powers, including to "give us intimations and hopes of a higher life," to unite "the best and noblest people," and to "raise men to the Godhead."[5] Consistently, through four decades, he connected his artistic purpose with a divine principle, seen as both the source and the goal of his creativity, affirming his faith in the transcendent purposes of art. For example, in 1792 or 1793 he wrote to his Bonn teacher, Christian Gottlob Neefe, of "my divine art" ("meiner göttlichen Kunst");[6] to the publisher Breitkopf & Härtel in 1812, of "my heavenly art, the only true divine gift of Heaven";[7] and, in his last decade, to another publisher, Bernhard Schotts Söhne, "before my departure for the Elysian fields I must leave behind what the Eternal Spirit has infused into my soul and bids me complete."[8] Such acknowledgment of the godhead is not unmixed with a sense of the godlike nature of his own creativity: in 1815 he wrote to a friend, "Have you already heard there [in Courland] about my great works? I call them *great*—but compared with the works of the All-highest all human works are small";[9] nor is it untouched by Beethoven's competitive spirit, for he described himself not merely as the recipient of God's gift but as an active creator along divine lines. Ultimately, Beethoven settled for a creative partnership with the deity: "There is nothing higher than to approach the Godhead more nearly than other mortals and by means of that contact to spread the rays of the Godhead through the human race."[10]

Beethoven's aesthetic comments often center on what he viewed as an antagonism between spiritual and material spheres: "Unfortunately," he wrote, "we are dragged down from the celestial element in art only too rudely into the earthly and human sides of life."[11] As for himself, he observed, "I much prefer the empire of the mind, and I regard it as the highest of all spiritual and worldly monarchies";[12] and again, "My kingdom is in the air. As the wind often does, so do harmonies whirl around me, and so do things often whirl about too in my soul."[13] It is noteworthy—and not without implications for his music—that these remarks are characterized by the use of spatial metaphors, and especially imagery of height and depth to represent value and judgment. He saw the conflict between the celestial and the earthly (and the subterranean as well) as a dialectic in which art attempts to escape from the world even as it is implicated in it: "A man's spirit, the active creative spirit, must not be tied down to the wretched necessities of life."[14] He imagined utopian havens where art could set up defenses against quotidian distraction, political censorship, and commercial necessity: "Art, when it is persecuted, finds asylum everywhere. Why, Daedalus when confined to the labyrinth invented the wings which lifted him *upwards* and out into the air. Oh, I too shall find them, these wings—."[15]

There is a suggestion in these remarks that music, by virtue of its ethereal natural medium ("the air"), occupies not merely a separate but a superior realm. Thus, although in his later years Beethoven dubbed himself a "Tondichter" ("tone poet") and infused musical form with unprecedented narrative and mythic strategies, he continued to see music as fundamentally distinct from the literary and pictorial arts:

> The description of a picture belongs to painting. And in this respect the poet too, whose sphere in this case is not so restricted as mine, may consider himself to be more favoured than my Muse. On the other hand my sphere extends further into other regions and our empire cannot be so easily reached.[16]

Similarly, even as he extended the imitative and symbolic potentialities of musical rhetoric, he continued to insist on their subordinate nature: "All painting in instrumental music is lost if it is pushed too far," he wrote in a sketchbook for the Pastoral Symphony. "Anyone who has an idea of country-life can make out for himself the intentions of the composer without many titles—Also, without any description, the whole will be recognized more as feeling than tone-painting."[17]

In his capacity as a working musician who was also an entrepreneur of his own musical commodities, Beethoven was preoccupied with the economics of art. "You know that I have to live entirely on the products of my mind,"[18] he wrote; it was a condition that he resented because it forced him to expend his energies on business negotiations. "To hell with the economics of music," summed up his feelings on this score.[19] In an unguarded letter to a composer-publisher with whom he shared political sympathies, he proposed to resolve the "tiresome" issues of artistic commodity exchange through a solution derived from French utopian and Babouvist sources: "I wish things were different in the world. There ought to be in the world a *market for art* to which the artist would only have to bring his works in order to take what he needed. As it is, one must be half businessman as well, and how can one be reconciled to that!"[20] In his enthusiasm for this utopian solution, Beethoven did not consider the possibility that economic independence might entail some cost in creative freedom. The influence of quasi-socialist concepts is apparent also in a draft introduction to a never-consummated complete edition of his works, in which he placed the issue of an author's compensation under the rubric of "human rights" and reiterated his resentment of the "greedy brainpickers" ("leckern Gehirnskoster") who line their pockets with profits from an author's work; he wrote: "The author is determined to show that the *human brain* cannot be sold either like coffee beans or like any form of cheese which, as everyone knows, must first be produced from *milk, urine* and so forth—The human brain is inherently inalienable."[21]

Throughout his life, Beethoven considered himself to be an adherent of Enlightenment rationalism, praising Reason, abjuring superstition, and disdaining libretti on magic or supernatural subjects: "I cannot deny that on the whole I am prejudiced against this sort of thing, because it has a soporific effect on feeling and reason—."[22] But, on a simultaneous yet separate track, he was drawn to Romantic restlessness, to Faustian striving for an unreachable objective, unnamable and mysterious: "Every day brings me nearer to the goal which I feel but cannot describe. And it is only in that condition that your Beethoven can live. There must be no rest—I know of none but sleep."[23] The Romantic conception of unceasing striving or yearning for "the infinite" ("das Unendliche") resonates throughout his conception of art:

> The true artist has no pride. He sees unfortunately that art has no limits; he has a vague awareness of how far he is from reaching his goal; and while others may perhaps be admiring him, he laments the fact that he has not yet reached the point whither his better genius only lights the way for him like a distant sun.[24]

If there were powerful neoclassicist undercurrents in his moralizing view of art's function and in his unswerving devotion to Reason, an amalgam of these with Romantic conceptions was underway as early as the later 1790s, when he wrote about the need "to strive towards the inaccessible goal which art and nature have set us."[25] While the language may be reminiscent of remarks in Kant's *Critique of Judgement* about "the unattainability of the idea by means of imagination," there is no real reason to connect Beethoven's descriptions of the inadequacy of his striving for artistic perfection with Kant's idea of the immeasurability and unreachability of the Sublime.[26] Beethoven's obscure goal, although it may be sublime, is not the Sublime, but creative achievement. Moreover, obscurity is itself an essential ingredient of the Sublime, as Edmund Burke knew when he wrote that "in nature, dark, confused, uncertain images have a greater power on the fancy to form the grander passions, than those have which are more clear and determinate."[27]

Still, Beethoven viewed the unknowable, the unreachable, and the infinite as territories to be conquered by rationality, spirit, and the abundant powers of art and wisdom.[28] Accordingly, as is shown in 1802 in his correspondence with Breitkopf & Härtel concerning the Piano Variations, opp. 34 and 35, he valorized originality as an essential ingredient of his art: "Both sets are really worked out in a wholly *new manner,* and each in a *separate and different way.* . . . I myself can assure you that in both these works the *method is quite new so far as I am concerned.*"[29] He was concerned about potential formal limitations on an oratorio that had been commissioned by the Gesellschaft der Musikfreunde: "I hope that I shall not be forbidden to deviate from the *forms which have been introduced until now into this type of composition.*"[30] Heedless of charges of "bizarrerie" that greeted his works in the classicizing music journals, he pursued the idea of the new in a multitude of formal, technical, and rhetorical innovations, insisting that each major work pose and solve a unique set of problems. It was reported by Karl Holz that when asked which among the String Quartets, opp. 127, 130, and 132, was the greatest, Beethoven responded with another Faustian remark, "Each in its way. Art demands of us that we shall not stand still." In these works, he continued, "You will find a new manner of partwriting and thank God there is less lack of fancy than ever before."[31]

Beethoven's defiant skepticism about compositional rules and conventions is well documented. When Ferdinand Ries, citing the prohibitions of the musical theoreticians, pointed out parallel fifths in one of Beethoven's opus 18 String Quartets, Beethoven closed the argument with the words, "And I allow them thus!"[32] According to Czerny, composer Anton Halm once tried to justify his own violations of the rules by alluding to precedent in Beethoven's works, to which the latter responded, "I may do it, but not you."[33] In a conversation book of November 1823, the violinist Ignaz Schuppanzigh wrote, "[Carl Maria von] *Weber* says, As God pleases; *Beethoven* says, As *Beethoven* pleases!"[34] A passage in a draft letter to his Russian patron Prince Nikolas Galitzin gives this issue an almost Wordsworthian turn: "[W]hen feeling opens up a path for us, then away with all rules—."[35] A candid statement of Beethoven's aesthetic Caesarism surfaced as early as 1798, when he wrote to his friend, Nikolaus von Zmeskall, "The devil take you, I refuse to hear anything about your whole moral outlook. *Power* is the moral principle of those who excel others, and it is also mine."[36]

Beethoven placed great value on the idea of progress in music: with Bach and Handel in mind, he wrote to Archduke Rudolph,

> [T]he older composers render us double service, since there is generally real artistic value in their works. . . . But in the world of art, as in the whole of our great creation, *freedom and progress* are the main objectives. And although we moderns are not quite as far advanced in *solidity* as our *ancestors*, yet the refinement of our customs has enlarged many of our conceptions as well.[37]

Thus, closely associated conceptions of modernity and progress in the arts are fundamental to Beethoven's aesthetic. He was skeptical about the ability of broad audiences to grasp his innovations: "Even if only a few people understand me, I shall be satisfied," he wrote as early as ca. 1796,[38] and at the end of his life, according to Ferdinand Hiller, he declared, "They say, 'Vox populi, vox dei'—I have never believed in it."[39] He once told Carl Czerny that in Mozart's String Quartet in A Major, K. 464, which offers an unprecedented array of dissociated forms, chromatic textures, and contrapuntal techniques, "Mozart was telling the world: 'Look what I could do if you were ready for it!'"[40] In his own career, Beethoven composed music for a wide range of audiences: centrally, of course, for serious music-lovers and musicians of every kind, but also potboilers or easy pieces for the layman and amateur, classicizing diversions and ostentatious occasional pieces for imperial tastes, and modernist works for the elite and avant-garde. Concerning one of his subtlest works, his String Quartet in F Minor, op. 95, he wrote, uncompromisingly, "The Quartett is written for a small circle of connoisseurs and is never to be performed in public."[41] He defended his later works against charges of excessive difficulty, writing "*what is difficult is also beautiful, good, great* and so forth. . . . [T]his is *the most lavish* praise that can be bestowed, since what is *difficult makes one sweat.*"[42] While striving to stretch the boundaries of musical discourse in his own time, the idea of reaching a future public had great appeal to him, for he saw it as providing the possibility of immortality: "*Continue to paint* and I shall *continue to write down notes,*" he wrote to a painter, "and thus we shall live—for ever?—yes, perhaps, for ever."[43]

There are several striking omissions in Beethoven's aesthetic remarks. He nowhere directly addressed issues of beauty or the Sublime, the judgment of taste, the sensuous substratum of art. Kant's conception of disinterested beauty may have been antithetical to Beethoven's own creed, though surely not to his actual creative practice.[44] Evidently he did not see—or would not acknowledge—the disinterested creation of beautiful works as fundamental to his lofty purposes. More surprisingly, Beethoven did not adopt Schiller's modification of Kantian perspectives and particularly his proposal that beauty has the capacity to reconcile the rational and the sensuous, to serve as an ideal projection of freedom and transcendent possibility. Nor did he give much weight to views of art as a fusion of pleasure and instruction; the rendering of delight and pleasure to audiences was not crucial to his aesthetics, even though he did acknowledge once, in passing, that for the artist himself, "there is no more undisturbed, more unalloyed or purer pleasure" than that which comes from rising "ever higher into the heaven of art."[45] Perhaps he shared Schiller's idea, in Letter 10 of the *Letters on the Aesthetical Education of Man,* that "the beautiful only founds its sway on the ruins of heroic virtues."[46] In letters of Beethoven's early and middle years there are occasional signs of an unmalleable earnestness, bordering on intolerance; and he was reported to have disapproved, on moral grounds, of the libretto to *Don Giovanni.*[47] To some extent, Beethoven shared the moralizing attitudes and didacticism of post-Rococo aesthetics, with its critique of hedonism; but his high praise for *Die Zauberflöte* suggests his awareness that there is no unalterable requirement for the artist to trade delight for virtue, wonder for reason.

Beethoven rarely referred to formal or structural issues, but he seems to have been affected by widely prevalent conceptions of the artwork as a coherent whole. This is implied by his saying to a British admirer in 1815, "I have always a picture in my mind, when I am composing, and work up to it";[48] by his remark about *Fidelio* that "my custom when I am composing even instrumental music is always to keep the whole before my eyes";[49] and by his comment to Breitkopf & Härtel that, "once one has thought out a whole work which is based even on a bad *text,* it is difficult to prevent this whole from being destroyed if individual alterations are made here and there."[50] One ought not to conclude from such remarks that Beethoven privileged Goethean or Coleridgean conceptions of organicism in art. Still, the subject was not foreign to him: on the autograph title page of his String Quartet in C-sharp Minor, op. 131, which he sent to Bernhard Schotts Söhne for engraving in August 1826, Beethoven jokingly described this extremely original and tightly structured quartet as "stolen together from a miscellany of this and that" ("zusammengestohlen aus Verschiedenem diesem u. jenem"),[51] thus affirming that aesthetic wholeness may derive from heterogeneity, paying tribute to the potential for coherence residing within the fragmentary and to the capability of the imagination to represent the unprecedented through the redeployment or transmutation of already-existing ideas and imagery.[52] Although on one occasion he wrote to Prince Galitzin, "Nature is founded on Art and, again, Art is founded on Nature,"[53] conceptions of art as imitation and of the artist as a percipient agent reflecting the external world had little resonance for Beethoven even during his years of apprenticeship. In his last years he made explicit his belief in the primacy of a productive, shaping imagination, seen as a distinct faculty of the mind to set alongside reason and understanding, capable of anticipating reality, creating rather than reproducing, emulating or rivaling divine creation rather than deferring to the deity's prerogatives. "The imagination, too, asserts its privileges," he reportedly remarked concerning his late quartets, "and today a different, truly poetic element must be manifested in conventional form."[54] To call upon several overworked metaphors, for him art was a beacon illuminating the chaotic reaches of as-yet-undiscovered worlds rather than a mirror of an ordered, mapped universe. In his later years, Beethoven began to see his creativity as an expression of both subjectivity and desire: "Gradually there comes to us the power to express just what we desire and feel; and to the nobler type of human being this is such an essential need."[55] Art involved self-revelation and implied an autobiographical dimension. Beethoven heard and responded to "the greater innate summons to reveal myself to the world through my works."[56]

It became an abiding article of Beethoven's faith that his personal creativity simultaneously involved and justified self-sacrifice. "Only in my divine art do I find the support which enables me to sacrifice the best part of my life to the heavenly Muses."[57] His intimate diary of 1812–18 contains several references to sacrificial imperatives of art, e.g., "For you there is no longer any happiness except within yourself, in your art"; "Everything that is called life should be sacrificed to the sublime and be a sanctuary of art";

"Live only in your art—for you are so limited by your senses.—This is still the *only existence* for you"; "Sacrifice once and for all the trivialities of social life to your art, O God above all!"[58] Toward 1815, under the influence of a mixture of Brahman and Masonic ideas of salvation through purification, he began to take such conceptions as prescriptions for life as well as art: "We finite beings, who are the embodiment of an infinite spirit, are born to suffer both pain and joy; and one might almost say that the best of us obtain *joy through suffering*."[59] A sacramental search for absolution and salvation ends in a fusion of divinity and art: "If afterwards I become darkened through passion for evil, I return, after manifold repentance and purification, to the elevated and pure source, to the Godhead.—And, to your art."[60] In the course of time, art increasingly became the main purpose of his existence, and the purpose of art almost tautologically became the creation of art, as when he referred to "the most important object of my art, namely, the composition of great works."[61] He was even willing to harness the demonic to his aesthetic mission: "I live entirely for my art and for the purpose of fulfilling my duties as a man. But unfortunately this too cannot always be done without the help of the powers of the underworld."[62] Along related lines is a remark embedded in an overwrought letter to Nannette Streicher about the domestic disorder in his household: "In the sphere of art even swamp and slime are of more use to a man than all that damned nonsense!!!"[63] Read literally, it seems possible that Beethoven here credited primordial matter with generative powers, or even that he glimpsed a dialectic in which hierarchical splits between "higher" and "lower" spheres could be reconciled or even reversed.

It may be that among Beethoven's most interesting aesthetic ideas are those which are not quite transparent and need to be understood in their "poetic" or "musical" implications. Another striking example appears in a literary quotation that Beethoven copied into a Conversation Book for 11 March 1820:

> The world is a king and desires flattery in return for favor; but true art is obstinate and will not yield to the fashions of flattery.
>
> Famous artists always labor under an embarrassment;—therefore their first works are the best, although they may have sprung from the dark womb.
>
> They say art is long, life is short—only life is long and art is short; may its breath lift us to the Gods—That is an instant's grace.[64]

One hesitates to impose too much of a sense of order upon such aphoristic and sometimes inchoate materials, to seek to reconcile Beethoven's conflicting ideas, or to situate his remarks within an evolutionary trajectory. Indeed, a more coherent set of aesthetic principles might well have become an impediment to his own creative efforts. Nevertheless, taken as a whole, Beethoven's aesthetic remarks are neither haphazard nor capricious. They exhibit an internal development which roughly parallels the evolution of ideas coming into play against the backdrop of the Habsburg Aufklärung, the French Revolution, the Napoleonic Era, and the post–Congress of Vienna years. They coincide with the emergence of Romantic tendencies among Beethoven's associates and contemporaries; it is possible to deduce a sympathy for Romantic music aesthetics from Beethoven's admiration for reviews of his works by E. T. A. Hoffmann and Adolph Bernhard Marx, as well as from his friendship with composer-critic Friedrich August Kanne, an advocate of Schleiermacher's ideas; at the very least, there seems to be a discernible shift in his aesthetic ideas toward Romanticist conceptions and imagery—emphasizing expression, inwardness, transcendental longing, and a drive to discover new ways of symbolizing extreme states of being. A Revolutionary Classicism gives way to an eclectic, un-reified Romanticism, which, however, never supersedes Beethoven's commitment to art as a moral force.

Perhaps more fundamentally, the weight of Beethoven's aesthetic formulations eventually shifts from the primacy of Reason to the primacy of the imagination. In his earlier years, a relatively unmediated adherence to Reason and virtue acted as a powerful organizing principle of his creativity as well as an eventual constraint on its further development. In the course of time, as the so-called "heroic style" (ca. 1803–13) moved toward exhaustion, Beethoven found a collateral organizing principle in the idea of the imaginative, seen as an adjunct to Reason, as an unfettered instrument of investigation invested with the power of representing a multitude of previously undescribed modes of being and strategies of transcendence.

Notes

1. Letter to the Directors of the Imperial and Royal Theaters in Vienna, before 4 December 1807; Emily Anderson, ed. and trans., *The Letters of Beethoven*, 3 vols. (New York: St. Martin's Press, 1961), 3:1444 (App. I [1]) [hereafter, *Letters*]. "[D]ie Veredlung des Geschmacks, und der Schwung seine *Genius* nach höheren Idealen und nach Vollendung"; Sieghard Brandenburg, ed., *Ludwig van Beethoven Briefwechsel Gesamtausgabe*. Beethovenhaus edition. 8 vols. (Munich: G. Henle Verlag, 1996—), 1:333 (no. 302) [hereafter, *Briefe*].

2. Letter to Franz Gerhard Wegeler, 29 June 1801, *Letters* 1:58 (no. 51). "[D]ann soll meine Kunst sich nur zum Besten der Armen zeigen"; *Briefe* 1:79 (65).

3. Letter to Hans Georg Nägeli, 9 September 1824, *Letters* 3:1139 (no. 1306). "[V]on Kindheit war mein größtes glück u. vergnügen für andere wirken zu können"; *Briefe* 5:362 (no. 1873).

4. Letter to Breitkopf & Härtel, 9 August 1812, *Letters* 1:384 (no. 380). "Göthe behagt die Hofluft zu sehr mehr als es einem Dichter ziemt. . . . Dichter, die als die ersten Lehrer der Nation angesehn seyn sollten"; *Briefe* 2:287 (no. 591).

5. Letter to Bernhard Schotts Söhne, 17 September 1824, *Letters* 3:1141 (no.

1308). "[D]ie unß ein höheres Leben andeuten u. hoffen laßen"; *Briefe* 5:368 (no. 1881). Letter to Karl van Beethoven, 18 July 1825, *Letters* 3:1221 (no. 1402). "[D]urch Kunst u wissenschaft sind ja die Besten edelsten Menschen verbunden"; *Briefe* 6:109 (no. 2012). Letter to Emilie M., 17 July 1812, *Letters* 1:381 (no. 376). "[E]rhöhen den Menschen bis zur Gottheit"; *Briefe* 2:274 (no. 585).

6. Letter to Christian Gottlob Neefe, between the end of October 1792 and 26 October 1793, *Letters* 1:9 (no. 6); *Briefe* 1:11 (no. 6). Max Rudolf (personal communication, from ca. 1978) suggested that "meiner göttlichen Kunst" could also be rendered as "my God-given art."

7. Letter to Breitkopf & Härtel, 28 February 1812, *Letters* 1:360 (no. 351). "[M]einer Himmlischen Kunst einziges wahres Göttergeschenk des Himmels"; *Briefe* 2:246 (no. 555).

8. Letter to Bernhard Schotts Söhne, 17 September 1824, *Letters* 3:1141 (no. 1308). "[M]uß ich vor meinem Abgang in die Elesaischen Felder hinterlaßen, was mir der Geist eingibt u. heißt vollenden"; *Briefe* 5:368 (no. 1881).

9. Letter to Karl Amenda, 12 April 1815, *Letters* 2:509 (no. 541). "[H]ast du schon von meinen großen Werken dort gehört? *groß* sage ich—gegen die werke des allerhöchsten ist alles klein"; *Briefe* 3:137 (no. 803).

10. Letter to Archduke Rudolph, July-August 1821, *Letters* 3:1095 (no. 1248, incorrectly assigned to 1823). "[H]öheres gibt es nichts, als der Gottheit sich mehr als andere Menschen nähern, u. von hier aus die strahlen der Gottheit unter das Menschengeschlecht verbreiten"; *Briefe* 4:446 (no. 1438). This can be read as a reference to Rudolph rather than to Beethoven.

11. Letter to Prince Nikolas Galitzin, ca. 6 July 1825, *Letters* 3:1225 (no. 1405), translation amended. "[L]eider wird man von dem überirrdischen der Kunst nur allzu unsanft in das irdische Menschliche hinabgezogen"; *Briefe* 6:96 (no. 2003). Compare Wackenroder: "Alas! there can be no doubt that, stretch our spiritual wings as we may, we cannot escape the earth, for it pulls us back with brutal force and we fall again among the most vulgar of vulgar people"; Wilhelm Heinrich Wackenroder and Ludwig Tieck, *Outpourings of an Art-Loving Friar,* trans. Edward Mornin (New York: Ungar, 1975), 118.

12. Letter to Johann Nepomuk Kanka, autumn 1814, *Letters* 1:474 (no. 502). "[M]ir ist das geistige Reich das liebste, und der Oberste aller geistigen und weltlichen Monarchien"; *Briefe* 3:64 (no. 747).

13. Letter to Franz Brunsvik, 13 February 1814, *Letters* 1:445 (no. 462). "[M]ein Reich ist in der Luft, wie der wind oft, so wirbeln die töne, so oft wirbelts auch in der Seele"; *Briefe* 3:8 (no. 696).

14. Letter to Johann Nepomuk Kanka, autumn 1814, *Letters* 1:473–74 (no. 502). "[D]er Geist der wirkende darf nicht an die elenden Bedürfnisse gefesselt werden"; *Briefe* 3:64 (no. 747).

15. Letter to Nikolaus Zmeskall, 19 February 1812, *Letters* 1:359 (no. 349). "Die Kunst die Verfolgte findet überall eine Freystadt, erfand doch Dädalus Eingeschlossen im Labirinthe Die Flügel, die ihn *oben* hinaus in die Luft emporgehoben, o auch ich werde sie finden diese Flügel—"; *Briefe* 2:244 (no. 553). Compare Schiller's "Man raised on the wings of the imagination leaves the narrow limits of the present, in which mere animality is enclosed, in order to strive on to an unlimited future"; Friedrich Schiller, *Letters on the Aesthetical Education of Man,* Letter 24, in *The Works of Friedrich Schiller: Aesthetical and Philosophical Essays,*

ed. Nathan Haskell Dole (New York: Bigelow, Brown & Co., Inc., 1902), 1:87–88. "Auf den Flügeln der Einbildungskraft verläßt der Mensch die engen Schranken der Gegenwart, in welche die bloße Tierheit sich einschließt, um vorwärts nach einer unbeschränkten Zukunft zu streben"; "Über die ästhetische Erziehung des Menschen, in einer Reihe von Briefen"; Letter 24, in *Schillers sämtliche Werke in zwölf Bänden* (Leipzig: Max Hesse, n.d.), 12:69.

16. Letter to Wilhelm Gerhard, 15 July 1817, *Letters* 2:689 (no. 788). "[D]ie Beschreibungen eines Bildes gehört zur Mahlerey, auch der Dichter kann sich hierin vor meiner Muse glücklich schätzen, dessen Gebiet hierin nicht so begränzt ist, als das meinige, so wie es sich wieder in andere Regionen weiter erstreckt und man unser Reich nicht so leicht erreichen kann"; *Briefe* 4:82 (no. 1141).

17. Translation amended from Alexander Wheelock Thayer, *Thayer's Life of Beethoven*, rev. and ed. Elliot Forbes, 2 vols in 1 (Princeton, N.J.: Princeton University Press, 1967), 436 [hereafter, Thayer-Forbes]. "Jede Mahlerei, nachdem sie in der Instrumentalmusik zu weit getrieben, verliehrt—Wer auch nur je eine Idee vom Landleben erhalten, kann sich ohne viele Überschriften selbst denken, was der Autor will—Auch ohne Beschreibung wird man das Ganze welches mehr Empfindung als Tongemählde erkennen"; Gustav Nottebohm, *Zweite Beethoveniana: Nachgelassene Aufsätze* (Leipzig: Rieter-Biedermann, 1887), 375. On a string part for the Symphony he added, "More the expression of feeling than painting" ("Mehr Ausdruck der Empfindung als Mahlerei"); Nottebohm, *Zweite Beethoveniana*, 378. Beethoven here closely parallels the theorist Johann Jakob Engel, who wrote, "the composer should always paint feelings rather than objects of feeling," in *Über die musikalische Malerey* (Berlin, 1780), in *J. J. Engel's Schriften: Reden und Ästhetische Versuche*, 12 vols. (Berlin: Mylius, 1844), 4:146, trans. Wye J. Allanbrook, "'Ear-Tickling Nonsense': A New Context for Musical Expression in Mozart's 'Haydn' Quartets," *The St. John's Review* 38 (1988): 10. For indications that Beethoven may have read Engel, see Adolf Sandberger, "'Mehr Ausdruck der Empfindung als Malerei,'" in his *Ausgewählte Aufsätze zur Musikgeschichte* (Munich: Drei Masken Verlag, 1921–24), 2:201–12. The influential theorist Johann Georg Sulzer also objected to naturalistic and imitative effects in music: "But such [tone] painting violates the true spirit of music, which is to express the sentiments of feeling, not to convey images of inanimate objects"; Johann Georg Sulzer, *Allgemeine Theorie der schönen Künste*, 2nd ed., 5 vols. (Leipzig: Weidmann, 1792–99), 2:357, cit. in *Aesthetics and the Art of Musical Composition in the German Enlightenment: Selected Writings of Johann Georg Sulzer and Heinrich Christoph Koch,* ed. Nancy Kovaleff Baker and Thomas Christensen (Cambridge: Cambridge University Press, 1995), 90.

18. Letter to Karl Wilhelm Henning, 1 January 1825; *Letters* 3:1165 (no. 1343). "Sie wissen daß ich bloß von den Erzeugnissen meines Geistes leben muß"; *Briefe* 6:3 (no. 1920).

19. Letter to Breitkopf & Härtel, 21 August 1810, *Letters* 1:284 (no. 272), translation amended. "Hol der Henker das ökonomisch-Musikalische"; *Briefe*, 2:148 (no. 465).

20. Letter to Franz Anton Hoffmeister, ca. 15 January 1801, my translation, *Letters* 1:48 (no. 44). "[I]ch wünschte, daß es anders in der Welt seyn könnte, es sollte nur ein *Magazin der Kunst* in der Welt seyn, wo der Künstler seine Kunstwerke nur hinzugeben hätte, um zu nehmen, was er brauchte, so muß man noch ein halber Handelsmann dabey seyn, und wie findet man sich darein"; *Briefe* 1:64 (no. 54).

See "Beethoven's *Magazin der Kunst*," in my *Beethoven Essays* (Cambridge: Harvard University Press, 1987), 193–204.

21. Translation combines those in *Letters* ["Draft Statement about a Complete Edition of His Works," undated [ca. 1822–25?], *Letters* 2:1450 (App. I, 6)], and Donald W. MacArdle and Ludwig Misch, eds., *New Beethoven Letters* (Norman: University of Oklahoma Press, 1957), 395–96 (no. 344). "[S]o will der Autor zeigen, daß das Menschengehirn weder Kaffeebohnen noch sonst wie Käse verkauft werden könne, welcher bekanntlich erst aus *Milch, Urin* etc. zustande gebracht wird. Das Menschengehirn ist an sich unveräußerlich—"; Emerich Kastner and Julius Kapp, eds., *Ludwig van Beethovens sämtliche Briefe*, 2nd ed. (Leipzig: Hesse & Becker, [1923]), 631–32 (no. 1051); *Briefe* 8, as yet unpublished.

22. Letter to Heinrich von Collin, autumn 1808, *Letters* 1:197 (no. 175). "[I]ch kann es nicht läugnen, daß ich wieder diese Art überhaupt eingenommen bin, wodurch Gefühl und Verstand so oft schlummern müßen—"; *Briefe* 2:21 (no. 332).

23. Letter to Franz Gerhard Wegeler, 16 November 1801, *Letters* 1:68 (no. 54). "[J]eden tag gelange ich mehr zu dem Ziel, was ich fühle, aber nicht beschreiben kann, nur hierin kann dein B. leben, nichts von ruhe—ich weiß von keiner andern als dem schlaf"; *Briefe* 1:89 (no. 70).

24. Letter to Emilie M., 17 July 1812, *Letters* 1:381 (no. 376). "Der wahre Künstler hat keinen Stolz; leider sieht er, daß die Kunst keine Gränzen hat, er fühlt dunkel, wie weit er vom Ziele entfernt ist und indeß er vielleicht von Andern bewundert wird, trauert er, noch nicht dahin gekommen zu sein, wohin ihm der bessere Genius nur wie eine ferne Sonne vor leuchtet"; *Briefe* 2:274–75 (no. 585). Arthur O. Lovejoy defined the Faustian aspect of Romanticism as a "demand for a perpetual transcendence of the already-attained, for unceasing expansion"; see his *The Great Chain of Being: A Study of the History of an Idea* (Cambridge, Mass.: Harvard University Press, 1936; reprint, New York: Harper Torchbooks, 1960), 306.

25. Letter to Christine Gerhardi, 1797 (written prior to 20 August 1798 at latest), *Letters* 1:29 (no. 23); "dem unerreichbaren Ziele, das unß Kunst und Natur darbeut, näher zu kommen"; *Briefe* 1:41 (no. 33).

26. Immanuel Kant, *The Critique of Aesthetic Judgement*, trans. James Creed Meredith (Oxford: Clarendon Press, 1911), 119.

27. Edmund Burke, *Philosophical Enquiry into the Origin of Our Ideas of the Sublime and Beautiful* (London: F. C. and J. Rivington, 1812), 104–5. He added (106–7, "a judicious obscurity in some things contributes to the effect of the picture." Compare Diderot's "Clarity is all right for convincing; it is of no use for moving. . . . Poets, speak incessantly of eternity, infinitude, immensity, time, space, divinity. . . . Be dark [soyez ténébreux]!" cit. in René Wellek, *A History of Modern Criticism: 1750–1950* (New Haven, Conn.: Yale University Press, 1955), 1:51.

28. Related ideas were widespread among followers of Schiller and the early Romantics: "In the creations of [the artist's] fantasy the dignity of human nature must be seen. From a lower sphere of dependence and limitation he must raise us up to himself and represent the infinite . . . in perceptible form"; Christian Gottfried Körner, "Über Charakterdarstellung in der Musik," *Hören* 5 (1795): 148, cit. in Edward Lippman, *A History of Western Musical Aesthetics* (Lincoln: University of Nebraska Press, 1992), 135.

29. Letter to Breitkopf & Härtel, 18 October 1802, *Letters* 1:76–77 (no. 62).

"[B]eyde sind auf eine wircklich ganz *neue Manier bearbeitet, jedes auf eine* andre
verschiedene Art. . . . [M]uß ich sie selbst versichern, daß die *Manier* in beyden
Werken ganz *neu von mir* ist—"; *Briefe* 1:126 (no. 108); see also the letter to Breitkopf
& Härtel, ca. 18 December 1802, *Briefe* 1:145 (no. 123); *Letters* 1:83–84 (no. 67).

30. Letter to Nikolaus Zmeskall, 9 February 1816, *Letters* 2:559 (no. 608).
"[W]ünsche aber nicht, daß es mir nicht vergönnt seyn soll, von den hierin *bisher
eingeführten Formen* abzugehn"; *Briefe* 3:223 (no. 898).

31. "Sie werden eine neue Art der Stimmführung bemerken . . . und an Fantasie
fehlt's, Gottlob, weniger als je zuvor!" Thayer-Forbes, 982; Wilhelm von Lenz,
Beethoven: Eine Kunst-Studie (Hamburg: Hoffmann & Campe, 1860), 5, part 4:217;
Alexander Wheelock Thayer, *Ludwig van Beethovens Leben*, rev. and ed. Hermann
Deiters and Hugo Riemann, 5 vols. (Leipzig: Breitkopf & Härtel, 1907–17), 5:318
[hereafter Thayer-Deiters-Riemann].

32. Franz Wegeler and Ferdinand Ries, *Biographische Notizien über Ludwig
van Beethoven* (Coblenz: Bädeker, 1838), 87; Thayer-Forbes, 367. "Und so erlaube
ich sie!" Thayer-Dieters-Riemann, 3:560.

33. According to Czerny, cit. in Thayer-Forbes, 629. "Ich darf das; Sie nicht";
Thayer-Dieters-Riemann, 3:527.

34. "*Weber* sagt, wie Gott will, *Bethowen* sagt, wie *Bethowen* [*sic*] will"; *Ludwig
van Beethovens Konversationshefte*, ed. Karl-Heinz Köhler and Grita Herre, with
Dagmar Beck, 11 vols. (Leipzig: Deutscher Verlag für Musik, 1968–2001), 4:268
(Heft 46, 34r, second half of November 1823) [hereafter Köhler-Herre]. A portrait
of Weber by Carl Christian Vogel von Vogelstein was engraved in 1823 with the
facsimile subscription, "Wie Gott will! Carl Maria von Weber"; Ibid. 4:379 n. 585.

35. Draft letter of 6 July 1825, in the De Roda sketchbook: "sobald das gefühl
unß—eine[n] weg eröfnert, fort mit allen Regeln—"; *Briefe* 6:98 (no. 2003). The
passage is not in *Letters* 3:1224–26 (no. 1405).

36. Letter to Nikolaus Zmeskall, 1798, *Letters* 1:32 (no. 30). "[H]ol' sie der Teufel,
ich mag nichts von ihrer ganzen Moral wissen, *Kraft* ist die Moral der Menschen, die
sich vor andern auszeichnen, und sie ist auch die meinige"; *Briefe* 1:43 (no. 35).

37. Letter to Archduke Rudolph, 29 July 1819, *Letters* 2:822 (no. 955). "[U]nß
die Alten zwar doppelt Dienen, indem meistens Reeller Kunstwerth, . . . allein
Freyheit, weiter gehn ist in der Kunstwelt, wie in der ganzen großen schöpfung,
zweck, u. sind wir neueren noch nicht ganz so weit, als unsere *altvordern* in *Festigkeit*,
So hat doch die verfeinerung unsrer Sitten auch manches erweitert"; *Briefe* 4:298
(no. 1318). Compare Schiller's "humanity cannot reach its final end except by
progress, and that the man of nature cannot make progress save through culture,
and consequently by passing himself through the way of civilization"; Friedrich
Schiller, "Naive and Sentimental Poetry," in *The Works of Friedrich Schiller:
Aesthetical and Philosophical Essays*, 1:307. "[D]as letzte Ziel der Menschheit nicht
anders als durch jene Forschreitung zu erreichen ist und der letztere nicht anders
fortschreiten kann, als indem er sich kultiviert und folglich in den ersteren übergeht";
"Über naive und sentimentalische Dichtung," in *Schillers sämtliche Werke*, 12:127.

38. Letter to Johann Andreas Streicher, 1796, *Letters* 1:25 (no. 18). "[W]enn
mich auch nur einige verstehen, so bin ich zufrieden"; *Briefe* 1:32 (no. 22).

39. "Man sagt: 'vox populi, vox dei'—ich habe nie daran geglaubt"; Ferdinand
Hiller, in *Die Erinnerungen an Beethoven*, ed. Friedrich Kerst, 2 vols. (Stuttgart:
Julius Hoffmann, 1913), 2:229.

40. Carl Czerny, *On the Proper Performance of All Beethoven's Works for the Piano*, ed. Paul Badura-Skoda (Vienna: Universal Edition, 1970), 8; translation amended. "Da sagte Mozart der Welt: 'Seht, was ich machen könnte, wenn für euch die Zeit gekommen wäre!'" *Die Erinnerungen an Beethoven* 1:51.

41. Letter to Sir George Smart, ca. 11 October 1816, written in English, *Letters* 2:606 (no. 664); *Briefe* 3:306 (no. 983).

42. Letter to Sigmund Anton Steiner, shortly after 9 January 1817, *Letters* 2:661 (no. 749). "[W]as schwer ist, ist auch schön, gut, groß, etc, . . . dieses *das fetteste* Lob ist, was man geben kann, denn das *schwere macht schwizen*"; *Briefe* 4:8 (no. 1061).

43. Letter to Alexander Macco, 2 November 1803, *Letters* 1:100 (no. 85). "*Mahlen sie*—und ich *mache Noten* und so werden wir—ewig?—ja vieleicht ewig fortleben"; *Briefe* 1:196 (no. 169). Compare Beethoven's citation from Pliny's *Epistulae* in his Tagebuch: "Nevertheless, what greater gift can be conferred on a man than fame and praise and eternal life?" Beethoven gives both the Latin and the German texts in his Tagebuch: "Tametsi quid homini potest dari majus quam gloria et laus et aeternitas?" / "Wiewohl was kann man einem Menschen größeres geben, als Ruhm und Lob und Unsterblichkeit?" See my "Beethoven's Tagebuch of 1812–1818," in *Beethoven Studies* 3, ed. Alan Tyson (Cambridge: Cambridge University Press, 1982), 265 (no. 114), and my *Beethoven Essays*, 282.

44. The term "Ästhetik" or its cognates appears only once in Beethoven's letters; in his letter to Hoffmeister of 8 April 1802 he wrote, "The *lady* can have a sonata from me, and, moreover, from an *aesthetic* point of view I will in general adopt her plan." [*Letters* 1:73 (no. 57)]. "[D]ie *dame* kann eine Sonate von mir haben, auch will ich *in Aesthetischer* hinsicht im allgemeinen ihren Plan befolgen"; *Briefe* 1:105 (no. 105).

45. Letter to Xaver Schnyder von Wartensee, 19 August 1817, *Letters* 2:700 (no. 803). "Es gibt keine ungestörtere ungemischtere reinenre [sic] Freude"; "immer weiter in den KunstHimmel hinauf zu versezen"; *Briefe* 4:99 (no. 1159).

46. Friedrich Schiller, *Letters on the Aesthetical Education of Man*, Letter X, in *The Works of Friedrich Schiller: Aesthetical and Philosophical Essays* 1:38. "[D]ie Schönheit nur auf den Untergang heroischer Tugenden ihre Herrschaft gründet"; "Über die ästhetische Erziehung des Menschen, in einer Reihe von Briefen," Letter 10, *Schillers sämtliche Werke* 12:29.

47. The main witnesses are composer Ignaz von Seyfried and poet Ludwig Rellstab. "*Don Giovanni* still has the complete Italian cut," reported Seyfried; "besides, our sacred art ought never permit itself to be degraded to the foolery of so scandalous a subject." ("*Don Juan* hat noch ganz den italienischen Zuschnitt, und überdieß sollte die heilige Kunst nie zur, Folie eines so scandalösen Sujets sich entwürdigen lassen"; Ignaz von Seyfried, *Ludwig van Beethovens Studien* [Vienna: Haslinger 1832], Anhang, 22.) And Rellstab claimed that he heard Beethoven say, "I could not compose operas like *Don Giovanni* and *Figaro*. I have an aversion to that." ("Opern wie 'Don Juan' und 'Figaro' könnte ich nicht componiren. Dagegen habe ich einem Widerwillen"; Ludwig Nohl, *Beethoven nach den Schilderungen seine Zeitgenossen* [Stuttgart: Cotta, 1877], 209.) Against these is a wholly favorable remark in Beethoven's own letter of 23 August 1811, to Gottfried Christoph Härtel: "The good reception of *Mozart's Don Juan* gives me as much pleasure as if it were my own work." *Letters* 1:334 (no. 323). "[D]ie gute aufnahme von *mozarts*

don juan macht mir so viel Freude als sey es mein eignes werk"; *Briefe* 2:211 (no. 519). Naturally, the letter should be given greater weight than the memoirs of acquaintances, but this would not be the only occasion on which Beethoven was able to hold opposing or even irreconcilable viewpoints in one hand.

48. Letter to Charles Neate, cit. in Thayer-Forbes, 620. "[I]ch habe immer ein Gemälde in meinen Gedanken, wenn ich am Komponieren bin, und arbeite nach demselben"; Thayer-Dieters-Riemann 3:506.

49. Letter to Georg Friedrich Treitschke, April 1814, *Letters* 1:454 (no. 479), translation amended. "[W]ie ich gewohnt bin zu schreiben, auch in meiner Instrumental Musick habe ich immer das ganze vor Augen"; *Briefe* 3:20 (no. 707).

50. Letter to Breitkopf & Härtel, 23 August 1811, *Letters* 1:334 (no. 323). "[A]ber hat man auch sich einmal aus einem schlechten *text* sich ein ganzes gedacht, so ist es schwer durch einzelne Änderungen zu vermeiden, daß eben dieses nicht gestört werde"; *Briefe* 2:211 (no. 519). Concerning his method of composition, Beethoven wrote (letter to Adolph Martin Schlesinger, 13 November 1821): "Now that my health appears to be better, I merely jot down certain ideas as I used to do, and when I have completed the whole in my head, everything is written down, but only once"; *Letters* 2:927–28 (no. 1060). "[J]etzt aber wo wie es scheint meine Gesundheit beßer ist, zeige ich wie sonst auch nur gewiße Ideen an u. bin ich mit dem ganzen fertig im Kopfe, so wird alles aber nur einmal aufgeschrieben"; *Briefe* 4:455 (no. 1446).

51. Thayer-Forbes, 983; Georg Kinsky and Hans Halm, *Das Werk Beethovens. Thematisch-bibliographisches Verzeichnis* (Munich: Henle, 1955), 397; Robert S. Winter, *Compositional Origins of Beethoven's Opus 131* (Ann Arbor, Mich.: UMI, 1982), 109. Cf. Thayer-Forbes translation (983): "Put together from pilferings from one thing and another."

52. In contrast to a "simple imagination" that apprehends "the whole object" all at once, Hobbes broached the idea of "a compound imagination" in which new images are formed from composites of existing ones. *Leviathan*, part 1, chapter 2.

53. Letter to Prince Nikolas Galitzin, ca. 6 July 1825, *Letters* 3:1224 (no. 1405). "[I]n der Kunst die Natur, u. sie wiederum die Natur in der Kunst gegründet ist"; *Briefe* 6:96 (no. 2003).

54. According to Holz, cit. in Lenz, *Beethoven: Eine Kunst-Studie*, 5, part 4:219. The original reads "die Phantasie will auch ihr Recht behaupten, und heut' zu Tage muß in die alt hergebrachte Form ein anderes, ein wirklich poetisches Element kommen."

55. Letter to Archduke Rudolph, 1 July 1823, *Letters* 3:1056 (no. 1203). "[N]ach u. nach ensteht die Fähigkeit gerade nur das, was wir wünschen fühlen, darzustellen, ein den Edlern Menschen so sehr wesentliches Bedürfniß"; *Briefe* 5:165 (no. 1686).

56. Letter to Bernhard Schotts Söhne, 10 March 1824, *Letters* 3:1114 (no. 1270), translation amended. "[D]en mir angebohrnen größern Beruf durch werke mich der welt zu offenbaren"; *Briefe* 5:278 (no. 1787); see also Thayer-Dieters-Riemann 5:102.

57. Letter to Hans Georg Nägeli, 9 September 1824, *Letters* 3:1139 (no. 1306). "[N]ur Sie die Göttliche Kunst nur in ihr sind die Hebel, die mir Kraft geben, dem Himmlischen Musen den besten Theil meines Lebens zu opfern"; *Briefe* 5:362 (no. 1873).

58. See Solomon, "Beethoven's Tagebuch of 1812–1818," 212, 229, 254, and 294 (nos. 1, 40, 88, 169); also Solomon, *Beethoven Essays*, 246, 258, 274, and

294: "für dich gibts kein Glück mehr als in dir selbst in deiner Kunst"; "Alles was Leben heißt sey der Erhabenen geopfert und ein Heiligthum der Kunst"; "Nur in deinem Kunstleben, so beschränkt du auch jetzt deiner Sinne halber bist, so ist dieses doch das *Einzige Daseyn* für dich"; and "Opfere noch einmal alle Kleinigkeiten des gesellschaftlichen Lebens deiner Kunst, o Gott über alles!"

59. Letter to Countess Marie Erdödy, 19 October 1815, *Letters* 2:527 (no. 563). "[W]ir endliche mit dem unendlichen Geist sind nur zu leiden und Freuden gebohren, und beynah könnte man sagen die ausgezeichneten erhalten *durch Leiden Freude*."; *Briefe* 3:161 (no. 827).

60. See Solomon, "Beethoven's Tagebuch of 1812–1818," 244 (no. 63); also Solomon, *Beethoven Essays*, 267: "Werd' ich nochmals durch Leidenschaft zum Bösen verdunkelt kehrte ich nach vielfacher Büßung und Reinigung zum ersten erhabenen reinen Quelle, zur Gottheit zurück."

61. Letter to Ignaz von Gleichenstein, February 1809, *Letters* 1:214 (no. 195). "[D]em Wichtigsten Zwecke meiner Kunst Große Werke zu schreiben"; *Briefe* 2:40 (no. 353).

62. Letter to Hans Heinrich von Könneritz, 25 July 1823, *Letters* 3:1068 (no. 1212). "[I]ch lebe nur für meine Kunst u. als Mensch meine Pflichten zu erfüllen, aber leider daß dieses auch nicht allzeit ohne die *Unterirdischen Mächte* geschehen kann—"; *Briefe* 5:198 (no. 1715). Italics canceled. This may be an allusion to a famous quotation from Virgil (*Aeneid*, Book VII, 1. 312): "Flectere si nequeo superos, Acheronta movebo" ("If I cannot bend the High Powers, I will move the Infernal Regions"). See Jean Starobinski, "Acheronta movebo," *Critical Inquiry* 13 (1987): 394–407.

63. Letter to Nannette Streicher, August 1817, *Letters* 2:705 (no. 810), translation amended. "Sumpf u. Schlamm sind im Kunstboden noch mehr werth, als all das Tuefelszeug für einen Mann!!!" *Briefe* 4:103–4 (no. 1163).

64. Thayer-Forbes, 747, translation amended. "Die Welt ist ein König, u. sie will geschmeichelt sejn, Soll sie sich günstig zeigen—Doch wahre Kunst ist eigensinnig, läßt sich nicht in Schmeichelnde Formen zwängen—Berühmte Künstler sind befangen Stets, drum ihre ersten werke auch die Besten: Obschon aus dunklem Schooße sie entsproßen. Man sagt die Kunst sej lang, kurz das Leben—Lang' ist das Leben nur, kurz die Kunst; Soll unß ihr Hauch zu den Göttern heben—So ist er eines Augenblickes Gunst—"; Köhler-Herre, 1:326 (Heft no. 9, 11ʳ), 11 March 1820. Beethoven's source is Franz Maria von Nell's tragedy, *Herostratos* (Vienna: Gerold, 1821), extracts from which appeared in the *Conversationsblatt* in March 1820. See *Köhler–Herre*, 2:452, following n. 788.

9

Schubert as Formal Architect: The *Quartettsatz*, D. 703

Lewis Lockwood

No Schubert finished or unfinished work—not even the B-Minor Symphony—speaks more eloquently or suggestively in varied voices than the C-Minor *Quartettsatz*, D. 703, written in December 1820.[1] The *Quartettsatz* has long been accepted as a mature Schubert classic, but few players know that this single movement, Allegro assai in 6/8, is not the sole survivor of the work as originally conceived. Partly finished is an A-flat-major Andante in 3/4, a slow movement that would have stood on the same high level as the first movement. Taken all in all, what remains implies a potential four-movement cycle that would have been the first of Schubert's late quartet masterpieces. Even standing alone, the first movement holds its own as a turning point in Schubert's career.[2]

In this essay I want to look at the Allegro movement in the light of its special place in Schubert's maturity as a quartet composer, and for what it reveals about his ways of shaping a sonata-form first movement. Its formal anomalies have generated much discussion, yet more remains to say. Furthermore, a substantial revision that Schubert made in the movement at the autograph stage shows his formal control, his sense of the inner proportions of the movement, and his self-critical effort to improve its larger sequential structure through a significant compositional change. It enhances the view that an older prevailing picture stressing Schubert's problems in the management of larger formal structures is long overdue for replacement by a new paradigm stressing his originality, as has begun to become clear in the recent literature. I also hope to furnish an example of the value of source studies for the analysis of content, an old-fashioned truism, advocated by Schenker and others, that bears reiteration in current musical scholarship.[3]

I

The opening of the movement, with its *pp* repeated-note descending fourth figure from *c* to *g*, symmetrically and incrementally adding repetitions at m. 3 (violin 2), m. 5 (viola), and m. 7 (lower octave, cello), initiates and builds an atmosphere of tension and expectation. Somewhat reminiscent of the second phrase of the first movement of the Unfinished Symphony (No. 8 in B Minor, D. 759) after the first theme in the cellos and basses, it differs in that the "tremolo" pattern in the *Quartettsatz* is not an obbligato accompaniment to a lyrical theme, as in the symphony, or an introductory flourish, but is in fact the primary thematic material of the opening of the movement.[4] It conveys the sense that its configurations contain important motivic ideas for the exposition and for the movement as a whole. Essential too is not simply its *misterioso* quality but a pattern of registral and dynamic expansion that emerges with the unfolding of the full shape of the first big paragraph (see example 9.1).

Example 9.1. Schubert, *Quartettsatz*, mm. 1–13.

At this point we will do well to outline the movement segment by segment, to establish its basic organizational plan.

Exposition, mm. 1–140

Exposition Segment 1, mm. 1–26

C minor; *agitato, pp, crescendo* to *f* and *ffz* and return to *pp*

Basic content: A descending-fourth figure (from 1 to 5) appears succes-
sively in sixteenth notes in all instruments in descending registral order,
leading through a crescendo to a first climax (*ffz*) at m. 9 (Neapolitan
sixth) and a cadence to C minor at m. 13. Although in some commentaries
the descending fourth is tagged the "Lamento" bass, there is no special
reason to think that Schubert was using the figure in that traditional association.[5] Probably more important would have been its intervallic affinities
with the opening of Beethoven's String Trio in C Minor, op. 9, no. 3, and
the opening descending then ascending fourth from 1 to 5 at the opening of
Beethoven's F-Minor Quartet, op. 95.

Further comments: A sense of growth emerges as the four instruments
enter one by one. Feeding that sense are several factors: 1) the *crescendos*
from *pp* to *f* at m. 7 and to a powerful *ffz* at m. 9, which coincides with an
arrival at the Neapolitan D-flat-major sixth chord, D-flat being a crucial
pitch for this movement; 2) the gradual filling-out of registers, from unison
to the minor third (*c/e♭*) at m. 3, to the upper octave *c–c'* at m. 5, to the
three-and-a-half-octave spread at m. 7, and to the temporarily culminating
four-octave span at m. 9. From here Schubert moves to the poignant *pp*
cadence at mm. 11–12 and to the new *pp* version of the theme that begins
at m. 13. The theme is now in a more comfortable three-octave registral
setting in which melody, inner parts, and bass all have room to breathe
more easily as the *agitato* sixteenth notes are replaced by rocking eighth-
note figures outlining the same descending fourth.

Exposition Segment 2, mm. 27–61

A-flat major; *dolce*; *p* with *pp* accompaniment

Basic content: An expansive and noble *dolce* melody in A-flat major
sweeps over the expressive terrain, shifting the balance firmly toward melodic beauty, while the inner voices accompany with a new version of the
"rocking" figure from Segment 1. The second phrase of the melody, beginning at m. 31, strikingly confirms the importance of the pitch D flat, already established through the climactic effect of m. 9 (see above), now not
as Neapolitan in C minor but as subdominant in A-flat. A parallel to the
registral growth of Segment 1 appears when at mm. 39–60, the theme and

all voices move up a full octave, so that the melodic crest at m. 44, the high ab'' is the same apex that had been reached in the first violin at m. 9.

Exposition Segment 3, mm. 61–93

agitato; much use of *fz* accents, *crescendos* and *decrescendos*; A-flat minor–C minor–G

Basic content: Here the *agitato* character returns but is newly developed through sixteenth notes in upward-sweeping scales with sharply accented points of arrival *(fz)*. This entire segment has the sense of a transition: it is harmonically mobile and has a series of strongly punctuated phrases. Its distraught character is in the strongest possible contrast to the serene Segment 2.

Dynamics: a series of short *crescendos* dominates: first from *p* through two measures to a climactic *fz,* then shortening the *crescendo* to one measure in an intensification of the same process (mm. 63–65, 67–69, 70–71, 72–73, 74–75, 76–77); thereafter in this segment the dynamic shades down to *p* and then to *pp* (mm. 81–93), with a *diminuendo* to close at the cadence into G at mm. 91–93.

Further comments: The sixteenth-note accompaniment figures in the cello at mm. 61–62 obviously derive from the opening of the movement and in turn develop into the chromatic "turning" figure in eighth notes at mm. 77–81. This figure in turn evolves rapidly into the rising *legato* figure at mm. 81–82 and 85–86, which has kinship with the figures at mm. 23–24 and 25–26 that had led into the great tune of Segment 2.

Exposition Segment 4, mm. 93–124

G major throughout

Basic content: A return to serenity and harmonic stability (G major prevails, intermingled with touches of G minor). Now the viola part brings a new and placid version of the chromatic descending fourth, stressing flat 7 and raised 6, articulating that primary interval in a way that recalls the second part of Segment 1 but now with groups of three eighth notes rather than two-plus-one. Above it, the first violin brings a new and pure G-Major melodic line (mm. 94–99/1) which is then repeated an octave higher (mm. 100–105/1). Then arrives the wonderful patch of mm. 105–112, which is also to be repeated at mm. 113–120 with the new effect of both a higher general register and the cello pizzicato. This marvelous moment, *ppp,* encapsulates much that we have heard before. It brings the descending fourth from 1 to 5 prominently in the upper line, chromaticizing it in a new way. It offers the "modal" harmonic effect of a pure G-major measure followed immediately by a pure F major and then by E-flat major and its dominant (m. 108), the whole leading now to the crucial return of the Neapolitan, A-flat major, at m. 109 (now in root position) and then the whole passage

Example 9.2. Schubert, *Quartettsatz*, mm. 105–112.

winds quickly back to its starting point by returning to G major. The passage is shown in example 9.2. Thereafter the final four measures of this segment make another move to the Neapolitan sixth at m. 117 (A-flat major) and set up a cadence that closes the segment.

Further comments: After the two-fold statement of the encapsulating figure at mm. 105–112 and 113–120 we have arrived at a late and final stage of the Exposition. And this is indeed a very important place on which to focus, since precisely here, after m. 120, Schubert in his autograph version of the work wrote a long passage of twenty-six measures for all instruments, of a very different character, which he then excised completely from the movement; we will come back to this passage shortly. The "Excerpt," as I shall call it, appears only in the Exposition, in full score, and is fully written out and then canceled with two strokes, showing that he composed it fully before removing it.[6] There is no trace of it in the Recapitulation, however, which may well mean that Schubert canceled the passage in a major pass through the Exposition before he got around to writing the Recapitulation.

Exposition Segment 5, mm. 125–140

closing segment of the Exposition; G major throughout

Basic content: Now the true feeling of a closing section envelops the movement. The harmony settles down to an ummixed G major, with none of Schubert's frequent hints of a major/minor mixture. The cello offers an ostinato figure that has still another and now simpler form of the "rocking" figure familiar from past events, and the upper parts move slowly and uniformly in pure dotted-quarter motion, with nothing but tonic and dominant harmonies. The material at mm. 124–130 is repeated an octave higher at mm. 131–137 in the upper strings, and the repetition steps down the dynamic from a placid *p* to a breathless *ppp*, holding this extremely soft level until the close of the whole Exposition at m. 139 plus its two descending first violin transition measures, which lead either back or onward.

From here on, it should not be necessary for my purposes to parse each successive segment of the Development, Recapitulation, and Coda. I will provide instead a bare outline of their segmentation and comment on a few salient points.

Development, mm. 141–194

The whole of the middle section, fifty-four measures in length, subdivides into three segments, as follows:

Development Segment 1, mm. 141–156 (16 mm.)

Harmonic layout: A-flat major—B-flat minor

Basic content: two 8-measure phrases—the first on A-flat major, the second on B-flat minor—project a continuation of the Exposition's last cello ostinato, with a new melodic figure formed of two-measure modules (mm. 143–144, 145–146) plus closing continuation.

Development Segment 2, mm. 155–172 (16 mm.)

Harmonic layout: D-flat major: I-vii/7; D-flat major: I-V/7 of B-flat minor

Basic content: two 8-measure modules, the first half of each consisting of an arpeggiation of the D-flat-major triad in first violin, reaching through a high two-octave span. This is followed by a contrasting low-register dominant unit in the second half of the phrase, then the first tonic phrase repeats in D-flat major, and now the second half moves upward a semitone to the dominant of B-flat minor and prepares the next segment.

Development Segment 3, mm. 173–194 (22 mm.)

Harmonic layout: B-flat minor—V/G minor . . .

Basic content: first an intensification of the tonic phrase of Development Segment 2, now in B-flat minor plus F minor; then the same in C minor plus G minor; then the same material sustains itself another fourteen measures (mm. 181–194), coming to rest on a firm V of G minor, as if to prepare the arrival of that key—and then at the last moment it reinterprets the *d* of the first violin as 3 instead of 5 and lands softly but firmly on B-flat major to start the entire next large phase.

Recapitulation, mm. 195–304

Recapitulation Segment 1, mm. 195–228

Harmonic layout and basic content: B-flat major (VII !) is the initial key of the recapitulation, a point of interest and controversy in the formal scheme of the movement, which now starts its Recapitulation with the lyrical theme of Exposition Segment 2.[7] It deviates harmonically and in phrase-repetition, however, at m. 206 (cf. m. 38) and now continues in E-flat major, to prepare the continuation. This shift, from the original unitary major-mode A-flat of the Exposition, to the two-tonic, B-flat/E-flat sequence of the Recapitulation, is one of those subtle shifts that most listeners hardly hear but which make all the difference between a master and a journeyman. The arrival of E-flat as a controlling tonic in this segment allows its subdominant, A-flat major, to appear again with this same melodic content, but now in a subordinate role (mm. 211–214). The large-scale motion to E-flat major also facilitates the return to a C-minor/major context for the remainder of the Recapitulation.

Recapitulation Segment 2, mm. 229–256

agitato, E-flat minor

Basic content: Almost identical to Segment 3 of the Exposition, but four measures shorter; the deviation occurs at mm. 240–241, where the two-measure occurrences of the *crescendo*-to-*sforzando* figure are reduced from four to two (cf. mm. 69–77).

Recapitulation Segment 3, mm. 257–288

C major/minor

Basic content: essentially the same serene material as Exposition Segment 4, now in C major/minor. A subtle and beautiful touch is that the viola now plays its version of the descending-fourth figure with the two-plus-one phrase-articulation that characterized the second half of Segment 1 of the Exposition, instead of the flowing *legato* of the parallel place in the Exposition, mm. 93–96. It thus conflates aspects of Segment 1 and Segment 2 of the Exposition.

Recapitulation Segment 4, mm. 289–304

C major

Basic content: Slightly reconfigured from the Exposition version, this quiet passage is nevertheless a true recapitulation of its predecessor; the shift in melodic contour in the cello, owing simply to its range, is a normal adjustment. The trailing-off of the upper voices at mm. 303–304 to let the cello continue contributes a sense of quiet uncertainty at the very end of this closing section, as one does not definitely know what is coming. But instead of any repeat of the large "seconda parte" of the form (the Development and Recapitulation taken together) we come to the final stroke.

Coda, mm. 305–315

C minor

Basic content: The long-awaited palindromic return of the opening *agitato* material: it literally reproduces mm. 1–8 in material, imitation, registral growth, *crescendo* at m. 5, and climax at m. 9. The climax is once more the Neapolitan, Db/6, in full strength, making its last appearance as a basic harmonic pole for this piece. The Neapolitan prepares the abrupt final cadence, Db/6-V-I in C minor, to bring the movement decisively to an end. It is of crucial importance that the *ffz* of the Neapolitan sixth at m. 313 sets up a *ff* dynamic for the entire last cadence, so that the movement ends *ff* and not *p* or *pp,* as it might have done.

II

We come now to what Schubert's autograph teaches us about his handling of form in this movement. To see the central point, a very brief synopsis of the larger form of the first movement is needed, despite my elaborate earlier discussion (or perhaps because of it). The form of the Exposition in basic terms is as follows:

EXPOSITION: five segments:
1) mm. 1–26
   agitato
   descending-fourth figure in sixteenth notes, then eighth notes, *pp–ffz–pp*
   C minor

2) mm. 27–60
   dolce
   flowing melody and accompaniment figures in eighth-note groups *p*
   A-flat major
3) mm. 61–93
   agitato
   sixteenth notes and upward scales
   fz [*crescendo–decrescendo*]
   A-flat minor–G major
4) mm. 93–124
   serene
   new version of descending-fourth figure
   ppp
   G major
5) mm. 125–140
   closing section
   ostinato in cello
   p–ppp
   G major

To this large-scale layout we can add the three-segment formal scheme of the Development (see above) and the parallel though not fully literal five-part layout of the Recapitulation (see above). The Recapitulation essentially mirrors the Exposition, but with the central difference that the opening *agitato* material is displaced to the very end so that the Recapitulation throws the "thematic" status of the opening into question as it begins with its "second theme," or rather what we have to call the lyrical theme that gives this movement so much of its special profile.

Starting at m. 121 of the Exposition, Schubert in his autograph composed the section twenty-six measures in length (the Excerpt), which he later cut from the movement entirely. In the final scheme of the movement this long section began four measures before the end of Segment 4, and it fitted in between mm. 120 and 121 of the final version. The whole segment was published and discussed by Werner Aderhold, editor of the work for the "Neue Schubert Ausgabe," in the appendix to his edition, and also in an article in the *Festschrift* for Arnold Feil, but since it is not easy of access for most readers, I include here a full transcription of the passage as example 9.3.[8] The passage surprises first of all by virtue of the *ff* outburst with which it begins: the rushing unison downward and upward scale passages in G minor lead to the *fp diminuendo* two-measure transition (example 9.3, mm. 4–5; the measures in the Excerpt are here renumbered to start from "1") that then cadences beautifully and for this piece characteristically in *pp* with a Neapolitan sixth preparing the dominant (example 9.3, mm. 6–7)—then repeats it up an octave, *ppp* (example 9.3, mm. 8–9). This gives way to an initially literal return of the rushing scales in G minor, but instead of a symmetrical continuation (as in mm. 4–9), the *fp* at m. 13

Example 9.3. Schubert, *Quartettsatz*, Canceled 26-mm. Passage from the Autograph (fits between mm. 120 and 121 of the Exposition). From Schubert's autograph, held in the Bibliothek der Gesellschaft der Musikfreunde, Vienna. Used by permission.

shifts subtly into C-flat major, colored by diminished seventh harmonies (mm. 15–16 and 19–20) that at last move to a new form of the Neapolitan sixth—V cadence at Excerpt mm. 24–26. It thus supplies an upper-octave version of the cadence at Final Version mm. 121–22 that anticipates the cadential preparation for the closing section.

The canceled passage warrants deep consideration. First, its strongly articulated rushing scale passages would have marked the first and only

Example 9.3. *(continued)*

sustained use of the dynamic *ff* in the movement, and certainly this would have been the only passage to have begun with a *ff* unison. The canceled passage is also marked by extreme contrasts of dynamics within its twenty-six-measure span, from *ff* to *fp* and to *pp* and *ppp* within a mere eight measures (example 9.3, mm. 1–8). This is a much more dramatic contrast of juxtaposed dynamic extremes than we find anywhere in the movement in its final form—the closest approach to it is in the *agitato* Segment 3 of the Exposition, with its successive *crescendo* units moving from *p* to *fz*, but elsewhere such immediate contrasts are reserved for the Development section, which they directly characterize, e.g., mm. 149 *ff* and 150 *p*.

Second, the canceled passage brings C-flat major into prominent relief, a key that is not otherwise employed in the movement. Thus the Excerpt augured a substantial complication of the harmonic range of the Exposition beyond the limits that Schubert finally set for it, emphasizing the leading tone of C minor (C-flat = B-natural) as a pitch for tonicization.

But, in my view, the most important function of the Excerpt was to cast the Exposition in a wholly different expressive light. Thus, the sequence of segments, affect by affect, would have been as follows:

Segment 1:   *agitato, pp*
        2:   *dolce,* flowing *p*
        3:   *agitato,* dynamics vary
        4:   serene, *pp, ppp*
[(Excerpt) 5:   extremely contrasting, from violent *ff* to *ppp*]
        6:   quiet closing section, *p, ppp*

Thus this canceled Excerpt, for all that it contributes to the richness of the movement (its thrust into C-flat major is only one such contribution) disturbs and complicates the emotional continuity of its Exposition. It upsets its surface smoothness in a way that, eventually, Schubert decided to avoid. It forces upon the final large part of the Exposition a culminating passage that is a climax for the Exposition and, in a sense, for the movement as a whole, by virtue of its extremes of contrast and immediacy of shift in dynamics. Omitting it meant that the two *agitato* segments of the Exposition could remain, respectively, introductory and transitional, leaving the great melody of Segment 2 as the centerpiece of the work, surrounded by a subtle chain of motivic derivations from the opening descending-fourth figure that progresses through the movement. Omitting the Excerpt also meant that the movement as a whole would be dominated by soft dynamics, with only occasional *fortes* and *fortissimos* breaking the surface.

Beyond this, the Excerpt added twenty-six measures to the Exposition; excising it helped to create a carefully balanced equilibrium between the larger segments of this part of the movement and the movement as a whole. Consider these dimensions, with and without it:

Exposition (with the Excerpt in place):
   Segment
     1   2   3   4   5   6
    26 34 32 32 26 16
   Total with Excerpt: 166
   Total without Excerpt: 140
Development:
   Segment
     1   2   3
    16 16 22
   Total: 54
Recapitulation:
   Segment
     1   2   3   4   5
    34 28 32 16 11
   Total: 121

With the Excerpt (leaving out the Exposition repeat) the proportions of the whole movement are 166:54:121, so that even in the absence of the repeat, the Exposition comes close to equaling the Development and Recapitulation combined (166:175). Without the Excerpt, the "second half" of the large form (comprising the Development and Recapitulation combined—this was the way in which composers of the time construed the large form)—takes on larger importance.[9] Now the proportions are 140:175.

It is important to see that Schubert constructs each segment of the piece from modules of two and four measures, avoiding the simplest larger symmetries except in the closing section of the Exposition and the first two segments of the Development. And equally interesting are his modest deviations in the Recapitulation from some of the segmental lengths of the Exposition.[10]

III

Why does the Recapitulation begin with the "second theme," and in the unusual key of B-flat major, ♭VII in C minor? Schubert's deviations from the "expected" in key structure and thematic order abound in some of his larger sonata-form movements, but this one calls for particular comment. I propose that the choice derives from Schubert's ways of integrating the whole movement.

The first way is by means of its sequence of basic aesthetic qualities, from one segment to the next, contrasting an *agitato* opening section with Segment 2 and its magnificent flowing melody, then returning to *agitato* in Segment 3 and passing on to the serenity of Segment 4. (All this is as discussed above, in relation to the Excerpt canceled in the autograph.)

The second is by means of its deep and intricate motivic development, for which the opening descending fourth, in repeated pairs of sixteenth notes, provides the basic model from which later intervallic units are shaped. The movement in the large continues to occupy itself with reformulating earlier figures into new ones, preserving enough of the previous shapes to make them recognizable.

The third arises from his use of the intervallic content of the descending fourth not only as a source for motivic derivation but as a pitch collection from which basic harmonic elements of the whole movement can be derived. Consider the basic keys of the Exposition:

1	2	3	4	5
C minor	A♭ major	A♭ minor–G major	G	G

and of the Recapitulation:

1	2	3	4	5
B♭/E♭ major	E♭ minor	C major	C major	C minor

Now if we look at the opening descending fourth as a diatonic pitch collection, we have most of the primary pitch centers that dominate each of the formal segments of the Exposition and Recapitulation: C–Bb–Ab–G (see Example 9.4). Though not in this order, these pitches serve as primary key

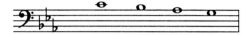

Example 9.4. Schubert, *Quartettsatz,* Initial pitch collection for opening motif: C–Bb–Ab–G.

centers. C and G are the basic keys for the C-minor tonal framework. A-flat and B-flat are the keys chosen for the lyrical melody of Segment 2. The prominence of B-flat (VII) to begin the Recapitulation directs attention to this set of pitches and picks up the only pitch of the descending fourth not yet given prominence. That Schubert then moves from B-flat to E-flat within the Recapitulation version of the melody is, as we have seen, a matter of large-scale formal necessity, to bring the framework back to the tonic, C major/minor. Thus his care in this movement to combine a wide expressive range, to maintain the cogency of thematic and motivic content, and to correlate rigorously harmonic structure and form with its basic opening idea exemplifies his command of formal architecture and musical integration. Just as we knew all along.

Notes

1. The definitive edition of the *Quartettsatz* and its unfinished slow movement is that in the "Neue Schubert Ausgabe," i.e., Walther Dürr, Arnold Feil, Christa Landon, et al., eds., *Franz Schubert: Neue Ausgabe Sämtliche Werke* (Kassel: Bärenreiter, 1964—), vol. V (1989), 3–14, plus Critical Notes, 173–75. This volume was edited by Werner Aderhold, who also published an important article on it ["Das Streichquartett-Fragment c-moll, D. 703," in *Franz Schubert, Jahre der Krise, 1818–1823: Arnold Feil zum 60. Geburtstag* (Kassel: Bärenreiter, 1985), 57–81] that presents the unfinished slow movement and the long passage in the Exposition of the first movement that was cut out of the autograph. Recent special commentaries on the *Quartettsatz* include Marianne Danckwardt, "Funktionen von Harmonik und tonaler Anlage in Franz Schuberts Quartettssatz c-moll, D. 703," *Archiv für Musikwissenschaft* 40 (1983): 50–60.

2. The chronology of Schubert's string quartets falls into two basic periods: 1) about fourteen works and fragments, ranging from the experiments of 1810/11, when he was fourteen and fifteen years of age, up to D. 353, the String Quartet in E Major, composed in 1816, when he was nineteen; 2) the late phase, beginning with this unfinished String Quartet in C Minor, D. 703 (*Quartettsatz*), of late 1820, through the string quartets D. 804 (A Minor, 1824), D. 810 (D Minor, 1824), D.

887 (G Major/Minor, 1826), and finally, though not a quartet, the String Quintet in C Major, 1828, D. 956.

3. By now source studies, especially of sketches and autographs in relation to formal and other compositional questions, has developed from its status as a still-promising sector of musicology to a venerable field. It was Heinrich Schenker who first insisted on it in his important "Erläuterungs-Ausgaben" of the late Beethoven piano sonatas and in other publications, and it has been followed up by many scholars, among them the honoree of this volume, Robert L. Marshall, in his book, *The Compositional Process of J. S. Bach* (Princeton, N.J.: Princeton University Press, 1972).

4. Schubert's way of intensifying the opening figure by dividing each eighth note as a pair of sixteenths, a procedure commonly miscalled "tremolo," is one of many instances of his discovery of new sonorities in his later chamber music. It is much more common in orchestral and dramatic music than in the quartet literature and is usually reserved for *f* or *ff* passages, as in Beethoven's Symphony No. 1 in C Major, op. 21, first movement, mm. 57–63 and 80–87, among other passages. *Misterioso* uses of it are harder to find in Beethoven: one example is the opening of the Presto finale of his String Quintet in C Major, op. 29, which Schubert probably knew.

5. On the "Lamento" bass see Aderhold, "Das Streichquartett Fragment," 57.

6. For a facsimile of the passage, see the *Neue Ausgabe*, V:xxi. The autograph, once Brahms's property, is in the Gesellschaft der Musikfreunde in Vienna; see the German edition of Otto Erich Deutsch, *Schubert: Thematisches Verzeichnis seiner Werke. Neuausgabe* (Kassel: Bärenreiter, 1978), 414. Deutsch calls it an "Erste Niederschrift." No other autograph survives, nor any sketches. The work was apparently not performed publicly before 1867 nor published before 1870.

7. For comments on this anomaly, see Danckwardt, "Functionen und Harmonik," 58–60. Danckwardt regards the reappearance of the lyrical theme in B-flat major not as the formal Recapitulation but as part of the Development section, the Recapitulation in her view not taking place until the return of C major at m. 257 ("T. 257 Reprisenbeginn"). But this is very late in the movement for a Recapitulation, and it leaves the thematic correspondence from m. 195 onward unexplained. For another view, see Hans-Joachim Hinrichsen, *Untersuchungen zur Entwicklung der Sonatenform in der Instrumentalmusik Franz Schuberts* (Tutzing: Hans Schneider Verlag, 1994), 134–38 (showing examples of Schubert bypassing the opening material of the Exposition at the moment of Recapitulation).

8. For the article and edition, see *Neue Ausgabe*, V:3–14, plus Critical Notes, 173–75; and Aderhold, "Das Streichquartett Fragment." For a published facsimile, see *Neue Ausgabe*, V:xxi.

9. On Beethoven's use of the term "seconda parte" in this meaning, see my *Beethoven: Studies in the Creative Process* (Cambridge, Mass.: Harvard University Press, 1992), 203–8, on op. 59, no. 1.

10. On aspects of modular form and symmetries in works by Haydn, Mozart, and Beethoven, see David M. Smyth, *Codas in Classical Form: Aspects of Large-Scale Rhythm and Pattern Completion* (Ann Arbor, Mich.: UMI, 1985). I am indebted to Professor Smyth for discussion of these matters during an NEH Summer Seminar on the Beethoven string quartets at Harvard University in 1989. See also his article, "Beethoven's Revisions of the Scherzo of the Quartet, Opus 18, No. 1," *Beethoven Forum* 1 (1992): 147–63.

10

Sex, Sexuality, and Schubert's Piano Music

Jeffrey Kallberg

Few arenas in modern musical scholarship are more fraught with controversy than the debates over Schubert's sexual proclivities and their possible relationship to his music. The issues strike many of us at gut level. Was he or was he not homosexual? Can listening to his music be affected by our answer to the first question? If not, are there other means by which sexuality can be musically expressed, and if so, how do we gain access to them?

But what is the issue here? The question must be raised, for these arguments have been debilitated by much talking at cross-purposes. As scholars have attempted to analyze Schubert's music in terms of sexuality (or have contributed to the dialogue on how one might—or if one should—achieve this goal), they have at times blurred the focus between historical meaning and present-day explanation.

This essay will look closely at some of the terms and issues under debate—particularly the concepts of "sexuality" and "sex"—from a more general historical perspective. It will suggest some ways that a more nuanced and historically informed understanding of these general concepts might affect how (and whether) we deploy them in connection with Schubert's piano music.[1] To this end, and by way of conclusion, it will explore how a more finely shaded and historicized reading of sex might be brought to bear on the Piano Sonata in A Minor, D. 845 (op. 42).

By accident of chronology, the case of Schubert raises a number of vexing problems from the standpoint of the history of sexuality. Indeed, the most troublesome of them is whether the phenomenon as it applies to Schubert should even be labeled sexuality at all. For sexuality, when understood in something like its modern sense—as a cultural production that configures the relationship between sexual practice and identity and that thus to some degree contributes to our personal, interior sense of self—proves to be an unstable term when examined historically. That is to say, sexuality should stand not for a fixed, transhistorical essence, but rather for a constructed phenomenon of relatively recent origin.[2]

To claim that sexuality emerged relatively recently means in part to distinguish between behavior and identity. Sexual acts and behaviors have obviously been with us forever. But, as Robert Padgug has observed, it is one thing to "commit" a sexual act of some type; it is another to "be" a homosexual, a heterosexual, or a transsexual.[3] To invoke sexuality is to call upon an entire nexus of institutions, desires, and acts that together endow an identity. Before this governing concept took shape, these institutions, desires, and acts either existed independently from one another or were linked in different sorts of ways. The distinctions between sexuality and what preceded it—"sex"—emerge clearly in marginal or unusual situations. Hermaphrodites provide an excellent example.[4] The long medico-legal tradition devoted to the dilemma posed by the ambiguous genitalia of hermaphrodites was, prior to the advent of sexuality, seldom concerned with finding a solution that might enable patients to obtain a measure of psycho-social stability in their identities as individuals. Instead treatises offered advice on how to determine the hermaphrodite's "true" sex in order to ascertain his or her civil status with respect to ownership or inheritance of property. Sexual characteristics and economic institutions interacted in ways foreign to our modern sense of identity; indeed, one literally could not "be" a hermaphrodite in this earlier system.

Plainly the development of sexuality marked a momentous and momentously complicated shift in the ways of conceiving human individuals, one that, as Lynn Hunt has argued, would seem to be intimately connected with the emergence of modernity, its attendant notions of individual, and its new versions of subjectivity.[5] And when did this shift take place? Here is where the matter becomes interesting and knotty with respect to Schubert, for different scholars argue for different dates both before and after the composer's lifetime. Sometimes, in fact, the same scholar argues for a variety of dates: at different moments in the first volume of *The History of Sexuality,* Foucault names the early seventeenth century, the early eighteenth century, the late eighteenth century, and the late nineteenth century as decisive moments in this shift. Other writers, when arguing for the precedence and significance of the emergence of different signs of sexuality, nearly always lobby for one of the moments articulated by Foucault. Thus Randolph Trumbach believes that the beginnings of a modern homosexual role ("role" here is perhaps not exactly congruent with "identity") should be traced to the "sodomitical subcultures" of early-eighteenth-century England, whereas Arnold I. Davidson contends that the notion of sexuality was the product of a "psychiatric style of reasoning" that arose around the middle of the nineteenth century.[6] Perhaps these scholars and others like them each describe important fragments—fragments distinct from one another both chronologically and geographically—of this massive and enigmatic concept. In other words, rather than argue that the concept of sexuality came into being relatively whole at a given moment in history, one might rather conclude that it emerged, unevenly and intricately in different times and at different places, over a century-and-a-half span from the early eighteenth century to the mid-nineteenth century. (One may productively read Foucault's variable positions just this way, not as evidence of an inconsistency in his argument.)

Hence, if sexuality figured into Schubert's life at all, it probably did so in a way that differs to some degree from the concept we know.[7] At most it would seem to have been a nascent, partially conceived force in the construction of identity. And Davidson's convincing arguments about the difficulty of conceiving of sexuality outside the context of a psychiatric mode of reasoning further suggest that any sexuality that was perceived around 1820 would have been quite unlike any present concept of it that we hold, perhaps most so at its boundaries with identity. (Indeed, the reception history of Schubert supports Davidson's claim, particularly in the way that the trope of Schubert as feminine and effeminate Other gained momentum as the nineteenth century progressed—we shall return to this point below.)

That sexuality and related categories like homosexuality may have been far from or differently construed in the minds of Schubert's contemporaries does not mean that they ignored sex. Of course the Viennese (and others) noticed, engaged in, gossiped, moralized, and otherwise circulated information about various sexual acts and activities, including those between people of the same sex. Speaking of the German-speaking states, Paul Derks copiously documents the manifold ways that same-sex passion figured into the wider literary public sphere between 1750 and 1850.[8] This evidence describes both stagings of same-sex love in novels, plays, and poems, as well as activities of authors, playwrights, dramaturges, and other participants in the German literary scene. This latter variety of evidence, I might note in passing, seems suggestive with respect to the debates about Schubert's own sexual tendencies: the kinds of same-sex social circles that Derks prolifically documents around authors like Johannes Müller and Emil von Platen resonate sympathetically with the largely homosocial milieu portrayed in the documentary record of Schubert's life.[9] Sometime the circles overlapped: Platen's name, for example, often surfaced in the discussions and activities of Schubert's personal coterie.

But if the similarities between Schubert's homosocial milieu and those of authors who unambiguously engaged in acts of same-sex love might be mustered on behalf of a reading of Schubert's sexual inclinations (a point that will hardly come as a surprise to those who have read the contributions to the debate by Maynard Solomon, Kristina Muxfeldt, and David Gramit[10]), the question still remains whether the sexually oriented activities of Schubert either by himself or together with his band of male friends were likely to have entered into the public sphere as did those of the literary notables described by Derks. There must have been a palpable difference between any interpretative situation that arose with Schubert's piano music and, say, the kind of public sexual scandal that surrounded August Wilhelm Iffland's refusal in 1810 to stage Heinrich von Kleist's *Käthchen von Heilbronn*. (Alluding to Iffland's love for men, Kleist complained in a personal note to Iffland that immediately became scandalous public knowledge that Iffland would have accepted the play had Käthchen been a young man.[11]) The distinction, of course, lies precisely in the vaunted semantic vagueness of Schubert's artistic product. Solomon addressed this issue in part when he wrote that "Schubert's music is not a diary of his own experience; his art is not circumscribed by his private obsessions and hungers."[12] Surely it is right to suppose that Schubert would not have construed his personal sexual practices as invested into the larger semantic domain that listeners might perceive in his music, particularly so if, as argued here, this sex life was not coupled to the larger interpretative field called sexuality.[13]

But Schubert's own perception of his practices is only part of the issue— the lesser part for those interested in questions of historical meaning during Schubert's life. The more pressing concern is how, or whether, his audiences construed sexual meanings in his music. In other words, did they— could they—hear sex or sexuality when they listened to his piano music? The question is not outlandish, for diverse, if sparse, evidence testifies that some listeners from around Schubert's time did explicitly link sex and music. Nothing more strangely links the two categories together than Karl Friedrich Zelter's startling description of Beethoven, written in a letter of September 1812 to Goethe:

> His works seem to me like children whose father is a woman or whose mother is a man. The last work of his that I encountered ("Christ on the Mount of Olives") seems to me like an unchaste thing whose basis and purpose are eternal death. . . . I know musical people who once found themselves alarmed, even indignant, on hearing his works and are now gripped by an enthusiasm for them like the partisans of Greek love.[14]

Just as remarkable is George Alexander Macfarren's 1842 interpretation of Mendelssohn's Symphony No. 3 in A Minor, op. 56, in terms of passionate love, the climax of which arrives in his almost Joycean evocation of the Allegro maestoso assai theme that enters toward the end of the last movement (m. 396):

> But then a new light bursts upon the mind, new oil is poured upon the flame, a rock is shifted from its base, and a world of waters is let loose upon the cataract. A new subject with a quite new feeling in A major, and in six-eight time, bursts like an eye-beam on the darkened heart, and says, in signs unquestionable and irrevocable, "Yes, ever yes," to all that undefinable craving to which the wildest

brain upon the pinnacle of its enthusiasm dare not, cannot give utterance. It is a joyous exultation, far beyond Hope's uttermost excitement . . . it is the pang of pleasure which a lover feels at knowing that his passion dream is realized.[15]

But whose sex or sexual experience is being heard in these responses? One would be hard pressed to identify it with the composers'. Macfarren's encomium makes no claim that the symphony (or the review) represents Mendelssohn's attitudes toward sensuous love. Zelter's comments are more complicated, but in brief, while he portrayed Beethoven's compositions as resulting from a kind of monstrous birth and evincing a kind of promiscuity, he did not relate the sex that he heard, and in particular the "Greek love," directly back to Beethoven himself. To the extent that listeners at this time were inclined to map narratives onto instrumental music, and to the even lesser extent that these narratives or associations concerned sex, it would have been unusual for listeners to have construed these associations as the composer telling something specific about himself. Hearing general human conditions and emotions in performances of instrumental music was not unusual in Schubert's day; ascribing specific emotions and acts to the creator of the instrumental work happened more commonly after the middle of the century.

The rhetoric of reviews around Schubert's time demonstrates this clearly. Expressions such as "the present Sonata appears to be such an effusion from the innermost heart" (the words are from A. B. Marx in 1824, in reference to Beethoven's Piano Sonata in A-flat Major, op. 110, and to the composer's heart) are common coin.[16] It is more rare for a reviewer to offer a precise summation of the content of such an effusion. Indeed, most critics in the first third of the nineteenth century celebrated the unique power of music to avoid evoking any concrete identification with the "outer sensual world," as E. T. A. Hoffmann put it in his essay on Beethoven's instrumental music.[17]

We may observe this strategy of avoidance in a review of the Fantasy in C Major, D. 760 ("Wanderer"), printed in the *Wiener Allgemeine musikalische Zeitung* in 1823. The anonymous critic devoted the first three paragraphs to a general assessment of the nature of the genre "Fantasy."

> A fantasy is a musical piece in which a composer may allow perfectly free deployment to the wings of his inventive spirit, unite the most curious forms into the greatest possible unity, and thus present our minds with a picture capable of laying claim to our perceptive faculty in a most interesting manner by means of vivacity of color, shape and arrangement as well as variety organized into a satisfactory whole.[18]

The reviewer's opening sally thus drew on conjoined tropes of free imagination and higher artistic unity that had configured the genre since at least the mid-eighteenth century. In the fourth paragraph, however, the discussion turned to Schubert in a way that would seem at first to allow a hermeneutics built around the composer's identity:

> Such a piece of music may for that reason be best suited faithfully to record and reproduce the feelings that inspired the composer at the time of its creation; nay, it may properly be regarded as a mirror of his depths.
>
> Seeing that a composer like Herr *Schubert,* who had already betrayed such profound sentiments in his generally esteemed songs, presents us with a soul-picture of this kind, the musical world can only rejoice.[19]

Schubert, the reviewer averred, offered up to his listeners a reflected image of his soul; the Fantasy somehow enabled the auditors to reproduce the deep feelings that motivated him when he composed.

And what did one find upon looking into the mirror of Schubert's depths? In fact, the reviewer remained silent on the issue: in the remainder of the article, he briefly sketched the overall shape of the Fantasy and drew special attention (as did many reviews of Schubert during his lifetime) to the composer's occasional "lapses" into harmonic license. While one might lament this silence—souls could be sexed places for the Romantics, as Susan J. Wolfson has recently reminded us—the critic's strategy conformed to the prevailing attitude that one should not place verbal limits on the expressive powers of music.[20] Schubert's soul as mirrored in the C-Major Fantasy offered a potential conduit through which to hear sex (and hence perhaps also the glimmerings of a nascent sexuality at work), but to bemoan the critic's failure to realize this potential would be to misconstrue a significant element of contemporary reception.

If, in the public sphere of the press, a review appears to sidestep the articulation of connections between Schubert's music and his soul, then perhaps we need to examine more private communications among the composer's intimates in order to find such correlations. And, indeed, we might be tempted to construe the following lines, from a letter that Anton Ottenwalt wrote to Josef von Spaun on 27 November 1825, as associating Schubert's creative output with something akin to his sexual identity:

> Von Schubert wüßte ich nichts Dir und uns Neues zu sagen, in seinen Werken offenbart sich der Genius, der Göttliches schafft, unverwüstlich durch die Affektionen einer lebhaft begehrenden Sinnlichkeit, und für Freunde scheint er ein wahrhaft treues Gemüt zu haben.[21]

But what exactly did Ottenwalt mean to say by conjoining remarks about Schubert's music and his sensual nature? Two published translations leave strikingly contradictory impressions of this relationship. According to Eric Blom in *The Schubert Reader,* Ottenwalt would claim that Schubert's music and his sensual passions were unconnected; the divine presence of the music remained unsullied by Schubert's sensual nature: "Of Schubert I could tell you nothing that is new to you and to us; his works proclaim a genius for divine creation, unimpaired by the passions of an eagerly burning sensuality, and he seems to have truly devoted sentiments for friends."[22] Compare Joshua Rifkin's translation, published in Christopher Gibbs's recent biography of Schubert, which yields an entirely different sense of Ottenwalt's intent in the central three clauses: in Schubert's works "the genius of divine creation reveals itself irreducibly through the passions of an ardently avid sensuality."[23] In this version, Ottenwalt would posit a link between Schubert's divine musical genius and his ardent sensual nature—although what precisely it might mean for "genius to reveal itself irreducibly through passions" remains obscure.

How we interpret the import of these murky phrases plainly hinges on how we understand both "unverwüstlich durch"—the difference between Blom's "unimpaired by" and Rifkin's "irreducibly through" largely determines the different tenors of their respective versions—and "Affektionen." And while neither translation appears to have rendered the German entirely accurately, the Rifkin/Gibbs version comes closer to the sense implied by the German original.[24] If we understand the basic structure of the original to parse as "Genius offenbart sich durch Sinnlichkeit," then a more literal translation of Ottenwalt's remarks might better resemble, "Of Schubert I am aware of nothing to tell that is new to you and us, in his works genius that creates something divine reveals itself, irrepressible thanks to the dispositions of an actively desiring sensuality, and for friends he seems to have truly loyal feelings."

In other words, Ottenwalt would appear simply to observe that Schubert's sensual nature abetted his musical genius. By reminding Spaun ("nothing that is new to you") that Schubert's well-known penchant for sensual pleasure (pleasure of all sorts: "Sinnlichkeit" here cannot be limited to the sexual sphere) was the engine that drove his musical genius, Ottenwalt did little more than invoke a hoary saw about the benefits to artistic creativity of a lust for life. Nothing in what Ottenwalt wrote can be construed as implying that listeners could perceive anything of Schubert's sensual nature in his music.

How, then, might the categories of sex and Schubert's piano music have converged in his day? Sexual tropes did not crop up very frequently in reactions to his piano music during his lifetime, but interestingly enough, the same piece, the A-Minor Sonata, op. 42, twice evoked sexual metaphors from critics. The first review of the Sonata, a lengthy rave in the *Leipziger Allgemeine musikalische Zeitung* from March 1826, replicated the structure (if not the size) of the review of the C-Major Fantasy. An involved series of musings over the title of the piece (here the critic opined that the Sonata would be better titled "Fantasy") led to a detailed consideration of the content of the Sonata. Describing "the predominant expression" ("der herrschende Ausdruck") of the first movement as "a suppressed but sometimes violently erupting somber passion, alternating with melancholy seriousness" ("eine niedergehaltene, zuweilen aber heftig hervorbrechende, düstere Leidenschaftlichkeit, wechselnd mit schwermüthigen Ernst"), the reviewer went on to portray the second movement as Haydnesque, and the third as Beethovenian, though without faulting Schubert's originality. He then continued, with respect to the fourth movement:

> What, to the stimulated mind, would be the most natural sequel after all these changing emotions? Surely an as it were generalized and elevated mood on the whole, not vehement but very lively, not sad but not light or merry either—a strong, manly, jovial mood, mixed of a greater part of seriousness and a smaller of jesting. And that is the very expression of the long, technically very well knit Finale—Allegro vivace, A minor, two-four time.[25]

An 1828 review in the *Wiener Zeitschrift für Kunst, Literatur, Theater und Mode* echoed these sentiments, but now with reference to the first movement:

> Just as Herr *Schubert* shows himself in his songs as a worthy connoisseur of harmony and knows how to season his melodies with a beautiful background of chords, he is here seen in an almost martial mood, in which a well-chosen change of harmonies accompanies the march-like middle theme in manifold variants. The moderate tempo is very well suited to the course taken by the ideas, and the composer keeps logically to the manly character he has once chosen.[26]

Both reviewers discovered epitomes of manliness in different aspects of Schubert's Sonata. Neither reviewer reached this conclusion by measuring the musical text against his sense of the composer's self (the "he" in the second review is plainly "Schubert the worthy connoisseur of harmony," not "Schubert the virile man"). Rather the manliness accrued to the generic referent in the first movement (martial music evokes the military, a distinctively masculine domain) and to the technical seriousness of the fourth movement (most likely a reference to the resolutely two- and three-part contrapuntal design of much of the movement). That "manliness" should in part derive from Schubert's evocation of the military world draws our attention to what was really at stake in this sexual category. As Linda Dowling, Alan Sinfield, and David Halperin have recently established, the term "manly," when used prior to the full flowering of the concept of sexuality, had more to do with civic capacity than with sexual demeanor.[27] In essence, then, to dub an artwork "manly" was to give it a gender, to interpret the sexual category in larger cultural and social terms.[28] By portraying the Sonata as "manly," the critics meant to call attention to its ability to sustain (in however small a way) the common political and national good. In other words, in these instances the sexual category of "manliness" was aligned with a political system of meaning, not with one that concerned individuality or personal identity. (And, it is important to add, the adjective "manly" could configure individuals irrespective of their preference in sexual partners. Thus, even if we were mistakenly tempted to read these remarks for evidence of Schubert's "identity," our reviewers' perceptions of manly qualities in the Sonata do not in any way provide evidence on contemporary perceptions of sexual practices.)

As the nineteenth century unfolded, the sense of the category changed sharply. "Manly," together with its antonym "effeminate" and its near-antonym "feminine," came increasingly to be employed in ways that helped conjoin sexuality to identity. A glance at the history of the terms "manly," "feminine," and "effeminate" in the reception of Schubert confirms this reading. For Schumann, the manliness of Schubert's music came into question in only one specific relational instance. Taken on its own, Schubert's music projected abundant masculinity: in his review of Schubert's *Grand Duo* (the source of all the terms cited here), Schumann noted the "boldness" and "free-spirited" character of the piece. But measured against Beethoven, Schubert became, for Schumann, the feminine Other:

> Schubert is a girlish character compared to the other, far more loquacious, softer ["weicher," also meaning "effeminate"] and broader, compared to the other a child who plays carefree under the giants. . . . To be sure, he brings in his powerful passages, he also summons masses; for all that he comports himself always as wife to husband, who orders, where the former pleads and persuades. But all this merely in comparison with Beethoven; compared to others, he is yet man enough; indeed, the boldest and most freethinking among the new musicians.[29]

In other words, Schumann's understanding of masculine and feminine hardly differed from the politically tinged sense we noted in Schubert's day. By dressing Schubert in girlish, wifely, effeminate garb, Schumann preserved the militaristic commanding role in the pantheon of German composers for Beethoven, the memory of whom Schumann and other critics cultivated, as part of their project of fostering a nascent sense of German national identity.[30]

During the second half of the nineteenth century (and continuing well into the twentieth century), ascriptions of feminine or effeminate characteristics to Schubert's music began to be likened to the composer's own psychical and physical make-up. David Gramit has fully documented how this process shaped Victorian constructions of Schubert.[31] The "feminine" in Schubert's music reflected feminine essences in the man. Hence Edward Wilberforce could imply parallels between Schubert's musical style and the purportedly "feminine organization" of his skull (which had been examined when his remains were disinterred in 1863); hence George Grove could suggest a kindred relationship between Schubert's "womanly" music and what Grove described as his shy, awkward, and girlish nature. It is no coincidence that artistic production and personal identity should be linked in this manner at more or less the same time that a psychiatric model of sexuality began to emerge from the work of great nineteenth-century sexologists like Heinrich Kaan, Carl Westphal, and Richard von Krafft-Ebing.

Can we talk about sexuality and Schubert's piano music? I have tried to suggest that if our concern is with the meanings that this repertoire might have enjoyed during Schubert's lifetime, the answer is largely no. But if our concern is with how our own sexualities might be measured against Schubert's instrumental music, then the answer is certainly yes.[32] Sexuality as a cultural construct joined to notions of personal and group identity did not much figure into Schubert's broader cultural context; to invoke it as a category of historical analysis is thus to risk anachronism. On the other hand, a historically appropriate category does exist, one that figured prominently in the public sphere around Schubert, and its name is sex. By appealing to sex rather than sexuality, we effectively and properly separate the issue from concerns with Schubert's life and with related ideas of subjectivity and focus instead on how listeners interpreted its relatively infrequent intersections with piano music. That the sexual category performed a perhaps unexpected bit of cultural work in a piece like the Sonata in A Minor—aligning it with notions of nascent German national identity—usefully reminds us of the curious gaps in experience that often still remain when we compare our experiences of this most familiar repertoire with those of Schubert's contemporaries.

Notes

1. The topic for this paper arose from an invitation to participate in an April 1995 symposium on Schubert's piano music hosted by the Westfield Center and the Smithsonian Institution.

2. In formulating the matter this way, I want both to acknowledge my debts to recent scholarship, most important that of Michel Foucault and David Halperin, and to signal that some scholars would challenge the claim that I am making: the late John Boswell was perhaps the most prominent figure to argue for an essential congruence between older and newer sexual categories. See Michel Foucault, *The History of Sexuality: An Introduction,* trans. Robert Hurley (New York: Pantheon, 1978); David M. Halperin, "One Hundred Years of Homosexuality," in his *One Hundred Years of Homosexuality and Other Essays on Greek Love* (New York: Routledge, 1990), 15–40, 154–68; Robert Hurley, "How to Do the History of Male Homosexuality," *GLQ* 6 (2000): 87–124; John Boswell, "Categories, Experience and Sexuality," in *Forms of Desire: Sexual Orientation and the Social Constructionist Controversy,* ed. Edward Stein (New York: Routledge, 1990), 133–73.

I have expressed some of the arguments in the following paragraphs in more condensed form in "Sex, Sexuality," *The New Grove Dictionary of Music and Musicians,* 2nd ed. (London: Macmillan, 2001), 23:178–80.

3. Robert Padgug, "Sexual Matters: On Conceptualizing Sexuality in History," in *Forms of Desire,* ed. Edward Stein, 43–67.

4. For a discussion of the relevance of hermaphrodites to an understanding of sex and sexuality in the early nineteenth century, see my *Chopin at the Boundaries: Sex, History, and Musical Genre* (Cambridge, Mass.: Harvard University Press, 1996), 81.

5. On "individual" as a modern formulation, see Lynn Hunt, "Foucault's Subject in *The History of Sexuality,*" in *Discourses of Sexuality: From Aristotle to AIDS,* ed. Domna C. Stanton (Ann Arbor: University of Michigan Press, 1992), 84–85. I have benefitted greatly from Hunt's critique of certain ahistorical gaps in Foucault's monumental project.

6. Randolph Trumbach has argued his position in several publications. In addition to his *Sex and the Gender Revolution,* vol. 1: *Heterosexuality and the Third Gender in Enlightenment London* (Chicago: University of Chicago Press, 1998), see his "Sodomitical Subcultures, Sodomitical Roles, and the Gender Revolution of the Eighteenth Century: The Recent Historiography," in *'Tis Nature's Fault: Unauthorized Sexuality during the Enlightenment,* ed. Robert Purks Maccubbin (Cambridge: Cambridge University Press, 1985), 109–21; his "Gender and the Homosexual Role in Modern Western Culture," in *Homosexuality, Which Homosexuality?,* ed. Dennis Altman (Amsterdam: An Dekker / Schorer, 1989), 149–69; his "London's Sapphists: From Three Sexes to Four Genders in the Making of Modern Culture," in *Body Guards: The Cultural Politics of Gender Ambiguity,* ed. Julia Epstein and Kristina Straub (New York and London: Routledge, 1991), 112–41; and "Sex, Gender, and Sexual Identity in Modern Culture: Male Sodomy and Female Prostitution in Enlightenment London," in *Forbidden History: The State, Society, and the Regulation of Sexuality in Modern Europe,* ed. John C. Fout (Chicago and London: University of Chicago Press, 1992), 89–106. Davidson makes his case in his "Sex and the Emergence of Sexuality," *Critical Inquiry* 14 (1987): 16–48.

7. This point is also made in two of the more interesting studies of the relationships between sexual categories and Schubert's music: Susan McClary, "Constructions of Subjectivity in Schubert's Music," in *Queering the Pitch: The New Gay and Lesbian Musicology,* ed. Philip Brett, Elizabeth Wood, and Gary C. Thomas (New York: Routledge, 1994), 205 and 228; and Lawrence Kramer, *Franz Schubert: Sexuality, Subjectivity, Song* (Cambridge: Cambridge University Press, 1998), 93–128.

8. Paul Derks, *Die Schande der heiligen Päderastie: Homosexualität und Öffentlichkeit in der deutschen Literatur, 1750–1850* (Berlin: Verlag Rosa Winkel, 1990). Derks's study actually dates from 1981 (see the author's statement on p. 17), which accounts for his failure to take into account the historiographical questions about the category of homosexuality that have been raised more recently by Halperin and Davidson. Nor does Derks mention Foucault, although the first volume of *The History of Sexuality* was translated into German in 1977.

9. On the homosocial nature of much of Schubert's life, see David Gramit, "'The Passion for Friendship': Music, Cultivation, and Identity in Schubert's Circle," in *The Cambridge Companion to Schubert,* ed. Christopher H. Gibbs (Cambridge: Cambridge University Press, 1997), 56–71, and Gibbs, *The Life of Schubert* (Cambridge: Cambridge University Press, 2000), 134–35, 152, and 188.

10. Maynard Solomon, "Franz Schubert and the Peacocks of Benvenuto Cellini," *19th-Century Music* 12 (1989): 193–206; Maynard Solomon, "Schubert: Some

Consequences of Nostalgia," *19th-Century Music* 17 (1993): 34–46; Kristina Muxfeldt, "Political Crimes and Liberty, or Why Would Schubert Eat a Peacock," *19th-Century Music* 17 (1993): 47–64; and David Gramit, "Constructing a Victorian Schubert: Music, Biography, and Cultural Values," *19th-Century Music* 17 (1993): 65–78.

11. On Kleist and Iffland, see Derks, *Die Schande der heiligen Päderastie*, 432–33.

One wonders if this aura of same-sex scandal had anything to do with the interest of members of Schubert's circle in this play. See the references to Moritz von Schwind's drawing of a scene from the play, to a performance of it, and to reading of it in Otto Erich Deutsch, *The Schubert Reader: A Life of Franz Schubert in Letters and Documents*, trans. Eric Blom (New York: W. W. Norton, 1947), 548, 578, 790, and 792.

12. Solomon, "Schubert: Some Consequences of Nostalgia," 46.

13. But whatever these personal sexual practices might have been, it is also surely right to insist that Schubert showed a strong inclination to explore the artistic resonances of sexual activity between men. See Kristina Muxfeldt, "Schubert, Platen, and the Myth of Narcissus," *Journal of the American Musicological Society* 49 (1996): 480–27; and Kramer, *Franz Schubert*, 101–2.

14. "Mir erscheinen seine Werke wie Kinder, deren Vater ein Weib oder deren Mutter ein Mann wäre. Das letzte mir bekannt gewordne Werk ('Christus am Ölberge') kommt mir vor wie ein Unkeuschheit, deren Grund und Ziel ein ewiger Tod ist . . . Ich kenne musikalische Personen, die sich sonst bei Anhörung seiner Werke alarmiert, ja indigniert fanden und nun von einer Leidenschaft dafür ergriffen sind wie die Anhänger der griechischen Liebe." *Briefwechsel zwischen Goethe und Zelter, 1799–1832*, ed. Max Hecker, 3 vols. (Frankfurt am Main: Insel Verlag, 1987), 1:352–53. Charles Rosen discusses these remarks by Zelter in his *The Frontiers of Meaning: Three Informal Lectures on Music* (New York: Hill & Wang, 1994), 69–71.

15. G. A. Macfarren, "Symphony in A Minor, of Dr. Felix Mendelssohn Bartholdy," *The Musical World*, 16 June 1842, 187.

16. "[D]ie vorliegende Sonate scheint ein solcher Erguss aus dem innersten Herzen zu sein." Marx's review is printed in Stefan Kunze, ed., *Ludwig van Beethoven: Die Werke im Spiegel seiner Zeit* (Laaber: Laaber Verlag, 1987), 369.

17. "Die Musik schließt dem Menschen ein unbekanntes Reich auf, eine Welt, die nichts gemein hat mit der äußern Sinnenwelt, die ihn umgibt, und in der er alle *bestimmten* Gefühle zurückläßt, um sich einer unaussprechlichen Sehnsucht hinzugeben"; "Beethovens Instrumental-Musik,"in E. T. A. Hoffmann, *Fantasiestücke in Callot's Manier; Werke 1814*, ed. Hartmut Steinecke, Gerhard Allroggen, and Wulf Segebrecht, *E. T. A. Hoffmann Sämtliche Werke* (Frankfurt am Main: Deutscher Klassiker Verlag, 1993), Bd. 2/1:52. "Music reveals to man an unknown realm, a world quite separate from the outer sensual world surrounding him, a world in which he leaves behind all *precise* feelings in order to embrace an inexpressible longing"; translation typographically modified from "E. T. A. Hoffmann's Musical Writings: Kreisleriana, The Poet and the Composer," in *Music Criticism*, ed. David Charlton, trans. Martyn Clarke (Cambridge: Cambridge University Press, 1989), 96.

18. "Eine Fantasie ist ein Tonstück, worin der Componist den Fittigen seines Erfindungsgeistes eine ganz freye Schwungkraft erlauben, die seltsamsten Formen

zur möglichsten Einheit verbinden, und so ein Bild vor unsere Seele stellen kann, das durch Lebendigkeit der Farbe, Gestalt und Gruppirung, durch Mannigfaltigkeit der zu einem schönen Ganzen vereinten Mittel unser Empfindungsvermögen auf eine hochst interessante Art in Anspruch nimmt"; *Wiener Allgemeine musikalische Zeitung*, 30 April 1823, as reproduced in *Franz Schubert: Dokumente, 1817–1830*, ed. Till Gerrit Waidelich (Tutzing: Hans Schneider, 1993), 157–58. I have slightly modified the translation of this document found in Deutsch, *The Schubert Reader*, 277–78.

19. "Ein solches Tonstück ist aus diesem Grunde wohl am meisten geeignet, die Gefühle, welche dem Tonsetzer bey der Erschaffung desselben beseelten, getreu in sich aufzunehmen und wiederzugeben, ja es kann füglich als ein Spiegel seiner Tiefe angesehen werden. Da nun ein Tonsetzer, wie Herr *Schubert*, der schon früher in seinen allgemein geschätzten Liedercompositionen ein tiefes Gemüth verrieth, mit einem solchen Seelengemählde auftritt, kann es der musikalischen Welt nicht anders als erfreulich seyn"; Waidlich, ed., *Franz Schubert: Dokumente*, 158. (I have again modified the translation found in Deutsch, *The Schubert Reader*, 277–78.)

20. Susan J. Wolfson, "A Lesson in Romanticism: Gendering the Soul," in *Lessons of Romanticism: A Critical Companion*, ed. Thomas Pfau and Robert F. Gleckner (Durham, N.C.: Duke University Press, 1998), 349–75.

21. Otto Erich Deutsch, ed., *Schubert: Die Dokumente seines Lebens* (Kassel: Bärenreiter, 1964), 326.

22. Deutsch, *The Schubert Reader*, 476.

23. Gibbs, *The Life of Schubert*, 95.

24. "Unverwüstlich" means neither "unimpaired" nor "irreducibly"; it is an adjective properly translated as "irrepressible," "inexhaustible," "indestructible," "durable," or "inveterate." And "Affektionen" means something more akin to "dispositions," "penchants," or "inclinations," rather than "passions." On "unverwüstlich," see *Langenscheidt's Encyclopedic Dictionary of the English and German Languages*, Part II: *German-English*, ed. Otto Springer, 2 vols. (Berlin: Langenscheidt, 1975; 5th ed., 1990), 2:1639; and Keith Spalding, *An Historical Dictionary of German Figurative Usage*, Fascicle 55 (Oxford: B. Blackwell, 1995), 2585–86, s.v. "verwüsten." On "Affektionen," see Jacob Grimm and Wilhelm Grimm, *Deutsches Wörterbuch*, rev. ed. (Leipzig: S. Hirzel, 1983), 1:cols. 1572–73; and Hans Schulz and Otto Basler, *Deutsches Fremdwörterbuch*, 2nd ed. (Berlin: W. De Gruyter, 1995), 1:174–77.

25. "Was würde im angeregten Gemüthen nach diesem Wechsel der Empfindungen am natürlichsten folgen? Doch wohl: eine, gleichsam verallgemeinerte, gehobene Stimmung überhaupt, nicht heftig, aber sehr lebhaft, nicht trübe, aber auch nicht leicht und lustig—eine kräftige, männlich-heitere Stimmung, gemischt aus Ernst zum grösseren, und aus Scherz zum kleineren Theile. Eben das ist der Ausdruck des langen, in technischer Behandlung sehr zusammengehaltenen Finale—Allegro vivace, A moll; Zweyvierteltakt." *Leipziger Allgemeine musikalische Zeitung*, 1 March 1826, as reproduced in *Franz Schubert: Dokumente*, 270–72. Again, I have somewhat modified the translation of this review found in Deutsch, *The Schubert Reader*, 512–15.

26. "So wie Hr. *Schubert* sich in seinen Liedern als tüchtiger Kenner der Harmonie zeigt, und seine Melodien durch eine schöne Folie der Accorde zu würzen versteht, so zeigt er sich hier in einer fast martialischen Stimmung, in welcher ein

wohlgewählter Harmonienwechsel das marschartige Mittelthema, in vielfältigen Veränderungen begleitet. Das moderate Tempo paßt sehr gut für den Gang der Ideen, und der Tonsetzer bleibt consequent in dem einmal aufgefaßten männlichen Charakter"; *Wiener Zeitschrift für Kunst, Literatur, Theater und Mode,* 14 August 1828, as reproduced in *Franz Schubert: Dokumente,* 428. English translation from Deutsch, *The Schubert Reader,* 799, modified slightly.

27. Linda Dowling, *Hellenism and Homosexuality in Victorian Oxford* (Ithaca, N.Y.: Cornell University Press, 1994), 5–12; Alan Sinfield, *The Wilde Century: Effeminacy, Oscar Wilde and the Queer Moment* (New York: Columbia University Press, 1994), 25–51; David Halperin, "How to Do the History of Male Homosexuality," 92–94. The arguments of these authors actually concern the term "effeminate," to which "manly" was ordinarily posed as the antonym. The sobriquet "effeminate" could be applied to men who engaged in sex with other men and also to men who overindulged their sexual passion for women. Both behaviors could equally debilitate the subject and render him unfit to serve a larger civic good. On the relationship between civil society and sexual behavior in Germany in the period just before Schubert, see Isabel V. Hull, *Sexuality, State, and Civil Society in Germany, 1700–1815* (Ithaca, N.Y., and London: Cornell University Press, 1996), 229–56.

28. On the relationship between sex and gender, see my article "Gender," in *The New Grove Dictionary of Music and Musicians,* 2nd ed., ed. Stanley Sadie and John Tyrrell (London: Macmillan, 2001), 9:645–47.

29. "Schubert ist ein Mädchencharakter, an jenen gehalten, bei weitem geschwätziger, weicher und breiter; gegen jenen ein Kind, das sorglos unter den Riesen spielt. . . . Zwar bringt auch er seine Kraftstellen, bietet auch er Massen auf; doch verhält er sich immer wie Weib zum Mann, der befiehlt, wo jenes bittet und überredet. Dies alles aber nur in Vergleich zu Beethoven; gegen andere ist er noch Mann genug, ja der kühnste und freigeistigste der neueren Musiker"; *Neue Zeitschrift für Musik,* 1838, as transmitted in Robert Schumann, *Gesammelte Schriften über Musik und Musiker,* ed. Martin Kreisig, 5th ed. (Leipzig: Breitkopf & Härtel, 1914), 1:330. I have modified the English translation found in Robert Schumann, *On Music and Musicians,* ed. Konrad Wolff, trans. Paul Rosenfeld (New York: Norton, 1969), 117. One wonders if Nikolaus Lenau felt the influence of Schumann's critique when he wrote to Maximilian Löwenthal on 19 November 1839 (the anniversary of Schubert's death): "Schubert's compositions are wearing thin. There is a certain coquetry, an unmanly effeminacy about them." ("Schuberts Kompositionen nützen sich ab. Es ist eine gewisse Koketterie, eine unmännliche Weichlichkeit in ihnen"; Otto Erich Deutsch, ed., *Schubert: Die Erinnerungen seiner Freunde* [Leipzig: Breitkopf & Härtel, 1957; reprint, Wiesbaden: Breitkopf & Härtel, 1983], 284.)

30. On this project, see Sanna Pederson, "On the Task of the Music Historian: The Myth of the Symphony after Beethoven," *repercussions* 2/2 (Fall 1993): 5–30. See also her "Beethoven and Masculinity," in *Beethoven and His World,* ed. Scott Burnham and Michael P. Steinberg (Princeton, N.J.: Princeton University Press, 2000), 313–31.

What needs also to be considered with respect to Schumann's pairing of Schubert against Beethoven is the manner in which the configuration of the relationship between these two composers changed after their deaths. That is, during Schubert's life, comparisons between the two composers—a relatively rare occurrence—generally placed them on equal footing (see, for example, the 1826 review of the A-

Minor Sonata cited above). After Schubert's death, the comparisons came more frequently and worked more often to Schubert's disadvantage (a good source is the collection of reviews in Otto Brusatti, *Schubert im Wiener Vormärz: Dokumente 1829–1848* [Graz: Akadem. Druck u. Verlagsanst., 1978]).

31. Gramit, "Constructing a Victorian Schubert," 71–73.

32. For one such exploration, see Philip Brett, "Piano Four-Hands: Schubert and the Performance of Gay Male Desire," *19th-Century Music* 21 (1997): 149–76.

11

"La Belle Exécution": Johann Nepomuk Hummel's Treatise and the Art of Playing the Pianoforte

Mark Kroll

Music instruction manuals have a long and colorful history. Typically written in the first-person singular, these treatises usually contain in equal measure concrete objective facts, eyewitness accounts of contemporary practices, and the author's highly personal opinions. They are therefore important sources of information, and also make for some interesting reading.[1] Some of the best known are those by Juan Bermudo, Tomás de Sancta María, and Girolamo Diruta in the sixteenth and seventeenth centuries, and Michel de Saint-Lambert, François Couperin, Johann Joachim Quantz, Leopold Mozart, and Carl Philipp Emanuel Bach in the eighteenth.[2] In the early decades of the nineteenth century, however, there was a virtual explosion of methods, particularly for the piano. This was the result of a variety of social, political, and cultural factors, including the rapid rise of the middle class, the dominance of the piano as the instrument of choice in the concert hall and in private homes, and the focus on the role of the individual in society.

Piano treatises established or reinforced the basic techniques of playing the instrument and its repertoire, but their relevance extends well beyond the music of their time. They heralded the era of the modern piano style, and developed the principles of piano playing which are, with some modifications, still valid today. Short methods were written by local teachers, and major treatises were published by eminent figures such as Daniel Gottlob Türk (1789/1802), Jan Ladislav Dussek (1796), Muzio Clementi (1801 and 1817–26), Louis Adam (1804), Carl Czerny (1839), Pierre-Joseph-Guillaume Zimmerman (1840)—and Johann Nepomuk Hummel (1827).[3]

Hummel's contribution to the genre is one of the most important. A renowned teacher, conductor, composer, and arranger, Hummel was considered during his lifetime to be the greatest pianist in Europe. His many tours took him as far as Poland and Russia, and he was particularly admired in England.[4] Hummel stands both as witness to and participant in the transformation from the classical to the romantic style. Here was a musician who was a student and friend of Mozart, a protegé of Haydn, and a colleague of Beethoven, but who also knew and was admired by Chopin and Schumann. Yet his accomplishments have been largely over-shadowed by those of his contemporaries, and his work is generally un-known today.[5]

Due to the connections of his father Johannes, Nepomuk had access early in his life to the most influential composers and pedagogues. Born in Bratislava in 1778, he moved to Vienna in 1785 or 1786 when Johannes became director of the Theater auf der Wieden. Shortly thereafter, father and son visited Mozart in the hope that he would accept the young Nepomuk as a student.[6] Not only did Mozart agree to teach the prodigy, but he also insisted that he live with him. These two years of instruction and life expe-rience between 1786 and 1788 determined Hummel's future artistic direc-tion and career. At the end of this period of apprenticeship, Mozart, per-haps recalling his own childhood experiences with *his* father, suggested that Johannes take his son on tour. In December of 1788 the pair em-barked on a trip that would last five years and take them through Ger-many, Denmark, the Netherlands, England, and Scotland. In England, Nepomuk studied with Muzio Clementi and established a close relation-ship with Joseph Haydn, who later would recommend him for the post of Konzertmeister to Prince Nikolaus Esterházy. He also studied composition with Johann Georg Albrechtsberger and Antonio Salieri in Vienna before assuming the post at Eisenstadt in 1804.

Hummel was successful at Esterháza, and was even entrusted there with the première of Haydn's *Die Schöpfung*.[7] But the young man was restless. He left the provincial court in 1811 and returned to Vienna, where he earned a living as a free-lance musician. During this period, he also contin-ued his association with Beethoven, whom he had met in Eisenstadt in 1807 (if not earlier) when Beethoven presented the Mass in C Major, op. 86, which had been commissioned by the Prince.[8] Even though the two virtuosos shared many of the same pedagogic influences, their personali-ties and artistic temperaments could not have been more different, and their relationship fluctuated between warm admiration and open hostility.[9] Leaving Vienna, Hummel served briefly as Kapellmeister to the Royal Württemberg Court (1816–18), but it proved too provincial for his taste. He resigned on 12 November 1818, and in 1819 moved to Weimar to accept the position of Kapellmeister to the Grand Duke of Saxe-Weimar, where he would remain for the rest of his life.

Weimar provided the ideal environment in which Hummel could realize his full potential. As director of the court chapel and theater, he conducted the latest symphonies, operas, and concertos by Mozart, Beethoven, Gluck, and others. These included some of the earliest performances of Weber's

Der Freischütz and, according to the *Chronik des Weimarischen Hoftheaters,* "50 performances of Mozart's *Don Giovanni.*"[10] Hummel thus was able to absorb the most current trends in style and composition. In addition, between 1820 and 1830 he transcribed many of the orchestral works he conducted for a chamber ensemble of piano, flute, violin, and cello. These delightful transcriptions provide important insights into the performance practices of this music, and into the musical and cultural life of Europe in the early nineteenth century. Moreover, their difficult keyboard parts give a clear indication of Hummel's virtuosity as a pianist.[11]

In an era of transition from royal patronage to a (relatively) free market system, Hummel the artist also proved to be an excellent businessman. His treatise and transcriptions, for example, clearly were written with an eye toward the mass market. Hummel's correspondence with publishers and sponsors shows him to have been an astute negotiator, and he lived in comfortable circumstances at his beloved home and garden in Weimar. Hummel's preference for bourgeois comforts can be seen in a letter to Peters of 29 November 1823, in which he wrote that "I have now been enjoying my lovely house, and I do not want to take any trips next year, but rather [want] to remain in Weimar."[12] He also was a tireless advocate for copyright protection for composers, and even attempted to establish the first composer's union in Germany.[13]

In Weimar, Hummel established himself as one of Europe's important and, not surprisingly, most expensive piano teachers. The leading pianists of the day, including Sigismond Thalberg, Ferdinand Hiller, Adolf Henselt, and Czerny, flocked to work with him. All that he learned as a pedagogue, composer, conductor, pianist, and arranger is revealed in one of his most important legacies, the monumental treatise *A Complete Theoretical and Practical Course of Instructions, on the Art of Playing the Piano Forte.*[14]

Published in English in 1827, German in 1828, and French in 1829, it was highly successful and popular. The present article offers a summary of its contents, placed within the context of its relationship to contemporary musical thinking.

Overview of Hummel's Treatise

The treatise begins with a "Preface" and "Preliminary Observations Addressed to Parents and Teachers of Music." This is followed by three parts, each divided into several sections and chapters. Part I, entitled "Elementary Instructions," contains chapters such as "On Sitting at the Piano-Forte" and "On Holding the Body, the Arms, the Hands and the Fingers," plus a complete curriculum on the fundamentals of music: an explanation of notation, a description of the layout of the keyboard, and lessons on note values, key signatures, time signatures, scales, and the words and symbols for tempo, rhythm, dynamics, and character. The format is similar to most other treatises of the period. Consistent with Hummel's nature, however, his treatise is almost numbingly thorough (and not without some pedantry). In fact, no other such publication contains as much material as that presented by Hummel. For example, he provides over 2,000 individual exercises covering everything that the fingers, the hand, and the musician will encounter in music. To cite a few instances, there are 144 exercises on rhythm, 241 on finger extensions, 234 on every finger combination imaginable, 286 exercises specifically dealing with the passage of the thumb above and below the other fingers, and even six on the performance of trills accompanied by other voices in the same hand. There are also footnoted comments for some of the individual exercises. Hummel's longer musical examples include both original compositions and excerpts from works by other composers, such as Haydn, Mozart, Beethoven, Clementi, and Dussek.

Part II is concerned with fingering, touch, articulation, and hand distribution (i.e., passages with hand crossings), and concludes with a separate chapter devoted to playing works in the "severe style" (i.e., fugues by Bach, Handel, and others), which Hummel considers the most difficult style of all.

Part III is perhaps of greatest interest and relevance to professional musicians. Here Hummel offers his observations on ornamentation, the subtleties and refinements of playing (the charming description in the French edition is "La Belle Exécution"), the differences between English and German (i.e., Viennese) piano actions, the use of pedals, the utility of Maelzel's metronome, improvisation, and tuning.

The Preface and "Preliminary Observations"

The Preface begins with Hummel's explanation for writing the treatise, and in this he follows a standard convention in which the author assumes an air of modesty and accommodation. As Hummel puts it, he wrote his treatise only "at the request of many friends and music-masters . . . adapted to the present newly commenced epoch of this instrument."[15] It is here that the authors usually make a claim for the superiority of their chosen instrument. Hummel therefore praises the piano for its leading role in contemporary musical life, writing that "the Piano-Forte is at present more generally cultivated than any other musical instrument" since "it is the least likely of any to prove injurious to the health of even the feeblest individual, and . . . the performer does not require the cooperation of any other instrument to produce the fullest and most perfect harmony."[16] He goes on to describe the dramatic changes in piano music that have occurred during his lifetime, in which "the great and increasing difficulties daily presented to the player, have rendered necessary a considerable change in the principles hitherto established."[17]

The treatise continues with advice on the choice of a suitable teacher and good pedagogy. Here again, Hummel follows the model of previous treatise authors. That is, money should be no object, the student must not overpractice, and the teacher must be diligent in the attention paid to his charges. For example, in the "Preliminary Observations" Hummel, ever the good businessman, urges parents to "direct their attention less towards cheapness of instruction" than to a competent teacher.[18] He then makes a good suggestion, which unfortunately would be impractical today: "For the first half year, and, if possible, for even the first entire year, every beginner requires one hours [*sic*] daily instruction." But the student should not practice too much:

> Many entertain the erroneous opinion that to arrive at excellence, it is necessary to practice for at least 6 or 7 hours every day; but I can assure them, that a regular, daily, attentive study, of at most three hours, is sufficient for this purpose; any practice beyond this, damps the spirits, produces a mechanical, rather than an expressive and impassioned style of playing, and is generally disadvantageous to the performer.[19]

Hummel was admired for his infallible sense of rhythm and uncanny ability to play in time. For example, Czerny remarked that "Hummel himself played his compositions in such a constant tempo that one could almost always have set the metronome beat to it."[20] It should therefore come as no surprise that from the outset Hummel twice urges the teacher to "give the pupil a clear and correct manner of marking time . . . and habituate the pupil to the strict observance of time, and to count while playing."[21]

Part I of the Treatise

Part I of Hummel's treatise begins with the proper position of sitting at the piano, and the correct use of the body, arms, hands, and fingers. Hummel's overriding principle was to maintain a natural and completely relaxed approach to playing the piano, in which the maximum effect is achieved with a minimum of motion and effort. Contemporary witnesses often observed this feature in his own playing.[22]

Hummel used and taught what is essentially a finger technique. The elbows are loosely held close to the body and are kept on the same horizontal plane as that of the wrists and hands, which are always quiet and relaxed. The fingers remain close to the surface of the keys, as if glued to them. He wrote, "In general, to attain the necessary facility, steadiness, and certainty . . . we must avoid every violent movement of the elbows and hands; and the muscles must not be exerted, beyond what a free and *quiet* position of the hand requires."[23] This approach was shared by most of the teachers and performers of the time, including Beethoven, Clementi, Adam, and Zimmerman. It also was true of Chopin. Drawings of Chopin at the piano by Jakob Götzenberger and Elisa Radziwill show him in Hummel's sitting position.[24] This position also recalls the harpsichord style of the eighteenth century, particularly in France (e.g., that of Couperin and Rameau), and it is the approach I teach to my students today.

There were some divergent opinions in the late-eighteenth and nineteenth centuries, however. Dussek wanted the hands to be free, the fingers elongated, and the wrist used freely as an integral part of the technique. An interesting problem arose regarding exactly where to sit at the piano, since the range of the instrument was being expanded from five to six and one-half octaves during this time. Hummel and others placed the pianist at middle C, but Kalkbrenner suggested that, because pianos now had a larger compass, one should sit at middle G.[25] On the other hand, the attitude of Franz Liszt was unique and unconventional. According to François-Joseph Fétis, Liszt "is the only pianist who has no fixed position . . . sometimes sitting left, sometimes right. His body is in a perpetual state of agitation."[26] Fétis observed, moreover, that "his talent is the most complete deviation . . . from the school of Hummel that one can imagine."[27]

Such a variety of opinions reflects a dramatic quantum shift in piano playing, which occurred between 1820 and 1830. The classical approach of Hummel, Beethoven, and others was replaced by Liszt and his followers with the "modern" style of pianism. Contemporary musicians and commentators were well aware that a major change was taking place in their midst. For example, Czerny laid out several basic styles: "Clementi's style," "Cramer and Dussek's style," "Mozart's school," and "the Beethoven style." He then added "the modern brilliant school founded by Hummel, Kalkbrenner and Moscheles," and noted that "out of these schools, a new style is just now beginning to be developed, which may be called a mixture of and improvement on all those which preceded it. It is chiefly represented by Thalberg, Chopin, Liszt and other young artists."[28]

The second and third sections of Part I deal with keys, scales, basic principles of rhythm, repeat signs, dynamics, and preparatory trill exercises. There are many interesting details here. For example, Hummel informs us that, if the last note in a measure contains an accidental and the first note in the next measure is the same pitch but contains no accidental, the previous accidental is retained (see example 11.1). Hummel demonstrates the two ways of phrasing sextuplets (see example 11.2). He also shows how to play septuplets without losing the basic beat (see example 11.3). Hummel also offers advice on how to play passages of two against three, urging the young pianist to first play the second eighth-note of the duplet figure together with the third eighth-note of the triplet figure, and only later to

Example 11.1. Hummel, *Complete Theoretical and Practical Course of Instructions, on the Art of Playing the Piano Forte* (London: T. Boosey, 1827), Part I, Section II, ch. 1, p. 19. Reproduced by permission of the British Library.

Example 11.2. Hummel, *Complete Theoretical and Practical Course of Instructions, on the Art of Playing the Piano Forte* (London: T. Boosey, 1827), Part I, Section II, ch. 2, p. 26. Reproduced by permission of the British Library.

Example 11.3. Hummel, *Complete Theoretical and Practical Course of Instructions, on the Art of Playing the Piano Forte* (London: T. Boosey, 1827), Part I, Section II, ch. 2, p. 27. Reproduced by permission of the British Library.

perform these multi-rhythms as notated. And he makes the good suggestion that one should first play the scale of the key in which a piece is written, as a kind of prelude, in order to accustom the ears and hands to the tonality.

As noted earlier, Hummel was very concerned about rhythm. He gives a clear description of metronomic time, tempo, time signatures, strong and weak beats, as well as basic conducting patterns which the student should use when practicing a work. He does not comment on the theory that time signatures and note values give clear indications about the tempo and character of a work.

Hummel's approach to articulation is generally consistent with that of his contemporaries, and also recalls practices from previous centuries. He describes three basic categories: *legato, staccato,* and *portamento.* To Hummel, *legato* is the basic touch, sometimes but not always indicated by a slur. This opinion was held by almost all the other pedagogues. For example, Nicolo Pasquali wrote that "the legato is the Touch that the Treatise endeavores to teach, being a general Touch fit for almost all Kinds of Passages."[29] Clementi stated that "the best general rule, is to keep down the keys of the instrument, the FULL LENGTH OF EVERY NOTE."[30] Adam wrote in particular detail about *legato* and the other varieties of touch. *Legato* was his "default" touch as well:

> Sometimes the composer indicates the musical phrase that ought to be slurred, but when he leaves the choice of legato or staccato to the taste of the performer, it would be better to use the legato and reserve the staccato, in order to apply to certain passages . . . the advantages of the legato.

To achieve this, "the hand must never leave the keyboard." "The liaisons are only done with the *fingers quite glued to the keys* [emphasis added]." Furthermore, Adam also suggested an articulation that is very familiar to harpsichordists, the technique of "overlegato": "[H]old down the first [note] and raise it after one-half the value of the second."[31] This technique, which I have dubbed the "digital damper," is a crucial aspect of performance practices of the period.[32] By using it, the pianist is not only able to achieve the most refined and varied legato, without the use of the pedals, but more importantly, he can highlight the melodic, harmonic, and structural elements of a composition. Almost every pianist in the eighteenth and early-nineteenth centuries practiced or taught this technique, including Beethoven (e.g., in his annotations to the Cramer *Etudes*). Adam, for example, wrote: "When the highest notes form a melody in those places where there is a slur . . . all the notes may then be held under the fingers."[33]

Hummel's treatise features a number of excellent examples of the use of overlegato and holding down notes. He writes, "There are certain groups of notes which include a melody, and which must not be played detached. . . . [T]he delivery of them must be connected, and the melody brought out."[34] He offers an example (see example 11.4).

Example 11.4. Hummel, *Complete Theoretical and Practical Course of Instructions, on the Art of Playing the Piano Forte* (London: T. Boosey, 1827), Part I, Section III, ch. 2, p. 60. Reproduced by permission of the British Library.

Hummel's *portamento*, notated by dots and slurs above the notes, follows standard practice. It is played with weight and some degree of separation, and is used primarily in "singing" passages. Here there is no disagreement among teachers.

Of particular note, however, is his interpretation of the two signs used for *détaché* or *staccato*, the dot (.) and the wedge ('). This was a source of confusion then, and remains so to the present day. Hummel uses only one symbol, the wedge, making no distinction between it and the dot. As one might expect, he strongly admonishes the player never to lift the hand when playing *staccato*, but rather to achieve the effect only with the fingers, which are pulled towards the interior of the hand.

Nevertheless, there is no unanimity of opinion among Hummel's contemporaries regarding the use of these symbols. Türk does agree that the two signs have the same meaning but he remarks that "some would like to indicate by the stroke that a shorter staccato be played than indicated by the dot." He also adds that "in playing detached notes one lifts the finger from the key when almost half the value of that note is past."[35] On the other hand, Adam holds that there are three basic articulations. Each is indicated by a different symbol, and each implies a distinctly different performance (see example 11.5).

Example 11.5. Adam, *Méthode de piano du Conservatoire* (1804; reprint, Geneva: Minkoff, 1974), Article 7, pp. 154–55. Reproduced by permission.

There was a similar lack of unanimity regarding the meaning of words for tempo. Hummel lists the following tempo indications, from slowest to fastest: *grave, largo, larghetto, lento, adagio, andantino, andante, allegretto, allegro, vivacissimo, presto,* and *prestissimo.*[36] Adam, on the other hand, considered *largo* to be slower than *grave* (as did Sébastien de Brossard [1703], Jean-Jacques Rousseau [1768], Johann Philipp Kirnberger [1779], and Türk [1789]), and he omitted *lento*.[37] Some composers did not consider *grave* a tempo at all, but rather a mood or character. Türk, for example, defined *grave* as "serious, therefore more or less slow."[38]

The term *andantino* was a particular source of controversy. Most musicians, including Rousseau (1768), Türk (1789), Clementi (1801), Justin Heinrich Knecht (1803), Adam (1804), and Friedrich Kalkbrenner (1830), agreed with Hummel that *andantino* was slower than *andante*. However, others like Heinrich Christoph Koch and Czerny defined *andantino* as faster than *andante*.[39] The confusion was so great that Beethoven pleaded in 1813:

> If among the airs that you may send me to be arranged in the future there are Andantinos, please tell me whether Andantino is to be understood as meaning faster or slower than Andante, for this term, like so many in music, is of so indefinite a significance that Andantino sometimes approaches an Allegro and sometimes, on the other hand, is played like Adagio.[40]

In frustration, some nineteenth-century composers wanted to give up tempo words altogether, as do many composers today. In a letter to Ignaz von Mosel around 1817, Beethoven wrote: "I have long been thinking of abandoning those absurd descriptive terms, Allegro, Andante, Adagio, Presto; and Maelzel's metronome affords us the best opportunity of doing so."[41] To resolve the controversy, Johann Adam Hiller called for a musical "parliament." No meeting seems to have been held.[42]

Hummel concludes Part I with a graded list of recommended pieces for study. His choices, which reflect both current musical taste and some political realities, include both the masters and lesser-known composers, and it is interesting that Hummel places J. S. Bach and Handel at the very top. The "Selections for the Beginner" include "6 pieces faciles" by Hummel, "18 pieces faciles" by Ignaz Pleyel, and works of Dussek, Friedrich Kuhlau, and Clementi. "In a more advanced stage," he suggests "easier works" by Pleyel, Hummel, Haydn, and Mozart. "When the Pupil shall have attained a still greater power of execution," Hummel says to "place before him Mozart, Clementi, Dussek, Beethoven," plus Clementi's *Gradus ad Parnassum* and Cramer's *Studies*. Finally, the student should play works by J. S. Bach and Handel "as a practice in the strict or fugue style of composition, and as a means of forming the taste for the loftiest departments of the art."[43]

Part II of the Treatise

Section I of Part II deals with fingering and ornamentation. Such an enormous topic cannot be summarized within the scope of this article, particularly in view of Hummel's exhaustive treatment. But let us consider a few of the essential points.

Hummel's approach to fingering is essentially the same as the modern system in use today. He begins with the observation that

> the diffusion of an increased facility of execution on the Piano-Forte, and the inventions of new passages and combinations of notes, have given rise to a more varied application of the fingers, and have rendered necessary a system of fingering more adequate to the modern and improved style of playing this instrument.[44]

He then provides detailed rules and copious exercises on every possible finger combination, such as: "Passage of the thumb under the other fingers, and of the other fingers over the thumb," "Omission of one or more fingers," "Substitution of one finger for another on the recurrence of the same note," "Extensions and skips," and "Use of the thumb and little finger on the black keys" (which he employed more often than did his colleagues). Consistent with his instructions in Part I, Hummel again reminds the reader to "keep the hand position quiet," especially with jumps and extensions. Repeated notes in the right hand are generally executed with the fingering 4-3-2-1-4-3-2-1. Many of the other fingerings are interesting as well, and range from the expected to some idiosyncratic combinations.[45]

Hummel's chapters on ornamentation are likewise thorough, covering all the signs and figures for ornaments. He first offers some technical advice on playing trills, recommending that the trill ("shake") be played by all five fingers, and offers an exercise for this purpose which was "communicated to me practically by MOZART himself."[46]

He then tackles the vexing question of the starting note for the trill. The conventional wisdom has held that the standard eighteenth-century practice of beginning a trill with the upper auxiliary gradually was superceded in the early nineteenth century by a main-note start. However, here we again find that there was no unanimity of opinion among Hummel's contemporaries. Early in the century Koch wrote:

> Music teachers do not agree in regard to the beginning of this ornament [the trill]; the majority maintain . . . that the beginning of the trill must be made with the upper auxiliary; others, on the contrary, assert that one should always begin it with the main note.[47]

Some other musicians also took the *laissez faire* approach. For instance, Nicolas Joseph Hüllmandel wrote that "the Shake begins indiscriminately with either of the two Shaken Notes, or sometimes by a Note under those of the Shake."[48] Early in the nineteenth century, violinists Pierre Baillot, Pierre Rode, and Rodolphe Kreutzer believed that the manner of starting was determined by the taste of the performer.[49] Although Adam wrote that he preferred a main-note start to a trill, a number of his printed examples indicate a preference for the upper auxiliary.[50]

Hummel's approach is clear and unequivocal: his trill begins on the main note. He writes:

> With regard to the shake, we have hitherto followed the practice of the ancient masters, and begun it always with the subsidiary note above; a custom to all appearances founded upon the earliest rules laid down for the voice in singing, and which were subsequently adopted for instruments. But . . . no reason exists that the same rules which were given for the management of the voice, must also serve for the piano-forte, without admitting of alteration or improvement.[51]

Therefore, "every shake should begin with the note itself, over which it stands, and not with the subsidiary note above, unless the contrary be expressly indicated."[52] Moreover, Hummel recommends that a termination should generally be added to a trill, even if not expressly notated. He follows with detailed realizations of almost every ornament.

Regarding the interpretation of appoggiaturas, Hummel conformed to a standard practice that was described by C. P. E. Bach and followed for the next fifty years: "The long or accented Appogiatura [*sic*] borrows one half the value of its principal note," and "Before a note with a dot, which by this means consists of three parts, the appogiatura borrows the whole value of the principal note which itself must be played to the dot" (see example 11.6).[53]

Example 11.6. Hummel, *Complete Theoretical and Practical Course of Instructions, on the Art of Playing the Piano Forte* (London: T. Boosey, 1827), Part III, Section I, ch. 6, p. 11. Reproduced by permission of the British Library.

Hummel ventures into the murky area of the difference between the long, variable appoggiatura and the invariable short appoggiatura. There was and continues to be confusion regarding the execution of these two types of appoggiaturas, and Hummel's contemporaries were not always in agreement or precise in their notation. In 1789 Türk wrote:

> Many copyists and probably even some composers still have the bad habit of notating all appoggiaturas alike, without regard for the following longer or shorter note, for example, by notating them as eighths or sixteenths, even though these

little notes should sometimes be notated as quarters or eighths. One should therefore not be misled by the note shape into playing an appoggiatura before a half note with only the value of a sixteenth, even when it is written in this way.[54]

This lack of clarity in notation was as frustrating then as it is today. Türk continued:

Perhaps music would be even better served if all long appoggiaturas were indicated by notes of usual size in the values they should have, as some composers are already doing. Why all composers do not make use of this more certain method of notation is something I do not understand. Many inaccuracies in execution could without doubt be avoided by this. It would certainly not be wrong to notate a composition as it is supposed to be played.[55]

Milchmeyer observed in 1797 that

as our taste in very many things has improved during the last twenty years, many of the best composers now generally write all the ornaments of their pieces with the usual large notes, according to the true value that each should receive. Personally I find that very good.[56]

Yet standard rules of performance practice were not the norm even during their supposed time of acceptance. This should not be surprising. Art is not science, and music has always been characterized by a wide range of players and personalities. As Zimmerman aptly put it in 1840:

It is diversity of talent which makes the charm of art. Would it not be tiresome if Kalkbrenner, Liszt, and Thalberg were to play in the same fashion? It is the completely different character of their talent which causes their great success.[57]

Part III of the Treatise

The conclusion of the treatise deals with aspects of achieving what Hummel terms, in the French edition, "La Belle Exécution." That is, Hummel attempts to bring the player to the highest levels of refinement and artistry. At the same time, he allows us a glimpse into the mind and the actual performance practices of a great artist. Part III is therefore the least pedantic and perhaps most interesting part of the book.

The best advice comes first. Hummel writes: "Learn beauty in taste by listening to the best performers and Singers."[58] He continues with some uncomplimentary observations about empty virtuosity, singling out C. P. E. Bach in particular: ". . . such dexterous players surprise the ear, (as Ph. Em. Bach expresses himself), but do not delight it; they astonish the under-

standing without satisfying it." And he warns against excessive ornamentation, the "capricious dragging or slackening of time," and, perhaps with
Liszt in mind, "unnatural elevations of the arm."[59] Once again Hummel
asks players to "never hurry the time in passages."[60] But one should not
infer from this that Hummel's playing was without rubato and flexibility.
The subtle manipulation of time and rhythm is an essential ingredient of
any artistic performance, and Hummel is no stranger to this concept. However, he cautions that this "must take place almost imperceptibly" and that
"the graces must . . . neither add to nor take from the strict time."[61] One of
the most interesting and important examples in the treatise is an extensive
excerpt from the Allegro of his own Concerto in A Minor, op. 85, in which
Hummel notates that which cannot be notated—a kaleidoscope of subtle
changes in time, dynamics, and touch (see example 11.7).

Example 11.7. Hummel, *Complete Theoretical and Practical Course of Instructions, on the Art of Playing the Piano Forte* (London: T. Boosey, 1827), Part III,
Section II, ch. 2, p. 49. Reproduced by permission of the British Library.

Hummel nevertheless remained a strong advocate for the use of the
metronome. He repeatedly emphasized the need to maintain a strict sense
of time earlier in the treatise, and here he devotes an entire chapter to the
metronome, stating that it will benefit both "Amateurs and even Artists,
who were in the habit of accelerating the time to excess." Amusingly,
Hummel the businessman could not resist a commercial suggestion:

Every Composer and Musician ought, by all means, to be in possession of a
Metronome. . . . This, it is hoped, would induce Maelzel to offer his metronome
to the Public at such a price as would enable every Musician and Amateur to
procure one.[62]

The relationship between rhetoric and music was widely discussed in the eighteenth and nineteenth centuries. It was recognized by composers such as J. S. Bach, Mozart, and Beethoven, theorists like Türk and Zimmerman, and many others, and it is an important but poorly understood aspect of musical interpretation. Hummel's explanation is clear and succinct: "As in speaking, it is necessary to lay an emphasis on certain syllables or words . . . so in music the same thing is requisite."[63] He further offers the valuable suggestion of placing imaginary words under a purely instrumental melody, in order to determine its natural phrasing and articulation.

Hummel's treatment of the pedals is quite conservative, and it is evident that they should be used with discretion when performing music for the early fortepiano. Not surprisingly, there was again a wide range of opinions about the application of the pedals during this period. The majority of pianists until the time of Liszt used them sparingly, particularly in Germany. As late as 1830, Kalkbrenner still reported that "in Germany the use of the pedals is scarcely known."[64] This is, admittedly, something of an overstatement. On the other hand, figures such as Daniel Steibelt and Milchmeyer were well known for their use (and abuse) of the pedals, and they often were accused of "charlatanism." Milchmeyer wrote extensively about the use of the damper pedal and the exploitation of every other possible "mutation" on the instrument. At one point he even offered unintentionally comic instructions on how to raise and lower the piano lid manually in order to create extreme dynamic effects.[65] Hummel's attitude about pedalling was simple and direct: "[A] truly great Artist has no occasion for Pedals to work upon the audience by expression and power," and they should be employed with discretion.[66] He then gives several musical excerpts showing when and how the pedal should be applied (see Example 11.8).

Example 11.8. Hummel, *Complete Theoretical and Practical Course of Instructions, on the Art of Playing the Piano Forte* (London: T. Boosey, 1827), Part III, Section III, ch. 3, p. 63. Reproduced by permission of the British Library.

The action and construction of the piano was changing rapidly during Hummel's lifetime, and he discusses some of the noteworthy attributes of the various types and styles prevalent at the time he was writing. In particular, he talks about the difference between English and German (i.e.,

Viennese) pianos. As a touring artist, Hummel encountered almost every style of piano, and readers today who have had the opportunity to play on both English and Viennese instruments of the time will immediately recognize the accuracy of his description. Hummel obviously preferred the Viennese action but knew that he had to be both practical and diplomatic. He wrote that, of the two styles, the German "is played upon with great facility as to touch," and the English "with considerably less ease." "The German piano," he continued, "allows the performer to impart to his execution every possible degree of light and shade, speaks clearly and promptly, has a round fluty tone, . . . and does not impede rapidity of execution by requiring too great an effort." Hummel, the frugal burgher, also commented on the price: "These instruments are likewise durable, and cost but about half the price of the English piano-forte." Not wishing to insult his English publishers and audience, however, he quickly added: "To the English construction however, we must not refuse the praises due on the score to its durability and fullness of tone, even though it . . . does not admit of the same facility of execution as the German; the touch is much heavier, the keys sink much deeper," and repetition is not as easy to achieve. Hummel then provided detailed advice on how best to negotiate the action of each instrument.[67]

A full chapter is devoted to tuning. The question of which temperaments are best for each musical style and era is indeed a difficult one, and the subject can often raise the blood pressure of scholars, historical performers, and instrument builders. The use of unequal temperaments in the music of earlier periods is certainly valid, but, because of the harmonic complexities and chromaticism of the music of Hummel and his contemporaries, the few advantages of using an unequal temperament are far outweighed by the utility of an equal system. Hummel's advice here is sound and pragmatic: he offers only one choice—equal temperament—because of the inadequacies of the "earlier systems" and the fact that they "cannot be so easily put into practice."[68] Finally, he even assures the reader that, if a tuner were to follow his instructions, the piano would remain in tune "not for a few hours or days, but for weeks or even months."[69] Considering the delicate nature of fortepianos and the vagaries of temperature and humidity, Hummel's claim seems overly optimistic.

Hummel also echoes the frequent complaint about the lack of a standard tuning and pitch—that, for example, one finds different systems in Dresden, Berlin, and Vienna. He wishes

> that a uniform mode of tuning were universally introduced. To what disagreeables [*sic*] are we not exposed, particularly with regard to wind instruments. . . . Would that in all countries they would at last agree upon some uniform system.[70]

Finally, Hummel even tries to teach musicians how to improvise. Hummel was as renowned for his skill in improvisation as he was for his performance of written compositions, and many of his concert programs ended with such a display. In fact, he seemed to prefer improvising to playing notated music: "I confess, I always felt less embarrassment in extemporizing before an audience of 2 or 3,000 persons than in executing any written composition to which I was slavishly tied down."[71] Hummel provides a clear and personal description about how he taught himself to improvise, and assures the student that he will be able to do the same if he follows this advice.

Johann Nepomuk Hummel's treatise opens a window onto a crucial period in the history of the piano. It also provides a compelling picture of the artist and the man, one who speaks to us today with the voice of exceptional authority—that of performer, teacher, businessman, composer, and friend to the greatest musicians. Its detailed instructions, lucid descriptions, and artistic philosophy enable one to enter into the world of nineteenth-century pianism and performance.

Notes

1. For a survey of many of the more interesting treatises, see Mark Kroll, "The Self-Help Bookshelf," *Early Music America* 8, no. 1 (spring 2002): 22–26.

2. Juan Bermudo, *Declaración de instrumentos musicales* (Osuna: Juan de Leon, 1550); Tomás de Sancta María, *El arte de tañer fantasía* (Valladolid: Impressor por F. Fernandez de Cordoua, 1565); Girolamo Diruta, *Il transilvano* (Venice: Vincenti, 1593 and 1609); Michel de Saint-Lambert, *Les principes du clavecin* (Paris: Christophe Ballard, 1702); François Couperin, *L'Art de toucher le clavecin* (Paris: Chés Mr. Couperin, 1716; rev. ed., 1717); Johann Joachim Quantz, *Versuch einer Anweisung die Flöte traversiere zu spielen* (Berlin: Voss, 1752); Leopold Mozart, *Versuch einer gründlichen Violinschule* (Augsburg: In Verlag des Verfassers, 1756); Carl Philipp Emanuel Bach, *Versuch über die wahre Art das Clavier zu spielen* (Berlin: In Verlegung des Auctoris, 1753 and 1762).

3. Daniel Gottlob Türk, *Klavierschule, oder Anweisung zum Klavierspielen für Lehrer und Lernende* (Leipzig and Halle: Schwickert, 1789; enlarged 2d ed., Leipzig and Halle: Schwickert, 1802); Jan Ladislav Dussek, *Instructions on the Art of Playing the Piano Forte or Harpsichord* (London: Corri, Dussek, 1796); Muzio Clementi, *Introduction to the Art of Playing the Piano Forte* (London: Clementi, Banger, Hyde, Collard and Davis, 1801) and *Gradus ad Parnassum* (Leipzig: Clementi, Banger, Hyde, Collard and Davis, 1817–26); Louis Adam, *Méthode de piano du Conservatoire* (Paris: Au Magasin de musique du Conservatoire royal, 1804); Carl Czerny, *Complete Theoretical and Practical Pianoforte School*, op. 500 (London: Cocks, 1839); Pierre-Joseph-Guillaume Zimmerman, *Encyclopédie du pianiste compositeur* (Paris: L'Auteur, 1840).

4. A review of "Hummel's Concert" in the 29 April 1830 issue of the English journal *The Athenaeum* stated:

> We had on Thursday the gratification of hearing, for the first time, the pianist who has long been spoken of as the greatest of his time. . . . [W]e certainly regard

it as the most sensible and best, consequently the most effective, pianoforte performance we have ever heard.

5. Hummel has experienced something of a revival lately, particularly with regard to his teaching and influence. See, for example, David Grayson, "Whose Authenticity? Ornaments by Hummel and Cramer for Mozart's Piano Concertos," in *Mozart's Piano Concertos: Text, Context, Interpretation,* ed. Neal Zaslaw (Ann Arbor: University of Michigan Press, 1996), 373–91; Helmuth Rudloff, "Johann Nepomuk Hummel o nauczaniu gry fortepianowej" ("Johann Nepomuk Hummel on Teaching Piano"), in *Aspekty muzycznego wykonawstwa (Aspects of Music Performance)*, ed. Janusz Krassowski (Gdansk: Akademia Muzyczna im. Stanislawa Moniuszki, 1993), 63–80; and Sergiei Grochotow, "Mozart und Hummel," *Acta Mozartiana* 40, nos. 3–4 (1993): 94–103. A number of recordings of his music have appeared recently, and I await a further revival of his solo and chamber music, as well as the concerti.

6. For a detailed account of this event, as recounted by the father Johannes, see Joel Sachs, "Hummel in England and France" (Ph.D. diss., Columbia University, 1968), 128–39.

7. Haydn wrote:

Liebster Hummel
Bedaure von Herzen, dass ich das vergnügen nicht haben kan, mein kleines Werck zum letztenmal selbst zu Dirigiren; indessen aber bin überzeugt, dass sich alle (keinesausgenohmen) die mühe geben werden Ihren alten Papa nach Kräften zu unterstützen, besonders da Sie den verdienstvollen Hummel zum Anführer haben.

(Dearest Hummel,
Trust me from the depths of my heart that I can take no pleasure in not being able to conduct my insignificant work for the last time, but it goes without saying that I am totally convinced that you will exert every effort to support your old Papa with dedication, especially since it will be the faithful Hummel who does it.)

Cited in H. C. Robbins Landon and Dénes Bartha, *Joseph Haydn: Gesammelte Briefe und Aufzeichnungen* (Kassel: Bärenreiter, 1965), 451. All translations are mine, unless otherwise noted.

8. Maynard Solomon, *Beethoven*, 2d rev. ed. (New York: Schirmer Books, 1998), 456 n. 15.

9. A moving description of their final encounter at Beethoven's deathbed is given in Anton F. Schindler, *Biographie von Ludwig van Beethoven*, 3rd ed., 2 vols. (Münster: Aschendorff, 1860). An English translation by Constance Jolly appears in Donald W. MacArdle, ed., *Beethoven As I Knew Him* (Chapel Hill: University of North Carolina Press, 1966), 387–90. Hummel served as a pallbearer at Beethoven's funeral.

10. Karl Benyovszky, *J. N. Hummel. Der Mensch und Künstler* (Bratislava: Eos Verlag, 1934), 90.

11. See my recording of two of these transcriptions (*Symphonies for Chamber Ensemble,* Mark Kroll, fortepiano, and the Parlor Philharmonic, Boston Skyline Records BSD 144 [1997]), and my editions of these works (Johann Nepomuk Hummel, *Mozart's Haffner and Linz Symphonies: Arranged for Pianoforte, Flute,*

Violin, and Violoncello, Recent Researches in the Music of the Nineteenth and Early Twentieth Centuries, vol. 29 [Madison, Wisc.: A-R Editions, 2000] and Johann Nepomuk Hummel, *Twelve Select Overtures: Arranged for Pianoforte, Flute, Violin, and Violoncello,* Recent Researches in the Music of the Nineteenth and Early Twentieth Centuries, vol. 35 [Middleton, Wisc.: A-R Editions, 2003]).

12. "Ich ben gesonnen nun mein hübsches Haus zu geniessen, und will daher nächstes Jahr keine Reise machen sondern in Weimar bleiben." Cited in Benyovszky, *J. N. Hummel,* 229.

13. For a comprehensive discussion, see Sachs, "Hummel in England and France," 178–94.

14. Johann Nepomuk Hummel, *A Complete Theoretical and Practical Course of Instructions, on the Art of Playing the Piano Forte* (London: T. Boosey, 1827); published in German as *Ausführliche theoretisch-practische Anweisung zum Pianoforte Spiel* (Vienna: T. Haslinger, 1828), and in French as *Méthode complète théorique et pratique pour le pianoforte* (Paris: A. Farrenc, 1829; reprint, Geneva: Minkoff, 1981). All citations are from the English edition.

15. Hummel, *Complete Course,* Preface, i.

16. Ibid.

17. Ibid.

18. Ibid., "Preliminary Observations," iii. This somewhat self-serving admonition can be found in many other manuals as well. For example, Türk writes that "it is believed that money can be saved and the cheapest teacher is engaged which results in actually costing far more than the most expensive teacher," but "one should not be misled by thriftiness and engage another who is cheaper" (Türk, *Klavierschule,* Introduction, article 15; *School of Clavier Playing,* trans. Raymond H. Haggh [Lincoln: University of Nebraska Press, 1982], 40). Even Chopin would not begin lessons until his students placed a twenty-franc coin on the mantelpiece.

19. Hummel, *Complete Course,* "Preliminary Observations," iii-iv. Zimmerman, Türk, and most of the other writers repeat this recommendation.

20. Czerny, *Complete Pianoforte School,* 31.

21. Hummel, *Complete Course,* Preface, v.

22. For example, in the 1830s the British pianist Charles Salaman remarked that Hummel played "with ease and tranquil, concentrated power; undeviating accuracy, richness of tone and delicacy of touch." Weber added his approbation: "His playing is extraordinarily sure, neat and pearly, as well as elegant." Cited in Benyovszky, *J. N. Hummel,* 199–202 and 41, respectively.

23. Hummel, *Complete Course,* Part I, Section I, ch. 2, pp. 3–4.

24. Chopin was a great admirer of Hummel, and once commented that he was one of the "masters we must recognize." Cited in Bronislaw Edward Sydow, ed., *Selected Correspondence of Fryderyk Chopin* (New York: McGraw Hill, 1963), 24. Chopin had attempted to write his own piano method, but unfortunately only a few sketches exist. Nevertheless, the surviving sketches testify to Chopin's support of Hummel's approach. See Jean-Jacques Eigeldinger, *Esquisses pour une méthode de piano F. Chopin* (Paris: Flammarion, 1993).

25. François-Joseph Fétis and Ignaz Moscheles, *Méthode des méthodes de piano* (Paris: M. Schlesinger, 1840), ch. 2, p. 6 n. 1. Kalkbrenner also invented the "guide-mains," a clumsy device placed on the keyboard to control wrist and arm movement. Henri Herz introduced a similar contraption, which he called the "dactylion."

26. Liszt "est le seul pianiste qui n'a pas de position fixe . . . se place tantôt plus à gauche, tantôt plus à droite. Son corps est d'ailleurs dans une perpétuelle agitation." Fétis and Moscheles, *Méthode des méthodes*, ch. 2, p. 6 n. 1.

27. "Son talent est la déviation la plus complète . . . qu'on puisse imaginer de l'école de Hummel." Ibid., Introduction, 3.

28. Czerny, *Complete Pianoforte School*, 100. Cited in David Rowland, *A History of Pianoforte Pedalling* (Cambridge: Cambridge University Press, 1993), 107.

29. Nicolo Pasquali, *The Art of Fingering the Harpsichord* (Edinburgh: R. Bremmer, 1758), Preface, 26.

30. Clementi, *Introduction to the Art of Playing the Piano Forte*, Introduction, x-xi.

31. "Quelquefois l'auteur indique la phrase musicale qui doit être liée, mais l'orsqu'il abandonne le choix du *legato* ou de *staccato* au gout de l'exécutant, il vaut mieux s'attacher au *legato* et reserver le *staccato* pour faire ressortir certains passages, . . . les avantages du *legato*." "[L]a main ne doit se déranger sur le clavier." "Les liaisons ne pouvant se faire qu'avec le doigts très serrés sur les touches." "[A]ppuyer un peu le doigt sur la première et le lever à la seconde en lui ôtant la moité de sa valeur." Adam, *Méthode de piano*, Article 7, p. 151.

32. See Mark Kroll, "As If Stroked with a Bow," in *The Beethoven Violin Sonatas: History, Criticism, Performance*, ed. Lewis Lockwood and Mark Kroll (Urbana: University of Illinois Press, forthcoming).

33. "Quand les notes les plus hautes peuvent former un chant dans les endroits où il y a une liaison . . . on peut tenir alors, toutes les notes sous les doigts." Adam, *Méthode de piano*, Article 7, pp. 151–52.

34. Hummel, *Complete Course*, Part I, Section III, ch. 2, p. 60.

35. Türk, *Klavierschule*, Chapter 6, article 36: "Bei den Tönen, welche gestossen werden sollen, hebt man den Finger, wenn fast die halbe Daner der vorgeschriebenen Note vorüber ist, von der Taste. . . ."; *School of Clavier Playing*, trans. Haggh, 342–43.

36. Hummel, *Complete Course*, Part I, Section III, ch. 5, pp. 68–69.

37. Adam, *Méthode de piano*, Article 9, 160–61.

38. Türk, *Klavierschule*, Chapter 1, Part V, article 70; *School of Clavier Playing*, 105.

39. Sandra Rosenblum, *Performance Practices in Classic Piano Music* (Bloomington: Indiana University Press, 1992), 316. For a full discussion of this issue, see 315–18.

40. Beethoven to George Thomson, 19 February 1813, *Beethoven's Letters*, trans. J. S. Shedlock (London: J. M. Dent, 1926; reprint, New York: Dover Publications, 1972), 140.

41. Cited in *Thayer's Life of Beethoven*, rev. and ed. Elliot Forbes (Princeton, N.J.: Princeton University Press, 1967), 555.

42. Johann Adam Hiller, *Anweisung zum Violinspielen* (Graz: Trötscher, 1795), 58. Cited in Rosenblum, *Performance Practices*, 316. Hummel remained undaunted, insisting that "the diminutive of the original word . . . implies a less degree of movement." Hummel, *Complete Course*, Part I, Section III, ch. 5, p. 68 n.

43. Hummel, *Complete Course*, Part I, Section III, supplementary chapter, 109–10.

44. Hummel, *Complete Course*, Part II, Introduction, 1.

45. Most of the other treatises take a similar approach to fingering. There are, however, as many exceptions as there are different shapes and sizes of the hand. For example, Adam suggests an atypical right-hand fingering 1-2-3-4-1-2-3-1-2-3-4-1-2-3 . . . for an ascending chromatic scale (Adam, *Méthode de piano*, Article 4, 33), and Fétis-Moscheles advocates the curious fingering 2-1-4-5-2-1-4-5 for playing repeated notes (Fétis and Moscheles, *Méthode des méthodes*, Article 7, p. 48).

46. Hummel, *Complete Course*, Part III, Section I, ch. 1, p. 2.

47. Heinrich Christoph Koch, *Musikalisches Lexikon* (Frankfurt: Hermann dem Jüngern, 1802), col. 1589. Cited in Rosenblum, *Performance Practices*, 244.

48. Nicolas Joseph Hüllmandel, *Principles of Music, Chiefly Calculated for the Piano Forte or Harpsichord* (London: The Author, 1796), 16.

49. Pierre Baillot, Pierre Rode, and Rodolphe Kreutzer, *Méthode de violon* (Paris: Magasin de musique de Conservatoire, 1803), 139–40.

50. Adam, *Méthode de piano*, Article 6, pp. 54–56.

51. Hummel, *Complete Course*, Part III, Section I, ch. 2, p. 2.

52. Ibid., Part III, Section I, ch. 1, p. 3.

53. Ibid., Part III, Section I, ch. 6, p. 11.

54. Türk, *Klavierschule*, Chapter 3, Part II, article 11; *School of Clavier Playing*, 201.

55. Ibid., Chapter 3, article 4; *School of Clavier Playing*, 195.

56. Johann Peter Milchmeyer, *Die wahre Art das Pianoforte zu Spielen* (Dresden: C. C. Meinhold, 1797), 37.

57. Zimmerman, *Encyclopédie du pianiste*, Chapter VII and Final, General Consideration, Advice to Professors, 68: "C'est la diversité des talents qui fait le charme de l'art. Ne serait-il pas fâcheux, que Kalkbrenner, Liszt, Thalberg se continuassent l'un l'autre? C'est même le caractère complètement différent de leur talent qui cause leurs grands succès."

Fétis, whose *Méthode* (with Moscheles) summarizes these viewpoints on ornamentation and remains an important compendium of all the practices of the previous fifty years, was a remarkably progressive and prophetic musician. For example, as early as 1840 he urged pianists to study the works of Frescobaldi and Froberger. His admonition that the performer must be conversant with all different styles and performance practices anticipates by over a century the approach of historical performance specialists today: "All good music has its time, its aesthetic, its conception. . . . Moreover, it is therefore the worst of all mistakes in the arts to obscure the distinction between styles, and to combine everything with one uniform [approach]. The ultimate in artistic perfection is to render [a work] as it is written." ("Toute bonne musique a sa destination, son principe, sa pensée. . . . C'est d'ailleurs effacer la distinction des styles, et ramener tout à l'uniformité, le pire de tout les défauts dans les arts. La comble de la perfection dans l'art est de rendre ce qui est écrit.") Fétis and Moscheles, *Méthode des méthodes*, ch. 11, p. 75.

58. Hummel, *Complete Course*, Part III, Section II, ch. 1, p. 39. This is one of the most valuable suggestions in the treatise, and for all performance of music. In view of Hummel's negative remarks about C. P. E. Bach, it is worth quoting Bach's comments on this subject: "Lose no opportunity to hear artistic singing. In so doing, the keyboardist will learn to think in terms of song. . . . This way of learning is of far greater value than the reading of voluminous tomes or listening to learned discourses." (Bach, *Versuch*, trans. and ed. William Mitchell [New York: W. W.

Norton, 1949], 151–52.)

In more recent times, it is interesting to note that the great piano virtuoso Vladimir Horowitz claimed that he owned and listened only to recordings of singers.

59. Hummel, *Complete Course*, Part III, Section II, ch. 1, p. 40.

60. Ibid., Part III, Section II, ch. 1, p. 41.

61. Ibid., Part III, Section II, ch. 2, p. 47. There was complete unanimity among keyboard pedagogues that the use of rubato must be subtle and refined. Adam wrote: "Without any doubt expression demands that one slow down or hurry certain notes of the melody, but these *ritards* should not be continual." ("Sans doute l'expression exige qu'on ralentisse ou qu'on presse certaines notes de chant, mais ces retards ne doivent pas etre continuels.") (*Méthode de piano*, Article 9, p. 160.) Czerny observed that "it is customary to drag a bit and depart somewhat from a strict observance of the bar," and suggested the use of a *ritard* "almost always where the Composer has indicated an espressivo" (*Complete Pianoforte School*, p. 35). Chopin was justifiably renowned for his rubato, but always within the context of a steady left hand. His student Carl Mikuli wrote in his edition of Chopin's mazurkas (New York: Schirmer, 1879; Leipzig: Kistner, 1880): "In his often described tempo rubato one hand—that having the accompaniment—always played on in strict time, while the other, that which sang the melody . . . was free of metrical time." Cited in Eigeldinger, *Esquisses pour une méthode*, 111–12.

62. Hummel, *Complete Course*, Part III, Section II, ch. 5, p. 65 n.

63. Ibid., Part III, Section II, ch. 2, p. 54.

64. Friedrich Kalkbrenner, *Méthode pour apprendre le pianoforte* (Paris: M. Schlesinger, 1830; English trans., *A New Method of Studying the Piano-Forte*, 3rd ed. (London: D'Almaine, 1837), 10. Cited in Rowland, *A History of Pianoforte Pedalling*, 35.

65. Milchmeyer, *Die wahre Art*, ch. 5, pp. 57–66; cited in Rowland, *A History of Pianoforte Pedalling*, 159–69.

66. Hummel, *Complete Course*, Part III, Section II, ch. 3, p. 62. Likewise, Adam believed that the pianist who abused the pedals was merely attempting to "cover up the mediocrity of his talent" ("couvrir la mediocrité de leur talent"). (*Méthode de piano*, Article 10, 218.) The incorrect application of the pedals during the early period of the piano was almost comical. The abuses ranged from using the pedal at every point where one wanted a forte, to holding it down for an entire movement regardless of the changes in harmony.

67. Hummel, *Complete Course*, Part III, Section II, ch. 4, p. 64.

68. Ibid., Part III, Section II, ch. 6, p. 69.

69. Ibid., Part III, Section II, ch. 6, pp. 71–72.

70. Ibid., Part III, Section II, ch. 6, p. 69 n.

71. Ibid., Part III, Section II, ch. 7, p. 74.

12

"For You Have Been Rebellious against the Lord": The Jewish Image in Mendelssohn's *Moses* and Marx's *Mose*

Jeffrey S. Sposato

Adolf Bernhard Marx first considered composing a work based on the subject of Moses and the Exodus at the age of fifteen, but was unable to find the time and means to tackle what he called his "old pet project" until 1832—seventeen years later. This new effort would not, however, be on the two-part opera he envisioned in his youth, but rather on a piece that would "have the outward form of an oratorio, and the Bible would have to provide the text." He confided this new oratorio plan to his friend of many years, Felix Mendelssohn Bartholdy, who in response mentioned that he too was planning an oratorio based on biblical texts. Marx excitedly replied, "That is a wonderful coincidence! . . . I was afraid that the business of looking for the text would take away the freshness from composing; now we are both saved. You put my libretto together for me, and I will do yours for you, and we shall both have a fresh start with our work." Mendelssohn happily agreed, despite some opposition from Marx when Mendelssohn requested a text on St. Paul, and quickly began assembling the libretto that was to catalyze the destruction of their friendship.[1]

The work on the libretto for Marx's oratorio *Mose* began as something of a joint effort, with Marx having already laid out an overall plan for the oratorio and begun construction of a first libretto draft. Once Mendelssohn agreed to take on the project, Marx handed these materials over; Mendelssohn then used them in the construction of a libretto he called *Moses,* which he delivered to Marx sometime after its 21 August 1832 completion date.[2] (For the purpose of this discussion, I shall use *Moses* to refer to the libretto Mendelssohn assembled for Marx, and *Mose* to refer to Marx's finished oratorio.) But despite the fact that Mendelssohn carefully modeled his libretto after Marx's own partially completed draft and covered most of the points listed in Marx's overall plan, Marx was greatly disappointed:

Now I held in my hands the text which my comrade in art assembled for me. As I read it through and read it again, I felt as though I was thunderstruck. "This, this then is *Mose!* of which you have for so long dreamed . . . and now you stand cold, emotionless before it! no heartbeat quickens for it, no vision dawns!" I felt, with true terror, that I could not compose the work. . . . Finally, though, I had to say to myself that . . . I would have to let the text fall. . . . Now it was clear to me how far our separate ways had drifted from one another, my friend and I. Certainly, . . . he had worked for me with loyalty and total conviction. He created the text as before us so many had created, and as had been simply accepted by the greatest masters without concern. The combination of narrative, lyrical outpouring, and dramatic elements were the standard forms of Handel and Bach; our favorite work, the [Bach] *St. Matthew Passion,* had the same design. Mendelssohn, therefore, was completely beyond reproach. If someone was deserving of reproach, it was I. Why did I neglect, or was unable to clearly show him the new form, which was so important to me?[3]

Marx continued by explaining that this "new form" centered around a sense of "living realism" ("lebendiger Wahrhaftigkeit"), which attempted to bring oratorio as close to opera as possible. (Indeed, a critic writing about the 1841 Breslau premiere of *Mose* for the *Neue Zeitschrift für Musik* described the piece as "a new star" in the history of the oratorio, with music so dramatic that one could easily envision "the changing of the scenes and people entering and exiting," and which—to his excitement—contained no narration or "delays from little moments of feeling.")[4]

Mendelssohn must have been equally disappointed by Marx's decision not to use his libretto and instead to assemble one of his own, especially given the pride Mendelssohn evinced in the work, as his letters to Karl Klingemann demonstrate: "I have put together for him [Marx] a text for an oratorio out of biblical passages, which I am exceptionally pleased with; a beautiful work must certainly come out of it."[5] And again a couple of weeks later:

Let the subject matter of his [Marx's] oratorio now be told to you, . . . it is Moses. In the first part, from the oppression of Israel to Moses' conversation with God in the burning bush. In the second part, Moses before Pharaoh, the plagues, the exodus, the miracle at the Red Sea through to Miriam's Song of Triumph. In the third, the desert, the uprisings, the golden calf, the wrathful Lord God, finally the ten commandments. I have assembled it completely from biblical passages, and the only thing that I have composed is: "In the evening, however," or "he said." That's why it's so beautiful.[6]

Mendelssohn's dismay at Marx's rejection presents itself unmistakably on Mendelssohn's copy of the libretto, whose cover page contains the inscription "*Moses* | ~~componiert~~ | ~~von~~ | ~~A. B. Marx~~," with the deletions so thorough as to make the underlying text barely readable.[7]

With Marx's rejection of the *Moses* libretto began a slow but steady breakdown in the relationship between the two composers, with written evidence of a change in Mendelssohn's attitude (aside from the dedication page alterations) appearing as early as an August 1834 letter to Julius Schubring, in which Mendelssohn noted for the first time that he "exceedingly disapprove[d]" of Marx's compositions.[8] The libretto was a turning point in the relationship for Marx as well, who later proclaimed it the source of their "inner division."[9] Like Mendelssohn, Marx was convinced that the two of them were destined to pursue different compositional paths, with the libretto itself serving as the final conclusive proof.

In the years that followed, Marx and Mendelssohn maintained the outward appearance of friends and continued to meet whenever the latter visited Berlin.[10] But this superficial display came to an abrupt end in 1839 when Marx approached Mendelssohn, the newly completed *Mose* in hand, to ask him to perform the work.[11] Marx's widow, Therese, later recounted the incident:

> It was now, 1839, when Marx was finally able to realize the dream of his youth, which he had carried with him his entire life. With jubilant, high spirits, he wrote his oratorio, *Mose*. His first thoughts after its completion were of his friend. He alone could help pave the way into the world for this child born of such painful labor.
>
> Filled with hope and anticipation, Marx traveled to Leipzig and sought out Mendelssohn. If he performed his work there, then—as Marx, perhaps wrongly, but definitely assumed—success was assured.
>
> With the plea: Help me, my work is finished, he approached his friend.
>
> Both sat at the piano and Marx played and sang the first part of the work from the score.
>
> After the completion of which, Mendelssohn rose and said coolly: "Do not take it amiss, but there is nothing I can do for this work."
>
> Marx, his hopes dashed, his confidence injured, without wasting another word, closed the score and left . . . .
>
> Marx returned from this failure very cross. The hopes, which he, at first, set solely upon Mendelssohn's help, were destroyed, the last bond of friendship broken. For a long time this pain continued to resonate in him; in fact he never got over it for the rest of his life.[12]

Shortly after Marx returned from Leipzig, he and Therese went for a walk in Berlin's Tiergarten, where from the Marschallsbrücke he took a packet full of all of Mendelssohn's letters to him and tossed it into the water.[13]

As Marx's memoirs and Mendelssohn's comments to Schubring suggest, the two composers had built their relationship upon the assumption that they were of equal caliber and would go through life as professional partners, each helping the other as need be. With Marx's rejection of the *Moses* libretto, however, both men began to suspect that this state of equality did not exist, a situation that chilled their relationship and finally led to Mendelssohn's total withdrawal of support from Marx. But the documents cannot be telling the whole story, for in Marx's account of his dissatisfaction with Mendelssohn's libretto, he never mentioned that he himself had written a great deal of the first two parts of the text (thus establishing a model for Mendelssohn to emulate). In fact, Marx's prose draft contained most of the first of the oratorio's three parts (Moses' call to service)—with some segments left blank where inspiration had not yet struck him—and the beginning of Part II (Moses and Pharaoh). As the partial transcription of the libretto draft in the left column of figure 12.1 reveals, the narrative formula that Marx complained of in his memoirs—complete with extensive scenic descriptions and monologue introductions such as "Er sprach"— stands at the core of the draft's structure. In assembling his own libretto, Mendelssohn followed this example and as a first step elaborated upon some of Marx's less-developed ideas before writing a coherent text for Part II and sketches for Part III (the journey in the wilderness). As the right column of figure 12.1 shows, even in his final libretto Mendelssohn continued to use Marx's original text as much as possible, probably out of concern for offending his friend by overcorrecting his work.

In addition to not acknowledging that Mendelssohn had followed his example in assembling a *Moses* libretto and despite his complaints about Mendelssohn's final product, in the end Marx did not, as he claimed, "let

Mose aber hütete die Schafe Jethor, seines Schwähers, des Priesters in Midian, und trieb die Schafe hinein in die Wüste und kam an den Berg Horeb. Und der Engel des Herrn erschien ihm in einer feurigen Flamme aus dem Busch. Und er sahe, daß der Busch mit Feuer brannte und ward nicht verzehrt.	Mose aber hütete die Schafe Jethor, seines Schwähers und trieb die Schafe tiefer hinein in die Wüste und kam an den Berg Gottes Horeb. Und er sahe daß der Busch mit Feuer brannte und ward doch nicht verzehrt.
Und sprach: ich will dahin und besehn dies große Gesicht, warum der Busch nicht verbrennet.	Und er sprach: Ich will dahin und besehn dies große Gesicht, warum der Busch nicht verbrennet?
Da aber der Herr sahe, daß er hinging zu sehen, rief ihm Gott aus dem Busch und sprach: Mose! Mose!	Da aber der Herr sahe daß er hinging zu sehn, rief ihm Gott aus dem Busch und sprach: Mose, Mose!
Er antwortete: Hier bin ich.	Er antwortete: Hier bin ich.
Er sprach: Tritt nicht herzu, ziehe deine Schuhe aus von deinen Füßen, denn der Ort darauf du stehest, ist ein heiliges Land.	
Und sprach weiter: ich bin der Gott deiner Väter.	Er sprach: Ich bin der Gott deiner Väter.

Figure 12.1. Opening of Part I, Scene 2, from Marx's prose libretto draft (left, Oxford Bodleian Library [Gb-Ob] MS M. Deneke Mendelssohn d. 30, no. 216a, f. 414^r) and Mendelssohn's final *Moses* libretto (right, Staatsbibliothek zu Berlin Preussischer Kulturbesitz [D-Bsb] MA MS 76, p. 4)

the text fall." Indeed, a comparison between Mendelssohn's *Moses* text and the one Marx eventually used for his oratorio *Mose* demonstrates that Marx continued to incorporate a considerable amount of Mendelssohn's version, especially those passages for which Mendelssohn found text from outside the Exodus narrative. To cite a single example, a comparison of the Egyptian persecution song ("Spottlied") in *Mose* (figure 12.2) with the passage for the same episode Mendelssohn took for his libretto from Lamentations 2:16 clearly indicates that Marx did not find this passage on his own, but borrowed it from Mendelssohn's supposedly "rejected" text. (This fact in itself could explain Mendelssohn's reaction to *Mose* when Marx requested a performance: there before him was much of the text Marx had rejected, now being appropriated without permission or credit.)

Figure 12.2. Egyptian "Spottlied" from Marx's *Mose* (left, published score, no. 4)

Ein Aegypter	*Knabenchor*
Das ist der Tag, deß wir haben begehret! Wir haben es erlangt, wir haben es erlebt: sie sind niedergestürzt und gefallen! wir aber stehen aufgerichtet!	Hah! Wir haben sie vertilgt! Das ist der Tag, deß wir haben begehrt. Wir haben es erlangt, wir haben es erlebt.

and Mendelssohn's *Moses* libretto (right, D-Bsb MA MS 76, p. 2)

Even Marx's stated excuse for abandoning Mendelssohn's libretto raises doubts, since transforming a responsorial narrative into a dramatic one would not have been excessively difficult—certainly not difficult enough to warrant starting from scratch. Therefore something else about the libretto must have bothered Marx. Eric Werner suggested the possibility that Mendelssohn's libretto was not Christological enough to suit the tastes of Marx, who was an eager convert to Lutheranism.[14] But as even a quick perusal of the text reveals, *Moses* clearly is Christological—indeed a great deal more so than Marx's *Mose*.[15] One of the most obvious examples of this appears in the transition between the first two scenes of Part I (figure 12.3). Here, at the point just before God calls Moses to service, two angels announce the people's coming "redemption" ("Erlösung")—not just physical salvation—in a manner clearly reminiscent of, and using text similar to, the angel's annunciation to the shepherds of Christ's birth.

Figure 12.3. The angels' pronouncement of the Israelites' coming redemption in

Zwei Engel	
Fürchte dich nicht! Denn ich habe dich erlöset, ich habe dich bei deinem Namen gerufen; du bist mein!	Fürchtet euch nicht; . . . Denn euch ist heute der Heiland geboren, welcher ist Christus der Herr, in der Stadt Davids.

Mendelssohn's *Moses* libretto (left, D-Bsb MA MS 76, pp. 3–4) and the annunciation of Christ's birth to the shepherds in Luke 2:10–11 (right, Luther Bible, 1824)

Mendelssohn continues to strengthen this image of Moses as a kind of Old-Testament Christ in Part III by having him experience and perform various Christ-like acts, building mostly on text taken from outside the Exodus narrative. Among the many examples are an attempted stoning (in which the crowd cries out an obvious adaptation of John 19:15), the betrayal of Moses by his closest "disciples," Aaron and Miriam, and Moses' attempt to take the sins of the people upon himself at the close of the work (figure 12.4).

Mose aber und Aaron fielen auf ihr Angesicht vor der ganzen Versammlung und sprachen: Fallet nicht ab vom Herrn, der Herr ist mit uns. Fürchtet Euch nicht.	But Moses and Aaron fell on their faces before the entire assembly and said: Do not abandon the Lord, the Lord is with us. Fear not.
Chor. Weg, weg mit denen. Steinigt sie! [*cf.* Jn. 19:15–Weg, weg mit dem! Kreuzige ihn!]	*Chorus.* Away, away with them. Stone them! [Num. 14:5, 9; John 19:15 (Away, away with him! Crucify him!)]

Und Mirjam und Aaron redeten wider Mose und sprachen: Redet denn der Herr allein durch Mosen? Redet er nicht auch durch uns?	And Miriam and Aaron spoke against Moses and said: Does the Lord only speak through Moses? Does He not also speak through us? [Num. 12:1–3]

Da wandte sich Mose und fiel nieder vor dem Herrn und sprach:	Then Moses turned and fell before the Lord and said:
[*Mose:*] Ach das Volk hat eine große Sünde gethan, und haben sich goldne Götter gemacht. Nun vergieb ihnen ihre Sünde, wo nicht so tilge mich auch aus deinem Buche, das du geschrieben hast.	[*Moses:*] Oh, this people have sinned a great sin, and have made for themselves gods of gold. Now forgive their sin—if not, blot me out of your book that you have written.
Der Herr aber sprach zu Mose: Was? Ich will den tilgen aus meinem Buch, der an mir sündigt.	But the Lord said to Moses: What? I will blot out of my book those who have sinned against me.
Mose: Ach vergieb ihnen ihre Sünde, Herr, Herr Gott, barmherzig und gnädig und geduldig und von großer Gnade und Treue. Und fiel vor dem Herrn nieder vierzig Tage und vierzig Nächte.	*Moses:* Oh, forgive their sin, Lord, Lord God, compassionate and merciful and patient and filled with mercy and faithfulness. And he fell before the Lord for forty days and forty nights.
Und der Herr sprach: Ich habe vergeben, wie du gesagt hast.	And the Lord said: I have forgiven, as you have said. [Exod. 32:31–33, 34:6; Deut. 9:18; Num. 14:20]

Figure 12.4. Three Christological moments in Mendelssohn's *Moses* libretto (D-Bsb MA MS 76): the attempted stoning of Moses and Aaron (p. 12), Aaron and Miriam's betrayal (p. 12), and Moses' taking of the Israelites' sins upon himself (p. 15)

But Mendelssohn's design of *Moses* as an intensely Christological work, while allowing him to portray his protagonist in a manner reminiscent of Christ, simultaneously necessitated that the Jews be portrayed as they are in the New Testament—in a predominantly negative light.[16] Moreover, Mendelssohn's depiction of the Jews ties into several common nineteenth-century stereotypes, including representations of them as greedy, slothful, and dependent on other peoples; as adhering to a religion based on some-times barbaric ritual, including the infamous "Blood Libel" or sacrifice of Christian children; and as a people incapable of true faith.[17] While Mendelssohn may not have consciously intended to invoke the full depth of the images that accompany these stereotypes, their appearance through-out the *Moses* libretto demonstrates a distinct lack of concern on his part for the safety of the Jewish image, something also visible (as I discuss else-where) in his oratorio *Paulus,* completed less than four years later.[18] Granted, the image of the Jews presented in the Exodus story is not exactly flatter-ing; but as was the case with most of the elements he used to make *Moses* Christological, Mendelssohn also imported negative imagery from outside the Exodus narrative, an act that demonstrates definite intent. Further-more, a comparison of these narrative segments in Mendelssohn's text to those same segments as finally set in Marx's *Mose,* where the Jews are treated more sympathetically, helps to place these images in sharp relief.[19] This comparison also suggests that Marx's disappointment with Mendelssohn's text was rooted in the latter's unflattering portrayal of the Jews, as well as demonstrates the very different relationship both compos-ers had with their shared Jewish heritage.

As with the Christological content of *Moses,* the negative imagery regard-ing the Jews is concentrated in Part III, but elements of it can be seen as early as the second scene of Part I. Here, during the conversation between God and Moses, Moses comments on the doubting quality of his people: "Moses answered [God] and said: See, they will not believe me, but instead will say: the Lord has not appeared to you" ("Mose antwortete und sprach: Siehe, sie werden mir nicht glauben, sondern werden sagen: der Herr ist dir nicht erschienen" [Exod. 4:1]). At this point, rather than have God em-power Moses' staff to become a symbol of proof (Exod. 4:2–3, where the staff becomes a snake), Mendelssohn instead has God confirm Moses' state-ment by bringing text from Isaiah 43:8–9 into the Exodus narrative: "The Lord said: Let this blind people come forth, so that they may hear and say: it is the truth" ("Der Herr sprach: Laß hervortreten das blinde Volk, so wird man es hören und sagen: es ist die Wahrheit"). Marx himself wrote Moses' statement ("See, they will not believe me. . . .") into his original libretto draft, but was apparently uncertain about it from the very begin-ning. At the time he gave his draft to Mendelssohn, he did not know how God should respond (and may even have been questioning whether to keep the statement at all), since after Moses speaks, he left a blank space—the only one on the page—between it and Moses' next complaint about his "heavy speech." When Mendelssohn completed the draft, he filled the space with God's call for "this blind people" to come forth. Marx, however, eventually decided against the entire passage. In no. 9 of *Mose,* the scene progresses from Moses asking for God's name, to his abdication ("My Lord, send whom Thou willst" ["Mein Herr, sende, welchen du senden willst"]), skipping this segment and the implication of unbelief that accompanies it.

Near the opening of Part II of his libretto, Mendelssohn confirms Moses' doubts of the Israelites' faith (figure 12.5). After Pharaoh throws Moses out of his chambers, he burdens the Israelites further, causing them to rise up against Moses and Aaron, almost exactly as the event appears in the Exodus narrative (Exod. 5:19, 21):

Und da die Kinder Israel sahen, daß es ärger ward, sprachen sie zu Mose und Aaron[:]	And when the children of Israel saw that they were in evil plight, they said to Moses and Aaron:
Chor. Der Herr sehe auf Euch und richte es; Ihr habt unsern Feinden das Schwert in die Hand gegeben, daß sie uns tödten.	*Chorus.* The Lord look upon you and judge; you have put a sword in the hand of our enemies, that they may kill us.

Figure 12.5. Excerpt of the opening scene of Part II of Mendelssohn's *Moses* libretto (D-Bsb MA MS 76, pp. 6–7)

Marx's original draft contains this first encounter with Pharaoh, up until the instant Pharaoh orders more labor for the Israelites, at which point the draft ends. That Marx stopped at precisely this moment suggests that he was again unsure about how to proceed, since the next step should have been simple: the very next sentence, Exodus 5:21, contains the Israelites' reaction to this encounter, exactly as Mendelssohn wrote it when he completed the libretto. But Marx likely questioned the suitability of this text, or he would have written it at the same time as the remainder of the scene. As before then, Marx seems to have hesitated when on the brink of having to portray the Jews in a negative light. This hypothesis is borne out in *Mose* (nos. 13–14), where Marx carefully avoids this negative portrayal: Moses and Aaron go to Pharaoh accompanied by numerous representatives of the people; in this way Marx avoids placing blame solely on the prophet and his brother. Once Pharaoh throws them out, a chorus of Egyptians announces that their "days of celebration will be turned into days of sadness!" ("Eure Feiertage sollen zu Trauertagen werden"). The people respond, "You [plural] have brought trouble upon us! Horror has come upon me!" ("Ihr habt uns Unglück zugerichtet! Grauen ist auf mich gefallen!").

The placement of the people's complaint immediately after the chorus of Egyptians (with no intervening statement from Moses) makes the subject of the complaint vague—it could be directed against either the Egyptians or the *group* who visited Pharaoh. If the latter, the attitude of the people is one of unhappiness and disappointment, not rebellion.

As in this first encounter, Mendelssohn sets the subsequent meetings between Moses and Pharaoh as they appear in Exodus, which again present the Jews in a negative light. In these later encounters, the image changes from unbelieving to greedy and, occasionally, cultish. After the plagues begin, Pharaoh begins to make concessions, but Moses continues to ask for more. During the hailstorm, Pharaoh agrees to allow the Jews to make their offering to God "in the land," but Moses insists that they must offer to God in the desert. After the plague of darkness, Pharaoh agrees to let them leave, on the condition that they leave their sheep and cattle behind. Moses replies, "You must also give us sacrifices and burnt-offerings, so that we may sacrifice to our God the Lord" ("Du mußt uns auch Opfer und Brandopfer geben, das wir unserm Gott dem Herrn thun mögen"). Here, the demand for offerings from Pharaoh not only portrays the Jews as dependent, but the mention of "burnt offerings" conjures images of cult-like barbarism.

Since Mendelssohn sets the actual Exodus text (Exod. 10:25) here, one should not fault him too much, but a comparison to Marx's setting demonstrates one possible alternative and serves as an example of the very different concept Marx had of the prophet and his people. Rather than set the Exodus text of Moses' final meetings with Pharaoh verbatim, Marx chose not to include the first of the two meetings (thus eliminating the repeated requests for assistance), and in his setting of the second meeting (no. 20), he modified Moses' text to create a more heroic character and to eliminate any possibility of either greed or cultishness being attributed to the Israelites. As seen in figure 12.6, rather than asking for (or even mentioning) offerings, Moses, in response to Pharaoh's demand that they leave their goods behind, instead forcefully announces that he and his people will take what is theirs—"What is ours shall go with us" ("Was unser ist, soll mit uns gehn"). Indeed, Marx's text even promotes an air of religious maturity and sophistication with its allusion to the term "Gottesdienst" (the modern German word for a religious service) in Moses' declaration that the Israelites will use their possessions "for the service of our God" ("zum Dienst unsers Gottes").[20]

Pharao	*Pharaoh*
Ziehet hin, ziehet hin! Vergebt mir meine Sünde und dienet dem Herrn! Ziehet hin!	Depart, depart! Forgive my sin and serve the Lord! Depart!

Mose	*Moses*
Rüstet euch! Hebet euch auf, von dannen!	Make ready! Rise up from there!

Pharao	*Pharaoh*
Allein— eure Heerden und Güter lasset hier!	Alone—leave your herds and goods here!

Mose	*Moses*
Was unser ist, soll mit uns gehn; denn von dem Unsern werden wir nehmen zum Dienst unsers Gottes.	What is ours shall go with us; for from what is ours we shall take for the service of our God.

Figure 12.6. Excerpt from Marx's *Mose*, no. 20

The image of the Israelites as cultish reappears in Mendelssohn's libretto in the final chorus of Part II, with their polytheistically flavored question, "Lord, who is like unto You among the gods?"[21] By omitting the mention of gods, Marx again eliminates such overtones in his version of the final Part II chorus (no. 21, figure 12.7), which otherwise uses most of Mendelssohn's text.

Ich will dem Herrn singen, denn er hat eine herrliche That gethan. Roß und Wagen hat er ins Meer gestürzt. *Herr, wer ist dir gleich unter den Göttern?* Wer ist dir gleich, der so mächtig heilig, schrecklich, loblich und wunderthätig sei? Der Herr wird König sein immer und ewig.	Sie sind niedergestürzt und gefallen! Wir aber stehen aufgerichtet!—*Wer ist dir gleich, O Herr?* so mächtig, so schrecklich, so wunderthätig, so heilig!—Ich will dem Herrn laut und fröhlich singen! Er hat fürwahr eine herrliche That gethan: Roß und Mann hat er ins Meer gestürzt! Herr ist sein Name.

Figure 12.7. Final Part II chorus from Mendelssohn's *Moses* libretto (left, D-Bsb MA MS 76, pp. 10–11) and Marx's *Mose* (right, published score, no. 21), emphasis added

Over the course of Mendelssohn's libretto, the image of the Jews steadily deteriorates to the point that Part III—the journey in the wilderness—focuses entirely on their negative qualities. Marx, telling basically the same story, presents an image which, while not depicting the Jews as blameless, is more positive and attempts to avoid common stereotypes, often incorporating a modified version of Mendelssohn's own text. As can be seen in figure 12.8a, for instance, Part III of *Moses* opens with an image of dependence and lack of faith, with the Israelites demanding water from Moses after three days in the wilderness ("Give us water so we may drink") and questioning the Lord's presence ("Is the Lord with us or not?"). Marx, on the other hand, opens Part III of *Mose* with two choruses of Israelites marching forth with confidence, one singing of their recognition of God's mercy to the righteous, and the other singing Psalm 114, "When Israel departed from Egypt" (figure 12.8b).

Und sie wanderten drei Tage in der Wüste, daß sie kein Wasser fanden. Da kamen sie gen Mara, aber sie konnten das Wasser nicht trinken, denn es war sehr bitter. Da murrete das Volk wider Mose und sprach: *Chor.* Was sollen wir trinken? *Mose.* Was zanket ihr mir? Warum versuchet ihr den Herrn? *Chor.* Gebt uns Wasser, daß wir trinken. Und murreten noch lauter und sprachen: *Chor.* Warum hast du uns lassen aus Aegypten ziehn, daß du uns alle Durstes sterben ließest? Ist der Herr unter uns, oder nicht?	And they wandered three days in the wilderness and found no water. Then they came to Marah, but they could not drink the water because it was very bitter. Then the people murmured against Moses and said: *Chorus.* What shall we drink? *Moses.* Why do you scold me? Why do you test the Lord? *Chorus.* Give us water so we may drink. And they murmured still louder and said: *Chorus.* Why have you allowed us to leave Egypt, only to allow us all to die of thirst? Is the Lord with us or not?
Mose schrie zum Herrn und sprach: Was soll ich mit dem Volke thun? Es fehlet nicht weit, sie werden mich noch steinigen.	Moses cried to the Lord and said: What shall I do with this people? They are almost ready to stone me.
Und Mirjam und Aaron redeten wider Mose und sprachen: Redet denn der Herr allein durch Mosen? Redet er nicht auch durch uns?	And Miriam and Aaron spoke against Moses and said: Does the Lord only speak through Moses? Does He not also speak through us?

Figure 12.8a: Opening scene of Part III of Mendelssohn's *Moses* libretto (D-Bsb MA MS 76, pp. 11–12)

Die eine Schaar Nun merk' ich, daß der Herr dem Gerechten hilft und erhöret ihn in seinem heiligen Himmel. Seine Hand hilft gewaltig.	*First Group* Now I know that the Lord helps the righteous and hears in his holy heaven. His hand helps mightily.
Die andre Schaar Da Israel aus Aegypten zog, das Volk aus fremdem Volk: da ward Juda sein Heiligthum, Israel seine Herrschaft. . . .	*Second Group* When Israel departed from Egypt, the people from a foreign people, Judah became his sanctuary, Israel his dominion. . . .

Figure 12.8b. Opening chorus of Part III of Marx's *Mose* (published score, no. 22)

As in Mendelssohn's libretto, the Israelites' dissatisfaction with their situation gradually begins to emerge in *Mose* as well, but at no time does Marx's text resonate with stereotypes of dependence or unfaithfulness. When the Jews complain of their thirst, Marx chooses the first of the two complaints used by Mendelssohn: "I am thirsty! What shall we drink?" ("Mich dürstet! was sollen wir trinken?"), which is merely an expression of distress, not a demand that someone obtain water for them. This same contrast between Mendelssohn's and Marx's text continues in the Israelites' complaint of hunger later in Part III: whereas Mendelssohn has them cry "Give us meat, so we may eat" ("Gieb uns Fleisch, daß wir essen"), Marx simply has them shout "Shall we all die of hunger?" ("Sollen Alle Hungers sterben?").

Marx continues to emphasize the steadfastness of the Israelites' faith throughout Part III, even in the rebellion scene (nos. 24–26). After the complaint of thirst, tension eventually builds to the point that one of the Israelites, Korah, is able to lead an uprising. But unlike Aaron and Miriam's rebellion in *Moses,* Korah's is against the authority Moses and Aaron have assumed, not against God. In fact, when Moses accuses the people of "testing" and "murmuring against" God, Korah protests, "You have gone too far; for the entire congregation is holy" ("Ihr macht's zu viel; denn die ganze Gemeinde ist überall heilig"). Marx then takes great care to retain this image of the Israelites' unyielding faith in God throughout the remainder of this segment of Part III by interspersing the episodes of discontent with arias from the faithful, such as the young boy's ("Jüngling") aria, "Gott der Herr ist Sonne und Schild!" ("God the Lord is sun and shield!"), which appears immediately after the thirst complaint. Similarly, after an old man ("Greis") loses his strength, his daughter reassures him: "Be patient! take courage, wait on the Lord and do not despair! He gives power to the faint, and ample strength to the powerless" ("Harre doch! sei getrost, harre des Herrn und sei unverzagt! Er giebt dem Müden Kraft, und Stärke genug dem Unvermögenden"). When the old man succumbs to his fears once again, the young boy responds, "He has given His angels charge over you, that they may protect you on all your paths" ("Er hat seinen Engeln befohlen über dir, daß sie dich behüten auf allen Wegen"), before reprising his previous aria.

In *Moses,* on the other hand, when the prophet and Aaron appeal to the people not to fall away from God, they reply, "Away, away with them. Stone them!" ("Weg, weg mit denen. Steinigt sie!"). Even the appearance of God's glory, which immediately follows, fails to make an impression. After the ground appears "like a beautiful sapphire and as the body of heaven, when it is clear," and Moses and Joshua depart to receive the commandments, not only do the people not comment on the event or on the falling of bread from heaven, but they instead turn almost immediately to Aaron and instruct him to make them a new god (figure 12.9).

Chor. Weg, weg mit denen. Steinigt sie!	*Chorus.* Away, away with them. Stone them!
Da erschien die Herrlichkeit des Herrn allen Kindern Israels; unter seinen Füßen war es wie ein schöner Saphir und wie die Gestalt des Himmels, wenn es klar ist.	Then the glory of the Lord appeared to all the children of Israel; [the ground] under their feet was like a beautiful sapphire and as the body of heaven, when it

Und das Ansehn der Herrlichkeit des is clear. And the appearance of the glory Herrn war wie ein verzehrend Feuer auf of the Lord was like a consuming fire on der Spitze des Berges. Und der Herr the peak of the mountain. And the Lord sprach zu Mose: said to Moses:

Wie lange lästert mich das Volk? Und wie How long will the people blaspheme lange wollen sie nicht an mich glauben? against me? And how long will they not Siehe, ich will euch Brod vom Himmel believe in me? Behold, I will allow bread regnen lassen, und ihr sollt inne werden, to rain from heaven for you, and they shall daß ich der Herr, euer Gott bin.—Du know that I am the Lord, your God.— Mose komm herauf zu mir auf den Berg, Thou, Moses, come up to me on the moun- daß ich dir gebe meine Gebote, die du sie tain, so that I may give you my command- lehren sollst. ments, which you shall teach to them.

Da aber das Volk sahe, daß Mose und But when the people saw that Moses and sein Diener Josua ~~vierzig Tage und vierzig~~ his servant Joshua failed to return from ~~Nächte~~ verzogen von dem Berg wieder zu the mountain ~~for forty days and forty~~ kommen, sammelte es sich wider Aaron ~~nights~~, they gathered together before und sprach zu ihm: Aaron and said to him:

Chor. Auf mache uns Götter, die vor uns *Chorus.* Arise, make us gods who shall hergehen. Denn wir wissen nicht, was go before us. For we do not know what diesem Mann Mose widerfahren ist, der has happened to this man Moses, who uns aus Aegyptenland geführet hat. led us out of Egypt.

Und er machte ein gegossen Kalb. And he made a molten calf.

Figure 12.9. Excerpt from the rebellion scene in Part III of Mendelssohn's *Moses* libretto (D-Bsb MA MS 76, pp. 12–13); cross-outs original

As the editorial markings in the libretto demonstrate, the immediacy of the Israelites' fall is the result of a last-minute deletion on Mendelssohn's part. Originally, Mendelssohn specified that Moses and Joshua had not returned from the mountain for forty days and nights, after which the Isra- elites turn to Aaron for new leadership. Mendelssohn then intensified the sense of unfaithfulness by deleting this reference before sending the final copy to Marx.

The episode of the golden calf naturally represents the outer extreme of the negative treatment of the Jews in Mendelssohn's libretto, and, as men- tioned earlier, also represents the completion of Aaron and Miriam's Christologically charged betrayal of both Moses and God. That Marx chose not to include this episode (which had been his original intention) and that Mendelssohn did is significant, since both choices further demonstrate the composers' concern, or lack thereof, for the Jewish image. For *Mose*, Marx instead imported Korah's rebellion, the largest in the Pentateuch, from Numbers 16 and 26:9–11, where the uprising occurs as the result of the restrictions Moses placed on the sons of Levi, restrictions that prohibited them from the office of the priesthood. But, as noted earlier, both the original biblical account and Marx's new setting of the rebellion leave God out of the equation entirely: the revolt is solely against Moses. In the golden calf episode (as it appears both in Exodus and in Mendelssohn's libretto), however, the Israelites turn away from *God* and ask Aaron to make a new deity for them.

Mendelssohn took the calf scene from Exodus verbatim with two exceptions: the chorus of praise to the calf, and a fiery aria for Moses following his destruction of the covenant tablets, a text Mendelssohn assembled from passages of Deuteronomy and Hosea (Deut. 32:6, 32:16–17; Hos. 8:7, 9:7; Deut. 9:24; Hos. 7:13; figure 12.10).

Dankest du also dem Herrn, deinen Gott, du toll und thörigt Volk? Durch Greu[e]ll erzürnst du ihn? Den Feldteufeln opferst du und nicht deinem Gott? Ihr säet Wind und werdet Ungewitter einerndten, die Zeit der Heimsuchung ist gekommen, die Zeit der Vergeltung. *Denn ihr seid ungehorsam dem Herrn gewesen solange ich euch gekannt habe.* Wehe euch, ihr seid von ihm gewichen.	Do you thus thank the Lord, you foolish and senseless people? With abominable practices do you provoke him to anger? You sacrifice to demons and not to your God? You sow wind, and shall reap the whirlwind, the days of punishment have come, the days of recompense. *For you have been rebellious against the Lord for as long as I have known you.* Woe to you, for you have strayed from him.

Figure 12.10. Moses' aria from Part III of Mendelssohn's *Moses* libretto (D-Bsb MA MS 76, p. 14), emphasis added

While the entire aria focuses on the faults of the Israelites, of particular interest is the inclusion of Deuteronomy 9:24, "For you have been rebellious against the Lord for as long as I have known you," the statement that, more than any other in the libretto, resonates most strongly with the stereotype of the Jews being incapable of true faith, and, even worse, declares that this has always been the case. Its presence here seems somehow inevitable, however, since it summarizes the image of the Jews Mendelssohn has cultivated throughout the course of the oratorio. But despite its harshness, Moses' accusation does little to change the Israelites' attitude. For even once Moses has destroyed the calf and God has announced his "day of vengeance," the Israelites do not repent. Instead, Moses pleads for forgiveness *for them*—a symbol of both his Christ-like sacrifice and the people's continuing dependence. Only once God grants His forgiveness do the people then thank Him for His kindness.

Mendelssohn's negative depiction of the Jews in the *Moses* libretto stems, I believe, from a desire to demonstrate his detachment from his Jewish heritage at this time in his life. Converted by his father from Judaism to Lutheranism at the age of seven and subsequently encouraged to separate himself from his Jewish past, Mendelssohn may have thought that a frankly positive representation of Jews might have led to doubts as to the sincerity of his conversion.[22] Even worse, it might have been construed as a particularly obvious declaration of a philo-Semitic agenda, especially since negative depictions in the oratorios of the early nineteenth century were fairly standard. Mendelssohn owned copies of several of these works, including Carl Loewe's *Die Zerstörung von Jerusalem* (*The Destruction of Jerusalem*, 1830).[23] Loewe's oratorio begins by portraying the Jews as a people of strength, rising up against their Roman oppressors, but this depiction changes radically once infighting among the Jews begins and especially once the Christians, who take the moral high-ground, are introduced. The oratorio's climax arrives after negotiations between Titus, the Roman governor, and the Jews fail, and the Romans begin their attack. As the Jews fight back, they cry with an almost animal-like fury, "I want to rage! I want to murder; I laugh; I laugh; Revenge" ("Rasen will ich! Morden will ich; Ich lache; ich lache; Rache"). Meanwhile, the Christians at Golgotha pray for the Jews, asking God to grant them the courage to bear their impending suffering. Once the Romans begin to gain the upper hand, Titus pronounces death for the Jews, but promises mercy for the Christians. With all nearly lost, a high priest cries out, "What sin, O Lord, has your poor people committed?" ("Was hat, o Herr, dein armes Volk verbrochen?"), to which "Spirit-voices" ("Geisterstimmen") respond, "His blood be upon us and our children" ("Sein Blut komme über uns und unsre Kinder!" [Matt. 27:25]). Their battle lost, the Jews cry out "Jehovah! Jehovah!," which, as a note in the score explains, indicates that they were convinced of their imminent destruction, since the sin of uttering the name of God was punishable by death.[24] The oratorio then closes with the chorus of prophets and Christians declaring that "For those are the days of revenge, which fulfilled what was foretold!" ("Denn das sind der Rache Tage, dass erfüllt sei, was verheissen!"). Thus Loewe characterized the destruction of Jerusalem as being the direct result of the Jews' rejection of Christ.

Equally negative is another work owned and known well by Mendelssohn, the passion oratorio *Des Heilands letzte Stunde* by Louis Spohr.[25] Based on a libretto by Friedrich Rochlitz (a mutual acquaintence of the two composers),[26] the text is a loose adaptation of the passion narrative, which allows it, among other things, to be considerably more anti-Semitic than the original biblical account. Of particular interest is the work's alignment with what Schleiermacher, in *Der christliche Glaube,* called the Jews' "limitation of the love of Jehovah to the race of Abraham, [which] betrays a lingering affinity with Fetishism."[27] This ideology is evident in the numerous segments of Spohr's oratorio in which the Jews not only claim to be the chosen people (a posture that would have seemed offensive to a Christian audience), but also maintain that God led them in their decision to crucify Christ.

While Mendelssohn's portrayal of the Jews in *Moses* may have stemmed from a fear that a positive depiction would have led to some kind of negative public response, as well as to accusations of his holding a secret philo-Semitic agenda, it remains uncertain whether this would in fact have occurred. For there were at least two composers—one Lutheran-born (Friedrich Schneider) and one converted Jewish (Marx himself)—who were able to include positive images of the Jews in their works, with no evidence that it adversely affected their careers. Friedrich Schneider's setting of the Exodus story in *Pharao* (1828), for example, portrays the Jews as nothing less than steadfast, and as a people who praise God at every opportunity. This heroic portrayal of the Jews, however, did not prevent the work from becoming one of Schneider's most oft-performed oratorios as well as the most popular of the century's settings involving Moses.[28] The oratorio begins just after the last of the ten plagues, with Israel celebrating while Egypt mourns and calls for revenge. Out of fear, however, Pharaoh allows the Jews to leave. In the second part, Israel continues to celebrate freedom and the promise of a "Fatherland," all granted by the grace of God. Egypt pursues, however, and for one brief instant, with their backs up against the Red Sea, the Jews' faith waivers. But with the parting of the sea, faith returns, and after crossing, they shout out, "Hosanna in the highest!"

Marx's highly positive depiction of the Jews in *Mose* likewise seems to have had little impact on the work's overall reception. As noted earlier, Gebhard von Alvensleben, a reviewer of the 1841 premiere in Breslau, heralded the highly dramatic work as a "new star" in the history of oratorio, a sentiment that was echoed in numerous other publications in the years that followed. In 1843, for example, Gustav Adolph Keferstein published a lecture he had delivered at the Academy of Sciences in Erfurt, in which he advocated "the idea of oratorio as a true, pure music drama," a concept he found well-executed in *Mose*. A year later, Gustav Heuser made a similar demand on the genre, and likewise lauded *Mose* as the perfect embodiment of this ideal. And in 1853, after Franz Liszt conducted the work in Weimar, reviewer Joachim Raff aptly summarized prevailing opinion by describing it as "a music drama in evening dress," and even questioned Marx's use of the label "oratorio," rather than "musical-dramatic poem."[29]

Given the public acceptance of other philo-Semitic oratorios at the time, that Mendelssohn could have provided a more benevolent depiction of the Jews in *Moses* but did not not only demonstrates his apparent desire to separate himself from his heritage, but also strikes at the heart of why Marx chose to reject the libretto. Marx commented in his memoirs that the libretto left him feeling "cold" because of its responsorial format. As Marx's initial prose draft demonstrates, however, Mendelssohn's choice of this format stemmed not only from his own personal leanings, but also from its being the same format Marx had used in his own version of the libretto. Marx may have realized this when he placed the blame for the libretto's inadequacies on himself, writing in his memoirs, "Why did I neglect, or was unable to carefully show him the new form, which was so important to me!"[30] But my comparison between *Moses* and *Mose* demonstrates that this was hardly the sole difference between the two libretti. Indeed, the most palpable difference between the works bears on the portrayal of the Jews, with that in *Mose* being far more positive than that in *Moses*. While Marx does not state outright that Mendelssohn's negative depiction was a factor in his rejection of the libretto, it is easy to imagine that he found it offensive, given his upbringing and attitude toward his Jewish heritage.

Like Mendelssohn, Marx was born into a Jewish family and converted during his youth. But unlike Mendelssohn, who had Christianity thrust upon him by his father, Marx found Christianity on his own, much to his father's dismay. Not that Marx's father, Moses, was a devout member of what Marx consistently referred to as the "old church" ("alte Kirche")—quite the contrary, in fact.[31] He was a textbook Rationalist, who adhered firmly to the teachings of Voltaire and who, despite being the son and grandson of rabbis, considered Judaism and Christianity to be faiths of superstition and ridiculed them both.[32] But, as Marx recalled, his father held it as a point of honor to remain a Jew (and even occasionally attended synagogue), despite the restrictions society placed upon him as a result. He was also literally dead set against his son's conversion, likely believing it to represent a rejection of his son's cultural and religious heritage. Once Marx had set his baptismal date, his father threatened that the bed from which he spoke would be his deathbed should Marx convert to Christianity. Marx, however, was resolved and followed through with his plan. (His father survived.)[33]

Knowing his father considered the choice between religions meaningless (in his eyes, they were all equally absurd), Marx was perplexed by his father's strong opposition to his conversion. But when considered in light of his father's other comments on the subject (which attack Judaism as a religion but never the Jews themselves) and his occasional visits to the synagogue despite his Rationalist leanings, one gets the sense that while his father abandoned Judaism, he retained a strong sense of Jewish cultural identity, one which he did not want to see his son forsake. Having raised his son as a non-observant Jew, Marx's father probably doubted the authenticity of his son's new-found Christian faith and believed the motivating force behind his conversion to be the improvement of his social status. Having himself been willing to forego the social advantages baptism would have provided—likely for the sake of preserving his cultural identity—such a superficial baptism would, in his mind, have been a cynical betrayal of that identity. But as Marx's frank discussion of the events of his youth reveal, not only was his conversion genuine, it never led him to deny his Jewish heritage.

What truly spurred Marx toward Christianity was Christian music: pieces such as Handel's *Messiah* and Mozart's Requiem led him to a passionate, zealous interest in the Bible. "Particularly inspiring to me were most parts of the Old Testament and from the New, the Gospels of Matthew and Luke," he wrote, adding that he found these particular writings more revealing of the true meaning of both Judaism and Christianity than the Epistles or any other theological writings known to him. Of the Gospels he noted that he was especially impressed by the Sermon on the Mount and by Christ's arguments with the Pharisees, and by what they each revealed of Christ's character and of the meaning of his coming.[34] Marx would later find that this new passion for Bible study would, "quite unexpectedly, show itself to have a great influence . . . on me as a composer and journalist."[35] This influence is particularly apparent in *Mose,* whose subject matter seems to have been central to his interest in the Bible. His mention of the gospel of Matthew in the same breath as the Old Testament is particularly revealing, as the gospel presents an image of Christ as the "New Moses" throughout.[36] That Marx was aware of this image of Christ is undeniable, given *Mose's* prophetic penultimate chorus with its adaptation of Deuteronomy 18:18—"Behold, I will send them a prophet, who shall speak to them all that I command him" ("Siehe, ich will einen Propheten ihnen senden, der soll zu ihnen reden Alles, was Ich ihm gebieten werde")—a text that contemporary Bibles connected with numerous points in the New Testament.[37] Marx's specific mention of his affection for the sermon on the mount, again in the context of his general attraction to the Old Testament and the direct parallel of the sermon (Matt. 5:17–48) to Moses' reception of the law on Mount Horeb (Ex. 31:18), further reveals the importance Moses held for Marx.

Despite the fervor of Marx's Lutheran faith, which perhaps even surpassed Mendelssohn's, Marx never attempted to disassociate himself from his Jewish heritage. Indeed, Marx spent the entire first chapter of his memoirs discussing his father's convictions, his own early experiences in the synagogue, and finally, the impetus for his conversion. Moreover, as Herzl Schumeli demonstrated in his documentation of Marx's attitudes toward Judaism and patriotism, Marx did not view his crossover into Christianity as a declaration that his former faith or its members were somehow inferior; Judaism may have been the "old church," but that made it and its adherents no less a part of the nation. Nor did he ever find it necessary to deny his heritage or attack the "old church" in order to proclaim either his patriotism or his faith.[38]

Mendelssohn, on the other hand, was not only led to the church by his father (who also converted), but was actively encouraged by him to disassociate himself from his Jewish heritage and the surname that signified it. As a result, those works written during Abraham's lifetime (that is, through the first version of *Paulus,* completed in early 1836) demonstrate

Mendelssohn's understanding of how best to disassociate himself from Judaism—namely, by disparaging it. It was not enough to prove the strength of his faith by filling *Moses* with Christian symbolism; it was also necessary—at least in Mendelssohn's mind—to demonstrate his complete separation from Judaism by aligning the work with the contemporary anti-Semitic standard, one defined at least partially in the works of the only two oratorio composers (aside from Marx) he knew personally: Carl Loewe and Louis Spohr.[39] Granted, there were other composers who successfully managed to portray the Jews favorably without reprisal, but these men did not bear the burden of being the grandson of the great Jewish philosopher and reformer Moses Mendelssohn—a name that was still of "great import" (to quote Abraham) to German Jews and was well-known to most Gentiles.[40] Indeed, throughout his life, Felix Mendelssohn—in biographies, publicity articles, and elsewhere—frequently heard his name uttered in the same breath as his grandfather's, a situation that may very well have led him to believe (and not unjustly) that he and his music were continually under the closest scrutiny by those who, as his father had warned him, felt that a Christian Mendelssohn was an impossibility.[41] As a result, Mendelssohn's tendency to attack the Jewish image and Marx's to protect it would continue in their collaboration on Mendelssohn's *Paulus,* which was completed before the total collapse of their relationship. Although Marx was less protective of the Jewish image in the *Paulus* libretto he assembled for Mendelssohn than he was in *Mose,* Mendelssohn would again reject Marx (and his libretto), bowing instead to the will of his family, friends, and professional associates, all of whom would, by word and example, continue to encourage him to leave his heritage behind. Eventually, the death of his father in autumn 1835 and the establishment of his career in Leipzig at roughly the same time would allow Mendelssohn to begin to reevaluate this attitude and to work toward developing a manner of proving the sincerity of his Christian faith without disparaging his Jewish heritage.

Notes

A shorter version of this article was read at the 1999 National Meeting of the American Musicological Society in Kansas City, Missouri. I would like to thank panel members K. M. Knittel, Michael Marissen, Klára Móricz, and Anne L. Seshadri and the conference participants for their comments. For their assistance and insights during the preparation of both the original paper and this article, I would also like to thank Ilse Andrews, Eric Chafe, Peter F. Cohen, Vera Deak, Ellen Harris, James Hill, Peter Ward Jones, Hans-Günter Klein, Robert L. Marshall, Diane Ota, Christian Schwirten, Darwin Scott, R. Larry Todd, and the Music Division of the New York Public Library for the Performing Arts. The research for this article was sponsored in part by the Fulbright Commission, the Spalding Trust, the Josephine de Kármán Foundation, and Brandeis University.

1. All citations in this paragraph are from Adolf Bernhard Marx, "From the Memoirs of Adolf Bernhard Marx," trans. Susan Gillespie, in R. Larry Todd, ed., *Mendelssohn and His World* (Princeton, N.J.: Princeton University Press, 1991), 212–13. For a discussion of Marx's libretto for Mendelssohn's oratorio *Paulus*, see Sposato, "Mendelssohn, *Paulus*, and the Jews: A Response to Leon Botstein and Michael Steinberg," *The Musical Quarterly* 83/2 (1999): 284–86.

2. For an in-depth discussion of the *Moses* sources, as well as transcriptions of Marx's outline, his prose draft, and Mendelssohn's subsequent drafts, see Sposato, "The Price of Assimilation: The Oratorios of Felix Mendelssohn and the Nineteenth-Century Anti-Semitic Tradition" (Ph.D. dissertation, Brandeis University, 2000), 1:146–52 and 2:7–46. The final version of the libretto has also been published in Edgar Kellenberger, "Felix Mendelssohn als Librettist eines Moses-Oratoriums: Erstedition mit Kommentar," *Musik und Kirche* 63/3 (1993): 126–39.

3. "Schon hielt ich in meinen Händen den Text, den mein Kunstgenoß für mich zusammengestellt. Als ich ihn durchlas und wieder las, fühlte ich mich wie vom Donner gerührt. 'Das, das also der Mose! von dem Du so lange geträumt . . . und jetzt stehst Du ihm kalt, fühllos gegenüber! kein Pulsschlag hebt sich für ihn, keine Anschauung dämmert empor!' Ich fühlte mit wahrhaftem Schrecken, daß ich das Werk nicht komponiren könne. . . . Endlich doch mußte ich mir sagen, daß . . . der Text fallen müsse. . . . Hier ward mir klar, auf wie weit geschiedenen Wegen wir gewandelt, der Freund und ich. Gewißlich, . . . hatte er in Treue und nach fester Ueberzeugung für mich gearbeitet. Er hatte den Text geschaffen wie vor uns so Viele geschaffen, und von den größten Meistern unbedenklich angenommen worden waren. Das Gemisch von Erzählung, lyrischem Erguß und dramatischen Momenten, war von Händel und Bach stehende Form; unser beider Lieblingswerk, die matthäische Passion hatte dieselbe Gestaltung. Mendelssohn also stand vollkommen vorwurfsfrei da. Wenn Einen ein Vorwurf traf, so traf er mich. Warum hatte ich versäumt, oder nicht vermocht, ihm die neue Form, die mir nothwendig war, deutlich vorzuzeichen!" Adolf Bernhard Marx, *Erinnerungen aus meinem Leben* (Berlin: Otto Janke, 1865), 2:171–73.

All translations are mine unless otherwise indicated.

4. Gebhard von Alvensleben, "Über die Idee dramatischen Fortgangs und Zusammenhangs im Oratorium. Bei Gelegenheit der Aufführung des 'Moses' von A. B. Marx," *Neue Zeitschrift für Musik* 16/19 (1842): 73.

5. Letter of 16 January 1833 from Mendelssohn to Karl Klingemann: "[I]ch habe ihm [Marx] aus Bibelstellen einen Text zum Oratorium zusammengestellt, der mir ganz ausnehmend gefällt; es muss ein schönes Werk daraus werden," *Felix Mendelssohn Bartholdys Briefwechsel mit Legationsrat Karl Klingemann in London*, Karl Klingemann II, ed. (Essen: G. D. Baedecker, 1909), 107.

6. Letter of 4 February 1833 to Klingemann: "Der Gegenstand seines [Marx's] Oratoriums werde Dir hiermit gesagt, . . . Moses ist es. Im ersten Teil die Bedrückung Israels bis zu Moses Gespräch mit Gott im flammenden Busch. Im zweiten Teil Moses vor Pharao, die Plagen, die Ausführung, das Wunder im roten Meer bis zum Triumphlied der Mirjam. Im dritten die Wüste, die Empörungen, das goldene Kalb, der grimmige Herr Gott, endlich die zehn Gebote. Ich habe es alles aus Bibelstellen zusammengestellt, und das einzige, was ich dazu gedichtet habe, ist: 'Des Abends aber' oder 'er sprach.' Drum ist's auch so schön;" Klingemann, ed., *Felix Mendelssohn Bartholdys Briefwechsel*, 109–10.

7. D-Bsb MA MS 76. Exactly how Marx handled his rejection of Mendelssohn's libretto remains unclear. The Staatsbibliothek zu Berlin manuscript, with its deletions, suggests at first glance that Marx returned the manuscript to Mendelssohn, who upon receipt crossed out the composer attribution in a fit of anger. The transcription of the very beginning and end of the manuscript in Marx's 1865 *Erinnerungen* (2:143–44), and, as will soon be seen, Marx's heavy use of the libretto in *Mose* (despite his claim of its unsuitability), as well as the lack of any of Marx's handwriting in the Staatsbibliothek manuscript, suggest, however, that Marx retained the libretto Mendelssohn sent him, and that MA MS 76 is Mendelssohn's own copy. That the manuscript contains some minor additions in Mendelssohn's hand further suggests that Mendelssohn wrote a presentation copy, decided on some last-minute changes, and then made a fresh, pristine copy which he sent to Marx, keeping this penultimate copy for himself. Once Marx announced he would not be using the libretto, Mendelssohn most likely pulled out his own copy and crossed out the attribution.

8. Letter of 6 August 1834 from Mendelssohn to Schubring. Paul Mendelssohn Bartholdy et al., eds., *Letters of Felix Mendelssohn Bartholdy from 1833 to 1847*, trans. Lady Wallace (Boston: Oliver Ditson and Co., 1863), 45. In her article on the relationship between Marx and Mendelssohn, Christina Siegfried charted the breakdown, noting that letters in which Mendelssohn voiced his doubts about the relationship begin in 1833. Christina Siegfried, "'Der interessanteste und problematischste seiner Freunde'—Adolph Bernhard Marx (1795–1866)," in Bernd Heyder and Christoph Spering, eds., *Blickpunkt: Felix Mendelssohn Bartholdy* (Cologne: Verlag Dohr, 1994), 41. The first example she includes, however, is the 6 August 1834 letter.

9. Marx, *Erinnerungen*, 2:138.

10. Therese Marx, *Adolf Bernhard Marx' Verhältniß zu Felix Mendelssohn Bartholdy, in Bezug auf Eduard Devrient's Darstellung* (Leipzig: Dürr'schen Buchhandlung, 1869), 22.

11. Eduard Devrient's account of this story indicates that Marx wanted him to arrange for a performance of *Mose* at the Lower Rhine Music Festival, which Mendelssohn would be directing in Düsseldorf in May 1839; see Devrient, *My Recollections of Felix Mendelssohn Bartholdy and His Letters to Me*, trans. Natalia MacFaran (New York: Vienna House, 1972), 98–99. Therese Marx's account (*Adolf Bernhard Marx' Verhältniß*, 22), printed here, indicates, however, that Marx was hoping for a performance in Leipzig.

12. "Da war es nun, 1839, wo Marx endlich seinen Jugendtraum, den er sein ganzes Leben mit sich herumgetragen, verwirklichen konnte. Er schrieb in glücklicher gehobener Stimmung sein Oratorium 'Mose.' Sein erster Gedanke nach der Vollendung war der an den Freund. Er allein konnte durch seine Hülfe diesem Schmerzenskind Eingang in die Welt verschaffen. Hoffnungsfreudig reiste Marx nach Leipzig und suchte Mendelssohn auf. Wenn der sein Werk dort aufführte, so war—wie Marx vielleicht irrig aber bestimmt annahm—der Erfolg entschieden. Mit der Bitte: Hilf mir, mein Werk ist vollendet, trat er dem Freunde gegenüber. Beide setzten sich an den Flügel und Marx spielte und sang den ersten Theil des Werkes aus der Partitur. Nach dessen Vollendung erhob sich Mendelssohn, und sagte kühl: 'Du darfst mir das nicht übel nehmen, aber für dieses Werk kann ich nichts thun.' Marx in seinen Hoffnungen getäuscht, in seinem Selbstgefühl verletzt,

verlor kein weiteres Wort, er schloß die Partitur und reiste ab. . . . Marx kam nach diesem Fehlschlage tief verstimmt zurück. Die Hoffnungen, die er anfangs allein auf Mendelssohn's Hülfe gesetzt, waren zerstört, das letzte Band der Freundschaft zerrissen. Lange klang dieser Schmerz in ihm nach, ja, er ist in seinem Leben nie darüber hinweg gekommen." Therese Marx, *Adolf Bernhard Marx' Verhältniß,* 22–23.

13. Ibid., 24.

14. Eric Werner, *Mendelssohn: A New Image of the Composer and His Age,* trans. Dika Newlin (London: Free Press of Glencoe, 1963), 40–41. Werner also claimed that Mendelssohn wrote the libretto in response to his rejection for the post of Berlin *Singakademie* director—a rejection due in part to his Jewish lineage. As discussed above, however, it was Marx who approached Mendelssohn with a proposed exchange. Also, Werner's dating is in error: the libretto was completed (21 August 1832) before the *Singakademie* vote (22 January 1833).

15. For nineteenth-century German theologians, all of the Old Testament's importance lay in its prophecies. As Friedrich Schleiermacher wrote, "everything [but prophecy] . . . in the Old Testament is, for our Christian usage, but the husk or wrapping of its prophecy. . . ." Oratorios written on Old-Testament subjects were written in accordance with this philosophy, and as a result made a point of including some connection (either direct or subtle) to the New Testament. This practice may be readily observed in the works of the era's foremost oratorio composers: Friedrich Schneider, Sigismund Neukomm, Louis Spohr, Carl Loewe, and Mendelssohn. Friedrich Schleiermacher, *The Christian Faith,* ed. H. R. Mackintosh and J. S. Stewart (Edinburgh: T&T Clark, 1989), 62; Schleiermacher, *Der christliche Glaube 1821/22: Studienausgabe,* ed. Hermann Peiter, 2 vols. (Berlin: Walter de Gruyter, 1984), 1:89. For a more in-depth discussion of Christology in the *Moses* libretto, as well as in Mendelssohn's *Elias,* see Sposato, "The Price of Assimilation," 1:159–82 and 351–423.

16. Although both Mendelssohn and Marx refer to the people in their texts as the "children of Israel" or "Israelites" (as is appropriate for this period in biblical history), contemporary German audiences would have viewed them as Jews. Therefore, the terms "Israelite" and "Jew" will be used interchangeably throughout this discussion.

17. Jacob Katz, *From Prejudice to Destruction: Anti-Semitism, 1700–1933* (Cambridge, Mass.: Harvard University Press, 1980), 150; Stephan Rohrbacher and Michael Schmidt, *Judenbilder: Kulturgeschichte antijüdischer Mythen und antisemitischer Vorurteile* (Reinbek bei Hamburg: Rowohlt Taschenbuch Verlag, 1991), 178–93, 289, 305–6, and 313–20.

18. See Sposato, "Mendelssohn, *Paulus,* and the Jews," 280–91.

19. In his study of Marx's *Mose,* Michael Zywietz too conducted a comparison between Marx's and Mendelssohn's texts (not including Mendelssohn's drafts). Michael Zywietz, *Adolf Bernhard Marx und das Oratorium in Berlin* (Eisenach: Verlag der Musikalienhandlung Karl Dieter Wagner, 1996), 269–82. Zywietz, however, focused on the handling of drama in the work.

20. Another reference to modern Christian services appears in no. 7 of *Mose.* The piece is a kind of proto-Kyrie, in which Aaron prays for the people; to each prayer they respond, "Lord, have mercy on us!" ("Herr, erbarme dich unser!").

21. The mention of "gods" here, and indeed Mendelssohn's entire depiction of

the Jews as cultish, may be a manifestation of Friedrich Schleiermacher's influence. Schleiermacher (*The Christian Faith*, 37) noted that Judaism was not fully monotheistic during Moses' lifetime or even for some time afterward: "Judaism, by its limitation of the love of Jehovah to the race of Abraham, betrays a lingering affinity with Fetishism; and the numerous vacillations towards idol-worship prove that during the political heyday of the nation the monotheistic faith had not yet taken fast root, and was not fully and purely developed until after the Babylonian Exile." A less detailed version appeared in Schleiermacher's first edition, *Der christliche Glaube*, 1:52.

22. For a discussion of Mendelssohn's relationship to his Jewish heritage, see Sposato, "Creative Writing: The [Self-]Identification of Mendelssohn as Jew," *The Musical Quarterly* 82/1 (1998): 190–96.

23. Margaret Crum and Peter Ward Jones, comps., *Catalogue of the Mendelssohn Papers in the Bodleian Library, Oxford*, 3 vols. (Tutzing: Hans Schneider, 1980–89), 3:77.

24. "Die Juden durften bekanntlich bei Todesstrafe das höchste Wesen nicht bei dem Namen nennen. Hier presst ihnen die Verzweiflung in der gewissen Ueberzeugung ihres Untergangs, den Ruf: Jehovah! aus." Carl Loewe, *Die Zerstörung von Jerusalem: Großes Oratorium in 2 Abtheilungen von G. Nicolai* (Leipzig: Fr. Hofmeister, 1832), 4.

25. That Mendelssohn was well acquainted with Spohr's oratorio is demonstrated in an unpublished letter of 6 October 1834 from Mendelssohn to his family (New York Public Library [US-NYpl] *MNY++): "Jetzt habe ich eben mit Spohr ein halbes neues Oratorium *[Des Heilands letzte Stunden]* von ihm durchgespielt, und wir haben dazu gesungen. . . ." ("Just now Spohr and I played through half of a new oratorio by him [*Des Heilands letzte Stunden*], and we sang along to it. . . ."). That the score of the work was part of Mendelssohn's library is documented in Crum and Jones, comps., *Catalogue of the Mendelssohn Papers in the Bodleian Library, Oxford*, 3:290.

26. Mendelssohn's relationship with Rochlitz, as well as his acquaintance with Rochlitz's libretto, is outlined in Louis Spohr, *Des Heilands Letzte Stunden*, ed. Clive Brown (New York: Garland Publishing, 1987), vi.

27. Schleiermacher, *The Christian Faith*, 37. Schleiermacher was, of course, speaking in general terms and not of *Des Heilands letzte Stunde*.

28. Howard Smither, *A History of the Oratorio*, 4 vols. (Chapel Hill: University of North Carolina Press, 2000), 4:99–101.

29. Gustav Adolph Keferstein, "Das Oratorium," *Allgemeine musikalische Zeitung* 45 (1843): cols. 922–23; Gustav Heuser, "Oratorium und Oper," *Neue Zeitschrift für Musik* 21 (1844): 162, 177, and 207–8; Joachim Raff, "Aus Weimar. Aufführung des Oratoriums *Mose* von Adolph Bernhard Marx am 3ten Juni 1853," *Neue Zeitschrift für Musik* 39 (1853), 6. These reviews are summarized in Smither, 4:71–72.

30. "Warum hatte ich versäumt, oder nicht vermocht, ihm die neue Form, die mir nothwendig war, deutlich vorzuzeichnen!" Marx, *Erinnerungen*, 2:173.

31. Marx never disclosed his father's name in his memoirs, but Zywietz (*Adolf Bernhard Marx und das Oratorium*, 120) revealed the name in his study. Marx's use of the term "old church" suggests that like many Jewish converts (including Abraham Mendelssohn), as well as many Christians, he saw Protestantism as the natural

successor to Judaism. A discussion of this view may be found in Michael A. Meyer, "Judaism and Christianity," in *German-Jewish History in Modern Times,* ed. Michael A. Meyer (New York: Columbia University Press, 1997), 2:168–79.

32. From what one can distill from Marx's memoirs, Marx's father seems to have been particularly attracted to Voltaire's Deist views of belief in a higher power, as well as his disdain for ceremony, ritual, and belief in the supernatural. Voltaire was, however, no friend to the Jews, as Jacob Katz (*From Prejudice to Destruction,* 34–47) demonstrated. While Voltaire's dislike of all organized faiths prevented him from calling for the Jews' conversion, he instead believed that "when the society of man is perfected, when every people carries on its trade itself, no longer sharing the fruits of its work with these wandering brokers, . . . [the Jews] will assimilate among the scum of the other peoples" (Ibid., 47). Marx's father, however, may not have been aware of Voltaire's views on this matter.

33. Marx, *Erinnerungen,* 1:1–10.

34. Ibid., 1:8-9. "Besonders waren es die meisten Theile des alten Testaments und vom neuen die Evangelien Matthäus und Lucas, welche mich erhoben" (9).

35. "Später erst, damals noch ganz unvorhergesehen, zeigte sich der große Einfluß, den die vertraute Bekanntschaft mit der Bibel auf mich als Komponisten und Schriftsteller äußern sollte." Ibid., 1:9–10.

36. For detailed discussions of the depiction of Christ as the "New Moses" in Matthew's gospel, see Howard Teeple, *The Mosaic Eschatological Prophet* (Philadelphia: Society of Biblical Literature, 1957), 74–83, and Dale C. Allison, Jr., *The New Moses: A Matthean Typology* (Minneapolis: Fortress Press, 1993).

37. For instance, a typical Bible from Mendelssohn's era (*Die Bibel, oder die ganze heilige Schrift des alten und neuen Testaments, nach der deutschen Uebersetzung Dr. Martin Luthers* [Berlin: Preußischen Haupt-Bibelgesellschaft, 1824]) indicates six parallels for Deut. 18:18 (John, 1:45, 7:16, 8:26, 8:40, and Heb. 3:2–3, 12:24).

38. Herzl Shmueli, "Adolf Bernhard Marx (1795–1866): Deutscher Musiker— Jüdische Herkunft (Eine Dokumentation)," *Orbis Musicae* 10 (1990/91): 224 and 226. Zywietz (*Adolf Bernhard Marx und das Oratorium,* 123) also provided evidence to demonstrate Marx's positive relationship to Judaism in later life.

39. For an overview of Mendelssohn's relationships with Loewe and Spohr, see Sposato, "The Price of Assimilation," 1:235–44.

40. Letter of 8 July 1829 from Abraham Mendelssohn to Felix Mendelssohn. Max F. Schneider, *Mendelssohn oder Bartholdy? Zur Geschichte eines Familiennamens* (Basel: Internationale Felix-Mendelssohn-Gesellschaft, 1962), 18.

41. Abraham's warning appears in his 8 July 1829 letter to Felix; ibid. Felix himself attested to his inability to separate himself from his grandfather's name in his 16 July reply, noting that during his current concert series in London, reviewers and concert promoters had repeatedly referred to him in connection with his grandfather and had even requested that he not require that "Bartholdy" be used when printing his name; ibid., 20–24. Likewise, in biographies written during his lifetime, Mendelssohn's descent from the great philosopher never failed to be mentioned. The 27 December 1837 issue of the *Allgemeine musikalische Zeitung* [col. 845], for example, contains an extensive Mendelssohn biography, which begins, "Felix Mendelssohn-Bartholdy, grandson of the philosopher Moses Mendelssohn, was born on 3 Febr. 1809 in Hamburg."

13

Andrea Maffei's "Ugly Sin": The Libretto for Verdi's *I masnadieri*

ROBERTA MONTEMORRA MARVIN

On 22 July 1847 Londoners attended the premiere of the first opera Verdi composed expressly for an audience outside Italy—*I masnadieri,* the setting of a libretto written by Andrea Maffei (1798–1885) based on Friedrich Schiller's *Die Räuber.*[1] The opera never achieved popularity, either in its day or after, and although several reasons may have accounted for the problems the work encountered, one prominent factor seems to have been the libretto. Despite the potential significance of the nature and shape of the text, however, no detailed study of the genesis of the libretto exists. Although the surviving documentation concerning the text is scanty, a contextualized reading of both old and new evidence can enhance our knowledge of the circumstances surrounding the work's creation. Drawing on extant documents, this essay reexamines the general nature of Verdi's and Maffei's collaboration on the opera, evaluates Maffei's attitude toward operatic texts, and assesses the role of his contribution in the reception of *I masnadieri.* It concludes by presenting information bearing on the nature of modifications Verdi and Maffei made to the libretto, specifically in the finale of the opera's second act.

Maffei's and Verdi's Relationship

We can gain preliminary insight into the nature of Verdi's and Maffei's relationship by reviewing their personal and professional history prior to *I masnadieri.* The composer and the poet had known each other from the early 1840s, when Verdi began frequenting the *salotto* (salon) of Andrea's wife, the Countess Clara Maffei. During the middle part of the decade, Andrea traveled with Verdi frequently: to Naples in autumn 1845 to hear *Alzira,* to Venice in spring 1846 for the premiere of *Attila,* and to Florence in spring 1847 for the first performance of *Macbeth.* On 16 June 1846 Verdi was a witness to the legal separation of Andrea and Clara, and soon thereafter Andrea accompanied Verdi to the spa at Recoaro, where Verdi was to undergo treatment for the illness he had suffered in Venice during the preparation of *Attila,* and where Maffei, in all probability, hoped to overcome the emotional trauma of separation from his wife. The idea for Maffei to write a libretto for Verdi based on Schiller's play *Die Räuber* was conceived during this summer respite, specifically between 3 July and 21 July 1846.[2]

In all probability, Maffei was responsible for the choice of subject, for he had recently completed his Italian translation of Schiller's *Die Räuber.*[3] Having agreed to supply Verdi with a libretto, Maffei likely set to work on the text shortly after returning to Milan.[4] Although it is not possible to establish precisely when Maffei began or completed the libretto, the surviving documents suggest that he may have embarked upon it as early as August 1846 and that he had likely finished a complete draft by mid-October 1846 (perhaps even earlier),[5] for on 23 October 1846 he confessed to his colleague Jacopo Cabianca: "I have committed an ugly sin . . . I have written a musical libretto: *I masnadieri.*"[6]

Verdi and Maffei collaborated on a variety of projects before working together on *I masnadieri.* Their first endeavor—a cantata that Verdi was to have composed for the Congresso degli Scienzati in 1844—turned out to be an unfruitful one, for at that time Verdi had found Maffei's text to be unsuitable for musical setting, due to inappropriate meter and scansion and lack of satisfactory divisions for duets, arias, etc.[7] In 1845 Verdi composed three romances for voice and piano setting Maffei's poetry, and, for at least one of these songs, the *brindisi* "Mescetemi il vino," the composer had requested the poet to write the text expressly for him.[8] In the operatic realm, Maffei may also have assisted Verdi with the sketch for *I due Foscari.*[9] Maffei evidently provided an *abbozzo* for *Attila* in 1845, and he may also have made alterations to the actual libretto.[10] And evidence exists to suggest that in 1846 he may have emended the libretto for *Il corsaro.*[11]

Most of these tasks suited the poet's literary talents, for they required a penetrating grasp of the essence of the literary sources and command of an eloquent and extensive vocabulary. On the other hand, a written synopsis of a source or adjustments to an existing libretto demanded only minimal acquaintance with the operatic medium, not the intuitive knowledge of effective dramatic pacing and the intimate familiarity with the conventional necessities involved in actually creating a text of operatic dimensions from a large-scale literary work. Even Maffei's often touted emendations to Francesco Piave's *Macbeth* text in late 1846 and early 1847 were not tantamount to writing the libretto for an entire opera. A close reading of many of the changes Maffei made in *Macbeth* reveals, as Francesco Degrada has suggested, that his work focused on replacing Piave's wordy verses with "more pertinent and precise locutions" and satisfying Verdi's desire for a more elevated poetic style by achieving subtlety of meaning or enhancing the rhetorical effectiveness of the declamation.[12] In *Macbeth,*

> Verdi turned to Maffei only because Piave had fallen short of even the most pessimistic predictions, and . . . Maffei's contribution was to be of a subordinate nature with respect to the overall conception. This in itself should be enough to lay to rest the notion that Maffei exerted a determining influence on the form of the libretto or on the "ideological" interpretation of Shakespeare's tragedy.[13]

In short, then, other than *I masnadieri,* Maffei's contributions to Verdi's operas were not ones of basic musical dramatic substance.

One other factor should be considered here. Maffei's literary skills were not universally admired. He was praised overtly by some nineteenth-century commentators for his abilities to reproduce accurately the essence of the works of foreign writers but criticized by those same commentators for his inability to imitate the style and accent of diverse poetic styles. His prose translations were admired for their classicism, force, and accuracy, but his poetic translations were often viewed as flowery and overly harmonious.[14] Nonetheless, because of the poet's supposed stature in Italian literary circles and as a consequence of the dearth of written documentation concerning the libretto for *I masnadieri,* more than one modern-day commentator has assumed that Maffei was granted much greater freedom in the writing of the text than Verdi afforded other collaborators.[15] Verdi normally dominated his librettists, however, and there is little reason to believe that, simply as a consequence of his presumedly unqualified respect for his friend, the composer did not make detailed suggestions to Maffei concerning the libretto for *I masnadieri.*[16] Moreover, the absence of written documentation is not indicative of the actual situation, for Verdi and Maffei were both residing in Milan during fall 1846 and spring 1847 and undoubtedly would have discussed the libretto in person. Indeed, the nature of the responsibilities Verdi had previously entrusted to Maffei and Maffei's inexperience as a librettist would seem to suggest rather strongly that Verdi would have needed to offer advice concerning the shape and structure of the text as well as its "singability" and suitability with regard to musical setting. It is altogether possible, however, that as a consequence of Maffei's derisive attitude toward his project and his insistence on adhering as closely as possible to his literary source (as discussed below), Verdi's suggestions about the text were at best not adequately heeded and at worst only superficially understood.

Maffei's Attitude and Its Consequences

Maffei was first and foremost a man of letters, a well-known and prolific translator of the works of Schiller, Heine, Goethe, Milton, Byron, and Shakespeare, with strong aesthetic convictions. Only unwillingly would he have reconciled the ideals of spoken drama or literary texts with librettistic needs. But it is not necessary to rely on assumptions in this matter, for Maffei pronounced his negative judgment of texts for musical setting quite forcefully in written form.[17] When compelled to write the previously mentioned cantata verses for Verdi, Maffei complained of being "condemned by those painful mutations demanded by the tyranny of the music."[18] He further expressed his contempt for writing texts to be set to music when he admonished Cabianca for having written an opera libretto:

> For goodness sake, leave that thievish task to the wretched quills of the theatrical writers, and persuade yourself that the needs of composers and singers are the death of sensible opera. . . . You ask me to excuse you, and I do so with plenary indulgence, but only under the inviolable condition that you never again commit such an ugly sin.[19]

Very shortly after reproaching his colleague, Maffei divulged his own transgression of having written *I masnadieri* (as cited on p. 281) and explained the steps he had taken to try to lessen the gravity of his literary violation:

> I have . . . put so much study into delineating the characters, capturing the most effective scenes, and versifying, that I hope, if nothing else, it will not be confused with so much [other] horribly disgusting trash.[20]

In the end, however, the only justification Maffei seemed to be able to find for having committed this "sin" was that he had done it for his friend Verdi: "But even if this were to be the fate of my *melodramma,* at least the satisfaction of having appeased the wishes of a friend will remain."[21]

To repent for the injustice he believed he had imposed upon the literary world, Maffei wrote a public apologia of sorts concerning his indiscretion in the form of a preface to *I masnadieri*:

> This melodrama is drawn from the celebrated tragedy by Friedrich Schiller: *The Robbers*; the first dramatic work to come forth from that divine intellect before maturity and the study of humanity tempered his too impassioned imagination. The struggles endured by the poet during his youth, combined with a temperament naturally inclined to melancholy inspired this horrifying drama which, as we know, so captivated the burning fantasies of the young men of his time that many ran away into the forests with the vision of bettering the world through crime and bloodshed. But if this frightening picture of society in part lacks truth as well as that penetrating insight into the heart that we admire in *Mary Stuart, William Tell,* and *Wallenstein*; it presents in contrast such vivid and heightened interest, such a wide range of emotions, and events so varied and intense, that I know of no other literary work that could offer situations so well suited to musical treatment.
> And it is to these situations, to this intensity of emotion, that one must primarily aim in undertaking the difficult task of writing for this genre [opera], whether one takes his plot from history or from fiction. Since the poet is confined to a very brief space, he cannot give to his thought the dimensions or the psychological

profundity the drama demands, but instead he must work in broad strokes and present the composer with little more than a skeleton, which will derive form, warmth, and life from the music rather than from the words.

In the end, he must reduce a vast conception to small dimensions without altering the original physiognomy, like a concave lens which reduces the size of objects while preserving their shape. As a result, the *melodramma* can be no more than the seed of a poetic creation that will come to its full maturity only through musical ideas.

Such things I have proposed to do in circumscribing in a few verses the profound tragedy of *The Robbers,* without hoping for nor claiming the specious appellation of literary for my labors. Even if the meagerness of my talent has yielded only a shadow of its many [original] supreme beauties, may the long study and the great love that I put forth in Italianizing the dramatic inspirations of this great German [poet] serve to pardon my guilt.[22]

In opening his disclaimer Maffei justified his choice of *Die Räuber* as a subject for operatic treatment, explaining how the elements he believed accounted for literary weaknesses in Schiller's brutally realistic work were precisely the qualities that made it so suitable for musical setting. Many *ottocento* commentators, however, disputed the propriety of the plot for the musical stage. Abramo Basevi, for example, expressed the opinion that *I masnadieri* was too vile to be set to music—where music should be made to express beauty, here it was made to express the base, ugly side of humankind.[23] And, in London, after hearing the premiere of the opera, the critic for *The Morning Herald* questioned whether "any musical interpretation at all could be given to [the] scenes of ruthless terror, or there was any probable chance of reflecting the metaphysical ideal which the hero presents."[24]

Maffei continued by explaining the difficulties with which a poet must contend in adapting a work to the musical stage and elaborating on the shortcomings of operatic dramas. Only here did Maffei even allude to the needs of musical drama, and one may be tempted to perceive his allusion as "lip service." The "skeleton" analogy is, in many ways, an appropriate one that is echoed in much commentary both then and now. But the question arises as to whether Maffei believed what he was saying. Given his scorn toward his libretto, we may wish to read his argument as a defense, especially since in concluding his commentary Maffei pleaded for pardon for having sinned against the literary gods.[25]

Maffei's published rationalization, which appeared in an English translation in the libretto prepared for the opera's premiere, had little effect on the London critics' judgment of the text.[26] Schiller had assumed a prestigious position in early nineteenth-century England.[27] Thus, commentators were familiar with his works in general and with *The Robbers* (*Die Räuber*) in particular. In light of their acquaintance with the German author's works, London journalists expressed strong conflicting opinions of Maffei's libretto. While admittedly it is not possible to evaluate these comments out of context, it is still possible to learn something about the English view of the opera (especially the text) from them.

The elements writers applauded were precisely the types of functional literary tasks in which Maffei would have excelled. The *Times* (23 July 1847) assessed the libretto as "exceedingly well constructed," in that the plot and nearly all of the situations had been preserved, noting in particular the "great tact and felicity" with which Maffei had worked into the recitatives "many points of the dialogue" and pointing out the poet's retention of "two of Schiller's songs." *The Musical World* (24 July 1847) praised the text quite similarly:

> The principal incidents [of Schiller's drama] . . . have been preserved with great tact by the Italian librettist, chevalier Maffei, who has omitted no point of interest except the incident of Kosinski, the introduction of which would doubtless have impeded the operatic effect by encumbering the musician with superfluous materials. The condensation of the dialogue has been managed with great discrimination, the loss of individual development of character (inevitable under the circumstances) being much less observable than would have been the case had the abbreviation been made with less judgment. As much of Schiller's dialogue as could be conveniently given in the recitatives has been preserved, and two of the original songs are cleverly imitated in the Italian version.

Such an emphasis on fidelity to the literary source surely would have pleased Maffei.[28]

Those commentators who were attuned to the requirements of works for the musical stage, however, were less enthusiastic about Maffei's accomplishment. They discussed how the libretto fell short in fulfilling the dramatic criteria for opera. For example, after having attended the premiere of *I masnadieri,* the critic for *The Athenaeum* (24 July 1847) evaluated the libretto as "awkward and deficient in its arrangement," and the writer for *The Morning Chronicle* (23 July 1847) informed readers that Schiller had been "cruelly treated by the Italian librettist" in that only "a shadow is supplied of the original conception." One critical evaluation of Maffei's work, the type he attempted to thwart with his preface, was that printed by the *Courrier de l'Europe* in late July 1847. Pointing to the evidence of the librettist's inexperience "in the choice, the cutting, the ordering and the setting into play [*mise en jeu*] of the dramatic elements," the journalist noted how "it was not possible to damage Schiller's drama any more completely and to make out of the logically progressing drama, proportioned artfully in its divine incidents, a more confused and disordered mess."[29] And Basevi criticized *I masnadieri* for not having any hint of the general *tinta* that characterized some of Verdi's most successful works. He attributed this weakness, in part, to the opera's being "various numbers sewn together" like "a canvas filled with different designs."[30]

Above all, it was in the dramatic design of the libretto that Maffei's principles and ideals, especially his insistent faithfulness to his source, seem to have prevented him from responding effectively to demands of the operatic medium. Indeed, as a comparison of the libretto with Maffei's translation of the play reveals, the librettist closely adhered to Schiller's ordering of scenes, omitted a few episodes he believed to be superfluous to the underlying dramatic premise or in some way underscoring a dramatic theme that was presented more effectively elsewhere, and conflated a few passages. This firm allegiance to the play proved, in many ways, problematic, however, in that Maffei made few concessions or adjustments to accommodate the special requirements of musical-dramatic pacing in an opera.

A summary of the basic events in the libretto serves to illustrate the shortcomings in dramatic pacing. Act I consists of three arias in three different venues in rapid succession—the first (which opens the opera in lieu of the traditional *introduzione*) for the hero Carlo, the second for the antagonist Francesco, and the third for the heroine Amalia—and concludes with a duet between Amalia and Massimiliano leading directly into the ensemble finale. Each of the scenes preceding the finale is primarily reflective and serves to introduce the singers and the characters. While there is some situating of characters, there is no true development of the drama until the finale. The real problem is that the gestures are not psychological or physical but intellectual, and everything serves simply as a backdrop for the events to come. The dramatic pacing in the act is static.

At first it seems as if Act II will compensate for the slow-moving Act I, and it certainly has the best layout of any of the four acts. But almost all of the dramatic development—Amalia's learning that her beloved Carlo is alive and Francesco's harassing encounter with the heroine—occurs in the beginning of the act (first two scenes/numbers). Although the action continues in the finale, it is relayed through a narrative chorus, arresting the quick dramatic pacing of the earlier scenes. The centerpiece of the finale is a reflective *romanza* sung by the hero Carlo (unnecessary to the development of the plot), followed by a very brief choral reprise to conclude the act. The finale is weak, and compared to other Verdi operas, the dramatic pacing in the act seems unbalanced.

Act III packs too many pivotal events into a brief span: the hero and heroine are reunited; the hero rescues his father Massimiliano who has been imprisoned (buried alive) by Francesco, and the Masnadieri swear to avenge their leader. While previous acts contained numbers in which internally the action developed slowly or not at all, here everything happens too quickly and in rapid succession. The dramatic pacing is too steady, lacking the necessary ebb and flow.

The drama continues to unfold steadily at the beginning of Act IV with the antagonist Francesco's narrative *sogno* and a powerful duet between Francesco and the Priest Moser—both highly effective musical-dramatic pieces. But because Maffei chose to retain *all* details from Schiller's final scenes, he included an encounter between Carlo and his father Massimiliano which provides an element of sentimentality but arrests the dramatic pace established in the first two numbers. The climax and denouement are quick, but the manner in which Maffei condensed the original scene leaves the motivations for the characters' actions so unclear that, as one English critic put it, the finale is "more provocative of hilarity than of tragic emotion."[31] The dramatic pacing is so economical that it becomes a bit disjointed.

In the *Ottocento* a competent librettist had to be a skillful versifier, but he also had to possess a talent for designing a scenario that would abide by the conventions of the era. To succeed in his undertaking, he had to adapt his subject to the structure and the sense of the musical forms and to ascertain what was most and least suitable for musical treatment.[32] As a consequence of Maffei's inexperience in the musical theater, he possessed few of these skills. In sum then, although Maffei may well have preserved the order of scenes and basic content of Schiller's story and in so doing preserved his literary independence and indulged his literary ideals concerning an efficiently and economically constructed spoken drama, the product of his labor is an unusually and, I would venture to say, ineffectively paced musical drama—too intellectual, and above all, too "literary" in dramatic focus, layout, and (as shall be discussed below) language.

Of course, Verdi had worked with unseasoned librettists before *I masnadieri*. Francesco Piave was a novice when he and Verdi worked together on *Ernani*. In this instance, however, "in the long term, . . . Piave's evident inexperience may . . . have been beneficial to the final result [for] it forced Verdi to take a far more active part in the dramatic planning."[33] And this, as well as Piave's receptiveness to Verdi's suggestions, resulted in libretti that were extremely well suited to Verdi's music because, "in detail as well as in general shape, Verdi himself composed them."[34] Unlike Piave, however, Maffei did not respect his task, and his low opinion of the literary quality of texts for the operatic medium may well have made him especially resistant to Verdi's recommendations concerning the libretto.

Verdi's and Maffei's Collaboration on *I masnadieri*

Unfortunately no correspondence survives relating Verdi's explicit suggestions for the libretto for *I masnadieri*, but two important letters dating from the latter stages in the opera's genesis are extant. In early April 1847 Verdi wrote to Maffei begging him to accept a gift, presumably in gratitude for his assistance with *Macbeth*, and explaining the sum of money he was to be paid for the rights to the text for *I masnadieri*. In closing his letter, Verdi requested Maffei to make a few changes in the libretto: "I would wish only that you retouch a few things in the second act, which is absolutely ineffective for the stage. If you want this libretto to achieve an effect as much as I do, it is necessary to make this final sacrifice. In any case, we shall talk about it in person."[35] Verdi's mention of a "final sacrifice" intimates that he had previously asked Maffei to make concessions, one may safely assume, for the sake of the requirements of the musical stage;

and that perhaps Verdi now anticipated that Maffei would make additional emendations only against his better judgment (hence the use of the word "sacrifice") and only with some coaxing.

Maffei's obsequious reply further hints that the road to the finished product had not been a smooth one. The conclusion of the librettist's letter suffices to illustrate its flavor:

> I am not so happy, dear Verdi; the solitude in which I find myself would be dear to an egoist, but not to me who needs friendship, mainly yours; by taking that away from me you could only pierce my heart. Do not speak of sacrifices when you wish something from me. My pen and my meager talent have been yours for a long time.[36]

Following on a lengthy text expressing many similar sentiments, the poet's expression of fear of Verdi's diminished affection and his offer of his literary expertise to accommodate the composer may be read as the words of one attempting to ingratiate himself with his colleague, and it thus may be that something less than congenial had transpired between the two men. The "indolence," "languor," "weariness," and "apparent impotence" that Gabriele Baldini sensed in Maffei's response, then, may not only be representative of the poet's tactics in ensnaring Verdi (as Baldini believed),[37] but may also be indicative of his resignation to the situation at hand, that is, to having to yield his literary principles to the requirements of the musical stage.

Emendations in Act II of the Libretto

However they may have come about, emendations were indeed made in Act II of the libretto, as Verdi requested. These modifications reveal an extraordinary attention to detail beyond dramatic considerations. Some of the minor alterations—omissions of verses, transpositions of text, substitutions of words—could easily have been made by Verdi, but those of poetic substance may have required Maffei's intervention. A comparison of several extant sources has revealed a number of smaller emendations and one large-scale revision—two different readings of a passage from the finale of Act II, which will be discussed presently.[38]

To set the scene: Carlo, the son of Count Moor, has been banished from his home, due to the intrigues of his conniving brother Francesco, and has become the captain of a band of brigands. The Act II finale finds the gang of bandits outside Prague (Carlo's home) discussing their leader's plans to rescue one of their group, Rolla, from the gallows and witnessing from afar Carlo's triumph (through the burning of the city). Upon Carlo's and Rolla's triumphant return one group of Masnadieri narrates the story of the rescue to which the rest respond with a cry of "viva." The two versions of the affected passage are printed in table 13.1; alterations are italicized.[39]

Table 13.1. Act II Finale Revisions.

(Verdi's stage directions in the autograph seldom match those in the printed libretto; thus the differences listed below cannot be taken as evidence of purposeful changes.)

Autograph Score: [II.4:]	London Libretto: II.4: LA SELVA BOEMA. PRAGA IN LONTANANZA MEZZO ASCOSA FRA GLI ALBERI. LA MASNADA.
A IL PRIMO CROCCHIO *(ENTRANO SUBITO IN SCENA)*: *Tutto quest'oggi le mani in mano[.]* *(ENTRANO ALCUNI MASNADIERI)* IL SECONDO CROCCHIO *(ACCORRENDO)*: *Oh non sapete?* I: *Che v'ha di strano?* II: Rolla è prigione! I: Prigion? che sento[!] II: Darà[,] vi dico[,] de' calci al vento[.] I: Che disse il capo[?] II: *Disse e giurò* *che far di Praga vuole un falò[.]* B ————————————	A ALC[UNI] M[ASNADIERI]: *Le mani in mano fin dall'aurora.* ALTRI:. *V'è noto il caso?* *[ACCORRENDO]* I: *Dite in mal'ora?* II: Rolla è prigione! I: Prigion! che sento? II: Darà, vi dico, de' calci al vento. I: Che disse il Capo? II: *Disse e giurò* *Che far di Praga vuole un falò.* B *Ardere un cero per tal convoglio*
I: Se l'ha giurato[,] lo manterrà[.] *Povera Praga[!]* II: *Tu n'hai pietà[?]* *Povero il Rolla che va tra poco.* *(VEDESI LA FIAMMA FRA GLI ALBERI)*	*Degno d'un morto che nacque in soglio.* I: Se l'ha giurato, lo manterrà. *Povera Praga!* II: *Tu n'hai pietà?* *Povero il Rolla che va tra poco.* [UNA FIAMMA LONTANA VEDESI ROSSEGGIARE FRA GLI ALBERI.]
Oh[!] non vedete quel vasto fuoco? I: Eccovi il cero[!] la non è fola[,] il Capitano tenne parola[.]	*Oh! non vedete quel vasto f[u]oco—* I: Eccovi il cero! la non è fola, Il Capitano tenne parola. [SCOPPIO SPAVENTOSO]
TUTTI: Che tuono orrendo[!] che mai segui? *(GRIDA INTERNE DI DONNE)*	TUTTI: Che tuono orrendo! che mai segui? [GRIDA INTERNE, QUINDI SBUCANO DAGLI ALBERI DONNE SCAPIGLIATI CON FANCIULLI.]
DONNE: La terra trema, s'abbuia il dì[.] *(ATTRAVERSANO LA SCENA FRA GLI ALBERI)* Oh noi perdute!*(ESCE LA SCENA)*— soccorso! aiuto!— Il finimondo certo è venuto.	DONNE: La terra trema, s'abbuia il dì. Oh noi perdute! —soccorso! aiuto!— Il finimondo certo è venuto. [SPARISCONO DI NUOVO FRA GLI ALBERI.]
[II.5:] *(ENTRA* ROLLA *COGLI ALTRI* MASNADIERI / *3° CROCCHIO)* MAS[NADIERI]: Morte e demonio! chi si fa presso? L'ombra del Rolla[?]—per Dio, gli è desso! D'onde ne vieni così serrato[?] ROLLA: Io? dalla forca dritto[,] filato.	II.5: ROLLA ED ALTRI MASNADIERI, POI CARLO MOOR. MAS[NADIERI]: Morte e demonio! chi si fa presso? L'ombra del Rolla?—per Dio, gli è desso! D'onde ne vieni così serrato? ROLLA (ANEL[LANTE]): Io? dalla forca dritto, filato.
Dell'aquavite! non reggo più. MAS.: Bevi, e poi narra! ROL.: Narrali tu.	Dell'aquavite! non reggo più. MAS.: Bevi, e poi narra! [GLI MESCONO UN BICCHIER D'ACQUAVITE.] ROL.(AD UNO DELLA MAS.): Narralo tu.

Table 13.1. *(continued)*

Autograph Score:	London Libretto:
MAS.: I cittadini correano alla festa[,]	MAS.: I cittadini correano alla festa,
e noi[,] lanciate più cánape ardenti[,]	E noi, lanciate più cánape ardenti,
gridammo: ["]al foco[!"] *da questa e da*	Gridammo: "al foco!" *da quella, da questa;*
quella;	
ed ecco pressa, tumulto, lamenti[—]	Ed ecco pressa, tumulto, lamenti—
la polveriera scoppiò con tempesta[,]	La polveriera scoppiò con tempesta,
e la paura confuse i sergenti[,]	E la paura confuse i sergenti,
C *Il duce allora piombò sulla folla,*	C *Allora il Capo fra lor s'avventò,*
e trasse il laccio dal capo del Rolla.	*E il prigioniero dal laccio salvò.*
ROL.: Sì[!] m'ha tirato fuor della fossa[.]	ROL.: Sì! m'ha tirato fuor della fossa.
MAS.: Eccolo[!]—ha l'aria mesta e	MAS.: Eccolo!—ha l'aria mesta e
commossa[!]	commossa!
	[CAR{LO} ENTRA PENSOSO E
	CONTEMPLA IL SOLE CHE TRAMONTA.]
MAS.: Capitano[!] qual è la tua mente!	MAS.: Capitano! qual è la tua mente?
CARLO: Noi partiam coll'aurora vegnente.	CARLO: Noi partiam coll'aurora vegnente.
D MAS.: *(PARTENDO / ALLONTANANDOSI)*	D ————————————
Viva! vittoria di braccio e pensier,	
chi gli sovrasti non ha il masnadier.	————————————
	[LA MAS{NADA} SI PERDE NELLA SELVA.]

The events that the band of *masnadieri* report, although they occur outside the action of the drama, are essential to the plot. It is not surprising, then, that the changes in the Act II finale reflect concern that the chorus's text be effective, concise, intelligible, and easily set to lyrical music.

In passage A in the table, the revised verses as Verdi set them (in the autograph score) facilitate the declamation of the words, slightly alter the verbal accentuation, change the musical-rhetorical emphasis, and provide a more authentic mode of expression for the Masnadieri. The early version contains numerous elisions—a common reason for text substitution elsewhere in the opera—which are eliminated in the revision. Easier to enunciate, the revised verses permit clearer declamation of the text when sung by multiple male voices.[40] The explosive sound of "tutto" provided the natural accentuation desirable on a downbeat vocal entrance, as Verdi set each verse in this section. "Tutto" is more forceful not only in sound but also in meaning: it evokes the bond among the Masnadieri; it also clarifies the import of the situation in which the group finds itself by specifying the lengthy period of time as *all* day. The change in the following line was precipitated, in all probability, by a need to adjust the rhyme scheme.[41]

In passage B Verdi excluded two verses from the musical setting of the opening dialogue. Omitting these lines not only focused attention on text emphasizing Carlo's heroic (if savage) leadership qualities but also allowed the action to unfold more expediently, insofar as the excised lines unnecessarily explained the rationale behind Carlo's menacing threats digressing from the action of the narrative. The deleted verses are also longer than those surrounding them; their inclusion may have destroyed the pace of conversational exchange that resulted from the short phrases. Poetic scansion and its implications for the melodic-rhythmic setting may also have played a role in the decision to delete these lines. The early reading of the entire text passage contains *doppi quinari* lines:[42]

4 *piano*–2 *tronco*–2 *piano*–2 *tronco*–4 *piano*–2 *tronco*–2 *piano*

When Verdi removed the 2 *piano* lines (B), he was left with a differently balanced arrangement of verses:

4 *piano*–4 *tronco*–4 *piano*–2 *tronco*–2 *piano*

a poetic scheme that he perhaps found more suitable for setting to music.

In the chorus's narrative *brindisi* Maffei rewrote two verses (C). The emendation not only adds a personal element, specifying the prisoner as "Rolla," it also narrates the action more vividly. Moreover, the revised version portrays Carlo as an active agent with lively description of his actions in Rolla's rescue. The adjustments to the poetic scansion are of even greater importance.[43] The original *tronco* (*doppi quinari*) verses would not easily have fit into the melodic-rhythmic declamation pattern suitable to the previous *piano* lines. But in revising the passage Maffei not only altered the final accent pattern of the verses, he changed their poetic scansion to *endecasillabo*, and, of even greater significance, he rearranged the syntactical structure. (Such differences in accentuation, syllable count, and syntax inevitably affected Verdi's musical setting; but without a musical setting for the original text it is impossible to determine the extent of the effects.)[44]

Following these two restructured verses, we find the *tronco* lines restored in the two added *endecasillabo* lines for the chorus (D)—the cry of "viva" uttered by the Masnadieri. The inserted verses augment the role of the chorus and color the scene. By expressing the Masnadieri's pride in their immoral lifestyle, the added text aptly prefaces Carlo's ensuing *romanza,* in which he ponders his desperate plight, trapped between his love for Amalia and his allegiance to the Masnadieri. The chorus's excessive joy spotlights his misery. Finally, the addition had a practical function: it accompanied stage movement. The added text enabled Verdi to frame the dialogue with a choral passage and escort the chorus musically from the stage to set the scene for Carlo's soliloquy.

Another omission and an alteration of verses worthy of note occur in Carlo's solo *romanza* (see table 13.2). Instead of "pesa più la mia catena / la mia pena—è più crudel," Verdi set the text "più mi duol la mia catena / la mia pena è più crudel." The accentuation is the same, and it is thus difficult to imagine a musical reason for the change. But in the verse he set

Table 13.2. Carlo's "Romanza," Act II, scene 6, Libretto from the London premiere.

[RECITATIVE]
    Come splendido e grande[a] il sol tramonta!
Degno ben che s'adori! In questa forma
Cade un eroe!—Natura! Oh sei pur bella!
Sei pur bella e stupenda; ed io deforme,
Orribile così!—Tutto è qui riso,
Io sol trovo l'inferno in paradiso!
[ARIA]
    Di ladroni attornïato,
Al delitto incatenato,
Dalla terra io son rejetto,
Maledetto—io son dal Ciel.
    Cara vergine innocente,[b]
Se mi corre a te la mente,
Pesa più la mia catena
La mia pena—è più crudel.
    Nè più mai rivederla degg'io?
Ah, si torni al castello natio!

[a]The original reading of this line was "Come splendido e bello il sol tramonta!" The "bello," found in an earlier layer, however, occurs two additional times in the following three lines. Moreover, the repeated "l" sounds in "bello il sol" or "o" sounds in "come splendido e bello il sol" may have provided additional reasons for the emendation.

[b]Verdi inserted an "Ah," at the beginning of this verse in the autograph.

the concept of causing pain gives Carlo a much more personal expression of his feelings and is thus much less "cold" in theatrical terms. Moreover, Verdi did not set the final two lines of Carlo's text (italicized in the preceding passage). A change in meter for these verses may well have accounted for part of the problem Verdi had with these lines: the recitative text consists of *endecasillabi*; the aria text is made up of *ottonari* with the exception of the lines Verdi eliminated, which are *decasillabi* and probably intended for recitative. It is, of course, possible that concern for dramatic propriety and musical-dramatic pacing accounted for the omission, for it is certainly quite effective for Carlo to be left in a state of despair and pain rather than pondering a return to his homeland. Nonetheless, a purely practical reason associated with stage convention may have prompted Verdi's decision; that is, allowing Carlo's number to conclude without recourse to recitative, which surely would slow the momentum. The presence of such "connecting verses" at the ends of solo and ensemble numbers (which occur elsewhere in the opera) may well have been a consequence of Maffei's inexperience in the genre.

Although none of Verdi's explicit suggestions about the *I masnadieri* libretto survives, assessing the rationale behind emendations such as these is far from arbitrary. Given that Verdi worked with Maffei on *I masnadieri* and *Macbeth* at about the same time, it is reasonable to assume that similar revisions incorporated into both libretti reflect, at least to some extent, similar dramatic, musical, and poetic considerations. In *Macbeth*, as

Francesco Degrada has shown, Verdi and his librettist revised the text to intensify the drama, to enhance the rhetorical effectiveness of the declamation, or to achieve greater subtlety of meaning. Verdi's interest in brevity and concision resulted in the removal of text that was repetitious, banal, or dramatically "inert." He excised text passages in order to concentrate attention on previous lines or to eliminate obstacles hindering the expedient unfolding of the action. Words and phrases were substituted and verses rearranged to heighten dramatic effect and even to emphasize musical and/ or textual, thematic, or symbolic ties. Verdi was also intent on creating an appropriate character by using certain verse types and choosing specific words in *Macbeth.*[45] Similar objectives are evident in the revisions Verdi and Maffei made in *I masnadieri,* both those in the finale of Act II and other minor changes scattered throughout the opera.

In sum then, Maffei's text may have spoken eloquently, but apparently it did not always sing well, and in some instances, Verdi substituted synonyms for Maffei's patrician words to eliminate multiple elisions, certain consonants, and repeated vowel sounds. Moreover, Verdi experienced some difficulty in deciding on an appropriate musical meter for setting Maffei's verses, due to some unusual metrical patterns. In addition, the literary decorum, beauty, and loftiness of the text does not always express the dramatic ideas directly enough or forcefully enough for a musical drama where concision, precision, and impact of the words and phrases is essential in conveying the message. In other words, Maffei's libretto is a bit "too poetic."[46]

Conclusion

There was every reason that *I masnadieri* should have been a successful opera. It represented Verdi's first attempt to compose a work expressly for a theater outside of Italy, it was written for a stellar cast, and its subject was drawn from a popular and profound drama and adapted by an established man of the literary world. But Maffei's libretto was "too meaty," for the librettist crammed in as many of Schiller's scenes as possible and ended up presenting Verdi with "a succession of indigestible dramatic units."[47] The reason for this was that "in spite of his poetic skills, [Maffei] was unsure of himself in dramatic pacing."[48] But perhaps it was more than uncertainty. Indeed, Maffei seems to have dismissed—maybe even, to some extent, disregarded—the delicate ebb and flow necessary in effective musical renditions of dramatic time in favor of his principles of literary propriety. Thus, although Maffei's *I masnadieri* could have been a viable adaptation as spoken drama, it did not fare quite so well as musical drama. And, inevitably, Verdi bore much of the blame for the opera's inadequacies.

Verdi's *I masnadieri* was deemed unsatisfactory by the majority of the English writers. Criticizing the opera as "lacking inspiration and originality"[49] in its "iterations of the commonest Italian [musical] forms,"[50] the journalists pronounced their judgment: Verdi had "not reached the height of the poet's [Schiller's] idea."[51] Thus, as one nineteenth-century French commentator remarked: "Although we can hardly measure the degree of influence that a bad libretto can have on the composer's spirit, or to what extent it can paralyze his inspiration, what we need to consider in this instance is Verdi's creative ability on such uneven and unsuitable terrain."[52]

Notes

1. Schiller's earliest version of the text was first published in 1781 in Stuttgart; a revised stage version was performed on 13 January 1782 at the Nationaltheater in Mannheim. For more information on the differing versions, see the preface to C. P. Magill and L. A. Willoughby, eds., *Schiller's "Die Räuber": Ein Trauerspiel*, (Oxford: Basil Blackwell, 1964).

2. On his return to Milan from Recoaro, Verdi reported to Clara Maffei (in a letter dated 3 August 1846): "It is not unlikely that he [Andrea] will write a libretto for me: *I masnadieri*." ("Non è difficile che Egli [Maffei] faccia per me un libretto: *I Masnadieri*.") Arturo Di Ascoli, ed., *Quartetto milanese ottocentesco: Lettere di Giuseppe Verdi, Giuseppina Strepponi, Clarina Maffei, Carlo Tenca, e di altri personaggi del mondo politico e artistico dell'epoca* (Rome: Archivi, 1974), document #30. As early as mid-August 1846 Verdi was seriously considering *I masnadieri* as the subject for his upcoming Florentine opera, as Emanuele Muzio reported to Antonio Barezzi (13 August): "The Maestro is considering the libretto for Florence; there are three subjects: [Grillparzer's *Die Ahnfrau*] *Avola*, [Schiller's *Die Räuber*] *I masnadieri*, and [Shakespeare's] *Macbeth*." ("Il signor Maestro si occupa del libretto per Firenze; i soggetti sono tre: *l'Avola, i Masnadieri, e Macbeth*.") Luigi A. Garibaldi, *Giuseppe Verdi nelle lettere di Emanuele Muzio ad Antonio Barezzi* (Milan: Treves, 1931), 258. This further suggests that Maffei's promise must have been in earnest and that he may well have started to work on the libretto by that time.

3. Maffei's Italian version of *Die Räuber* appeared in 1846 as one of the volumes in the series *Friedrich Schiller: Tragedie tradotte da Andrea Maffei*, published by Pirola in Milan (1842–52). Maffei's translation of the play parallels Schiller's *Schauspiel* of 1781 (the *Trauerspiel* of 1782) closely, though not exactly. His libretto is drawn from his translation.

Surely Verdi easily accepted a Schillerian plot. Schiller's works were gradually achieving popularity in *ottocento* Italy, in part because they were closely aligned with the philosophy of the Risorgimento. Verdi had already written an opera based on Schiller, *Giovanna d'Arco* (1845), on a libretto by Antonio Solera, drawn from Schiller's *Die Jungfrau von Orleans* (1801). For additional information on Schiller and Italian opera in general, see Ethery Inasaridse, *Schiller und die italienische Oper* (Frankfurt: P. Lang, 1989) and Lavinia Mazzucchetti, *Schiller in Italia* (Milan: Ulrico Hoepli, 1913).

4. Guglielmo Barblan ("*I masnadieri* di Verdi," unpublished manuscript, *Atti del convegno su Verdi-Schiller* [Parma: Istituto di Studi Verdiani, 1973]) assumed

that Verdi himself, as was his custom, drew up an outline of Schiller's tragedy; but Barblan presented no evidence for his speculation.

5. By 9 November 1846 Muzio had evidently read Maffei's verses; for in a letter to Barezzi (Garibaldi, *Giuseppe Verdi*, 292, cited in part in note 16 below), he praised the poetry.

By 4 October 1846 Verdi claimed he had finished almost two acts (presumably one and two) of *I masnadieri* (see Muzio's letter to Barezzi of 4 October 1846, in ibid., 283). Verdi had evidently been composing *I masnadieri* while he was in negotiation with Lanari concerning the possibility of composing an opera for Florence. This does not, however, preclude the possibility that Maffei had not finished the libretto by that date, since Verdi often began composing an opera before the versification was completed.

6. "Ho commesso un brutto peccato . . . ho scritto un libretto per musica: *I Masnadieri.*" Maffei's letter to Cabianca, 23 October 1846, in Angelo Foletto, "Poeta 'assai distinto'; librettista dilettante?" *L'ottocento di Andrea Maffei* (Riva del Garda: Museo civico del comune di Riva del Garda, 1987), 92.

7. For additional information on the cantata, see, for example, "Un inno quarantottesco ed alcune lettere di Andrea Maffei," *Rassegna nazionale* 34/187 (1912): 536–48.

In a letter to Antonio Barezzi dated 24 June 1844, Emanuele Muzio wrote, citing *Il Figaro*: "Maestro Verdi did not find the poetry of Cavalier Maffei suitable for musical setting in the cantata for the Congresso degli Scienziati." ("Il signor Maestro Verdi non ha ritrovato musicabile la poesia del cav. Maffei da servire per cantata nel Congresso de' Scienziati.") Garibaldi, *Giuseppe Verdi*, 167–68. In a subsequent letter, dated 30 June 1844, Muzio elaborated on this comment, noting that although Maffei's verses were "beautiful, as sublime as ever, . . . the breath of the Eternal," they were "definitely . . . not suitable for musical setting"; for "there were *versi sciolti* here, *terzine* there, *quartine* in another place; above all, there was no dialogue; and Maestro Verdi was unable to divide this poetry into sections so that he could have the chorus sing in one spot and the soloists in another; he wanted it to be dramatic." (The text was "bella, sublime quanto mai, era il fiato dell'Eterno, . . . ma decisamente non era musicabile; erano ora versi sciolti, ora terzine, ora quartine; insomma non vi era dialogo; ed il signor Maestro Verdi non poteva dividere in pezzi questa poesia per far cantare ora i cori ora le prime parti; voleva che avesse del drammatico.") Garibaldi, *Giuseppe Verdi*, 169–70.

8. In a letter to Clara, dated 29 May 1871, Andrea noted: Verdi "forgets having wonderfully set the *brindisi* in *Macbeth,* the one in *I masnadieri,* and the one I wrote at his request 'Mescetemi il vino.'" (Verdi "dimentica d'aver musicati stupendamente dei brindisi nel *Macbeth,* nei *Masnadieri,* e quello che scrissi a sua preghiera: 'Mescetemi il vino.'") Raffaello Barbiera, *Verso l'ideale: profili di letteratura e d'arte* (Milan: Libreria editrice nazionale, 1905), 241. The other two romances with Maffei's poetry are "Il tramonto" and "Ad una stella." All three were published by Francesco Lucca in 1845 as part of a set of six songs titled *Album: Sei Romanze.*

9. Foletto ("Poeta," 95) speculated on this idea.

10. In a letter from early 1845 Verdi wrote to Piave: "Maffei will do the sketch of *Attila* for me." ("Maffei mi farà lo sbozzo dell'*Attila.*") Franco Abbiati, *Giuseppe Verdi*, 4 vols. (Milan: Ricordi, 1959–63), 1:585. Gabriele Baldini (*The Story of*

Giuseppe Verdi, trans. Roger Parker [Cambridge: Cambridge University Press, 1980], 104) suggested that Maffei may also have made additions to the libretto for *Attila*.

11. Verdi's letter to Piave of 22 August 1846: Pierpont Morgan Library, New York [US-NYpm], Koch Coll. 783, box 103; cited by Evan Baker, "Lettere di Giuseppe Verdi a Francesco Maria Piave 1843–1865," *Studi Verdiani* 4 (1986–87): 152; and also G. Elizabeth Hudson, introduction to *Il corsaro* in *The Works of Giuseppe Verdi*, Series I, vol. 13 (Chicago: University of Chicago Press; Milan: G. Ricordi, 1998), xiii-xiv.

It is also possible that in late 1847 Verdi may have considered Maffei as the translator of *Jerusalem* (Paris, 1847) into Italian. See Muzio's somewhat cryptic reference to Maffei in his letter to Tito Ricordi, dated 22 December 1847, unpublished, Archives of Casa Ricordi, Milan [I-Mr].

12. Francesco Degrada, "Observations on the Genesis of Verdi's *Macbeth*," in *Verdi's "Macbeth": A Sourcebook*, ed. David Rosen and Andrew Porter (New York: W. W. Norton, 1984), 168–69.

13. Ibid., 157.

14. For additional opinions of Maffei's literary activities, see Luigi Baldacci, ed., "Andrea Maffei," *Poeti minori dell'Ottocento*, 2 vols. (Milan: Riccardo Ricciardi, 1958), 1:451–73; Mazzucchetti, 159–71; Enrico Nencioni, "Andrea Maffei," *La domenica del Fracassa*, 1885, cited in *Saggi critici di letteratura italiana* (Florence: Le Monnier, 1898), 293–301; and Emilio Teza, "Andrea Maffei," *Atti della Reale accademia della crusca* (Florence: M. Cellini, 1887), 49–68.

15. See, for example, Baldini, *The Story of Giuseppe Verdi*, 127–28; Julian Budden, *The Operas of Verdi*, 3 vols. (New York: Oxford University Press, 1973), 1:319–20; and Virginia Cisotti, *Schiller e il melodramma di Verdi* (Florence: La Nuova Italia, 1975), 50–51.

16. Verdi's view of Maffei's skills in the operatic realm was not unequivocal. Consider, for example, Muzio's comment to Antonio Barezzi (9 November 1846) about *I masnadieri*: ". . . a more beautiful libretto has never been written. Those of Romani are nothing in comparison. Suffice it to say that Maffei is the premier Italian poet." (". . . non è mai stato scritto un più bel libro. Quelli di Romani sono un nulla a confronto. Basti il dire che Maffei è il primo verseggiatore italiano . . .") Garibaldi, *Giuseppe Verdi*, 291–93. On the surface, these words appear to express unqualified praise for the poet's creation, but Muzio continued: "with his works he [Maffei] has earned the *croce di cavaliere*, and even more important, lots of money." ("colle sue opere si è guadagnato la croce di cavaliere, e quello che conta di più, dei gran denari.") Muzio's words, which often echoed Verdi's own, ring with a certain sarcasm.

17. Despite Maffei's attitude toward opera libretti, in 1850 he wrote another text for Vincenzo Capecelatro. *David Riccio* received its premiere on 9 March 1850 at the Teatro alla Scala, Milan. *L'Italia musicale* (13 March 1850) printed a scathing review of Maffei's text:

> Maffei's drama is without a doubt poorly conceived and poorly versified; besides being too long, in places it is shallow and trivial. Moreover, it lacks situations, grandeur, antagonism, contrast, and sentiment; and finally it has no originality, and no lyrical, elegiac, or tragic power. Nor is the meagerness of the work, the absence of dramatic instinct, or the paucity of action redeemed by the

splendor of the form or veiled by the enchantment of the overabundance or the voluptuousness of the language or imagination that occurs frequently in Maffei's poetry, which overflows with oriental color, heavenly scent, angelic harmonies, and shining gems: of course all taken or borrowed from French or English authors.

(Il dramma di Maffei è senza contraddizione mal concepito e male verseggiato; oltrecchè troppo lungo, e qua e là basso, triviale. Poi v'ha difetto in esso di situazioni, di grandiosità, d'antagonismo, di contrasto, di sentimento; finalmente nessun invenzione, nessun potenza lirica, elegiaca o tragica. Nè la pochezza del lavoro, l'assenza di ogni istinto drammatico, la povertà dell'azione è redenta dallo splendore della forma, velata dall'incantesimo del numero, dalla volutà della parola e dell'immaginazione, come accade non rado nelle poesie del Maffei, in cui abbondano colore orientale, profumo di cielo, armonie angeliche e gemme rilucenti: ben inteso tutta merce presa e prestito da autori francesi ed inglesi.)

18. Maffei wrote to Cabianca in 1844: "I thought about my idea [for the cantata text] for several days and before versifying it I consulted the oracle of a teacher of counterpoint in order not to be condemned by those painful mutations demanded by the tyranny of the music." ("Pensai più giorni sul mio concetto e prima di verseggiarlo interrogai l'oracolo d'un professore contrappuntista per non essere poi condannato a quei dolorosi mutamenti comandati dalla tirannia della musica.") Foletto, "Poeta," 93.

19. Cabianca's libretto was for Nicola Vaccai's *La sposa di Messina*. Sometime before 23 October 1846 Maffei wrote to his colleague: "Lascia per carità quel ladro mestiere agli affamati schinca penne di teatro, e persuàditi che l'esigenza dei maestri e dei cantanti è la morte d'un ragionevole melodramma. Tu chiedi il mio perdono ed io te lo concedo con plenaria indulgenza ma sotto la inviolabile condizione di non ricadere più in quel brutto peccato." Ibid.

20. "Vi ho messo . . . tanto studio nell'improntare i caratteri, nel cogliere le scene di maggior effetto e nella verseggiatura ch'io spero, se non altro, non verrà confuso con tante solennessime porcherie." Maffei to Cabianca, 23 October 1846, ibid., 92.

21. "Ma se toccasse pure al mio melodramma questo destino, mi rimarrà la soddisfazione d'aver appagato un amico." Ibid.

22. The translation is mine; the original Italian preface to *I masnadieri* reads:

Questo melodramma è tratto dalla celebre tragedia di Federico Schiller: *I Masnadieri;* il primo drammatico lavoro uscito da quel divino intelletto avanti che l'età matura e lo studio dell'uomo ne temperassero la troppo ardente immaginazione. I duri contrasti di cui fu travagliata la prima gioventù del poeta ed un'anima naturalmente inclinata al dolore gli ispirarono questo dramma terribile, il quale, com'è noto, sedusse le calde fantasie di molti giovani a cacciarsi per le foreste nell'intento sognato di migliorare i costumi coi misfatti e col sangue. Ma se questa spaventosa pittura della società manca in parte di vero e di quella sapiente cognizione del cuore che ammiriamo nella Stuarda, nel Tell e nel Wallenstein, presenta a riscontro un interesse così vivo e crescente, ed uno svolgersi di affetti e di avvenimenti così vario ed efficace, che non saprei qual altro lavoro di penna potesse offrire situazioni più accomodate alla musica.

E a queste situazioni, a questa forza d'affetti deve principalmente mirare che si mette all'ardua prova di scrivere per quest'arte, sia che o la storia o l'invenzione gliene dia l'argomento; giacché confinato il poeta in brevissimo spazio, non può dare al pensiero le proporzioni e il discorso psicologico voluti dal dramma, ma lavorare a gran tratti, e presentare al maestro poco più di uno scheletro che aspetti dalle note, anziché dalle parole, le forme, il calore, la vita.

Insomma egli deve ridurre un vasto concetto in piccola dimensione senza mutarne l'originale fisionomia, come una lente concava che impicciolisce gli oggetti e ne conserva tuttavia la sembianza. Il melodramma per tanto non può essere che il germe di quella creazione poetica che riceve dal pensiero musicale la sua piena maturità.

Le quali cose io mi sono proposto nel circoscrivere in pochi versi l'ampia tragedia dei Masnadieri, senza sperare nè pretendere alla mia fatica lo specioso titolo di letteraria. Che se lo scarso mio ingegno non avesse pur resa una larva di tante sovrane bellezze, vagliano a perdonarmi la colpa il lungo studio e il grande amore ch'io posi nel far italiane le drammatiche ispirazioni di questo sommo alemanno.

23. "Such a subject, whatever Maffei may assert to the contrary, is not a fitting one for musical treatment, because . . . the purpose of music is fondness for the beautiful. In *I masnadieri,* one would wish to be fond of the vile. Not even the character of Amalia, who represents virtue, suffices to save the dignity, nobility, and purity of the human consciousness in this work." ("Tale argomento, checchè in contrario asserisca il *Maffei,* non punto acconcio alla musica, perchè, . . . il fine della musica è l'amore del bello. Ne' *Masnadieri* si vorrebbe far amare il turpe; nè vale il personaggio di Amalia, che rappresenta la virtù, a salvare in questo componimento la dignità, la nobilità, e la purezza della coscienza humana.") Abramo Basevi, *Studio sulle opere di Giuseppe Verdi* (Florence: Tofani, 1859), 112–13.

24. *The Morning Herald* (23 July 1847): "Schiller's cumbrous and inhuman tragedy was far from being an appropriate subject for Verdi to grapple with. No one but a Beethoven should have dared to meddle with a theme of such gigantic proportions—that is, if any musical interpretation at all could be given to its scenes of ruthless terror, or there was any probable chance of reflecting the metaphysical ideal which the hero presents, of honour in the midst of guilt, and moral sublimity in an atmosphere of atrocity. It may be easily inferred that the leading incidents, in their naked deformity, could only be taken; and that we have a polite version of a fearful story, with but a small glimmering of the deeply-seated passion, and head-long superstition in the operations of destiny, which Schiller has evolved with such repugnant force."

25. Maffei's critique of his libretto may well have appeased Italian critics who were, at least temporarily, enthralled by his reputation. Although the libretto received little attention from contemporary Italian writers, the comments expressed by Luigi Toccagni, writing for the *Gazzetta musicale di Milano* (18 August 1847), are noteworthy. This commentary by and large echoed Maffei's preface. While it is impossible to glean the true Italian perspective from a single review, we should consider that in Italy, with regard to *I masnadieri,* Maffei may well have been resting on his established reputation as a translator.

26. Maffei's text is reprinted in the Critical Commentary for *I masnadieri* in *The*

Works of Giuseppe Verdi, Series I, vol. 11, ed. Roberta Montemorra Marvin (Chicago: University of Chicago Press, 2000), 20.

27. For additional information on the popularity of Schiller in England, see Frederic Ewen, *The Prestige of Schiller in England, 1788–1859* (New York: Columbia University Press, 1932); and Thomas Rea, *Schiller's Dramas and Poems in England* (London: T. Fisher Unwin, 1906).

28. Other London newspapers reported in a similar vein. *The Morning Herald* (23 July 1847) noted: "The events of the drama are reproduced with but few deviations from the original. . . . The Italian text has been adapted from the original by the Chevalier Maffei with considerable cleverness, so much so as to entitle him to the warmest praise." Having read the libretto but not having seen the opera, the critic for *The Morning Post* (19 July 1847) reported that Maffei had "cleverly and faithfully translated and adapted" Schiller's play.

29. The report was reprinted in the program issued for the third performance of *I masnadieri* at Her Majesty's Theatre in London on 29 July 1847: "De tous les sujets empruntés par les librettistes italiens, celui d'*I Masnadieri* accuse le plus d'inexpérience de la part de l'arrangeur, dans le choix, la coupe, l'ordonnance et la mise en jeu des éléments dramatiques. Il n'était pas possible de gâter plus complétement le drame de Schiller, et de faire, d'une oeuvre nette dans sa marche, et graduée habilement dans ses diverses incidents, un gâchis plus confus et plus desordonné."

30. "Nei *Masnadieri* non vediamo traccia di questa tinta generale, e sembra di scorgervi vari pezzi cuciti insieme, anzichè una tela continua con differenti disegni." Basevi, *Studio sulle opere*, 115–16.

31. *The Morning Chronicle*, 23 July 1847.

32. Discussions concerning the work of librettists in the nineteenth century can be found in Gilles De Van, *Verdi's Theater: Creating Drama through Music*, trans. Gilda Roberts (Chicago: University of Chicago Press, 1998), esp. chapter 3; Carl Dahlhaus, "Il mestiere del librettista," in *Storia dell'opera italiana*, ed. Lorenzo Bianconi and Giorgio Pestelli, 6 vols. (Turin: EDT/Garzanti, 1987—), 4:92–93; and Scott Balthazar, "Aspects of Form in the *Ottocento* Libretto," *Cambridge Opera Journal* 7/1 (1995): 23–35.

33. Roger Parker, "Levels of Motivic Definition in *Ernani*," *19th-Century Music* 6 (1983): 142–43.

34. Baldini (*The Story of Giuseppe Verdi*, 71) wrote: Piave's "libretti are in fact those best suited to Verdi's music—even from a literary point of view they are much finer, in the sense of being better finished, than Boito's—simply because, in detail as well as in general shape, Verdi himself composed them."

35. "Desidererei solo che tu ritocassi [*sic*] alcune cose del secondo atto il quale è assolutamente freddo per la scena, e se tu ami al pari di me che questo libretto ottenga effetto è necessario fare quest'ultimo sacrifizio. Nel caso ne parleremo a voce." Ascoli, ed., *Quartetto milanese ottocentesco*, document #44.

36. "Io sono poco felice, caro Verdi; la solitudine in cui mi trovo sarebbe cara a un egoista, ma non a me che ha bisogno dell'amicizia e della tua principalmente; tu non potresti levarmela che lascerandomi il cuore. Non parlar di sacrifici quando desideri alcuna cosa da me. La mia penna e il poco mio ingegno sono da gran tempo cose tue." Ibid., document #45.

37. Baldini, *The Story of Giuseppe Verdi*, 129.

38. Other minor emendations are found elsewhere in the opera.

39. In the autograph score column of table 13.1 I have placed appropriate punctuation (ordinarily omitted by Verdi) in brackets according to the printed libretto.

40. The early version appears only in the printed libretto source, and the revision is the only version appearing in the musical sources. The sources included in this study are the libretto printed by Her Majesty's Theatre in London for the opera's 1847 premiere, Verdi's autograph score, the manuscript full score prepared for the opera's premiere, and Francesco Lucca's first-edition piano-vocal score.

41. In this context "*mal'ora*" is a contraction of "*male*" and "*ora*." When sung, this might easily be confused with the noun "*malora*" ("ruin") or the idiomatic use of the word in a phrase such as "*va in malora!*" ("go to the devil!") or even with "*malore*" ("faintness" or "malaise"). A similar problem arises with "*caso*" ("case," "chance," "fate," "vicissitude," "opportunity"; "*al caso*" ["eventually"], "*in caso*" ["by chance"], "*a caso*" ["at random"]) and "*casa*" ("house"). When written, read, or perhaps even spoken, these words would not present a problem, but when sung, mispronunciation and misunderstanding of the text would have been much more common (a result of Maffei's inexperience). To avoid obscuring the subtleties in the text, then, Verdi may have requested Maffei to rewrite these verses.

42. A verse is *piano* if it ends with an accent on the penultimate syllable; *tronco* if it ends with an accent on the final syllable. A *quinario* line consists of five syllables with an accent on the fourth and on the first or second syllables. A *doppio quinario* chains together two *quinari*. An *endecasillabo* line contains eleven syllables with an accent on the tenth syllable and one or two accents earlier in the line.

43. Rewritings such as "Arminio . . . un altro ascolto!" ("Arminio . . . someone else I hear!") for "Arminio!—oh Ciel!—che ascolto!" ("Arminio!—oh Heavens!—what do I hear!") in the Act III finale and "A Praga pugnò quell'ardito / finchè del corpo fù tutto ferito" ("In Prague this bold one fought / until his body was full of wounds") for "A Praga pugnò quell'ardito / fin chè da mille percosso, ferito" ("In Prague this bold one fought / until beaten by a thousand, wounded") in the Act I finale also fall into this category. Unfortunately, no musical settings of the earlier texts survive.

44. It is conceivable, of course, that Verdi planned to set the *tronco* verses to the same music he ultimately used for the *piano* verses. (A few minor rhythmic alterations in the existing setting make this feasible; but such a setting is, at the least, awkward.) In that case, fitting these verses (which were at one time the final two verses of the chorus's *racconto* before the tenor's *romanza* in the Act II finale) to the rhythmic, metric, and melodic contour Verdi had used for the preceding lines would have accounted, in part, for the text revision. But since the early version of the text appears only in the libretto sources and not in any of the musical sources, it is probable that Verdi never set the early version of the text at all.

45. I have formulated my comments based on a study of the *Macbeth* libretto as reproduced by Degrada in "The 'Scala' *Macbeth* Libretto: A Genetic Edition," in *Verdi's "Macbeth"*, ed. Rosen and Porter. Cf. also Degrada's observations concerning the revisions in his "Observations on the Genesis," in ibid.

46. Many other emendations in the libretto are discussed in detail in my "The Genesis and Reception of Verdi's *I masnadieri*" (Ph.D. diss., Brandeis University, 1992). The details are also included in Marvin, *I masnadieri*, Critical Commentary and Introduction to the full score.

47. Budden, *The Operas of Verdi*, 1:322.

48. Roger Parker, "*I masnadieri*," *New Grove Dictionary of Opera*, 4 vols. (London: Macmillan, 1992), 3:252.

49. *The Morning Chronicle*, 23 July 1847.

50. *The Morning Herald*, 23 July 1847.

51. *The Illustrated London News*, 31 July 1847.

52. *Courrier de l'Europe*, July 1847, cited from the 29 July 1847 program for *I masnadieri* at Her Majesty's Theatre in London.

14

Mozart's Piano Concertos and the Romantic Generation

Claudia Macdonald

The body of Mozart piano concertos that remains in the repertory today numbers twenty-one. The earliest of these were composed in 1776 in Salzburg (K. 238 in B-flat Major, K. 246 in C Major, and K. 271 in E-flat Major), and were played by Mozart over the next two years in Munich, Mannheim, and Paris as he sought employment in each of those cities as a court musician. He moved instead to Vienna in 1781 and there embarked on a career as a freelance musician. Central to establishing his reputation in Vienna as a leading keyboard virtuoso were the large academies, or subscription concerts, he gave for his own benefit. For these he invariably composed a concerto, producing twelve during his peak years, from 1784 to 1786.[1]

Today Mozart's piano concertos are considered among his greatest contributions to the repertory. Yet, in his own day one might say they were, at least in one sense, ephemera. Most were composed for his own use, then performed soon after they were completed, only to be superseded by yet another concerto within a few months, or sometimes only weeks or days. Only some six to nine, or at most fewer than half of the twenty-one, were published during his lifetime. Of these, three were specifically composed for sale in manuscript copy (K. 413/387a in F Major, K. 414/385p in A Major, and K. 415/387b in C Major), and for them Mozart intentionally chose a style he did not consider his most brilliant.[2] This, of course, does not mean that there was little contemporary interest in Mozart's concertos beyond their premier performances, only rather that their status as an obligatory part of all piano players' equipment was still in the future. Often enough Mozart had copies made for patrons, for fellow professionals who were the recipients of dedications, or for skilled students who then gave their own performances.[3] Among the latter was Johann Nepomuk Hummel, who came to Mozart in 1786 at age seven, studied with him for two years, then was taken by his father on an extended tour that eventually brought him to England, where on 5 May 1792 he played a "new concerto by Mozart."[4]

During the two decades immediately after Mozart's death in 1791, many of his works, including at least ten concertos, were given their first publication by Johann Anton André, beginning in 1792.[5] Then, as part of their complete works edition, from 1800 to 1804 Breitkopf and Härtel published a series that ran to twenty concertos, issued, as was the normal practice of the day, in instrumental parts only.[6] Naturally, there were those who responded to this wider dissemination of the concertos. Among them was Beethoven, who admired particularly Mozart's D-Minor Concerto, K. 466, and played it in 1795 at a concert arranged by Mozart's widow, Constanze. He may have played it again in 1796. Later still Beethoven wrote two, by now well-known, cadenzas for the D-Minor Concerto, most likely to give his piano student, Ferdinand Ries.[7] Another admirer of Mozart's concertos was August Eberhard Müller, cantor of St. Thomas's in Leipzig, who, as early as 1796, published a *Guide to the Accurate Performance of Mozart's Piano Concertos Principally with Respect to Correct Fingering.*[8] Müller's wife, Maria Catharina, regularly played Mozart's concertos with the Gewandhaus Orchestra in Leipzig.[9] Indeed, during the time the Müllers were in Leipzig, from 1794 to spring 1810, the city seems to have reached a high-water mark in performances of Mozart concertos with forty-four performances on Gewandhaus subscription concerts alone.[10] After the Müllers left Leipzig, the frequency of performances of Mozart concertos dropped sharply. Still, there remained in the city admirers of Mozart who continued to play his concertos, among them Friedrich Schneider, who held various musical posts until his departure from Leipzig in 1820.[11] And on 21 February 1820, the city heard Franz Xaver Mozart (who adopted the name Wolfgang Amadeus, Jr.) play a concerto in C major by his father, as well as one of his own.[12]

Nonetheless, 1820 marks the end of the first phase in the posthumous spread of Mozart's concertos, a phase that involved the dissemination of these works in their earliest editions, and their performance by those who came to know and admire them through these publications. In Leipzig, at least, the last decade of this phase was marked by fewer performances of Mozart's concertos. Of course one should keep in mind that in Leipzig and throughout Europe, the number of performances of Mozart's concertos was outstripped by the number of performances of newer concertos by younger composers, particularly in 1810–20.[13] The same is also true of the second phase, beginning in the decade of the 1820s. The most popular concertos of this decade were not by Mozart, but by Hummel, Ries, Ignaz Moscheles, and Friedrich Kalkbrenner. At the same time, it was also during the 1820s that many musical centers, notably Berlin, Paris, and London, began to experience an upsurge of interest in music by composers of earlier generations—in Beethoven's music particularly, but also Mozart's and Bach's. In Paris, performances by François-Antoine Habeneck of Beethoven's works at his Conservatory Concerts beginning in March 1828 set off a wave of interest in the composer. This sent the great virtuosos of the city scurrying to perform piano concertos by not only Beethoven, but also Mozart. In June 1828 the brilliant Parisian pianist and Chopin's early idol, Friedrich Kalkbrenner, played his arrangement of Mozart's Concerto in C Major, K. 503, at a Conservatory Concert. Ferdinand Hiller followed with a concerto in C Major by Mozart, performed at the Conservatory Hall on 15 December 1833.[14] Though already in 1818 Kalkbrenner had played his arrangement of K. 503 in London, the champions of Mozart's concertos in that city were John Baptist Cramer and Cipriani Potter, who played them regularly on the London Philharmonic Society's concerts beginning in 1820.[15] In Berlin Mozart's concertos were seldom heard in the 1820s.[16] Then, beginning in 1830, they were played by the local pianists Wenceslas Hauck, Wilhelm Taubert, and Felix Mendelssohn at concerts presented by Karl Möser, concertmaster of the Berlin *Hofkapelle,* in honor of Mozart's birthday, and in 1833 Kalkbrenner came to town with his arrangement of K. 503.[17] The wave finally hit Vienna—where the correspondent for the *Allgemeine musikalische Zeitung* reported no performances of Mozart's piano concertos during the 1820s—when the touring artists Ignaz Tedesco and Mozart, Jr., and local celebrity Carl Maria von Bocklet performed concertos by the elder Mozart during the 1830s.[18]

With this increased interest in Mozart's concertos came a need for new editions, and it is a discussion of these, and of the second phase in the posthumous spread of Mozart's concertos, that brings us to the main subject of this essay. These editions, for solo piano or piano accompanied by a small chamber ensemble, were characterized by an effort at modernizing Mozart to suit newer instruments, techniques, and tastes. Arguments for such arrangements fell into two disparate categories, both of which sought to woo the uninitiated. One, paradoxically, raised the question of authenticity: additions to Mozart concertos were necessary because Mozart himself made them in performance. The other saw propaganda value in the embellishment of the solo part for performances in a concert setting, and also in arrangements of the concertos for home music-making. Proponents of the first argument liked to point to such arrangers as Mozart's pupil, Hummel, or Clementi's pupil, Cramer: each composer had credentials in the past that were impeccable, and each also had a command of newer practices that favored reinforced basses, expanded treble range, and more brilliant passagework. A leading proponent of the second argument was Gottfried Weber. For him, André's 1800 edition of *Six grands concertos,* Op. 82 (i.e., K. 246, 450, 467, 489, 488, and 491), represented Mozart's concertos in their "true and original form" ("ursprünglichen echten Gestalt"). Still, writing in 1832, he advocated arrangements acceptable to modern tastes as suitable for gradually introducing Mozart's concertos "into salons and private circles, into the very practice room of the piano player" ("in Salons und Privatzirkeln, ja im Uebungszimmer des Clavierspielers"), and thereby gaining them entrance into larger concert halls. In other words, his scholarly view was tempered by what is in fact a realistic assessment of the tolerance limits of modern tastes and programming practices.[19] In Paris Mendelssohn performed Beethoven's G-Major Concerto with the Conservatory Orchestra on 18 March 1832, but his performances of Mozart's concertos were in private homes with quartet accompaniment.[20] And in Leipzig the *Allgemeine musikalische Zeitung* reported as late as April 1835 that Emil Leonhardt's performance two months earlier of Mozart's C-Minor Concerto "did not seem generally to please."[21] The reviewer gave no further details, but might have agreed with a report in the *Haude- und Spenersche Zeitung* of the performance of Mozart's D-Minor Concerto by Hauck in Berlin on 27 January 1830: "It was extremely interesting, for once to hear finally one of Mozart's pianoforte concertos, which are still completely alien to our modern virtuosos, because there is not enough passagework in them."[22]

The first new editions of Mozart's concertos were commissioned by J. R. Schultz in the early 1820s and prepared by Johann Nepomuk Hummel.[23] Beginning in 1828 and up to 1842, after his death in 1837, seven of Hummel's versions of Mozart's concertos were published by Chappell in London and by B. Schott in Mainz, Paris, and Antwerp (in order, K. 466 in D Minor; K. 503 in C Major; K. 365/316a in E-flat Major, for Two Pianos; K. 491 in C Minor; K. 537 in D Major ["Coronation Concerto"]; K. 482 in E-flat Major; and K. 456 in B-flat Major). These were arranged for piano, flute, violin, and cello, and were also available for piano alone. In 1823 Schultz expanded his commission to Hummel, which was to reach twelve concertos, to include arrangements by Kalkbrenner and Moscheles and thereby bring the number to twenty.[24] Kalkbrenner published only one edition, of K. 503, the same concerto he played in June 1828 at the Paris Conservatory (École Royale de Musique). Moscheles, too, produced only one, of the Two-Piano Concerto in E-flat Major, K. 365, which was not published until 1861. Neither was part of Schultz's series as originally planned.[25]

From 1825 to 1835 another person, John Baptist Cramer, also arranged six of Mozart's concertos (K. 459 in F Major; K. 450 in B-flat Major; K. 467 in C Major; K. 482 in E-flat Major; K. 466 in D Minor; and K. 491 in C Minor—all published by Addison and Beale in London) for piano, violin, flute, and cello—and, again, they could alternatively be played by the piano alone. Three of the concertos Cramer arranged were the same as those arranged by Hummel.

The title pages of Cramer's editions boldly state one of the main purposes for undertaking these arrangements: "Mozart's Celebrated Concertos, Newly Arranged for the Piano Forte with Additional Keys." By 1830 pianos had a wider range than those used by Mozart—in the treble, as much as a full octave more (f'''' vs. f''')—and the new editions were intended to take advantage of the extra keys. Furthermore, not only had the range of pianos increased but their sound too was bigger, whether they were of Viennese or English manufacture. Piano virtuosos, accordingly, cultivated a bigger, more brilliant style. To put it succinctly, in 1830, neither Mozart's piano nor the style of his writing for piano was up-to-date. Indeed, when Schultz expanded his original commission, Moscheles understood that the purpose of these arrangements was to enrich the solo. This entailed reinforcing the closing passagework of both the exposition and the recapitulation to increase their brilliance, and occasionally even adding extra measures. Moscheles wrote to Hummel:

> *Herr* Schultz's project: To bring out a selection of Mozart's concertos with enriched solo, reinforcement, [especially in the] closing passagework, seems of special interest to me. If you undertake this enterprise, you cannot fail to succeed. Would you kindly just explain the following points further: 1) if in the tuttis and the obbligato parts the accompaniment ought not to be written out for the piano in small notes (as in your concerto). 2) If occasionally due to the increased brilliance, a few measures could not be added to the principal passages. 3) If it would not be better to retain the designation concerto (not sonata). 4) Would you please indicate which concertos you will arrange, because Herr Kalkbrenner and I would gladly attach ourselves to this work and then choose.[26]

What did Hummel's, Cramer's, and Kalkbrenner's arrangements sound like? Generally, Hummel's and Cramer's editions of the Mozart concertos feature a reinforcement of the solo part, particularly in the bass, that is meant to substitute for, and often transcribes exactly, the missing orchestra part. They also include many changes in the solo part that are intended to modernize the passagework, by taking it higher, making it fuller and more ornate. Cramer's editions have first-movement cadenzas for only three of the six concertos (E-flat Major, K. 482, D Minor, and C Minor); for the other three, no fermata indicates where a cadenza would fall. But cadenzas were not commonly heard in concertos of the day either. However, Kalkbrenner's and five of Hummel's (the exceptions are K. 365 and 537) do give first-movement cadenzas. And all three composers elaborate Mozart's slow movements. Today, the composition of a first-movement cadenza by a performer, or at the very least, the appropriation of a cadenza composed by someone else is *de rigueur,* and elaborations of the slow movement are not uncommon. Both have a long history: cadenzas (including Mozart's own) as well as ornaments for the slow movements of Mozart's concertos were printed as early as 1801 by André and Artaria.[27] But the remainder of this essay will concentrate on changes that are not heard in the concert hall today, changes in the concertos' first movements.

Our examination of Hummel's and Cramer's changes overlaps to a certain extent with David Grayson's, particularly with respect to the first movement of Mozart's Concerto in D Major, K. 537 ("Coronation").[28] Grayson writes,

This particular arrangement is of special interest because Mozart's autograph omits the left-hand part where it is essentially accompanimental; the version generally heard today, serviceable but not particularly imaginative, derives from the posthumously published first edition of 1794, so Hummel's alternatives are especially welcome.[29]

Example 14.1 shows the second phrase of the solo entrance, a cadenza-like passage, in Hummel's version (Hummel, mm. 82–92; Mozart, mm. 89–99). Hummel reinforces the bass, expands the range of the right hand by replacing Mozart's scales with arpeggios, and in the final four measures thickens Mozart's single line with brilliant octaves, broken octaves, and

Example 14.1. Hummel's adaptation of Mozart, "Coronation" Concerto, K. 537, mvt. 1, mm. 82–92. From *Concertos de Mozart arrangés pour Piano à 2 mains par J. N. Hummel*, Collection Litolff (Braunschweig: Henry Litolff's Verlag, n.d.).

arpeggios that reach to the high and low extremes of the piano. Similar changes transform other passages as well, with the most extreme alterations coming before the closing trill. At this point in the exposition Hummel replaces Mozart's sixteenth-note arpeggios and scales with odd groupings (twenty-one or twenty-two sixteenths to the measure), and lengthens the final trill from one to two measures (Mozart, mm. 210–216). For Kalkbrenner, in his reworking of K. 503, the norm is to extend any dominant preparation by one or more measures, adding further arpeggios, scales, or trills. In his hands the four measures of a single-line scale that leads to the second theme of the second group became seven, ranging both higher and lower than Mozart's original (see example 14.2).

Example 14.2. Kalkbrenner's adaptation of Mozart, Concerto in C Major, K. 503, mvt. 1, mm. 166–170. Bibliothèque nationale de France. Used by permission.

Changes in the passagework were intended to bring Mozart's concertos more in line with the style of virtuoso concertos of the day. Their emphasis, as is only natural in arrangements intended for unaccompanied solo performance, is on solo brilliance. Indeed, this endeavor is consistently pushed to the point where, in the solo versions of these concertos, important melodies played by one or another of the orchestral choirs are suppressed altogether and replaced by enhanced obbligatos that change the phrase rhythm.

A case in point is mm. 172–175 in K. 537. In Mozart's original this passage is the repeat of the antecedent phrase of the second theme in the second group, played by the strings. In Hummel's version (mm. 165–169) the melody is not heard at all. What stands in for it is a newly-composed solo obbligato, whose pair of two-measure gestures makes it sound like a cadential suffix rather than a phrase (see example 14.3). This preference for short-breathed, formulaic gestures is a feature of the modern virtuosic

Example 14.3. Mozart, "Coronation" Concerto, K. 537, mvt. 1, mm. 172–176; and Hummel's adaptation. From *Concertos de Mozart arrangés pour Piano à 2 mains par J. N. Hummel*, Collection Litolff (Braunschwieg: Henry Litolff's Verlag, n.d.).

style, and can also be seen in Cramer's editions. An example is provided by a phrase in Mozart's Concerto in B-flat Major, K. 450 (from the upbeat to m. 79, to m. 86; see example 14.4). It comes early in the first solo, being preceded only by a long flourish (mm. 49–70) and the solo statement of the first eight measures of the principal theme (mm. 71–78, also the tutti's opening theme). The passage begins with a threefold repetition of a metri-

Example 14.4. Mozart, Concerto in B-flat Major, K. 450, mvt. 1, mm. 78–86; and Cramer's adaptation. The British Library, h. 321. r. Used by permission of The British Library.

Example 14.4. *(continued)*.

cally displaced version of the first motive of the principal theme, played by the woodwinds and accompanied by piano obbligato. It is then completed by the solo with elaborations of the obbligato motive. In the Mozartean scheme the passage is a full I-V-I phrase, serving as an "afterphrase" (to use William Rothstein's term) of the principal theme.[30] In Cramer's version the woodwind motive is suppressed and the obbligato is entirely recomposed, transforming it into short-breathed virtuosic flourishes that have nothing to do with Mozart's motivic material. In sum, Cramer does away with the motivic connections to the principal theme, and thus with the phrase structure of the passage. His version is no longer the afterphrase of the theme but merely a string of cadential gestures—in Rothstein's terms, a series of suffixes to that theme.[31]

Both Hummel and Cramer also make changes to the melodic areas of Mozart's concertos to make them conform to the modern style. In stark contrast to the single-line melody and Alberti bass accompaniment at the solo's first entrance in Mozart's Concerto in F Major, K. 459, in Cramer's version the solo plunges in with full chords, just as it would in almost any virtuoso concerto of the day (see example 14.5).[32] In his arrangements of first movements Hummel retains much of the bare simplicity of Mozart's

Example 14.5. Cramer's adaptation of Mozart, Concerto in F Major, K. 459, mvt. 1, mm. 72–79. The British Library, h. 321. r. Used by permission of The British Library.

thematic areas, and thereby heightens the brilliance of his newly composed, modern passagework. Yet he does elaborate Mozart's melodies somewhat, and, often enough, takes them an octave higher. Cramer treats Mozart's melodies similarly, though he is more ample in his addition of ornaments, chromatic notes, and octave doublings. All these features can readily be seen in a melody from the second group in the exposition of the first movement of Mozart's Concerto in E-flat Major, K. 482 (see example 14.6).

  Naturally, such changes to Mozart's concertos derived from performance practices of the 1820s and 1830s, whether the performance was of a new concerto by Hummel or an older one by Mozart. Indeed, one prominent champion of the music of Beethoven, Mozart, and other earlier composers—Adolf Bernhard Marx of Berlin—seemed not to notice the many changes wrought by Hummel on Mozart's concertos. In a review of Hummel's edition of the D-Minor Concerto, Marx noted that "the piano part alone offers . . . a reproduction without any essential omission."[33] He made no comment on the modernized passagework, the extensive elaboration in the middle movement, or the fact that the opening of the first movement is played without syncopation until mm. 14–15 (and mm. 53–57 are eliminated altogether). Similarly, Ludwig Rellstab characterized Kalkbrenner's rendition of K. 503, which he performed in Berlin on 15 June 1833, as "arranged with much taste and great discretion."[34] Cramer is known to have played his editions in public concerts in London, and even to have combined two movements of his own Concerto in C Minor, Op. 48 (composed in 1807), with the last movement of Mozart's Concerto

Example 14.6. Cramer's adaptation of Mozart, Concerto in E-flat Major, K. 482, mvt. 1, mm. 152–171. The British Library, h. 321. r. Used by permission of The British Library.

in the same key, presumably with his own elaborations.[35] Moscheles called this tasteless.[36] But when other elaborated performances of Mozart's concertos in London, by Cipriani Potter and Felix Mendelssohn, were recalled by George Macfarren in 1884, Macfarren considered them authentic, even citing Mozart as their source. While one may dispute Macfarren's belief that these changes reflect Mozart's practice, what is certain is that performers of the 1830s included them to suit modern tastes and instruments—the very reason Moscheles understood that Schultz solicited them from Hummel. Macfarren tells us:

Example 14.6. *(continued).*

When Potter returned to England he again played at the Philharmonic, and the piece in which he made his reappearance was the Concerto of Mozart in D minor [on 12 March 1821]. He had learnt, perhaps in Vienna, and from the particular explanations of [Thomas] Attwood, who had witnessed Mozart's performance of his concertos [and was also a student of Mozart], the fact that the printed copies are but indications of the matter which Mozart himself used to play, and he had gathered from Attwood and others what was the manner in which Mozart used to amplify the written memoranda in his performance. It almost amounted to a re-composition of the part to fill it out with such pianoforte effects as would do justice to the original intention, and it was with such amplification that Potter presented the D minor concerto. It was in such wise that at a later time Mendelssohn made his first appearance as a pianist here with the same concerto [on 13 May 1833], and with that kind of treatment of the printed sketches.[37]

Grayson cites other English critics who, similarly, viewed Cramer's and Hummel's arrangements as in keeping with Mozart's style. He also quotes one German critic, Gottfried Wilhelm Fink, who "welcomed [Kalkbrenner's] new, ornamented edition [of K. 503] on both historical grounds—the evidence that Mozart himself embellished his concertos—and on aesthetic and practical grounds—the observation that Mozart's bare notes were not expressive to contemporary audiences."[38] But there were, of course, those who differed with Macfarren's and Fink's ideas about authentic Mozart performance. In his 1832 review of Hummel's arrangement of the C-Minor Concerto, Gottfried Weber called Hummel's alterations "not so much an arrangement of a Mozart Concerto reduced to a more modest accompaniment, but rather much more a Hummelian recasting of a Mozart Concerto."[39] For the Concerto in its "true and original form" he referred the reader to André's 1800 edition of the concerto in parts, and for the sake of comparison even headlined his essay with the titles of both André's *édition*

Example 14.7. Hummel's adaptation of Mozart, Concerto in C Minor, K. 491, mvt. 1, mm. 135–147. From *Concertos de Mozart arrangés pour Piano à 2 mains par J. N. Hummel*, Collection Litolff (Braunschwieg: Henry Litolff's Verlag, n.d.).

and Hummel's *arrangement*.[40] To prove his point, Weber listed many changes made by Hummel to the C-Minor Concerto. The first involves mm. 135–146 where, "instead of the sixteenth-note runs of the right hand alone, both hands are changed to scales together in sixths or octaves, and in general the entire passage, twelve bars long, is very freely altered" (see example 14.7).[41]

Unquestionably Weber feels that the player should know Mozart in his "original purity" ("ursprüngliche Reinheit"). At the same time, he is by no means suggesting that this is the form in which the C-Minor Concerto should be performed. Like Fink, he understands the necessity of performing Mozart's work in a manner suitable to modern tastes, and he laments instead

that the arranger [Hummel] did not retain the piano part exactly as Mozart wrote it and did not simply show what he added of his own or what he completely altered in smaller notes or on a special supplementary staff. In this form the edition would have had the incomparably higher, double value of bringing in view the work of the great glorified master in its original purity together with the modern additions, and of according the player the freedom to use from the latter as much or as little as might seem good to him.[42]

In fact, Weber sees the primary purpose of Hummel's enterprise as the reintroduction of Mozart's concertos (which by then, he says, had disappeared from the concert repertory) into salons and private circles, into the very practice room of the piano player. They would thereby gain recognition and entrance once again into the larger concert halls. Only secondarily does Weber believe the enterprise's purpose is "to dress up somewhat the solo voice according to the latest fashion's taste in playing and performance, and to give the player an opportunity through the execution of prodigious difficulties to shine with the taste one is used to hearing these days."[43]

Weber says that he does not "blame or censure" Hummel's editions, but rather points to Hummel's alterations "for the sake of the truth, for those who do not know it, namely that Mozart concertos do not sound this way but very differently."[44] Nonetheless, I know of no evidence that Weber ever heard Mozart play. His pronouncement on the "sound" of Mozart's concertos is based on acquaintance with the printed pages of an edition produced by André, which he considered to be authoritative. He may also have known an earlier performance tradition exemplified in Müller's 1796 *Guide to the Accurate Performance of the Mozartean Piano Concertos,* which also seems to rely on the printed page.[45] Müller himself was admired in Leipzig for his performances of Mozart concertos, and he was one of the first pianists to publish cadenzas for them.[46] While he hoped that "great crowds of connoisseurs, amateurs, and virtuosos" ("ganze Schaaren von Kennern, Liebhabern und Virtuosen") would adopt his view that these concertos were viable in the concert hall, the specific purpose of his book was to present for the amateur "*all* the important and difficult passages of *all* the Mozartean concertos that are published" ("alle bedenkliche und schwierige Stellen aller Mozartschen Konzerte, die öffentlich erschienen sind").[47] Only the first volume of his projected two-volume book ever appeared. It gives examples from the Concertos in A Major (K. 414), F Major (K. 413), C Major (K. 415), D Major (K. 451), and B-flat Major (K. 595)— the first four published in 1785, the last in 1791. Müller cites Mozart as an authority, confidently proclaiming in one instance that "Mozart himself used this fingering" ("Selbst Mozart bediente sich in solchen Fällen dieser Appl[icatur]").[48] But as with Weber, there is no evidence that he had any personal contact with Mozart.[49] That Müller's own performances, and those by his wife, of Mozart's concertos were not overly elaborated can be inferred from the comment of a Leipzig critic who, after hearing Mme. Müller play a Mozart concerto in 1820, concluded that the composer's concertos "seem to have been set aside by our virtuosos, perhaps because they are too easy for them" ("unsere Virtuosen bey Seite gelegt zu haben scheinen, wahrscheinlich weil sie ihnen zu leicht sind").[50] The expectation of a different performance style for Mozart's concertos is further underscored by this critic when he rebukes Wolfgang Amadeus Jr. for introducing tempo changes into his father's concerto, even though he considered these appropriate for the younger Mozart's own work.[51] Such changes of tempo were expected and often written into the scores of contemporary concertos, and, one might add, are clearly suggested in Kalkbrenner's, Hummel's, and Cramer's later adaptations of the senior Mozart's concertos.

What, finally, different pianists did play when they performed a Mozart concerto in the 1830s is difficult to know.[52] When Hauck played Mozart's D-Minor Concerto at the Berlin concert celebrating the composer's birthday in 1830, the correspondent for the *Allgemeine musikalische Zeitung* noted that "one must not be too particular about the mixing-in of the modern style"—that is, of Hummel's style in his cadenzas (which the audience applauded), alongside Mozart's—while adding that he would rather be left "the undisturbed joy of the magnificent tutti areas, likewise the sparkling instrumentation."[53] Yet, one can imagine that Hauck may well have made many other additions to the concerto beyond the two cadenzas, and these may have been suggested either by his teacher, Hummel, or have been those already published by Hummel in his 1828 version of the D-Minor Concerto. Indeed, Hauck's cadenzas, which were by his teacher, may have come from this very edition. Of course, it may also have been the case that Hauck played Mozart's concerto as it was published in early editions by André (1796) or Breitkopf and Härtel. If so, the reviewer's comments about the necessity of mixing-in the modern style would accord with those of a colleague writing in another issue of the same volume of the *Allgemeine musikalische Zeitung,* about J. P. Schmidt's edition of Mozart's Concerto in D Minor for piano four hands. The latter reviewer cites players who say that "Mozart does not offer the virtuosos enough to do with respect to the level of today's piano playing as regards skillfulness, artistry, difficulty, and striking effects in technical execution." Like Gottfried Weber, he recommends that, until audiences can force virtuosos to perform more concertos by Mozart, they should acquaint themselves with these works at home. To this end Schmidt's edition will serve them well, either as "preparation for or recall of" ("zur Vorbereitung oder Wiedererinnerung") whatever public performances may come about.[54] The edition is a rather conservative transcription, with the occasional reinforcement of the parts that four-hand playing allows, and, at times, displacement of the passagework upward into a higher octave. It is, in other words, much different from what an audience was likely to hear in a concert-hall performance of Mozart at the time.

As for Mozart himself, ultimately whatever additions he did or did not make to the manuscripts of his concertos when he performed them is a

subject for another study. Though stories that Mozart occasionally or generally played his piano concertos from incompletely notated parts do not
seem tenable, Frederick Neumann has provided ample evidence that he
elaborated what he recorded in the solo part, which at times was notated in
shorthand.[55] Be that as it may, what must be said here is only that tastes
change, and that by mid-century they had changed again. This brings us to
the third phase of the posthumous spread of Mozart's concertos. Hummel's
editions were reprinted as late as the 1890s by Litolff. But already by mid-
century—as the first editions of the concertos in score began to be printed,
in Offenbach by André, and in Paris by Richault—the fashion for performing embellished versions of Mozart's concertos seems to have passed. By
1852 Friedrich Wieck, the father and teacher of Clara Wieck, was explaining that Mozart's piano compositions had been "bowdlerized" in the hands
of Kalkbrenner and Hummel, while admitting that, under the influence of
the Parisian virtuosos, his daughter, too, had at one time "excited much
applause owing to Mozart's piano concertos arranged in such a manner."
Nonetheless, he remained more ambivalent about the practice than we might
today: he still justified it on the grounds that Mozart himself had enriched
the compositions of Handel, and because, whatever the form of his
daughter's additions to Mozart, they were part of what he considered a
"serious development."

> It could not fail, then, that as a result of such newer, more brilliant, more sono-
> rous tonal effects [from modern pianos] that one either neglected, or indeed, as
> Hummel and Kalkbrenner did with the concertos of Mozart, completely bowd-
> lerized the, albeit classic, yet simpler and less challenging piano compositions of
> Handel, Mozart and Haydn. One played them in the modern way, that is, more
> brilliantly, more virtuosically, in a faster tempo, more passionately and more
> forcibly accentuated, in a word, in the "modern concert fashion," and wronged
> fully the piety due these masterworks. . . . Just as Hummel and others corrupted
> the old piano compositions, so Mozart and [Ignaz Franz von] Mosel did earlier
> with instrumental things when they decked out the oratorios of Handel with
> richer orchestration. I myself, too, and my daughter Clara devoted ourselves
> zealously to this new, brilliant manner of playing. It was truly a serious develop-
> ment, not an insidious one as our most recent artists have made it. It was not
> foolish virtuosic extravagance, no twisted presentation of good pieces of music,
> because the method, in itself simple enough, did not permit the dazzling superfi-
> cialities which a few years later the public admired as manifestations of genius.
> My daughter, Clara, at that time excited much applause owing to Mozart's pi-
> ano concertos arranged in such a manner, to be sure not in her homeland, not in
> Leipzig, at least not until she returned to her native city from Paris with the
> laurels wreaths she had won there.[56]

However she may have played Mozart's concertos in her youth, like her
father, Clara Wieck Schumann, too, took a "serious" and pious attitude
toward them. Already in 1845 she condemned a performance of Mozart's

D-Minor Concerto by her friend Ferdinand Hiller, who, she thought, "did not play with the respect such as one can demand from a good artist." On the other hand, she said, Mendelssohn executed works like Mozart's with "love and mastery."[57] Perhaps Mendelssohn did play Mozart's concertos with "scrupulous exactness . . . without a single addition or *new reading* of his own," as *The Harmonicon* reported after his 1833 performance of the D-Minor Concerto in London.[58] But it might be that Macfarren (b. 1813), speaking from the perspective of some years later, was correct in saying that Mendelssohn in fact amplified the score. Under the circumstances it is difficult to know in just what way the Berlin reviewer heard Mendelssohn's performance of Mozart's C-Minor Concerto in 1833 as "finished and expressive in the *spirit* of the magnificent composition" (emphasis added).[59]

By the end of the century, opinions about the best way to perform Mozart's concertos had changed once again. By 1890 Breitkopf and Härtel had published new editions of Mozart's complete piano concertos, twenty-eight altogether including the Concert Rondo in D Major, K. 382, with "accurate rendition of the original piano parts in the first piano" ("genau bezeichneten Original-Klavierstimmen, als erstes Klavier"), though with added fingerings and expression marks by Carl Reinecke, and a second piano part arranged by Louis Maas. In his book, *Zur Wiederbelebung der Mozart'schen Clavier-Concerte,* Reinecke noted that, with the exception of the two in D Minor and C Minor, Mozart's concertos were seldom played any more, even though earlier the public had heartily rejoiced at performances by Clara Schumann, Hiller, and Taubert (at least the first two of whom, he recalled, elaborated Mozart's score, just as did Mozart himself).[60] Reinecke also advocated elaborations to Mozart's passagework, and gave many examples. It should be added that these are slight in comparison with Hummel's changes, for which he expressed a distaste.[61] They involve mostly extensions of the register, or reinforcement of certain right-hand passages with the left hand for greater brilliance.[62] Like Weber, Reinecke feels that the performer should work from Mozart's original score, not for the purpose of piously following it note-for-note, but rather in order to determine how to realize the best modern performance from it.[63]

Some of what we have said here resonates with responses to Mozart in our own day: the call for "original" editions with small notes showing editorial additions; the notion that we should assume a certain manner when approaching Mozart's music, perhaps showing due respect by not playing too emphatically or ardently; or the idea that it is possible to play "in the spirit" of Mozart. Whereas, like Reinecke, we probably feel that Clara Schumann's ideal Mozart performance is closer to our own than Hummel's, Cramer's, or Kalkbrenner's, nevertheless, we need to keep in mind that today, just as in the 1830s, not only modern instruments but also modern tastes have changed what we hear and what we expect to hear in a performance of a

Mozart piano concerto. We have rejected the solutions that performers of the 1820s and 1830s arrived at for presenting old music to a contemporary audience—quite obviously so, since Hummel's, Cramer's, and Kalkbrenner's arrangements of Mozart are no longer performed. Yet we still face the same questions as did that earlier century: What exactly did Mozart play as compared with what he wrote down? How does our view of what he played affect what we play? Just how are we going to achieve a brilliant effect with his concertos? The answers are as diverse as the many recorded renditions of Mozart's concertos now available, both on modern and on older-style instruments. And the answers will continue to change, as will historical perceptions, audience tastes, and performance venues.

While I do not foresee a return to the performance practices of the 1830s (or the 1890s, for that matter) in the near future, after this essay was presented in its original version for the Allen Memorial Art Museum's series "Images and Sound" in fall 1996, Kimi Kawashima played Hummel's solo version of the recapitulation of the first movement of Mozart's Concerto in D Major, K. 537.[64] I am sure that this was an Oberlin, Ohio, premiere. Afterward, members of the audience came to me and, like Gottfried Weber, noted that what they heard certainly was not the Mozart they knew. What they could not gainsay, however, was that their response to this splendid performance had been enthusiastic and immediate—their applause brought down the house.

Notes

1. According to the eighth edition of Ludwig Köchel's catalog (*Chronologisch-thematisches Verzeichnis sämtlicher Tonwerke Wolfgang Amadé Mozarts*, ed. Franz Giegling, Alexander Weinmann, and Gerd Sievers [Wiesbaden: Breitkopf and Härtel, 1983]), these are: K. 449 in E-flat Major (dated 9 February 1784; performed by Barbara Ployer, for whom it was composed, on 23 March, and by Mozart on 17 March at an academy); K. 450 in B-flat Major (dated 15 March 1784; performed by Mozart on 24 March); K. 451 in D Major (dated 22 March 1784; performed by Mozart on 31 March); K. 453 in G Major (dated 12 April 1784; performed by Ployer on 10 June at an academy in which Mozart participated); K. 456 in B-flat Major (dated 30 September 1784; performed by Mozart on 13 February 1785 at a concert given by the singer Luisa Laschi, and apparently played later by Maria Theresia von Paradis in Paris); K. 459 in F Major (dated 11 December 1784; performed by Mozart on 15 October 1790 in Frankfurt as part of the coronation festivities for the Emperor Leopold II); K. 466 in D Minor (dated 10 February 1785; performed by Mozart on 11 February at a subscription concert); K. 467 in C Major (dated 9 March 1785); K. 482 in E-flat Major (dated 16 December 1785; performed by Mozart in December 1785 during the intermission of a theater performance); K. 488 in A Major (dated 2 March 1786; performed by Mozart in early 1786 at a subscription concert); K. 491 in C Minor (dated 24 March 1786; per-

formed by Mozart on 3 April at a subscription concert and again on 7 April at an academy); K. 503 in C Major (dated 4 December 1786; performed by Mozart at an Advent academy on 5 December 1786 and again at an academy on 7 March 1787).

2. Three of the concertos published during Mozart's lifetime are K. 451 (ca. 1785 in Paris by Boyer [?]); K. 453 (ca. 1787 in Speyer by Boßler, and in Bonn by Simrock); K. 595 in B-flat Major (by August 1791 in Vienna by Artaria). On three more, those composed for sale in manuscript copy (K. 413, 414, and 415), see Köchel, 8th ed., under no. 385p = 414, p. 425. Mozart first offered these concertos for sale in January 1783; Artaria published them by January 1785. Concerning them, Mozart wrote his father Leopold on 28 December 1782, "The concertos are a thing halfway between too light and too difficult. They are very brilliant and pleasing to the ear, without being vacuous. Here and there the connoisseur alone will be gratified, yet in such a way that those lacking knowledge are bound to find them satisfying, without knowing why" ("Die Concerten sind eben das Mittelding zwischen zu schwer, und zu leicht—sind sehr Brillant—angenehm im die ohren—Natürlich, ohne in das leere zu fallen—hie und da—können auch kenner allein satisfaction erhalten—doch so—daß die nichtkenner damit zufrieden seyn müssen, ohne zu wissen warum").

While in Paris in September 1778 Mozart planned to publish three other concertos, K. 238, 246, and 271, with François-Joseph Heina. According to Köchel, 8th ed., the publisher may have issued one of the concertos by 1779 (see under no. 271, p. 277).

3. According to Köchel, 8th ed.: Mozart performed K. 438 at an academy in Augsburg on 13 February 1777, then on 12 February 1778 his student Rose Cannabich performed it in Mannheim; he composed K. 246 for the Countess Antonia Lützow, who may have been a student of Leopold Mozart; he composed K. 271 for the French pianist Mademoiselle Jeunehomme; K. 365/316a, the Concerto for Two Pianos in E-flat Major, he composed for himself to play with his sister Maria Anna, and he then played it with Josephine Auenhammer on 23 November 1781 and 26 May 1782 in Vienna; he composed K. 449 and 453 for Ployer; he offered K. 449, 453, 456, 459, and 488 to Prince Joseph Wenzeslaus von Fürstenberg on 8 August 1786; he gave K. 456 to Paradis to take with her on a concert tour to Paris and other European cities.

4. Karl Benyovszky, *J. N. Hummel. Der Mensch und Künstler* (Bratislava: EOS Verlag, 1934), 44–45.

5. In the absence of complete information on the publications of Heina (see note 2), Köchel, 8th ed., lists the following first editions by André: K. 271, 449, 456 (1792); 459, 537 (1794); 466 (1796); 246, 467, 482, 488, 491 (1800); 365 (1804). For more about first publications by André, see Köchel, 8th ed., Anhang E ("W. A. Mozarts Verleger"), 943. Otherwise, Köchel, 8th ed., lists K. 238 (which may have been published by Heina) as first published in Berlin and Amsterdam by J. J. Hummel (1792); K. 450 as first published by Artaria (1798); and K. 503, by Constanze Mozart (1798). See pp. 941, 944, 946.

6. The order of the concertos in the series is (1) K. 467; (2) K. 488; (3) K. 459; (4) K. 450; (5) K. 415; (6) K. 482; (7) K. 491; (8) K. 466; (9) K. 453; (10) K. 414; (11) K. 456; (12) K. 413; (13) K. 451; (14) K. 449; (15) K. 595; (16) K. 503; (17) K. 365; (18) K. 238; (19) K. 271; (20) K. 537.

7. The first performance by Beethoven of Mozart's D-Minor Concerto was on

31 March 1795 during the intermission of the opera *La clemenza di Tito*. A second performance may have been at an academy on 8 January 1796. See Georg Kinsky, *Das Werk Beethovens. Thematisch-Bibliographisches Verzeichnis*, ed. Hans Halm (Munich and Duisberg: G. Henle, 1955), 504 (WoO 58). Kinsky-Halm further suggests that Beethoven's cadenzas were written for Ferdinand Ries—whose family possessed the autograph of the cadenza for the first movement until the late nineteenth century—in either 1802–5 or 1808–9.

8. On the *Guide*, see Nathan Broder, "The First Guide to Mozart," *The Musical Quarterly* 42 (1956): 223–29. It was published in Leipzig by Breitkopf & Härtel.

9. Alfred Dörffel, *Die Gewandhauskonzerte zu Leipzig: 1781–1881* (Leipzig: Breitkopf & Härtel, 1884; reprint, Leipzig: Breitkopf & Härtel, 1980), "Chronik," 28. The Leipzig subscription concert series normally began on 29 September, or *Michaelistag*, each year. Madame Müller appeared regularly on the opening concerts from 1796 through 1809. A comparison of Dörffel's listing of her appearances with his listing of performances of Mozart concertos suggests that she played a Mozart concerto at nearly every opening concert (Dörffel, "Statistik," 43 and 90). A similar comparison suggests that her husband played concertos by Mozart on 22 November 1798, 23 January 1800, 12 February 1801, and 24 February 1803. Further, on 3 December 1807, an all-Mozart concert was given, and Madame Müller played Mozart's K. 466 (Dörffel, "Chronik," 34); and on 8 March 1810, she played Mozart's Concerto in C Minor ("Nachrichten. Leipzig," *Allgemeine musikalische Zeitung* 12, 9 May 1810, col. 507; cf. Dörffel, "Statistik," 43). Madame Müller returned to open the Gewandhaus series on Michaelmas 1820 with a Mozart concerto in C major. By then her husband had died, in 1817.

10. Dörffel, "Statistik," 43. Dörffel's first listing is in 1796.

11. Schneider played K. 491 with the Gewandhaus Orchestra on 3 December 1812 for a memorial concert marking the day of Mozart's death, then performed a Mozart concerto again on 29 September 1816, at a benefit concert for the singer Anna Neumann-Sessi (Dörffel, "Chronik," 64, 203). The organist Wolfgang Riem, a friend of Schneider's, performed Mozart's Concerto in D Minor on 13 December 1810 ("Nachrichten. Leipzig," *Allgemeine musikalische Zeitung* 13, 23 January 1811, col. 65; cf. Dörffel, "Statistik," 43), and a concerto in E-flat by Mozart on 6 October 1811 ("Nachrichten. Leipzig," *Allgemeine musikalische Zeitung* 13, 30 October 1811, col. 442; cf. Dörffel, "Statistik," 43). Dörffel lists only one other performance of a Mozart concerto at a Gewandhaus subscription concert from the time the Müllers left Leipzig up until 1820, namely, on 2 October 1814 ("Statistik," 43). This brings the total number of performances of Mozart's concertos from late 1810 through 1819 to five.

12. "Nachrichten. Leipzig," *Allgemeine musikalische Zeitung* 22, 29 March 1820, col. 219. The report reads, in part, "Herr Mozart played the splendid concerto of his father in C Major, the same one that was engraved by Breitkopf & Härtel immediately after his death, and which, at least so the oldest members of the orchestra maintain, the great man himself is supposed to have played here thirty years ago" ("Hr. M. spielte das vortreffliche Concert seines Vaters aus C dur, das gleich nach dessen Tode bey Breitkopf und Härtel gestochen worden ist, und das, wie wenigstens die ältesten Mitglieder des Orchesters behaupteten, vor dreyssig Jahren der grosse Mann hier selbst gespielt haben soll"). An account by Friedrich Rochlitz of the concert by the elder Mozart on 12 May 1789 reads, "In the second half he played

the most gorgeous and most difficult of all his concertos that are known so far, in C major, which was published by his wife after his death" ("Im zweyten Theile spielte er das prachtvolleste und schwierigste aller seiner bisher bekannt gewordnen Concerte aus C dur, das seine Gattin nach seinem Tode herausgegeben hat") ("Biographieen. Anekdoten aus Mozarts Leben," *Allgemeine musikalische Zeitung* 1, 21 November 1798, col. 113). K. 503 was published by Mozart's widow in 1798. However, I believe a case could be made that even though this was the concerto that Rochlitz says the elder Mozart played, it was in fact K. 467, the more popular of these two C-Major concertos, which his son played in 1820. The latter was published by Breitkopf & Härtel in 1800 as the first in its series of twenty concertos. Horst Heussner considers the Breitkopf & Härtel edition of K. 467, and not the one published that same year by André, to be the first (Mozart, *Neue Ausgabe sämtlicher Werke,* ser. V [concertos], work group 15 [concertos for one or more pianos and orchestra with cadenzas], vol. 6 (Kassel: Bärenreiter, 1986), f/48 [K. 467, "Quellen"]).

The elder Mozart played two concertos on the 1789 Leipzig concert. According to Rochlitz, the second was K. 456 in B-flat Major. On this and on the veracity of Rochlitz, see Maynard Solomon, "The Rochlitz Anecdotes: Issues of Authenticity in Early Mozart Biography," in *Mozart Studies,* ed. Cliff Eisen (Oxford: Clarendon Press, 1991), 1–7, 24–25.

13. While it may be the case that in Leipzig from 1800 to 1810 the number of performances of concertos by Mozart equaled or even exceeded the number by other composers, from 1810 to 1820 this certainly is not true. On the other hand, Terese Ellsworth has shown that in London performances of concertos by other composers are far more numerous than performances of Mozart's concertos, beginning already in 1801 ("The Piano Concerto in London Concert Life between 1801 and 1850" [Ph.D. diss., New York University, 1973], 244–51 [appendix 1, "Piano Concerto Performances in Order by Date"]).

14. Geraldine Keeling, "Liszt's Appearances in Parisian Concerts, 1824–44, Part 1: 1824–1833," *Liszt Society Journal* 11 (1986): 33. Note, though, that Jeffrey Cooper says Mozart's piano concertos were "discovered" in Paris in the 1840s, when the D-Minor Concerto became especially popular (*The Rise of Instrumental Music and Concert Series in Paris, 1828–71* [Ann Arbor, Mich.: UMI Research Press, 1983], 127).

15. See Ellsworth, "The Piano Concerto in London," 251–57. Up until 1818, Ellsworth notes only four performances of Mozart's piano concertos in London (pp. 115, 303).

16. Mozart Jr. played a concerto by his father on his concert of 1 February 1820, and the nine-year-old Albert Schilling played Mozart's D-Minor Concerto on 10 January 1825. I have found no other reports of performances of Mozart's piano concertos from the correspondent for the *Allgemeine musikalische Zeitung.* On these two performances, see that journal under "Nachrichten. Berlin," vol. 22, 15 March 1820, cols. 182–83; and vol. 27, 15 February 1825, col. 116. In 1829, after hearing a performance of a Beethoven concerto, the correspondent hoped for performances of the best Mozart concertos, for example the one in D Minor, in the coming season (vol. 31, 3 June 1829, col. 367).

17. Wenceslaus Hauck (1801–34) was a pupil of Hummel. On his performance, see "Nachrichten. Berlin," *Allgemeine musikalische Zeitung* 32, 3 March 1830, col. 137. On Wilhelm Taubert, Wilhelm Neumann wrote, "In the course of time,

through his repeated public appearances, especially through his performance of Mozart's and Beethoven's piano concertos—heard often and with pleasure from him at Möser's soirées—he earned the place nearest his teacher Berger as the most respected and sought after piano teacher in Berlin" ("Im Laufe der Zeit erwarb er sich durch wiederholtes öffentliches Auftreten, namentlich durch die in den Soiréen Möser's oft und gern von ihm gehörte Ausführung der Klavierkonzerte Beethoven's und Mozart's die Stellung des nächst seinen Lehrer Berger geachtetsten Virtuosen und gesuchtesten Klavierlehrers Berlins") (*Carl Wilhelm Taubert. Ferdinand Hiller,* Die Componisten der neueren Zeit, 43 [Kassel: Ernst Balde, 1857], 6). The correspondent for the *Allgemeine musikalische Zeitung* reported three performances by Taubert as part of the Mozart birthday celebrations—in 1831 (K. 271), 1834 ("ein kleineres Pianoforte-Concert"), and 1835 (K. 466) ("Nachrichten. Berlin," *Allgemeine musikalische Zeitung* 33, 23 February 1831, col. 127; 36, 5 March 1834, col. 157; 37, 25 March 1835, col. 196). Mendelssohn performed Mozart's C-Minor Concerto in 1833 ("Nachrichten. Berlin," *Allgemeine musikalische Zeitung* 35, 20 February 1833, col. 126). Other performances by Mendelssohn were of Mozart's C-Minor Concerto for a *Sonntagsmusik* at the Mendelssohn home on 14 November 1824, and of his D-Minor Concerto at a concert with Anna Milder-Hauptmann in Berlin on 24 October 1832 (Peter Ranft, *Felix Mendelssohn Bartholdy. Eine Lebenschronik* [Leipzig: Deutscher Verlag für Musik, 1972], 13, 33). Both Taubert and Mendelssohn were pupils of the Berlin piano teacher Ludwig Berger. Another student of Berger was Heinrich Dorn, who performed Mozart's D-Minor Concerto in Leipzig, where he was music director of the theater, on 24 November and 1 December 1831, as part of the fifty-year jubilee celebrations of the Gewandhaus concerts (Dörffel, "Chronik," 77–78).

Kalkbrenner's performance was on 15 June 1833 ("Nachrichten. Berlin," *Allgemeine musikalische Zeitung* 35, 7 August 1833, col. 521). See also Hans Nautsch, *Friedrich Kalkbrenner. Wirkung und Werk,* Hamburger Beiträge zur Musikwissenschaft 25 (Hamburg: Karl Dieter Wagner, 1983), 81.

18. "Nachrichten. Wien," *Allgemeine musikalische Zeitung* 37, 10 June 1835, col. 380 (Ignaz Tedesco performing a C-Major concerto by Mozart); 38, 20 July 1836, col. 248 (Carl Maria von Bocklet performing Mozart's C-Minor Concerto); 41, 5 June 1839, col. 447 (Mozart Jr. performing his father's D-Minor Concerto).

19. Gottfried Weber, review of No. 3 in C Minor from *Six grands concertos pour le Pianoforte,* Op. 82, by W. A. Mozart (édition faite d'après la partition en manuscrit), and of No. 4 in C Minor from *Douze grands concerts,* by W. A. Mozart, arranged for piano solo, or piano with accompaniment of flute, violin, and cello, with cadenzas and ornaments composed by J. N. Hummel, in *Caecilia, eine Zeitschrift für die musikalische Welt* 14, no. 56 (1832): 310, 311.

20. Ranft, *Felix Mendelssohn Bartholdy,* 20. Ferdinand Hiller, *Felix Mendelssohn-Bartholdy. Briefe und Erinnerungen* (Cologne: M. Du Mont-Schauberg, 1874), 17.

21. "Nachrichten. Leipzig," *Allgemeine musikalische Zeitung* 37, 22 April 1835, col. 267. The concert was on 26 February 1835 (Dörffel, "Chronik," 72).

22. "Höchst interessant war es, wieder endlich einmal eines der Mozartschen Pianoforte-Concerte zu hören, welche unsern modernen Virtuosen ganz fremd bleiben, weil es nicht Passagen-Werk genug darin giebt." *Haude- und Spenersche Zeitung,* 1 March 1830. Citation from Klaus Kropfinger, "Klassik-Rezeption in Berlin (1810–30)," in *Studien zur Musikgeschichte Berlins im frühen 19. Jahrhundert,*

ed. Carl Dahlhaus, Studien zur Musikgeschichte des 19. Jahrhunderts, 56 (Regensburg: Gustav Bosse, 1980), 375.

23. Joel Sachs, "Authentic English and French Editions of J. N. Hummel," *Journal of the American Musicological Society* 25 (1972): 205–9.

24. Benyovszky, *J. N. Hummel*, 231–33 (letter to Hummel from J. R. Schultz, 15 April 1823).

25. Kalkbrenner's manuscript for this performance, later owned by Nadia Boulanger, is now part of the collection of the Bibliothèque nationale de France. The publication was by Probst; it probably appeared in 1829, when it was reviewed in the *Allgemeine musikalische Zeitung* by Gottfried Wilhelm Fink (31, 19 August, cols. 541–45). The title page read, "arranged for 6-octave pianos with a cadenza and performed in Paris at a concert of the Royal Conservatory of Music" ("arrangé pour les Pianos à 6 Octaves avec un Point d'Orgue et exécuté à Paris au Concert du Conservatoire Royal de Musique"). See also Hans Nautsch, who equates the Paris performance, a later one in Berlin (mentioned above), and the Probst publication (Nautsch, *Friedrich Kalkbrenner*, 239). Moscheles made no essential changes to the piano parts of Mozart's concerto, but added his own cadenzas in his edition of K. 365/316a, published by Breitkopf & Härtel in 1861.

26. "Herr Schulzes Projekt: eine Auswahl der Mozart'schen Concerte mit Bereicherung der Hauptstimme, Verstärkung, Schluß-Passage, heraus zu geben, scheint mir von besonderem Interesse. Wenn Sie diese Unternehmen beginnen, kann der gute Erfolg nicht ermangeln. Wollten Sie nur folgende Punkte gütigst näher erklären: 1.) ob die Tuttis u. obligaten Stellen der Begl. nicht mit kleinen Noten fürs Klavier ausgeschrieben werden müssen (wie in Ihrem Concert). 2.) Ob nicht zuweilen zur Vermehrung der Brillance einige Takte in den Haupt-Passagen zugesetzt werden könnten. 3.) Ob es nicht besser sei den Nahmen Concert bey zu behalten, (nicht Sonate). 4.) Wollten Sie gefälligst anzeigen welche Concerte Sie bearbeiten würden, denn H. Kalkbrenner u. ich wollen uns mit vergnügen zu dieser Arbeit anschließen u. dann wählen." Benyovszky, *J. N. Hummel*, 312–13 (letter to Hummel from Moscheles, 23 April 1823). Moscheles's letter is an addendum to an appeasing letter written by Schultz on 15 April (cited above in note 24).

27. According to Köchel, 8th ed., Artaria published eighteen of Mozart's own cadenzas in 1801; this set was enlarged to thirty-five by André in 1804 (see under no. 626a = 624, pp. 732–33). Also in 1801, André published a set of cadenzas for the six concertos designated by him as op. 82 (K. 503, 595, 491, 482, 488, and 467), and, in a separate set, elaborated versions of the solo parts of the slow movements of the same concertos. The cadenzas and elaborations of the two sets were composed by Philipp Carl Hoffmann. In 1959 Hinrichsen published a modern edition of these, edited by A. Hyatt King. See King's introductory essay, "Philipp Karl Hoffmann: His Cadenzas to Some of Mozart's Piano Concertos and Elaborations of Their Slow Movements," in *Klavierkonzerte* (London: Hinrichsen, 1959). King notes that in 1818, A. E. Müller published cadenzas to Mozart's concertos (K. 456, 459, 466, 482, 488, 491, 503, and 537), and that Hummel's op. 4 comprised cadenzas to seven of Mozart's concertos. The latter were offered for sale in 1798 but no copies have been preserved. Some or all of the cadenzas may have been incorporated into the seven arrangements of Mozart's concertos that Hummel published beginning in 1828.

28. David Grayson, "Whose Authenticity? Ornaments by Hummel and Cramer

for Mozart's Piano Concertos," in *Mozart's Piano Concertos: Text, Context, Interpretation,* ed. Neal Zaslaw (Ann Arbor: University of Michigan Press, 1996), 373–91, esp. 380–83.

29. Ibid., 380. K. 537 was first published in 1794 by André, who also fully realized the parts, including the solo, which was incomplete at times. See Mozart, *Neue Ausgabe sämtlicher Werke,* ser. V, work group 15, vol. 8, ed. Wolfgang Rehm (Kassel: Bärenreiter, 1960), xxiii-xxiv ("Zum Vorliegenden Band"). This edition prints the left-hand notes of mm. 89–99 in small type.

30. William Rothstein, *Phrase Rhythm in Tonal Music* (New York: Schirmer, 1989), 18–19.

31. Ibid., 70–73.

32. In the first movement, Cramer changed many of the triplet eighth notes in the solo (and in the orchestral accompaniment) to groups of four sixteenth notes. For the second movement, he substituted the Andantino of Mozart's Concerto in E-flat Major, K. 449.

33. "Die Klavierstimme allein bietet . . . ein Abbild ohne wesentlich Lücke." A. B. Marx, review of Beethoven, Symphony in C Minor, and Mozart, Concerto in D Minor, arranged by Hummel, *Berliner allgemeine musikalische Zeitung* 5, 19 March 1828, 90.

34. ". . . mit vielem Geschmack und grosser Discretion." "Nachrichten. Berlin," *Allgemeine musikalische Zeitung* 35, 7 August 1833, col. 521. On the identification of the critic and date of the concert, see Nautsch, *Friedrich Kalkbrenner,* 81, 239.

35. The performance with the London Philharmonic took place on 23 February 1835. Stephan D. Lindeman calls Cramer's first seven concertos (composed from 1792 to 1816) "quite conservative, especially in comparison with the work of his contemporaries" ("Formal Novelty and Tradition in the Early Romantic Piano Concerto" [Ph.D. diss., Rutgers University, 1995], 180–82). The passagework of his C-Minor Concerto uses the scales and arpeggios typical of the classical style. In fact, it conforms quite closely to the few elaborations he wrote for the finale of the Mozart Concerto.

36. *Aus Moscheles' Leben. Nach Briefen und Tagebüchern,* ed. Charlotte Moscheles, 2 vols. (Leipzig: Duncker and Humbolt, 1872), 1:289.

37. George Macfarren, "Cipriani Potter: His Life and Work," *Proceedings of the Musical Association* 10 (1883–84): 46. Note that the first Mozart concerto Potter played with the Philharmonic on his return to England was in E-flat Major, probably K. 482, on 20 March 1820 (Ellsworth, "The Piano Concerto in London," 40, table 2). Mendelssohn's performance of Mozart's D-Minor Concerto in 1833 did not, of course, mark his first appearance in London as a pianist or with the Philharmonic, both of which took place in May 1829. Nor was it even the first time he played a Mozart concerto in London, since he had already performed the Concerto for Two Pianos in E-flat Major, K. 365/316a, with Moscheles on 1 June 1832. Mendelssohn composed two long cadenzas for the occasion (Ranft, *Felix Mendelssohn Bartholdy,* 20, 32). As for Potter's additions to Mozart's piano concertos, Cecil B. Oldman, with reference to Potter's editions of Mozart's piano works, writes: "The inclusion of an arrangement of the Piano Concerto in A [K. 488] is also something of an oddity; it was presumably inspired by, and intended as a supplement to, the similar arrangements by Cramer and Hummel, neither of whom had

produced a version of this particular concerto. [On the title page Potter takes credit for having been the first to perform this concerto in England, at his Benefit Concert, on 2 June 1837.] Intruder though it may be, it is welcome for the light it throws on contemporary methods of performance; it is a fully 'realized' version and the cadenzas are of special interest" (Oldman, "Potter's Editions of Mozart's Pianoforte Works," in *Festschrift Otto Erich Deutsch zum 80. Geburtstag am 5. September 1963*, ed. Walter Gerstenberg, Jan LaRue, and Wolfgang Rehm [Kassel: Bärenreiter, 1963], 126).

38. Grayson, "Whose Authenticity?" 378–80. The English reviews he cites are from the *Quarterly Musical Magazine and Review* (1827) and *Repository of Arts, Literature, Commerce, Manufactures, Fashions and Politics* (1827). Fink's remarks appeared in the *Allgemeine musikalische Zeitung* 31, 19 August 1829, cols. 541–45.

39. ". . . nicht sowohl ein auf kleinere Begleitung reducirtes arrangirtes Mozartisches Concert, sondern vielmehr eine Hummelsche Umarbeitung eines Mozartschen Concertes . . ." Weber, review of Mozart's Concerto in C Minor (see note 19), 311.

40. Ibid.

41. "statt der Sechzehntelläufe der rechten Hand allein, in Läufe beider Hände zugleich in Sexten oder Octaven, verwandelt, und überhaupt die ganze Stelle, zwölf Tacte lang, ganz frei verändert." Ibid.

42. ". . . dass der Herr Bearbeiter die Clavierstimme nicht ganz so wie Mozart sie geschrieben, beibehalten und dasjenige, was er von Seinigem hinzuthat oder gänzlich abänderte, nicht entweder blos in feinerer Notenschrift, oder in einer besonders beigefügten Notenzeile hinzugefügt hat, in welcher Gestalt die Ausgabe den ganz unvergleichlich höhern doppelten Werth gehabt hätte, das Werk des verklärten grossen Meister in seiner ursprünglichen Reinheit, und zugleich die modernen Zuthat zu Gesichte zu bringen, und dem Spieler die Freiheit zu gewähren, von Letzterer so Viel oder so Wenig, als ihm gut schiene, zu benutzen." Ibid., 312.

43. ". . . die Principalstimme einigermassen im Geschmacke der neusten Spiel- und Vortragmode aufzuputzen und dem Spieler Gelegenheit zu geben, durch Ausführung gewaltiger Schwierigkeiten, in dem Geschmacke, wie man sie in neuesten Zeiten zu hören gewohnt ist, zu brilliren." Ibid., 311.

44. "Nicht als Tadel, nicht als Rüge, führen wir dieses alles an, wohl aber in der zwiefachen Absicht: Erstens um, der Wahrheit zur Steuer, denen, welche es nicht wissen, zu sagen, dass so nicht die Mozartschen Concerte laufen, sondern viel anders." Ibid., 312.

45. A. E. Müller, *Anweisung zum genauen Vortrage der Mozartschen Clavierconcerte hauptsächlich in Absicht richtiger Applicatur* (Leipzig: Breitkopf & Härtel, 1796).

46. See note 27.

47. Broder, "The First Guide to Mozart," 225, 227. Emphasis added by Broder.

48. Ibid., 228.

49. Ibid., 223–29.

50. "Nachrichten. Leipzig," *Allgemeine musikalische Zeitung* 22, 29 March 1820, col. 222.

51. Ibid., cols. 219–20, 222.

52. In conjunction with the work of Katharine Ellis on pianistic repertory in

nineteenth-century Paris, I would like to note that this is yet another reason why the categorization of "the dazzling virtuosity of Liszt and Thalberg" as masculine, and Mozart, among others, as "stereotypically feminine" is "unstable." Mozart's concertos were reinvented by virtuosos—nearly always male—for public display alongside their own compositions, while at the same time being advocated as suitable for chamber performance—a more usual domain for women and a place where less soloistic approaches were expected—or given to children to learn (e.g., the nine-year-old Albert Schilling, or the young Clara Wieck). See Ellis, "Female Pianists and Their Male Critics in Nineteenth-Century Paris," *Journal of the American Musicological Society* 50 (1997): 362, 364–65, 378. On Clara Wieck's repertory, see Berthold Litzmann, *Clara Schumann. Ein Künstlerleben*, 3 vols. (Leipzig: Breitkopf & Härtel, 1923, 1925; reprint, Hildesheim: Georg Olms, 1971), 3:615–16 ("Studienwerke und Repertoire," 1827).

53. "Insofern muss man es mit der Vermischung des modernern Styls nicht so genau nehmen. Blieb uns doch der ungestörte Genuss der herrlichen Tuttisätze wie der geistreichen Instrumentirung überhaupt." "Nachrichten. Berlin," *Allgemeine musikalische Zeitung* 32, 3 March 1830, col. 137.

54. "Mozart gibt den Virtuosen bey weitem nicht genug zu thun für die jetzige Höhe des Pianofortespiels in Hinsicht auf Fertigkeit, Künstlichkeit, Schwieriges und Frappantes im Mechanischen der Ausführung." Review of Concerto No. VIII [K. 466] by W. A. Mozart, arranged for four hands by J. P. Schmidt, *Allgemeine musikalische Zeitung* 32, 8 December 1830, cols. 792–95.

55. Solomon, "The Rochlitz Anecdotes," 25–26; and Frederick Neumann, *Ornamentation and Improvisation in Mozart* (Princeton, N.J.: Princeton University Press, 1986), 240–56 ("The Special Case of the Piano Concertos").

56. "Es konnte also nicht fehlen, daß man in Folge so neuer glänzender und volltönender Klangeffekte die obschon klassichen, aber doch einfacheren und weniger herausfordernden Klavierkompositionen von Händel, Mozart, Haydn entweder vernachlässigte, oder wohl gar verballhornisirte, wie Kalkbrenner und Hummel mit den Konzerten von Mozart gethan.—Man spielte sie auf moderne Weise, d. h. brillanter, bravourmäßiger, im schnelleren Tempo, leidenschaftlicher und heftiger akzentuirt, mit einem Worte: 'modern konzertmäßig' und versündigte sich somit gegen die diesen Meisterwerken schuldige Pietät. . . . Wie Hummel und Andere mit den alten Klavierkompositionen verfuhren, so thaten es in Instrumentalsache früher Mozarts und von Mosel, als sie die Oratorien von Händel mit reichere Instrumentation ausschmückten. Auch ich selbst und meine Tochter Clara ergaben uns mit Eifer dieser neuern, glänzenden Spielweise. Es war wirklich ein ernster Fortschritt, kein trügerischer, wie ihn unsere neuesten Künstler gemacht haben, es war kein geckenhafte Virtuosenthuerei, keine verzerrte Darstellung guter Musikstücke, denn die an sich einfache Methode ließ keine verblendenden Aeußerlichkeitern zu, die wenige Jahre später das Publikum als Manifestationen des Genies bewunderte. Meine Tochter Clara errang damals durch die auf solche Weise arrangierten Mozart'schen Klavierkonzerte vielen Beifall, freilich nicht in der Heimath, nicht in Leipzig, sondern erst, als sie aus Paris mit dem dort errungenen Lorbeerkranze in die Vaterstadt zurückkehrte." Friedrich Wieck, *Klavier und Gesang. Didaktisches und Polemisches*, 3rd ed. (Leipzig: F. E. C. Leuckart, 1878), 148–49. It is difficult to know which concerts of Clara's are being referred to by Wieck. Her program books show no public performances of Mozart concertos until 1 January 1857, when for the first

time she played the D-Minor Concerto with a cadenza by Brahms (Litzmann, *Clara Schumann*, 3:17). That would not, however, seem to invalidate Wieck's remarks about performance practice.

57. ". . . doch nicht mit dem Respekt spielte, als man es von einem guten Künstler verlangen kann." Litzmann, *Clara Schumann*, 2:95 (quoted from her diary, 9 December 1845).

58. "Philharmonic Concerts," *The Harmonicon* 11 (1833): part 1, p. 135. The report also notes that Mendelssohn played the Concerto from memory and with two cadenzas of his own composition.

59. ". . . fertig und ausdrucksvoll im Geiste der grossartigen Composition vor." "Nachrichten. Berlin," *Allgemeine musikalische Zeitung* 35, 20 February 1833, col. 126. The reviewer notes further how much Mozart's Concerto differs from the "latest unfeeling, mechanical products of nimble fingers" ("neuesten herzlosen, mechanischen Fingerfertigkeits-Fabrikaten"), among which, however, he says concertos by Hummel, Kalkbrenner, and Moscheles are not to be counted.

60. Carl Reinecke, *Zur Wiederbelebung der Mozart'schen Clavier-Concerte. Ein Wort der Anregung an die clavierspielende Welt* (Leipzig: Gebrüder Reinecke, [1891]), 6–7, 27.

61. Ibid., 17–18.

62. Ibid., 26–27. The greater part of Reinecke's book is devoted to suggestions for performance of the "Coronation" Concerto, K. 537.

63. Ibid., 7–8, 24–25.

64. Recently, though, Mozart's "Linz" and "Haffner" Symphonies have been recorded in Hummel's arrangement for piano, flute, violin, and cello by Mark Kroll, John Solum, Carol Lieberman, and Arthur Fiacco on the Boston Skyline label. A review by Bernard Holland calls the reduction an "historical document of everyday life," yet persists in asking the question, "Is it Mozart?" ("Mozart, in Hummel's Fluoroscope," *New York Times*, 6 July 1997, sec. 2, p. 26).

15

"Wo die Zitronen blühn": Re-Versions of *Arie antiche*

Margaret Murata

If we truly wanted to perform historically, we would begin by imitating early-twentieth-century recordings of late-nineteenth-century music and extrapolate back from there. . . . The pioneers extrapolated—from very soft evidence bolstered by very firm desiderata—a style of performing Renaissance and Baroque music, and from then on it has been a matter of speculative forward encroachment.
—Richard Taruskin, "The Modern Sound of Early Music"

Needing the realization of its *basso continuo* line, the score of a Baroque composition is usually more complete than a jazz lead sheet but more incomplete than a classical operatic aria. What must always be discovered for a Baroque performance are textures and rhythms, and at times, the harmonies. A *basso continuo* line can yield strumming on a guitar that exaggerates or elaborates the meter, or it might sound as the luxuriant, widely spread resonance of a harp or chitarrone. When the continuo part supports a contrapuntal texture, its harmonically connected sonority can glue vagarious lines together. The choice of continuo instruments also affects tempo, articulation, and ultimately, the character of a work. Whether thought of as "filling in" a score or developing and "filling it out," whatever the continuo does, its role is not optional. For both music historians and performers, therefore, finding new scores of Baroque music has also meant hunting for instructions on how to execute continuo lines in various musical genres.

In current practice, after more than a century of musicological discussion, editors of Baroque scores generally leave the responsibility for realizing the continuo part to their informed reader-performers. Publishers bringing out editions for performers in the nineteenth century, however, were obliged to provide complete parts for the chordal instruments. These were usually prepared by composer-arrangers whose assignments were never exclusively "old" music. A recent introduction to historical performance attributes "some of the most extravagant 'performing editions'" to "the middle of the nineteenth century" and describes some as "more closely" approximating "arrangements than editions."[1] Whether an old edition or a modern performance yields a "version" of a piece or an "arrangement" of it, examining continuo realizations in all their variety is one way to "read the readers" of Baroque scores.[2] All versions of a score indicate obliquely how a bit of music writing is "pronounced" in various musical "dialects." At the end of the twentieth century, one could read a range of such executions of Baroque scores, from musical examples in teaching manuals to orchestral arrangements by Leopold Stokowski to re-scorings for voice and string quartet or for Japanese kōtō ensemble. These do not, however, simply form a geography of *Wirkungsgeschichten*. In a postmodern world, the past is not just another country.

One Baroque repertory has had a continuous presence in modern times, as evidenced by a long history of pirated, newly edited, and, in recent decades, photoduplicated anthologies. Italian solo songs and arias from the seventeenth and eighteenth centuries have been heard on the concert stage and in the voice studio for the past two hundred years. New editions of the same "standards" continue to appear.[3] Each aria has had a different journey from its original source to one of the numerous modern editions for voice and piano that first began to appear in London in the early nineteenth century.[4] In some cases, written prefaces to the editions reveal the aesthetics and aims of their editors. More telling, however, are the piano accompaniments that served as realizations of continuo lines or, more often, as substitutes for them.

At first this repertory of "ancient music" consisted mainly of eighteenth-century operatic arias heard in public concerts with their orchestral accompaniments, sometimes with modernized instrumentation. When earlier continuo arias began to be programmed, equivalent orchestral parts were invented for them. Late Baroque arias by Alessandro Scarlatti, Giovanni Legrenzi, and Giovanni Bononcini formed a largely tonal repertory alongside arias by composers such as Leonardo Vinci, Giovanni Paisiello, Tommaso Traetta, and Christoph Willibald Gluck. When these *arie antiche* were sold as sheet music, their piano parts were both orchestral reductions and keyboard accompaniments. Charles Santley was renowned for his performances of Verdi operas. The edition containing his rendition of an aria by Alessandro Scarlatti undoubtedly represents the singer's operatic persona, for all other mid-century editions of the same aria were less "extravagant" (see example 15.1).

Arias that did not come from operas were added to this repertory later in the nineteenth century, in English, French, and German publications. In 1877, for example, T. Ridley Prentice produced an edition of cantatas and motets by Giacomo Carissimi.[5] It included an optional harmonizing alto line to be performed on the cello. Typically, however, the piano parts for sheet-music editions reflected contemporary song styles. Varieties of persistently subdivided, broken-chord figurations for the right hand are common. In some editions with pedagogical intent, though, the piano accompaniments might be kept simple.[6] None of the editions suggests that

Example 15.1. From Alessandro Scarlatti, "O cessate di piagarmi," romanza sung by Mr. [Charles] Santley (London, [between 1866 and 1871]), *Gemme d'Antichità*, no. 72; taken from Carl Banck, ed. and arr., *Zwei Liebeslieder . . . von Aless. Scarlatti* (Leipzig and London, [1863–64]). Aria originally from *Il Pompeo* (Rome, 1683).

music originally from chamber cantatas should be sung differently from operatic music (as indeed no such distinction was made during the Seicento).

By 1885 this repertory was well along in a process of "re-genrification," from arias for professionals to solo-arias-as-songs. Recitatives that had been performed in concert in the 1840s were omitted in publication; and from cantatas, only brief arias were published, excised from their original contexts. When Italians musicians and scholars finally took note of their own "heritage," it was initially in reaction to the excesses and vocal demands of the newly emerging *verismo* opera. The intent of Alessandro Parisotti's first two anthologies of *arie antiche* for Ricordi, published in 1886 and

1890, was conservative and neo-classicistic, even if to us the style of his piano parts does not seem to be.[7] His first volume was an attempt at neither scholarship nor re-appropriation, since most of its twenty-nine items came from previous German, French, and English editions. The collection, with few exceptions, represents Parisotti's choices from among the north European canon of music from the late Baroque and classical periods.[8]

Along with the shift to a largely piano-accompanied existence for *arie antiche* and the increased appearance of chamber solos, the end of the nineteenth century also saw a rise in music from before the era of "common-practice" harmony. Parisotti's second volume (1890) included two obscure early-seventeenth-century composers, Andrea Falconieri and Raffaello Rontani, whose music he culled from prints of 1616 and 1623. He also published a facsimile from a manuscript source, in order to show how he "used the themes of different compositions to develop the preludes according to the style of the time and the accompaniments."[9] Instead of his previous reliance on foreign editions, Parisotti now sought for old music in Italy, aided by the librarians of the Accademia di Santa Cecilia in Rome, the Museo Civico in Bassano, and by Cesare Pollini, called "collector" of the Contarini manuscripts in Venice, all of whom he acknowledges. In 1892 Ricordi issued a third anthology by Parisotti, his *Piccolo album di musica antica,* which has been generally ignored. This volume departed from precedent by offering seven compositions from before the mid-seventeenth century.[10] In 1894 Leipzig-trained Luigi Torchi brought out his first anthology of early Italian solos, *Eleganti canzoni ed arie italiane del secolo XVII: Saggi antichi ed inediti della musica vocale italiana / raccolti, annotati e trascritti per canto e pianoforte.* Most of these, too, are "early," with only five of twenty-three pieces dating from the last quarter of the Seicento.[11] At the same time, as editor of the new *Rivista Musicale Italiana,* Torchi published two discursive articles about this repertory, one on instrumental accompaniment for early Italian opera and the other on solo *canzoni ed arie.*[12] Torchi's historical approach to the solo repertory as well as his insistence on "collecting, annotating, and transcribing" from original sources challenged Parisotti to issue a third volume in the series of *arie antiche* in 1898 that was different from his first two.[13] Its forty items extended from Giulio Caccini to the late eighteenth century, with fourteen pieces from before 1675 balancing eighteen from the Settecento.[14] More than a decade after his plea for classical Italian vocal technique, in this last volume Parisotti made a veiled appeal for its retention outside the opera house. "Many years have passed," he observed in its preface, "since the publication of the first [volume of *Arie antiche*], and in this period, Italian chamber music has once again fallen silent."[15]

With Torchi drawing on Bolognese sources and Parisotti on prints and manuscripts from Florence and Rome, it fell to Maffeo Zanon to borrow from Venetian sources in his 1908 edition of operatic arias by Francesco

Cavalli for a publisher in Trieste.[16] This publication gave all non-original pitches in small type (see example 15.2b), and it appears to be the most source-oriented or "text-centric" Italian edition to date.[17] Zanon did point out, however, that since the sources give no indications for tempo or nuances of dynamics and phrasing ("colorito"), "all the editorial marks"—which he did not hesitate to add—"are susceptible of modification, according to the taste of the performers" ("Si tenga pure presente che non esistendo nei manoscritti originali alcun accenno nè al tempo nè al colorito, tutte le indicazioni introdotte sono suscettibili di modificazione secondo il gusto degli interpreti"). Six years passed before Ricordi issued a second Zanon collection of arias "by various seventeenth-century authors" ("di vari autori del secolo XVII"). Twenty of the twenty-four pieces come from operas dating from 1666 to 1681, three come from cantatas by Alessandro Stradella, and one is said to be from a cantata by Alessandro Scarlatti, though it actually is from an opera of 1679.[18]

Issued in separate fascicles as well as in collected anthologies, these Italian editions were intended to be practical, not scholarly. It appears, nevertheless, that in the thirty years encompassed by Parisotti's first volume, Torchi's work, and Zanon's "24," the Italians were, in principle, well on their way to expanding the repertory of *arie antiche* in a historically conscious manner. The editions by these three pioneers, however, are not alike. Born in 1858 and older than both Claude Debussy and Richard Strauss, Luigi Torchi had been studying in Germany at the time that Wagner's music made its first impact. Though he was among the first to seek out original sources and to edit them with knowledge from early treatises on continuo practice, a comparison of arioso passages in triple meter as realized by Torchi and Zanon (twenty-four years Torchi's junior) reveals an editorial divide that can be marked, perhaps, by the year 1900 (see examples 15.2a and 15.2b).

Example 15.2. Four Italian editions:

Example 15.2a. From [Pietro] Cesti, "Sì, sì, voglio morir," in Luigi Torchi, ed., *Eleganti canzoni ed arie italiane del secolo XVII* (Milan: G. Ricordi, [1894]), 61. From the cantata *Alpi nevose e dure,* probably edited from I-Bc MS Q.47.

Example 15.2a. *(continued)*.

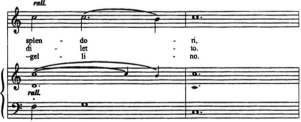

Example 15.2b. From Francesco Cavalli, *Aria di Lidio* ("Or che l'aurora spargendo") from *Egisto* (Venice, 1643), in Maffeo Zanon, ed., *Venti arie . . . di Francesco Cavalli* (Leipzig and Trieste: C. Schmidl & Co., [1908]), 8.

Example 15.2c. From Giulio Caccini, "Amarilli mia bella," in Claudio dall'Albero and Marcello Candela, eds., *Celebri arie antiche* (Milan: Rugginenti Editore, 1998), 5; accompaniment for lute transcribed from Robert Dowland, *A Musicall Banquet* (1610). The piano accompaniment is from Alessandro Parisotti, *Arie antiche*, vol. 2 (Milan: G. Ricordi, [1890]), 20. Originally in Caccini's *Le nuove musiche* (Florence, 1602).

Note especially the local "sighing" motive invented by Torchi that opens with a rising minor sixth. Also in contrast to Torchi is the version of Caccini's "Amarilli, mia bella" in Parisotti's 1890 volume.[19] Apart from octave doublings in the piano bass, its harmonization and texture resemble the straightforward and plain recent edition based on a 1610 version for lute (see example 15.2c; also example 15.6a). But given Zanon's "clean" 1908 edition, how is it that his 1914 accompaniments were so much more extensively composed, contrapuntal, and wide-ranging? Was the path toward the literal modern edition so quickly abandoned?

Between Zanon's two volumes, Ricordi issued *Antiche gemme italiane / Gems of Old Italy,* collected by Vittorio Ricci.[20] This practical anthology does not present *arie antiche* as part of the classical Italian repertory or as archaeological finds. It also is not an "urtextliches" project. Rather it can be seen as an "early music" edition—with Taruskinian implications, because Ricci's aim is to present what is modern in the arias. His "Introductory Remarks" point out their metric irregularity, the not-tonal harmony and asymmetrical phrasing, and above all, their emotional charge (he does not use the label "Baroque").[21] Furthermore, for Ricci, "ancient" music is more transparent than the classical. For him, its variety and difference signify that its emotional content is less mediated by convention. His comments reveal an early modernist's belief that more authentic expression emanates from the "primitive":

> The Editor trusts that the present Collection of Italian Songs by Composers of the 16th, 17th, and early 18th Centuries will meet with the favour of both the lovers of old music, and also of those who, although fully appreciating the gorgeous beauties of the modern style, find a new source of pleasure in the refreshing melodies written in those times, when Art was characterised by graceful simplicity, spontaneous brightness, and true sentiment. Such peculiar features common to all *primitives,* are evident in these Airs, where the deep sorrow of departure is so forcibly expressed in Bottegari's song, and a plaintive love note languidly moans in Gagliano's, Vitali's, Scarlatti's, and in one song by Marcello, whilst a spirited and somewhat ironical mood seems to pervade the two songs by Steffani, Strozzi, and one by Rontani.[22]

He praises the irregularities of this earlier music compared to the classical:

> A simple perusal of these songs will be sufficient in fact to show first of all that a much larger variety of rhythm and harmony was used at the birth of music in comparison with the rhythmical uniformity and harmonic poverty characterising the style which subsequently prevailed, expecially [*sic*] in Italy. Further, the musical phrase, which afterwards was constantly moulded in the same symmetrical form, appears here to be shaped, . . . so as to follow strictly the words, the sentiment of which it vividly expresses; thus assuming more resemblance to the modern style of phrasing than to the one in fashion at Rossini's time.[23]

The English remarks are milder than the parallel Italian observations, which blame the circular progressions of tonal harmony and its series of "closed periods" for causing later Italian music to atrophy into a miserable state. Ricci's embrace of old Italian vocal music and his rejection of the classical reverses the original aim of Parisotti's first volume, which was to set aside the neurotic excesses of post-bel-canto singing and to restore healthy, that is, classical, tradition. Parisotti had recommended singing with simplicity and tranquility, in a style "at once calm, elegant, correct, and expressive, yet without coldness or heaviness."[24] Ricci's collection offered "deep sorrow" and languid moans.

Reading the differing aims of early-twentieth-century Italian editions against the general observation by Lawson and Stowell cited earlier that "the period during which some of the most extravagant 'performing editions' appeared and were most readily accepted was around the middle of the nineteenth century," one would expect these Italian editions to project the simplicity, brightness, and depth of expression of which Ricci spoke. In their modes of being anti-romantic, the conservatism of both Ricci and Parisotti could be considered modern. But they belong to a stage prior to 1920 and to Taruskin's characterization of the modernity of early music performance as "literalistic," "impersonal," and "leery of the profound or sublime."[25]

"Primitive" for Ricci, however, is only a relative term. Unadorned, arpeggiated chords project the "deep sorrow of departure" in Cosimo Bottegari's "Mi parto" by insistent quarter-note repetition (see example 15.3a). In a simple canzonetta by Filippo Vitali (that had already been edited by Gevaert in 1868), Ricci emphasized the meter by irregular barring, but he also created a new musical motive and re-composed the bass to exploit it. In some cases, Ricci warns his readers that he has added "a few bars of introduction or conclusion, founded upon the theme of the song," or as the Italian text states, "in harmony with it." These additions were supposed to be signaled in the edition between asterisks, as in examples 15.3a and 15.3d. The asterisks were forgotten, however, in the arietta by Barbara Strozzi, "E che diavol sarà questo?" Here Ricci introduced increased rhythmic participation on the part of the piano, by extrapolating from a closing cadential figure in the *basso continuo* (transcribed in example 15.3b). In the second section of the cantata, in triple meter, he reiterated the third "beat" of a modern 3/4 measure and gave it harmonic emphasis, ignoring the swing of the original 6/2 notation (see examples 15.3b and 15.3c). Even more inventive is the introduction he created for a *da capo* aria attributed to Alessandro Scarlatti (see example 15.3d). Anticipating the first four bars of the *basso continuo,* Ricci constructed a late-Baroque-style instrumental figuration above it, which incorporated the principal tones of the vocal line. Its sixteenth-note motion then continues after the voice enters. Such a continuo realization no longer qualifies either as "primitive" or as modern. As mentioned earlier, a similar increase in continuous, contrapuntal textures appears in Zanon's "24" of 1914.

Despite notions of the modern that inspired Ricci's edition, its accompaniments also reflect new historicist influences from Germany. One of

Example 15.3a. From Cosimo Bottegari, "Mi parto, ahi, sorte ria." In Vittorio Ricci, *Antiche gemme italiane* (Milan: G. Ricordi & Co., [1909–10]), 1.

Parisotti's first main sources had been the Leipzig song arrangements by Carl Banck (see note 8). Quite different are the piano accompaniments in Hugo Riemann's *Kantaten-Frühling (1633–1682),* an edition of fourteen Italian works.[26] Not only did the title announce a genre other than "song" or "aria," but "cantata" signaled the importance and restoration of recitative, while "spring" implied that the contents were the beginnings of a genre with a future development. A composer, arranger, scholar, and founder in 1908 in Leipzig of the first German institute for musicology, Riemann also discussed the Italian cantata repertory in his *Handbuch der Musikgeschichte.* The *Handbuch* gives several examples of solo cantatas in short score, including some that appear in the *Kantaten-Frühling.* What is

Example 15.3b. From Barbara Strozzi, "E che diavol sarà questo?" From her *Cantate, ariette e duetti*, op. 2 (Venice: Gardano, 1651), 18.

Example 15.3c1. From Strozzi, "E che diavol sarà questo?" In Vittorio Ricci, *Antiche gemme italiane* (Milan: G. Ricordi & Co., [1909–10]), 15.

Example 15.3c2. From Strozzi, "E che diavol sarà questo?" In Vittorio Ricci, *Antiche gemme italiane* (Milan: G. Ricordi & Co., [1909–10]), 16.

Example 15.3d. From "Tu lo sai." Attributed to Alessandro Scarlatti in Vittorio Ricci, *Antiche gemme italiane* (Milan: G. Ricordi & Co., [1909–10]), 20. Ricci's source is unknown.

clear from both publications is that for Riemann one of the hallmarks of musical progress was what the continuo part had to offer. He rejected the notion that only simple chords would have been executed. In discussing Caccini, he concluded "that the performance of the accompaniment is in no way bound to the asceticism sought after in principle with respect to pure monodies" ("dass die Ausführung des Akkompagnements in keiner Weise zu der für die reinen Monodien im Prinzip erstrebten Askese verpflichtet ist"). After faulting Hugo Leichentritt for missing the earliest example of imitation between voice and bass in the new monodies, Riemann declares, "We have already shown how quickly strict contrapuntal work returns in the music of the monodists" ("wir haben ja . . . gezeigt, wie schnell die ernste kontrapunktische Arbeit wieder Eingang in die Werke der Monodisten fand"). Where Ricci saw the liberation of the present in the primitive, Riemann saw promise only in progress. He demonstrated the result of his beliefs in a complete four-part setting of Orfeo's lament from Act II of Monteverdi's *L'Orfeo*. Riemann presented "Tu sei morta" as an example "of a more contrapuntal realization of the continuo part, together with a presentation of the actual metric relationships hidden behind the common-time signature (C)," which, in the light of his discussion, "needed no further justification."[27]

In the outer, transcribed parts, apart from the reduction of the note values by half, as he himself pointed out, Riemann altered the original regular barring by the breve (as in the 1615 print of *L'Orfeo*), in order for syllable stress to coincide with downbeats. He created a pseudo-counterpoint by repeating tones in subdivision in the tenor or alto parts and by giving them a rising or falling motion when the voice is static. The passage is unfigured in Monteverdi's score. Example 15.4a gives just a few measures from Riemann's version of the entire solo. Four first-inversion chords (G♯dim6, Gm6, F6, Edim6) slide to a dominant, a passage which Riemann made more harmonically eventful with a C♯ passing note (marked in the example with an asterisk) and with a struck, dissonant second that makes a ii4/3 chord, which then moves to an unlikely Dm 6/4 instead of to F6. The repeated Fs that delay the 5̂–4̂–3̂–2̂ descent in the voice receive a rising, stepwise line in the piano part. Contrary to the voice's illustration of the "king of the shades," perhaps it was meant to suggest the softening of Pluto's heart (or Orfeo's hope from sensing it). The main point of this example, however, is not to decry Riemann's harmonic invention, but rather to take note of Riemann's rhythm and resultant texture. Riemann's "uncovering" of the true metric relationships ("Die wirklichen Taktverhältnisse herauszuschälen") made visual the mixed meters that Ricci saw as "modern." Above all, the eighth notes with ornamental groups of two passing sixteenths occur persistently. In comparison, Max Spicker's 1910 edition of the same solo limits itself to half-note block chords (see example 15.4b).[28] Moreover, Spicker instructs the pianist to play "con canto." Riemann envisions little declamatory flexibility on the part of the singer.

Riemann's predilection for more complex accompaniments can be seen in other examples in the *Handbuch*.[29] An aria published as one by Stradella, for example, becomes a three-part keyboard sinfonia.[30] Where the bass and voice are not imitative, Riemann often creates a duet in the style of a trio sonata between the voice and the pianist's right hand. Some passages,

Example 15.4a. Passage from Claudio Monteverdi, "Tu sei morta" from Act 2, scene 1 of *L'Orfeo* (Mantua, 1607), in Hugo Riemann, *Handbuch der Musikgeschichte*, vol. 2, pt. 2 (Leipzig: Breitkopf & Härtel, 1912), 200–203. Bottom staff reduced from the 1615 print of *L'Orfeo* (facs. ed., Kassel: Bärenreiter, 1998), 39.

however, are unexpectedly in lieder styles. Some recitatives are set to common-practice, sustained block chords; for others, however, the piano creates an almost *brisé*, quasi-Straussian screen of sound (see example 15.5a). For other recitatives, song-style accompaniments transform them into "ariosi" (see example 15.5b).

We could attribute Riemann's accompaniments to his having an ear like Luigi Torchi's—that is, one steeped in a musical language acquired over more than a half-century of experience—and to a creativity born of an interpretive response to the text and score before him. (By 1910 he had published sixty-eight opuses of his own compositions and prepared seventy-five editions of "fremder Werke.")[31] It is also inevitable that these realizations should be considered deliberate or unconscious anticipations

Example 15.4b. The same passage edited by Max Spicker in *Voices from the Golden Age of Bel Canto*, ed. Henry Edward Krehbiel (New York: G. Schirmer, 1910); this "Monologue" ©1909 (English text omitted).

of later German Baroque music. "Basic to the value and meaning" of song, Lawrence Kramer has written with regard to the nineteenth-century lied, "is the interplay between the singing voice and the independent, always compelling, sometimes authoritative musical voice constituted by the accompaniment."[32] Baroque chamber music is unusual in the space it demands the continuo performer—or performer-editor—to occupy. Riemann occupied it with authority, projecting more loudly to his listeners than to those who sang. He believed that Italian music did not unduly influence the native German style that arose after Heinrich Schütz and, according to him, replaced the musical "hegemony" of the Italians.[33] By publishing earlier Italian works with accompaniments in a later "German" style, Riemann's editions "predicted" the later replacement of the Italian hegemony by the German. The appearance of Carissimi and Cesti in the *Kantaten-Frühling*, dressed at times as J. S. Bach and at times in the garb of late-romantic lieder, appropriated this Italian repertory into the then-present history of German music. At the same time, Riemann's cantatas offered a different language of "antiquity" in their pseudo-contrapuntal accompaniments. His editions do not offer the immediacy of expression sought by Ricci, an Italian hearing the projection of Italian text. Riemann instead provided a translation in which Kramer's "imaginary voice" of the music is not in the vocal

Recitativo

Example 15.5a. Opening recitative from "Al tramontar del giorno." Attributed to Giacomo Carissimi, in H. Riemann, *Kantaten-Frühling,* 2:3. Probably edited from a copy of Paris, Biblothèque du Conservatoire [F-Pc] Rés. F.935, 171–79. The cantata is most likely by Bernardo Pasquini; see three sources in the *Wellesley Edition Cantata Index Series,* fascicle 5b (Wellesley, Mass.: Wellesley College, 1966).

line, but in the keyboard part. In fact, in his discussion of Schubert, Riemann pointed out that

> it should not be forgotten that in operas and cantatas, the artfully accompanied melody had long ago (as far back as the last decades of the seventeenth century) also evolved with characteristic tendencies toward tone-painting. The mechanism with which Schubert worked is not really new.[34]

What Riemann did find new in Schubert was the original shaping of musical form to the meaning of each poem, creating "something individual with distinct character" ("ein Individuum von ausgesprochenem Charakter"). He followed this statement with a direct reference to his owncontinuo realizations:

> I hope that I have succeeded in demonstrating, through the examples offered of seventeenth-century art songs, especially by the completely edited ones in the collection *Kantaten-Frühling,* that it [the cantata] also—after overcoming the

Example 15.5b. Internal recitative from [Pietro] Cesti, *La corte di Roma* ("Era l'alba vicina"), *Kantaten-Frühling*, 2:33.

worst impediments of aesthetic theory—has occasionally found this way to the free realization of a poem. Without shrinking back from assigning an important role to an accompaniment sketched only as a bass line and completed in the hands of a master thoroughly schooled in counterpoint—whose right or, more often, whose duty is without doubt—one would not be able to recognize the close relationships between pieces such as Dom Paolo's "Fra duri scogli" (before 1400), Benedetto Ferrari's "Premo il giogo delle Alpi" (1637), and perhaps Schubert's "Wanderer."[35]

The arranger who puts the hybrid nature of Riemann's accompaniments into clear relief is Pietro Floridia, an Italian who had no interest in Germanizing *arie antiche*. His "concert versions" are the most Puccinian and extroverted, and wonderfully contrary to the ideals of Parisotti, Ricci, or Riemann, as well as being a flamboyant exception to Lawson and Stoller's generalization about extravagant editions (see examples 15.6a and 15.6b).[36]

In sum, when "purists" of the 1920s and later turned their attention to this repertory, there were two legacies of "romanticism" that could be cleared away. One was Pietro Floridia. The other was represented in different degrees by Riemann and by Ricci, whose creations in a proto-modern heterotopia (notwithstanding the universalist ideals that prompted them) only

Example 15.6a. From Andrea Falconieri, "Bella porta di rubini," in Alessandro Parisotti, *Arie antiche,* vol. 3 (Milan: G. Ricordi, [1898]), [1]. Original in his *Quinto libro delle musiche* (Florence, 1619).

Example 15.6b. The same in Pietro Floridia, *Early Italian Songs and Airs,* vol. 1 (Boston: Oliver Ditson Co., [1923]), 12, a "modern concert transcription."

now speak again to the last decades of the twentieth century, after the dissolution of high modernism and the dispersal of its avant-gardes.[37]

   Present-day pluralism does more than tolerate revisiting these earlier publications of "ancient" music, though not necessarily in the spirit of rehabilitation. In the years since Richard Taruskin wrote "The Modern Sound of Early Music," early music performance has become less literal, much more personal, and certainly less "lightweight." Sonority—from period instruments—has broadened and deepened; tempos have slowed down or sped up tremendously; in some genres sculptural shaping by *messa di voce* has replaced any sense of tactus; everywhere improvised ornamentation, whether Italian, French, or Moroccan, draws attention to the performer and not to any "infallible composer-creator."[38] In Baroque repertories, the most competent performers ignore published "editions" and perform from facsimile sources. Often this has little to do with getting "closer to the composer's intent" and is more about having the same open field from which to create performances as did earlier musicians. Just as Riemann may have had J. S. Bach in his fingers and ears, a harpsichordist today may have fifteen years of twentieth-century d'Anglebert and both Couperins as his second musical language, along with a degree in musicology. The variety of recent continuo practices in another melody-plus-continuo genre is exemplified by a 1996 discussion by Peter Walls of recordings of Arcangelo Corelli's solo violin sonatas. He noted especially that

> Jesper Christensen's approach to his role as a harpsichord continuo player is arresting—and he can point to historical justification for much of what he does. His use of saturated chords laden with *acciacature* is, on the face of it, the sort of thing practised by Pasquini and approved of as a "full, rich style" by Gasparini. Christensen precedes the third movement (Adagio) of Sonata no. 2 with a short prelude. This sounds fine in itself—but as the movement continues—the activity in the harpsichord part reduces the violinist's freedom to be declamatory. This happens time and time again, where Christensen adopts a more active rhythm than the bass line prescribes.[39]

When Riemann, Zanon, and Ricci published their editions, the fine distinctions in style between fifteen-year periods of the Seicento were inconceivable, and obviously no one could hear reproductions of old music in recordings. Today, the languages in which historical repertories are performed are learned by doing and hearing (historically, an authentic procedure) and not from reading editions.[40] Daniel Leech-Wilkinson has observed that, in many successful cases, performers make "a new style" that "works for us today; and it is the major achievement of the last 12 or 13 years . . . that we no longer need to claim its historical authenticity."[41] The transmission of such "new styles" has been amplified by the sheer number of people and projects vested in the present world of early music, though this is only a tiny sector of the global economy tied to culture.

In trying to establish how music in the West is a performing art, Peter Kivy posited that "the performer is an artist, somewhat akin to a composer or, better, 'arranger' of musical works." He also pointed out, from Lydia

Goehr's arguments, that we owe the notion of the musical work as a fixed object to the late nineteenth century.[42] Conceiving of a score more as a script than as a text, as many performers of Baroque music do these days, loosens the fixity of the object and opens it toward multiple possibilities, the essence of performance. Michael Chanan has observed that the "authoritative identification of the musical work with the text is a rationalization of fairly recent origins, which already shows signs of dissolution."[43] The editor of a musical score, then, has a range of possible functions that lie somewhere between those of a conservator and of a performer, any of which may yield a diversity of musical results. Riemann's Italian cantatas did not survive their northern grafts, but the piano accompaniments of Carl Banck, his contemporary in Leipzig, survived and flourished after Parisotti transplanted them to the South. Banck's arrangements were orchestrated for Janet Baker, when she recorded them in 1978, in an eerie reversion to London practice of the 1840s.[44] They were scored up in 1993 for string ensemble by Albert Vinci in volumes with a painting by Sir Edward Burne-Jones on the covers.[45] When all is said and done, it is the versions that were popular from around 1875 to 1890 that have remained "canonical," chosen by generations of teachers and students of voice, despite the efforts of subsequent editors to push them backward or forward in time. Few have ventured to perform them—in any historical style—either as complete cantatas in which the singer does the work of interpretation or as lieder in which the "impalpable plenitude" of meaning comes from the piano.[46]

Notes

1. Colin Lawson and Robin Stowell, *The Historical Performance of Music: An Introduction* (Cambridge: Cambridge University Press, 1999), 37 (in a section titled "The Application of Primary Sources: The Role of Editions"). The authors also observe that such editions may "constitute valuable sources of information about the . . . performing practices of their era." Similarly, Nicholas Kenyon has pointed out how transcriptions "are precious evidence of how creative figures actually heard the music of the past" ("Time to Talk Back to Treatises!" *Early Music* 25 [1997]: 555).

2. For a discussion of the continuum from "version" to "arrangement," see Peter Kivy, *Authenticities* (Ithaca, N.Y.: Cornell University Press, 1995), 128–35. With respect to Baroque music, he concentrates more on varied melodic lines than on continuo practice. For a brief historical series of arrangements of early music, see Antje Müller, "Die Wiederentdeckung alter Musik," in *Musikalische Metamorphosen. Formen und Geschichte der Bearbeitung*, ed. Silke Leopold, Bärenreiter Studienbücher Musik, 2 (Kassel: Bärenreiter, 1992), 147–56.

3. See, for example, Giancarlo Chiaramello's edition of *Arie antiche: Twelve Italian Baroque Arias* for tenor and piano (Boca Raton, Fla.: Masters Music Publications, 1998), for which orchestral parts are available, and Claudio dall'Albero

and Marcello Candela, *Celebri arie antiche / Famous Ancient Airs* (Milan: Rugginenti Editore, 1998), perhaps the most scholarly of recent popular editions.

4. See Margaret Murata, "Four Airs for Orontea," *Recercare* 10 (1998): 249–62; and her "Dr Burney Bought a Music Book . . . ," *Journal of Musicology* 17 (1999): 76–111.

5. T. Ridley Prentice, *Six Cantatas by Carissimi* (London: Lamborn Cock, [1877]). An exemplar is GB-Lbl H.57. Prentice's sources for the four Italian cantatas were likely all manuscripts extant in England, since two of them are found in the Harley Collection in the British Library and two others in GB-Och MS 51. All four were reedited in Pietro Floridia, *Early Italian Songs and Airs,* vol. 1 (Boston: Oliver Ditson Co., [1923]), and one, "Filli, non t'amo più," which is known only in two English sources, is the first example of a cantata by Carissimi in Riemann's *Handbuch der Musikgeschichte,* vol. 2, pt. 2: "Das Generalbasszeitalter" (Leipzig: Breitkopf & Härtel, 1912), 69–72. Riemann cites Prentice as a source on p. 371. (The cantata is more reliably attributed to Carlo Caproli in I-Rc ms. 2480.)

6. This is especially true of L[orenzo] Pagans, ed., *Échos d'Italie,* vol. 6 (Paris: Durand, Schoenewerk et Cie., [1874]).

7. See Murata, "Four Airs." Parisotti's first two volumes were issued during an obscure period of Italian opera, between Verdi's *Aïda* and *Otello,* between Scapigliatura and musical *verismo,* when young composers were absorbing current French and German movements, especially the music of Richard Wagner. Ricordi published Puccini's first opera *Le villi* in 1885, after its premiere in Milan in 1884.

The approximate dating of Ricordi publications can now be checked against the publisher's registration numbers given in Bianca Maria Antolini, ed., *Dizionario degli editori musicali italiani, 1750–1930* (Turin: Edizioni ETS, 2000), s.v. "Ricordi" (hereafter abbreviated *DdEMI*). The preface to Parisotti's first volume is dated November 1885; its registration number is 50251 (early 1886). Its contents were also issued in separate fascicles, numbered 51924 to 51953—that is, in 1887, most likely in the latter part of the year.

8. Alessandro Parisotti, *Arie antiche,* vol. 1 (Milan: G. Ricordi, [1886]). Among his printed sources were Carl Banck, *Arien und Gesänge älterer Tonmeister* (Leipzig: F. Kistner, n.d.), which he acknowledges; François-Auguste Gevaert, *Les Gloires d'Italie,* 2 vols. (Paris: Heugel, 1868); and realizations derived from, if not taken directly from, Pagans, ed., *Échos d'Italie,* the English series *Gemme d'Antichità* (London: C. Lonsdale, [ca. 1834–77?]), and *Cäcilia. Geistliche und weltliche Arien und Lieder älterer Meister für eine Singstimme mit Begleitung des Pianoforte, bearbeitet und übersetzt von Prof. A. Schimon, Ferd. Gumbert, u. Ä.* (Offenbach am Main: J. André, [1875]). Parisotti's only Italian source was Salvatore Palumbo, ed., *Sei arie inedite del cavaliere Alessandro Scarlatti* (Naples: Stab. Musicale Partenopeo, n.d.). This important print dates from between 1853 and 1856; see *DdEMI,* s.v. "Girard," 176.

Three compositions in Parisotti's first volume appear to have come from original manuscripts in the library of the Accademia di Santa Cecilia: "Deh, più a me non v'ascondete" from Giovanni Bononcini's *Eraclea* (Rome, 1692), possibly from I-Rsc G. ms. 392 (Lowell Lindgren, private communication); and two arias from Antonio Caldara's *La costanza in amore vince inganno* (Macerata, 1710): "Sebben crudele" and "Selve amiche." Parisotti's prefatory notes clearly indicate that he has seen the complete orchestral score of the latter. All the other arias come from earlier editions, with the exception of the famous "Se tu m'ami" attributed to Pergolesi, for which no musical source prior to Parisotti's edition has yet been found.

9. "Riproduco in questo volume il *fac-simile* delle pagine, da cui furono tratte tre arie della collezione e per curiosità bibliografica e perchè si vegga come mi sia servito dei temi delle diverse composizioni per isvolgere i preludi secondo lo stile dell'epoca e gli accompagnamenti. In ogni riduzione poi l'originale fu da me scrupolosamente rispettato." Preface to Alessandro Parisotti, *Arie antiche,* vol. 2 (Milan: G. Ricordi & C., [1890]), [i].

10. Alessandro Parisotti's *Piccolo album di musica antica* (Milan: G. Ricordi & C., [1892]) included two pieces published by Andrea Falconieri, and one each composed by Jacopo Peri (1610), Domenico Visconti (1616), Francesca Caccini (1618), Girolamo Frescobaldi (1630), and Barbara Strozzi (1651). Of the works for which Parisotti gave no source, "Dolce Amor, bendato dio" from *Massenzio* (1673) had been published by Charles Burney under the name of Cavalli (see Murata, "Dr Burney," 80–81), and Stradella's "Così, Amor, mi fai languir" from *La forza dell'amor paterno* (1678) had already appeared in four modern editions between 1855 and ca. 1874 (see Carolyn Gianturco and Eleanor F. McCrickard, eds., *Alessandro Stradella (1639–1682): A Thematic Catalogue of His Compositions* [Stuyvesant, N.Y.: Pendragon Press, 1991], 125–26).

11. Luigi Torchi, ed., *Eleganti canzoni ed arie italiane del secolo XVII* (Milan: G. Ricordi, n.d.), issued as separate fascicles with registration nos. 97573 through 97595. All twenty-three were also available together as no. 97596. Torchi noted that both manuscript and printed sources for the songs and arias were in the conservatory library in Bologna; he became its librarian in 1895. The later Seicento composers are Stradella, Legrenzi, Giovanni Battista Mazzaferrata, Bernardo Gaffi, and Francesco Supriani.

12. Luigi Torchi, "L'accompagnamento degl'instrumenti nei melodrammi italiani della prima metà del Seicento," *Rivista Musicale Italiana* 1 (1894): 7–38; 2 (1895): 666–71; and Torchi, "Canzoni ed arie italiane ad una voce," *Rivista Musicale Italiana* 1 (1894): 581–656. F. T. Arnold's magisterial survey of sources on thoroughbass practice did not appear until 1931.

13. *Arie antiche,* vol. 3 (Milan: G. Ricordi, n.d.). This third volume never appeared in America, and most of its pieces are less well known outside of Italy. According to *DdEMI,* 310, the Ricordi registration nos. 101918–101958 require emending to 1898 the date of 1900 traditionally given for this volume.

14. The early pieces include four by Falconieri and an anonymous work that Parisotti thought resembled Falconieri; two by Caccini; and one each by Peri, Raffaello Rontani, Claudio Monteverdi, Cavalli, Carissimi, Giovanni Battista Fasolo, and Stradella.

15. "Molti anni sono corsi dalla pubblicazione del primo e in questo periodo la musica da camera italiana ha taciuto ancora." *Arie antiche,* vol. 3 [1898], v. This introduction no longer appears in the Ricordi reprint.

16. Maffeo Zanon, *Venti arie (1 voce in chiave di Sol) tratte dai drami [sic] musicali di Francesco Cavalli (Pier Francesco Caletti Bruni, 1599–1676) raccolte su manoscritti dell'epoca e trascritte con accompagnamento di pianoforte da Maffeo Zanon* (Leipzig: C. Schmidl & Co., [1908]), 1, from the preface dated Venice, 27 July 1908. Ricordi had taken over Schmidl in 1901, when both opened branches in Leipzig; see *DdEMI,* 323. The series "Tesori musicali d'Italia," in which Zanon's

volume appeared included Ottorino Respighi's orchestration of Monteverdi's "Lamento d'Arianna."

17. "Text-centricity" is one aspect of the modern early-music movement in Richard Taruskin's characterization, along with "impersonality" and avoidance of the "profound or the sublime." See Richard Taruskin, *Text and Act: Essays on Music and Performance* (New York: Oxford University Press, 1995), 167.

18. Maffeo Zanon, *Raccolta di 24 arie di vari autori del secolo XVII, scelte ed armonizzate* (Milan: G. Ricordi & Co., 1914). He laments the lack of attention to the Contarini sources, heretofore edited only by Hugo Goldschmidt and by Alessandro Parisotti in "a few brief excerpts" ("qualche piccolo brano"). The Stradella excerpts are identified and their sources given in Gianturco and McCrickard, *Alessandro Stradella*, 325. Zanon's earliest excerpt is from Cesti's *Tito*. Goldschmidt's *Studien zur Geschichte der italienischen Oper im 17. Jahrhundert* (Leipzig: Breitkopf & Härtel, 1901; reprint, Hildesheim: G. Olms, 1967) gives no realizations of the continuo lines.

19. Parisotti's version is based on its apparently first modern appearance in the 1868 anthology of *Les Gloires d'Italie* by Gevaert, who once had been director of the Paris Opéra (see n. 8 above).

20. The English title is *Gems of Old Italy: Six Ariettes, Four Duets and One Trio of the XVI, XVII and XVIII centuries. Edited and provided with pianoforte accompaniment by Vittorio Ricci* (Milan: G. Ricordi & Co., n.d.). The Ricordi registration no. is 113053, by which it can be dated to the end of 1909 or in 1910; see *DdEMI*, 310. This clarifies my own citation in Murata, "Four Airs," 260 n. 26.

21. Ricci describes some of the same features that made early music attractive after the 1960s to soloists and small ensembles that specialized in performing both early and contemporary music.

22. "Col presentare al pubblico questa piccola Raccolta di Canzoni Italiane del XVI, XVII e principio del XVIII secolo, credo di far cosa grata non solo a coloro che serbano un culto speciale per il passato; ma a quelli ancora che, mentre subiscono tutto il fascino che emana dalle complesse e sfolgoranti bellezze della musica moderna, amano rinfrescarsi ogni tanto nell'onda purissima di una melodia liberamente sgorgata, quando l'arte era fatta di grazia ingenua, di festività e di sentimento sincero. Tali qualità intrinseche, comuni del resto a tutti gli artisti primitivi, si rispecchiano infatti luminosamente in queste pagine; dove amaramente piange col Bottegari il dolore della separazione, o rassegnata sospira la musa amorosa del Gagliano, e flebile si lamenta quella del Vitali e del Marcello, o spensierato ride l'amore del Rontani, o, non si sa bene se sul serio o per celia, ma certo con una grazia civettuola ed una tal punta d'ironia, protesta quello di Barbara Strozzi e dello Steffani." Ricci, "Osservazioni preliminari"/"Introductory Remarks," *Antiche gemme*, [i].

23. "È di non poco interesse . . . di osservare come questi sentimenti sieno espressi . . . specialmente nelle canzoni più antiche, ancora con una varietà tale di accenti, di ritmi e di armonie, con un fraseggiare così libero (direi quasi melopeico) sempre strettamente legato alla parola e una forma così indipendente, da mostrare fino all'evidenza il danno prodotto dalla successiva costante adozione del periodo chiuso e dall'uso quasi esclusivo di quel limitato giro armonico, che costrinsero, atrofizzarono, immiserirono la musica italiana in tempi posteriori." Ibid.

24. From the preface to the American edition of *Anthology of Italian Song of the*

Seventeenth and Eighteenth Centuries, selected and edited with biographical no-
tices by Alessandro Parisotti, 2 vols. (New York: G. Schirmer, 1894), 1:iii.
    25. See n. 17 above.
    26. Hugo Riemann, *Kantaten-Frühling (1633–1682),* 2 vols. (Leipzig: C. F. W.
Siegel's Musikalienhandlung, [1912?]), pub. nos. 15512–15513. The compositions
are by Bendetto Ferrari, Francesco Manelli, Francesco Cavalli, Maurizio Cazzati,
Luigi Rossi, Giacomo Carissimi, Marc'Antonio Cesti (i.e., Pietro Cesti), Alessandro
Stradella, and G. B. Bassani.
    A rare work with recitative had been published earlier in Torchi's *Eleganti canzoni,*
an "Aria in istile recitativo (1660)" by Giovanni Francesco Tenaglia that begins
"Non è mai senza duol chi vive amante." Torchi gives Tenaglia "the honor of having given a strong impulse toward the cantata from monody" ("l'onore di aver dato
un forte impulso alla monodia della *Cantata*") and adds, "His style is admirable for
its forcefulness and the élan of its dramatic *pathos*" ("Il suo stile è ammirevole per
la forza e lo slancio del *pathos* drammatico"). The work also has, however, two
prominent passages *in aria,* an opening in "compound duple" time that returns at
the end, after two lines in triple time.
    27. "Der folgende Versuch einer mehr kontrapunktischen Ausführung des
Continuo, zugleich mit Herausstellung der sich hinter dem C verbergenden effektiven
Taktverhältnisse, bedarf nach unsern bisherigen Erörterungen wohl keiner weitern
Rechtfertigung." Hugo Riemann, *Handbuch der Musikgeschichte,* 2 vols. (Leipzig:
Breitkopf & Härtel, 1904–22), II/2:200. Vol. II/2 appeared in 1912; its 2d ed. in
1922, edited by Alfred Einstein. Riemann, *Handbuch,* II, ¶79 (both eds.), 199, 200:
"We have also no reason to assume that songs like these would have been accompa-
nied only by block chords, under a ban against all contrapuntal fashioning. . . . The
idea that this song would have been thought to be accompanied only with meager
chords is to be firmly rejected" ("Wir haben auch keinerlei Grund anzunehmen,
dass dergleichen Gesänge unter Verzicht auf alle kontrapunktische Gestaltung des
Akkompagnements nur mit Akkordschlägen begleitet worden wären. . . . Der
Gedanke, dass dieser Gesang nur mit mageren Akkordanschlägen begleitet gedacht
wäre, ist entschieden abzuweisen"). The setting of Orfeo's solo is on pp. 200–203;
Riemann's general discussion of continuo practice is in ¶75, 72–85.
    28. Henry Edward Krehbiel, ed., *Aus dem goldenen Zeitalter des Bel Canto.
Eine Auswahl von 26 Gesängen des XVII. und XVIII. Jahrhunderts aus
Manuskripten und frühen Drucken zugesammengestellt,* 2 vols. (Mainz: B. Schott's
Söhne; New York: G. Schirmer, 1910), 104. All of the piano accompaniments are
by Max Spicker, who arranged and edited many vocal anthologies for Schirmer.
    29. See the examples from Marco da Gagliano (pp. 221–23), Benedetto Ferrari
(pp. 226–29), and "Alessandro Stradella" (pp. 400–402) (see n. 30).
    30. Riemann edited "Già nell'Indo emisfero" in its entirety in the *Kantaten-
Frühling,* where it has a much more elaborate piano part than even the version in
the *Handbuch.* The attribution to Stradella in D-Dlb Mus. 1/I/2 was considered
"unreliable" by Owen Jander, in the *Wellesley Edition Cantata Index Series,* fascicle 4b (Wellesley, Mass.: Wellesley College, 1969), no. B 249; it was retained as a
doubtful work in Gianturco and McCrickard, *Alessandro Stradella,* 255. Jander
lists a concordance in GB-Lbl Add. ms. 14207 (dated 1737), where it is attributed
to "Giovanni veneziano."
    31. See the list in the volume compiled by Hugo Socnik for Riemann's sixtieth

birthday, *Riemann-Festschrift. Gesammelte Studien* (Leipzig: M. Hesse, 1909; reprint, Tutzing: Verlag Hans Schneider, 1965), xxxvi-xl. Among Riemann's editions were the Two- and Three-Part Inventions, the Well-Tempered Clavier, keyboard concertos, and the Art of Fugue by J. S. Bach; *Altmeister des Klavierspiels* (with seventy pieces); numerous keyboard pieces by Rameau; and volumes of lieder by Franz Schubert, Robert Schumann, Carl Maria von Weber, and others.

32. Lawrence Kramer, "The Lied as Cultural Practice," in his *Classical Music and Postmodern Knowledge* (Berkeley: University of California Press, 1995), 148.

33. Riemann, *Handbuch,* 2d ed., ¶89: "The Passing of Musical Hegemony to Germany: 'Into the hands of a Master always comes forth something bequeathed by his model'" ("Der Übergang der musikalischen Hegemonie auf Deutschland: 'Unter den Händen eines Meisters kommt dabei allemal etwas heraus, was das Vorbild hinter sich lässt'" [492]). "What Spitta still primarily called 'expressive declamation' is quite certainly not, however, something that descended from the monody of the Florentines, but rather something that was already characteristic of the era of imitative vocal music, something that indeed expresses one's innermost being" ("Das, was Spitta in erster Linie noch nennt, die ausdrucksvolle Deklamation, ist aber eben nicht etwas der Monodie der Florentiner Entstammtes, sondern das, was auch schon der Periode des durchimitierenden Vokalstils eigentümlich ist, ja deren innerstes Wesen ausmacht" [494]).

34. "Vor allem ist doch nicht zu vergessen, daß in den Opern und den Kantaten der kunstvoll begleitete Liedsatz viel weiter zurück (bis in die letzten Dezennien des 17. Jahrhunderts) auch mit charakteristischen tonmalerischen Tendenzen entwickelt worden ist. An dem Apparat, mit welchem Schubert arbeitet, ist eigentlich nichts neu." Riemann, *Handbuch,* II/3 (1922), ¶106, 210–11. He had drawn the parallel a few pages earlier: "The true art song of the seventeenth century turned out to be the aria of opera and cantata. . . . The many collections of opera arias . . . that have survived prove that tuneful operatic songs were also treasured off the stage and that along with contemporary chamber cantatas and chamber duets, they quite certainly represent the art song of the era" ("Das eigentliche Kunstlied des 17. Jahrhunderts ist eben die Arie in Oper und Kantate geworden. . . . Die vielen erhaltenen meist handschriftlichen Sammlungen von Opernarien überwiegend italienischener aber französicher, deutschen u. englischer beweisen aber, dass man auch ausserhalb der Bühne die liedartigen Operngesänge wohl zu schätzen wusste, und dass eben sie und die mit ihnen parallel gehenden Kammerkantaten und Kammerduette das Kunstlied dieser Zeit repräsentieren" [207]). Kramer discusses the valences of solo song and its "imaginary voice" in terms of its means of "constructing subjectivities"; see Kramer, "The Lied as Cultural Practice," 145–48.

35. "Ich hoffe, daß es mir gelungen ist, durch die mitgeteilten Proben der Liedkunst des 17. Jahrhunderts (besonders durch die vollständig ausgearbeiteten in der Sammlung *Kantaten-Frühling*) zu erweisen, daß auch sie nach Überwindung der schlimmsten Hemmnisse ästhetischer Theorien gelegentlich diesen Weg zur freien Nachschöpfung des Gedichtes gefunden hat; scheuet man nicht davor zurück, dem nur durch den Bass skizzierten Akkompagnement unter den Händen der gründlich im Kontrapunkt geschulten Meister eine bedeutsam ergänzende Rolle zuzuweisen—wozu die Berechtigung oder vielmehr die Verpflichtung außer Zweifel steht—, so wird man nicht umhin können, die nahe Verwandtschaft von Stücken wie Dom

Paolos 'Fra duri scogli' (vor 1400), Benedetto Ferraris 'Premio il giogo delle Alpi' (1637) und etwa Schuberts 'Wanderer' zu erkennen." Ibid.

36. Floridia, *Early Italian Songs,* 2 vols.

37. For utopian and heterotopian conditions with respect to European aesthetics, see Gianni Vattimo's extended essay *La società trasparente* (n.p.: Garzanti Editore, 1989).

38. See Taruskin, *Text and Act,* 167: "A closer look will reveal the ironic links binding at least the first two [text-centeredness and impersonality] with the romantic enthronement of the autocratic and infallible composer-creator, divorced from real-time music making."

39. Peter Walls, "Performing Corelli's Violin Sonatas, Op. 5," *Early Music* 24 (1996): 133–42; quotation from 136–37. The CD of the first six sonatas in opus 5, with (besides Christensen) Chiara Bianchini, violin, Luciano Contini, archlute, and Käthy Gohl, cello, is Harmonia Mundi France HMA 1951307 [1989].

40. Modern performers have also been reading historical instruction manuals and treatises. An evaluation of their use vis-à-vis the changes in performing early music is beyond the scope of this essay.

41. Daniel Leech-Wilkinson, "Early Music—Observations and Predictions," *Early Music* 25 (1997): 564.

42. Kivy, *Authenticities,* 261, and Lydia Goehr, *The Imaginary Museum of Musical Works: An Essay in the Philosophy of Music* (Oxford: Clarendon Press, 1992), cited by Kivy on 262.

43. Michael Chanan, *Musica Practica: The Social Practice of Western Music from Gregorian Chant to Postmodernism* (London: Verso, 1994), 72.

44. *Arie amorose,* LP disk Philips 9500 557 [1978]; Dame Janet Baker accompanied by the Academy of St. Martin-in-the-Fields.

45. Mary Sue Hyatt, ed., *Italian Songs and Arias of the Eighteenth Century, for voice and string quartet (or string orchestra),* 4 sets (Boca Raton, Fla.: Masters Music Publications, 1993).

46. Kramer, "The Lied as Cultural Pratice," 145.

16

Material Culture and Postmodern Positivism: Rethinking the "Popular" in Late-Nineteenth-Century French Music

Jann Pasler

Recently we have come to think of the proliferation of "pop music" and its implications as products of the twentieth century. But a preoccupation with "popular" culture also drove much of the musical world of late-nineteenth-century Paris. This period saw the rise of music hall entertainment and big exotic spectacles as well as more intimate café-concerts and cabaret. The former dazzled audiences with their endless variety; the latter offered simpler escapism and sometimes social critique. In part to combat their influence, those committed to serious art music—composers and performers, publishers and concert-organizers, private patrons as well as State officials—were driven by the desire to reach large audiences. They wished to popularize music that would elevate public taste. This meant finding a balance between pleasing listeners by catering to what they liked—thereby seeing their numbers grow—and educating them while shaping their taste.

This story about the popularization of art music has many surprises. These come to light only in rethinking our assumptions and scholarly methodologies. First, we know that people at the time looked to opera and opera singers to confer distinction on their consumption in part because of opera's traditional association with elites. Workers rarely had the chance to see an opera staged, even if the government periodically attempted to provide cheap seats. Contrary to what this may imply, not only did the lower classes have access to art music, including operatic music (albeit in transcriptions), they also participated in the supply as well as the demand. Moreover, performing and listening to this music provided new opportunities for self-expression and self-development in addition to the possibility of imitating the upper classes. Elites were not alone, therefore, in determining the evolution of musical tastes.

Second, as we shall see, boundaries were fluid in this musical world, throwing into question our concepts of not only center and periphery, but also the serious and the popular. Musicians and repertory migrated from venue to venue. For example, concerts at the Bon Marché department store often presented performers and music from the Opéra. And instead of taking years, their organizers chose some excerpts only months after their Opéra premieres, other works even before these premieres. Such practices force us to reconsider "trickle-down" theories about cultural hegemony.[1] A close look at concert life of the time also reveals how heterogeneous musical experiences often were. At the Bon Marché, as well as in prestigious private salons, audiences could hear humorous monologues and comic scenes by star cabaret performers interspersed with the art music. Moreover, the heterogeneity of Bon Marché concerts extended to a public that included employees as well as potential customers. These juxtapositions of musicians, repertory, and publics suggest that, despite what some elites may have preferred, in some contexts music helped mediate class and cultural differences.

Third, the struggle over what would become "popular" in France after 1871 did not concern principally the emergence of a canon of Western musical classics as we conceive of it today. Rather, it supported and perhaps even fueled a renaissance in French contemporary music. The example of France is important. It forces us to reexamine our presumption that dead composers dominated concert life in the late nineteenth century and that music's domestication necessarily implied learning the German canon. French audiences of all types were strikingly tolerant of the unfamiliar, even drawn to it, and this included new music. Moreover, many composers, including the most illustrious, were committed to helping amateurs perform and understand their music.

Such conclusions come from studying a wider array of primary sources than those related to scores, composers' manuscripts, letters, and first editions. Of course, critical reviews and other print journalism of the time are a good place to start. Lesser-known sources, however, can also be immensely helpful, even those usually dismissed as of transient value. This essay seeks to expand our notion of archival research by suggesting how useful popular music magazines, sheet music reproduced in newspapers, military band transcriptions, and especially concert programs can be in investigating the growing taste for art music in the French populace.

To understand concert life in Paris—the best evidence of what was popular—it is also important not to focus exclusively on elite cultural organizations, as many scholars have done in studying cities. Of course, the two Opéras and the Société des Concerts (the professional orchestra of the Conservatory) maintained a certain prestige in the social status of their publics and the quality of their performances. The government expected as much in return for generous subsidies. But when other institutions, such as the Concerts Colonne, were praised as equally good, competition some-times forced the former into following rather than leading, especially when it came to presenting new French compositions. In the 1890s, when elite institutions were museums more than trend-setters, even concerts at the zoo performed more music by living composers than did the Conservatory. Concerts in a wide range of venues—from public spaces like the zoo and city gardens, to private ones such as department stores and salons—tell us much about what became "popular." Investigating the network of rela-tionships connecting them, as I shall do through *Samson et Dalila,* sheds important light on the process of popularization at the time.[2]

Definitions of the Popular

What gave rise to a pronounced interest in the popular in late-nineteenth-century Paris and what attracted large, diverse audiences to music? To an-swer these questions, we must understand that the *populaire* was neither a single nor a reified concept. When it came to music, there were three cat-egorical definitions. The first comes from the Latin *populus,* the inhabit-ants of a State as distinct from its rulers.[3] *Populaire* was sometimes associ-ated with large numbers of people. In music this was significant for, with the population of Paris rising fifty percent between 1860 and 1896, audi-ences for music were bound to grow. Generally speaking then, *populaire* could mean having broad appeal, something that could be understood or at least appreciated by many people, or else representing, being associated with, or standing as an emblem for many people.

The genre *chanson populaire* (indigenous folk song) points to the inherent complexity of this concept. Throughout Europe in the late nineteenth cen-tury, musicians and scholars combed the countryside seeking to find and write down such music. Many associated it with what was meaningful and authen-tic in culture, what persevered beyond politics, not as during the French Revo-lution when popular songs often concerned social critique or resistance. Be-ginning in the 1880s, French Republicans advocated teaching *chansons populaires* in the primary schools as a way to inculcate a shared sense of identity. Because children in the various provinces spoke different languages and had somewhat different cultures, *chansons populaires* could serve as a common language, especially to the extent that they were transcribed into French. That people of different social and political orientations used this genre at the end of the century to argue for mutually contradictory social goals—including as a way to insist on differences in regional identity—suggests that intense controversy surrounded this meaning of the word and that "the people" could be used to refer to various interests.

For most Republicans, *populaire* referred to a utopian sense of the lower classes developed during the Revolution. In their attempts to address the enormous divisions and inequalities within the nation, it came to imply a kind of righteousness associated with the lower classes and a debt which elites owed to them because of having a special place in God's eyes (according to Catholic tradition) or having been victimized, exploited, or alienated (according to Socialist tradition).[4] *Populaire* also referred to the need in a democracy to assimilate these classes through education in order to produce informed citizens who would support the political order. In the nineteenth century then, *populaire* could mean not so much what was produced by the lower classes, as what was given to them for their consumption to bring their ideals into conformity with those of their leaders. Education of the lower classes thus was a crucial element of the *populaire*. The historian Jules Michelet saw politics and education as synonymous: to make a democracy was to educate its people, and that education should last a lifetime. Educating social sentiments, in particular, would allow identification with the general interest of the country. This meant domesticating passions and elevating desires.[5]

This "top-down" aspect of the *populaire* was especially important when it came to music. Many believed in the ancient Greek practice of education through music. This art was thought to be the "direct translation of moral feelings," capable of teaching feelings as well as of "softening one's manners, raising man to the level of his intelligence . . . [and] making him understand the precious resources that nature has given him." Participation in choral singing was believed to help people "control their passions themselves" while serving as a "respite from their problems, a relaxation from their work, and a remedy to all their suffering." Municipal music societies, made up of workers, were called "conservatories of the people" because they not only taught singing "within the limits of their hearts and purses," but also "habituated them to loving, or at least respecting, social institutions." In this context, music was considered the "most human, the most social" art because it often needs groups and depends on collaboration.[6] By 1876, François-Auguste Gevaert claimed that "no art plays a more important role in modern life, none fascinates [*passionne*] the public and the masses more than music, this art which is democratic by its very nature." He believed music would help lead to the "moral and ideal perfection of humanity."[7]

Still, the popular did not always refer just to workers or peasants, even if it was rural culture that maintained the tradition of the *chansons populaires*. In his influential text, *Le peuple* (1846; 1866), Michelet described suffering in all classes of society: peasants, machine workers, manufacturers, bureaucrats, and even the rich. *Populaire* sometimes referred to all classes, or their coexistence, though this usually meant a conscious attempt to include the lower ranks. Those in government trying to make a democratic society out of disenchanted monarchists, religious conservatives, provincial traditionalists, and hopeful socialists valued music for its capacity to cross class lines and bridge political differences, even within the various classes, e.g., the elites who attended the Opéra or the Société des Concerts. Republican politicians supported music generously for this reason, linking their subsidies to the requirement that certain concerts and low cost tickets be made available to those could not otherwise attend. As might be expected, "the people" who actually benefited were less often the urban poor than the bourgeois middle class.

The second category of the *populaire* extends this notion of something shared to a public. Building a public meant turning the contagious emotions of a crowd into a sense of solidarity through shared experiences. This implied getting people to develop tastes, have opinions, and participate as the early Revolutionaries dreamed they might—a collective body acting in the interests of the whole. This definition points to the culture of sociability at the heart of the *populaire* in France. It suggests that people in groups affect one another reciprocally. The late-nineteenth-century sociologist Gabriel Tarde considered the public the social group of the future and defined it not by the people or classes that made it up, but rather as "a purely spiritual collectivity, of which the cohesion is entirely mental." He felt that "social evolution begins and ends in games and *fêtes*" and that "the communion of ideas" shared by a public would form "the basis for a new social morality," similar to what Durkheim called "conscience collective." Tarde explained the process of becoming a public, of forming opinions, as "assimilation by collective contagion." For him, the purpose of public opinion is "to turn the reason of today into the tradition of tomorrow."[8]

The composer Louis Bourgault-Ducoudray alluded to this function in his first lecture as historian at the Conservatory. After preaching how instruction turns people into "real men" by "rendering their judgement free," he concluded:

> The public is the majority, and the majority rules. If public taste is raised, if it has noble aspirations, art rises. If public taste is lowered, the level of art goes down. It can be said that public taste is a touchstone that makes it possible to assess the value and strength of production of an age.
>
> The public makes art and the artists what they are.
>
> Therefore, nothing is more useful in the interest of art than for public taste to rise and its aspirations to grow.[9]

To the extent that this public embraced, appreciated, and came to respect French music, they attached prestige to it. This prestige—an important element of the *populaire*—carried its own self-generating authority, the first stage of becoming a tradition. A tradition represents the transformation of public opinion into belief, or what Michelet called faith. These beliefs, once formed, determine the trend of ideas. As such, Gustave Le Bon considered them "the indispensable pillars of civilizations"; they determine the trend of ideas.[10] When French music became increasingly *populaire*, it had the capacity to become a tradition, not only to represent the nation but also to influence the future by feeding nationalist pride.

The third definition of the *populaire*, associated with the growing commodification of music as a consumer product, refers to both generating and responding to a demand. Composers and music publishers popularized a work by making it as accessible as possible, that is, by producing transcriptions of it for diverse instrumental combinations and getting it reproduced in multiple print sources. Conductors and performers popularized music by repeating it immediately as a *bis,* at the end of a concert, or on later concerts. Any *première audition* that audiences liked might reappear as a *deuxième audition,* noted on the subsequent program. To hear a work performed twice not only signaled some success for a composer, it informed listeners of others' approval or at least desire to hear it again, indicated also by the expression *redemandé.* To give a *troisième audition* carried the hope of general acceptance. Colonne's orchestra made Berlioz's *La damnation de Faust* popular by performing it on successive Sundays, threatening that each would be the last, until they no longer had a sold-out hall. In the late 1870s, this meant seven or eight times in a row. By the late 1890s, they had done it one hundred times. This tactic allowed the orchestra to stay solvent while assuming the financial risk of performing new works. It also helped Colonne build a loyal following and encourage a taste for Berlioz.

The power of repetition was well recognized. As Le Bon pointed out, "The thing affirmed comes by repetition to fix itself in the mind in such a way that it is accepted in the end as a demonstrated truth."[11] Extensive repetition plants the work in the unconscious, making possible subsequent reflection. Multiple performances of works such as *La damnation de Faust,* especially in the context of competition with other orchestras doing the same work sometimes the same day, pushed musicians to play it better, both technically and musically. The saturation of repeated performances allowed assimilation into the general music culture where a work could become "popular" in the American sense.

Rethinking Leisure

New attitudes toward leisure contributed significantly to music's appeal. The pressures and pace of life under industrialization brought a need for the renewal and recreation associated with leisure activities. According to the urban historian Peter Bailey, some Victorians thought that "men were encouraged to seek recreations that provided the greatest contrast to their normal occupation." As he pointed out, however, work and play in this period were "antithetical in form only. . . . Play was change *of* work, as much as change *from* work."[12] This attitude had several implications.

First, and crucial when it came to the marketing of music, was the association of "amusement" with "instruction," as if they should go hand in hand. "To amuse, to interest, and to instruct" was the emblem of not only numerous family magazines of the 1880s and 1890s, but also Colonne's orchestral concerts when *La vie de famille* was publishing his programs. To say that a leisure activity could address these simultaneously was the ultimate draw for consumers.

The development of program notes during this period reflects this increasing preoccupation. Programs of Emile Pasdeloup's orchestral Concerts Populaires in the 1860s—famed for successfully attracting "all classes" of society—usually consisted of a single page. Beyond giving the list of works, composers, and performers, they tended to include more information only for titles of multi-movement works or programs for dramatic works (e.g., overtures drawn from those by Wagner, Schumann, Beethoven). In the 1870s, with the increased prevalence of French music on concert programs, these often increased to two pages to reproduce the long descriptive programs of Saint-Saëns's symphonic poems or the extended texts of Berlioz's dramatic symphonies as well as *drames lyriques* by various French contemporaries. Program notes presenting historical details about composers and short analyses of their works did not appear until the 1880s. At the Concerts Colonne, these increased to twelve pages in the late 1890s, as education became an explicit reason to attend concerts and orchestral concerts took to presenting chronological successions of works as a "history of music."[13] Programs provide a fascinating record of not only what audiences heard, but also what they were supposed to listen for, especially when notes evolved over time or differed from venue to venue. They also give remarkable and, for the most part, accurate performance and reception histories of the works, presented in part to offer audiences a basis of comparison.

In general, there is little evidence that non-orchestral music societies provided such notes, although both amateurs and professionals distributed free programs listing works and performers. One exception is significant: *Le petit poucet,* a pocket-sized military-music magazine (see figure 16.1). Its purpose was to announce the programs for the military-band concerts in Paris. After its first season in 1895, it too entered the business of education. Each issue thereafter began with a three-page biographical essay about a French musician. Composers varied in age, professional stature, occupation, and gender, ranging from Thomas, Bizet, and Charpentier to Charles Bordes, Cécile Chaminade, and Augusta Holmès. Conductors included Lamoureux, Gabriel Marie, and those leading the major military bands. Biographies of lesser-known musicians often provide information that would be difficult to learn elsewhere. To accompany one military-band concert each week, the magazine added analytical program notes specially written for them. Typically three to four pages in length, these are every bit as

3ᵉ Année   Dimanche 13 Juin 1897   Numéro 11

Le Petit Poucet

JOURNAL DES CONCERTS MILITAIRES

ADMINISTRATION — 63, Avenue du Roule, 63 — NEUILLY-s/-SEINE

Augusta HOLMÈS

Augusta - Mary - Anne Holmès est née à Paris de parents irlandais résidant en France. Elle fut élevée à Versailles dans un milieu artistique : son père, après avoir été un brillant officier, était devenu un savant distingué, et sa mère cultivait avec passion la peinture et la littérature.

Dès l'enfance, ses dispositions musi-

LE PORTRAIT DE LA SEMAINE

cales s'éveillèrent, et, à l'âge où les fillettes ne songent qu'à la poupée, elle se serait adonnée au piano si on lui en avait laissé la liberté.

Mais sa mère, qui détestait la musique et déplorait que sa fille consacrât à cet art une ardeur qu'elle eût souhaité voir s'appliquer à la peinture, l'arrachait à son instrument et l'installait devant un chevalet. Poussée par la force

---

13 Juin 1897   ## Place de la Nation   De 4 à 5 h.

89ᵉ D'INFANTERIE — Chef : M. SUZANNE

1. **Isabelle-Marsch** (pas redoublé)................ ....   Pétrowski

2. **Les Noces de Figaro** (ouverture ....   Mozart

3. **Coppélia** (valse lente)................... ......   L. Delibes

4. **Lakmé** (fantaisie).. ... .   L. Delibes

Basse, M. July ; bugle, M. Depardav ; cornet, M. Blanchetière.

5. **Polka du Cheval** ... .   Lecocq

Figure 16.1. A example of *Le petit poucet*, a journal of military music featuring biographies of musicians, concert programs for performances in Parisian gardens, and extensive program notes. Used by permission of the Bibliothèque Nationale.

informative as those for the Concerts Colonne. They discuss previous performances and reception, often citing what the composer or major critics have written. They also explain the original source of any excerpts as well as the dramatic context or texts underlying the music. When a cover was added in 1899, *Le petit poucet* became a veritable music journal, with the occasional concert review by major critics, such as Alfred Bruneau on Charpentier's *Louise* and Paul Dukas on Richard Strauss. These suggest that by 1900 popular audiences were keen to follow the latest developments in avant-garde art music.

After 1870 and the frivolous abuses of the Second Empire, those espousing Republican ideals also wished to redefine the function of leisure, conceiving it as a fundamental component of the "good life" for all classes. Even aristocrats such as Georges d'Avenel endorsed the idea of "equalizing enjoyments, rather than money," thereby "approving a vast delusion whereby human inequalities are masked by material appearances."[14] The unprecedented abundance of leisure activities expanded free will among the lower and middle classes, giving them a "mobility and anonymity that removed them from supervision by their fellows."[15] However, this abundance also raised new issues: How to educate people's desire? How to seduce them away from the dangerous frontier zones of certain kinds of entertainment and provide them with "healthy" alternatives? As Bailey put it, "leisure constituted a threat to the discipline and cohesion of the bourgeois world," even as it "tested the elasticity of class mores."[16]

Many looked to music for help in negotiating these challenges. Like other consumer goods, music helped people "contemplate the possession of an emotional condition, a social circumstance, even an entire style of life."[17] To the extent that all classes developed similar tastes, as Tarde put it, ideally they would come to resemble one another internally, for tastes express one's inner desires. In his analysis of the fashion world, George Simmel saw this process as unidirectional, with "subordinate social groups" seeking new status claims by imitating the tastes of "superordinate groups." He called this "trickle-down."[18] From this perspective, the dominant classes could use the dissemination of taste (and moral values) through art music to expand their influence over the lower classes. To the extent that the appropriation of certain musical practices and tastes resulted from envy, however, this imitation by the lower classes could involve a kind of interaction with their social superiors rather than passive receptivity. For Tarde, this was the symptom of a "socal transformation." If he was right in believing that "unseen and mental imitation lessens the psychological distance between superior and inferior," then shared musical experiences could, ideally, constitute "a form of democratization."[19] Exploring the meaning of shared musical experiences in more recent years, Christopher Small also makes the analogy to play as a model for social transformation.[20]

Workers' musical societies, of which there were hundreds, illustrate well the domestication and democratization of art music in Paris at the time. Learning to sing or to play an instrument demonstrated to the world liberation from the assumptions one might make about workers. The acquisition of musical skills suggested certain virtues—evidence of devotion, study, self-discipline, and interest in "the finer things in life," including charm and grace. Knowledge of art music also allowed for performance of another kind of social identity, something workers could use to trade up socially, possibly to marry better, or at the least to command respect from superiors and co-workers. The allure of respectability, considered by many "a principal prerequisite for true citizenship," was central to the appeal of performing art music.[21] It not only encouraged some among the lower classes to feel part of bourgeois society, it also provided for differentiation, or distinction, within these classes.

Membership in these societies served other, more tangible functions as well. Not just a medium for social imitation, they also constituted a form of fraternity. Although some societies bemoaned frequent turnover in their membership, those who stayed were known for their *esprit de corps*. (This may have contributed to the emerging class consciousness underlying the rise of trade-unionism.) Workers joined for other reasons too. Besides serving as outlets for their creativity, participation in these societies held the promise of release from the grind of daily life. All organizations held annual banquets and offered the possibility of travel to the provinces. Moreover, performing as a soloist, with one's name in concert programs, or winning prizes in city or national competitions brought public recognition, something otherwise utterly lacking in workers' lives. Competitions also brought workers into contact with a wide range of their peers across the country. And because the competitions often involved commissions from contemporary composers, they insured that workers learned to perform new music and had opportunities to compare their performances with those of others. Such personal, social, and musical benefits were undoubtedly unobtainable outside such contexts.

The Usefulness of Transcriptions

Except for those who could afford a subscription at the Opéra or Opéra-Comique or who produced operas in their own homes—the musical manifestation of luxury for its producers and consumers—most people got to know art music through some virtual representative, whether an excerpt or, more often, a transcription. Transcriptions, in particular, blurred the boundaries between classes, as did consumer goods at department stores, which likewise helped domesticate luxury products and encourage desire for them. Most Parisians could afford to purchase only cheap imitations of the real thing, be it furs, jewelry, or music. Transcriptions allowed for performances by and for people from a wide range of classes and orientations and in a diversity of venues.[22]

Two forms of transcription dominated in the late nineteenth century—piano and wind-band. Since increasing numbers of people had pianos in

their homes—rentals were only ten francs per month—piano transcriptions were by far the most numerous. Whether for piano solo, piano four
hands, two pianos four hands, two pianos eight hands, or piano and voice
scores, they ranged in difficulty from those for "easy piano" to those requiring pianistic virtuosity. Such scores could be purchased directly from
the publisher or acquired through music magazines for sale at newspaper
kiosks, train stations, and bookstores.[23] They also could be borrowed from
one of the many municipal lending libraries, located in both wealthy and
poor neighborhoods.

Professionally oriented journals, produced by music publishers, regularly included a piano or piano-vocal score with each bimonthly issue. These
reflect what publishers wished to promote. To coincide with important
premieres of works they published, their magazines often reproduced several excerpts. For example, in 1882 *Le ménestrel,* published by Heugel,
printed nine transcriptions from Ambroise Thomas's *Françoise da Rimini*
and in 1883 six from Leo Delibes's *Lakmé.* That Massenet's music appeared disproportionately—in ten out of twenty-four issues in 1892, 1894,
and 1899—suggests his popularity with the public as well as his status
with the publisher.

Despite the relatively high level of its reporting and the musical training
expected of its readers, *Le ménestrel* also published light works. These included polkas by Philippe Fahrbach and Joseph Gung'l, *quadrilles* and cornet solos by Jean-Baptiste Arban, waltzes by Johann Strauss, and sentimental religious works by the composer / Opéra singer Jean-Baptiste Faure.
This suggests that at least some of *Le ménestrel*'s readers had enough interest in this repertory to want to perform it themselves. Some of these composers and works also turned up on concerts in popular venues. Heinrich
Strobl's polka, "La machine à coudre" (The Sewing Machine), appeared in
Le ménestrel (17 December 1876) and was performed at the Bon Marché
department store (7 July 1877). Such juxtapositions defy any strict separation between the serious and the popular, even in one of the period's most
prestigious publications.

Other music magazines (less cited by scholars) tell us more about the
emerging taste for art music.[24] The weekly *Le journal de musique* (1876–
1882) was one of the most sophisticated and varied in terms of its repertory. Each issue featured three to five works for piano or piano and voice.
As in *Le ménestrel,* the scores signaled the latest developments in concert
life. In addition to including not only music from opera premieres, but also
"fragments of almost all lyric works, whether important or light, that had
success on Parisian stages," they consciously varied "genres" and "degrees
of force" [i.e., difficulty?] to satisfy "all whims, all levels of knowledge . . .
all ages and all tastes."[25] In 1877–1878, this meant transcriptions of orchestral music at the Concerts Populaires, an oratorio at the Société des
Concerts, military marches of the Garde Républicaine, a chorus written for

an Orphéon competition, polkas in the ball repertory, *chansons populaires* from other countries, and exotic music at the 1878 Exposition. Besides giving access to a full range of what Parisians might be hearing, these transcriptions provided a broader context for understanding works gaining popularity. For example, just as *La damnation de Faust* was taking orchestral audiences by storm—its Hungarian march encored at virtually every performance—in spring 1877 and throughout 1878 *Le journal de musique* published numerous Hungarian marches and songs, including other versions of the Rakoczy tune Berlioz borrowed, sometimes accompanied by explanatory articles. One was from a gypsy performance at the 1878 Exposition. For this service, readers paid only forty centimes per issue, or eighteen francs per year.

Another, even cheaper bimonthly music magazine from the 1870s and 1880s, *Le mélomane,* is a good source for studying the tastes of a less musically cultured audience, or those who could afford only ten to twenty-five centimes per issue (one penny in England). Some works reproduced in *Le mélomane* also appeared in *Le journal de musique*—evidence of their broad appeal. Some, such as Rameau's "Le tambourin," were published in *Le mélomane* (1877) before *Le journal de musique* (1879). The magazine offered its subscribers not only classics—by Beethoven, Bach, Gluck, Donizetti, Rossini, and others—but also music performed in popular venues (such as skating rinks). Beginning in 1885, "unpublished music" became their explicit focus (as indicated at the top of each cover). At this point, *Le mélomane* offers a context for studying what new music meant in such a setting. Some pieces derived from their annual "International Composition Competition" for the best (1) prelude, fugue, or minuet, (2) romance without words, and (3) dance music, all for piano. Contestants were exhorted to seek "grace, elegance and originality, but not difficulty." The winners—including little-known women, Conservatory instructors, and the future director of the Garde Républicaine, Gabriel Parès—were awarded medals and publication of their winning composition in the magazine. These works reveal which aspects of art music—genres, styles, and aesthetics—were increasingly appreciated.

Newspapers (and illustrated Sunday supplements, very popular in the 1890s) also reproduced piano or piano-vocal transcriptions. In terms of amusing, interesting, and instructing their publics, these were like short stories or reproductions of paintings. They are also important records of taste and concert life. *Le figaro,* one of the most respected Parisian dailies, reproduced two to four pages of scores each Wednesday from the 1870s through the 1890s. In many ways, the paper tried to be balanced and thoughtful about its choices by not giving undue advertising advantage to any one music publisher, theater, style, composer, or performer. Piano-vocal scores dominated (sometimes almost two to one with piano scores), with songs often outnumbering opera excerpts. Orchestral works occasionally

appeared in transcriptions for two pianos. Light genres such as polkas and
other dances were rarer because, more than any other collection of scores
from the time, *Le figaro*'s transcriptions documented important performances or musical events. These included premieres in Paris, the French
provinces, and abroad; cantatas winning the annual Prix de Rome; and
piano pieces written for the Conservatory's annual sight-reading exam (perhaps included to inform future potential candidates of the level required
for admission to the Conservatory's piano class). Short explanatory notes
sometimes indicated what to expect in performing this music. This suggests that the scores were not just news items, but also part of the popularization of serious music. Through them, readers could participate vicari-
ously in the musical world.

Another medium through which the French got to know art music was
the wind-band transcription. Whereas some were for small groups called
fanfares, most called for around thirty woodwind and brass instruments.
Some of the best transcribers, like Louis Mayeur and Gabriel Parès, were
conductors as well as authors of orchestration treatises and instrumental
method books. These men helped liberate wind-band transcriptions from
being restricted to martial-type music or certain tonalities. Increasingly,
thanks to their treatises, transcribers were able to reproduce the effects of
orchestral music and present works in their original keys. Parès wanted to
make wind bands the equal of symphonic orchestras, especially in "trans-
lating a composer's inspiration." In his volume, dedicated to his composition teacher, Théodore Dubois, Parès explained that he wished to "charm
the listener and [sometimes] give the illusion of a string orchestra (the most
perfect creation of the musical art)." To translate a full range of sentiment,
he advocated learning to produce not only power and brilliant sonorities,
but also variety and sweetness.[26] Such language and the intentions underlying it most likely were meant to bring wind-band transcriptions closer to the
original music and to the composer's intended expression. However, ironically, they also upset the gender stereotypes associated with band music and,
by underlining feminine as well as masculine sentiments, suggested the kind
of bi-musicality inherent in larger forms such as symphony and opera.

Indeed, during this period, military bands as well as amateur wind bands
(*harmonies*) performed not only marches and polkas, but also transcriptions of overtures, symphonic poems, and opera—music that called for a
wide range of expressivity. Opera transcriptions were called "fantasies"
and "mosaics." They resemble piano fantasies in that both string together
a selection of excerpts, most with a strong melodic or rhythmic allure, not
necessarily in the original order. As in Disney's *Fantasia,* material could
also return (possibly for the sake of musical closure) even if this did not
take place in the original. In their program notes, *Le petit poucet* increasingly indicated where the opera's excerpts are in the piano-vocal scores,
implying that some military-band fans might own these scores.

The typical transcription, in full score for the conductor, is over thirty pages long. Individual instruments—such as the bugle, cornet, and trombone—perform singers' arias. Lyrics are sometimes printed below the notes. Parès's mosaic for Bruneau's *Messidor* (Opéra, 1897) was performed by the Garde Républicaine in 1899. The story of overt class conflict between a peasant family and a factory-owner is resolved by the love between the peasant hero, Guillaume, and the industrialist's daughter, Hélène. Their dialogue appears in the score and in *Le petit poucet*:

> Trombone—But I love you! I want you today as I wanted you yesterday. And aren't you mine, since here you are poor?
> Cornet—O how wonderful to be loved! I have always loved you, dear spouse, I have never loved anyone but you.
> Trombone and Cornet—Like two flames that come together, let our hearts burn all our lives.[27]

Such works, especially newer works with more complicated rhythms and timbral interrelationships, served as occasions for performers to practice expressivity as well as coordination.[28] They also suggest that military-band audiences may have been open to newer French works because of the ideologically subversive content some promoted.

This repertory reached diverse audiences and made works accessible to the public sometimes years before they were heard on the stage. Often it was the only form in which audiences in the provinces or colonies could hear certain music. As *Le petit poucet* pointed out (14 June 1899), it was in the provinces that Parès first popularized his fantasies based on music by Wagner, Reyer, Saint-Saëns, Massenet, and others. Because the journal saw popularizing art music as the role of wind-band orchestra, *Le petit poucet* wished that more contemporary composers would write for them.

How to explain the success of such replicas? One should remember this was the era of reproduction—the early years of the phonograph, the wax museum (founded in 1882), and the craze for panoramas representing current events, modern life, and imaginary tours of the world. Parisians were used to blurred lines between fantasy and reality. In *Spectacular Realities,* the historian Vanessa Schwarz argues that illusion itself was a source of consumer pleasure, especially the illusion of voyage.[29] The sociologist Rosalind Williams concurs. In *Dream Worlds,* she cites Des Esseintes from Joris-Karl Huysmans's novel, *À Rebours,* as someone who consciously pursues the "pleasure of self-deception." For him, inner vision is what counts, not the thing itself, and one achieves visions through self-deception. Des Esseintes believes that, as in religious practice, the validity of an experience depends on the "quality of faith in the consumer, not on the quality of the product used to stimulate the experience."[30] Agreeing with him, I would go further and suggest that the object, or signified of musical transcriptions, was not necessarily the thing itself, the original form of a work—I do not think transcriptions always functioned as iconic signs. Rather, their object may have been what they evoked in the listener, whether this meant, for Parès, the wind band as string orchestra, or, for others, feelings or ideas they might link to music. McCracken called this their displaced meaning, often "an idealized version of life as it should be lived."[31] To the extent this was true, success—or popularity—may have de-pended on what people associated with certain music as much as the music itself.[32]

Concerts, Popular Venues, and Their Publics

Interesting and informative documents, concert programs have also been too long ignored by scholars. These provide a wealth of information about repertory, premieres, performers, and concert venues as well as the nature of musical production and consumption at the end of the nineteenth century. Their first function was to attract as well as to inform audiences. Programs were sent through the mail, published widely in the press, and distributed free at virtually all public concerts, regardless of venue. For concert societies, they were evidence of the organization's performance history—a form of collective memory—of particular value to concert-organizers and program-annotators.[33]

Some programs preserved at the Bibliothèque Nationale and elsewhere contain handwritten notations. Comments may refer to works a listener liked or disliked—which they found "pretty," "charming," "mediocre," or "too long." Other indications point to how the general public responded. An 11 February 1866 program of the Concerts Populaires, for example, tells us that at the orchestra's first performances of these works, audiences demanded encores of the minuet from Haydn's Symphony in C Minor and the prelude from Wagner's *Lohengrin* and that, after his performance of Mendelssohn's Violin Concerto, Joachim gave four curtain calls. This suggests that listening was often accompanied by recording aesthetic judgments from the individual as well as public perspective. Concert programs are thus important records of audience reception and demonstrate self-consciousness in the French as to their musical tastes.

Concerts that reached the largest audiences were those given by military bands. Each summer in the gardens and squares of the city, Parisians could hear twenty to thirty such concerts per week. In provincial villages and colonies, military bands were the mainstay of musical life. Demand was such that in 1899 the Ministry of War increased the number of military bands from 177 to 195. Military-band programs, often printed in local newspapers, are a treasure for studying the works to which the masses had easy access and for tracing the evolution of public taste.

The most prestigious military band was the Garde Républicaine. Many of its seventy-nine members had earned first prizes from the Paris Conservatory. Unlike other military-band performers who were soldiers, Garde musicians were hired as professionals with civil contracts. Most of the Garde also played with the principal Parisian theater orchestras or those of Colonne or Lamoureux.[34] Between 1855 and 1873, Georges Paulus turned the Garde into a prestigious institution of excellent musicians, who, in their wildly successful ninety-three-day tour of the United States in 1872, were hailed as the best of their kind in the world. His standards of performance were quite high, helping to inspire the notion that this band could help restore French pride and glory. Adolphe Sellenick, assistant conductor under Paulus, took over when Paulus reached retirement, and Gustave Wettge followed when Sellenick retired in 1884. Several concurrent developments helped their successor, Gabriel Parès, a saxophonist-member of the Garde, turn the organization into one even more valued for its seriousness of purpose and musical achievements. In 1893, when Parès took over, the Garde got a new building conceived specifically for music. There they could rehearse three times per week. Parès put this to good use in expanding their repertory. He, together with M. Émile Leblan, conductor of the twenty-eighth military band regiment, considered it their duty to promote modern music.

Upon their retirement, two of the Garde's conductors, Paulus and Wettge, took positions conducting the wind band of one of the city's most important department stores, the Bon Marché. At first a small drapery and notions store, Aristide Boucicault took it over in 1853 and began the transformation immediately. When the store expanded into a whole city block in 1872, including dorms, dining hall, and recreation areas for his employees, Boucicault began to offer them free music lessons (voice as well as wind instruments) along with free courses in English and fencing. With an explicitly educational purpose in mind, he hoped to "encourage a taste for study" and wanted to do everything he could to help his male as well as female employees "use their evenings in an instructive and attractive manner." Besides conceiving of the store and its employees as a "big family," he hoped to produce a new kind of employee. Music lessons taught discipline and personal competitiveness, useful attributes in an effective sales force. After passing solfège classes, employees were allowed to join the choral society, or in the case of men only, the Harmonie, their wind band. All employees of the store could become members of the society, either as performers or as honorary members.[35] The former, of which there were about sixty at any one time, rehearsed two evenings per week; the latter were given a special concert each spring. Each paid one franc per month in dues, a standard amount for workers' societies. Both groups encouraged loyalty and commitment, virtues Boucicault needed when training employees for long careers. Although the Société Chorale and the Harmonie remained strictly amateur ensembles, their concerts—whether within the store itself

Table 16.1. Conductors of the Garde Républicaine, the Société Chorale et Harmonie du
Bon Marché, and the Concerts at the Jardin zoologique d'acclimatation.

La Garde Républicaine	Société Chorale et Harmonie du Bon Marché	Concerts at the Jardin zoologique d'acclimatation
G. Paulus (1855–1873)	L. Mayeur (1872–1877)	L. Mayeur (1872–1893)
A. Sellenick (1874–1884)	G. Paulus (1877–1894)	L. Pister (1893–1896)
G. Wettge (1884–1893)	G. Wettge (1895–1900+)	J. Lafitte (1896–1900+)
G. Parès (1893–1910)		

in winter, outside in the square in summer, or in competitions in Paris and the provinces—gave the store a way to advertise its efforts and largesse, build good will, and attract customers. Their concerts, documented on the programs stamped with police approval and now in the store's private archives, offer the modern scholar a window onto the participation of workers in the concert life of the city.[36] They also provide an important basis for comparison with other groups their conductors directed and with amateur groups from the upper classes (see table 16.1).

The first conductor of the Bon Marché concerts, Louis Mayeur, a clarinetist and saxophonist at the Opéra, also landed the job as director of a new concert series at a city zoo.[37] The Jardin zoologique d'acclimatation opened in 1855 as a place to introduce, domesticate, and reproduce animals and plants from foreign lands. Administrators sought to understand their use-value in the West and to render them popular by exhibitions and sale. After the Franco-Prussian war, when people were tired and needed places of leisure, the Jardin continued to encourage the study of natural history, but added recreation and amusement. To attract people to the park on days of low attendance, in 1872 they began to give concerts on Thursday afternoons . The idea was to excite the interest of a broader public than would otherwise visit the Jardin. The success of these concerts financially, as demonstrated by an increase in admissions on Thursdays, led in 1873 to giving two concerts per week and to constructing a kiosk for music. In 1893, so performances could be given all year long, they built the Palais d'hiver. This was an immense structure containing a large concert hall and a 50-x-25-meter palm-tree-lined "Palmarium" to which chairs could be brought. The administration also hired Louis Pister, who had worked under Pasdeloup at the Concerts Populaires, and asked him to recruit their musicians from the most prestigious institutions in town—the Société des Concerts du Conservatoire, the Opéra, and the Opéra-Comique. As the level of performance rose, the music grew more serious, and Sunday concerts began to be listed in *Le ménestrel*, as if an alternative to those of Colonne and Lamoureux.

Each of these societies contributed significantly to the expansion of the public for serious music, and all relied on their venue to facilitate this.

Military bands played all over the city five days per week for an hour, beginning at 4:00 or 5:00 p.m. They could be heard in poor neighborhoods in eastern Paris, such as the Buttes Chaumont in the nineteenth *arrondissement* and the Place des Nations in the twelfth, and in wealthy ones in the west, such as Place du Ranelagh in the sixteenth and the Parc Monceau in the seventeenth. Such concerts were occasions for people from different classes and backgrounds to mix. As a critic recounted in 1898, one such concert in Montmartre "overflowed with women and children and on the sidewalks, a crowd of men, both bourgeois and workers, salespeople (*calicots*) and artists, all of whom stood to hear the music."[38] Whereas in the 1880s, the Garde Républicaine performed at up to seven venues all over town, in the late 1890s they restricted themselves to twice a week at the city's central, prestigious gardens—those of the Tuileries, Palais du Luxembourg, or Palais Royal. These attracted foreign visitors, students, and occasionally aristocrats. On 21 July 1899 *Le petit poucet* noted that, while visiting their favorite shops in the Palais Royal, elegant female Opéra subscribers mixed in with "humble music-lovers." The press often reported 5,000 to 6,000 people at military-band concerts, regardless of the weather, and sometimes up to 15,000 for the Garde Républicaine. In 1905, one publisher bragged that they printed 150,000 programs for military-band concerts that season. Audience behavior at these concerts was not necessarily what one might expect. As the end of the century neared, critics praised Parès for getting his listeners to pay attention silently, although many still liked to beat the measure with their bodies.

The ten to thirteen summer concerts of the Bon Marché wind band, occasionally accompanied by the choral society, resembled those of military bands except that they took place on Saturdays at 8:30 p.m. in the square beside the store. Typically 1,000 programs were printed for each concert. The press, however, reported that sometimes 6,000 people attended. Interestingly, the largest type on their programs is always the name of the store, as if the Bon Marché itself was the main attraction (see figure 16.2).

The indoor concerts of the Bon Marché, which began three years earlier in January 1873, were quite different. In the beginning, they were called "musical meetings" (*réunions musicales*), as if intimate gatherings. By 1880, however, the store began to take them seriously. For the two or three choral concerts that took place within the main hall of the store each winter, the merchandise was cleared out; oriental rugs, curtains, exotic plants, and lighting were brought in; and the space was turned into a huge luxurious salon. Six thousand invitations were sent for one concert in 1881. This included 300 pink ones for female employees, 2,000 green ones for male employees, and the balance presumably for customers and invited guests. In all, 4,000 free programs were printed. After 1881, they decided the first concert should take place between the exhibition of new coats and the end of the fall season, and the second should coincide with the January white

SAISON D'ÉTÉ

CONCERT DU SAMEDI 21 JUILLET

5me Audition

dans le Square

à 8 heures ½ du soir

PAR

L'HARMONIE

DU

BON MARCHÉ

SOUS LA DIRECTION

de **M. Paulus** ✱ ***ex-chef de musique de la Garde Républicaine***

PROGRAMME

1° **Marche du Figaro** . . . . G. WITTMANN.

2° **Samson** et **Dalila**. . . . . SAINT-SAËNS.

3° **Anna Bolena** . . . . DONIZETTI.

4° Fragments de **Rienzi**. . . . . R. WAGNER.

5° **Solo de Cornet,** par M. PRIALOUX . . J. MELLÉ.

6° **Mystères des bois** . . . . L. ITASSE.

FINALE

La prochaine audition aura lieu le Samedi 4 Août

Figure 16.2. The program of a concert given by the wind band of the Bon Marché department store in the square outside the store on Saturday evening, 21 July 1894. Used by permission of the Bon Marché department store.

Cours de Musique des Magasins du BON MARCHÉ

CONCERT

Du Samedi 27 Janvier 1883.

Programme

1° **La Somnambule**. . . . . BELLINI.
  Fantaisie exécutée par l'HARMONIE.

2° **Duo** concertant pour flûte et hautbois . . . . GATTERMAN.
  Exécuté par MM. CANTIÉ & SAUTET.

3° **Hérodiade**, chœur des Romains. . . . . MASSENET.
  Exécuté par l'HARMONIE et le CHORAL.

4° Prière de **Rienzi**. . . . . R. WAGNER.
  Chanté par M. BOSQUIN de l'Opéra.

5° Air des **Saisons** . . . . V. MASSÉ.
  Chanté par Madame BRUNET-LAFLEUR.

6° ⟨ (A) **Premier amour** . . . . PAUL BILHAUD.
  ⟩ (B) **Paris**. . . . . GRENET DANCOURT.
  Monologues dits par M. COQUELIN Cadet.

7° **Grenade** (Chœur). . . . . LAURENT DE RILLÉ.
  Exécuté par le CHORAL.

8° **Solo** de Cornet. . . . . ARBAN.
  Exécuté par M. MELLET.

9° Fantaisie sur **Aïda** (Verdi), *arrangée par* . . . . M. PAULUS.
  Exécutée par l'HARMONIE.

10° Septuor d'**Ernani**. . . . . VERDI.
  Exécuté par l'HARMONIE et le CHORAL.

11° Air du **Comte Ory** . . . . ROSSINI.
  Chanté par Madame BRUNET-LAFLEUR.

12° ⟨ (A) Barcarolle de **Polyeucte** . . . . GOUNOD.
  ⟩ (B) Couplets de **Rigoletto** . . . . VERDI.
  Chantés par M. BOSQUIN de l'Opéra.

13° **Mira la blanca Luna**. . . . . ROSSINI.
  Duo chanté par Madame BRUNET-LAFLEUR & M. BOSQUIN.

14° ⟨ (A) **Le nouveau Tabarin**, scène comique . . . X***
  ⟩ (B) **La Revue du Régiment**, scène militaire . LHUILLIER.
  Jouées par M. FUSIER.

15° **Final**, par l'HARMONIE. . . . . X***

L'HARMONIE sera dirigée par M. PAULUS, ex-chef de musique de la Garde-Républicaine. — Les **CHŒURS**, par MM. DELAFONTAINE & ESBIN, professeurs de la ville de Paris.
Le Piano sortant des ateliers de MM. PLEYEL, sera tenu par M. L. JACOB.

Figure 16.3. The program of a concert given by the choral society and the wind band of the Bon Marché department store in the main hall of the store on Saturday evening, 27 January 1883. Used by permission of the Bon Marché department store.

sale, a marketing tactic invented by Boucicault. Ads for the white sale were occasionally inserted in the programs. To attract a sophisticated audience, in January 1883 they began to invite Opéra stars, such as M. Jules Bosquin and Mme Marie-Hélène Brunet-Lafleur and Comédie-Française actors like M. Ernest Coquelin Cadet (see figure 16.3). This coincided with printing "CONCERT" in capital letters at the top of its programs, perhaps to imply the increasingly public nature of these events or the credibility to which they espoused. In 1885 the invitation list included Baronness de Rothschild and in 1887 Colonne and Gounod.

Of the various concert societies in Paris, the Jardin became the most conscious of the diversity of its potential publics and the need to serve each of them. Each summer in the 1870s and 1880s, fifty concerts were held in their outdoor kiosk. A subscription cost twenty-five francs for men, but only ten francs for women and children, perhaps to make it easier for the latter to attend. In 1893, however, as the construction of the Palais d'hiver led the Jardin to reconceive its musical activities, a decision was made to provide concerts for three types of public. The Sunday concerts, performed in the main hall, continued with works by the "best-known masters," or what was considered "easy and likeable music"—overtures, fantasies, genre pieces. Besides the price of entry to the zoo (one franc), concert admission cost only twenty centimes to one and a half francs. Four days a week, from 3:00 to 5:00 p.m., the Jardin also initiated concerts for twenty centimes in the Palmarium—Promenade concerts. Listeners were invited to relax and converse with friends under the shade of the palm trees while their children played. With the warm temperature, evergreen trees, and fresh flowers, the idea was a big salon giving the illusion of eternal spring. The Jardin began a new third concert series on Wednesdays with advanced music, which their advance publicity noted would be addressed to a "more initiated" public, those interested in the "progress of art." They hoped the public would enjoy the historical part of their programs and works by young composers. For these, they increased the size of the orchestra from sixty to ninety musicians, occasionally invited guest soloists—pianists, organists, and opera singers—and, to cover the increased expenses, raised ticket prices to from one to four francs. In 1896 they bragged that they had been able to attract the high society of Paris as well as the middle class, business men, and government employees, though not yet much of the working class.

These examples suggest that several strategies aided in making music available and appealing to a wide range of people. First, it was brought to their neighborhoods. Second, it was performed in familiar settings, not only local squares and gardens, but also indoor spaces transformed into salons. The latter made the bourgeoisie feel comfortable, as if at home, at the same time that they offered those of lesser means access to the bourgeois lifestyle and an aristocratic model of consumption. Third, concerts were accompanied by printed programs, turning the listening experience into more than entertainment.

Repertory

Given the huge number of people listening to concerts in popular venues, we should take seriously what was performed. The extent to which repertory was shared or overlapping in diverse venues suggests the emergence of both a "popular culture" that included art music and a national culture that transcended the crude, divisive nationalisms troubling France at the end of the century.

Most concerts, of any type, embodied an aesthetic of variety. This underlies the almost obligatory alternation of genres; the often eclectic juxtaposition of styles, periods, and composers; and the variation in a group's programs from week to week. As they hoped to "amuse, interest, and instruct," most concert organizers too were mindful not to tire listeners. Concerts were to provide a succession of experiences, like parts of a meal. Lighter works, such as marches or polkas, came at the end, as if "desserts," with the middle reserved for more difficult music, "main courses."

The formula for military-band concerts was four or five pieces, starting with a march or other military music, followed by an overture, dance, opera fantasy or mosaic, and then a polka or other dance (see figure 16.1). What filled this formula, however, changed over the years. Although Paulus popularized his transcription of the prelude from *Lohengrin*, in the early 1870s under Sellenick and in the 1880s under Wettge, the works most frequently performed by the Garde Républicaine were Sellenick's marches, fantasies on Gounod's *Faust*, and Auber's overtures, followed by fantasies from operas by Thomas, Meyerbeer, Verdi, and Adam. Wettge gradually added more works by French contemporaries, especially Delibes and Saint-Saëns. In summer 1896, Massenet joined Gounod and Thomas as the favorites, followed by Verdi, Meyerbeer, Messager, Auber, Delibes, and Wagner. Increasingly, there were also fantasies on French operas recently premiered in Paris, such as Massenet's *Navarraise, Esclarmonde,* and *Le cid*; Bruneau's *Attaque du moulin* and *Messidor*; Saint-Saëns's *Ascanio* and *Samson et Dalila*; and Vidal's *Maladetta*. The 1890s also show more and more French symphonic music in transcription, such as the tone poems of Saint-Saëns and Massenet, Bourgault-Ducoudray's *Rapsodie cambodgienne,* and Grieg's *Peer Gynt*. Excerpts from Wagner's *Ring* and *Parsifal* could also be heard here in transcription, especially in the 1890s. In August 1898, Parès even added opera singers to a concert, and in 1899 the Eighty-Second *Régiment de ligne* performed a complete transcription of Massenet's *Eve,* one of the only long, complex works in their repertory not consisting of excerpts. In the provinces and colonies, military bands often performed more recent French music than local orchestras or theaters did. This should give us pause not to underestimate the level of popular interest in art music, the capacity of the general public to appreciate it, and the ability of amateurs to perform it.

Beginning in January 1873, Bon Marché concerts within the store consisted of fourteen or fifteen short pieces, typically ten to fifteen minutes in length, with alternating solos and chorus (see figure 16.3). These lasted two hours and twenty minutes—the same as a typical concert by Colonne's orchestra. From the beginning, the programs juxtaposed art music (mostly opera overtures, choruses, and solo excerpts) with popular genres (chansonnettes, monologues, and comic scenes). Occasionally these included recent works, such as excerpts from Charles Lecocq's *Kosiki,* performed by the wind band on 10 February 1877, only four months after its premiere at the Théâtre de la Renaissance. That concert ended with a spoof, "Titi at a performance of Robert-le-diable," suggesting that at least some of their public could identify with the experience of attending the Opéra. These concerts are a fascinating example of concerts shared by professionals and amateurs, for even with the addition of stars from the Opéra, the Comédie-Française, and the most famous Parisian cabarets, employees performed in at least half of the works presented.

The summer concerts of the Bon Marché resembled military-band concerts in length and repertory. Most presented six works and included an overture, an air, an instrumental solo, and one to three opera fantasies (increasing to three to five in 1887) (see figure 16.2). Marches began many concerts; polkas ended them, as in military-band concerts. The repertory was chosen by the conductor and an elected committee of four to eight member-performers. Beethoven, Mozart, and Berlioz are absent from the programs until 1896. Wagner first appears on their concerts in 1879, coinciding with the return of his music to the Concerts Pasdeloup after a two-year hiatus. Like military bands, the Harmonie included recently composed French works, as well as music by Méhul, Grétry, and Rameau. From the 1870s through the 1890s, eighteen opera fantasies they performed were based on new works. For example, they did Saint-Saëns's *Henry VIII* in July 1883 after its premiere at the Opéra that March and his *Phryné,* a year after its Opéra-Comique premiere in May 1893. The Bon Marché band played a fantasy on Massenet's *Hériodiade* the summer after its premiere in Brussels, almost two years before its Paris premiere. Only months after premieres or recent revivals at various Parisian theaters, they also performed fantasies on Gounod's *Roméo et Juliette,* Massé's *Paul et Virginie,* Offenbach's *La fille du tambour major* and *Belle Lurette,* Paladilhe's *Patrie,* Planquette's *Les voltigueurs* and *Rip,* and Serpette's *Madame le diable,* and two years after their premieres, Reyer's *Sigurd* and Massenet's *Le cid* and *Esclarmonde.* Most of these remained in their repertory, suggesting wide-ranging aesthetic tastes. Perhaps a product of the store's interest in fashion,

Table 16.2. Concerts in the Square of the Bon Marché.

1870s: Donizetti (9), Verdi (9), Lecocq (6), Meyerbeer (4), Rossini (3), Auber (3), von Suppé (3), Guiraud (3), Bellini (2), Rameau (2), Wagner (2), plus miscellaneous solos, polkas, waltzes, etc.

Italian opera	39% (23 of 59 on this list)
living French composers (14)	24%

1880s: Verdi (17), Rossini (16), Donizetti (14), Gounod (14), Offenbach (12), Meyerbeer (11), Planquette (10), Auber (9), Joncières (9), Wagner (9), Massenet (7), Paladilhe (7), Lecocq (5), Halévy (5), Delibes (5), Bizet (5), Hérold (5), Reyer (5), Chabrier (5), Thomas (4), Liszt (4), etc.

Italian opera	25% (53 of 209)
Gounod	7%
Wagner	4%
living French composers	40% (83 of 209)

1890s: Gounod (27), Wagner (25), Meyerbeer (13), Verdi (12), Thomas (11), Delibes (11), Saint-Saëns (10), Donizetti (10), Rossini (8), Massenet (8), Bizet (8), Auber (6), Chabrier (6), Bellini (5), Offenbach (4), Hérold (4), Paladilhe (4), etc.

Italian opera	16% (34 of 213)
Gounod	13%
Wagner	12%
living French composers	47% (98 of 213)

Bon Marché concert organizers were astutely aware of what elite institutions were performing and were intent on keeping their audiences abreast of the newest developments.

Bon Marché concerts allow us to examine changes in audiences' tastes from the 1870s through the 1890s (see table 16.2). Early on, Italian opera fantasies dominated their programs. Other works (e.g., by Meyerbeer and Auber) coincided with what was being performed in theaters and by military bands. In the 1880s, under Paulus and Wettge, however, the focus of the repertory shifted. Music by living French composers (e.g., Gounod, Massenet, Paladilhe, Delibes, Reyer, and Chabrier) rose to forty percent, with Italian opera fantasies dropping to twenty-five percent. As elsewhere, music by living French composers grew still more prevalent in the 1890s, rising to forty-seven percent. Gounod's presence also increased over this decade, as did Wagner's. Perhaps reflecting a more general decline in their popularity, performances of Italian operas dropped to sixteen percent.[39] Further study of the precise repertory shared with Parisian theaters will shed light on the meaning of this evolution in musical tastes.

In the 1870s and 1880s, the Sunday concerts at the Jardin zoologique d'acclimatation had a similar formula, only the programs were twice as long. Most, presenting eight to ten works, started with a march, ended with a light work such as a dance, and included opera fantasies and overtures. This was the case without exception during the 1881 season:

Part I	*Part II*
march	potpourri opera / march / other
overture	polka / solo
opera fantasy	opera fantasy
waltz (Mayeur)	dance / march

That summer the most frequently performed composers were Mayeur himself, followed by Auber, Sellenick, Rossini, Meyerbeer, Donizetti, Verdi, and Strauss. Massenet, Gung'l, and Fahrbach also appeared. In the 1890s, after the construction of the Palais d'hiver, the zoo's concerts became a home for more serious music. The Wednesday concerts presented symphonies and Opéra singers for the first time. On 5 April 1893, audiences heard Saint-Saëns's Symphony no. 3 (C Minor, op. 78), and on 17 May Beethoven's Symphony no. 1 (C Major, op. 21). Pister also began promoting more French music, especially by his contemporaries, on all of his concerts. The press followed his Wednesday series with particular excitement. In addition to Saint-Saëns, Massenet, and Widor, lesser-known composers Paul and Lucien Hillemacher and a young Prix de Rome winner Pierre Letorey appeared there to conduct their own music. In 1895 Pister fashioned the Sunday concerts to compete with the contemporary music series at the Opéra, offering some of the same repertory. Later in the century, Jacques Lafitte initiated one-composer festivals with large choruses and opera singers, a formula popularized by Colonne and Lamoureux.

Thus, to understand how music was used to mediate differences of class and culture, we need to understand how those contexts overlapped; which works appeared in elite, bourgeois, and working-class venues; and what those works meant to multiple publics (a study beyond the scope of this essay). This entails examining a broad range of data, much of it derived from transient material culture, and interrogating its social as well as musical significance. We also need to see that women, through their magazine consumption, use of piano transcriptions, and choral societies, were not the only ones domesticating art music. Men too, especially through wind bands, contributed to blurring the boundaries of art and consumer society. And, to the extent that Parès got his way, men explored feminine as well as masculine forms of expressivity in their performances. We also need to admit that using music for commercial ends had some benefits. Concerts used to attract people to commercial venues made art music—even operas and symphonic poems by living French composers—available to the masses as well as to elites. Just as consumer goods in department stores became "instruments of instruction and politics," so too could concerts play an important role in promoting social change.[40]

Perhaps the most striking conclusion of this study is the dramatic increase of new music on concert programs in the 1890s. We know that in 1891 the government forced the Opéra, through its Cahier de Charges, to perform more new works. Despite this, elites increasingly gravitated to music representing the distant past, seeking to shelter their hopes and ideals from the realities of the bourgeois Republic. Those hoping to improve their lot in life, by contrast, remained focused on the present. Whether they were roused by Auber's, Meyerbeer's, or Rossini's overtures to operas about great men, or preferred *Patrie, Henry VIII,* and *Messidor* about the social and political aspirations of common people, we cannot know how the lower classes understood this music. Still this study has shown that they willingly performed and listened to new works as well as to traditional favorites. We should not assume that ordinary people liked only what they already knew, or that the march of progress meant the march of the classical German canon. The ideal of using music and musical tastes as a form of democratization had some success, especially in disseminating modern French music to the general public. Perhaps just as important as the elites' increasingly embrace of museum culture, this fusion of art and consumer culture set the stage for modernist reaction.

Samson et Dalila: Becoming Popular

Saint-Saëns's opera *Samson et Dalila* offers a good example of how a work became popular and raises important questions about the process of popularization. The Théâtre National de l'Opéra did not lead the way, and yet by the time the Opéra finally produced the opera in 1892, it was already hailed as the composer's most popular work. The story of how this paradox emerged leads us to examine other aspects of the musical world—performers, transcriptions, and popular venues. Without pressure from them, the Opéra may never have performed *Samson et Dalila*.

The first performance took place as excerpts, a piano transcription of Act II with the composer accompanying Pauline Viardot in her salon, purportedly in 1868 and 1874. The Opéra's director may have heard one of these, but refused to stage the work, finding it more oratorio than opera. Colonne gave the first orchestral performance of Act I on Good Friday in March 1875. Clearly he meant to do the composer a favor, scheduling it with Beethoven's ever-popular Ninth Symphony on a day when everyone went to concerts. The concert was indeed well attended—ticket sales at the door were the highest for the season. The success led Colonne to program the "Dance of the Priestesses" the following January and may have convinced Durand to publish Saint-Saëns's piano transcription of it later that year. When Weimar agreed to produce the opera in 1877, with the composer conducting, Durand published a piano-vocal score of the entire opera in French and German for fifteen francs and an eleven-page piano fantasy based on the work, called "Reminiscences," by Henri Cramer.

The story of why Weimar took on the opera goes beyond Liszt's intervention and is worthy of closer examination. In short, Saint-Saëns had enjoyed a good career in Germany as a respected performer of Austro-German music, especially the works of Mozart. Although Frenchmen disagreed, some Germans considered him an alternative to Wagner, "one of the few not taken in" by him.[41] *Le journal de musique* contextualized this premiere abroad by comparing it to Delibes's *Sylvia* in Vienna and by finding glory in the export of French music. In part to draw attention to it, in August 1877 they reproduced a piano transcription of the "Dance of the Priestesses." Colonne repeated this for orchestra in November, while Pasdeloup did the "Bacchanale." The following year Ernest Guiraud made a version of both excerpts for piano four-hands. Already by 1877 then, both publishers and performers had perceived the "Dance of the Priestesses" and the "Bacchanale" as excerpts capable of achieving popularity, despite the absence of dancers.

Before its French theatrical premiere in 1890, French audiences got to know *Samson et Dalila* through multiple performances of these orchestral excerpts, as well as piano transcriptions and airs. In the 1880s Colonne performed fragments of the work on four concerts, with Saint-Saëns conducting selections from Act III on Good Friday in 1880. Lamoureux, too, performed excerpts. Opéra singers, such as Mme Gabrielle Krauss and Mme Marie-Hélène Brunet-Lafleur, sang airs in private homes, e.g., at the Countess Élisabeth Greffuhle's in April 1884.

On 3 March 1890, the Rouen premiere at the Théâtre des Arts, known for supporting new works, stimulated a new wave of interest as did the Paris premiere that October at the Eden Theater, famous for its exotic spectacles, but not for opera. Both settings attracted the musical cognoscenti, but few others. Thankfully, critics embraced the work immediately, calling it Saint-Saëns's best for the theater. Others helped draw attention to it as well: *Le figaro* published "Dalila's Song" on 19 March 1890 (see figure 16.4), and fantasies for easy piano, for piano and violin, and for wind band followed. Colonne opened his concert season the following fall again with the "Bacchanale" and the "Dance of the Priestesses," repeating the "Bacchanale" a month later. Amateurs also began to perform the work widely. The piano students of Mme Bosquet-Luigini, for example, played piano four-hand versions of it in their recital that May. Military bands performed excerpts in September and October 1890, and the Bon Marché wind band opened its 1891 season that June with the wind-band transcription.

Still, it took until 1892 before the Paris Opéra produced the work, and pressure from previous productions in the provinces (Bordeaux, Toulouse, Nantes, Dijon, and Montpellier) and abroad (Geneva, Monte Carlo, Algiers, New York, and Florence). When the Opéra did program it, beginning on 23 November, Colonne conducted it from memory, Mme Blanche Deschamps-Jehin was unconvincing as Dalila, her talents perceived as "a little too bourgeois."[42] Moreover, throughout that December, another new work, of far less significance, Alix Fournier's one-act opera, *Stratonice*

Figure 16.4. "Chant de Dalila" from Saint-Saëns's *Samson et Dalila*, reproduced in the newspaper *Le Figaro* (19 March 1890). Used by permission of the Bibliothèque Nationale.

(1892), was performed before it.[43] For reasons I explain elsewhere, however, the work caught on. Sixty-one performances followed in two years, as did transcriptions for other instrumental combinations. Interestingly, after being produced as an opera, *Samson et Dalila* left the repertory of the major orchestras, but joined that of military and wind bands (see figure 16.2). From July 1892 through 1894, there were over sixty-one military-band performances in more than a dozen Parisian gardens. No one in Paris was deprived of hearing the work. Indeed it would be hard to imagine anyone not having been familiar with some aspect of it by the time the Opéra gave its hundredth performance in 1897.

This example suggests that theaters did not always determine which operas the public heard and came to appreciate. Even after *Samson et Dalila* entered the Opéra's repertoire, other musical organizations, especially military bands, may have done more to popularize it. Such circumstances challenge the direction, tempo, and dynamics of Simmel's trickle-down theory, together with any notions we may have about the Opéra's hegemony or its mechanisms of control. Repertoire moved in multiple directions, both up and down as well as across organizational categories, defying differences not only in musical genre, but also in class, education, politics, and location of listeners. To understand this, one must acknowledge connections and dialectical relationships within the musical world and ask a broader range of questions than modernists have been willing to consider. When works like *Samson et Dalila* were performed by and for amateurs as well as professionals, provincials as well as Parisians, and in a wide diversity of venues, both private and public, they lived up to the three definitions of the popular discussed here. We may not know exactly how such music was understood, but we know how, when, and where it was performed, in other words, how it was used.

What is a work in the context of so many diverse uses? This essay proposes that not only do discourses help to articulate the musical object, so do its mediators—performances in whatever form or format, venues, and publics. The identity of the work, then, is not just musical, but also social, and like all social identities, as Tia de Nora points out, "emerges from its interaction and juxtaposition to others, people and things."[44] It is from this perspective that *Samson et Dalila* was part of a shared tradition, and because French, one associated with the nation.

Notes

1. Georg Simmel, "Fashion," *International Quarterly* 10 (1904): 130–55.

2. Preparation for this essay has entailed research in private archives and participation in conferences. I am very grateful to the following individuals for permission to consult their materials: Lt.-Col. François Boulanger, conductor of the Orchestra of the Garde Républicaine, and Lt.-Col. Verdy of their public relations; Guy François, Secrétaire général of the Bon Marché and their archivist Elizabeth Russo; and Valérie Magnier of the Jardin zoologique d'acclimatation. Portions of this paper have appeared previously in "Music in Service of Public Utility in Four Late Nineteenth-Century French Concert Societies" at the conference *Concert et publics en Europe entre 1700 et 1900,* Göttingen, Germany (26 March 1999); "Popularizing Classical Music in Paris, 1870–1913: The Contribution of Popular Venues" at the National Meeting of the American Musicological Society, Kansas City (4 November 1999); "Ideologies of the Popular: Morality and Ethics in the Music Culture of Late Nineteenth-Century Paris" at the University of California, Santa Barbara (3 February 2000) and the University of California, Los Angeles (29 February 2000); and "Democracy, Ethics, and Commerce: The Concerts Populaires in Late Nineteenth-Century France" at the conference, *Les sociétés de musique en Europe, 1700–1920.*

Structures, pratiques musicales et sociabilités, Zurich, Switzerland (7 October 2000). I devote fuller discussion to these organizations and their concert repertory in my book, *Useful Music, or Why Music Mattered in Third Republic France*, to be published by the University of California Press.

3. The word *populaire* does not translate well into English in part because of differences between French and Anglo-American socio-political cultures. For an excellent discussion of the etymological origins and use of *populaire* and *le peuple*, see Geneviève Bollme, *Le peuple par écrit* (Paris: Seuil, 1986), chapter 1.

4. For this insight, I am grateful to my research assistant, Jean-Louis Morhange.

5. Jules Michelet, *Le peuple* (Paris: Hachette, Paulin, 1846).

6. Marcel de Ris, *L'orphéon*, 1 October 1855; J. F. Vaudin, "Les orphéons devant l'histoire," *L'orphéon*, 1 January 1859 and 1 September 1865. All translations from the French are my own unless otherwise noted.

7. François-Auguste Gevaert, "De l'enseignement public de l'art musical à l'époque moderne," *Le ménestrel*, 8 October 1876, 356–59, and 15 October 1876, 364–65.

8. These citations from Gabriel Tarde's *La psychologie économique*, 2 vols. (Paris: Alcan, 1902) and *L'opinion et la foule* (Paris: Alcan, 1901) are borrowed from Rosalind Williams, *Dream Worlds: Mass Consumption in Late Nineteenth-Century France* (Berkeley: University of California Press, 1982), 374–77 and 425 n. 82. Emile Durkheim developed the idea of "*conscience collective*" in several books cited in *Dream Worlds*, including *The Division of Labor in Society*, trans. George Simpson (New York: Free Press, 1965); *The Elementary Forms of the Religious Life*, trans. Joseph Ward Swain (New York: Free Press, 1965); and *Suicide: A Study in Sociology*, trans. John Spaulding and George Simpson (New York: Free Press; London: Collier Macmillan, 1951).

9. Louis Bourgault-Ducoudray, "Cours d'histoire générale de la musique, séance d'ouverture," *Le ménestrel*, 1 December 1878, 3.

10. Although his study is highly critical and focused on crowds, a fear of rising socialism, and a belief that the opinion of crowds was becoming "the supreme guiding principle in politics," some of the conservative Le Bon's *Psychologie des foules* (trans. as *The Crowd, A Study of the Popular Mind* [London: Ernest Benn, 1896]) is helpful in reflecting on the nature of musical publics in the late nineteenth century, including Bourgault-Ducoudray's notion of opinion as "free judgment." Le Bon defined prestige as "a sort of domination exercised on our mind by an individual, work, or idea. This domination entirely paralyzes our critical faculty, and fills our soul with astonishment and respect. . . . It is easy to imbue the mind of crowds with a passing opinion, but very difficult to implant therein a lasting belief. However, a belief of this latter description once established, it is equally difficult to uproot it" (130, 142).

11. Ibid., 125.

12. Peter Bailey, *Popular Culture and Performance in the Victorian City* (Cambridge: Cambridge University Press, 1998), 24–25. In her *Music in Everyday Life* (Cambridge: Cambridge University Press, 2000), Tia De Nora also described music as a "place or space for 'work,'" which she defined as "meaning or lifeworld making" (40). See also her "How is Extra-Musical Meaning Possible? Music as a Place and Space for Work," *Sociological Theory* 4 (1986): 84–94.

13. For more on this, see my "Building a Public for Orchestral Music: Les Concerts Colonne," in *Concert et public: mutation de la vie musicale en Europe de*

1780 à 1914, ed. Hans-Erich Boedeker, Patrice Veit, and Michael Werner (Paris: Éditions de la Maison des Sciences de l'homme, 2002).

14. Williams, *Dream Worlds*, 105.

15. Bailey, *Popular Culture*, 20.

16. Ibid., 21, 29.

17. Grant McCracken, *Culture and Consumption: New Approaches to the Symbolic Character of Consumer Goods and Activities* (Bloomington: Indiana University Press, 1988), 110.

18. In his *Culture and Consumption*, McCracken (93) explained that this theory puts fashion diffusion in a social context, which helps determine fashion's "direction, tempo, and dynamics."

19. See Williams, *Dream Worlds*, 356. Underlying this ideal is Tarde's belief that there was no line between society and the individual, between internal feelings and external constraints. He conceived them as in a dynamic relation of role-setting and role-following. See Gabriel Tarde, *Les lois de l'imitation, étude sociologique*, 3rd ed. (Paris: Alcan, 1900).

20. See Christopher Small, *Musicking: The Meanings of Performing and Listening* (Hanover, N.H.: Wesleyan University Press, 1998), 63.

21. Bailey, *Popular Culture*, 32. For an illuminating summary of the latest thinking on working-class respectability, see his chapter 2.

22. See also Thomas Christensen, "Four-Hand Piano Transcription and Geographies of Nineteenth-Century Musical Reception," *Journal of the American Musicological Society* 52/2 (1999): 255–98.

23. Magazines also occasionally rented their issues. In 1895, *La quinzaine musicale*, which published the music of many women composers, lent their scores for three days in Paris, or eight days in the provinces.

24. Some, such as *La musique des familles*, began earlier in the century and were explicitly oriented toward families.

25. "A nos lecteurs," *Le journal de musique*, 19 May 1877, 1.

26. Gabriel Parès, *Traité d'instrumentation et d'orchestration à l'usage des musiques militaires, d'harmonies, et de fanfares* (Paris: Lemoine, 1898), 111.

27. "Programme analytique du concert de la Garde," *Le petit poucet*, 19 September 1899, 4. Among other descriptive passages and scenes presented by various instruments, this one ends:

> Trombone—Mais je t'aime! je te veux aujourd'hui comme je te voulais hier. Et n'es-tu pas à moi, puisque te voilà pauvre?
>
> Cornet—O délices d'être aimée! je t'ai toujours aimé, cher époux, je n'ai jamais aimé que toi.
>
> Trombone et Cornet—Comme deux flammes qui se rejoignent, que nos coeurs brûlent pour la vie entire!

28. A mosaic of Berlioz's *La damnation de Faust*, performed in 1898, is evidence of the degree of difficulty that ensembles and their public could handle by the end of the century.

29. Vanessa Schwarz, *Spectacular Realities: Early Mass Culture in Fin-de-Siècle Paris* (Berkeley: University of California Press, 1998).

30. Williams, *Dream Worlds*, 142–45.

31. McCracken, *Culture and Consumption*, 104–17. I agree with McCracken's critique of Williams, who assumes that people consume only out of superficial

motives, and I also think we should consider other cultural meanings inherent in consumption.

32. André Michael Spies makes this point about Opéra audiences as well, arguing that aristocratic subscribers embraced Wagner when they began "to identify with the heroic outsider as a symbol of opposition to the corrupt, vacillating—in short, bourgeois—Third Republic;" see his *Opera, State, and Society in the Third Republic, 1875–1914* (New York: Peter Lang, 1998), 86.

33. Using the press, the industrious scholar can reconstruct programs that are no longer extant. The process is valuable, for which newspaper or magazine published an organization's programs tells us about their public, their relative reputation, and their peer groups.

34. "Historique de la musique de la Garde républicaine," *Le petit poucet,* 25 July 1897, 7.

35. Michael B. Miller argued that department stores did much to give "shape and definition to the very meaning of a bourgeois way of life"; see his *The Bon Marché: Bourgeois Culture and the Department Store, 1869–1920* (Princeton, N.J.: Princeton University Press, 1981), 182. It is not clear, however, that they did much for workers (*ouvriers*). Employees, many of whom were from the lower middle class in the provinces, received fixed salaries and could earn additional commissions on sales in the store. *Ouvriers*—those in the workshops and the women who cut catalogue samples—were paid hourly or daily wages. As part of "the family," employees could receive music lessons; workers, excluded, could not.

36. I am grateful for a small note in the appendix to Miller's *The Bon Marché,* 241, indicating the existence of a "trunk containing concert documents" and to the Bon Marché for permitting me to consult and organize its documents.

37. Mayeur brought both organizations the prestige of the Opéra as well as practical understanding of musical life as author of saxophone method books and opera transcriptions.

38. "Musiques militaires," *Le monde musical,* 15 July 1898, 102.

39. As with new French works, Bon Marché performances of Italian opera sometimes followed premieres in various Parisian theaters. For example, they did fantasies from *Aida* only months after the Opéra premiere in 1880, *Rigoletto* soon after performances there in 1885, and *La traviata* after those of 1886. In *Le Ménestrel,* 10 January 1892, a critic pointed to declining taste for Italian opera in Europe, noting that the number of troupes performing it in Italy as well as elsewhere decreased from twenty-eight in 1883 to nineteen in 1892 (14).

40. McCracken, *Culture and Consumption,* 28.

41. Hans von Bülow, "*Samson et Dalila,*" *La renaissance musicale,* 7 May 1882, 145. This was written after the Hamburg premiere and originally published in *Allgemeine deutsche Musik-Zeitung.*

42. F. Regnier, "Premières représentations. Opéra. *Samson et Dalila.*" *Le journal,* 24 November 1892.

43. Émile Eugène Alix Fournier (1864–97), a pupil of Delibes, won a Deuxième Second Grand Prix de Rome in 1889. Louis Gallet wrote of the libretto of his one-act opera, *Stratonice,* published by Paul Dupont in 1892. It had recently won the Crescent Prize.

44. De Nora, *Music in Everyday Life,* 31.

17

Otto Gombosi's Correspondence at the University of Chicago

Laurence Libin

The year 1939 held great promise for the future of American musicology, for it saw the arrival in the United States of such prominent Central European scholars as Manfred Bukofzer, Alfred Einstein, Erich Hertzmann, Kathi Meyer-Baer, Paul Nettl, Dragan Plamenac, and the harpsichordist Edith Weiss Mann, among other wartime émigrés who helped shape our discipline.[1] One of the most gifted of this 1939 cohort was Ottó János Gombosi (b. Budapest, 23 October 1902; d. Natick, Massachusetts, 17 February 1955), an exceptionally versatile musicologist and brilliant teacher.[2]

Otto Gombosi's scholarship earned respect, even from those who questioned his innovative and controversial methods, while his engaging personality and wholehearted commitment to teaching inspired lasting affection among his students.[3] His legacy includes a substantial body of hitherto overlooked correspondence relevant to the history of American musicology during a crucial phase of its development. I wish to call attention to these sources, comprising dozens of letters and other documents spanning the years 1936–50 preserved in the University of Chicago's Joseph Regenstein Library, Department of Special Collections.

Guided by pack-rat instinct, I had the good fortune to discover this material in 1967, when, as an impecunious University of Chicago graduate student, I tried to salvage objects of value that remained in the university's vacated music building on Woodlawn Avenue at 58th Street (which was scheduled to be demolished). The correspondence turned up in a cardboard box in a closet of the building where Gombosi formerly had his office. Hans Lenneberg, the university's music librarian at the time, confirmed the letters' significance and deposited them in Regenstein Library in two batches, in August and September 1969. Unless otherwise noted, all documents cited below are in the Otto Gombosi Papers, box 1.

The following remarks about Otto Gombosi's life and career provide a context for the correspondence and help sustain the memory of this remarkable scholar, who would have celebrated his one-hundredth birthday in 2002.[4] Otto was born into a Hungarian Jewish family. His father, József, prospered as a wholesale stationer; his mother, Elizabeth, was a pianist, who gave Otto his first music lessons. The eldest of four brothers, Otto was the only one to emigrate. His parents and one of his siblings, György (1904–45), an art historian, perished during World War II; another brother, Endri, was deported to Russia at the end of the war.[5] In an undated (probably 1943) job-application draft, Otto credited his maternal grandfather, the mathematics professor Samuel Bogyó, with inspiring his fascination with numbers, later expressed in his analyses of rhythm and form.

After having studied piano further with Sándor Kovács at the Fodor Conservatory and composition with Leó Weiner and Albert Siklós at Budapest's Royal Academy of Music, in 1921 Otto entered the University of Berlin to pursue musicology and secondarily art history and philosophy.[6] Under Johannes Wolf's tutelage in Berlin, Gombosi received his Ph.D. in 1925 with a style-critical dissertation on Jacob Obrecht, based on Wolf's recently completed edition of Obrecht's works.[7] When the published dissertation evoked no job offers, Gombosi returned to Budapest where, for most of the time from 1926 through 1928, he pursued independent research, reviewed concerts, and became the founding editor of the music magazine *Crescendo.* In summer 1926, however, he took classes in music history with André Pirro in Paris. There, he made the acquaintance of a fellow student, Geneviève Thibault, later Comtesse de Chambure, a founder of the Société de Musique d'Autrefois and a notable collector of old instruments and manuscripts, who became his lifelong friend. Thibault arranged for posthumous publication of Gombosi's best-known work, *Compositione di meser Vincenzo Capirola: Lute-Book (circa 1517).*[8] Gombosi participated in the first International Musicological Society meeting in Vienna (1927) and another in Cambridge, England (1933). There he met his future wife, the Swiss-born violinist Anne (Annie) Tschopp, a performer with the Schola Cantorum Basiliensis; they married in 1937, the year Gombosi converted to Christianity.

The subjects of Gombosi's journalistic and scholarly writings from 1926 to 1928 in Budapest and from 1929 to 1933 as a freelancer in Berlin ranged from Renaissance subjects to the newest compositions of Bartók, whom he admired. His first important music edition, prepared in collaboration with his former Berlin classmate Hans Albrecht, was of sacred works by Thomas Stoltzer (another composer previously investigated by Wolf).[9] Independently, in 1931 Gombosi became a "principal collaborator" with *Acta musicologica,* a position he held until 1954. In 1935 he became a Fellow of the Royal Dutch Musicological Society and also held a fellowship at the Hungarian Historical Institute in Rome, where he studied late medieval liturgical music. His book on the German-Hungarian composer Bálint (Valentin) Bakfark, issued in 1935, reflected his deep interest in sixteenth-century lute and dance repertoire.[10]

Hitler's ascendancy to power no doubt discouraged any hope Gombosi might have had of returning to Berlin, and in 1936, at Anne Tschopp's prompting, he moved to Basel, Anne's home town, where from 1937 to 1939 he lectured as a guest at the University of Basel's Institute of Musicology, a center for early music study and performance involving such proponents as Jacques Handschin, Paul Sacher, and August Wenzinger.[11] For the fourteenth International Art Historical Congress in Basel, Gombosi prepared a choreographic and musical reconstruction of Renaissance court dances, with instrumental performance by the Schola Cantorum under Wenzinger's direction (on 4 September 1936) and program notes, which introduced art historians to various early dance forms.

In 1936 Gombosi seems to have intended to apply for a position in the United States; this is attested by several letters of recommendation written for him in English. His references were Jacques Handschin, a distinguished organist as well as professor of musicology at the University of Basel, who particularly respected Gombosi, Johannes Wolf, Curt Sachs, and Paul Henry Lang.[12] (Significantly, Sachs wrote a separate recommendation for Anne, stating that she "would be a valuable asset to the United States."[13])

Gombosi's next major publication, *Tonarten und Stimmungen der antiken Musik,* a response and extension, based on archaeological evidence, to Sachs's broad studies, appeared in 1939.[14] In this connection, on 28 July 1939 Gustave Reese (then secretary of the American Musicological Society [AMS], associate editor of *The Musical Quarterly,* and Sachs's colleague at New York University) invited Gombosi to speak on ancient Greek music at the International Congress for Musicology that was to be held in New York from 11 to 16 September 1939.[15] Reese's invitation offered $100 toward expenses and help in finding accommodation with an AMS member for two weeks. Reese met Otto and Anne Gombosi when they arrived in New York, and a warm collegial relationship ensued.[16] The Gombosis expected to remain in America for only six or eight weeks before returning to neutral Switzerland. In anticipation of this sojourn, Otto had arranged several excursions, including a trip to Boston's Museum of Fine Arts to see a Greek vase painting of a kitharist, to discuss Greek lyres, and to visit the museum's musical instrument collection with its cataloguer, Nicholas Bessaraboff. He had also asked the museum about lecture opportunities in Boston and was referred to Harvard University's Archibald T. Davison, a contact that later proved invaluable.[17]

Once in New York, eager to advance his and Anne's careers, Gombosi sought further lecture engagements for himself and performances for his wife; Harold Gleason at the Eastman School of Music, Otto Kinkeldey at Cornell University, Edward N. Waters at the Library of Congress, and Carleton Sprague Smith at the New York Public Library responded to his overtures, several of which bore fruit, but no cash.[18] Notably, on 11 October he approached Glenn Haydon of the University of North Carolina at Chapel Hill, who replied that he could not arrange a paid lecture but invited Gombosi to address the Washington-Baltimore Chapter of the American Musicological Society on 4 November.[19] One thing led to another, and in November the archaeologist David M. Robinson invited Gombosi to speak on ancient music at Johns Hopkins University.[20] Also, Reese happily notified Gombosi that Carl Engel had accepted the first of his important writings in English, "The Melody of Pindar's 'Golden Lyre,'" for publication in *The Musical Quarterly*.[21]

Gombosi was an enthusiastic correspondent. In a letter dated 9 November to "Verehrtester Herr Professor" (probably Handschin), Gombosi vividly described his brief experience in the United States. He was charmed by the warm reception he had received: "People, at least professional colleagues, are just simply charming. Overall, I can say nothing against Americans; I have really met only nice people."[22] The "very cheerful" ("recht lustig") congress delighted him with excellent lectures and concerts: "The biggest sensation was the Metropolitan Museum's Cristofori piano, which Sachs has just had restored."[23] Above all, he recognized the potential of the impressive libraries and universities he visited: ". . . in a few decades [America] will offer ideal work opportunities for music historians."[24]

Finding ideal American working conditions was to preoccupy Gombosi for years, because at the end of their intended stay, he and his wife found themselves stranded and nearly broke when their ship was not allowed to depart due to hostilities abroad. As Gombosi plaintively explained to Prof. Jothan Johnson of *Classical Weekly* and the University of Pittsburgh, "I should buy new tickets [for the Italian Line], and that would cost for two persons about 350 dollars. I must confess, that it is too much for me, because I was provided with money for only two months. So I have to stay here and to see how to live."[25] On 10 November the Immigration and Naturalization Service informed Gombosi that he had to pay a "head tax" to extend his temporary visa; fortunately, on 15 November he obtained a $25 advance for his "Pindar" article, making it possible to pay the tax, and his visa was extended until 5 May 1940. The couple moved from their temporary quarters in Brooklyn to Manhattan near Columbia University, where Gombosi gave a lecture probably arranged by Lang.

Worried by the worsening conflict in Europe and realizing that his return might be indefinitely delayed, in the winter Gombosi redoubled his efforts to find employment for the duration of the war. Compounding his anxiety was the impending expiration of his Swiss residency permit (at the end of 1939).[26] Anne considered returning to Switzerland alone, but decided against it. In addition to these problems, Gombosi could obtain no more copies of his *Tonarten,* because the printer, Sutter & Cie., had not been paid and therefore impounded the edition in Rixheim, behind the Maginot Line; a proposal to Scribner's for an English edition led nowhere.[27]

On 22 November 1939 (the same day he wrote to Jothan Johnson), Gombosi appealed for advice from his fellow émigré Alfred Einstein, a

senior scholar hired as guest professor at Smith College. Einstein responded
just two days later, counseling patience—"American mills are like the mills
of God in that they work slowly but hopefully and also surely"[28]—referring him to the Oberlaender Trust, a Philadelphia organization under auspices of the Carl Schurz Memorial Foundation that offered placement assistance to foreign scholars, with which Otto Albrecht, the University of
Pennsylvania's music librarian, was connected. In response to another appeal, Judge Charles Klein of Orphans' Court in Philadelphia suggested that
Gombosi contact Hugo Leichtentritt at Harvard, head of another organization that placed experts in the field of music.[29]

Gombosi also pursued summer teaching opportunities, but neither Warren D. Allen at Stanford nor Archibald Davison at Harvard could honor
his requests to teach upcoming summer school courses.[30] All Otto Kinkeldey
could offer was a place to stay at his house in Ithaca.[31] To remain in the
United States legally and to find regular employment, the Gombosis had to
obtain "good conduct" statements from every country in which they had
lived. According to Lawrence H. Moe, the expense of this documentation
and of other immediate needs was generously borne by the Philadelphia
lawyer and amateur musicologist Henry S. Drinker.[32] On 20 February 1940,
Otto Albrecht, president of the newly formed Philadelphia chapter of the
AMS, invited Gombosi to speak on the music of Crete and Mycenae at the
chapter's first meeting; Drinker's wife, Sophie, a feminist music historian
and secretary of the chapter, provided hospitality at their home where the
meeting was held, paid the Gombosis' round-trip fare, and eagerly questioned Otto about "girl choirs of ancient Greece."[33]

In New York, the Gombosis met Otto K. Rinderspacher, an early music
performer based in the Midwest. In several subsequent letters written from
Kansas, Iowa, and Nebraska, Rinderspacher insistently sought a closer
connection with the Gombosis; for example, he proposed forming an ensemble with Anne, although apparently nothing materialized.[34] Notes scattered among the Gombosi correspondence indicate, however, that about
this time Anne performed in New York with the harpsichordist Ralph
Kirkpatrick, and the Gombosis counted the harpsichordists Alice Ehlers,
Yella Pessl, and Blanche Winogren, the conductor Antal Dorati, the pianist
Andor Földes, the violinists Yehudi Menuhin and Feri Roth, the violinist
and composer Tibor Serly, the Trapp family, and many other professional
musicians among their friends.

Within a few months of his arrival, Gombosi had sized up the current
state of American musicology and thought he knew where it was headed
and how he could fit in. While insisting that performers and audiences
should benefit from musicological research, he favored separating gradu-
ate-level music-history programs from the hegemony of music departments,
in which, he felt, musicology too often formed an insignificant appendage
to practical studies. Not surprisingly considering his interest in classical

antiquity, he regarded music history rather as a subdiscipline within the history of culture and ideas; here, he believed his field would receive its due. He made this view explicit in a letter, introducing himself to Prof. Alice M. Baldwin of Duke University's history department:

> History of Music as an academic discipline is in an intermediate stage in this country nowadays. Some of the leading Universities (Harvard, Yale, Cornell, Columbia, Princeton, North Carolina, Wisconsin, Smith College) have fully acknowledged Musicology. At Cornell and Yale[,] Musicology has obtained the right place within the Department of History, Languages, and Philosophy, and not, as mostly has happened, within the Music Department. The further development certainly will promote the acknowledge[ment] of this common field of History and Music. Universities claiming for [themselves] a leading role will be forced to introduce Musicology, as they already have introduced History of Art and related subjects. Within a short time, Duke University also will have to face this problem. It seems to me, however[,] that the situation at Duke University will be much more favorable than at many other places, because there is no danger that Musicology will be only a more or less unsignificant [*sic*] part of the Music Department, and because you as a historian will be able to realize the right place and importance of this historical discipline rather than [as] people in charge of musical affairs at other Universities do. I think you will agree with me that an [*sic*] University with an excellent Department of History would need and could use somebody who would be able to teach competently this branch of History of Human Culture."[35]

With this somewhat awkward letter he enclosed his curriculum vitae and an impressive list of references that included, in addition to ten musicologists, the archaeologist David Robinson, the classicist Caspar Kraemer, Jr., of New York University, and his friend, the Hungarian "music ethnologist" George Herzog of Columbia University's anthropology department (another devotee of Bartók).

Searching for work and suffering from rheumatism aggravated by bad weather, Gombosi, nonetheless, continued writing and sending proposals to publishers. On 19 April 1940, music editor Howard Taubman accepted his article, "The Art of the Hungarian Composer Bartok" for publication in *The New York Times*. But other endeavors, such as a proposed book on Renaissance dance, met with rejection. His thoughts about these rejections are reflected in his letter to the authors' agent Frances Pindyck: "I am not surprised by the reluctant attitude of the publishers; I have not expected anything else. It is a glorious feeling and a great consolation to be a part or better one of the smallest objects of the world disaster. I try, however, to make the best out of it."[36]

In spring 1940, while awaiting an additional six-month visa extension, the Gombosis toured the Midwest pursuing employment leads furnished by the Oberlaender Trust. Writing to a friend "Frank" at Bryn Mawr before the trip, Otto was pessimistic about its outcome, but admitted that prospects on the East Coast were equally dim: "Worst of all is that the big colleges, for example around Philadelphia, are mostly Quaker institutions and therefore somewhat anti-musically inclined."[37] The trip to the Midwest was unfruitful, and the couple left the University of Chicago and Northwestern University empty-handed, as Anne told Otto Rinderspacher, but they had not wasted their time in Chicago.[38] Gombosi had been captivated by the Capirola lute manuscript at the Newberry Library, and Anne met the harpsichordist Gavin Williamson, with whom she planned some performances. The psychologist Carl Seashore welcomed the couple at the University of Iowa; Anne was well received at Grinnell College; and Central College in Pella, Iowa, actually offered Otto a job, with the Oberlaender Trust to fund his full salary. By the time Central College formalized its offer in July, however, Grinnell College had hired Anne, and Otto was exploring a promising opportunity at the University of Washington.

Back in New York before his wife's appointment was confirmed, Gombosi wrote a glum letter to Otto Kinkeldey about their Midwestern experience:

> It was very interesting and it seems that something may be worked out for us both, although some of our hopes died before being born. We have the intention to take anything, because we have no other choice. . . . We are in a terrible mood right now. The situation in Hungary and in Switzerland is really too bad, and we have our families there. By the way, my whole material, collected in nearly twenty years, is in our apartment in Basel. I fear it is lost for ever.[39]

At the same time, Gombosi reluctantly asked Charles Klein for a personal loan. Klein demurred, but put Gombosi in touch with the Mastbaum Loan System in Philadelphia, a predominantly Jewish, non-profit corporation that (on 4 June) advanced him $300, the maximum allowed.[40] Gombosi proferred Curt Sachs's daughter Judith, a librarian at Swarthmore College, as a reference, and Klein and Henry Drinker guaranteed the loan.

At the suggestion of Gustave Reese, Gombosi contacted the University of Washington's music department head, Carl P. Wood, about an opening there.[41] Wood's blunt response reveals both the obstacles facing many foreign scholars and the attitude of some American academics with whom they competed for scarce jobs. Wood inquired of Reese:

> What is the policy of the Oberlander [sic] Trust with respect to the renewal of contract? Would they expect a university to assume the salary of a man originally subsidized by them, or would they spread their support over two or more years? Our administration would not wish to be obligated to continue such an appointment.
>
> My other question as you may have guessed has to do with race. We already have some Jewish and other "refugees" on our general faculty, and the administration will perhaps feel that it has gone far enough in this direction for the present. Naturally the music faculty has its share of qualms.[42]

Reese, who was Jewish, answered Wood coolly:

> Dr. Gombosi is not a refugee. He came to this country on invitation of the American Musicological Society . . . [which] thanks to a grant from the Carnegie Corporation, was able to contribute towards his expenses. The Society was anxious to have a delegate from Hungary, and Dr. Gombosi is doubtless the most distinguished musicologist that country has at present. The other questions will have to be answered by Dr. Gombosi himself .[43]

Remarkably, Gombosi never considered himself a target of anti-Semitism, according to his son Peter. Still, he hastened to assure Wood that he and his wife were Presbyterians.[44]

On 2 August 1940, the University of Washington finally appointed Gombosi Lecturer in Music. He accepted a salary of $1500 for the academic year 1940–41 (half of Bartók's salary at Columbia), with $600 coming from the Oberlaender Trust.[45] Yet the issue of immigration and naturalization remained unresolved, since to obtain immigrant status the Gombosis would have had to leave the country and reenter, at considerable personal expense. On 18 August Gombosi requested a letter of recommendation from Kinkeldey (an American by birth), saying, ". . . we are in a mouse trap and need your friendly help very badly."[46] The following day he cabled Senator Louis B. Schwellenbach in Washington, D.C.: "Am here on visitor's visa. Must leave country and return. Have all necessary papers but badly need advice."[47] Soon thereafter, Gombosi thanked Schwellenbach for making it possible to immigrate from nearby Canada rather than Cuba,[48] and the couple reentered the U.S. from Victoria, B.C., on 11 October 1940. At the same time, Gombosi wrote a long overdue letter to Johannes Wolf, bringing Wolf up to date on his activities and conveying reservations about the challenge ahead: "Work in Seattle will be a hard slog, without a reasonably equipped library . . . and right now I don't know how the human aspect will be."[49] Seattle surely represented a step down after Berlin and Basel, but at age 38 Gombosi was glad to have his first regular faculty appointment.

Once settled in his new position, Gombosi formulated ambitious plans. His main responsibilities were to build up the music library and the graduate musicology program, and to this end he wanted to start a collegium musicum as a means of drawing public attention and funding to his department. Soon he became involved with organizing a Northwest chapter of the AMS—on 16 December 1940 Reese notified him of his election to AMS membership—and he proposed to Carl Engel that the firm of G. Schirmer should initiate a new quarterly journal for essays longer than those in *The Musical Quarterly,* focusing on music's place in the history of culture and ideas.[50] Curt Sachs endorsed Gombosi's proposal in principle and insisted that the budget should include authors' honoraria; he pointed out that, in these hard times, it was difficult to interest students in pursuing research just for fun.[51]

Since Anne had already accepted Grinnell College's offer to teach violin for the school year 1940–41, the couple separated temporarily. In September 1940 while in Grinnell visiting Anne, Otto wrote to the Newberry Library requesting a microfilm of the Capirola manuscript in order to prepare a transcription that he proposed to publish in place of the Newberry Library's planned facsimile; this project, like many that he undertook, proved more complicated than he anticipated and occupied him on and off for years.[52]

Reunited in Seattle, where their first son, Peter, was born in December 1941, the new parents befriended Lawrence Moe, a young musicologist who often stayed at their home and baby-sat; Gombosi set Moe on the path to his Harvard doctorate and became his main thesis advisor.[53] Imogene Horsley, Paul J. Revitt, and John Milton Ward stood out among Gombosi's Seattle graduate students, and Gombosi saved cordial letters from Revitt and Ward relating their wartime experiences; Revitt, a draftee, wrote from boot camp in Florida that he had brought along Sachs's *History of Musical Instruments*.[54]

During this period Gombosi immersed himself in American folk and popular music; he analyzed all of Stephen Foster's songs and many works by lesser composers of the Civil War era.[55] His comprehensive knowledge and appreciation of this homespun repertory may reflect the folkloristic influence of Bartók and Kodály. (Possibly it was Gombosi who prompted the University of Washington to offer Bartók a position as a researcher of American Indian music. Bartók declined the offer, but letters from Bartók's manager, Andrew Schulhof at Boosey & Hawkes in New York, show Gombosi acting on Bartók's behalf.) In November 1940 Schulhof asked Gombosi, "Would it not be advisable at this time to write a book about Bartok? You would really be the right man for this."[56] And in December, regarding Bartók's engagement, Schulhof wrote:

> As I could not set a fee lower than two hundred and fifty dollars, I spoke to Mr. Bartok, and he was willing to do, for the same amount of money, not only a recital on March 4th, but also a lecture on March 3rd [1941]. . . . Mr. Bartok was very pleased because he will be in Seattle for the weekend previous . . . and could be with you. I am glad that this affair is settled and I hope you will have time to talk over with Mr. Bartok your opinion and suggestions regarding the book which you want to write about him. . . . Perhaps it would be possible to get Bartok as a lecturer and teacher for advanced piano students?[57]

Gombosi's insightful and eloquent memorial to Bartók, who was his son's godfather, reveals a close spiritual affinity; clearly, Bartók's tribulations struck a sympathetic chord in the younger man.[58]

Another letter from this time, from the Gombosis' friend Friede F. Rothe, also concerns Bartók:

> I had an interview with Schönberg when he came here to conduct his Pierrot Lunaire. He told me that he admires Bartok very much and is only sorry that in all these years they have never met. I told this to Bartok and he said he was very sorry too, and hoped on his way west this might at last come to pass, seeing that somehow Budapest, Vienna and Berlin were divergent places. . . . Annie tells me you have at one time made an analysis of [Bartók's *Music for Strings, Percussion and Celeste*]. I would be very grateful if you could send it to me immediately airmail, as I need it for the program notes which I am writing for the New School concerts."[59]

Even as he craved repose, Gombosi became restless in Seattle and began seeking a different position. A letter (from May 1941) from Anne H. Webb, supervisor of the extension division of the Boston Museum of Fine Arts, thanked Gombosi for

> the contribution for our program . . . . Indeed, I am giving it early today to Miss Laura Taylor [a specialist in Byzantine music at the New England Conservatory], who would like to see you come to Boston in some university capacity . . . she was very much interested to have your bibliography, suggesting that she would like to take it to Dumbarton Oaks . . . . You asked about Boston University. Miss Taylor tells me that not one but two people in the Department of Music have passed on there within the past year. It seems to me that it would be quite worth your while to write to President Daniel L. Marsh, giving him such references as you think desirable. I met Professor [Henri] Gregoire in New York recently and he spoke enthusiastically about your work. . . . If you would care to have him call me, I should also be glad to tell him of your help to us.[60]

Following Webb's suggestion, at the end of May Gombosi wrote to Daniel Marsh, explaining that his "research [was] suffering from lack of adequate library facilities."[61] No reply survives, and a month later he contacted the Clark-Brewer Teachers Agency in Chicago, seeking any sort of music teaching job.[62]

Throughout this period Gombosi tried to stay in touch with his family in Budapest, although a letter he wrote to them in November 1941 was returned because mail service to Hungary had been suspended. Some contact must have been maintained, however, because in March 1942, through the Red Cross, Gombosi received his father's congratulations on his son Peter's birth. Later that year, communication with family evidently ceased for a long time, perhaps until 3 December 1945, when a cable from his brother Geza starkly informed him, "PARENTS GEORGE DISAPPEARED ANDY [Endri] BLANCHE MARY GEZA ELIZABETH JOHNES KATHERINE GEORGES SECOND WIFE VERA WITH HER DAUGHTER ANNE ARE ALLRIGHT LETTER FOLLOWS SEND MONEY."

Many letters in Hungarian followed, one of them enclosing his father's funeral notice from 1944.[63]

On 21 March 1942, the University of Washington reappointed Gombosi for the coming summer term at a salary of $250, but in June he was unexpectedly dropped from the faculty for the next fall. He wrote urgently to Frederic B. Stiven at the University of Illinois at Urbana:

> The declaration of war between the U.S. and Hungary puts me in a strange situation. Both my wife and I applied for citizenship as soon as it was possible, and got our first papers. Our son, of course, is an American citizen. But technically, we are still Hungarian citizens and thus shall be classified as enemy aliens, facing eventual evacuation from the west Coast. . . . For the present, we still have the choice of leaving voluntarily ~~instead of being put into a concentration camp~~. During the past two years, I have built up a nice class here. I have planned to stay here, unless our plans in Urbana could be realized. But the situation has changed now. I am looking for an emergency solution that would enable me to stay with my work and make a living for my family. I wonder whether you would see any possibility for me in Urbana. I do not mean a work restricted to musicology or to graduate study. Perhaps you have lost or are going to loose [sic] some of your younger faculty members; I would be glad to teach history of music, or appreciation or harmony classes as well.[64]

At the same time, Gombosi struggled to retain his place at the university. In July 1942 he wrote to Wilbur K. Thomas, secretary of the Oberlaender Trust:

> In spite [of] the most urgent recommendation of the School of Music and the Dean of the Graduate School, the President made up his mind to discontinue the work in musicology. Dean Padelford told me that he had a two hours fight with the President and did not succeed in convincing him that the work I was doing was not "creative art" and that his theory regarding "rotating influences in creative art" could hardly be applied to this case. Dr. Sieg, our president, is a physicist, has very little understanding for things outside his field and is one of the most stubborn men I ever have met.
>
> Of course, the war created a very difficult situation here; many departments lost several members and not one is going to be replaced. But the School of Music has not lost any member yet and thus the president has refused to continue the appointment of the two temporary teachers. This means, of course, that the graduate work will be stopped entirely. I am sorry for the work I have put into these courses; I feel it was a good beginning. I finished Summer School yesterday and will work, unofficially, with the four students who want to take their degrees this quarter.
>
> I do not know yet what I am going to do next year. It is very late for looking for another job. I have contacted everybody in the field but I am not very hopeful. It was of course not very fair to delay the decision until the middle of June. But I cannot help it. It seems the only job I could get in Seattle would be some laborer's job and I am going to take it no matter what it will be.[65]

Thomas replied sympathetically, saying that he had received an inquiry from the University of Tampa but adding:

> However, I believe that unless you get something very good, that promises permanency and an adequate income for your family, you will be better off to stay in Seattle. Mrs. Gombosi is getting a real start and I believe that in time you will be able to build up enough private work until you can add materially to your income. It is better to be rooted than to be moving around constantly. You perhaps know that Dr. [Willi] Apel was dropped from Harward [*sic*], but they have stayed on and have really found a place for themselves in a private school. . . . I believe that you and Mrs. Gombosi have a real contribution to make to the cultural life of America—and the west is the place to make it.[66]

However unfair it seemed, Gombosi's dismissal was part of a general contraction; as Harold Gleason told Gombosi, "A large part of [Eastman's] theory work will be eliminated in favor of mathematics, physics, etc."[67] Between August and October 1942, Gombosi corresponded with Miss Roxy Grove of Baylor University in Waco, Texas, who considered hiring both Otto and Anne, but because of the university's strict behavior codes, required assurances about their smoking and drinking habits. This and other dismal efforts to acquire a new position failed, despite friendly assistance from several colleagues. Howard Nostrand, one of Gombosi's associates in Seattle, sent Gombosi a copy of a letter he had received from Douglas Moore at Columbia University, saying in part:

> I have discussed the matter of helping Gombosi with Paul Lang and he, who knows the field much better than I, is very pessimistic. Naturally at this time there is less opportunity for graduate work everywhere. However, he is going to take up the matter with Gustave Reese and see if there is anything he can suggest. Mr. Lang has a high opinion of Gombosi's importance as a scholar.[68]

In the event, Gombosi's fear of internment proved unfounded. He first took a job tarring roofs, then moved up to running newsboys for the Seattle *Star*. (Lawrence Moe was "always astounded at the good grace with which he handled the job."[69]) At least these experiences enhanced his command of colloquial English; Reese complimented him on his "remarkable improvement."[70] Fortunately, Anne was able to earn some money as an orchestral violinist in Takoma, as first violinist of the Seattle String Quartet, and from 1942 as an instrumental teacher and chamber music coach at the Cornish School of Music and Art and at the University of Washington's summer school. In addition, she directed an "all-girl" orchestra on a local radio program. Although their own resources were scant, especially after the birth of their second child, Elizabeth Claire Christiana, in 1943, the Gombosis sent aid packages to Johannes Wolf in Germany and to friends in Hungary.[71]

The tedious job hunt continued. Southern Methodist University inquired about hiring Otto and Anne in June 1943, but no offer resulted. In July 1944 Paul Henry Lang informed Gombosi of an opening for a music critic at the Louisville (Kentucky) *Courier-Journal,* and Edward Lowinsky told him about possibilities at Converse College and Fisk University, to no avail.[72] An undated (probably 1943) draft of a letter on University of Washington stationery shows Gombosi trying other tacks. In this letter he pointed out to the unnamed recipient that he was

> interested in other musicological fields such as psychology of music, folklore, and acoustics. I am perfectly willing to descend from the orphic sphere of musicology . . . and teach theoretical subjects . . . but I feel I am somewhat incompetent in teaching subjects [that] demand a touch of creative spirit, such as orchestration or composition.

Regarding his willingness to teach theory, Gombosi wrote to Ernest Bacon at Converse College, "I do not see any hard and fast rule dividing theory and musicology. After all, our present theory is very much *historic* theory."[73] Here he disagreed with Sachs, who had stated flatly in 1940 that "The theory of music is not in the domain of musicologists."[74]

Disappointments notwithstanding, Gombosi remained active professionally. Anne's affiliation with the Cornish School paid off in a small way when Eleanor King offered Otto $25 to speak on Renaissance dance in a lecture series that also featured the leading choreographers Katharine Dunham and Anthony Tudor.[75] In October 1943 Reese asked Gombosi to contribute a chapter on Hungary to his *Music in the Renaissance* (1954)[76]—a task that took Gombosi years to complete, occasioning many plaintive reminders from Reese—and in November 1943 Gombosi was invited to join the American Association for the Advancement of Science.[77] On 4 July 1944, Walter H. Rubsamen asked him to participate in a four-day "Institute on Music in Contemporary Life" at UCLA;[78] Gombosi addressed a session on music libraries, offering "Some ideas regarding the musical and musicological training of music librarians," and also participated in a forum devoted to "Musicology, its contributions and influence."

In Seattle on 19 July 1946 the Gombosis became naturalized citizens, and at last Fortuna seemed to smile on them. After a long break from teaching, through the American College Bureau placement service Gombosi secured a position as assistant professor in the powerful department of literature and fine arts at Michigan State College in East Lansing, where the younger Berlin-trained musicologist Hans Nathan was already teaching; John Ward joined them on the faculty in 1947 and Milton Steinhardt in 1948.[79] Gombosi had applied for the Michigan position in part because he wanted to move closer to the University of Michigan's library at Ann Arbor.[80] Although the institution initially passed him over in favor of Lazlo

J. Hetenyi,[81] he finally landed the job, although Anne and their children had to remain in Seattle for the first school year. Gombosi helped to organize an AMS Midwest chapter meeting at Michigan State in May 1947; the harpsichord builder John Challis was among those who heard Gombosi speak on that occasion.[82] (Another speaker was his older friend from Budapest, the renowned piano pedagogue Margit Varró, then living near the University of Chicago.[83])

In Michigan Gombosi made slow progress on his project with the Capirola manuscript, but he discussed it before the American Musicological Society in Boston on 30 December 1947.[84] The previous April he had again proposed his edition of the manuscript to Stanley Pargellis of the Newberry Library; unfortunately this correspondence was misplaced and his proposal was accepted only on 20 September. He could not immediately complete the work, however, for, as he explained to Pargellis: "my correspondence and notes are packed away and stored with different friends."[85]

By September 1947 Gombosi was again exploring other teaching prospects, and by December he had been asked to teach summer school the following year at the University of Chicago. In April 1948, however, he won a Guggenheim Fellowship to study "popular patterns of Renaissance music and of their tradition in England and America from Elizabethan times to the present." An undated draft of his Guggenheim application specifies his intent to follow the thread of tradition connecting early 16th-century Italian court music to blues and boogie-woogie. Before taking up the fellowship Gombosi found time to judge the annual Mu Phi Epsilon musicological research contest, and he agreed to do the same in 1949.

Few letters from Gombosi's fellowship period survive in the Regenstein Library, but one concerning his Bartók book, from Betty Randolph Bean at Boosey & Hawkes, refers to his poor state of health.[86] Nevertheless, he traveled widely with his growing family (a third child, Martin George, had been born in Basel), among other places to London where he saw his cousin Györgyi, a dance and exercise instructor and a composer.[87] In summer 1949 he spoke on Greek music theory at the fourth congress of the International Musicological Society in Basel[88] and lectured in Bern; on 29 August, S. Heinimann of the University of Bern philosophy faculty thanked him for his "... work on Bern's currently so arid soil" ("Arbeit auf dem gegenwärtig so trockenen Berner Boden").[89]

While in Aeschi and after his return to the United States, Gombosi corresponded at length with Armen Carapetyan, founder in 1945 of the American Institute of Musicology, concerning the outrage felt by some musicologists in America, notably Bukofzer and Lang, over Carapetyan's professional collaboration with scholars tainted by evil actions and associations during the war, and over his perceived high-handed organization of his so-called American institute, which was based in Italy.[90] In the midst of this bitter and protracted controversy, Gombosi, who was admired by colleagues on both sides, played a conciliatory role. His frank but sympathetic letters to Carapetyan and Lang—whom he did not hesitate to scold—deserve a separate article, but extracts from a long, handwritten letter to Carapetyan convey Gombosi's straightforward tone:

> I am a politician to an even smaller degree than you. My wife is certainly right in thinking that in such matters I am an outright naif. But, perhaps even because of this naiveté, I often see things in simple contours and get to the truth by a short-cut. I am so much outside the closely knit musicological machine that my knowl-edge of details is equal to zero. . . . There are only two points in your letter which I would like to take exception to. One is the question of politics. You say, in the case [of Guillaume] de Van [born William Devan in Memphis, Tennessee; chief of music collections at the Bibliothèque Nationale during the Vichy government] it was his character, rather than his political views that should have warned you. May be so. But if politics becomes a question of character, you cannot lightly dismiss it. This is the salient point. Now, if you have no nose to smell a rat—just as I have not—, a little more precaution would be in your best interest. . . . my naïve view of this whole question is this: since people are touchy—and for good reasons—, and since you do not want to mix into politics, why don't you have a small group of let us say three people, if possible of the older generation, who could be of help to you in screening? It is no use running up against a wall of ill-will, if it can be avoided in a simple way. . . . [Secondly,] there is a general misconception in the minds of European scholars about the character, the aims and the scope of the Institute, and also about your role. The latter point is not without importance in this world of ours where nearly everybody is fighting like mad for more influence and for more pies to stick their fingers into. . . . Yet I am afraid the real seat of all the trouble, of this 'Sturm in einem Wasserglas' is to be sought much deeper. . . . In your earlier statements people resented the 'totalitar-ian' approach; perhaps it would have been wiser to announce your publication plans as you went along. People had the feeling that you, in a way, expropriated a few centuries, and nobody knew that you were seeking the collaboration of people who had been working in the field for many years. This was the source of much animosity. . . . You know that I do not claim to have discovered the stone of wisdom and that I do not seek power or influence. I have my work and my plans are laid out for years. But I am deeply interested in your undertaking, for both selfish and unselfish reasons. . . . As to your kind suggestion of a short trip to Florence: we would be glad to accept it. What we would like, however, is the assurance, that you do not consider it essential to keep up the royal and tri-royal style. As a simple university teacher, I belong to the working class and I am not used to courtly etiquette.[91]

In fall 1949 Gombosi became assistant professor at the University of Chicago, and almost at once (25 October) he was approached by Paul M. Oberg, head of the University of Minnesota's music department, regarding an anticipated vacancy there. Having at last found a suitable situation for himself and his family, for once Gombosi did not need the job. Hyde Park, the university's immediate neighborhood, had an eclectic, if fragmented, musical tradition thanks to the activities there of such notables as Henry Clay Work, Arnold Dolmetsch, the harpsichord duo of Philip Manuel and Gavin Williamson, Margit Varró, and Arnold Schoenberg; thus, Gombosi's interests in nineteenth-century American popular song, early music performance, pedagogy, and modern composition were not out of place.[92] His music department colleagues included Grosvenor Cooper, Scott Goldthwaite, Siegmund Levarie, and Howard Talley; among his graduate students were Leonard B. Meyer (a Ph.D. candidate and teaching assistant) and Leo Treitler. Gombosi's most significant publication during this brief but fertile period dealt with Machaut;[93] other projects he had underway included the Capirola edition and the as yet (and never to be) completed book about Bartók. According to Meyer, Gombosi sought to elucidate durational relationships in Bartók's music, and perhaps his analyses of Obrecht and Machaut shaped his ideas in this respect.[94]

Aaron Asher, who audited one of Gombosi's classes at the University of Chicago, recalls his teacher's having shown him a small copybook that had belonged to Bartók and that contained pencil sketches for the *Concerto for Orchestra,* as well as bird songs that Bartók had notated in Asheville, North Carolina, during winter 1943–44.[95] László Somfai believes that Asher saw the so-called Turkish fieldbook (now number 80FSS1) in the private archives of Peter Bartók in Homosassa, Florida, and at one time lent to Gombosi from the composer's estate;[96](apparently the bird songs were in a separate notebook).[97] No reliable documentation of these loans seems to survive, but Gombosi obviously considered Bartók's manuscripts to be no less worthy of serious study than were the extant primary sources of Renaissance music.

The Chicago years were typically unsettled, with the family having to move five times in seven months;[98] furthermore, Gombosi was being dunned by the IRS for back taxes from 1946. On 13 September 1949, Isabel Pope wrote to him on behalf of Adolfo Salazar in Mexico City, requesting a copy of the English translation of *Tonarten,* which Pope had proposed to Harvard University Press for publication; she was under the impression that the translation existed in manuscript.[99] The issue of the sequestered copies of *Tonarten* still had not been resolved, with Sutter & Cie. holding out for payment and threatening otherwise to destroy the books. Gombosi's Danish publisher spelled out his choice: either pay the printer, or let them dispose of the books and undertake with the publisher, Munksgaard, to issue a photographic reprint with corrections; he chose the latter course.[100]

During winter 1949–50 Gombosi stayed in close touch with Lang (who had succeeded Reese at G. Schirmer after Reese had moved to Carl Fischer) over other publication projects including the Bartók book, and W. W. Norton paid him $200 for his "very useful labors on the [Oliver] Strunk manuscript, *Source Readings in Music History.*"[101] Antal Dorati, another former student of Leó Weiner's, invited Gombosi to a concert by the Minneapolis Symphony Orchestra in January, featuring Bartók's *Concerto for Orchestra,* and Donald J. Grout, then editor of *JAMS,* sought his advice concerning the Carapetyan affair. Meanwhile he nearly finished editing the Capirola study, having received Carapetyan's encouraging offer of assistance.[102]

For the moment Gombosi seemed optimistic. Carapetyan told him, "For your desire of making Chicago the 'damned best graduate institute' you have at all events only my damned best wishes and hopes. I think that you ought to be able to realize it—and God knows the country needs it."[103] Gombosi wrote back, "Life around here is becoming worth living. We bought a house and shall be moving at the end of May. In the meantime I took my books out of storage and I hope to . . . submit something to you regarding the Ghizeghem-Frottola plan very soon."[104]

Gombosi seemed inclined to stay in Chicago, but on 29 June 1951 he accepted an unanticipated and irresistible offer; he wrote excitedly to Ward that day, "We are moving again! This time to Cambridge. Harvard made a very nice offer, full professorship and so [on],—and Chicago could not match it. I just accepted this morning."[105] A day earlier, Gombosi had informed Gustave Reese: "I want you to be the first to know: from Oct. 1 on I shall be at Harvard. I got a very nice offer, full professorship and everything, out of a blue sky."[106]

Markedly informal in manners and dress and disdainful of academic snobbery, Gombosi was hardly the image of an Ivy League gentleman as represented by, say, Randall Thompson. By all reports, Thompson openly disliked Gombosi, who, ironically, filled the slot vacated at Harvard when Thompson became that university's first Walter B. Rosen Professor. The family's move to the Boston area opened many opportunities for Anne, a versatile performer and a formidable early music specialist in her own right. (Anne had been closely involved since 1929 with the conductor Paul Sacher through his Basler Kammerorchester and had played and taught historical bowed instruments with the Schola Cantorum Basiliensis from its founding by Sacher and August Wenzinger in 1933 until her marriage.)[107]

Resuming her career in the Boston area, Anne played with the harpsichordist Erwin Bodky and his Cambridge Collegium Musicum and collaborated with Narcissa Williamson, keeper of musical instruments at the Museum of Fine Arts, and advisors, including Melville Smith (director of the Longy School of Music) and Leo Schrade, in organizing the Boston Camerata.[108] From 1959 to 1974 Anne directed the All-Newton Music School, an important suburban cultural resource.

In his new position at Harvard, initially as Visiting Lecturer, Gombosi "hit the ground running." He delivered a paper titled "The Beginnings of Renaissance Music" to the New England AMS chapter on 26 November 1951, participated in a conference on "Music in Contemporary American Civilization" held at the Library of Congress under auspices of the American Council of Learned Societies Committee on Musicology on 13–14 December, took part in an AMS symposium on "Principles of Editing and Transcribing Music before 1700" at Eastman on 27 December, and the following day was installed as vice-president of the AMS, whose Council he had joined in 1950 during the presidency of Curt Sachs.

Gombosi quickly won praise from Tillman Merritt, his department chairman, "for having been of the 'greatest help' in the 'direction of a peak load of work of graduates,'" and in accord with expectations he was appointed full professor in spring 1952.[109] His Harvard and Radcliffe students included some of the most successful musicologists and teachers of the next generation, from Howard Mayer Brown (who wrote his senior honors thesis on Bartók's string quartets and later played with the Boston Camerata) to Victor Fell Yellin, and including Bathia Churgin, Frank D'Accone, Victoria Glaser, James Haar, Daniel Heartz (another Camerata performer), Imogene Horsley, David G. Hughes, Owen Jander, Lawrence Moe, Claude Palisca, H. Colin Slim, Miloš Velimirović, and Ivan Waldbauer (son of the Hungarian violinist and Bartók proponent Imre Waldbauer); the composers Billy Jim Layton and Claudio Spies likewise took his classes.

Heartz, who regarded Gombosi's teaching as "exuberant and inspiring and without which I never would have done well," dedicated a publication to his memory.[110] Churgin says, "It was Gombosi's course in the history of Western music—which just managed to get up to 1600—that inspired me to go into musicology. He was not only a brilliant lecturer but music was always the focus, not just reading about it."[111] Victoria Glaser recalls that Gombosi's stimulating teaching continued after class at a nearby doughnut shop, where every week or two he joined a group of his students for informal discussion;[112] he had done the same, over beer, in Seattle and Chicago. Frank D'Accone remembers ". . . going to his office hours, often as lunch was approaching, and one time as he pulled out a sandwich he offered me a bite without even thinking twice."[113]

Victor Fell Yellin was also "bowled over" by Gombosi:

> The first classes he gave were virtuoso performances. Everything he said came directly from his memory, history, theory, anecdotes, personal and otherwise. He was absolutely without guile or political sophistication. There were no topics about which he had no specific knowledge. He had studied everything and experienced everything musical. . . . When people used to complain about the language examinations all graduate students used to face, he would come back with [t]he riposte that after the fifth *all* languages were easy. Easy for a Hungarian to say!"[114]

Frank D'Accone concurs:

> I remember Gombosi as a very simpatico person, with no pretenses, who seemed to like his students, all of them, including the untutored first-year ones . . . . [I]n

the one course in Middle Ages that I managed to have with him, he was so full of information—and so digressive—that we never got much beyond the Notre Dame School. But who noticed or cared, he was so brilliant.[115]

His students remember him as charming, kind, amusing, and generous as well as intellectually exciting, but personal troubles dogged him and no doubt contributed to his restlessness. Whether Gombosi would have remained at Harvard or, following a pattern of frequent moves, would have sought yet another position cannot be known, but according to his son Peter, by 1955 the thought of returning to Europe had crossed his mind.[116] According to Peter, the loss of family and homeland left his father "tortured in spirit"; he never disclosed his Jewish ancestry to his children, perhaps out of fear of future victimization, and he detested military authority.

In a touching obituary, Curt Sachs alluded to his former student's "often militant attitude" and his sometimes difficult temperament: "Often he crossed swords with opponents . . . he was never inclined to accept without the closest examination other men's thoughts, opinions, or interpretations, even when he himself had to offer not facts but interpretations of his own."[117] Indeed, Sachs had sparred with Gombosi over the *ballo* and *bassadanza*,[118] yet Sachs warmly endorsed Gombosi's ideas on the architectonic quality of Machaut's Mass.[119]

Yellin remarks further that Gombosi "demonstrated that musicology could be an exciting field, that even with the advent of 'scientific' standards of credibility there was still a lot of received opinion based upon ignorance, prejudice, and sloth to be cleared away. One can easily see how such a man could be a thorn in many sides."[120]

Gombosi might have been describing himself when he characterized his revered teacher Johannes Wolf as a "non-conformist."[121] Apparently his unconventional teaching style (for example, his dislike of examinations and grades), his provocative arguments and tart criticisms, not to mention his intimacy with students, antagonized some of his less broadminded peers.[122]

But he labored under other stresses, too, including illness and domestic disruption. Explaining his absence from the 1952 IMS meeting in Utrecht, he wrote to Thurston Dart: "on the train to Chicago I was taken by a heart attack and spent most of the time flat on my back. I don't know what I would have done had the silly thing happened in Europe."[123] In January 1953 he wrote to Daniel Heartz: "I am running out of time, since at present I am cook, nursemaid, cleaning woman, etc., in addition to my *sinecura* at Harvard. My wife had to take off for a while and get a good rest with some medical attention."[124] Otto himself took medical leave in fall 1953, but suffered a fourth heart attack, during class, in June 1954. That summer his marriage fell apart, and one day after he obtained a divorce in Reno, Nevada, he wedded his Radcliffe student Marilyn Purnell; the Reno divorce and remarriage were not recognized outside Nevada, however, and occasioned a minor scandal in Boston. Gombosi died before his and Marilyn's son was born.

Gombosi's Harvard *Nachlass,* now in the Eda Kuhn Loeb Music Library, consists mainly of research notes, charts, transcriptions, bibliographic references, and related working materials. Other notes, drafts, and letters remain in the possession of Gombosi's eldest and youngest sons and some of his students. Moe remembers that Gombosi avoided accumulating things, keeping only what he needed; Moe attaches no special significance to Gombosi's abandoning the letters in Chicago.[125] It is hard to imagine that Gombosi did not miss them later, particularly those from his family; nevertheless, he did not recover them when he returned to Chicago for Leonard Meyer's doctoral examination in 1954.

Despite his private insecurities, in his scholarship, teaching, and other professional activities, Otto Gombosi displayed great confidence and resourcefulness. His personal troubles put the annoying politics of musicology into perspective. Cut off for a decade from European libraries and archives, he explored sources in America that others had overlooked. The correspondence in Chicago offers a fuller understanding of Otto Gombosi's passions and the circumstances that constrained him and thus enriches the history of American musicology.

Notes

1. I have relied on *The New Grove Dictionary of Music and Musicians,* 2nd ed., ed. Stanley Sadie and John Tyrrell (London: Macmillan, 2001) for these names. See also Reinhold Brinkmann and Christoph Wolff, eds., *Driven into Paradise: The Musical Migration from Nazi Germany to the United States* (Berkeley: University of California Press, 1999).

2. The dedicatee of this volume, Robert L. Marshall, was born in 1939; Gombosi was one of Marshall's predecessors at the University of Chicago.

3. See John M. Ward, "Otto John Gombosi (1902–1955)," *Acta musicologica* 28 (1956): 57–59. Claude Palisca regarded the "schools" founded by Gombosi at Harvard University and by Leo Schrade at Yale University to be the most productive of those initiated by émigré scholars; see Frank LL. Harrison, Mantle Hood, and Claude V. Palisca, *Musicology* (Englewood Cliffs, N.J.: Prentice-Hall, 1963), 199.

4. See further Hans Albrecht's tribute to Gombosi in Friedrich Blume, ed., *Die Musik in Geschichte und Gegenwart* (Kassel and Basel: Bärenreiter, 1956), 5:cols. 509–12.

5. Like Otto, György was a precocious scholar; in 1926 he already published a style-critical study of the painter Spinello Aretino (ca.1350–1410). I am especially grateful to Otto's son Dr. Peter Gombosi for information about his family and for permission to quote from his father's materials.

Lawrence H. Moe (personal communication, 1 May 2001) understood from Otto Gombosi that his father was conscripted into the Hungarian army and then disappeared, and his distraught mother one day wandered into the city and was never found; however, a funeral notice preserved among Otto Gombosi's papers gives the date of his father's death, 5 November 1944, and does not list Elizabeth among the survivors. A letter dated 8 July 1946 from his brother Bondi finally informed Otto that their parents had separately been murdered by Hungarian Fascists of the Arrow Cross Party. The fate of György, who was in Paris when war broke out, was likewise sealed when he loyally returned to Hungary; he died in a boxcar en route to a concentration camp.

6. As one of the first Hungarian musicologists and an earlier matriculant of Berlin, Kovács could have been a model for Gombosi's far-ranging interests; Kovács wrote his 1907 doctoral dissertation on the evolution of music, contributed thoughts on Renaissance music to the *Allgemeine musikalische Zeitung* in 1911, and in that same year, together with Béla Bartók and Zoltán Kodály, helped organize the Hungarian Society for New Music.

7. Otto Gombosi, *Jacob Obrecht: Eine stilkritische Studie* (Leipzig: Breitkopf & Härtel, 1925). An incomplete list of Gombosi's publications appears in Curt Efram Steinzor, *American Musicologists, c. 1890–1945; A Bio-Bibliographical Sourcebook to the Formative Period*, Music Reference Collection, no. 17 (New York and Westport: Greenwood Press, 1989), 97–102. Among the items missing from Steinzor's list are "Koessler János," *Crescendo*, September 1926, 1–3; "Nyílt levél a magyar muzsikáról," *Crescendo*, October 1926, 16–19; "Stoltzer Tamás," *Crescendo*, January 1927, 9–16; "A bécsi Beethoven ünnepség," *Crescendo*, April 1927, 9–12; "A parlandóról," *Crescendo*, March 1928, 1–4; "Gyermekek kompozíciói és az elemi tananyag," *Crescendo*, April-May 1928, 15–24; "Elvi megjegyzések a Händel-renaissanceról," *Crescendo*, June-July 1928, 19–23; *Kovács Sándor Dr. hátrahagyott zenei írásai Popper Irma és Gombosi Ottó a mester növendékei közremuködésével összeállította Molnár Antal* (Budapest: Rózsavölgyi és Társa Kiad, 1928); review of *Adrian Willaert in der weltlichen Vokalmusik seiner Zeit*, by Erich Hertsmann, *Zeitschrift für Musikwissenschaft,* 16 (1934): 54–56; review of *Die in deutscher Lautentabulatur überlieferten Tänze des 16. Jahrhunderts,* by Jenny Dieckmann, *Zeitschrift für Musikwissenschaft* 17 (1935): 118–20; review of *Aufführungspraxis alter Musik in Deutsche Literaturzeitung,* by Arnold Schering, *Deutsche Literaturzeitung* 52 (27 December 1931): cols. 2476–82; "Music in Hungary" in *Music in the Renaissance,* by Gustave Reese (New York: W. W. Norton, 1954), 714–27.

8. Otto Gombosi, ed., *Compositione di meser Vincenzo Capirola: Lute-Book (circa 1517)* (Neuilly-sur-Seine: Société de Musique d'Autrefois, 1955).

9. Thomas Stoltzer, *Sämtliche lateinische Hymnen und Psalmen*, in *Denkmäler Deutscher Tonkunst* (hereafter *DDT*), XLV, Hans Albrecht and Otto Gombosi, eds. (Leipzig: Breitkopf & Härtel, 1931). Wolf's edition of Stoltzer's *Newe deudsche geistliche Gesenge* appeared in 1908 (*DDT*, XXXIV).

10. Otto Gombosi, *Bakfark Bálint élete és müvei (1507–1576)*, Musicologia Hungarica II (Budapest: Az Orsz. Széchenyi könyvtäi kiadása, 1935).

11. Basel was also the site of the first postwar international musicological congress in 1924 and became the headquarters for the International Musicological Society (founded in 1927), which "[i]n its early years . . . maintained close relations

with musical performance and composition" (Rudolf Häusler, "International Musicological Society," *The New Grove Dictionary of Music and Musicians,* 2nd ed., 12:495). Johannes Wolf had addressed the significance of historical performance practice in a paper ("Über den Wert der Aufführungspraxis für die historische Erkenntnis") for the 1925 Leipzig musicological congress. Gombosi's editorial methods too, which reflect his own interest in performance and compositional issues, aimed to clarify form and structure for performers.

12. Paul Henry Lang (another of Weiner's students in Budapest) and Curt Sachs (one of Gombosi's teachers in Berlin, who also left the city in 1933) were already teaching in New York. The letters are dated as follows: Handschin, 18 May 1938; Wolf, 1 April 1938; Sachs, 10 April 1938; Lang, 28 April 1938.

13. The recommendation was dated 10 April 1938.

14. Otto Gombosi, *Tonarten und Stimmungen der antiken Musik* (Copenhagen: Ejnar Munksgaard, 1939) was dedicated to Johannes Wolf. (Munksgaard also published *Acta musicologica.*) Curt Sachs's most relevant publications up to that time were *Musik des Altertums* (1924) and *Die Musik der Antike* (1928).

15. Reese's letter to Gombosi in Berzona, Val Onsernone, 28 July 1939. Gombosi's paper appeared as "New Light on Ancient Greek Music" in *Papers Read at the International Congress of Musicology* [1939] (New York: Music Educators National Conference for the American Musicological Society, 1944), 168–83.

16. Bathia Churgin, personal communication with the author, 9 May 2001. According to John M. Ward (personal communication with the author, 7 July 2001), Johannes Wolf planned to travel with the Gombosis but returned to Germany when war broke out on the day their ship sailed from France.

17. L. D. Caskey's letter to Gombosi, 18 August 1939.

18. The dates of the responses are 7 October 1939, from Gleason; 9 October 1939, from Kinkeldey; 10 October 1939, from Waters; and 11 October 1939, from Smith.

19. Haydon's letter to Gombosi, 23 October 1939.

20. Robinson's letters to Gombosi, 14 November 1939.

21. Reese's letter to Gombosi, 17 October 1939.

22. Gombosi's letter of 9 November to "Verehrtester Herr Professor": "Die Leute, wenigstens die Fachkollegen, sind ja einfach reizend. Ueberhaupt kann ich nichts gegen Amerikaner sagen, ich habe wirklich nur liebenswürdige Leute angetroffen."

23. Ibid.: "Die grösste Sensation war der Cristofori-Flügel des Metropolitan Museum, den Sachs jetzt restaurieren liess."

24. Ibid.: ". . . in einigen Jahrzehnten wird es auch für Musikhistoriker ideale Arbeitsmöglichkeiten geben."

25. Gombosi's letter to Johnson, 22 November 1939.

26. Gombosi's letter to Kantonale Fremdenpolizei Basel, 5 December 1939, and the reply of 22 December.

27. Gombosi's letter to Scribner's, 1 September 1940.

28. Einstein's letter to Gombosi, 24 November 1939: ". . . auch die americanischen Mühlen gleichen den Mühlen Gottes darin, dass sie langsam arbeiten, und aber hoffentlich auch darin, dass sie sicher arbeiten."

29. Klein's letter to Gombosi, 28 November 1939. Educated both at Harvard and in Berlin, Leichtentritt left Berlin and returned to Harvard in 1933.

30. Gombosi's letters to Allen, 28 December 1939, and to Davison, 31 December 1939.

31. Kinkeldey's letter to Gombosi, 9 January 1940.

32. Lawrence Moe, personal communication with the author, 1 May 2001.

33. S. Drinker's letter to Gombosi, 25 February 1940.

34. Rinderspacher's letter to the Gombosis, 13 February 1940.

35. Gombosi's letter to Baldwin, 29 March 1940.

36. Gombosi's letter to Pindyck, 17 July 1940.

37. Gombosi's letter to "Frank," 20 March 1940: "Das allerschlimmste ist, dass die grossen Colleges z.B. um Philadelphia herum meistens Quaeker-Gruendungen sind und deswegen etwas anti-musikalisch eingestellt sind."

38. Anne Gombosi's letter to Rinderspacher, undated.

39. Gombosi's letter to Kinkeldey, 16 May 1940.

40. Klein's letter to Gombosi, 29 May 1940.

41. Gombosi's letter to Wood, 5 June 1940.

42. Woods's letter to Reese, 11 July 1940. Compare Hans Joachim Moser's remark to Theodor Kroyer (28 May 1927) regarding Alfred Einstein's hope for employment at Heidelberg University: ". . . the fact is that there are already so many Jews here that the ministry would hesitate to increase the number." Quoted by Pamela M. Potter, "From Jewish Exile in Germany to German Scholar in America: Alfred Einstein's Emigration," in Brinkmann and Wolff, *Driven into Paradise*, 303.

43. Reese's letter to Wood, 16 July 1940.

44. Gombosi's letter to Wood, 17 July 1940.

45. The Oberlaender Trust renewed the grant on 2 June 1941.

46. Gombosi's letter to Kinkeldey, 18 August 1940.

47. Gombosi's letter to Schwellenbach, 19 August 1940.

48. Gombosi's letter to Schwellenbach, 7 Sepetember 1940.

49. Gombosi's letter to Wolf, 7 September 1940: "Die Arbeit in Seattle wird ein boeses Holzhacken, ohne eine eiginermassen aussgeruestete Bibliothek . . . und vorlaeufig weiss ich nicht, wie das Menschenmaterial sein wird."

50. Gombosi's letter to Engel, undated.

51. Sachs's letter to Gombosi, 29 August 1941.

52. Gombosi's letter to the Newberry Library, 16 September 1940.

53. Moe, personal communication with the author, 28 May 2001.

54. Letter from Revitt to Gombosi, 8 November 1942.

55. See Gombosi's "Stephen Foster and 'Gregory Walker,'" *The Musical Quarterly* 30/2 (April 1944): 133–46 (an outgrowth of his lecture to the Northwest Chapter of the American Musicological Society in Seattle, 22 November 1941), and "The Pedigree of the Blues," *Proceedings of the Music Teachers National Association* 40 (1946): 382–89. According to John Ward (personal communication with the author, 30 July 2001), "Gombosi was attracted to those aspects of American music that had European roots . . ."

56. Schulhoff's letter to Gombosi, 25 November 1940.

57. Schulhoff's letter to Gombosi, 13 December 1940.

58. "Béla Bartók (1881–1945)," *The Musical Quarterly* 32/1 (January 1946): 1–11.

59. Rothe's letter to Gombosi, 1 December 1940. Anne had been in New York to play viola d'amore in a Bach concert with the New School Chamber Orchestra under Otto Klemperer. The orchestra performed Bartók's work under Rudolf Kolisch's direction on 11 December 1940.

60. Webb's letter to Gombosi, 22 May 1941.

61. Gombosi's letter to Marsch, 26 May 1941.

62. Gombosi's letter to Clark-Brewer Teachers Agency, 29 June 1941.

63. See note 5.

64. Gombosi's letter to Stiven, 4 June 1942.

65. Gombosi's letter to Thomas, 23 July 1942.

66. Thomas's response to Gombosi, 27 July 1942.

67. Gleason's letter to Gombosi, 24 August 1942.

68. Nostrand's letter to Gombosi, 11 July 1942.

69. Moe, personal communication with the author, 28 May 2001.

70. Reese's letter to Gombosi, 15 March 1944.

71. A card dated May 1946 from Mrs. György Lévai thanked Otto and Anne for two parcels containing clothes, shoes, and coffee. (Anne later performed with the pianist György Lévai in Boston.)

72. Lang's letter to Gombosi, 13 July 1944; Lowinsky's letter to Gombosi, 16 July 1944.

73. Gombosi's letter to Bacon, 4 August 1944.

74. Quoted by Palisca, *Musicology*, 98.

75. King's letter to Gombosi, 18 September 1943.

76. Reese's letter to Gombosi, 21 October 1943.

77. Letter from an unidentified author to Gombosi, 10 November 1943.

78. Rubsamen's letter to Gombosi, 4 July 1944.

79. According to Ward (personal communication with the author, 7 July 2001), "For a time there were more musicologists teaching at this institution than anywhere else in the country."

80. See his letter of 3 July 1946 to an unidentified recipient.

81. John F. A. Taylor's letter to Gombosi, 31 August 1946.

82. Already in 1929 Michigan State's Institute of Music offered harpsichord instruction.

83. Varró's letter to Gombosi, 14 April 1947.

84. Abstracted as "A Manuscript in the Newberry Library," *Journal of the American Musicological Society* 1/1 (spring 1948): 58.

85. Gombosi's letter to Pargellis, 27 September 1947.

86. Randolph's letter to Gombosi, 7 March 1949, addressed to Chalet Lindenegg in Aeschi near Basel.

87. Györgyi published *Six Simple Hungarian Dances: For Use in Girls' and Women's Physical Recreation Composed and Set to Traditional Airs by Georgie Bogyo* (London: Central Council of Recreative Physical Training, 1941).

88. "Key, Mode, Species," summarized in *Société internationale de musicologie congrès* (Basel: Bärenreiter, 1949), 133–34, and published in full in *Journal of the American Musicological Society* 4/1 (spring 1951): 20–26.

89. On 6 August Heinimann had requested Gombosi's opinion of Sándor Veress, a composer and associate of Bartók's, who came to Bern as guest professor of folk music in 1949.

90. Further, see Edward E. Lowinsky, "Homage to Armen Carapetyan," *Musica Disciplina* 37 (1983): 9–27.

91. Gombosi's letter to Carapetyan, 23 August 1949.

92. Work, whose music Gombosi studied, had lived in one of the oldest houses

still standing in Hyde Park. Intending to live permanently in America, Dolmetsch rented an apartment near the campus in 1905. Schoenberg lectured at the University of Chicago in 1946.

93. "Machaut's *Messe Notre-Dame*," *The Musical Quarterly* 36/2 (April 1950): 204–24.

94. Personal communication from Meyer, 25 April 2001. Gombosi's drafts for the Bartók book are in the Budapest Bartók Archives; see László Somfai, "A Major Unfinished Work on Bartók," *New Hungarian Quarterly* 22/82 (summer 1981): 91–99.

95. Asher, personal communication with the author, 15 April 2001.

96. Somfai, personal communication with the author, 17 April 2001.

97. See also László Somfai, *Béla Bartók: Composition, Concepts, and Autograph Sources* (Berkeley: University of California Press, 1996), 92 and 318. Gombosi showed John Ward Bartók's short score of the whole *Concerto for Orchestra*, probably the same source seen by Asher.

98. Gombosi's letter to W. W. Norton, 25 May 1950, explaining delays in his work.

99. Pope's letter to Gombosi, 13 September 1949.

100. Sutter and Co.'s letter to Gombosi, 4 October 1949.

101. W.W. Norton's communication to Gombosi, 10 November 1949. This work is not acknowledged in Strunk's 1950 book and might have been unknown to him.

102. The first proofs arrived on 17 October 1952.

103. Carapetyan's letter to Gombosi, 25 February 1950.

104. Gombosi's letter to Carapetyan, 31 March 1950.

105. Gombosi's letter to Ward, 29 June 1951, courtesy of John M. Ward.

106. Gombosi's letter to Reese, 28 June 1951, courtesy of Bathia Churgin.
        One of Churgin's graduate students gave her several of Gombosi's letters to Reese; these had been found in a book that had once belonged to Reese and that had been discarded by the Jewish National and University Library (Jerusalem). Gombosi was not Harvard's first choice for the position, but Manfred Bukofzer, the preferred candidate, chose to remain at Berkeley (John M. Ward, personal communication with the author, 7 July 2001). Like Gombosi, Bukofzer had studied in Berlin, lectured in Basel in 1937, and died prematurely in 1955.

107. Jürg Erni, *Paul Sacher Musiker und Mäzen* (Basel: Schwabe & Co., 1999), 41, 103, and 110; *Alte und neue Musik: 25 Jahre Basler Kammerorchester* (Zurich: Atlantis, 1952), passim.

108. Wenzinger's Harvard lectures on historical performance practice in spring 1953 (reportedly instigated by Anne) gave impetus to the Camerata, which Anne frequently directed from 1954 to 1959.

109. Elliot Forbes, *A History of Music at Harvard to 1972* (Cambridge: Harvard University Department of Music, 1988), 97–98 and 100.

110. Heartz, personal communication with the author, 24 April 2001. Daniel Heartz, *Preludes, Chansons and Dances for Lute, published by Pierre Attaingnant, Paris (1529–1530)* (Neuilly-sur-Seine: Société de Musique d'Autrefois, 1964).

111. Churgin, personal communication with the author, 9 May 2001.

112. Victoria Glaser, personal communication with the author, 15 May 2001.

113. Frank D'Accone, personal communication with the author, 23 May 2001.

114. Victor Yellin, personal communication with the author, 26 April 2001.

115. D'Accone, personal communication with the author, 23 May 2001.

116. Peter Gombosi, personal communication with the author, 10 May 2001.

117. Curt Sachs, "Otto Gombosi 1902–1955," *Journal of the American Musicological Society* 8/1 (spring 1955): 1. Incidentally, Sachs mistakenly implied that Gombosi had studied with Bartók.

118. Recounted by Manfred F. Bukofzer, *Studies in Medieval and Renaissance Music* (New York: W. W. Norton & Co., 1950), 190 and 201–4.

119. Curt Sachs, *Rhythm and Tempo: A Study in Music History* (New York: W. W. Norton & Co., 1953), 180.

120. Yellin, personal communication with the author, 26 April 2001.

121. Otto Gombosi, "Johannes Wolf (1869–1947)," *The Musical Quarterly* 34/2 (April 1948): 149–54.

122. See Gombosi's dismissal of Paul Nettl's *The Story of Dance Music* in *The Musical Quarterly* 34/4 (October 1948): 622–27.

123. Gombosi's letter to Dart, 22 August 1952; courtesy of John M. Ward.

124. Gombosi's letter to Heartz, 11 January 1953; courtesy of Daniel Heartz.

125. Moe, personal communication with the author, 1 May 2001.

Contributors

LAWRENCE F. BERNSTEIN is Karen and Gary Rose Term Professor of Music at the University of Pennsylvania. His research interests focus on the French chanson, the music of Ockeghem and Josquin, and, most recently, on the symphonies of Joseph Haydn. He has served as editor-in chief of the *Journal of the American Musicological Society* and as founding editor of the American Musicological Society Monographs.

Professor Bernstein and the publishers are grateful to Universal Edition, Vienna and European American Music Distributors LLC for permission to reproduce the music examples from the H. C. Robbins Landon Critical Edition of the Haydn Symphonies.

STEPHEN A. CRIST, contributing co-editor of this volume, is Associate Professor and chair of the Music Department at Emory University. He is editor of *Bach in America* and his writings on Johann Sebastian Bach have appeared in *The Cambridge Companion to Bach* and the *Journal of the American Musicological Society*, among other publications. His work has been supported by several grants, including a NEH Fellowship for University Teachers.

ELLEN T. HARRIS is Class of 1949 Professor at MIT, where she previously served as Associate Provost for the Arts and Head of the Music and Theater Arts Section. Her most recent book, *Handel as Orpheus: Voice and Desire in the Chamber Cantatas*, won the 2002 Otto Kinkeldey Award from the American Musicological Society and the 2002–3 Louis Gottschalk Prize from the Society for Eighteenth-Century Studies. She has published numerous articles and reviews in the area of Baroque opera and vocal performance practice in publications such as the *Journal of the American Musicological Society*, *Händel Jahrbuch*, *Notes*, and the *New York Times*.

JEFFREY KALLBERG, Professor of Music History at the University of Pennsylvania, has published widely on the music and cultural contexts of Chopin. He also wrote the articles on "Gender" and "Sex, Sexuality" for *The New Grove Dictionary of Music and Musicians*, 2d ed.

RICHARD KRAMER is the author of *Distant Cycles: Schubert and the Conceiving of Song*, awarded the Otto Kinkeldey prize of the American Musicological Society and an ASCAP-Deems Taylor prize, and *Beethoven: A Sketchbook from the Summer of 1800*. He has served as editor-in-chief of the *Journal of the American Musicological Society*. A fellow of the American Academy of Arts and Sciences, Kramer is Distinguished Professor of Music at the Graduate Center of the City University of New York.

MARK KROLL, one of the world's leading harpsichordists and fortepianists, has written on a variety of musical topics that include seventeenth- and eighteenth-century keyboard music, performance practices in Beethoven's music, and contemporary music. He is currently writing a biography of Hummel and recently published two editions of Hummel's chamber ensemble arrangements. Kroll is Professor Emeritus at Boston University, where he served as Chair of the Department of Historical Performance and Director of the Early Music Series.

LAURENCE LIBIN has been Research Curator at The Metropolitan Museum of Art since 1999, where he previously directed the Department of Musical Instruments for twenty-six years. An advisor to cultural institutions from Mexico to Russia, he has also taught at Columbia University and New York University. Recent publications include a series of articles on music iconography for *BBC Music Magazine*.

LEWIS LOCKWOOD is the author of *Beethoven: The Music and the Life*. His future projects include a volume of essays on Beethoven's violin sonatas, jointly edited with Mark Kroll, and a book on aspects of Beethoven's string quartets.

CLAUDIA MACDONALD is Associate Professor of Musicology at Oberlin College. Her articles on Robert Schumann, the piano concerto, music criticism, and women musicians have appeared in various journals. She is currently completing a book titled *The Piano Concerto and Robert Schumann*.

MICHAEL MARISSEN holds a B.A. from Calvin College and Ph.D. from Brandeis University. He joined the Swarthmore College faculty in 1989, where he is Daniel Underhill Professor of Music and department chair. He has also been a visiting professor at Princeton University and Oberlin College. His publications include *The Social and Religious Designs of J. S. Bach's Brandenburg Concertos, Lutheranism, Anti-Judaism, and Bach's St. John Passion,* and articles in the *Harvard Theological Review* and the *New York Times*.

ROBERTA MONTEMORRA MARVIN, contributing co-editor of this volume, focuses her scholarship on the music of Verdi and Rossini. She is editor of the critical edition of *I masnadieri* for *The Works of Giuseppe Verdi* and co-editor of *Verdi 2001*. Her recent work on Verdi's music in Victorian London has been supported by NEH and Howard Foundation fellowships, and her project on Verdi's educational activities was awarded the 1991

Premio Internazionale "Giuseppe Verdi." She has been on the faculty of the University of Iowa since 1997.

MARGARET MURATA, Professor at the University of California, Irvine, took her first course with Robert Marshall when she was an undergraduate. She has served as president of the Society for Seventeenth-Century Music and vice-president of the American Musicological Society; she has published extensively on Italian Baroque vocal music.

JESSIE ANN OWENS is Louis, Frances and Jeffrey Sachar Professor of Music at Brandeis University. Former President of the American Musicological Society and President-elect of the Renaissance Society of America, she became a Fellow of the American Academy of Arts and Sciences in 2003. A specialist in Renaissance music, her interests include music historiography, theory and analysis of early music, and compositional process; at present she is working on a book about tonalities in early modern England.

JANN PASLER, Professor of Music at the University of California, San Diego, has published widely on French and American contemporary music, cultural life in Paris at the turn of this century, and modernist/postmodernist issues in music. She has also produced two video documentaries on music and ritual in Bali, *Taksu: Music in the Life of Bali* and *The Great Ceremony to Straighten the World*. Pasler is currently completing a book titled *Useful Music, or Why Music Mattered in Third Republic France*.

MAYNARD SOLOMON is author of *Mozart: A Life* and four books on Beethoven, most recently *Late Beethoven: Music, Thought, Imagination*. He has held visiting appointments in music at CUNY Graduate Center, SUNY Stony Brook, Columbia, Harvard, and Yale Universities. He is currently on the Graduate Faculty of the Juilliard School of Music and is working on a biography of Schubert.

JEFFREY S. SPOSATO is Assistant Professor of Music at the University of Pittsburgh at Greensburg, where he teaches music history and directs the collegiate chorale. His current research, which examines Felix Mendelssohn's relationship to his Jewish heritage, has appeared in *The Musical Quarterly*; he has a forthcoming book, titled *The Price of Assimilation: Felix Mendelssohn and the Nineteenth-Century Anti-Semitic Tradition*.

RUSSELL STINSON is the Josephine Emily Brown Professor of Music and College Organist at Lyon College in Arkansas. His numerous publications on the music of J. S. Bach include monographs on the *Orgelbüchlein* and the Great Eighteen Organ Chorales. He is currently writing a book titled *The Reception of Bach's Organ Works from Mendelssohn to Brahms*.

Index

Eastman Studies in Music

(ISSN 1071–9989)

Historical Musicology:
Sources, Methods, Interpretations

Edited by Stephen A. Crist and Roberta Montemorra Marvin

How do we know what notes a composer intended in a given piece?—how those notes should be played and sung?—the nature of musical life in Bach's Leipzig, Schubert's Vienna?—how music related to literature and other arts and social currents in different times and places?—what attitudes musicians and music lovers had toward the music that they heard and made (including in the bourgeois parlor)?

We know all this from primary sources: musical manuscripts and prints, opera libretti, composers' letters, reviews in newspapers and magazines, archival data, contemporary pedagogical writings, essays on aesthetics, and much else. Some of these categories of sources have, for over a century, served as the bedrock of music history and musicology. Others have begun to be examined only in recent years.

Furthermore, musicologists—including biographers of famous composers—now explore these various kinds of sources in a variety of ways, some of them richly traditional and others exciting and novel.

The seventeen contributors to this volume are all renowned specialists in their respective repertoires: the Renaissance and Baroque, Mozart, Beethoven, Mendelssohn, Verdi, Debussy, and much else. Their essays, all newly written for this book, use a wide array of source materials to probe issues pertaining to a cross section of musical works and musical life from the sixteenth through the twentieth centuries.

Taken together the essays provide models reflecting the pluralistic profile of musicology at the beginning of the twenty-first century. It will prove welcome to anyone fascinated by the problems of reconstructing—reimagining, sometimes—the evanescent musical art of the past and pondering its implications for musical life today and in the future.

Contributors: Lawrence F. Bernstein, Stephen A. Crist, Ellen T. Harris, Jeffrey Kallberg, Richard Kramer, Mark Kroll, Laurence Libin, Lewis Lockwood, Claudia Macdonald, Michael Marissen, Roberta Montemorra Marvin, Margaret Murata, Jessie Ann Owens, Jann Pasler, Maynard Solomon, Jeffrey S. Sposato, Russell Stinson.

Praise for Historical Musicology:

"In this book some of the best minds in current musicology explore untrodden territory. They show that the classic source study and the traditional methods of musical analysis are not only alive and kicking, but generating rich new ideas—some of them controversial, all of them stimulating."

—Nicholas Temperley, Professor of Musicology (Emeritus), University of Illinois, and author of *Bound for America: Three British Composers.*

"Striding onto the stage of the 'New Musicology,' the seventeen contributors to *Historical Musicology* proceed to kick in the footlights. Out of the broken glass, they manage to create an approach to the scholarly study of music that recognises that musical scholarship (whatever its methodological imperatives) remains rooted in the study of primary sources, and go on to demonstrate brilliantly how the benefits of the 'New' can be combined with the 'Old.'"

—Mark Everist, Professor of Music, University of Southampton, UK, and co-editor of *Rethinking Music.*

"When musicologists combine source study, critical analysis, and interpretation, they effectively dissolve the unproductive dichotomy between 'traditional' and 'new' musicology. The studies in Crist and Marvin's *Historical Musicology* brilliantly demonstrate the effectiveness of an integrated approach, illuminating a wide swath of musical territory from Renaissance Italy to Debussy's Paris and beyond."

—Mary Sue Morrow, Professor of Musicology, College-Conservatory of Music, University of Cincinnati, and author of *German Music Criticism in the Late Eighteenth Century.*

LaVergne, TN USA
02 March 2011
218604LV00003B/71/P